treehouse

CSS3
Foundations

treehouse™

CSS3
Foundations

Ian Lunn

WILEY

A John Wiley and Sons, Ltd, Publication

This edition first published 2013

© 2013 Ian Lunn

Registered office

John Wiley & Sons Ltd, The Atrium, Southern Gate, Chichester, West Sussex, PO19 8SQ, United Kingdom

For details of our global editorial offices, for customer services and for information about how to apply for permission to reuse the copyright material in this book please see our website at www.wiley.com.

978-1-118-35654-8

A catalogue record for this book is available from the British Library.

ISBN 978-1-118-35654-8 (paperback); ISBN 978-1-118-42516-9 (ebook); 978-1-118-42514-5 (ebook); 978-1-118-42515-2 (ebook)

Printed in the U.S. at Command Web Missouri

About the Author

IAN LUNN (DEVON, UK) is a Freelance Front End Developer, passionate about building the future of the web using technologies such as CSS3 and HTML5. With a Higher National Diploma in Internet Technology, Ian combines his education with expertise in CSS, HTML, JavaScript, and WordPress to build creative and effective websites and applications. Ian's enthusiasm for utilizing cutting edge technologies is matched by his dedication for advocating them; sharing his knowledge with the community, in the form of blog tutorials and open source projects.

Follow @IanLunn on Twitter (www.twitter.com/IanLunn) where he shares links and ideas about web design and development.

Publisher's Acknowledgements

Some of the people who helped bring this book to market include the following:

Editorial and Production

VP Consumer and Technology Publishing Director:
Michelle Leete

Associate Director–Book Content Management:
Martin Tribe

Associate Publisher:
Chris Webb

Assistant Editor:
Ellie Scott

Development Editor:
Brian Herrmann

Copy Editor:
Chuck Hutchinson

Technical Editor:
Nick Elliott

Editorial Manager:
Jodi Jensen

Senior Project Editor:
Sara Shlaer

Editorial Assistant:
Leslie Saxman

Marketing

Associate Marketing Director:
Louise Breinholt

Marketing Executive:
Kate Parrett

Composition Services

Compositor:
Andrea Hornberger
Jennifer Mayberry

Proofreaders:
Linda Seifert

Indexer:
Ty Koontz

Contents

part 2: Learning CSS Syntax and Adding Presentational Styles

part 3: Building a Solid and Adaptable Page Structure

part 6: Preparing for Multiple Browsers and Devices

CHAPTER FIFTEEN

Testing Across Multiple Browsers

CHAPTER SIXTEEN

Making Your Website Look Great Across Multiple Devices

Introduction

YOU'RE READING *CSS3 FOUNDATIONS* at an exciting time. Right now, the way in which the web is styled is undergoing changes, and with the constant advancement of technology, that doesn't look to end any time soon. The web is already a beautiful place, but with more features allowing you to style a page than ever, the possibilities of what can be created are endless.

Who Should Read This Book?

CSS3 Foundations is for those completely new to styling web pages, but also makes as a great reference for those familiar with CSS too—particularly when you want to remind yourself of the newest CSS features that you may not have committed to memory.

Ideally, you have a basic understanding of HTML (Hypertext Markup Language) but it's not essential. The HTML that makes up the web page built upon throughout *CSS3 Foundations* is provided for you and described in Chapter 2. So, whether you've chosen to start learning CSS before HTML, or vice versa, you'll be gently eased into both technologies.

If you're a hobbyist, somebody looking to make a career change into the wonderful world of the web industry, an owner of a website that is need of restyling, or a web designer/developer looking to upgrade your skills to the most recent techniques and methods in use today, *CSS3 Foundations* is for you.

What You Will Learn

CSS3 Foundations aims to get you not just hitting the ground running, but hopping, stepping, and jumping too!

You'll go from the very basics of styling a web page; changing the background color, the size of text, and so on, all the way through to more advanced topics such as animations and media queries, which allow you to change a page's layout for different sizes of device.

Although the easiest topics come first and slowly progress to reach the more advanced chapters, the way in which *CSS3 Foundations* is laid out represents the workflow I, and many other people in the web industry use to create a website. So, as well as learning CSS, you'll also learn a "best practice" approach that can be applied to real-world projects, to make pages not just great to look at, but easy to update and robust enough to be viewed on a wide range of devices too (such as desktop computer and mobile phone).

You'll also learn methods and techniques not described in the CSS specification (the official technical document that explains CSS), which web designers and developers have relied on for years to make the most of CSS.

How to Use This Book

In Chapter 2, I'll introduce you to a fictitious company that has asked you to create a web page—there's no pay but the experience is golden! You'll be able to download the necessary project files to get started. This download contains updated project files for each chapter (which are sometimes broken into milestones for the bigger chapters). I'll let you know when a milestone is reached and you can either use the project files to compare to your own work, or switch to that milestone's project files in case you didn't follow the steps that came before it.

Depending on your current experience with CSS, you may decide to jump ahead to the chapters that interest you most -- that's fine, the beginning of each chapter will let you know which project files to start with.

Once you've finished reading *CSS3 Foundations*, it'll make a great desktop companion for when you need to remind yourself on how to use a feature or solve a particular problem. Each property description includes useful information for quick reference, such as the property's initial value, browser compatibility, and so on. If you're unfamiliar with those terms, I'll explain those too!

Using This Book with Treehouse

By no means do you need to be a member of Treehouse to make the most out of *CSS3 Foundations*, but the two sit nicely together. Although both aim to be extensive, there's certainly always something extra to learn.

What's more, Treehouse's video courses are often followed by fun, interactive challenges that put what you've learned to the test. You can redo a challenge as many times as you like until you feel comfortable with the topic being covered.

Treehouse also has a great community (which I am pleased to be a part of), so if at any time you have a question or want to show off your CSS skills, come and join in!

part 1
Introduction

chapter one

Understanding CSS and the Modern Web

IN THIS CHAPTER, you'll learn what the modern web is and why CSS is so important to it.

What Is the Modern Web?

Most importantly, the web today is what it has always been—accessible information. Unlike the early days of the web, though—when it was just a collection of text files—the modern web has grown to support many differing media formats and now, more than ever, many differing ways to access information.

No longer do you just sit at a desktop computer to "log on." Nowadays, you sit on a beach reading the news on a tablet device, you go to a coffee shop with laptop in hand to chat with friends in different countries, and you try to refrain from laughing at pictures of cats playing keyboards while viewing a smart phone on a train journey. The information on the web is practically infinite (more content is created than you could ever consume), and the way in which you access that information continues to grow.

The modern web is an exciting media to be a part of. It is continuously growing and so too are the technologies behind it.

What Is CSS?

Cascading Style Sheets (CSS) is a simple language defining styles that can be applied to HTML. Where HTML describes the structure of a web page, CSS describes its presentation.

An international community called the World Wide Web Consortium (W3C) writes and maintains the CSS specifications that define and standardize the way in which people should write the CSS language and browser vendors (the people who make web browsers) should implement it. Because the CSS specification has grown since its introduction in 1996, the latest version, CSS3, has been broken up into modules so that each defines a part of CSS, making the overall specification easier to maintain.

You can find the CSS specifications at www.w3.org/Style/CSS/. Because these specifications are very much technical and in depth, you may find them off-putting. I know I do! Although they are useful to refer to from time to time, by no means do you need to read them. *CSS3 Foundations* takes a much more simple and friendly approach to your understanding of CSS3.

Before you take a closer look at what CSS can offer, you should first understand the current state of CSS. You may have noticed I referred to both CSS and CSS3. What's the difference?

CSS refers to all three levels of the specification: CSS Level 1 (CSS1), CSS Level 2 (CSS2), and CSS Level 3 (CSS3). Each level of CSS builds on its predecessor. CSS2 had a shaky start and many issues came to light, leading to a revision of this specification and the release of CSS2.1. So, CSS3 contains aspects of its predecessor CSS2.1, and CSS2.1 contains aspects of CSS2 and CSS1.

Although each CSS level builds on its predecessor, where relevant, a level recommends a particular feature from its predecessor no longer be used and thus deprecated. This means that when referring to CSS3, one is actually referring to all the features made available throughout CSS, except those that have been deprecated.

In *CSS3 Foundations*, you learn CSS3, which includes not just the newest of features, but also those from the previous CSS levels that experienced designers and developers have relied on for years.

The Role of CSS

The main purpose of CSS is to separate structure (HTML) from presentation (CSS). Figure 1-1 shows a web page that consists only of HTML, without any CSS.

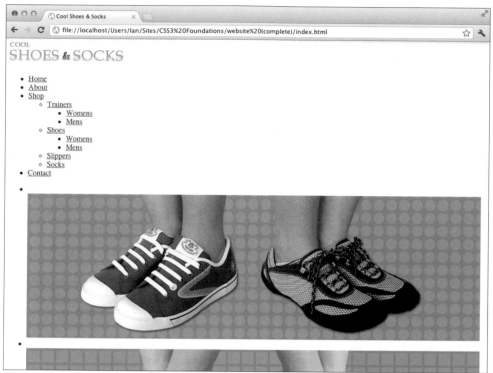

FIGURE 1-1 A web page without any CSS.

Figure 1-2 shows the same web page *with* CSS applied to it—a huge difference, one that makes the page much more attractive.

In the early days of styling web pages, structure and presentation were mixed together. Presentation was directly applied to structure, meaning that maintaining pages became an arduous task. If, for example, somebody decided that the main title on each page of a website should be changed from black to blue and that site consisted of 10 pages, you had to change the style for that title 10 times.

By separating structure and presentation, you gain numerous advantages:

- A Cascading Style Sheet can be shared across multiple web pages.

- Sites are easier to maintain and become more flexible.

- The styles applied to a web page can be tailored to suit multiple devices/environments.

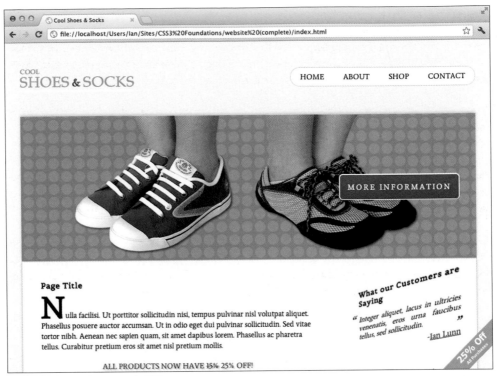

FIGURE 1-2 A web page with CSS.

In the modern web, the role of CSS is more important than ever. As technology has advanced and the ways in which you access the web are more diverse, CSS must evolve to accommodate both users wanting to access information over the web and developers wanting to present that information in a particular way. I say *developers,* but really I mean anyone. The web is not just for the technically minded. Open information is for everyone, and CSS aims to be as easy and open to use as possible, allowing anyone to style information.

The most important aspect of CSS is backward compatibility. Because each new level of the specification builds on the last, CSS remains backward compatible. Although features may become deprecated, they still work in existing browsers because new levels only add new functionality or refine existing definitions. By working backward first, the specification then has the opportunity to pave a solid path into the future.

CSS3 offers many new features to push the web forward and help improve the accessibility and presentation of information. With the emergence of multiple ways to access the web, one of CSS3's most important features is the Media Queries module, which builds on media types.

When CSS2 was developed, it became apparent there was a need to serve different styles based on how web pages were being accessed, so media types were introduced. These media types allowed for specifying different styles for particular devices, such as screen (intended for color computer displays), print (intended for printers and printed documents), and hand-held (intended for small screen devices with limited bandwidth).

With such a varied range of handheld devices on the market today, defining those devices within the handheld category certainly isn't descriptive enough. Likewise, desktop displays differ greatly in features too.

CSS3's Media Queries module builds on media types, allowing a developer to query particular aspects (such as width and height) of the device and environment on which a web page is being viewed and specify styles to be applied only when certain conditions are met.

The specification also adds new presentational features such as gradients and rounded corners to make easier some of the tasks developers have been doing for years, more ways to select the elements to be styled (called Selectors), and web fonts, which sees the number of fonts you can safely use go from tens to thousands—if not tens of thousands!

Working Draft and the CSS Process

At the time of writing, the overall CSS3 specification is incomplete. To make reading and implementing it easier, the specification is broken up into modules. While some of these modules are complete, others are still being written or tested. Modules go through varying stages to determine how far from being complete they are and also serve as an indication of whether you should use them:

- **Working Draft**—A module that is incomplete and still being worked on.
- **Last Call**—A module that is considered to be complete. This module will move toward Candidate Recommendation unless significant issues arise.
- **Candidate Recommendation**—All known issues are resolved and the features of the module are ready to be implemented into web browsers.
- **Proposed Recommendation**—Features of the module are implemented in at least two web browsers and the module is reviewed by W3C Members one last time.
- **Recommendation**—The module is complete.

When implementing features from modules that are Working Draft or Last Call, those features should be used with a vendor prefix; this ensures you are using experimental features in a way that prevents incompatibilities should there be changes to modules in the future.

You'll learn exactly what a vendor prefix is and how to use them in Chapter 5.

More information about the CSS process can be found at www.w3.org/Style/2011/CSS-process#rectrack.

All in all, CSS3 makes creating web pages easier and more exciting than ever. So, at the time of writing, as the specification is in Working Draft status, can you use it yet?

Absolutely! Modern browsers already have great support for CSS3 because the sooner you start using it, the sooner you can provide feedback and improve the future of CSS. The W3C consists not only of member organizations and its full-time staff but the public, too. By using CSS3 today, you can have your say in its future. Just by using a feature of CSS3 is giving your stamp of approval to it.

Throughout *CSS3 Foundations*, you learn to use CSS3 in a safe way that is compatible with both existing browsers that have some or no CSS3 support and future browsers, in the case of features being redefined prior to the specification reaching its Recommendation status.

Modern Browsers

A web browser is, at its core, an engine that renders HTML, CSS, and other technologies, turning them into a functional web page. Browsers also offer features such as bookmarking, history management, developer tools and many others, including support for add-ons that allow for extending a browser's capabilities.

So, which browser should you use to create your website? All of them! Okay, you don't need to download them all right now, but it is important to test the websites you build in a range of browsers (and devices).

Today's Major Browsers

Five major browsers are available today. These browsers are created by organizations—often referred to as browser vendors or vendors for short—and are made free to download and use.

- Google Chrome (`www.google.com/chrome`)
- Apple Safari (`www.apple.com/safari`)
- Mozilla Firefox (`www.mozilla.org/firefox/new`)
- Opera (`www.opera.com`, both browser and vendor are referred to as Opera)
- Microsoft Internet Explorer (`http://windows.microsoft.com/en-US/internet-explorer/downloads/ie`)

I personally like to create websites using Chrome. I feel its web developer tools are the most useful for the way I work, and it is often ahead of the rest when implementing the latest CSS features.

Throughout the book, I use Chrome as my main browser (and test other browsers in Chapter 15). I recommend avoiding Microsoft Internet Explorer versions 7–9 as a browser to use while creating a web page because its features aren't as consistent as the others listed, but if you'd like to use Safari, Firefox, or Opera, feel free. The development tools, which I use and refer to, are similar between browsers, and I don't use a feature if it doesn't exist in another browser.

At the time of writing, Microsoft Internet Explorer 10 is available as a preview but hasn't officially been released.

Browser Engines (Layout Engines)

Knowing which engine these browsers support is also useful:

- **WebKit** (www.webkit.org/)—Both Google Chrome and Apple Safari use this open source engine. Although these browsers use the same engine, they may have implemented it in a slightly different way, so you shouldn't expect one to render the page exactly the same as the other. Always test in both to make sure. That said, in most cases, consistency between these browsers is very good. Android Browser also uses WebKit, which together with Safari (used on Apple's iPhone, iPad, and iPod products) makes it the most-used browser engine on mobile devices.

- **Gecko** (www.developer.mozilla.org/en/Gecko)—Mozilla Firefox uses Gecko, another open source project.

- **Presto** (www.opera.com/docs/specs/)—Available only as a part of Opera products.

- **Trident** (www.en.wikipedia.org/wiki/Trident_(layout_engine))—Available only as a part of Microsoft's products.

These engines are used not only by desktop and mobile browsers but also by other products such as e-mail clients and word editing software.

What Is Open Source Software?

Open source software is that which is made available for use and modification completely free. This is a great way to open up a project to everybody and, in turn, enhance the project by having many people improving it at the same time. *CSS3 Foundations* uses a few open source projects, and no doubt, you'll come across many on your own in the future.

Browser Usage Statistics

Although browsers are free to download and use, the web browser market is very much a competitive place. As mentioned, vendors are all trying to push the web forward, but they also stand to gain a lot from people using their particular browser. Some vendors have other products that they want to profit from. The bigger their share of the market, the more they are able to push these products and services.

Tables 1-1 and 1-2 present the usage statistics provided by www.netmarketshare.com in July 2012 (the time of writing).

Table 1-1   Desktop Browser Usage

Browser	Total Market Share
Internet Explorer	54.02%
Firefox	20.06%
Chrome	19.08%
Safari	4.73%
Opera	1.60%
Others (below 1%)	0.34%

Table 1-2   Mobile/Tablet Browser Usage

Browser	Total Market Share
Safari	65.79%
Android Browser	19.17%
Opera Mini	10.45%
BlackBerry	1.45%
Others (individually below 1%)	2.56%

Older Browsers on the Modern Web

Unfortunately, the modern web—with all its fancy new features—comes with excess baggage in the form of older web browsers that are still in use today. Although the W3C, browser vendors, and the web community/industry are working to push the web forward, there are many web users who are either unaware of or unable to embrace this change.

Before looking at which of the browsers still in use today could be deemed as being old, Table 1-3 shows the breakdown of market share into individual version numbers.

Table 1-3   Desktop Browser Usage by Version Number

Browser	Total Market Share
Internet Explorer 8.0	26.65%
Internet Explorer 9.0	17.96%
Chrome 19.0	15.56%
Firefox 12	7.76%
Firefox 13	6.33%
Internet Explorer 6.0	5.92%
Safari 5.1	3.63%
Internet Explorer 7.0	3.10%
Firefox 3.6	1.38%
Opera 11.x	1.04%

Like me, you may find these statistics to be surprising. Internet Explorer 8 has the biggest market share, over 25%? There are a few reasons for this. Internet Explorer comes packaged with Microsoft Windows, which is the most-used operating system. Many people access the web via Internet Explorer unaware that other browsers even exist. They also don't upgrade their browser because either they don't know that option is available or the technology they have is too outdated to do so. You should note that Internet Explorer 9 is available only to users of Windows Vista and Windows 7. Many users are still using Windows XP, which is restricted to Internet Explorer 8. This may explain why it is the number one web browser, despite Internet Explorer 9 being on the market since 2011.

Here's where I drop the bomb: Internet Explorer 6, 7, and 8 are old browsers, despite all having significant market share. Although each is superior to the next, their support of standardized CSS is poor. Versions 6 and 7 implement CSS 2.1 but not particularly well. Version 8 has good support for CSS 2.1 but little for CSS3.

There is light ahead though. Although Internet Explorer 6 has around a 6% share according to these statistics, many of its users are Asian based, so if your website is not targeting that audience, you may find those statistics greatly drop. Internet Explorer 6 is such an old browser, and so troublesome to the future of the web that even Microsoft is trying to make its users aware that they can upgrade, with the site www.ie6countdown.com. This site also confirms that Asia (in particular, China, with a 22.4% share) greatly contributes to that 7% global statistic.

Aside from Internet Explorer versions 6, 7, and 8, the only other old browser with a share greater than 1% is Mozilla Firefox 3.6. It has good support for CSS2.1 and CSS3 and is not a problem browser by any means, but at the time of writing, Firefox is in the double figures, at version 14. You would be forgiven for thinking you didn't have to test in 3.6 then because it's so outdated, but testing in Firefox 3.6 is something I highly recommend due to its having a market share higher than 1% (generally a browser with a market share less than 1% is deemed as being redundant), and you do just that toward the end of *CSS3 Foundations*.

So how do you deal with older browsers because they are still very much a part of the modern web?

It is important to remember that the web is open information and it is the person's job that is making that information available as accessible to as many as possible. You shouldn't ignore users of old web browsers, but it's unrealistic to provide them the same levels of features you would provide somebody using a modern web browser. You would still like them to be able to see the beauty of the page you've created, just at the level their browser can support.

Say you've used some of CSS3's features such as rounded corners and background gradients. An older browser doesn't understand these features, so it can't display them. Instead, that browser just shows square corners and a solid background, as shown in Figure 1-3 and Figure 1-4.

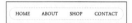

FIGURE 1-3 An element with rounded corners.
Copyright © 2012, Eduardo Tunni (http://www.tipo.net.ar), with Reserved Font Name "Average."

FIGURE 1-4 The same element viewed in a browser that doesn't support CSS3's rounded corners.
Belgrano font designed by Daniel Hernández and Latinotype in 2011. All rights Reserved.

This is known as *graceful degradation*. In a browser that doesn't support CSS3, it simply falls back to what it does support. The user of that browser still sees a nicely styled web page and is none the wiser to the fact that in a modern browser, he could be seeing a few extra niceties. Nothing appears broken to him, and the way in which he is interacting with your web page isn't affected.

There is also another technique similar to this known as *progressive enhancement*, but what's the difference? Although graceful degradation starts with modern browsers in mind first and then provides workarounds for older browsers later, progressive enhancement does the opposite: it starts with an older browser and then later adds new features for modern browsers.

Which approach should you use? With all the work being done to push the web forward, it would be a shame for that to go to waste. By using graceful degradation, you are putting the future of the web first but making sure there is support for the part of the web that is yet to catch up, too.

In the case of Internet Explorer 6, you may decide to just ignore it completely, simply because it's such an old and troublesome browser to provide fixes for. Rather than spending *x* number of hours fixing it, in Chapter 15, you'll apply basic CSS to Internet Explorer 6, which still makes the content of the web page perfectly accessible, it just won't be styled as much. This saves you work (and if you're creating a web page for a client, it saves money), but the user can still see all the information on the page because, after all, CSS is just presentation.

Of course, if you're creating web pages for a paying client, now or in the future, you would need to discuss browser support. By analyzing the latest usage statistics for browsers, as well as the client's existing statistics on their own website (should they already have one), you can determine what browsers your client's users are using to view the site and aim to support those browsers with the site you're creating.

Throughout *CSS3 Foundations*, I advise you when a feature isn't available in an older browser, and you learn to test and examine alternatives for these browsers in Chapter 15.

Tools for Building and Styling the Modern Web

As the web has grown, so too has the number of tools available to build it. You can easily become overwhelmed by choice, but you should remember that, at its core, the web is just text. To start building a web page, you need only a web browser and a text editor.

Tools range in price anywhere from completely free to several hundred dollars, but by no means are the most expensive ones necessarily the best. You can get started with some great tools having spent no money whatsoever.

Web Developer Tools

Each of the latest web browsers has its own version of web developer tools that make creating websites easier and more efficient.

Web developer tools allow you to quickly look at HTML elements and the CSS applied to them. You can also make live alterations to CSS within a browser's web developer tools, often a quicker way to experiment with styles. Figure 1-5 shows Google Chrome's web developer tools.

You use these tools later in the book, but for now, you might want to familiarize yourself with opening them in your chosen browser.

FIGURE 1-5 The web developer tools open in Google Chrome.

Opening Web Developer Tools in Desktop Browsers

Browser	Web Developer Tool's Name	Mac Shortcut	Mac Menu Navigation	Windows Shortcut	Windows Menu Navigation
Chrome	Developer Tools	Option + Command + I	View → Developer → Developer Tools	Ctrl + Shift + I	Settings icon (wrench) → Tools → Developer Tools
Safari	Web Inspector	Option + Command + I	Develop → Show Web Inspector	Ctrl + Alt + I	Menu icon (page) → Develop → Show Web Inspector*
Firefox	Firebug (Add-on; see following note)	N/A	View → Firebug	F12	Firefox → Web Developer → Firebug

Browser	Web Developer Tool's Name	Mac Shortcut	Mac Menu Navigation	Windows Shortcut	Windows Menu Navigation
Opera	Dragonfly	Option + Command + I	View ➜ Developer Tools ➜ Opera Dragonfly	Ctrl + Shift + I	View ➜ Developer Tools ➜ Opera Dragonfly
Internet Explorer	F12 Developer Tools	N/A	N/A	F12	Settings icon (cog) ➜ F12 Developer Tools

*Safari's Develop menu must first be switched on under Preferences ➜ Advanced.

Prior to version 10, Firefox didn't come with built-in developer tools. I highly recommend an add-on called Firebug both in the absence of tools prior to version 10 and in place of the built-in tools available from version 10 onward. Firebug has more features than the built-in tools and is more consistent with those available in other browsers.

To install Firebug, in Firefox, click Tools ➜ Add-Ons to open the Add-Ons Manager. Search for Firebug and then click the Install button. After it is downloaded, click Restart Now (or close and reopen Firefox manually) to complete the installation.

Text Editors

A text editor is the tool used to write CSS. Text editors also allow for writing HTML, JavaScript, and many other languages that make up the web.

Text editors allow you to do just that—edit text. You would expect them all to be quite similar, but actually, text editors come with many differing features. Most come with features that speed up your writing of CSS (and other web technologies). Some come with File Transfer Protocol (FTP) clients and What You See Is What You Get (WYSIWYG) editors.

A WYSIWYG editor allows you to build a website without your having any knowledge of code. Although this idea sounds great, in reality, it's not! When you are using these tools—dragging elements into the positions you want—the editor is given the responsibility of generating the code for you. These types of editors are rarely up to date with the latest coding standards and can never do as good a job of coding a website as you or I. Generated code is almost always bloated (more code than needed) and doesn't exercise the best practices you learn in this book, leading to a poor experience for the visitors to your website. Should your text editor also come with a WYSIWYG editor (such as Adobe Dreamweaver), that's fine; just choose to ignore it and make use of the text editor feature instead.

If you don't already have one, I recommend using a basic text editor to begin with. TextEdit (for Mac users) or Notepad (for Windows users) already come installed on your computer and are perfectly acceptable to use. They don't offer any features beyond editing your text, but that's all you need to start.

Throughout *CSS3 Foundations,* I use a text editor for Mac called Espresso (`www.macrabbit.com/espresso/`).

Summary

The web could exist without CSS, but it would never be as accessible or pretty as it is today. Its importance—in particular the new features introduced in CSS3—grows significantly as the ways in which people access the web change. CSS continues to advance, with many exciting features being introduced. Now is a great time to jump in and start learning how to use it.

With the necessary tools to begin creating CSS and web pages, in the next chapter you will get started with the project files built on throughout *CSS3 Foundations*. You'll take the page seen in Figure 1-1, and turn it into the styled page seen in Figure 1-2.

chapter two
Getting Started

AS YOU MAKE your way through *CSS3 Foundations*, you learn CSS from the basics to the more advanced topics, all the while adding to an overall project that will eventually become a fully featured web page.

Often, I find the best way to learn new things is to create a scenario with particular restrictions and an end goal. In doing this, you can focus on reaching that end goal by limiting the number of choices you have to make (an infinite number of choices is often scary and off-putting, so it's always good to define boundaries!). This approach to learning also means you have to make some real-world decisions to get the best possible outcome for the project.

So, without further ado, I'd like to introduce you to the fictitious company Cool Shoes & Socks (CSS for short—get it?).

The folks at Cool Shoes & Socks have asked you to style the company's website for them. This web-savvy company, like the name says, sells cool shoes and socks. The staff have given you the go-ahead to use CSS3 on the website; their only caveat is that you must make the website gracefully degrade in browsers that don't support CSS3. The company is also very aware that the web is accessed on many different types of devices (and its underfunded research department has determined socks will be able to access the web in the near future), so having a Responsive Web Design is very important to everyone involved.

Cool Shoes & Socks has already had the HTML of the site written and handed it to you to begin implementing CSS and modifying the HTML should that be necessary.

Getting Started with the Project Files

In a moment you will download the Cool Shoes & Socks project files that are built on throughout *CSS3 Foundations*. At specific milestones in the book, the most up-to-date project files are made available for you to reference or in case you want to skip a section and start at a different point. These milestones are marked in the book, along with the project file number and a link to where you can download it.

Downloading the Project Files

Go to www.wiley.com/go/treehouse/css3foundations in your web browser, where you can download the project files. The project files are contained within a Zip file that you should unzip into the location of your choosing.

Example, I unzipped the files to the following directories:

- Windows: C:/Users/Ian/Sites/CSS3 Foundations/
- Mac: Users/Ian/Sites/CSS3 Foundations/

Folder Structure and Good Practices

When you unzip the downloaded file, you are presented with folders named *website* followed by a chapter and milestone number, such as *(ch02-00)*, representing the first milestone of Chapter 2 (the one you begin with). Each website folder contains the project files that are worked on throughout *CSS3 Foundations*. My personal recommendation is to keep the files within the website folder. So, my folder structure looks like this:

Users/Ian/Sites/CSS3 Foundations/website (ch02-00)/

Often, you might want to save files that aren't part of the website but relate to it (such as notes, instructions from a client, images that have yet to be edited), so it's a good idea to have a *website* folder within the project folder to keep it separate from those extra files.

Within the *website (ch02-00)* folder, you find the following folders and files:

- css
- fonts
  - Average-OFL.txt
  - Average-Regular.eot
  - Average-Regular.woff
  - Belgrano-OFL.txt
  - Belgrano-Regular.eot
  - Belgrano-Regular.woff
- images
  - banner-25percent.png
  - banner-shoes.jpg
  - banner-socks.jpg
  - banner-trainers.jpg
  - bdr-footer.png
  - bg-blog.png
  - bg-body.jpg
  - bg-footer.jpg
  - bg-newsletter.png
  - check.png
  - icon-newsletter.png
  - logo-small.png
  - logo.png
  - socks-horses.png
- index.html

A good practice is to separate external files (those separate from the main HTML files, known as *assets* or *dependent files*) into their own folders. Being organized in this way speeds up your workflow and makes managing a website easier.

Another good practice is to follow consistent naming conventions for your images. For example, bg-body.jpg and bg-footer.jpg are so called because they are applied as backgrounds (*bg,* meaning background). Multiple versions of the company logo exist, all beginning with the prefix *logo-,* which keeps them together alphabetically. As a website grows, using naming conventions such as these makes finding your files quicker.

Of course, these are only my personal preferences; you may like to use different naming conventions or folder structures that work better for you.

Understanding the HTML Template

The web page template (index.html) is written in HTML5. Because you will build on and style one page in *CSS3 Foundations,* links to other pages are only included to represent and demonstrate a real-world web page. `href` links are given the value #, which means the page only refers to itself. Should you wish to add more pages in the future, feel free to change the links. index.html in all of its glory:

```
<!DOCTYPE html>
<html lang="en">
  <head>
      <meta charset="utf-8" />
      <title>Cool Shoes &amp; Socks</title>
      <!--[if lt IE 9]>
      <script src="http://html5shiv.googlecode.com/svn/trunk/html5.
js"></script>
      <![endif]-->
  </head>
  <body>
      <header id="header" class="group" role="banner">
          <a href="#" title="Return to the front page">
              <img class="logo" src="images/logo.png" alt="Cool
Shoes &amp; Socks" />
          </a>

          <nav role="navigation">
              <ul>
                  <li>
                      <a href="#" title="Return to the front
page">Home</a>
                  </li>
                  <li>
                      <a href="#" title="About Company
Name">About</a>
                  </li>
                  <li class="products">
                      <a href="#" title="Visit our shop">Shop</a>
                  </li>
```

```
            <li>
                <a href="#" title="Contact us">Contact</a>
            </li>
        </ul>
    </nav>
</header>

<div class="showcase">
    <img src="images/banner-trainers.jpg" alt="Some of our
cool trainers" />
    <a class="button purchase" href="#" title="Purchase
product">
        More Information
    </a>
</div>

<div id="main" class="group">
    <div id="content" role="main">
        <h1>Page Title</h1>
        <p>Nulla facilisi. Ut porttitor sollicitudin nisi,
tempus pulvinar nisl volutpat aliquet. Phasellus posuere auctor
accumsan. Ut in odio eget dui pulvinar sollicitudin. Sed vitae
tortor nibh. Aenean nec sapien quam, sit amet dapibus lorem.
Phasellus ac pharetra tellus. Curabitur pretium eros sit amet
nisl pretium mollis.</p>
        <p class="offer">
            All products now have <span class="strike">15%</
span> 25% off!
        </p>
        <p>Nulla facilisi. Ut porttitor sollicitudin nisi,
tempus pulvinar nisl volutpat aliquet.</p>
        <img class="product" src="images/socks-horses.png"
alt="Horse Socks" />
        <p>Nulla facilisi. Ut porttitor sollicitudin nisi,
tempus pulvinar nisl volutpat aliquet. Phasellus posuere auctor
accumsan. Ut in odio eget dui pulvinar sollicitudin. Sed vitae
tortor nibh. Aenean nec sapien quam, sit amet dapibus lorem.
Phasellus ac pharetra tellus. Curabitur pretium eros sit amet
nisl pretium mollis.</p>
        <p>Nulla facilisi. Ut porttitor sollicitudin nisi,
tempus pulvinar nisl volutpat aliquet.</p>
        <div class="benefits">
            <h3>Why Choose Cool Shoes &amp; Socks?</h3>
            <ul>
                <li>World's Largest Range of Shoes &amp;
Socks</li>
```

```
                          <li>Next-Day Free Delivery</li>
                          <li>Money Back Guarantee</li>
                    </ul>
              </div>
        </div>

        <div class="sidebar" role="complementary">
              <aside>
                    <h3>What our Customers are Saying</h3>
                    <ul class="testimonials">
                          <li>
                                <blockquote>
                                      <p>Integer aliquet, lacus in
ultricies venenatis, eros urna faucibus tellus, sed
sollicitudin.</p>
                                            <cite>
                                                  <a href="http://www.ianlunn.co.
uk/" title="Visit Ian Lunn's website">Ian Lunn</a>
                                            </cite>
                                </blockquote>
                          </li>
                    </ul>
              </aside>

              <aside class="post">
                    <h3>
                          <img src="images/bg-blog.png" alt="Latest
Blog Post" />

                          Latest Blog Post
                    </h3>
                    <p>Nulla facilisi. Ut porttitor sollicitudin
nisi, tempus pulvinar nisl volutpat aliquet. Phasellus posuere
auctor accumsan. Ut in odio eget dui pulvinar sollicitudin. Sed
vitae tortor nibh. Aenean nec sapien quam, sit amet dapibus
lorem. Phasellus ac pharetra tellus. Curabitur pretium eros sit
amet nisl pretium mollis.</p>
                    <p>Nulla facilisi. Ut porttitor sollicitudin
nisi, tempus pulvinar nisl volutpat aliquet. Phasellus posuere
auctor accumsan. Ut in odio eget dui pulvinar sollicitudin. Sed
vitae tortor nibh. Aenean nec sapien quam, sit amet dapibus
lorem. Phasellus ac pharetra tellus. Curabitur pretium eros sit
amet nisl pretium mollis.</p>
              </aside>
```

```
                <aside>
                    <form id="newsletter" action="#">
                        <h3>Newsletter</h3>
                        <p>Sign up for news and special offers
    delivered to your inbox monthly.</p>
                        <label>Name: </label>
                        <input type="text" placeholder="Your Name" />

                        <label>Email: </label>
                        <input type="email" placeholder="Your Email
    Address" />


                        <input class="button" id="submit-newsletter"
    type="submit" value="Sign Up" />
                    </form>
                </aside>
            </div>
        </div>
        <footer id="footer" role="contentinfo">
            <ul class="container">
                <li class="small-logo">
                    <a href="#" title="Return to the front page">
                        Cool Shoes &amp; Socks
                    </a>
                </li>
                <li class="back-to-top">
                    <a href="#header" title="Go back to the top of
    the page">
                        Back to Top
                    </a>
                </li>
            </ul>
        </footer>
    </body>
</html>
```

So, what does this code mean?

The first line, `<!DOCTYPE html>,` specifies the type of markup the *document* (the technical term for a web page) will use; in this case, it uses HTML.

Next is the <head>, which is the location where you place metadata about the web page. The template's <head> contains the charset (which tells the browser what character encoding to use) and the title of the page. You also use <head> to add resources such as stylesheets and

JavaScript, among other metadata. Because the template is built using HTML5 elements—which isn't supported by Internet Explorer 6, 7, and 8—a script is referenced here that makes those browsers understand HTML5. Conditional comments are used to make the script apply only to Internet Explorer versions below version 9. Conditional comments are explained in Chapter 15.

```
<head>
    <meta charset="utf-8" />
    <title>Cool Shoes &amp; Socks</title>
    <!--[if lt IE 9]>
        <script src="http://html5shiv.googlecode.com/svn/trunk/
   html5.js">
        </script>
    <![endif]-->
</head>
```

The <body> tags follow the closing </head> tag. Here, you place the structure and content of the page:

```
<body>
    ...
</body>
```

Inside the <body> tags is the header of the web page:

```
<header id="header" class="group" role="banner">
    <a href="#" title="Return to the front page">
        <img class="logo" src="images/logo.png" alt="Cool Shoes
   &amp; Socks" />
    </a>

    <nav role="navigation">
        <ul>
            <li>
                <a href="#" title="Return to the front page">Home</
   a>
            </li>
            <li>
                <a href="#" title="About Company Name">About</a>
            </li>
            <li class="products">
                <a href="#" title="Visit our shop">Shop</a>
            </li>
            <li>
                <a href="#" title="Contact us">Contact</a>
```

```
        </li>
      </ul>
    </nav>
</header>
```

The header <header> is given the ID header, the class group and the role banner. IDs, classes, roles, and other additional information within element tags are known as *attributes*. In CSS, you can select elements based on their attributes.

The role attribute lets screen readers (software used by people with disabilities such as visual impairment) know that this particular section of the page is a banner, defined as being "a region that contains mostly site-oriented content, rather than page-specific content" (www. w3.org/TR/wai-aria/roles#banner). The roles model is another specification being developed by the W3C, which aims to improve the accessibility of web pages for persons with disabilities. For more information, see www.w3.org/TR/wai-aria/.

The header also contains the Cool Shoes & Socks logo and site navigation.

Underneath the header is a *product showcase*:

```
<div class="showcase">
    <img src="images/banner-trainers.jpg" alt="Some of our cool
  trainers" />
    <a class="button purchase" href="#" title="Purchase product">
        More Information
    </a>
</div>
```

The product showcase contains one large image and a call to action that links to more information about the product. A *call to action (CTA)* is an area of the page that aims to grab the attention of web page visitors and lead them through to achieving a particular goal. The product showcase is the place where Cool Shoes & Socks can show off its best products and latest offers; the CTA aims to lead visitors through to finding out more information about the products and potentially buying some shoes or socks. Employing calls to action is a classic technique used across many sites on the web. A CTA often stands out from the rest of the page to draw visitors' eyes to it, leading them to complete an action. Using CSS, you can make this button stand out from the rest of the page to achieve that goal.

After the product showcase is the main content of the page. First, look at the main structure of this section:

```
<div id="main" class="group">
    <div id="content" role="main">
        . . .
```

```
        </div>

        <div class="sidebar" role="complementary">
            <aside>
                …
            </aside>
        </div>
    </div>
</div>
```

The line `<div id="main" class="group">` contains the content of the page as well as a sidebar that holds customer testimonials, the latest blog posts and a newsletter sign up form. The preceding code shows only the structure of this main section. As you make your way through *CSS3 Foundations*, you learn how to create columns, placing the content on the left, with the sidebar to its right. Again, this code uses role attributes to assist screen readers.

Finally, prior to the closing of the `</body>` and `</html>` tags, you see the pages footer:

```
<footer id="footer" role="contentinfo">
    <ul class="container">
        <li class="small-logo">
            <a href="#" title="Return to the front page">Cool Shoes
    &amp; Socks</a>
        </li>
        <li class="back-to-top">
            <a href="#header" title="Go back to the top of the
    page">Back to Top</a>
        </li>
    </ul>
</footer>
```

The footer holds a link to the front of the page and a link to the top of the page.

Figure 2-1 shows index.html when viewed in a web browser. The template doesn't much resemble a web page yet, does it? All the information is there and so too is the navigation, but it doesn't look that great.

In Figure 2-1, notice that the content of the page is gibberish. This sort of text is known as *Lorem Ipsum*. It's dummy text that can be used to fill out a web page with content, prior to real content being put in place. By using dummy text, you can see how a page will look and function before you get any real content.

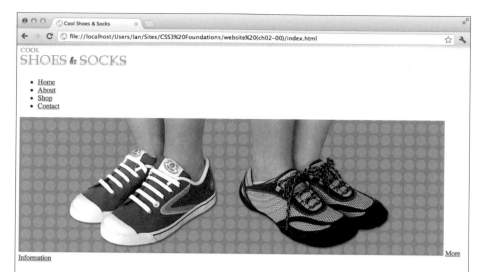

COOL
SHOES & SOCKS

- Home
- About
- Shop
- Contact

Information   More

Page Title

Nulla facilisi. Ut porttitor sollicitudin nisi, tempus pulvinar nisl volutpat aliquet. Phasellus posuere auctor accumsan. Ut in odio eget dui pulvinar sollicitudin. Sed vitae tortor nibh. Aenean nec sapien quam, sit amet dapibus lorem. Phasellus ac pharetra tellus. Curabitur pretium eros sit amet nisl pretium mollis.

All products now have 15% 25% off!

Nulla facilisi. Ut porttitor sollicitudin nisi, tempus pulvinar nisl volutpat aliquet.

Nulla facilisi. Ut porttitor sollicitudin nisi, tempus pulvinar nisl volutpat aliquet. Phasellus posuere auctor accumsan. Ut in odio eget dui pulvinar sollicitudin. Sed vitae tortor nibh. Aenean nec sapien quam, sit amet dapibus lorem. Phasellus ac pharetra tellus. Curabitur pretium eros sit amet nisl pretium mollis.

Nulla facilisi. Ut porttitor sollicitudin nisi, tempus pulvinar nisl volutpat aliquet.

Why Choose Cool Shoes & Socks?

- World's Largest Range of Shoes & Socks
- Next-Day Free Delivery
- Money Back Guarantee

What our Customers are Saying

- Integer aliquet, lacus in ultricies venenatis, eros urna faucibus tellus, sed sollicitudin.

  Ian Lunn

Latest Blog Post

Nulla facilisi. Ut porttitor sollicitudin nisi, tempus pulvinar nisl volutpat aliquet. Phasellus posuere auctor accumsan. Ut in odio eget dui pulvinar sollicitudin. Sed vitae tortor nibh. Aenean nec sapien quam, sit amet dapibus lorem. Phasellus ac pharetra tellus. Curabitur pretium eros sit amet nisl pretium mollis.

Nulla facilisi. Ut porttitor sollicitudin nisi, tempus pulvinar nisl volutpat aliquet. Phasellus posuere auctor accumsan. Ut in odio eget dui pulvinar sollicitudin. Sed vitae tortor nibh. Aenean nec sapien quam, sit amet dapibus lorem. Phasellus ac pharetra tellus. Curabitur pretium eros sit amet nisl pretium mollis.

Newsletter

Sign up for news and special offers delivered to your inbox monthly.

Name: [Your Name]   Email: [Your Email Address]   [Sign Up]

- Cool Shoes & Socks
- Back to Top

FIGURE 2-1 The index.html file when viewed in Google Chrome.

Getting Started with CSS

To create a new stylesheet file, follow these steps:

1. In your text editor, create a new file and name it styles.css.

2. Save the file in the css folder of your website project.

You must now reference that stylesheet in the web page.

Adding CSS to a Page

As you saw in the HTML template, the <head> is the place where you add metadata and reference the resources on which the page relies.

In the <head> section of index.html, reference the stylesheet you just created as follows:

```
<head>
    <meta charset="utf-8" />
    <title>Cool Shoes &amp; Socks</title>
    <link rel="stylesheet" href="css/styles.css" type="text/css"
media="all" />
    <!--[if lt IE 9]>
        <script src="http://html5shiv.googlecode.com/svn/trunk/
html5.js">
        </script>
        <![endif]-->
</head>
```

Here, you add a link for which the relationship (rel) to this page is a stylesheet. The hypertext reference (href) points to the place where that stylesheet is located within your project files and is of type text/css. This stylesheet will be utilized across all media types. More on media types shortly. Note that when a page is using the HTML5 doctype <!DOCTYPE html>, specifying the type is optional.

Often, you require multiple stylesheets per page. To do this, you can simply add another <link>:

```
<link rel="stylesheet" href="css/styles.css" type="text/css"
  media="all" />
<link rel="stylesheet" href="css/styles2.css" type="text/css"
  media="all" />
```

Alternatively, within a stylesheet, you can use the @import rule, which is a reference from one stylesheet to another and can be added anywhere within a stylesheet:

```
@import url("styles2.css");
@import url("styles3.css");
```

Which approach is better? `<link>` performs better over `@import` (you can find out more about the performance impact of `@import` at: www.stevesouders.com/blog/2009/04/09/dont-use-import/) but on a live web page (on the web and viewable by everyone), neither approach is best!

When you're creating a web page, separating styles into multiple sheets is a good idea to make managing styles easier. However, when a site is live, ideally, you should have only one stylesheet. This is best practice, making a web page more efficient. Whether you choose to use multiple `<link>` references within the HTML or use `@import` in your main stylesheet is entirely your choice. Just remember for good practice, you should merge all stylesheets into one when it's time for a web page to go live. This is something you'll do in Chapter 17.

Using Media Types

As mentioned in Chapter 1, you can apply a stylesheet to specific media types, such as screen, print, and handheld. Note that if a media attribute isn't specified, a browser treats that referenced stylesheet as applying to all media types, like so:

```
<link rel="stylesheet" href="css/styles.css" type="text/css" />
```

This is a safe (it works in all browsers) and slightly quicker way of referencing a stylesheet.

What about multiple stylesheets for different media types? No problem. Assume styles.css is the main CSS file applied to all media types, but you decide you want to add an extra stylesheet that is only applied when you print the web page. You can do that like so:

```
<link rel="stylesheet" href="css/styles.css" type="text/css" />
<link rel="stylesheet" href="css/print.css" type="text/css"
  media="print" />
```

Here, the first `<link>` references a stylesheet to be applied to all media types (because you haven't specified a media type). However, the second `<link>` references a stylesheet specifically for print. The main stylesheet still applies to all media types (including print), but the additional print stylesheet applies only to the print media type.

Sometimes styles within the print stylesheet can override the ones in the main stylesheet. Most of the time this will be intentional, but sometimes you get conflicts. The next chapter covers specificity and importance that determines which styles should be applied when style conflicts occur.

Much like using the @import rule for adding additional stylesheets into another stylesheet, you can also use the @media rule for defining styles for specific media types within a stylesheet.

Assume you have just one main stylesheet, like the following:

```
<link rel="stylesheet" href="css/styles.css" type="text/css" />
```

Rather than adding another <link> to reference a print stylesheet, within styles.css, you can add the following with the main stylesheet:

```
@media print{
    /*print styles here*/
}
```

Any styles within this @media rule are applied only to printed web pages. Anything outside this rule is applied to all media types.

You may find using media rules more desirable because it means referencing only one stylesheet, which is more efficient.

Inline Styles

In the earlier days of the web, it was possible to use inline styles, forgoing the need for a referenced stylesheet. In fact, you still are able to use inline styles today, *but* it's advisable that you don't.

Inline styles are those applied directly to HTML, as follows:

```
<body style="color: blue; margin: 10px;">
```

By applying styles in this way, you lose all the benefits previously mentioned. No longer can styles be shared across pages, pages become more difficult to maintain, and styles can't be tailored to suit differing types of devices and environments.

Although the web has, fortunately, moved away from inline styles, e-mail hasn't. E-mails are also created using HTML and CSS, but unlike the web, the standards and technologies haven't moved forward.

E-mail clients are in the unfortunate position of relying on old technologies with a lack of standardization, and because of that, they often don't support the CSS used in today's modern web. Therefore, if you want to create an HTML/CSS-based e-mail, it is better to use inline styles.

User Agent Stylesheets

Before you begin applying styles to a page, it's important to understand that browsers apply their own default stylesheet to every web page—often referred to as a *user agent stylesheet*.

User agent stylesheets add default styles to HTML elements. These styles make an HTML page without any custom CSS applied to it instantly readable. When creating a web page using these stylesheets, you don't have to apply all the default CSS styles as defined by the CSS specification to elements yourself.

Figures 2-2 and 2-3 show the web page in Chrome and Internet Explorer 9, respectively. You may notice differences between the two. For example, the logo in Internet Explorer 9 has a blue border around it, but in Chrome it doesn't. The reason is that these two browsers use different user agent stylesheets. Microsoft, the vendor of Internet Explorer 9, made the decision that a linked image should have a border around it; otherwise, you have no visual indication that it's a link. Microsoft makes a fair point; but in most cases, this border is undesirable, and furthermore, no other modern browser does that.

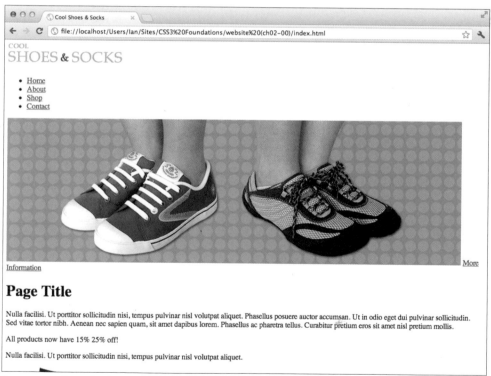

FIGURE 2-2 The index.html file when viewed in Google Chrome.

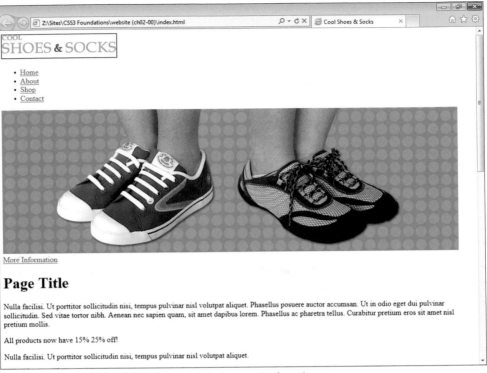

FIGURE 2-3 The index.html file when viewed in Internet Explorer 9.

In modern browsers, user agent stylesheets are similar, making creating cross-browser-compatible (pages that work in all browsers) pages easier, but particularly in older browsers, consistency isn't so good. You can be thankful that there's an easy solution to fix these inconsistencies.

Using a CSS Reset for Better Browser Consistency

A CSS Reset is a set of styles that overwrite user agent styles, making the default styles as consistent as possible across all browsers. Eric Meyer (www.meyerweb.com/eric/), an industry leader, has worked on improving this technique over many years, producing a small set of styles that make writing CSS much easier from the start.

By using a CSS Reset, you must add a few default styles back into your own CSS, because they are almost certainly required, but that is a small task when you consider how much easier it is to begin with consistent styles across all browsers.

To add a CSS Reset to the web page, follow these steps:

1. Copy and paste Eric Meyer's CSS Reset from www.meyerweb.com/eric/tools/css/reset/

2. Create a new file and name it reset.css.

3. Paste the CSS Reset into reset.css.

4. Save reset.css into your css folder (which should already contain styles.css).

5. In styles.css, add the following:

   ```
   @import url("reset.css");
   ```

6. Save styles.css.

You've now added an additional stylesheet and imported it into the main stylesheet. Remember, using multiple stylesheets when you create your web page makes for a more efficient workflow, but before you make a website live, it's good practice to add all stylesheets into one. If you'd like to do that now, simply paste Eric Meyer's CSS Reset into the top of styles.css instead of a new file.

Eric Meyer's CSS Reset as of July 2012:

```
/* http://meyerweb.com/eric/tools/css/reset/
   v2.0 | 20110126
   License: none (public domain)
*/

html, body, div, span, applet, object, iframe,
h1, h2, h3, h4, h5, h6, p, blockquote, pre,
a, abbr, acronym, address, big, cite, code,
del, dfn, em, img, ins, kbd, q, s, samp,
small, strike, strong, sub, sup, tt, var,
b, u, i, center,
dl, dt, dd, ol, ul, li,
fieldset, form, label, legend,
table, caption, tbody, tfoot, thead, tr, th, td,
article, aside, canvas, details, embed,
figure, figcaption, footer, header, hgroup,
menu, nav, output, ruby, section, summary,
time, mark, audio, video {
    margin: 0;
    padding: 0;
    border: 0;
```

```css
        font-size: 100%;
        font: inherit;
        vertical-align: baseline;
}
/* HTML5 display-role reset for older browsers */
article, aside, details, figcaption, figure,
footer, header, hgroup, menu, nav, section {
        display: block;
}
body {
        line-height: 1;
}
ol, ul {
        list-style: none;
}
blockquote, q {
        quotes: none;
}
blockquote:before, blockquote:after,
q:before, q:after {
        content: '';
        content: none;
}
table {
        border-collapse: collapse;
        border-spacing: 0;
}
```

You come to understand this CSS in the following chapters.

After you add a CSS Reset, compare the web page in Chrome and Internet Explorer 9 again (see Figures 2-4 and 2-5). They're much more consistent now, right? The blue border has been removed from the logo in Internet Explorer 9 and the spacing between elements is almost exactly the same.

In these figures, you may notice that a lot of the spacing between elements has been removed, but you add that again shortly.

FIGURE 2-4 The index.html file in Chrome with a CSS Reset applied to it.

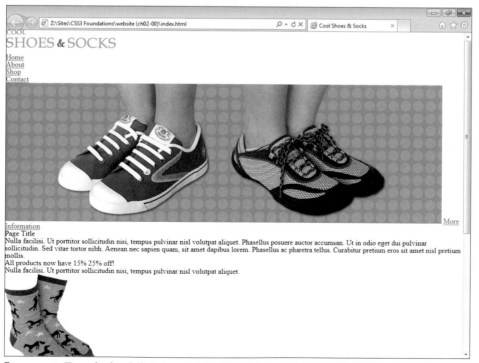

FIGURE 2-5 The index.html file in Internet Explorer 9 with a CSS Reset applied to it.

Summary

In this chapter, you've set up the project files that are worked on throughout *CSS3 Foundations*. By adding a CSS Reset to the project, you've given yourself a more consistent base to begin working from.

In the next chapter, you'll learn about the syntax of CSS (the rules of how it should be written), and start selecting elements to be styled using Selectors.

part 2

Learning CSS Syntax and Adding Presentational Styles

chapter three

Mastering the Power of CSS Selectors

IN THIS CHAPTER, you will learn to master the power of CSS selectors, which allow you to select any HTML element to be styled. Selectors have a very friendly learning curve and are easy to start with but can become more advanced as and when you are ready.

Writing Your First Styles

CSS is a collection of *rule sets* (also called *rules*), which consist of a selector and a declaration.

A *selector* is used to select the element you want to apply styles to, and a *declaration* is the combination of a property and a value for that element, as shown in Figure 3-1. You learn about property values in the next chapter and properties from Chapter 5 onward.

Selector Property Value

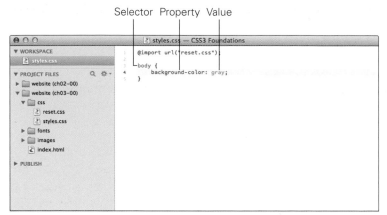

FIGURE 3-1 A rule set that changes the background color of the <body> element, written in Espresso text editor.

You end a declaration with a semicolon; this way, you are able to add multiple declarations within the same rule set.

Project Files Update (ch03-00): If you haven't followed the previous instructions and are comfortable working from here onward or would like to reference the project files up to this point, you can download them from www.wiley.com/go/treehouse/css3foundations.

Go ahead and add the style shown in Figure 3-1 to the page.

1. Open styles.css and add the following:

```
body {
    background-color: gray;
}
```

2. Save styles.css.

To see the affect of this rule, open index.html in your browser of choice. Whenever you save a modification made to styles.css, index.html, or any other file, you should refresh the browser to see the most up-to-date version of the page.

The rule you just added to styles.css tells the browser to select the <body> HTML element and apply the background color gray to it.

What if you want to add another style to the <body> element? Rather than add another body selector, you can simply define a second declaration within this rule, as shown here:

1. Inside the `body` selector, below the `background-color` declaration, add the following:

   `background-image: url("../images/bg-body.jpg");`

2. Save styles.css

Note that in CSS, a word followed by parentheses is known as a *function*. A function requires at least one *argument* (depending on the function being used), which, in the case of the `url()` function, is the path to an image. In Chapter 5 you will learn more about `background-image` and what exactly those two dots mean in the path.

You now see a background image applied to the body of the page, as shown in Figure 3-2. What happened to the background color? Don't worry; it's still there! The browser sees that you've added both a background color and background image to the same selector. The browser knows that a background image has more detail than a background color and is the preferred choice. So why add a background color if it's hidden behind an image? In some cases, the browser may not download images (a user can turn them off, for example, or a technical issue may prevent the image from being downloaded and displayed). If this happens, the page still has a background color similar to that of the image. Also, an image may be too small to cover the whole background; the areas that it doesn't cover show the background color.

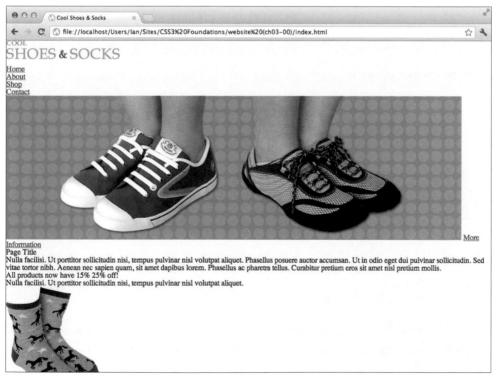

FIGURE 3-2 The page with a background image applied to it.

If you've had a good look through the project files, you may have noticed that the image bg-body.jpg is small (only 40 × 40 pixels), yet the background image when viewed in the browser covers the whole page. The reason is that a background image, by default, repeats, so when viewing the page in a browser, the background image is repeated multiple times to cover the whole page. More on background images in Chapter 5.

Inheritance and the Relationship Between Elements

Just before you begin selecting elements to style, it's a good idea to understand CSS inheritance and the relationship between elements.

When applying a style to an element, depending on the property being used, that style may be inherited by other elements. The following rule set makes text in the <body> element blue:

```
body {
    color: blue;
}
```

Assume this is applied to the following HTML (a simplified version of index.html):

```
<body>
    <div id="main" class="group">
        <h1>Page Title</h1>
        <p>Nulla facilisi. Ut porttitor sollicitudin nisi, tempus
  pulvinar nisl volutpat aliquet.</p>
    </div>
</body>
```

Although the <body> element doesn't contain any text itself, the text within <h1> and <p> will still have the blue color applied to them. This is because the color property is inherited. From Chapter 5 onward, *CSS3 Foundations* explains properties in greater depth and points out whether each is inherited.

What is meant by inherited, though? Because <body> in the HTML example contains the <h1> and <p> elements, they are known as the *descendants* of <body>. An inherited property is one that is passed down and applied to descendant elements, unless that element overrides it with a property of its own.

Descendants can also be referred to as *children*, but only when an element is the direct descendant of another. For example: the <h1> and <p> elements are descendants of <body> and children of <div id="main" class="group">. Likewise, <div id="main" class="group"> is a child of <body>.

An element that contains other elements may be called the *parent*, and two elements at the same level (such as the <h1> and <p> in the example) are called *siblings*.

More advanced selectors allow you to select an element based on its relationship with others, which you will see shortly.

Selectors

Selectors are the conditions of a CSS rule set. The true power of selectors comes from their capability to be combined, allowing you to create very specific conditions, applying styles only to the exact element or elements you want.

Universal Selector

The *universal selector* is represented by an asterisk (*) and selects every element that makes up a web page:

```
*  {
    color: black;
}
```

In this example, every element is given a black text color. Note that this isn't a very effective method of applying this style, though. Because styles are inherited, rather than apply a style to *every* element, you could apply it to a body selector instead, which would give the exact same result, but a little quicker. Because each rule set is an action the browser carries out to turn HTML and CSS into a beautiful page, this sort of consideration means a browser can work faster and the user can see a page quicker. So, because it's not always the most efficient approach to styling multiples elements, universal selectors tend to be used with a combination of other selectors to make them apply only to specific elements rather than all of them. More on combining selectors shortly.

Type Selector

When you added a background color to the <body> element, you used a type selector to do that. A *type selector* is the name of an HTML element. A type selector can be used as follows:

1. In styles.css, add the following rule set:

```
h1 {
    font-weight: bold;
}
```

2. Save styles.css.

Here, you select the <h1> element—a type selector. This declaration makes the <h1> bold. Changing the font style is covered in more detail in Chapter 11.

 Unless otherwise specified, add new rule sets below others you've already added.

ID and Class Selectors

IDs and classes, which are attributes of an HTML element, allow you to be more specific when styling elements.

As you saw in the project files, some elements already have IDs and class attributes. The main content area, for example, is a <div> with an ID of main and class of group:

```
<div id="main" class="group">
```

If you use a type selector for this element to make its background color white, for example, you add the following to the CSS:

```
div {
    background-color: white;
}
```

The problem here is that although the main content area is now white, so too is every other <div> on the page. By using an ID selector instead, you can select just that particular <div>.

Go ahead and change the main content area's background color to white:

1. In styles.css, add the following:

```
#main {
    background-color: white;
}
```

2. Save styles.css.

A Note on Using and Naming Classes

The purpose of a class is modularity. When writing styles, you should ask yourself: "Could I use this style elsewhere?" If elements are to share similar styles, rather than write out two similar rule sets, you can use a class and apply that class to both elements.

When creating classes, also put some thought into their names. Although you're free to call a class whatever you like, consider whether the name of a class represents its purpose. If you come back to work on your web page in six months (or somebody else does), will your class names make sense then?

These are best practice approaches that you learn to use throughout *CSS3 Foundations*.

The hash or pound symbol (#) represents an ID. An ID should be used only once per page. Consequently, it allows you to be very specific when applying styles.

Similar to the ID is the less specific *class selector*. When elements on a page (or across a website) need to share the same styles, you should use a class selector. Unlike IDs, classes can be used on a page as many times as you want.

You will eventually apply quite a few styles to the call to action button described in Chapter 2 (remember its purpose is to attract the user's eye) and will use it multiple times on the same page. Because of this, it makes sense to use the button class for elements representing a button.

Style any element with the button class like so:

1. In styles.css, add the following:

```css
.button {
    background-color: hotpink;
    color: white;
}
```

2. Save styles.css.

The full-stop, period, or dot represents a class. Here, you make the background color hot pink and make the text of the button white. You take a closer look at these property values, known as *color keywords*, in the next chapter.

Grouping Selectors

Sometimes you may want to apply a style to more than one element. You recently made the text of the <h1> element bold but what if you want the subtitle elements such as <h2>, <h3>, and <h4> to be bold too? You could write a rule set that selects each element individually, but a quicker way is to group those selectors instead.

Cross Browser Compatibility for Advanced Selectors

Up to now, the selectors demonstrated are supported in all browsers in use today. However, the more advanced selectors have a varying level of support, which will be stated in the description of each selector.

That said, this lack of support for some advanced selectors can be corrected using a free script called Selectivizr, found at `www.selectivizr.com`. When completed, the Cool Shoes & Socks page will only use selectors with full browser support. Visit the Selectivizr website for installation instructions should you choose to use advanced selectors now or in the future.

1. In styles.css, find the h1 rule set:

```
h1 {
    font-weight: bold;
}
```

2. Modify the rule set to include other title elements, like so:

```
h1, h2, h3, h4 {
    font-weight: bold;
}
```

3. Save styles.css.

By separating each selector with a comma, you can apply the same styles to multiple elements.

Combinators

Combinators allow you to apply styles to elements based on their relationship with other elements. All the selectors you've learned up to now can be used with combinators to make even more specific selectors.

Descendant Combinators

A descendant selector describes the descendant of an element. Descendant combinators are great for styling elements that exist inside of other elements.

1. In styles.css, add the following:

```
blockquote p {
    font-style: italic;
}
```

2. Save styles.css.

In this example, only <p> elements that are descendants of <blockquote> will be made italic. By using a descendant combinator, you can be more specific about which elements you want to select.

Child Combinators

Sometimes, a descendant combinator isn't quite strict enough for your purposes. Follow these steps to use a child combinator:

1. In styles.css, add the following:

```
aside > h3 {
    font-weight: bold;
}
```

2. Save styles.css.

A child combinator is a greater-than character (>) placed between two selectors. With the selector you just added, the <h3> title element that is a child of the <aside> element will be made bold.

Child combinators are unsupported in Internet Explorer 6.

Sibling Combinators

CSS Level 3 introduces sibling combinators, allowing you to create selectors for elements when at the same level.

Adjacent Sibling Combinator

You can use the adjacent sibling combinator to style elements that share the same parent, providing one element immediately follows the other:

1. In styles.css, add the following:

```
p + .offer {
    color: red;
}
```

2. Save styles.css.

An adjacent sibling combinator is a plus symbol (+) placed between two selectors. With the selector you just added, the element <p class="offer"> is made red, *only* when it follows another <p> element.

Adjacent sibling combinators are unsupported in Internet Explorer 6.

General Sibling Combinator

Like the adjacent sibling combinator, elements making use of the general sibling combinator share the same parent; however, because their relationship is "general," one element doesn't have to immediately follow the other to be selected:

```
p ~ h2 {
    color: black;
}
```

Where an adjacent sibling selector selects only the element that immediately succeeds it, the general sibling selector in this example selects all <h2> elements that succeed a <p> element.

A general sibling combinator is a tilde symbol (~) placed between two selectors.

General sibling combinators are unsupported in Internet Explorer 6.

Attribute Selectors

Attribute selectors allow you to select elements by referring to their attributes, such as ID, class, title, src, and so on. "But wait," you cry! "Didn't you just cover IDs and classes?" Yes! Technically, the ID and class selectors you just learned about are their own unique types of selectors. You can also select IDs and classes using attribute selectors.

When you made the background color of the main section white, you used this rule set:

```
#main {
    background-color: white;
}
```

You can accomplish exactly the same goal using an attribute selector, like so:

```
div[id="main"] {
    background-color: white;
}
```

Which should you use? Because attribute selectors aren't supported in Internet Explorer 6, and ID and class selectors are just a little quicker to type anyway, I'd suggest using those instead.

Of course, elements can have a lot of other attributes you could use to create a selector. Here's an example:

1. In styles.css, add the following:

```
input[type="text"], input[type="email"] {
    border: none;
}
```

2. Save styles.css.

Here, you select the newsletter input fields with attribute types `text` and `email` and declare these elements should have no border.

The power of attribute selectors doesn't just end there.

Selecting Elements with an Attribute, Regardless of Its Value

This example selects an element such as `<a title="More information">`. As long as it has a title, it is selected regardless of the title's value:

```
a[title] {
    color: blue;
}
```

Selecting Elements with Multiple Attributes

The following example selects an element that has both of the attributes `type="submit"` and `class="button"`:

1. In styles.css, add the following:

```
input[type="submit"][class="button"] {
    font-size: 1em;
}
```

2. Save styles.css.

This will give the newsletter sign up button `<input class="button" id="submit-newsletter" type="submit" value="Sign Up" />` a font size of 1em. More on `font-size` in Chapter 11.

Other Attribute Selectors

Attribute selectors don't just stop there, but the remainders tend to be for more special use case situations, so they aren't covered in *CSS3 Foundations*.

These other attribute selectors allow you to select an element that:

- Contains multiple attribute values
- Has an attribute value list of hyphen-separated words
- Has an attribute value starting with, ending with, or containing a certain string of text

If the sound of those takes your fancy, I'd recommend reading more about them at reference.sitepoint.com/css/attributeselector.

Pseudo-Classes

Sometimes, a part of a web page isn't made up of a physical element, meaning it can't be selected through the use of a normal selector; this is where *pseudo-classes* come in use. Note that, unfortunately, pseudo-classes are not supported in all browsers and each of the following descriptions will state which browsers a pseudo-class is not be supported in. In *CSS3 Foundations*, you don't rely on too many pseudo-classes, and any issues that may occur in browsers that don't support these pseudo-classes are addressed in Chapter 16.

Dynamic Pseudo-Classes

Dynamic pseudo-classes allow you to style an element when it is interacted with—when a user hovers over it, for example.

At present, when a user hovers over links on the Cool Shoes & Socks page, the links don't change. You can use pseudo-classes to make it so:

1. In styles.css, add the following below the body rule set:

```
a:link {
    text-decoration: underline;
}

a:hover {
    text-decoration: none;
}
```

2. Save styles.css.

A pseudo-class consists of a colon (:) followed by the name of the pseudo-class. Here, you add two pseudo-class rule sets: one for an unvisited link and another for when a user is hovering over a link. An unvisited link is underlined, and when hovered over, that underline is removed. When the cursor moves away from the link (and is no longer being hovered over), the underline is applied again.

You can use other dynamic pseudo-classes along with `:hover`:

1. In styles.css, add the following:

```
a:visited {
    color: black;
}

a:active {
    color: red;
}

a:focus {
    outline-color: black;
    outline-style: dotted;
    outline-width: 1px;
}
```

2. Save styles.css.

The `:visited` styles indicate—you guessed it—a link that has been visited. When you make this link a different color, a user can quickly scan a page he is returning to should he wish to find where he navigated previously.

The `:active` style is applied when an element is activated by the user—that is, when the user presses the mouse button down on a link. Hold down your mouse button on a link, and you see its color change to red, until you release the mouse button.

Focus is when an interactive element is deemed to have the user's attention—when an input text box is clicked, for example. With the `:focus` pseudo-class, you add a very important style: the `outline` property. It may not seem that important at the moment, but it's crucial for accessibility. You take a deeper look at `outline` and its importance in Chapter 5.

It's possible for elements to have more than one pseudo-class at a time. A link can be both `:visited` and `:active`, for example. If you want to style a link such as that, you could use the following:

```
a:visited:active {
    color: orange;
}
```

Structural Pseudo-Classes

Structural pseudo-classes are used when you want to select elements based on generic criteria, such as the second <p> element amongst three.

Selecting Child Elements

The pseudo-class `:nth-child()` allows you to select a particular child element based on its position relative to its siblings within a parent element:

```
p:nth-child(1) {
    background-color: lightblue;
}
```

You should place an argument within the parentheses of `:nth-child()` to specify an element that is the *n*th element relative to its siblings; this can be either a number or the words odd or even. By selecting only odd or even elements, you can create an alternating color for rows within a table, for example (making the table easier to scan with the eye). Figure 3-3 shows this style applied to the Cool Shoes & Socks page.

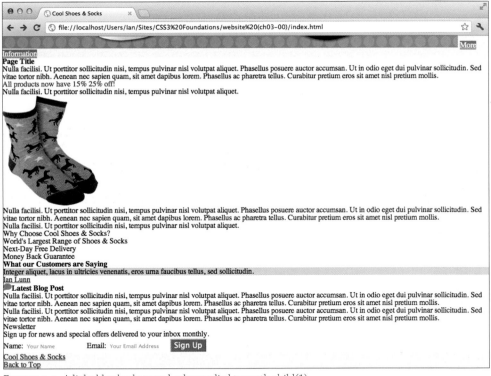

FIGURE 3-3 A light blue background color applied to p:nth-child(1).

The `<p>` element within the "What Our Customers Are Saying" section is given a light blue background because that is the only `<p>` element to be a first child among its siblings. The first child `<p>` elements within the content and newsletter sections are headings and not paragraphs, which is why the first paragraphs in those particular sections are not given the same background color.

Be aware that :nth-child(1) represents the first element, which can also be expressed as :first-child. Similarly, you can use :last-child to select the last element, or if you want to start counting from the last child, you can use :nth-last-child(), where :nth-last-child(1) is the last element and :nth-last-child(2) is the element next to the last.

You can also select an element if it is the only child of its parent (it has no siblings), using :only-child.

nth-child() isn't supported in Internet Explorer versions 6, 7, and 8.

Selecting Child Elements of a Particular Type

Where :nth-child() selects a child element based on its position among its siblings (regardless of what types of element they are), :nth-of-type() does the same but counts only siblings of the same type:

```
p:nth-of-type(1) {
    background-color: lightblue;
}
```

Figure 3-4 shows this style applied to the Cool Shoes & Socks page, in place of the :nth-child(1) rule. Now, three <p> elements are given a background color of light blue.

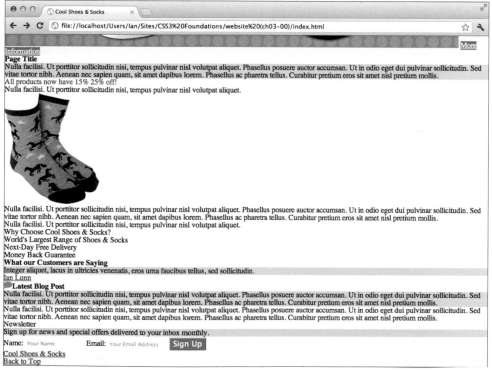

FIGURE 3-4 A light blue background color applied to p:nth-of-type(1).

As with `:nth-child()`, `:nth-of-type()` has similar variants. `:nth-last-of-type()` allows for counting elements of the same type from the last child. `:first-of-type` selects the first element of a specific type, and `:last-of-type` selects the last element of a specific type. Finally, `:only-of-type` selects an element if it is the only child of the specified type (it *can* have siblings, but only those that aren't of the same type).

`:nth-child()`, `:first-of-type()`, `:last-of-type()`, and `:only-of-type()` aren't supported in Internet Explorer versions 6, 7, and 8.

Selecting Empty Elements

Usually, you should aim to avoid having empty elements on a page (although they are sometimes used for dynamic sites where content is added after the browser or a user carries out a particular action). To select an empty element, use the `:empty` pseudo-class.

`:empty()` isn't supported in Internet Explorer versions 6, 7, and 8.

Selecting the Root Element

The root of a web page can be selected using `:root`, which most often is the `<html>` element.

`:root()` isn't supported in Internet Explorer versions 6, 7, and 8.

The Target Pseudo-Class

You are able to place an anchor link on a page that refers to a section on that same page.

At the bottom of the Cool Shoes & Socks page, there is a Back to Top anchor link, which links to the element with an ID of `header`. When the user clicks that link, the browser moves back up to the header element (at the top of the page). The header is the target of this link.

If a user clicks on an anchor link, you can style its target to make it stand out, like so:

```
:target {
    color: red;
}
```

The UI Element States Pseudo-Classes

The `:enabled` and `:disabled` pseudo-classes are used to select elements in enabled and disabled states. For example, on a dynamic page, a form may contain input fields irrelevant to a particular user and can be disabled to prevent the user from interacting with that field.

You disable a field in the HTML, as follows:

```
<input disabled type="email" placeholder="Your Email Address" />
```

A field that isn't disabled is considered enabled. If you want to prevent user frustration when disabling an input field, it's a good idea to change its color to represent that, like so:

```
:disabled {
    background-color: lightgray;
}
```

Another element state pseudo-class is `:checked`, which again relates to input forms—this time, check boxes and radio buttons. When an element is checked, it can be styled as follows:

```
:checked {
    background-color: green;
}
```

`:enabled()`, `:disabled()` and `:checked()`, aren't supported in Internet Explorer versions 6, 7, and 8.

The Language Pseudo-Class

You can use the `:lang` pseudo-class to declare styles based on the language of an element. Assume, for example, a quote is in French, like this:

```
<blockquote>
    <p lang="fr">Integer aliquet, lacus in ultricies venenatis,
 eros urna faucibus tellus, sed sollicitudin.</p>
</blockquote>
```

The HTML specifies the quote is of a French language (`lang="fr"`). To apply a style to only elements of French language, you can use the following:

```
:lang(fr) {
    color: blue;
}
```

`:lang()` isn't supported in Internet Explorer versions 6 and 7.

The Negation Pseudo-Class

The negation pseudo-class, `:not()`, allows you to select elements that do not represent its argument. As you saw with the language pseudo-class, you can style an element if it matches a particular language, but what if you want to style all languages except French? Rather than add each language code to the language pseudo-class, you can do the following:

```
:not(:lang(fr)) {
    color: blue;
}
```

Now *all* elements that *aren't* of the French language have blue text.

`:not()` isn't supported in Internet Explorer versions 6 and 7.

Pseudo-Elements

Pseudo-elements are parts of a web page that have physical form but aren't defined by an element—the first line of a paragraph, for example.

Officially, a pseudo-element is made of two colons (::) followed by the name of the element. When you use *two* colons, pseudo-elements are visually distinguishable from pseudo-classes (with their *one* colon). However, using one colon is also acceptable, so the choice is yours. I use just one colon throughout *CSS3 Foundations*.

Selecting the First Line

To select the first line of text, use the pseudo-element `:first-line` (or `::first-line` if you're going with two colons), like so:

```
p:first-line {
    font-weight: bold;
}
```

Selecting the First Letter

To select the first letter, use the pseudo-element `:first-letter`, as shown in the following steps:

1. In styles.css, add the following:

   ```
   #content p:first-of-type:first-letter {
       font-size: 4em;
       font-weight: bold;
   }
   ```

2. Save styles.css.

Here, you combine quite a lot of the selectors you've learned so far. You use a descendant combinator to select only <p> elements within the <div id="content" role="main"> element. You also combine the `:first-of-type` pseudo-class with `:first-letter`, which has selected the first element of type <p>, and then select only the `:first-letter` from that.

By using this selector, you style the first letter of the content section with a large and stylish typographic letter (as shown in Figure 3-5), much like an old book! You learn what an *em* is in the next chapter and font styles such as font weight in Chapter 11.

FIGURE 3-5 The first letter of the content area styled to be bigger and bolder than other text.

Generating Content Before and After an Element

Sometimes, you might want to add a style before or after an element that doesn't warrant using another element within the HTML to do that. For this, you can use :before and :after pseudo-elements.

Using :before and :after, add some quotation marks to the customer testimonials:

1. In styles.css, below the blockquote p rule set, add the following:

```
blockquote p:before {
    content: "\201C";
}
```

2. Save styles.css.

Here, you use another descendant combinator to select only <p> elements within <blockquote> elements and then tell the browser to create a pseudo-element before the <p> element and give it the content "\201C". What on earth is \201C?! It's an American Standard Code for Information Interchange (ASCII) value, which is a scheme used by computers to understand text. The \201C represents an opening quotation mark ("). You can find more ASCII codes at www.ascii.cl/htmlcodes.htm.

As you see, this CSS rule adds a quotation mark before the quote. In Chapter 5 you see more uses for the content property, *and* if you're thinking "what place does content have in CSS?" I explain that too.

The :after pseudo-element works in the same way:

1. In styles.css, below the blockquote p:before rule set, add the following:

```
blockquote p:after {
    content: "\201D";
}
```

2. Save styles.css.

This time, \201D represents a closing quotation mark.

The :before and :after pseudo-elements have huge potential. Because they are non-physical elements (they're not a part of the HTML), you can do a lot with them without having to change the structure of your web page.

 Sometimes you may want to use a pseudo-element to apply styles to the page but not have to put content inside the element using the content property. Because pseudo-elements don't work in the absence of the content property, you can simply use the declaration content: ""; to trick the browser into showing the pseudo-element. You'll see an example of this in Chapter 8.

Selector Specificity and the Cascade

Now that you've learned about selectors, you probably realize that they are certainly powerful things, often with more than one way to select the same element. For example:

```
header#header > nav[role="navigation"] {
    color: blue;
}

nav {
    color: red;
}
```

These selectors both select the navigation element <nav role="navigation">.

The question is: Because these rules select the same element but try to apply different styles to it, which gets used?

Quite simply, the most specific selector wins. Because I've gone over the top with the first selector (I'm just showcasing my selector superpowers, but in the real world, the less your selectors consist of the better), the browser applies the first style.

This is known as *specificity*, and it is calculated in a points system, as follows:

- Count the number of ID selectors in the selector
- Count the number of class selectors, attribute selectors, and pseudo-classes in the selector
- Count the number of type selectors and pseudo-elements in the selector
- Ignore the universal selector

IDs are deemed to be very specific (because they are unique to the page) and count as 100 points. Each class, attribute, and pseudo-class selector counts as 10 points, and each type or pseudo-element selector counts as 1 point.

So, out of the two selectors in the example, `header#header > nav[role="navigation"]` gets 112 points and `nav` gets only 1!

If the first rule should be more important than the other, I could be more sensible and just make it `header nav` (giving it 2 points). This is better for performance and makes CSS more manageable in the future; plus, you can still clearly see this rule is more specific, without going to the lengths of calculating specificity!

What if both rules are as specific as each other? For example:

```
nav {
    color: red;
}

nav {
    color: blue;
}
```

In this case, the latter rule always wins.

This attribution of importance is known as the *cascade*—where the *C* in CSS comes from.

The !important Rule

If you're the type of character who doesn't play by the rules and that's how you want your CSS to be, let me introduce you to `!important`.

You've learned the rules of the cascade, but sometimes you might need to make a selector that has less specificity more important than those with higher specificity.

The `!important` rule is ideal during development when you just want to see a style applied to the page, regardless of specificity. It's arguable whether `!important` should be used in production at all because it's better for performance that you respect the cascade. Here is a good use case, though:

```
.error {
    color: red !important;
}
```

This approach tends to be used on dynamic sites. Imagine a contact form in which the user hasn't added all the required details. It's important that the color of the error message be red (above any other color potentially being applied to this element through other selectors) so that the user knows he's made a mistake and his eye is drawn to it.

The `!important` rule should start with an exclamation mark (!) and be placed after a property value before the closing semicolon.

Summary

Although you've seen a lot of selectors in this chapter, the key is to keep them as simple as possible. While you're learning how to create and style web pages, there is nothing wrong with just using type, class, and ID selectors until you feel comfortable enough to try others.

The reason there are so many selectors available is to allow for creating CSS that is more efficient, modular, and robust. That doesn't mean, however, that if you don't use advanced selectors your pages will be slow. A well-considered selector against a more beginner-friendly one may shave a few milliseconds off the time it takes a browser to render a page—something that only really pays off on bigger websites with heavy amounts of user traffic.

In the next chapter, you learn the different types of values that can be used with properties to style a page just the way you want!

chapter four

Creating Styles Using Property Values

SO FAR, YOU'VE used a handful of properties to add styles to the page, such as background-color, background-image, and color. You learn more of these properties from Chapter 5 onward. Before that, take a look at the different types of values that can be used with properties, allowing you to apply the exact styles you want to a page.

Color Keywords

You've already added some colors to the page, which all made use of color keywords, like so:

```
#main {
    background-color: white;
}
```

White is one color keyword of 16 that CSS defines:

- Black
- Silver
- Gray

- White
- Maroon
- Red

- Purple
- Fuchsia
- Green
- Lime
- Olive

- Yellow
- Navy
- Blue
- Teal
- Aqua

In CSS Level 3, another 146 color keywords have been added. I don't list them all here, but you can find them at www.w3.org/TR/css3-color/#svg-color.

So, as those extended color keywords were introduced in CSS Level 3, does that mean they won't work in older browsers that don't support CSS3? Not quite. This is one of those times when CSS3 was updated to match what was already being implemented by browsers. The extended colors, known as *X11 colors,* are originally from another browser technology—SVG. SVG has been supported in browsers for many years, and because of that, so too have most of the extended colors. I say "most" because you may find some browsers don't support all 146 extended colors.

Having 162 colors isn't that breathtaking, is it? The web would be a boring-looking place if you had access to only that many colors.

What if you're creating a website for somebody else and she asks you for "a color similar to hot pink, except not quite hot pink, more like a dark strawberry color, except closer to a raspberry red"? First, I sympathize with you! Second, no, that's not a color keyword, but with the possibility to use more than 16 million colors, you'll be glad to hear that there are not 16 million color keywords.

Color Values

You can also use other color values and functions to access more than 16 million colors; they are RGB and HSL.

RGB (Hexadecimal)

RGB stands for Red, Green, Blue, and in its hexadecimal (hex for short) form, it consists of a hash or pound symbol (#), followed by either three (RGB) or six (RRGGBB) hexadecimal characters. Hexadecimal characters are 0–9 and A–F.

I mentioned previously that you should make a background color closely match the background image. The gray color you applied earlier looks a lot darker than the gray (as shown in Figure 4-1) of the background image though, right?

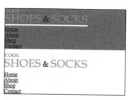

FIGURE 4-1 The dark background color compared to the background image applied in Chapter 3.

You can change that using RGB:

1. In styles.css, find

    ```
    body {
        background-color: gray;
    }
    ```

2. Change the `gray` keyword to `#f5f5f5`.

3. Save styles.css.

Because the background image still takes precedence over the background color, you might want to comment out the background image to see the change you just made (See the sidebar Using Comments and "Commenting Out"). Remember to uncomment it again after you view the change.

Example:

```
body {
    background-color: #f5f5f5;
    /* background-image: url("../images/bg-body.jpg"); */
}
```

Using Comments and "Commenting Out"

Comments are text you can add to CSS to, well, comment! A browser ignores comments, so they aren't displayed in a web page but they do appear in the CSS file that's downloaded to a user's computer. You may like to add comments to keep notes about why you used a particular style, for example.

To let the browser know you are using a comment that it can ignore, use the following syntax:

```
/* Hi Mom. I made this web page! */
```

You should prefix a comment with a forward slash and an asterisk and suffix it with an asterisk followed by a forward slash. Comments can be used either outside or within CSS rule sets.

You can also use comments for "commenting out" styles. If you added a style to a page but want to see the page without that style for a moment, rather than delete the style, you can make it a comment, causing the browser to ignore it.

When a hex value is `#000000`, it has no color, making it black, and at the opposite end of that range, `#ffffff` is white. Your background color should now closer match the color of the background image, but how on earth do you determine `#f5f5f5` is a gray color? To get the exact color, you need to use a tool, often known as a *color picker*; see the sidebar "Color Pickers."

To make writing hexadecimal values a little quicker, when a value has repeating characters (such as `#ffffff`), you can write `#fff` instead. Three character values are expanded to six by replicating each character. For example, `#fb0` expands to `#ffbb00`.

Unfortunately, you can't shorten `#f5f5f5`.

Color Pickers

Many graphics editors come with color pickers (such as Adobe Photoshop and Fireworks). If this is something you don't already have, here are some free ones you can use:

Colors for Mac—www.mattpatenaude.com/.

ColorPix for Windows—www.colorschemer.com/colorpix_info.php.

Colorzilla Browser Add-on for Chrome and Firefox—www.colorzilla.com/.

RGB (Integer Range)

RGB can also be specified via an integer range from 0 – 255 or 0 – 100%. Much like hex, the bottom of the range (0) represents black, and the top (255/100%) is white.

To set the background to white, for example, you can use the following:

```
body {
    background-color: rgb(255, 255, 255);
}
```

`rgb()` is a function, and its arguments are the red, green, and blue values.

You can specify the same gray color as the background as follows: `rgb(245, 245, 245)`. Many color pickers will be able to give you these values.

RGBA

In CSS Level 3, you can specify an alpha argument along with the red, green, and blue arguments. Alpha allows an element to take on a level of transparency.

To select the main content area of the page and make its background white, with a slight transparency, follow these steps:

1. In styles.css, find the following:

   ```
   #main {
       background-color: white;
   }
   ```

2. Add another `background-color` declaration, like so:

   ```
   #main {
       background-color: white;
       background-color: rgba(255, 255, 255, 0.6);
   }
   ```

3. Save styles.css.

Here, you select the element with an ID of `main` and give it two `background-color` declarations, but why? Because RGBA is a part of the CSS Level 3 specification, it is implemented only in modern browsers. When a browser sees these declarations, if it doesn't understand `rgba()`, it renders only the first declaration, making the background color white. If it understands both declarations (in the case of modern browsers), it renders the latter (remember this is how the cascade works), setting `background-color` to `white` (255, 255, 255) with a `0.6` (60%) transparency. This is a safe way to use CSS Level 3 features, providing graceful degradation for older browsers.

HSL and HSLA

Having read about RGB, you may be thinking that specifying colors in that way is unintuitive, and you'd be right. Although you can guess at a value for a particular color, that guess will be far from accurate.

CSS Level 3 aims to make guessing color values more intuitive with the introduction of the HSL function. HSL stands for Hue, Saturation, and Lightness.

Imagine a color wheel with red at the top (0° or 360°). As you move clockwise around that color wheel, the colors fade between yellow (60°), green (120°), cyan (180°), blue (240°), magenta (300°), and then back to red. (See Figure 4-2.)

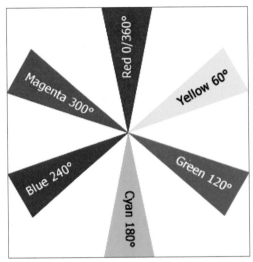

FIGURE 4-2 The position of the main colors on a color wheel.

Assuming you want a red color, you choose the hue value 0 or 360.

Next, you choose the saturation value, which is a percentage value. The higher the value, the brighter the color of red you get.

Finally, you can increase the red color's lightness using a percentage value again. Using 0% makes the color completely black, whereas 100% makes it completely white.

HSL might not sound that intuitive, but unlike RGB, it allows you to select a base color quicker and then tweak it to your needs.

Much like RGBA, an HSLA function also exists; it allows you to change the opacity of a color by using the alpha argument—a decimal value between 0 and 1, 0 being transparent, 1 being opaque.

Again, because HSL is implemented only in modern browsers, you need to add a declaration that older browsers can understand, like so:

```
body {
    background-color: #f5f5f5;
    background-color: hsl(0, 0, 0.961);
}
```

This approach is rather convoluted, though. The purpose of using HSL is to make choosing colors easier. Because older browsers require a color property they understand, you would have to go to the effort of using a color picker to determine the hexadecimal equivalent of the HSL value, defeating its purpose. Because of this, I recommend you stick with using the RGB property instead; you need to use a color picker either way!

Code Challenge: Add More Colors to the Page

In styles.css:

1. Add a rule set with the selector #newsletter and the declarations color: white; background-color: #00ACDF;.

2. Add a rule set with the selector #footer and the declarations background-color: #ccc; background-image: url("../images/bg-footer.jpg");.

3. Add a rule set with the selector .showcase .button:hover and the declaration background-color: #00ACDF;.

4. Below the rule set input[type="submit"][class="button"], add a new rule set with the selector input[type="submit"][class="button"]:hover and the declaration background-color: #d4326d;.

> Project files update (ch04-01): If you haven't followed the previous instructions and are comfortable working from here onward or would like to reference the project files up to this point, you can download them from www.wiley.com/go/treehouse/css3foundations.

Units

A *unit* is a measurement consisting of a number immediately followed by a unit identifier, such as 5cm or 20%, used for properties such as height, width, and font-size. Only when a unit of length is 0 can the unit identifier be omitted. There are numerous types of unit; percentages, lengths, and time to name a few.

Percentages

By using a percentage, you tell the browser how much space an element should take up, relative to its containing element. To change the width of the content area:

1. In styles.css, add the following:

```
#content {
    width: 65%;
}
```

2. Save styles.css.

At present, the content area is contained in the `div` with ID of `main`, which has a default width of 100%. This means the main area will fill the full size of the viewport (the area in which the page is rendered). Now that you've given the content area a width of 65%, try resizing your web browser to see that area expand and shrink to always be 65% of the viewport width.

Using percentages is a great way to make an element's size relative to another element's size. When making a responsive layout, you rely on percentages to allow for the changing of a web page's structure so it best fits the device on which it is being viewed.

You can apply percentages to many different types of properties: `width`, `height`, and `font-size` being just a few.

You use more percentage values and add structural CSS in Chapter 6.

Units of Length

There are two types of unit of length: absolute and relative. Absolute units consist of physical units (inches, centimeters, millimeters, points, and picas) and pixel units. Relative units consist of ems, rems, and exs.

Absolute Units

Absolute units are fixed and don't relate to one another, meaning they aren't inherited. They can be a little tricky to understand due to screens having different pixel densities (pixels are the tiny dots that make up a screen).

Physical Units

Physical units are anchored using the measurements of a device, assuming the pixel density of that device is 96dpi (96 dots per inch/pixels per inch).

Sample usage of physical units:

```
width: 10in;
width: 25.4cm; /* 1 inch = 2.54cm */
```

```
width: 254mm;
width: 720pt; /* 1 inch = 72pt */
width: 60pc; /* 1pc = 12pt */
```

If a device has 96dpi and you declare the width of an element should be 1 inch, that element is 96px wide. The problem is, not all devices are 96dpi, and therefore, physical units are not particularly useful for the web. They are, however, more useful for print stylesheets. You don't use physical units in *CSS3 Foundations*.

Pixel Units

Pixels are possibly the most common unit used for the web.

Sample usage:

```
width: 960px; /* 1px = 0.75pt */
```

Pixels are commonly relied on because they are easy to use, the downside being that you can't scale them in relation to each other.

If a user requires that the contents of a page become bigger so he can better see it, many browsers nowadays have a zoom feature that makes the whole page bigger. In this instance, the fact that pixels don't scale doesn't matter—because the page is zoomed and *everything* becomes bigger. In older browsers, this zoom feature isn't available, but in its place is a text resize feature. Users of older browsers aren't able to utilize this feature if you choose to use pixels. Furthermore, because you will want to change the size of text for mobile devices, using relative units called *ems* makes it easier in the long run, allowing you to manipulate the overall scale with just one change to the CSS.

Relative Units

Relative units are those that relate to each other, being inherited from their parent element.

Working with Relative Units

Whilst relative units are very much a part of styling the modern web, they can be a little difficult to work with due to the fact they relate to each other. When specifying a `font-size` should be 1em, what exactly does that mean? How long is a piece of string?

When specifying a relative unit or percentage, the browser will take that value and run some calculations based on other values. This is known as the *computed value*.

Say an element has a width of 500px, and you specify its child element should be 50% wide, the browser will do the calculation: 250px = 500px × 0.5.

continued

continued

When a page consists of lots of elements, these calculations can be difficult for the person styling the page to keep up with.

Using the web developer tools of a browser, you can find the calculated value of any element:

1. Open your browsers web developer tools as described in Chapter 1.

   a. The Element Inspector in all web developer tools consists of two panes: the *Document Object Model* (DOM) and the properties. The larger pane on the left (by default) is the DOM, which consists of the rendered HTML in a tree view. The smaller pane on the right (by default) is the properties, which consists of *noncomputed* and *computed styles,* and you may find your browser has other features too, which *CSS3 Foundations* doesn't cover.

   b. Noncomputed styles are those that have been taken directly from your stylesheet. Computed styles are those that the browser has calculated based on the relative and percentage units in your stylesheet. To see an example of these computed styles:

2. Navigate through the DOM by clicking the + or triangle symbols to open parent elements that contain the <h1>.

3. Once you've found it, click the <h1> element.

4. In the right-hand pane, click Computed or Computed Style (browser dependent).

Here you can see all of the computed styles applied to this element. There are quite a lot of them because this includes styles inherited from the user agent stylesheet described in Chapter 2. None of these properties are relative units or percentages because they have all been computed. Knowing the computed style often makes doing your own calculations easier.

Em

The W3C defines an *em* unit as "the computed value of the `font-size` property of the element on which it is used." Not particularly straightforward, is it? Use an em unit as follows to better understand it:

1. In styles.css, add the following to the body selector:

   ```
   font-size: 1em;
   ```

2. Save styles.css.

If you view the page now, you notice nothing has changed! The default font size of the <html> element is 16px, and because font size is inherited, the font size of the body is also 16px. By declaring a font size of 1em, you tell the browser you want the font size to be 16px (16px = inherited value (16px) × 1em). Ems get slightly trickier when font sizes are inherited.

Now consider a list as an example to demonstrate inheritance:

```
<ul>
    <li>Item 1</li>
    <li>Item 2
        <ul>
            <li>Item 3</li>
        </ul>
    </li>
</ul>
```

Say the <body> element has a font size of 16px and you give a list item a font size of 2em, like so:

```
li {
    font-size: 2em;
}
```

In this case, Item 1 and Item 2 in the list have a calculated font size of 32px, but because Item 3 is a child of Item 2, it first inherits the calculated font size of 32px. Then the browser calculates 32px × 2em, giving it a font size of 64px.

To avoid this, you could just set the font size on the <ul>, like so:

```
ul {
    font-size: 2em;
}
```

Setting the size this way makes each list item inherit the same font size, and they all become 32px. Sometimes this result isn't avoidable, though, and you need to do the following to adjust Item 3:

```
li {
    font-size: 2em;
}
li li {
    font-size: 1em;
}
```

Here, Item 1 and Item 2 are 2 em, making them 32px (32px = inherited value (16px) × 2em). Item 3 inherits the font size of 32px; then the browser calculates 32px × 1em, giving it the same font size as its parent element.

Although ems may sound troublesome at first, they're key to creating responsive websites. They allow you to quickly scale text (and other elements) in size, which is essential for making a website accessible across many different devices. In older versions of Internet Explorer, a web page that uses ems allows users to scale text themselves via built-in browser options.

There is a nice trick you can use to make working with ems a little easier:

1. In styles.css, find the font size you applied to the body selector:

   ```
   font-size: 1em;
   ```

2. Change its value to 62.5%:

   ```
   font-size: 62.5%;
   ```

3. Save styles.css.

Here, you tell the browser to make the body's font size 62.5% of its default size (inherited value (16px) × 0.625 = 10px). Now 1 em is the equivalent of 10px, 1.2em is 12px, and so on. Figure 4-3 shows this in action.

FIGURE 4-3 The Cool Shoes & Socks page with a font size of 62.5% (10px).

Yikes! As shown in Figure 4-3, the text is much smaller now! You can fix that:

1. In styles.css, below the rule set for the body selector, add the following:

```
#header, #main, #footer {
    font-size: 1.6em;
    /* inherited value (10px) x 1.6em = 16px */
}
```

2. Save styles.css.

Ems can be used for many more properties. You will see examples of this later in the book.

Rem

CSS Level 3 introduces a new unit called *Rem* (Root em). The W3C is aware of the difficulties when dealing with inherited values and em, so it introduced rem. Rem inherits its value only from the root element, that being the `<html>` element. So, in the em unit example, Item 3 inherited the value of its parent—causing its font size to double; when you use rem, this wouldn't happen because each element inherits only the same font size from the root.

Although this is an easier way to use ems, unfortunately, it isn't supported in all browsers yet, so for the moment, you cannot use rems to create a cross-browser-compatible website.

Ex

Ex refers to the x-height of a font (the height of the lowercase *x*) but unfortunately isn't particularly reliable. Because of this, it is less commonly relied on for creating web pages; therefore, you don't use this unit in *CSS3 Foundations*.

Other Units

The CSS3 specification lists other units that haven't been covered in this chapter. You will learn to use angle units in Chapter 12 when rotating elements, and time units in Chapter 14 when animating elements.

The specification also includes frequency and resolution units, which tend to have more of a special use-case and viewport-percentage length units that, as yet, are unsupported in browsers.

If you'd like to know more about these unit types, please see the CSS3 Values module at: www.w3.org/TR/css3-values.

Summary

Getting to know the different types of property values means the way in which you style a page can become more diverse and you can commit your design ideas to screen quicker, with greater accuracy.

In the next chapter, you'll learn many new presentational properties on which to use the values described in this chapter. The Cool Shoes & Socks page will really start to transform into something that closer resembles a modern day web page.

chapter five
Adding Presentational Styles

IN THIS CHAPTER, you take a deeper look at some of the properties you've already used, learn how to use shorthand properties and property values, and learn many more properties to make Cool Shoes & Socks really stand out!

Before you begin reading about presentational styles, first set up the page to give it a little more structure:

> Project Files Update (ch05-00): If you haven't followed the previous instructions and are comfortable working from here onward or would like to reference the project files up to this point, you can download them from www.wiley.com/go/treehouse/css3foundations.

1. In styles.css, find the body rule set and add the following declarations:

   ```
   margin: 0 auto;
   max-width: 960px;
   ```

2. Save styles.css.

These properties—that center the web page as shown in Figure 5-1—are covered in Chapters 6–9. It's kind of looking more like a web page now, right?

These properties—that center the web page as shown in Figure 5-1—are covered in Chapters 6–9. It's kind of looking more like a web page now, right?

Property Definitions

In *CSS3 Foundations*, each property definition begins with key information about that property, which consists of:

- The property's initial value
- Whether the value is inherited
- Which elements the property can be applied to
- Whether the property is from the CSS2.1 or CSS3 specification
- Which browsers the property is supported in

A property's initial value is that which is applied to an element prior to your changing it via CSS. For example, many elements have an initial background color of `transparent`.

If a property is inherited, it is passed down to the child elements of the element to which it is applied. For example, when you gave the `<body>` a `font-size` of `62.5%` in Chapter 4, that `font-size` was inherited by all the elements contained within the `<body>`.

If, by default, a property is not inherited, you can give a child element a property with the value `inherit` to tell the browser to apply the same property value used for the element's parent.

Not all properties can be applied to all elements. The `table-layout` element, for example, can be applied only to table and inline-table elements such as `<table>` and `<td>`.

If a property is from the CSS2.1 specification, unless otherwise stated, it is safe to use in all browsers. Properties from the CSS3 specification may not be safe to use in all browsers—particularly Internet Explorer versions 6, 7, and 8; if this is the case, I explain how best to work around that. Furthermore, experimental properties from CSS3 may require vendor prefixes, which you learn how to use shortly.

Each property definition also includes a list of browser versions that support that property, both with and without vendor prefixes where necessary.

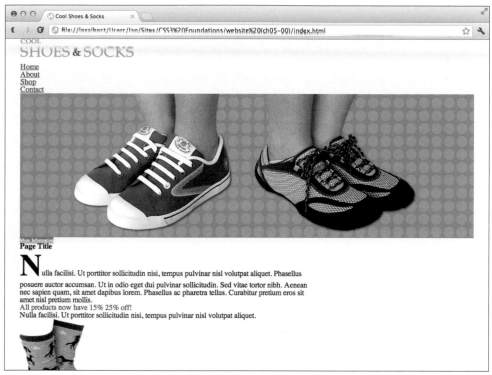

FIGURE 5-1 The web page centered and with a defined width of 960 pixels.

Using Experimental Properties Safely

In Chapter 1, I mentioned that some of the CSS3 modules are incomplete and at various stages prior to reaching the Recommendation status.

With many of CSS3's modules still being written, browser vendors are constantly updating their browsers to better support CSS3's new features. The more they can implement, the more they and their users can test and provide feedback on, so it is very important for a browser to keep up with the latest web technology.

To make implementing experimental features as safe as possible, it was decided that each browser should have its own prefix to be placed before a CSS property. That way, if two browsers do implement a feature in a different way, that feature viewed in one browser doesn't appear broken in the other; they both refer to the same feature but may have their own unique implementation of it. When a feature becomes official, the vendor-prefixed property then becomes obsolete, and the official property is relied on instead.

So, what exactly are vendor prefixes and how do you use them?

One example of an experimental property is `transition-duration`, which you will learn to use in Chapter 14. A `transition-duration` declaration may be written like so:

```
transition-duration: 2s;
```

This is the official property name that is described in the CSS3 Transitions module. However, as at the time of writing, that module is a Working Draft, for the safest implementation, `transition-duration` should be written with a vendor prefix for each browser, like so:

```
-webkit-transition-duration: 2s;
-moz-transition-duration: 2s;
-ms-transition-duration: 2s;
-o-transition-duration: 2s;
transition-duration: 2s;
```

These vendor prefixes apply to the following browsers:

- `-webkit-` — Google Chrome and Apple Safari (they use the WebKit Layout Engine)
- `-moz-` — Mozilla Firefox
- `-ms-` — Microsoft Internet Explorer
- `-o-` — Opera

The vendor-prefixed properties should be followed by the official, unprefixed property, which ensures that when this property does become official, the standardized property will be used—instead of the vendor-specific one.

In the preceding example, the same property is repeated five times. If you're anything like me, typing it that many times sounds like a hassle. It's important to use vendor prefixes, though!

You can be thankful that there are free tools that allow you to write only one vendor prefix during development, and they will fill in the rest for you. When you use vendor prefixes throughout *CSS3 Foundations*, write one only for the browser in which you've decided to create your web page (I use `-webkit-` for Google Chrome), and in Chapter 15, you use a tool that adds the other vendor prefixes to your CSS automatically.

When a property should be used with vendor prefixes, I'll let you know. However, as the web is constantly evolving, if you'd like to be certain of whether a property still requires a vendor prefix or not, I recommend visiting a website called When can I use... (`www.caniuse.com`). Not only will When can I use... tell you which properties are supported in which browsers, it'll also show whether you need to use vendor prefixes for that property.

At the time of writing, browser vendors are making a push toward removing vendor prefixes from the more established CSS3 properties and as time goes on, fewer vendor prefixes will be required, until they eventually become obsolete.

Using vendor-prefixed properties when they are no longer necessary won't cause any problems and it is better safe than sorry. A browser will simply skip over a vendor-prefixed property that it may no longer support and instead use the official property. So, providing you place the official property below the vendor-prefixed ones, your CSS will remain future proof.

Borders

Borders are graphical elements that are applied around the edge of an element.

border-color

Initial value: the value of `color` | Inherited: No | Applies to: All | CSS2.1
Browser support: IE 4+, Firefox 1+, Chrome 1+, Opera 3.5+, Safari 1+

As you would expect, `border-color` specifies the color of a border and can be given a variety of values, such as RGB, RGBA, HSL, HSLA, and color keywords.

1. In styles.css, find the #main rule set and add the following declaration:

   ```
   border-color: #ccc;
   ```

2. Save styles.css.

This gives the border around the main content container `<div id="main" class="group">` a gray border color. *However*, for borders to work, you need to specify a `border-style` and `border-width` along with the `border-color` property. Because the initial value of `border-style` is none, you cannot see the border yet.

In the CSS2.1 specification, the initial value for `border-color` is the same as that of the `color` property. So if a `border-color` isn't specified and the `color` is red, then the `border-color` will be red too. In CSS3, the initial value is the keyword `currentColor`, which achieves exactly the same—the `border-color` will be the same as the `color`. The introduction of this keyword is just to allow you to specifically show you want the `border-color` to be the same as the `color`. If you were working in a team with multiple people working on the same stylesheet for example, the following clearly shows you intend to have the `border-color` be the same as the `color`, whereas without the `border-color` declaration, it may look like you forgot to add that style:

```
body {
    color: red;
    border-color: currentColor;
}
```

Although `currentColor` is a CSS3 keyword and may not work in older browsers, those older browsers will simply ignore it and just apply the same `color` value to the `border-color` property anyway, so it can be safely used across all browsers.

border-style

Initial value: `none` | Inherited: No | Applies to: All | CSS2.1
Browser support: IE 4+, Firefox 1+, Chrome 1+, Opera 3.5+, Safari 1+

`border-style` styles the border of an element, unless that element also has a `border-image` declaration.

1. In styles.css, underneath the `border-color` declaration you just added to the `#main` rule set, add the following:

    `border-style: solid;`

2. Save styles.css.

The values you can use with the `border-style` property are `none`, `hidden`, `dotted`, `dashed`, `solid`, `double`, `groove`, `ridge`, `inset`, and `outset` (see Figure 5-2).

The none keyword can be used with many properties and will remove a style that is inherited in the cascade or for example when you wish to have a style removed when an element is hovered over.

FIGURE 5-2 The dotted, dashed, solid, double, groove, ridge, inset, and outset border styles each with a border-color of white and border-width of 8px.

The border styles page can be found in the project files ch05-00, named `border-styles.html`.

You'll be able to see the border after you specify a `border-width`...I promise!

border-width

Initial value: `medium` | Inherited: No | Applies to: All | CSS2.1
Browser support: IE 4+, Firefox 1+, Chrome 1+, Opera 3.5+, Safari 1+

The `border-width` property sets the thickness of a border.

1. In styles.css, underneath the `border-style` declaration, add the following:

   ```
   border-width: 1px;
   ```

2. Save styles.css.

Now finally, you can see a thin border applied around the main content area.

For `border-width`, you can specify all values of length as well as the keywords `thin`, `medium`, and `thick`.

border (Shorthand)

Browser support: IE 4+, Firefox 1+, Chrome 1+, Opera 3.5+, Safari 1+

When CSS properties share similarities, you can use one shorthand declaration in place of multiple declarations.

The `border` property is a shorthand way of writing the three properties you just added. Go ahead and change those declarations into just one declaration:

1. In styles.css, in the #main rule set, remove the following declarations:

   ```
   border-color: #ccc;
   border-style: solid;
   border-width: 1px;
   ```

2. Add the shorthand `border` declaration:

   ```
   border: #ccc solid 1px;
   ```

3. Save styles.css.

The `border` property requires three values (in any order), separated by spaces. By adding this shorthand declaration, you achieve the same effect using less code and less time!

Now, if you're wondering how you style the border of just one side of an element, you can do that using `border-left-width`, `border-top-style`, and so on. This means that `border-color`, `border-style`, and `border-width` are shorthand properties too; they apply styles to all four borders of an element in one go.

Try styling just one side of an element using a shorthand property:

1. In styles.css, find the `#footer` rule set, and below its other declarations, add the following:

   ```
   border-top: #999 dotted 4px;
   ```

2. Save styles.css.

Here, you style the top border of the footer element with a dark gray dotted border (see Figure 5-3). You use a shorthand property, which is the equivalent of:

```
border-top-color: #999;
border-top-style: dotted;
border-top-width: 4px;
```

Cool Shoes & Socks
Back to Top

FIGURE 5-3 The footer area with a dotted border applied only to the top.

I like things to be as simple as possible. It's not that I'm lazy...honest! If you like the simplicity of shorthand properties, you'll be pleased to know CSS has quite a few more like these, which are covered as you make your way through *CSS3 Foundations*.

border-radius

Initial value: 0 | Inherited: No | Applies to: All, except internal table elements when `border-collapse is collapse` | CSS3

Unprefixed browser support: IE 9+, Firefox 4+, Chrome 4+, Opera 10.5+, Safari 5+

Prefixed browser support: Firefox 1+, Chrome 0.2+, Safari 3.0+

`border-radius` enables you to give elements rounded corners. It is supported in all modern browsers but not Internet Explorer 6, 7, and 8. Because it's a visual effect and nothing more, the fact that old versions of Internet Explorer don't render rounded corners isn't a problem; they just remain square.

1. In styles.css, find the `#newsletter` rule set, and below its other declarations, add the following:

   ```
   border-radius: 8px;
   ```

2. Save styles.css.

Here you give the newsletter box very subtle rounded corners (see Figure 5-4). Because the CSS3 Backgrounds and Borders Module (`www.w3.org/TR/css3-background/`), which this property is a part of, is a "Candidate Recommendation," you can use `border-radius` without vendor prefixes.

Newsletter
Sign up for news and special offers delivered to your inbox monthly.
Name: Your Name   Email: Your Email Address   **Sign Up**

FIGURE 5-4 The newsletter box with subtle rounded corners.

Although you haven't given the newsletter box a style, `border-radius` still applies (because whether or not an element has styled borders, the border of an element still exists).

`border-radius` is shorthand for `border-top-left-radius`, `border-top-right-radius`, `border-bottom-left-radius`, and `border-bottom-right-radius`. By specifying one value of 8px for the `border-radius`, you tell the browser you want all four corners to be 8px. What if you want each corner to have a different value?

```
border-radius: 8px 12px 16px 20px;
```

This declaration gives the top-left corner a radius of 8px and then works clockwise from there, giving the top-right a 12px radius; bottom-right, 16px; and bottom left, 20px.

You also are able to create corners that aren't perfectly round by specifying two values for a corner, one for the horizontal radius, and the other for the vertical radius, like so:

```
border-top-right-radius: 8px 20px;
```

If this declaration is applied, the top-right corner of an element has a horizontal curve of 8px, going into a vertical curve of 20px.

If you want this noncircular radius to apply to all corners, you can use the shorthand `border-radius` property, first specifying the four horizontal values, followed by a slash / and then the four vertical values, like so:

```
border-radius: 8px 8px 8px 8px / 20px 20px 20px 20px;
```

Or, because those values are repeating, an even shorter way would be to write

```
border-radius: 8px / 20px;
```

Border Images

If none of the border styles covered so far takes your fancy, CSS Level 3 introduces border images, which allow you to use your own images in place of the basic styles described previously. Border images are unfortunately at various states between browsers at the moment. Google Chrome has good support, Firefox partial, Internet Explorer versions 6–9 have no support at all, and other modern browsers support only the shorthand property `border-image`.

Because border image is another visual style, it doesn't particularly matter that Internet Explorer doesn't show a border image. Let's look at the longhand properties for border images and then convert them to shorthand so the style works in the majority of browsers.

border-image-source

Initial value: none | Inherited: No | Applies to: All, except internal table elements when `border-collapse is collapse` | CSS3

Unprefixed browser support: Firefox 15+, Chrome 15+

`border-image-source` enables you to specify an image to use for the border by using a `url()` function with a path to the image (the source) as an argument. You take a closer look at the `url()` function and its arguments in the `background-image` definition shortly.

Figure 5-5 shows the custom border to be used on the Cool Shoes & Socks website. Although you apply it only to the top border of the footer section, the image to be used should still consist of four sides.

FIGURE 5-5 The image to be used for the border of the newsletter box.

1. In styles.css, below the other declarations in the #footer rule set, add the following:

   ```
   border-image-source: url("../images/bdr-footer.png");
   ```

2. Save styles.css.

As you saw with the other border declarations, it takes a few of them to work together before you get a result.

border-image-slice

Initial value: 100% | Inherited: No | Applies to: All, except internal table elements when `border-collapse is collapse` | CSS3

Unprefixed browser support: Chrome 15+

When the browser knows which image you want to use, it slices it into nine parts; four corners, four edges, and one center piece. How that slicing occurs depends on the `border-image-slice` property.

1. In styles.css, below the `border-image-source` declaration, add the following:

   ```
   border-image-slice: 4;
   ```

2. Save styles.css.

The `border-image-slice` property can be given up to four number values. Here, `border-image-slice: 4;` is the same as `border-image-slice: 4 4 4 4;`, the first value being the top and then working clockwise from there.

Note that unless using percentage values, the `border-image-slice` value should not be given a unit identifier (such as px). This is because the values represent pixels when using a raster image and co-ordinates when using a vector image (a file ending with a .svg extension).

As shown in Figure 5-6, a `border-image-slice` of 4 will slice the raster image 4px from the edge of the image.

FIGURE 5-6 The border image is sliced with the border-image-slice property set to 4.

border-image-width

Initial value: 1 | Inherited: No | Applies to: All, except internal table elements when `border-collapse is collapse` | CSS3

Unprefixed browser support: Firefox 13+, Chrome 15+

`border-image-width` determines the width of the image applied to the border.

In most cases, you don't need to specify a `border-image-width` because its initial value of 1 along with the use of the `border-width` property is usually adequate. The border already has a width of 4px, which you specified on the `#footer` element earlier, like so:

```
#footer {
    background-color: #ccc;
    background-image: url("../images/bg-footer.jpg");
    border-top: #999 dotted 4px;
}
```

The `border-image-width` can be either a percentage value (or four percentage values for the top, right, bottom, and left), which causes the border's width to be a certain percentage of the element it is applied to, or a number (or four numbers for top, right, bottom, and left), which is a multiplication of the calculated `border-width`. If you specify a `border-image-width` of 4, the `border-image-width` is 16px = 4px × 4.

As shown in Figure 5-7, the border image is now applied to the footer in Google Chrome (other browsers don't work until the shorthand `border-image` property is added). At the moment, though, the border image is stretched because the `border-image-repeat` property's default value is `stretch`. You can fix that...

Cool Shoes & Socks
Back to Top

FIGURE 5-7 The border image stretched across the footer.

border-image-repeat

Initial value: `stretch` | Inherited: No | Applies to: All, except internal table elements when `border-collapse is collapse` | CSS3

Unprefixed browser support: Firefox 15+, Chrome 15+

The reason the border image is currently stretched is that the initial value of border-image-repeat is stretch.

1. In styles.css, below the border-image-slice declaration, add the following:

   border-image-repeat: repeat;

2. Save styles.css.

This tells the browser to take each of the nine slices and repeat them where necessary (see Figure 5-8). Because you're applying only this border image to the top border, the top edge slice (or tile) of the nine slices is repeated until it fills the area.

FIGURE 5-8 The border image repeating across the footer.

The Backgrounds and Borders module also describes two other values that can be used: round and space. Note that at present no browsers support these values. round repeats the image, but if the repeated tile does not fill the area using a whole number of tiles, it rescales the image so it does. space also repeats, but if the tile does not fill the area in the same way, the extra space is distributed around the tiles.

border-image-outset

Initial value: 0 | Inherited: No | Applies to: All, except internal table elements when border-collapse is collapse | CSS3
Unprefixed browser support: Chrome 15+

Another option for border images is the outset, which specifies how far outside an element the border should be positioned:

border-image-outset: 20px;

This example causes the border image to be 20 pixels outside the element it is applied to (see Figure 5-9). The border-image-outset can be any unit of length, and as with values for the other border image properties, you can specify up to four, representing the top, right, bottom, and left borders.

Element border

Border image outset by 20px

FIGURE 5-9 An element with a border-image and border-image-outset of 20px applied to it.

If you're a fan of math, you can use a multiplication number too, just like the border-image-width number, which is a multiplication of the computed `border-width`.

border-image (Shorthand)

Unprefixed browser support: Firefox 15+, Opera 11+

Prefixed browser support: Firefox 3.5+, Chrome 7+, Opera 10.5+, Safari 3+

As with the other border properties, border image properties have a shorthand property too and, as mentioned, at present, most browsers support only the use of the `border-image` property. Therefore, it's wise to use that property in place of the other border image properties.

The shorthand property should take the following syntax:

```
border-image: border-image-source border-image-slice border-image-
width border-image-outset border-image-repeat
```

When any of the preceding values are omitted, the properties initial value is used.

1. In styles.css, find the `#footer` rule set and remove the following declarations:

```
border-image-source: url("../images/bdr-footer.png");
border-image-slice: 4;
border-image-repeat: repeat;
```

2. Add the shorthand declaration in their place:

```
-webkit-border-image: url("../images/bdr-footer.png") 4 repeat;
```

3. Save styles.css.

Rather than use three properties here, you use one; specifying the `url()`, followed by the slice value and then the repeat value.

As mentioned earlier in this chapter, during the creation of the Cool Shoes & Socks website, I use the `-webkit-` vendor prefix because I am using Google Chrome. If you are using a different browser, use the vendor prefix for that browser.

In Chapter 15, you use a tool that automatically adds the other vendor prefixes to the CSS, saving you from having to write five different vendor-prefixed properties now.

box-shadow

Initial value: none | Inherited: No | Applies to: All | CSS3
Unprefixed browser support: IE 9+, Firefox 4+, Chrome 10+, Opera 10.5+, Safari 5.1+
Prefixed browser support: Firefox 3,5+, Chrome 1+, Safari 3+

The `box-shadow` property applies a drop shadow to an element.

You can add a subtle drop shadow (see Figure 5-10) to the main content area:

1. In styles.css, find the `#main` rule set and add the following below the other declarations:

```
box-shadow: 0 3px 8px 0 #ccc;
```

2. Save styles.css.

FIGURE 5-10 The main content area with a subtle box shadow.

The first four values of the box-shadow property can be any unit of length and modify the shadow as follows:

- The first value of a drop shadow represents its horizontal offset: how far the shadow is from the right of the box, a negative value to its left. The shadow you added doesn't have an offset.

- The second value is the vertical offset. A positive number goes below the element and negative goes above. The shadow you added is offset 3px vertically from the main content element.

- The third value is the blur of the shadow. A value of 0 here would make the edges of the shadow sharp, whereas 8px gives it a mild blur.

- The fourth value is the spread distance, which determines how far the shadow should spread on all sides of the element.

Following on from the shadow values is an optional color. By default, a shadow is black, but the shadow you added has a light gray color to match the border.

You also are able to make box shadows inset so the shadow appears inside the element:

1. In styles.css, find the rule set for input[type="text"], input[type="email"] and add the following:

   ```
   box-shadow: -3px 3px 2px 0 #ccc inset;
   ```

2. Save styles.css.

Adding this declaration gives the input fields of type text and email an inset shadow. An inset shadow is often a good visual indication of an input field.

It's also possible to add more than one shadow to an element (see Figure 5-11), by separating shadows with a comma:

```
box-shadow: 0 3px 8px 0 #ccc, 0 3px 8px 0 red inset;
```

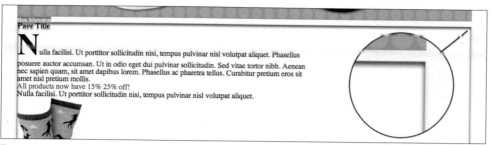

FIGURE 5-11 The main content area with a subtle gray box shadow and red inset box shadow.

Code Challenge: Add More Border and Box Shadow Styles

In styles.css, do the following:

1. Add a declaration of `border: rgba(0,0,0,0.1) solid 5px;` to the `#newsletter` rule set.

2. Add a declaration of `border-radius: 8px;` and `border: 2px solid white;` to the `.button` rule set.

3. Add a new rule set for `#header nav > ul` with the declarations `border-radius: 20px;` and `border: #ccc solid 1px;`.

4. Add a new rule set for `.showcase` with a declaration of `box-shadow: 0 -3px 8px 0 #ccc;`.

Project files update (ch05-01): If you haven't followed the previous instructions and are comfortable working from here onward or would like to reference the project files up to this point, you can download them from `www.wiley.com/go/treehouse/css3foundations`.

Backgrounds

In the preceding chapter, you applied a background color to a couple of elements, as well as a background image to the body of the page. CSS has many other properties to allow you to style a background.

background-color

Initial value: `transparent` | Inherited: No | Applies to: All | CSS2.1

Browser support: IE 4+, Firefox 1+, Chrome 1+, Opera 3.5+, Safari 1+

As you saw in the preceding chapters, you specify a background color using the `background-color` property and can give it a variety of values, such as RGB, RGBA, HSL, HSLA, and color keywords:

```
body {
    background-color: #f5f5f5;
}
```

By default, `background-color` is `transparent`, meaning it is see-through, allowing elements below it or containing it to show through.

background-image

Initial value: `none` | Inherited: No | Applies to: All | CSS2.1

Browser support: IE 4+, Firefox 1+, Chrome 1+, Opera 3.5+, Safari 1+

`background-image` accepts a `url()` function or `none` as its value. As you saw in the `border-image-source` explanation, the `url()` function takes a URI as its argument.

A URI (also referred to as a source, link, or path) within the `url()` function can optionally be wrapped with single or double quotation marks. Previously, you added this style:

```
background-image: url("../images/bg-body.jpg");
```

This style is just as acceptable written without the quotation marks and with optional whitespace inside the brackets:

```
background-image: url( ../images/bg-body.jpg );
```

The choice is yours.

You may be wondering what the two dots mean in the URI. The two types of URI you can use are relative and absolute. This type is known as relative.

An absolute URI is complete and in its entirety. For example, if you want to view the image `bg-body.jpg` directly, in your browser, you can navigate to `http://www.cool shoesandsocks.com/images/bg-body.jpg`. To make the URI of the background image apply to the body, you use the following declaration:

```
background-image: url("http://www.coolshoesandsocks.com/images/
  bg-body.jpg");
```

Avoid Hot Linking

Linking from your own web resource to another that you don't own via an absolute URI is known as *hot linking*. Say I like an image I've seen on someone else's website and I make it the background image of my web page via an absolute link. Not only may that person be upset with me because I don't have her permission to do that, but I'm also using the bandwidth of her server. It is common that web hosting is priced based on the amount of bandwidth a website uses, so potentially, by hot linking that image, I could be costing the person money!

If the owner of the image is kind enough to give you permission to use an image, you should upload that image to your own server and link to it from there, ideally via a relative URI.

Absolute URIs tend to be used when you're linking to an external resource—on another domain, for example. Although they can be used internally too, it is good practice to use relative URIs instead as they can make a web page quicker to load.

A relative URI is a path (source or link) that is relative to the document it is within. When you added the relative URI `../images/bg-body.jpg` in styles.css, you told the browser to go up one directory (denoted by `../`) into the `images` directory and then use the image bg-body.jpg from there.

Following are a few rules when using relative URIs:

- Links to resources in the same directory should consist only of the filename and file extension: `bg-body.jpg`

- Links to subdirectories consist of the subdirectories' names (without a preceding slash), followed by the filename and extension: `images/bg-body.jpg`

- To go up a directory, use two full stops (dots or periods) followed by a slash, then the subdirectory (if required), and then the filename and file extension: `../images/bg-body.jpg`

You may have noticed I refer to a *URL* and a *URI.* What's the difference? You might be sorry you asked, but I hope this explanation clears up matters! The name *URL* means Uniform Resource Locator and, as the CSS specification states, the `url()` function requires a URI (Uniform Resource Identifier) as its argument. A URL and URN (Uniform Resource Name) are subclasses of a URI (they can be both referred to as URIs). However, a URN has no use in CSS, so although it's technically true that the `url()` function does take a URI as its argument, only a URL is of use (hence the function being called `url()` rather than `uri()`). This distinction is not necessarily something you need to be concerned about, but you may have been curious!

background-repeat

Initial value: `repeat` | Inherited: No | Applies to: All | CSS2.1

Browser support: IE 4+, Firefox 1+, Chrome 1+, Opera 3.5+, Safari 1+

When you applied the background image to the body in Chapter 3, as you saw, that image was only 40px × 40px, but the browser repeated the image to make it fill the whole body. This is the default behavior of a background image, but by using the `background-repeat` property, you can change that.

Add a background image to the newsletter form:

1. In styles.css, find the `#newsletter` rule set and add the following:

   ```
   background-image: url("../images/icon-newsletter.png");
   ```

2. Save styles.css.

Figure 5-12 shows that the little image of the envelope has repeated across the entire newsletter box. Looks a bit over the top, doesn't it?

FIGURE 5-12 The background image repeating across the newsletter box.

Because you have not yet specified a `background-repeat` declaration, the initial value of repeat is applied. So, what other values can you use?

- `background-repeat: repeat-x`—causes an image to repeat only horizontally.
- `background-repeat: repeat-y`—causes an image to repeat only vertically.

Although these values are useful, this image would look better if it wasn't repeating.

1. In styles.css, below the `background-image` declaration you added to the `#newsletter` rule set, add the following:

   ```
   background-repeat: no-repeat;
   ```

2. Save styles.css.

Figure 5-13 shows the result of applying `no-repeat`.

FIGURE 5-13 The background image of the newsletter box, now with no-repeat specified.

Now, the background image doesn't repeat, and you see only one image applied to the newsletter box.

background-position

Initial value: 0% 0% | Inherited: No | Applies to: All | CSS2.1
Browser support: IE 4+, Firefox 1+, Chrome 1+, Opera 3.5+, Safari 1+

The background image is currently in its initial position of 0% 0%. The first 0% is the horizontal position, relative to the left of the parent element, and the second 0% is the vertical position, relative to the top of the parent element.

When specifying a background-position value, you can use all the length unit types as described in Chapter 4, percentages, pixels, ems, and so on. You can also use the keywords left, right, top, bottom, and center.

Because the background image is currently sitting underneath the text, making the text hard to read, change its position:

1. In styles.css, below the background-repeat declaration you added to the #newsletter rule set, add the following:

   background-position: right top;

2. Save styles.css.

As shown in Figure 5-14, the background image is now positioned to the far right and at the top of the newsletter box. This declaration is the equivalent of background-position: 100% 0%. It's just a little nicer to read and write a declaration like this when it's written using keywords!

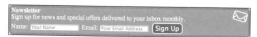

FIGURE 5-14 The background image positioned to the right and at the top of the newsletter box.

If only one of the background-position values is specified, the missing value is assumed to be center, so if you use the declaration background-position: right, the background image is positioned to the right of the newsletter box but vertically centered.

The position of the background image might not make a huge amount of sense at the moment, but when you give the page more structure in Chapters 6–9, it will!

In preparation, give the background image a more accurate position that will better suit the newsletter box when it has more structure:

1. In styles.css, change the `background-position` declaration to

   `background-position: 91% 2%;`

2. Save styles.css.

background-attachment

Initial value: `scroll` | Inherited: No | Applies to: All | CSS2.1
Browser support: IE 4+, Firefox 1+, Chrome 1+, Opera 3.5+, Safari 1+

By default, when you scroll the viewport or an element that can scroll (you learn how to make an individual element scrollable using the `overflow` property in Chapter 9), a background image moves with the scrolling of the viewport or element.

```
body {
    background-color: #f5f5f5;
    background-image: url("../images/bg-body.jpg");
    background-attachment: fixed;
    font-size: 62.5%;
}
```

For example, giving the background image applied to the <body> element a declaration of `background-attachment: fixed` causes the background image to remain in place when you scroll the page (as opposed to the background image moving with the scrolling).

If you want to try this example yourself, depending on your screen size, you might need to give the body selector a temporary declaration of `height: 2000px` to make the page tall enough to require scrolling.

Applying Multiple Background Images

Browser support: IE 9+, Firefox 3.6+, Chrome 1+, Opera 11+, Safari 1.3+

CSS Level 3 introduces multiple background images per element. Multiple background images are supported in all modern browsers, but not in Internet Explorer versions 6, 7, and 8. Because of this, it's best to use multiple background images only if they're not important, such as those used for decorative purposes.

Add another background image to the newsletter box:

1. In styles.css, change the `background-image`, `background-repeat`, and `background-position` declarations in the `#newsletter` rule set to

   ```
   background-image: url("../images/icon-newsletter.png"),
   url("../images/bg-newsletter.png");
   background-repeat: no-repeat, repeat;
   background-position: 91% 2%, 0;
   ```

2. Save styles.css.

Here, you specify two `url()` functions for the `background-image` and separate them with commas, which now apply two background images to the newsletter box. Likewise, you give the `background-repeat` and `background-position` declarations secondary values, again, by separating them with commas.

So, the secondary background image repeats (filling the whole newsletter box) and is given a position of 0 (it's set to repeat so the position doesn't matter).

Background Gradients

Prior to CSS Level 3, a gradient (an image that blends from one color to another) had to be made in a graphics application such as Adobe Photoshop or Fireworks, but now you can do it using nothing but CSS! Technically, a gradient is an image that the browser generates so it can be applied to—and in place of—any element that accepts the `url()` function.

Just like background images, provided that you specify a basic background color to fall back to, you can use gradients safely.

Gradients come in two flavors: linear and radial. A *linear* gradient is the blending of colors from one point to another, whereas a *radial* gradient starts from a center point and blends outward.

Unfortunately, gradients are in a state of disarray, with varying support and syntaxes across browsers.

Internet Explorer versions 6, 7, 8, and 9 have no support for official gradients. That said, they do actually support a different type of gradient using an unofficial `filter` property that Microsoft added before they concerned themselves with following the standardized specifications.

For more information about the unofficial `filter` property, visit `msdn.microsoft.com/en-us/library/ie/ms530752(v=vs.85).aspx`.

Linear gradients in other browsers are supported either using the official syntax or an outdated one. You'll learn both syntaxes to be able to achieve the most supported and future-proof approach to linear gradients.

Radial gradients have an even wider level of varying support. Because of this, *CSS3 Foundations* doesn't cover radials. Should you wish to learn more, I'd recommend reading the CSS3 Image Values and Replaced Content module which contains the Candidate Recommendation explanation of radial gradients, found at www.w3.org/TR/css3-images/#radial-gradients. The Candidate Recommendation will almost certainly be the finalized syntax, which is already supported unprefixed in Internet Explorer 10+ and Firefox 16+.

If you'd rather just create a radial gradient effect and not worry about how the code works, you can use a code generator, such as the one found at www.colorzilla.com/gradient-editor/ (which can also generate linear gradients).

Linear Gradients

Unprefixed browser support: IE 10+, Firefox 16+, Opera 12+

Prefixed browser support: Firefox 3.6+, Chrome 10+, Opera 11+, Safari 5.1+

Start by applying a linear gradient to the buttons on the page before taking a closer look at how to write them:

1. In styles.css, find the rule set for .showcase .button:hover and above it, add the following rule set:

```
.showcase .button {
    padding: 20px;
    background-image:
-webkit-linear-gradient(top, #FB3876 0%, #d4326d 100%);
    background-image:
-moz-linear-gradient(to bottom, #FB3876 0%, #d4326d 100%);
    background-image:
-o-linear-gradient(to bottom, #FB3876 0%, #d4326d 100%);
    background-image:
linear-gradient(to bottom, #FB3876 0%, #d4326d 100%);
}
```

2. Save styles.css.

When using gradients, the vendor prefix is prefixed to the property value rather than the property.

First, you add 20px of padding to the showcase button, which places space between the border of the box and the content. You learn about this property in Chapter 7. The purpose of this padding is just to make the area a little bigger so you can see that fancy gradient better!

I mentioned previously you wouldn't have to write all of the vendor-prefixed properties yourself but just to demonstrate the safest way to use gradients, you've done so in this rule set. The -webkit- property uses the outdated syntax for gradients, which you'll look at in a moment. The -moz- property applies to Firefox versions 3.6 to 15. The -o- property applies to Opera 11 and the official, unprefixed property applies to Internet Explorer 10+, Opera 12+, and Firefox 16+, it will eventually apply to future versions of WebKit browsers too. Note that because Internet Explorer 9 doesn't support gradients at all and Internet Explorer 10+ only supports the official unprefixed property, a prefixed -ms- property is not required. Should you include it, though, it won't affect anything.

So, now you know how to achieve gradients in the widest amount of browsers, what does the linear-gradient() function do?

As evident in Figure 5-15, linear-gradient() specifies the gradient line (the direction of the gradient) and two color stops, which consist of a color and the position of that color.

— #FB3876

— #D4326D

FIGURE 5-15 The linear gradient applied to the showcase button, starting with a hot pink, going into a darker pink at the bottom.

Gradient Line

The default argument for the gradient line is the keyword to bottom, so technically in this example, to bottom can be omitted and the same effect would be achieved. The keyword to bottom starts the gradient from the top and ends at the bottom. Other gradient line keywords are to top (going from bottom to top), to right (going from left to right), and to left (going from right to left).

Note that WebKit doesn't understand these keywords and instead opts for top, bottom, left, and right (the outdated syntax), which denote the starting point of the gradient and are the equivalents of to bottom, to top, to right, and to left.

If you would like something other than a straight gradient line, you can specify an angle in degrees. The preceding keywords each represent an angle; to top is 0deg, to right is 90deg, to bottom is 180deg, and to left is 270deg. You can also combine these keywords to create a gradient line that goes from corner to corner; `to bottom right` goes from the top left to the bottom right, for example. You'll be pleased to know that WebKit, does understand gradient lines when expressed as degrees in the same way that Firefox does, so to make things more consistent, you could rely on degrees instead of keywords.

Color Stops

A color stop is composed of a color value (using any of the color property values described in Chapter 4), followed by an optional stop position, which can be defined by a value type such as percentages or pixels. You can specify as many color stops as you need, separating each with a comma to create a multicolored gradient. If you specify a color value but not an optional stop position, the browser assumes the stop position should be placed exactly in between the other stop positions. So, `linear-gradient(#fff, #000)` creates a gradient going from top to bottom with the top being white, fading into black as it reaches the bottom.

Figure 5-16 shows how `linear-gradient(#fff, #ff0000, #000)` creates a gradient going from top to bottom with the top being white, the center being red, and the bottom being black.

FIGURE 5-16 The linear gradient applied to the showcase button, starting with white, changing into red at the center, and then changing into black at the bottom.

 When you are adding a gradient to a web page, sometimes it's better to look at a visual representation of the gradient you're trying to create, to get it exactly as you want it. Many free tools are available that make working with gradients easier. My personal recommendation is ColorZilla's gradient editor, which you can find at www.colorzilla.com/gradient-editor/.

background-clip

Initial value: `border-box` | Inherited: No | Applies to: All | CSS3
Browser support: IE 9+, Firefox 4+, Chrome 1+, Opera 10.5+, Safari 3+

`background-clip` determines the "painting area" of an element, the area of the element to which a background should be applied. By default, the `background-clip` value is `border-box`, which makes the painting area start from the edges of an element, where the border starts.

Looking at Figure 5-17, you can see the background image of the newsletter box reaches the edges. Earlier in the "Add More Border and Box Shadow Styles" code challenge, you gave this element a black border with a transparency of `0.1`, but note that the border actually looks like a dark blue color. The reason is that the background image appears behind the border and shows through the partially transparent border.

FIGURE 5-17 The newsletter box, with a background-clip of border-box.

If you want the painting area to start inside the border, you can apply the following to the `#newsletter` rule set:

```
background-clip: padding-box;
```

The "padding" of an element starts inside an element's border. In Figure 5-18, you can now see the border is black with a `0.1` transparency (making it gray because the white of the main content area shows through).

FIGURE 5-18 The newsletter box, with a background-clip of padding-box.

Padding, which is covered in Chapter 7, adds space between the edge of an element and the elements or contents it contains.

Add padding to the newsletter box:

1. In styles.css, add the following declaration to the `#newsletter` rule set:

   ```
   padding: 6%;
   ```

2. Save styles.css.

There is now a significant space between the edges of the newsletter box and its content. What if you want the painting area to be only the background of the content? In that case, you can use the final `background-clip` value, `content-box`, as shown in Figure 5-19.

FIGURE 5-19 The newsletter box with a background-clip of content-box and 6% padding.

Note that if you want to use multiple background images, as with the other background properties, you can separate multiple `background-clip` properties with a comma.

background-origin

Initial value: `padding-box` | Inherited: No | Applies to: All | CSS3
Browser support: IE 9+, Firefox 4+, Chrome 1+, Opera 10.5+, Safari 3+

In Figure 5-19, you may have noticed the newsletter icon disappeared. With a declaration of `background-clip: content-box`, the icon was positioned outside the content area and got clipped. `background-origin` allows you to change the background positioning area.

In Figure 5-20, I changed the `background-clip` back to `border-box` and gave it a `background-position` of 92% 0. As you can see, the newsletter icon still sits 92% to the right of the box but starts perfectly where the padding box does—the default value for `background-origin`.

FIGURE 5-20 The newsletter icon in relation to the newsletter box with a background-clip of border-box and a background-position of 92% 0.

When you change the `background-origin` to `border-box`, the newsletter icon touches the top of the border, as shown in Figure 5-21.

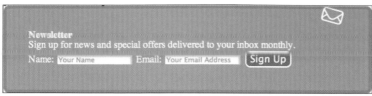

FIGURE 5-21 The newsletter icon in relation to the newsletter box with a background-origin of border-box applied to it.

Can you guess what happens when `background-origin: content-box` is applied? The position of the newsletter icon starts within the content area, as shown in Figure 5-22.

FIGURE 5-22 The newsletter icon in relation to the newsletter box with a background-origin of content-box applied to it.

background-size

Initial value: `auto` | Inherited: No | Applies to: All | CSS3

Unprefixed browser support: IE 9+

Prefixed browser support: Firefox 3.6+, Chrome 1+, Opera 9.5+, Safari 3+

The `background-size` property was introduced in CSS Level 3, which allows you to change the size of a background image. As with `background-position`, you can use all value types, percentages, pixels, ems, and so on. Percentages are relative to the background positioning area, a concept explained in the descriptions for the previous properties.

```
background-size: 50% 100%;
```

In this example, two values are specified: one for the width, one for the height. A background image with this declaration is 50% the width of the element to which it is applied and 100% its height.

If you use the declaration `background-size: 50%`, the second value is assumed to be `auto`. When `auto` is used, the browser calculates the height based on the specified width to maintain the image's aspect ratio.

You can also use two keyword values: `cover` and `contain`.

`background-size:` `contain` scales a background image to fit inside the background positioning area, making it as large as possible while respecting the image's aspect ratio.

`background-size:` `cover` scales a background image to the smallest size so that both the image's height and width cover the background positioning area while respecting the image's aspect ratio.

background (Shorthand)

Browser support: IE 4+, Firefox 1+, Chrome 1+, Opera 3.5+, Safari 1+

Much like the border properties, background properties also have a shorthand property, simply called `background`.

Rather than have up to eight declarations to style a background, you can use the background shorthand with the following syntax:

```
background: background-image background-position background-size
repeat-style attachment background-origin background-clip
background-color
```

When you use multiple background images, you should specify `background-color` only on the last layer of a background.

1. In styles.css, find the `#newsletter` rule set and remove the following declarations:

    ```
    background-color: #00ACDF;
    background-image: url("../images/icon-newsletter.png"),
    url("../images/bg-newsletter.png");
    background-repeat: no-repeat, repeat;
    background-position: 91% 2%, 0;
    ```

2. Add a shorthand declaration:

    ```
    background: url("../images/icon-newsletter.png") no-repeat
      91% 2%,
    url("../images/bg-newsletter.png") repeat 0 #00ACDF;
    ```

3. Save styles.css.

The shorthand declaration achieves the exact same styles as was originally achieved. Because the newsletter box had two background images applied to it, a comma separates the two shorthand values. Finally, although you can have multiple background images, you can have only one background color, so you add `background-color` at the end of the last background layer.

CSS Image Replacement

Sometimes, you may want to show an image in place of text. Take the Cool Shoes & Socks link in the footer of the page for example. At the moment, it's just text, but really, it would look nicer if it was a small version of the logo.

Add a background image to the footer link:

1. In styles.css, add the following rule set:

```
.small-logo a {
    background: white url("../images/logo-small.png") no-repeat
  center;
    display: block;
    min-height: 11px;
    width: 162px;
    padding: 5px;
}
```

2. Save styles.css.

   This rule set adds a small version of the Cool Shoes & Socks logo as a background image, makes the `<a>` element a block to fill a space of 11px × 162px and gives it a small amount of padding (`padding` is covered in Chapter 7 and `display` in Chapter 9).

   The problem with doing this is that the text sits on top of the background image, which doesn't look right, as shown in Figure 5-23.

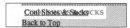

FIGURE 5-23 The footer link text conflicting with the background image.

   You could just remove the text from the HTML and put an `<img>` element in its place. However, as the footer logo is more of a style than content, it's a best practice to make it a background image instead.

To work around the clashing of text and background image, you can use a technique commonly referred to as Image Replacement.

3. In the newly added `.small-logo` a rule set, add the following declarations:

```
font: 0/0 a;
text-shadow: none;
color: transparent;
```

4. Save styles.css.

You will learn about `text-shadow` and `font` properties in Chapter 11. For now, know that the `font` property makes the font size and line height zero. Any shadow that may be applied to the text is removed and the color is made transparent. These three properties together hide text in all browsers (see Figure 5-24) so now, although the text is still in the HTML, it can't be seen, allowing just the background image to show. If CSS is disabled in the browser, the text will be shown in place of the background image. Ideal!

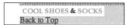

FIGURE 5-24 The footer link with hidden text, allowing the background image to show through.

Code Challenge: Add More Background Properties

In styles.css, do the following:

1. Add a new rule set for `#header nav > ul > li` with the declaration `background: white;`.

2. In the `#footer` rule set, change the `background-image` and `background-color` declarations to use the `background` shorthand property.

3. In the `.showcase` rule set, add the declaration `background: #f5f5f5;`.

 Project files update (ch05-02): If you haven't followed the previous instructions and are comfortable working from here onward or would like to reference the project files up to this point, you can download them from `www.wiley.com/go/treehouse/css3foundations`.

opacity

Initial value: 1 | Inherited: No | Applies to: All | CSS3
Browser support: IE 9+, Firefox 1+, Chrome 1+, Opera 9+, Safari 1.2+

opacity, introduced in CSS Level 3, gives elements a level of transparency.

```
opacity: 0.5;
```

The value for opacity is a number, ranging between 0 and 1, to one decimal place. In the preceding example, the opacity of an element is 50%.

Unlike when you use a background color with an alpha value (which is a color with a transparency), opacity applies to the element and *all* its children. So say you use the following:

```
body {
    opacity: 0.7;
}
```

Here, the entire web page has a 70% transparency, which isn't very sensible!

The opacity property works in all modern browsers except for Internet Explorer versions 6, 7, and 8. However, as with gradients, these older versions of Internet Explorer support a filter property that achieves the same effect. For more information about the unofficial filter property, please see msdn.microsoft.com/en-us/library/ie/ms530752 (v=vs.85).aspx.

In Chapter 15, you learn how to use a tool to automatically write vendor prefixes you haven't included during the creation of the Cool Shoes & Socks website. It also adds the alternative filter properties to make any instance of opacity work in older versions of Internet Explorer.

visibility

Initial value: visible | Inherited: Yes | Applies to: All | CSS2.1
Browser support: IE 4+, Firefox 1+, Chrome 1+, Opera 4+, Safari 1+

Using opacity: 0 to hide an element works visually, but it's not necessarily the best way to hide an element. The visibility property can be given three values: visible, hidden and collapse. All elements, by default, are visible. visibility: hidden hides an element, but how does that differ from opacity: 0, which also hides elements?

Assume for a moment that you want to hide the "About" link on the Cool Shoes & Socks web page. When hiding the link, you use opacity, like so:

```
nav ul li:nth-child(2){
    opacity: 0;
}
```

In Figure 5-25, the "About" link is no longer visible on the page, but you can still see an empty space where that link should be. If you hover over that empty space, you can still click the "About" link, even though the element has an opacity of 0.

FIGURE 5-25 The blank area where the "About" link is positioned.

When `visibility: hidden` is applied:

```
nav ul li:nth-child(2){
    visibility: hidden;
}
```

The "About" link is still rendered (you can see the empty space, as in Figure 5-25); however, this time, you can't click it! So both methods of hiding an element still render that element, but `visibility: hidden` has no events—such as clicking—whereas `opacity: 0` does.

What if you want to have an element hidden and not even rendered? An element that exists in the HTML but doesn't show an empty space when it's hidden?

Using `display: none` achieves that, as shown in Figure 5-26:

```
nav ul li:nth-child(2){
    display: none;
}
```

FIGURE 5-26 The "About" link is no longer rendered on the page when it is given the declaration display: none.

Because `display` relates to structure, it is covered in Chapter 9.

cursor

Initial value: `auto` | Inherited: Yes | Applies to: All | CSS2.1
Browser support: IE 4+, Firefox 1+, Chrome 1+, Opera 7+, Safari 1.2+

The `cursor` property allows you to change the type of cursor displayed when hovering over an element. The initial value of `auto` means the user agent stylesheet determines the cursor.

Changing the cursor is a great way to show users how they can interact with a particular element.

1. In styles.css, find the rule set for `input[type="submit"][class="button"]` and add the following declaration:

   ```
       cursor: pointer;
   }
   ```

2. Save styles.css.

Now, when you hover over the Sign Up button in the newsletter box, the cursor changes to a pointer, letting the user know the button can be clicked.

The look of the cursors differs based on the operating system they are being viewed on. The following values can be used: `crosshair`, `default`, `pointer`, `move`, `e-resize`, `ne-resize`, `nw-resize`, `n-resize`, `se-resize`, `sw-resize`, `s-resize`, `w-resize`, `text`, `wait`, `help`, and `progress`.

If these cursors don't take your fancy, you can also use the `url()` function (as you did with the `background-image` property) to use a custom cursor.

outline (Shorthand)

Browser support: IE 8+, Firefox 1.5+, Chrome 1+, Opera 7+, Safari 1.2+

You applied styles in Chapter 3 to give every element that has focus an outline. Giving elements an outline is important for accessibility. Assume a visitor to your web page can't use a mouse (he may have a disability that prevents him from doing so or, quite simply, the batteries in his mouse ran out). To browse your web page, that user needs to use his keyboard. To move between elements of a web page using a keyboard, you can use the Tab key. With each press of the Tab key, starting from the top left of the page, elements are given an outline style, which lets the user know where on the page he is.

Because this is an important property that aids navigation, many browsers have this style built in to their default styles via the user agent stylesheet. If you want to change those default styles, you can use the outline-color, outline-style, and outline-width properties.

Do those property names ring a bell? That's right; they work in the exact same way as border-color, border-style, and border-width. You can use the shorthand outline in the same way as the shorthand border too!

Because you already added outline styles to the a:focus pseudo-class in Chapter 3, you don't need to add any more. However, you can change those properties into one shorthand property:

1. In styles.css, find the pseudo-class a:focus and remove the following declarations:

```
outline-color: black;
outline-style: dotted;
outline-width: 1px;
```

2. Add the shorthand declaration:

```
outline: black dotted 1px;
```

3. Save styles.css.

content

Initial value: auto | Inherited: No | Applies to: :before and :after only | CSS3
Browser support: IE 8+, Firefox 2+, Chrome 4+, Opera 9+, Safari 3.1+

In Chapter 3 you used the content property to give quotation marks to the customer testimonials. content can be applied only to :before and :after pseudo-elements.

Now try another example:

1. In styles.css, below the three blockquote related rule sets, add the following:

```
blockquote cite:before {
    content: "- ";
}
```

2. Save styles.css.

This adds a hyphen before the customer's name, showing that a testimonial belongs to her. This is just a visual style, and in its absence, the content of the page isn't affected. These sorts of styles are the purpose of content, which I hope answers the question raised in Chapter 3: What place does content have in CSS? CSS, after all, is supposed to separate style from content and structure, so why would you want to include content in your CSS?

Characters such as quotation marks and hyphens are arguably presentational styles as opposed to content. You may have a website containing 50 quotation marks, and one day decide you want to change the style of them. If those quotation marks were included in the HTML page as physical characters, you would have to go into each page and change them individually. If you generate those characters via the content property, changing their style is a simple case of changing one property value.

Summary

In this chapter, you learned to use many of CSS's visual styles. With the inclusion of CSS Level 3's most recent and exciting features, border and backgrounds alone are enough to give a page a unique look.

Properties such as opacity, visibility, cursor, and outline allow you to give a page certain styles when interacted with, helping a user navigate through your web site.

You've also learned how to implement experimental properties safely using vendor prefixes. As you make your way through *CSS3 Foundations*, you'll rely on vendor prefixes again, to be used with the latest CSS3 properties.

Now that you've added styles to make elements stand out and give the page its own personality, you're ready to move on to giving the page structure.

part 3

Building a Solid and Adaptable Page Structure

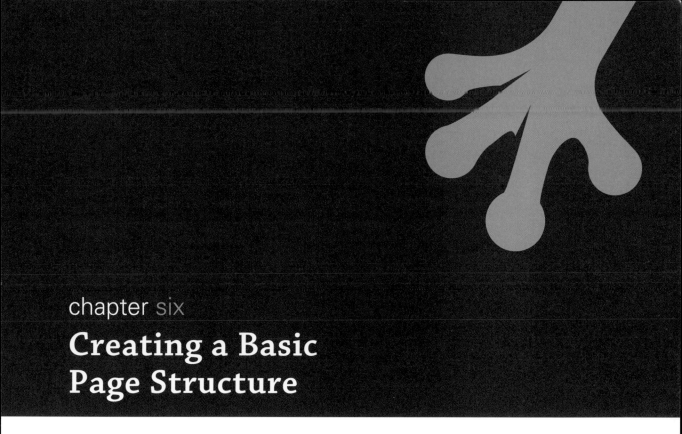

chapter six
Creating a Basic Page Structure

IN THE PRECEDING chapters, you added presentational styles to the Cool Shoes & Socks web page, but as yet, the page doesn't have much structure other than the basic top-to-bottom layout of elements. In this chapter, you learn about fixed and fluid page layouts, plus a hybrid of the two that will help to make Cool Shoes & Socks responsive, so a layout can respond to the device on which it is being viewed.

Structure Types

Structure types aren't necessarily something described in the CSS specification. They are a method of combining multiple CSS properties to create page structures that suit particular tasks.

In the early days of web pages, structure types tended to be fluid, meaning a web page stretched and resized as the browser did to always fill the viewport. This is where the "fluid" name comes from: It fills every area of the web page regardless of its size, just like a fluid fills its container.

As the web moved forward and design became more elaborate, web designers wanted more control over web pages. If a fluid page stretched depending on the browser window size, designers would have a difficult job designing a web page because they couldn't be sure how that page would look to the users. The majority of the web started making use of the fixed-width layout, which is still the most-used structure type today.

117

Although fixed-width layouts are the most used today, with new technologies such as CSS3 and HTML5, and in particular the CSS3 media queries, the web is moving toward responsive layouts that start with a fluid structure but then change that layout based on the size of a device—something that couldn't be done when fluid layouts were first in use.

In this chapter, you look at fixed and fluid layouts but actually use a hybrid of the two, and then in Chapter 16, you add media queries to make the layout responsive!

 Project files update (ch06-00): If you haven't followed the previous instructions and are comfortable working from here onward or would like to reference the project files up to this point, you can download them from `www.wiley.com/go/treehouse/css3foundations`.

Fluid

A web page, by default, is fluid. The reason is that the initial value for an element's width is `auto`, which tells the browser to work out the width itself, based on the unused space around that element. Without any CSS applied to a page—other than the user agent stylesheet—`width: auto` is the equivalent of `width: 100%`.

Before you gave the `<body>` element a `max-width` in the previous chapter, the Cool Shoes & Socks web page was completely fluid.

Fluid-width websites are often used when a page has a lot of information and the designer wants to make the most of the space available.

Fixed

Fixed-width layouts are made by giving the element that contains the rest of the page's elements—in the case of Cool Shoes & Socks, the `<body>` element—a `width` property. The `width` property is usually a pixel value such as 960px, which makes the `<body>` element always 960px, regardless of the size of the browser.

Why a width of 960px? When the web was accessed by fewer types of devices (mainly the only consideration was differing desktop display sizes), it was wise to use a width of 960px because the most-used screen resolution was 1,024 × 768, meaning that 960px would fit nicely into a 1,024px display (as shown in Figure 6-1), as well as anything bigger than that. If a web page is 1,260px wide and is viewed on a screen 1,024px wide, the browser has to show horizontal scroll bars to allow the user to move across to see the full page. Likewise, if viewing a web page that is 960px wide on a screen or in a browser window less than 960px, horizontal scroll bars appear. Although you can't control the size of the browser window, you can make a web page a size that fits in the majority of screen sizes. The choice of the browser window size and whether a horizontal scroll bar appears is then left to the user.

So, what's wrong with horizontal scroll bars? Because users expect a web page to be navigated vertically, the addition of a horizontal scroll bar can make navigation around a web page feel awkward. For the sake of good usability, you should avoid horizontal scroll bars where possible.

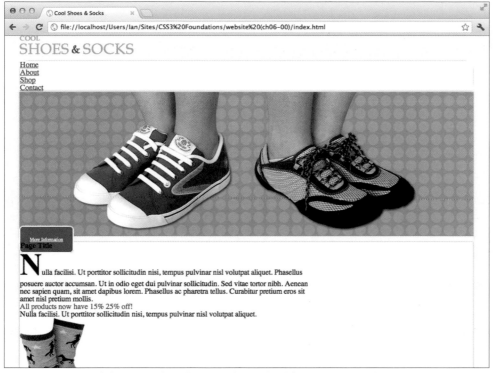

FIGURE 6-1 The Cool Shoes & Socks web page with a fixed width of 960px, viewed on a 1,024 × 768 resolution.

Further to this, 960 is a nice round figure that can be divided into round values when using columns, making a web page of 960px easier to lay out and more pleasing to the eye.

A page being centered using the following declaration on the element that contains all other elements is another common characteristic of fixed-width layouts:

```
margin: 0 auto;
```

If a centered, fixed-width layout is viewed on a screen with a width greater than the page width, the page is still centered. This is another technique often used in fixed-width layouts.

That's fixed-width layouts in a nutshell. Note that when referring to fixed, fluid, and hybrid layouts, I am referring only to the width of the layout. Although you can have lots of control over the width of a layout, because content can be resized—either by the device viewing that page or the user—the height of a layout is always an unknown, and as a best practice, you should avoid declaring specific heights on any element of a page.

Hybrid Layout for Responsive Design

In the previous chapter, you made the page a hybrid layout, by adding the following rule set to styles.css:

```
body {
    . . .
    margin: 0 auto;
    max-width: 960px;
}
```

Let's start with the obvious: `max-width` is the maximum width an element should be. Here, you specified the `<body>` element should get no bigger than `960px`. Because a `width` isn't specified, the default width of the `<body>` is `100%` unless your browser is narrower than `960px`, in which case the `<body>` element is the same width as your browser.

This layout is a hybrid. Although you fixed the maximum width of the page to 960px, it is still fluid below those 960 pixels.

Technically, a layout doesn't have to be a hybrid (a mixture of fixed and fluid) to be responsive; it just needs to be fluid. The reason you make Cool Shoes & Socks a hybrid—fluid below 960px and fixed above—is to make sure the site scales down to size on mobile devices but doesn't grow so big that it looks messy on displays with a large resolution. Currently, the biggest screen resolution available is 2,560px wide. If the page is allowed to stretch 100% across a screen of that size, sentences become very long and there is a lot of white space between elements, neither of which is great for readability and usability. Of course, a 960px wide site on a 2,560px wide screen leaves a lot of empty space on either side of the site, so you might want to make the `max-width` wider to better accommodate. I leave that choice to you, but for *CSS3 Foundations*, I stick with 960px.

You also added the declaration `margin: 0 auto`, so what does that do? The `margin` property is similar to `padding`, but rather than adding space between the borders of an element and its child elements, `margin` adds space between the borders of an element and its parent element. The layout of elements in this way is known as the *box model*, which is covered in Chapter 7. The margin you added to the `body` rule set specifies two values: the first being the top and bottom values; and the second, the left and right. So, the `<body>` element has no margin on the top and bottom, but the left and right are half of the remaining space between the `<body>` and `<html>` element—in other words, centered!

Now that the page has a hybrid layout, if you reduce the size of the browser, the page shrinks to fit. However, the smaller the browser becomes, the less room elements have and everything starts to look crammed. In Chapter 16, you learn to use media queries to change the style of elements based on the size of the browser window or device on which the page is being viewed, making the page responsive.

Fluid Images

If you're keen of eye, you may have noticed that although the Cool Shoes & Socks page is now a hybrid layout, while most of the webpage shrinks to fit the browser window below 960px, the showcase image doesn't.

As you can see in Figure 6-2, when a browser is shrunk below 960px, a horizontal scroll bar is added to the page so the user can move across to see the overflow.

Horizontal scroll bar

FIGURE 6-2 Cool Shoes & Socks viewed in Google Chrome at a width of 500px.

When scrolling horizontally to the right, you can see the page doesn't look too great; in fact, it looks broken, as shown in Figure 6-3. Although the container of the page is 500px—the same size as the browser window—the showcase image sticks out like a sore thumb. The reason is that the natural size of the showcase image is 960px × 301px, and the browser has respected those dimensions so the image doesn't look stretched or shrunken.

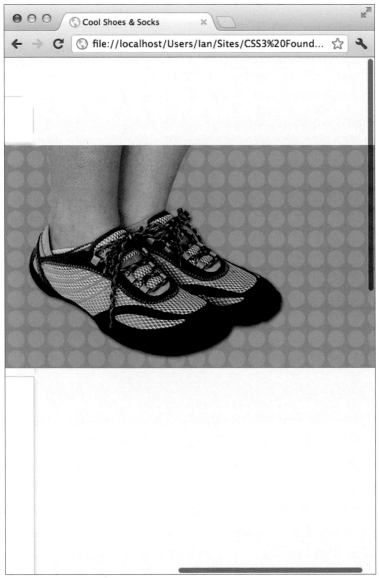

FIGURE 6-3 The overflow of the Cool Shoes & Socks page when viewed in Google Chrome at a width of 500px.

Go ahead and fix that:

1. In styles.css, underneath the body rule set, add the following rule set:

```
img {
    max-width: 100%;
}
```

2. Save styles.css.

This is a rule set very common to responsive design and doesn't just fix the showcase image, but makes all images on the page scale based on the width of the element they are contained within.

With this rule set, the showcase image can now only be the same size as the `<div class="showcase">` element it is contained within. Now, no matter what the width of the browser window, the image is fluid, just like the rest of the page, as shown in Figure 6-4.

Adaptive Design

If *responsive design* is something you've heard of before, you may have heard about *adaptive design,* too. What's the difference?

Where a responsive design uses a fluid layout and media queries to make a web page change its layout for every different width, an adaptive design uses a fixed layout and media queries to change the layout only when specific width conditions are met. A responsive design changes its layout for every different pixel width, whereas an adaptive design may change its layout several times: one for mobile, one for tablets, and one for desktop/laptops, for example.

FIGURE 6-4 The image is now rescaled to fit perfectly in the browser window with a width of 500px.

Mobile First Design

While on the subject of responsive and adaptive design, let's cover another buzz phrase you may have heard of: mobile first design.

The purpose of mobile first design is to begin creating a website with mobile devices in mind first.

This mobile first mindset forces you to think about what is the most important content to display in the space available. You can then slowly build up the less relevant content as and when you have more space to play with. This approach has performance benefits too—for mobile devices that typically have less processing power and generally less bandwidth than other devices.

Because a responsive site unavoidably has some styles on a web page that need to be overwritten to change the layout appropriate for the device on which it is being viewed, it is better to begin with a mobile layout. This way, the mobile device doesn't have to process styles or download images that it doesn't need. Instead, you can leave the overwriting of styles to devices with more processing power and bandwidth, where speed and efficiency aren't quite as critical.

So why isn't this type of design practiced in *CSS3 Foundations*? Well, for a few reasons. First, not every website needs to be responsive, so it is better to learn how to create a web page as you are doing now—by building the desktop version first. In the future, you may find that if you are creating web pages for clients or other people, they request only a desktop version of a website but then later ask you to modify it to be more efficient and accessible for mobile devices. Although "mobile first" is *best* practice, "desktop first" is a real-world practice, too, especially during this time when the web is transitioning from fixed to responsive layouts. You can apply the method of adding media queries, which you do in Chapter 16, in the same way if you decide to try a "mobile first" approach in the future. So by learning the "desktop first" approach, you don't miss out on any techniques, and learning is more efficient.

Summary

In this chapter, you learned about the various layouts that are commonly used for web pages; you also learned what a few of the web industry's most recent buzz phrases mean. The Cool Shoes & Socks web page now has a hybrid layout, and the contents within that layout are scaling relatively to it. With this new overall page structure applied to the page, in the next chapter, you learn about the box model and box-sizing, concepts which are used to structure the elements within the main page.

chapter seven

Creating Space and Understanding the Box Model

THE BOX MODEL describes the layout of elements on a web page. In this chapter, you learn how `margin`, `padding`, and `border` affect the layout of the box model, making structuring a page easier.

Project files update (ch07-00): If you haven't followed the previous instructions and are comfortable working from here onward or would like to reference the project files up to this point, you can download them from `www.wiley.com/go/treehouse/css3foundations`.

The Box Model

In Chapter 5, you used `padding` to create some space between the content and border of the newsletter box and changed the `border` properties. By making these changes, you affected the box model of the main newsletter element `<form id="newsletter" action="#">`.

Now add some margin and padding to the footer to better understand these properties:

1. In styles.css, below the other declarations in the `#footer` rule set, add the following:

   ```
   margin-top: 2.5em;
   padding: 1.4em 0;
   ```

2. Save styles.css.

Here, you change the box model of the `<footer id="footer" role="contentinfo">` element, as shown in Figure 7-1.

Before:

After:

FIGURE 7-1 The footer element before and after adding the margin and padding properties.

Because the box model is invisible—it changes the visual layout of an element, but you can't see the boundaries that make up that element—Figure 7-2 shows exactly how the `margin-top` and `padding` property change the box model for the footer.

FIGURE 7-2 The way the box model of the footer element is laid out.

Look familiar? Figure 5-19 in Chapter 5 showed the content area and padding area to demonstrate `background-clip` and `background-origin`. In Figure 7-2, the margin area is also shown, which adds space outside the footer element.

Figure 7-3 shows how the content, padding, border, and margin areas relate.

- The content area is that which contains the content.
- The padding area, which is optional and 0 by default, is the area between the content area and the inner edge of the border.
- The border, which is optional and none by default, is the visual edge around an element (in Figure 7-3 I made the border 27px so it can be clearly seen).
- The margin area, which is optional and 0 by default, is the area outside the border.

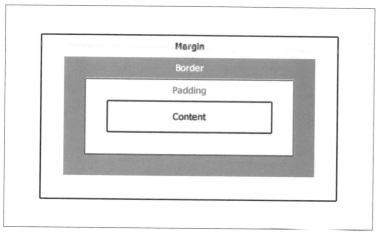

FIGURE 7-3 A simplified version of the box model.

Using Web Developer Tools to Better Understand the Box Model

Sometimes working with the box model can be troublesome. Although manipulating the box model affects elements visually, you can never be sure where the boundaries of the content, border, padding, and margin areas are.

A handy little trick is to apply a temporary border around an element to see exactly how it is laid out, by using the following declaration on the element you are working on:

```
border: red solid 1px;
```

Of course, because this is only a temporary style for your use during the creation of a web page, you can make the border style whatever you want. Sometimes I find myself using temporary border styles each with a different color on multiple elements.

Although seeing the border of an element is helpful, it doesn't show the margin area, and you can only guess at where the content and padding areas are.

Many web developer tools make working with the box model easier, by showing the areas that make up the box model.

In Figure 7-4, I right-clicked on the footer element and selected Inspect Element to use Google Chrome's web developer tools.

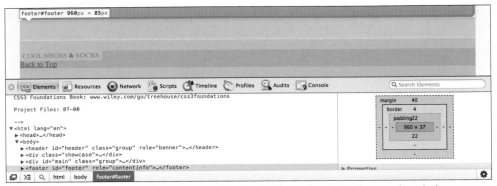

FIGURE 7-4 The footer element being inspected in Google Chrome's web developer tools with the simplified box model in the smaller pane to the right.

Chrome, Firefox (when using Firebug), Safari, and Opera show a visual representation of the box model directly on the page. All browsers (including Internet Explorer 9+) show a visual representation along with measurements in the side panel under "Layout" (or "Metrics" in Chrome and Safari).

In Chrome and Safari 6+, each particular area that makes up the box model is color-coded. The blue area is the content area; green, the padding; yellow, the border; and orange, the margin.

Opera and older versions of Safari don't color-code the areas. Just remember that the content area is the innermost, followed by the padding, and then margin areas.

When using Firebug for Firefox, you must right-click an element and select Inspect Element. Firebug doesn't show the box model until you hover over the element in the DOM window, though. It colors the content area blue, the padding purple, and the margin green.

Internet Explorer 9's equivalent of the Inspect Element feature is called Select element by click, which you can find in the F12 Developer Tools, represented as a white cursor. After you select that, you can then click on the element you want to inspect.

margin

Initial value: 0 | Inherited: No | Applies to: All except elements with table display types other than table-caption, table, and inline-table | CSS2.1

Browser Support: IE 3+, Firefox 1+, Chrome 1+, Opera 3.5+, Safari 1+

As you saw in the box model explanation, `margin` applies space outside an element. A margin can be a value of any length type, such as pixels, percentages, and ems. You also can use the auto keyword to make the browser determine the margin of an element based on the unused space around that element.

Using margin is a great way of adding *white space*—also known as *negative space*—between elements on a web page. White space is an empty area and doesn't necessarily mean a space is white in color. It is used to give web pages design aesthetics such as rhythm and balance, making for a better user experience.

You may agree at the moment that the Cool Shoes & Socks page doesn't have much rhythm or balance; all the elements are squashed together because they have margins of 0. You can change that:

1. In styles.css, find the following declaration in the body rule set:

    margin: 0 auto;

    This is the declaration you added in Chapter 5 to make the page centered.

    The margin property is actually shorthand for the properties margin-top, margin-right, margin-bottom, and margin-left. By specifying two values for the shorthand margin property, you tell the browser the top and bottom of the <body> element should have no margin and the left and right should have a margin of auto.

2. Change the margin value of the body rule set to the following:

    margin: 2.5em auto 0 auto;

3. Save styles.css.

Now the <body> has a margin-top of 2.5em, a margin-right of auto, a margin-bottom of 0, and a margin-left of auto. The <body> is still centered but now with some white space above it so the logo no longer touches the top of the window.

You also are able to achieve the same effect using just three values, like so: margin: 2.5em auto 0. In this case, the margin-top is 2.5em, the margin-left *and* margin-right are auto, and the margin-bottom is 0.

Code Challenge: Add More Margins to Elements

In styles.css, do the following:

1. Add a new rule set for #header with the declaration margin: 0 0 2em 0;.

2. Add a new rule set for #header .logo with the declaration margin: 2.4em 0;.

3. Add a new rule set for #header nav with the declaration margin-top: 2em;.

4. Add the declaration margin: 0 auto; to the #content rule set.

5. Add a new rule set for .container with the declarations max-width: 920px; and margin: 0 auto;.

6. Add the declaration margin: 2em auto 1em; to the input[type="submit"] [class="button"] rule set.

7. Add a new rule set for aside with the declaration margin: 0 0 2em 0;.

8. Add the declaration margin: 0 0 1.6em 0; to the rule set aside > h3.

9. Add a new rule set for #content h1, #content h2, #content h3, #content h4 with the declaration margin: 0 0 1.6em 0;.

10. Add a new rule set for #content p, #content ul with the declaration margin: 0 0 1.25em 0;.

11. Add a new rule set for blockquote cite with the declaration margin: 0.625em 0 0 0;.

12. Add a new rule set for #newsletter h3 with the declaration margin: 0 0 1em 0;.

13. Add a new rule set for #newsletter label with the declaration margin: 1.5em 0 0 0;.

14. Add a new rule set for .aside with the declaration margin: 0 0 2em 0;.

15. Add a new rule set for .post h3 with the declaration margin: 0 0 1em 0;.

16. Add a new rule set for .post img with the declaration margin: 0 .5em 0 0;.

Project files update (ch07-01): If you haven't followed the previous instructions and are comfortable working from here onward or would like to reference the project files up to this point, you can download them from www.wiley.com/go/treehouse/css3foundations.

padding

Initial value: 0 | Inherited: No | Applies to: All except table-row-group, table-header-group, table-footer-group, table-row, table-column-group and table-column | CSS2.1

Browser Support: IE 4+, Firefox 1+, Chrome 1+, Opera 3.5+, Safari 1+

padding works in a similar way to margin but instead applies to the inside of an element prior to the border, rather than the outside of the element after the border.

The value of padding can be a percentage or any unit of length, but with it, unlike margin, you can't use the auto keyword.

In Chapter 5, you added padding to the newsletter box, like so:

```
#newsletter {
    ...
    padding: 6%;
}
```

This value gives each side of `<form id="newsletter" action="#">` a 6% padding, which is a percentage relative to the overall width of the newsletter box.

Now, because you haven't defined a width for the newsletter box, its width by default is `auto`. This `auto` setting, as explained previously, tells the browser to calculate an element's width based on the unused space. The width is calculated after the padding, so the calculated width of the newsletter box is `88%`. Why so? Because each side of the newsletter box has a `6%` padding, meaning in total the left and right have 12% padding, leaving that figure 88%. The way in which the box model is calculated seems—to me at least—more difficult than it needs to be, and I expand on this issue shortly so it doesn't catch you out.

As with `margin`, you can specify one to four values for `padding`:

- One applies to all four sides of an element.
- The first value of two applies to top and bottom and the second left and right.
- The first value of three applies to the top, the second to left *and* right, and the third to the bottom.
- Four values apply to top, right, bottom, and left, respectively.

Code Challenge: Add More Padding to Elements

In styles.css, do the following:

1. Add the declaration `padding: 2.5em;` to the #main rule set.

2. Add the declaration `padding: 1em;` to the .button rule set.

3. Remove the declaration of `padding: 20px;` from the .showcase .button rule set.

4. Add the declaration `padding: .8em;` to the input[type="submit"][class="button"] rule set.

5. Add a new rule set for .testimonials with the declaration `padding: 1em 0 0 0;`.

6. Add the declaration `padding: .4em 1em;` to the input[type="text"], input[type="email"] rule set.

Project files update (ch07-02): If you haven't followed the previous instructions and are comfortable working from here onward or would like to reference the project files up to this point, you can download them from `www.wiley.com/go/treehouse/css3foundations`.

The Pitfall of the Box Model and Working Around It

In the definition of the `padding` property, I mentioned the box model can sometimes be harder to work with than it needs to be. Let's take a deeper look at this issue so you can avoid any confusion in the future, or if you are in the fortunate position of not needing to support anything but modern browsers, a way around these difficulties altogether.

When creating a page, you may decide to declare that an element should have a width of 100%. Do that now for the newsletter box:

1. In styles.css, find the `#newsletter` rule set and add the following:

   `width: 100%;`

2. Save styles.css.

As shown in Figure 7-5, the newsletter box has a width greater than 100%, even though you told it to be 100%!

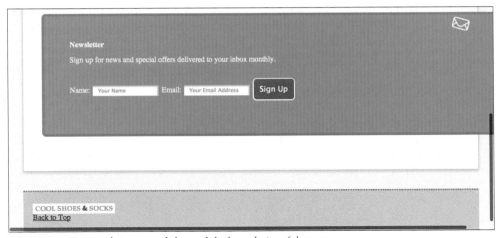

FIGURE 7-5 The newsletter extends beyond the boundaries of the page.

The reason is that, by default, the width of an element is applied only to the content area. The `#newsletter` rule set declares that the newsletter box should have a border width of 5px, a padding of 6%, and a width of 100%:

```
#newsletter {
    color: white;
    border-radius: 8px;
    border: rgba(0,0,0,0.1) solid 5px;
    background:
```

```
        url("../images/icon-newsletter.png") no-repeat 91% 2%,
        url("../images/bg-newsletter.png") repeat 0 #00ACDF;
padding: 6%;
    width: 100%;
}
```

The width of the newsletter box is now

- 10px (5px for the left border and 5px for the right) +

- 12% (for the left and right padding) +

- 100% (for the content area)

Although the browser can easily do these calculations, it makes your job styling elements a little harder because you have to do the math, too. It's not a very human-friendly way of working with the box model, is it? You'll be glad to hear that the W3C is aware of this issue, and CSS Level 3 introduces the box-sizing property, which allows you to change how the box model works. Unfortunately, because it's a CSS Level 3 feature, it isn't supported in Internet Explorer versions 6 and 7. If you have the privilege of not needing to support these older browsers, I cover box-sizing in a moment, but because the Cool Shoes & Socks scenario requires Internet Explorer 7 support, you need to fix the newsletter box so it *does* fit into the page properly:

1. In styles.css, change the width declaration of the #newsletter rule set:

    width: 88%;

2. Save styles.css.

This solution is still not completely perfect. You've changed the width of the newsletter box to account for the 12% of padding, but the calculated width is still 88% + 12% + 10px, meaning the newsletter box is still 10px bigger than 100%. Because the border is specifically 5 pixels on each side, you can't adjust the width again to account for the border, as you can't use percentages with the border-width property.

As you can see in Figure 7-6, the newsletter box isn't quite centered. The left of the newsletter box has a space of 40px, and the right is 32px. This 8px difference is due to the 10px border on the newsletter box (minus 2px for the border on #main).

FIGURE 7-6 The amended newsletter box that is no longer centered with a width of 88%.

To fix this, do the following:

1. Add a `margin` declaration to the `#newsletter` rule set:

   `margin-left: -4px;`

2. Save styles.css.

By giving the newsletter box a left margin of `-4px`, you forcefully pull it over to the left to balance out the space, making each side 36px. You may feel a little strange doing that. It kind of feels as though you are forcefully yanking the newsletter box back over to the left—fighting against the browser. As you gain experience with CSS, though, you'll find that from time to time these little "hacks" give you the control you need to make everything look perfect.

box-sizing

Initial value: `content-box` | Inherited: No | Applies to: All elements that accept width and height | CSS3

Unprefixed browser support: IE 8+, Chrome 9+, Opera 7+, Safari 5.1+

Prefixed browser support: Firefox 1+, Chrome 1+, Safari 3+

The `box-sizing` property, which was introduced in CSS Level 3, gives web page creators the choice of how they want the box model to work. The initial value for `box-sizing` is `content-box`, which has been used throughout *CSS3 Foundations* up to this point and is the described box model in this chapter.

In a nutshell, with `box-sizing` set to `content-box`, when you are specifying a width and height, those properties are applied to the content area of an element, and then the padding and border are applied outside those dimensions, as shown in Figure 7-7.

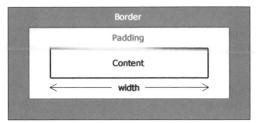

FIGURE 7-7 The way the areas of the box model are laid out when the box-sizing is content-box.

By changing the `box-sizing` to `border-box`, you, like me, may find the box model easier to work with. Before I explain, remember that `box-sizing` works in all modern browsers, as well as Internet Explorer 8, but not versions 6 and 7. For this reason, you use `box-sizing: border-box;` for only a few elements that don't need to be perfect in older versions of Internet Explorer.

`border-box` applies padding and borders inside an element with a specified width and height, as shown in Figure 7-8.

FIGURE 7-8 The way the areas of the box model are laid out when the box-sizing is border-box.

So, if the newsletter box has a specified width of 100%, you don't have to work around the centering issues you saw. These styles caused the newsletter box to appear bigger than the width of the page:

```
#newsletter {
    color: white;
    border-radius: 8px;
    border: rgba(0,0,0,0.1) solid 5px;
    background:
        url("../images/icon-newsletter.png") no-repeat 91% 2%,
        url("../images/bg-newsletter.png") repeat 0 #00ACDF;
    padding: 6%;
    width: 100%;
}
```

If you were to give the #newsletter rule set the declaration box-sizing: border-box;, the browser would make the newsletter box 100% and then apply the padding and border inside that, meaning the newsletter box wouldn't get any bigger than the defined 100%. Woohoo! Such a simple property makes working with the box model so much easier. No more math!

Again, box-sizing isn't supported in Internet Explorer 6 and 7, so you should use it only if you're not supporting those browsers or use it on noncritical styles. Now add a noncritical style to the page and make use of box-sizing: border-box in doing so:

1. In styles.css, find the rule set for input[type="text"], input[type="email"] and add the following:

    width: 100%;

2. Save styles.css.

The input fields with type text and email (which are in the newsletter box) now have a width of 100%, *but* because those elements also have padding, the same issue occurs as with the newsletter box itself.

In Figure 7-9, you can see that the input fields have a width of 100% + 2em because of the declaration padding: .4em 1em;.

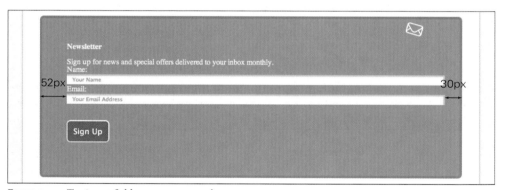

FIGURE 7-9 The input fields are not centered.

Rather than adjust values and use that negative margin-left hack as you did before, use the box-sizing property to change how the box model is laid out instead:

1. In styles.css, add the following to the rule set input[type="text"], input[type="email"]:

    box-sizing: border-box;

2. Save styles.css.

As yet, Firefox does not support the unprefixed `box-sizing` property. If you are using Firefox as your development browser, please use `-moz-box-sizing: border-box;` instead. If using a different browser, you will provide support for Firefox in Chapter 16.

And now, the input fields are exactly 100% wide and not a single pixel more, as you can see in Figure 7-10. You don't even need to do any math. Freedom!

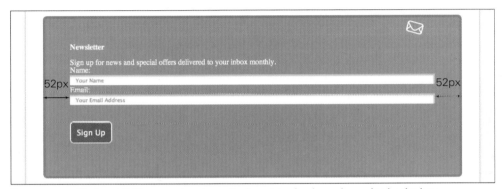

FIGURE 7-10 The input fields are centered now the box-sizing has been changed to border-box.

You may remember `content-box` and `border-box` from the `background-clip` and `background-origin` definitions in Chapter 5. You may also remember a third value those properties accepted, called `padding-box`, which at present is included in the CSS3 User Interface Module, where `box-sizing` is described (www.w3.org/TR/css3-ui/).

`padding-box` works in a similar way to `border-box`. Where `border-box` draws a border and padding inside the specified width and height of an element, `padding-box` draws the padding only on the inside and the border remains on the outside. I'm not sure why you would choose this property over the original box model `content-box` (because it's just as unintuitive to start with, if not more so) or the newer and easier to use `border-box`. This is obviously an opinion shared by browser vendors and the W3C, too, because not all browser vendors have implemented `padding-box`, and the W3C has suggested `padding-box` might be removed from the specification in the future.

Summary

In this chapter, you learned about the mysterious box model—the way in which browsers determine the layout of elements. The box model is an important concept to understand if you really want to achieve well-laid-out pages that can not only change in size based on the device a page is being viewed on but will also remain robust and modular as you continue building and styling a page. As you saw in the code challenges, a page will often have many padding and margin properties applied to it. Spending a little extra time carefully considering padding and margin during the layout stage can often save you a lot of time in the future.

With this knowledge under your belt, you're close to completing the layout of the Cool Shoes & Socks page. In the next chapter, you learn to make elements "float" next to each other, creating a multicolumn layout.

chapter eight

Creating a Multicolumn Layout

ONE OF THE most common layouts in web design is a multicolumn layout. By giving a web page columns, you can separate content into relevant sections, making better use of the space available.

Multicolumn layouts are most commonly achieved using the `float` property, which technically was never added to the CSS specification for the purpose of creating robust, multicolumn layouts. Its true purpose is actually quite a simple one: to allow one element to flow next to another. Creating multiple columns via the use of `float`, `clear`, and other properties is really a "hack"—you're making use of something in the way it wasn't intended—but it's a hack that is needed because CSS, as yet, offers very little in terms of enabling the creation of multicolumn layouts.

CSS Level 3 sees the introduction of flexbox (`www.w3.org/TR/css3-flexbox`) and regions (`www.w3.org/TR/css3-regions`), modules that aim to improve how columns and content areas are created on a web page. Unfortunately, both of these modules are in working draft and have little to no support in modern browsers, so they can't be used on a working website.

Currently, each element on the Cool Shoes & Socks web page vertically follows the next. In this chapter, you learn the basics of the `float` and `clear` properties and then combine these properties along with others to place elements side by side to make better use of the horizontal space available.

Project files update (ch08-00): If you haven't followed the previous instructions and are comfortable working from here onward or would like to reference the project files up to this point, you can download them from `www.wiley.com/go/treehouse/css3foundations`.

float

Initial value: `none` | Inherited: No | Applies to: All unless `display` in none or `position` is absolute | CSS2.1

Browser Support: IE 4+, Firefox 1+, Chrome 1+, Opera 7+, Safari 1+

At present, the product image of those irresistible horse socks—positioned in the main content of the Cool Shoes & Socks page—breaks the flow of text and takes up more space than necessary. By floating that image, you can make the text flow alongside it:

1. In styles.css, below the `#main` rule set, add a new rule set:

```
.product {
    float: left;
}
```

2. Save styles.css.

As shown in Figure 8-1, the product image now floats to the left of the containing element, and following elements that were vertically positioned below that element now flow to its right. By floating the elements this way, you utilize some of that unused space, and the image looks as though it relates to the text now.

Of course, you can float elements to the right of the containing element too, by declaring `float: right;`, which makes elements flow to the left of that floated element.

`float` also accepts the value none, which means an element should not float.

When using `float`, you can style a floating element just as you would when it's not floating. Although having the text flow to the side of the product image is desired, at the moment there's not much space between the image and text. You can change that:

1. In styles.css, add the following to the `.product` rule set:

```
margin: 0 1em 1em 0;
```

2. Save styles.css.

The image now has a small amount of white space to its right as well as below it.

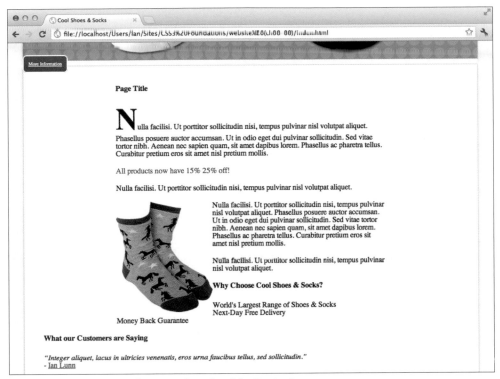

FIGURE 8-1 The main text flowing to the right of the floating image.

clear

Initial value: `none` | Inherited: No | Applies to: Block-level elements (covered in Chapter 9) | CSS2.1

Browser support: IE4+, Firefox 1+, Chrome 1+, Opera 3.5+, Safari 1+

You may notice that now the product image is floating and the text flows to its right, so too does the "Why Choose Cool Shoes & Socks" title and list items below it (contained with the `<div class="benefits">` element). Assume the "Why Choose Cool Shoes & Socks" content is to appear below the product image, it can be pushed down by clearing the float.

`clear` works in tandem with the `float` property and accepts the values `left`, `right`, `both`, and `none`.

1. In styles.css, add a new rule set for `.benefits`, like so:

```
.benefits {
    clear: left;
}
```

2. Save styles.css.

By clearing the left side of the `<div class="benefits">` element, you tell the browser this element shouldn't have a floating element to its left. When you declare `clear: left;`, the browser positions a cleared element to make sure its top border is below the bottom border of the floating element, pushing that element down, as shown in Figure 8-2.

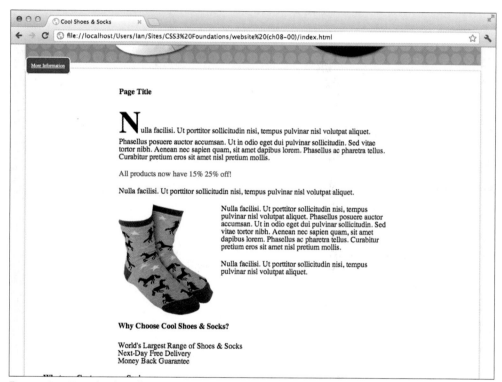

FIGURE 8-2 The `<div class="benefits">` element clearing any floating elements to its left.

Likewise, if you need to clear the right side, you can declare `clear: right;`, or to clear both sides, you can declare `clear: both;`.

If you give the `.benefits` rule set the declaration `clear: both;`, because no elements are floating to the right, the same visual effect is achieved.

Floating Multicolumns

The `float` and `clear` properties work together to allow for placing elements next to each other. When `float` and `clear` were introduced to CSS, it became apparent that they could be used beyond their intended purpose for creating multiple columns that can sit aside each other.

The sidebar was intended to sit to the right of the main content on the Cool Shoes & Socks web page, so set that up now:

1. In styles.css, find the #content rule set and add the following:

    ```
    float: left;
    ```

2. Save styles.css.

    Note that the `<div id="content" role="main">` element was originally centered via the declaration `margin: 0 auto;`, but this no longer applies because the `float` declaration takes precedence, and as shown in Figure 8-3, the content box now floats to the left of its containing element `<div id="main" class="group">`.

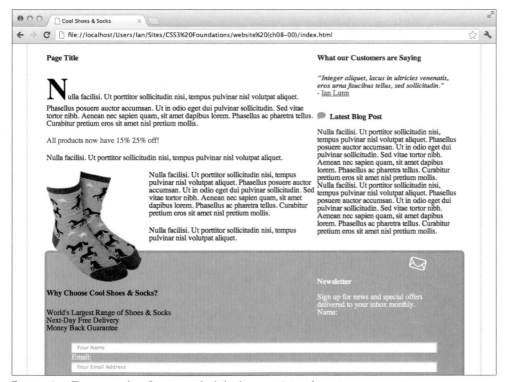

FIGURE 8-3 The content box floating to the left of its containing element.

3. In styles.css, add a new rule set:

```
.sidebar {
    float: right;
    width: 25%;
}
```

4. Save styles.css.

As you can see in Figure 8-4, although you created two columns, the layout isn't quite right. The reason is that now all the elements within the main element are floating; there's nothing clearing the elements below it. Consequently, those elements are trying to flow to the sides of the columns.

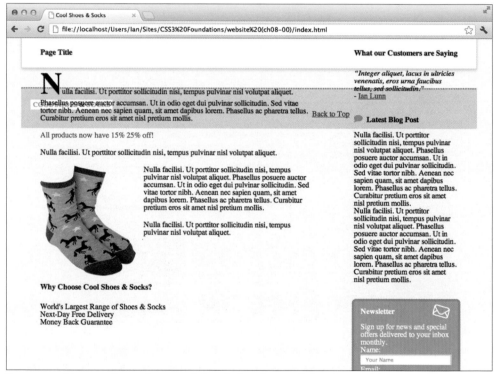

FIGURE 8-4 The two columns floating side by side, but elements below that aren't being cleared.

This is the "hacky" nature of creating columns with floats, and you can find many ways around this issue.

You may think that clearing the footer `<footer id="footer" role="contentinfo">` element would seem to work because that is the element that follows on from the floating elements.

To do that, you could add the following to the `#footer` rule set:

```
clear: both;
```

Although this technique does as expected—the footer clears below the floating columns—an unexpected behavior occurs, too: The main container doesn't appear to be aware of the size of the columns and is no longer wrapped around them, as shown in Figure 8-5.

The main container doesn't wrap around the columns

The footer, now clearing the columns

FIGURE 8-5 The browser window zoomed out to show the footer is now cleared, but the height of the main container isn't right.

You might be tempted to specify the height of the main container to make it *appear* to contain the columns, but doing so is a bad practice because you can't guarantee the main container or its contents will always be the same height. This solution is a no-go.

You could add an empty HTML element below the two floated elements:

```
<div id="main" class="group">
    <div id="content" role="main">
        ...
    </div>
    <div class="sidebar" role="complementary">
        ...
    </div>
    <div class="clear"></div>
</div>
```

Then use CSS to select the empty element to clear it:

```
.clear {
    clear: both;
}
```

Figure 8-6 shows this solution works perfectly in all browsers, but it means adding an empty element to the page, which goes against best practice. So is there a better technique?

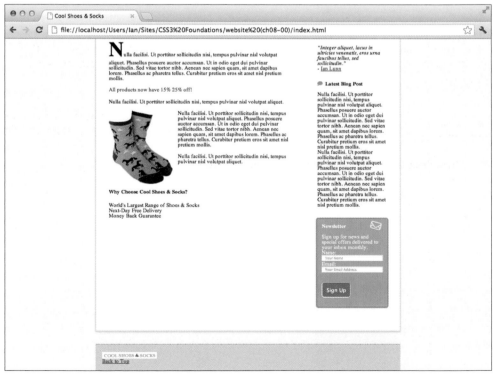

FIGURE 8-6 The browser window zoomed out to show the columns cleared by an empty HTML tag.

I could show you many different ways to work around this situation, and if you were to ask a few web designers and developers, they all would probably give you a different answer as to which technique they use. Remember that `float` and `clear` weren't created for the purpose of columns, so there's no explanation in the CSS specification of how to achieve this effect. Ideally, the best technique is the easiest to implement while not breaking any rules of good practice. With this in mind, I personally use and recommend a technique that has evolved over time and eventually been given the name *micro clearfix hack* by Nicolas Gallagher, who has worked to make this particular technique as small and efficient as possible. You can read about his work on it at `http://nicolasgallagher.com/micro-clearfix-hack`.

The micro clearfix hack in all of its glory:

```
.group:before, .group:after {
    content: "";
    display: table;
}
.group:after {
    clear: both;
}
.group {
    zoom: 1;
}
```

You may see this code used elsewhere on the web with the class name "clearfix" or "cf" for short. I personally prefer to call the class "group" to show that it contains a group of elements (acting as columns).

By using this CSS, you can give an element containing floating elements the class named `group` to fix the issue. The main container already has the class `group`, so add this fix to the CSS:

1. In styles.css, below the `body` rule set, add the following:

```
.group:before, .group:after {
    content: "";
    display: table;
}

.group:after {
    clear: both;
}

.group {
    zoom: 1;
}
```

2. Save styles.css.

The page now looks as intended, as it did in Figure 8-6 but with a more robust clearfix solution applied to it, but what exactly is that CSS doing?

It's using some properties yet to be covered:

```
.group:before, .group:after
```

First, pseudo-elements are placed before and after the `.group` element.

```
content: "";
display: table;
```

The pseudo-elements are given an empty content declaration, which, as explained in Chapter 3, is required to get pseudo-elements working.

These pseudo-elements are told to display as if they were tables. The `display` property is covered in the Chapter 9. When you make them act as tables, margin-collapse is prevented, which is to say any margins on elements before and after these elements are still respected.

```
.group:after {
    clear: both;
}
```

The pseudo-element that is placed after the `.group` element is then cleared on both sides, which makes the main container the correct height—so it actually contains the floating elements—and pushes the footer down below the main container.

These rule sets alone create a clearing effect that fixes the issue seen in Figure 8-6. However, as is often the case, this fix doesn't work in Internet Explorer versions 6 and 7 without one final tweak:

```
.group {
    zoom: 1;
}
```

As explained with the `filter` property in Chapter 5, Microsoft used to be in the habit of adding unofficial properties to its browsers. `zoom` is another of those properties, but here you can use it to get Internet Explorer versions 6 and 7 to clear the floating elements correctly. By using `zoom`, you can work around a bug in these browsers that make the clear fix work as expected.

Now this CSS is in place, whenever an element contains floating elements, you can give that containing element a class of `group` to make the container clear them properly.

With the sidebar now floating to the right of the page and with a width of 25%, you can see that all those styles you added to the newsletter box finally make sense. No longer is the newsletter box stretched right across the page with lots of padding; instead, it's a nice-looking box that draws the users' eyes in an attempt to persuade them to sign up for the newsletter.

You may have noticed the header also has a class of `group`; the reason is that the logo and navigation float side by side, just like the content and sidebar.

1. In styles.css, find the `#header .logo` rule set and add the following:

   ```
   float: left;
   width: 240px;
   ```

2. Find the `#header nav` rule set and add the following declaration:

   ```
   float: right;
   ```

3. Save styles.css.

By floating the logo to the left and navigation to the right, as shown in Figure 8-7, you make better use of the horizontal space available. At the moment, the navigation still looks a little messy, but in Chapter 9, you learn about `display` properties to better align those navigation links.

FIGURE 8-7 The logo and navigation links now float side by side.

Code Challenge: Make the Footer Elements Float Side by Side

In styles.css, do the following:

1. Add a new rule set for `#footer li:nth-child(1)` with the declaration `float: left;`.

2. Add a new rule set for `#footer li:nth-child(2)` with the declaration `float: right;`.

3. Add the declaration `float: right;` to the `blockquote cite` rule set.

Summary

After you make the footer elements float, you may notice that the footer isn't being cleared. In the next chapter, you use a different method to change how the footer is displayed, so clearing it isn't necessary.

In this chapter, you've given the Cool Shoes & Socks page a multicolumn layout by floating elements, then clearing any elements that should sit below those columns.

In the next chapter, you complete the main layout of Cool Shoes & Socks. You change the layout of the navigation links using the `display` property and learn about manipulating the position of elements in the flow of the document.

chapter nine

Understanding Display, Position, and Document Flow

IN THIS CHAPTER, you complete the main layout of Cool Shoes & Socks, making use of the `display` and `position` properties. Plus, you learn about the flow of a document. Later in the chapter, you use some of the more advanced CSS selectors that were covered in Chapter 3, to create a drop-down menu that will appear when users hover over the "Shop" link.

Project files update (ch09-00): If you haven't followed the previous instructions and are comfortable working from here onward or would like to reference the project files up to this point, you can download them from `www.wiley.com/go/treehouse/css3foundations`.

Document Flow

A *document* is the fancy name for a web page. A web page has a flow, which determines the layout of elements. Prior to the preceding chapter, in which you made elements float, the entirety of the Cool Shoes & Socks page had a "normal flow."

All elements on a web page, by default, have a normal flow, referred to as being "in flow." This means the position of one element affects the next. Figure 9-1 shows how the Cool Shoes & Socks page looked at the end of Chapter 7, where all elements were in flow—each element following the next.

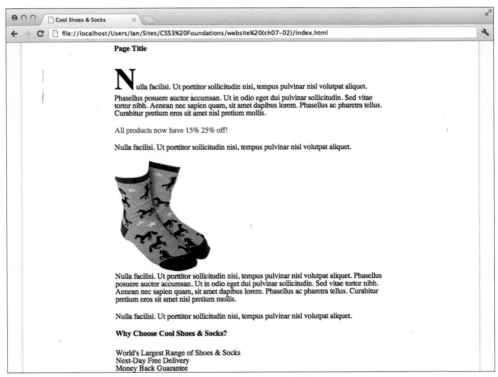

FIGURE 9-1 The Cool Shoes & Socks page as it was at the end of Chapter 7.

Assume you have a page with two paragraphs of content (whether they are on a web page or a word processing document, which also has a normal flow). When you add a new paragraph in between the other two, the second paragraph is pushed down to accommodate the new paragraph. This happens because the document has a normal flow and elements are positioned relative to each other.

Using CSS, you are able to take an element "out of flow," using the position: absolute; declaration. When you do this, an element no longer affects or is affected by the elements around it. This capability has an endless number of uses, and when an element doesn't need to be in flow, it allows for greater control over the position of that element.

The beauty of this capability is that a containing element can be in flow but its child elements can be out of flow—useful for web page features such as drop-down menus (shown in Figure 9-2), which you add to the page later in this chapter.

The normal flow and absolute position are types of positioning schemes that affect the document's flow. *Float* is another form of positioning scheme, which essentially is a hybrid of normal flow and absolute positioning. Floats are first laid out according to the normal flow (affecting the elements relative to it) and then taken out of the flow of the document, being absolutely positioned, typically to the left or right of its containing element.

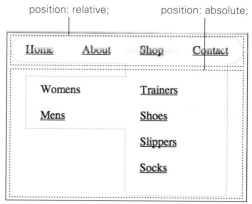

position: relative;   position: absolute;

FIGURE 9-2 A menu positioned relative and "in flow," with a drop-down submenu positioned absolute, "out of flow."

You already used the float positioning scheme in the preceding chapter, so now take a look at the normal flow and how you can manipulate elements within that scheme.

display

Initial value: `inline` | Inherited: No | Applies to: All | CSS2.1
Browser support: IE 4+, Firefox 1+, Chrome 1+, Opera 7+, Safari 1+

The `display` property determines the type of box an element generates and has values such as `block`, `inline`, `inline-block`, `list-item`, `none`, and quite a few different values relating to the display of tables.

block

Most elements are given the declaration `display:  block;` by a browser's default stylesheet. An element that is a block—referred to as being block-level—doesn't have other block-level elements to the side of it, which, as shown in Figure 9-1, is why elements only appear one after the other vertically rather than side by side.

By default, block-level elements usually have some white space around them, but this is something you removed when adding the CSS Reset in Chapter 2 for better consistency across browsers.

Figure 9-3 shows two <div> elements, which are block-level and 100% wide by default.

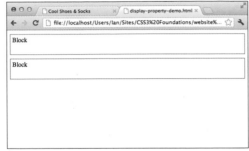

FIGURE 9-3 Two block elements with a default width of 100% and specified height of 40px.

This display properties demonstration page can be found in the project files ch09-00, named display-property-demo.html

On the Cool Shoes & Socks page at present, the Sign Up button in the newsletter box is an inline-block element. While the margin top value of 2em and margin bottom value of 1em of the Sign Up button are being rendered, the margin left and right value of auto are not. The reason is that inline and inline-block elements don't have a defined width; they are simply the width of their contents—more on this shortly. So, when the browser sees that margin left and right value of auto, it can't determine the unused space around that element because it doesn't know how wide that element is, and as such, the button doesn't get centered. To work around that problem, make the Sign Up button block-level instead:

1. In styles.css, find the rule set for input[type="submit"][class="button"] and add the following declaration:

   display: block;

2. Save styles.css.

Now the Sign Up button is block-level, the margin declaration margin: 2em auto 1em; takes full effect, and the button is horizontally centered relative to the newsletter box.

Code Challenge: Make the Newsletter Labels Block-level

In styles.css, do the following:

Add a new rule set for label below the #newsletter label rule set with the declaration display: block;.

inline

An element with the declaration `display: inline;` is only the size of the content it contains and positions itself inline, meaning it doesn't attempt to push itself away from, or below other elements.

In Figure 9-4, I placed two inline-level elements in between two block elements. Because the element above the inline-level elements is a block, it can't have elements to its side, so the inline elements are placed below it. The inline elements don't form new blocks, so they sit side by side and are only as wide as the contents they contain. Because of this, properties that affect the layout of an element can't be used on inline elements, such as `width`, `height`, and `margin`. In Figure 9-4, each element has a height of 40px, but this is ignored for the inline-level elements.

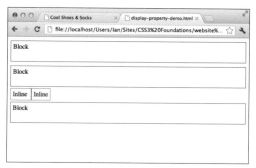

FIGURE 9-4 Two inline elements among two block elements.

By default, elements such as anchors `<a>`, images `<img>`, and quotes `<q>` are inline-level.

List of Inline Elements

The following elements are inline by default:

- `<b>`, `<big>`, `<i>`, `<small>`, `<tt>`
- `<abbr>`, `<acronym>`, `<cite>`, `<code>`, `<dfn>`, `<em>`, `<kbd>`, `<strong>`, `<samp>`, `<var>`
- `<a>`, `<bdo>`, `<br>`, `<img>`, `<map>`, `<object>`, `<q>`, `<script>`, `<span>`, `<sub>`, `<sup>`
- `<button>`, `<input>`, `<label>`, `<select>`, `<textarea>`

Prior to giving the Cool Shoes & Socks page a `max-width` declaration in Chapter 5, you may have noticed some inline-level elements.

Figure 9-5 shows that the image and More Information button in the product showcase are both inline-level, positioning them side by side (the More Information button breaks onto a new line because the page isn't wide enough for both the image and link). The fact that these elements are inline is not as obvious when you give the page a maximum width because there isn't enough room for the elements to sit beside each other.

FIGURE 9-5 Some of the inline-level elements prior to Chapter 5.

Later in this chapter, you use the `position` property to position the More Information button over the top of the showcase image.

Some elements that display well as inline-level are the navigation links, which are currently `display: list-item;`. Change that as follows:

1. In styles.css, find the `#header nav > ul > li` rule set and add the following declaration:

   `display: inline;`

2. Save styles.css.

When you make each navigation list item inline-level, those links line up horizontally, as shown in Figure 9-6. This arrangement makes better use of the horizontal space available.

COOL
SHOES & SOCKS   Home About Shop Contact

FIGURE 9-6 The navigation links positioned inline.

inline-block

Sometimes you might want an element to be inline but still give it dimensional values such as height and margin. These types of elements can be given the declaration `display: inline-block;`.

In Figure 9-7, I added two inline-block elements to a page. These properties take on attributes of both inline-level and block-level elements. First, they take on an inline-level, being positioned next to each other. Unlike inline-level elements, though, they are then formatted as a block-level, allowing them to be given dimensional properties. As you can see, these inline-block elements have taken on the height declaration of 40px, just like the block-level elements have.

FIGURE 9-7 Inline-block elements in relation to block and inline elements.

Aside from the height and margin of the inline-block elements, can you see what else is different about them when compared to the inline-level elements? Inline-block elements are horizontally separated by 4 pixels of white space. This is an intended behavior although, admittedly, an annoying one! I show you how to fix this behavior in a moment.

Although you made the navigation links inline, you will shortly add `margin` properties to them, so instead make them inline-block:

1. In styles.css, change the display declaration of `#header nav > ul > li` to

   `display: inline-block;`

2. Save styles.css.

As you can see in Figure 9-8, `inline-block` elements are separated by 4 pixels, and although the width of the navigation links isn't critical (there's plenty of room for the navigation links to stretch out), it's often easier to get rid of these additional 4 pixels, especially when you know some elements are going to have quite a few different styles applied to them.

FIGURE 9-8 The navigation links now being displayed as inline-block.

These 4 pixels aren't actually caused by the CSS but instead the white space in the HTML (the spaces that separate the `<li>` elements).

1. In index.html, find the unordered list in the header:

```
<nav role="navigation">
    <ul>
        . . .
    </ul>
</nav>
```

2. Remove any white space between the top level closing `</li>` and opening `<li>` elements, so

```
<li><a href="#" title="Return to the front page">Home</a></li>
<li><a href="#" title="About Company Name">About</a></li>
```

becomes

```
<li><a href="#" title="Return to the front
page">Home</a></li><li><a href="#" title="About Company
  Name">About</a></li>
```

and so on. You should only need to remove three amounts of white space between four list items.

3. Save index.html.

When you do this, the HTML that makes up the navigation links is a little more difficult to read but it at least removes the 4 px of white space, as shown in Figure 9-9.

COOL
SHOES & SOCKS   HomeAboutShopContact

FIGURE 9-9 The navigation links with no space between them.

Note that Internet Explorer versions 6 and 7 don't support `display: inline-block;`. However, they fortunately treat `display: inline;` in the same way that other browsers—that better support the CSS specification—treat `display: inline-block;`. So, when an element is required to be inline-block, you can simply specify the declaration `display: inline;` only for Internet Explorer 6 and 7. You learn how to create a stylesheet specifically for the use of older versions of Internet Explorer in Chapter 15.

list-item

List items—the `<li>` elements that are placed within either ordered `<ol>` or unordered `<ul>` lists—have the declaration `display: list-item;` by default. When an element is a list-item, it generates a block box *and* a marker box—if that element has a visual representation of being a list item in the form of a bullet point or other graphical element. Styling lists are covered in Chapter 11.

Displaying Tables

When a page contains a table, using the HTML element `<table>`, it, by default, has the declaration `display: table;`. Aside from the hack you saw in the preceding chapter, where `display: table;` was used to prevent the margins of an element from collapsing (a trait of tables), and one other hack to achieve vertical alignment—which you see later in this chapter—`display: table;` tends to be used only for tables, suprisingly! Because the `<table>` element already has this display value written into user agent stylesheets, you most likely don't need to use it in your own CSS. This, too, goes for the other table display values; `inline-table`, `table-row`, `table-row-group`, `table-header-group`, `table-footer-group`, `table-column`, `table-group-column`, `table-cell`, and `table-caption`.

If you would like to find out more about these table values, see the CSS Table Model at www.w3.org/TR/CSS21/tables.html#value-def-table.

none

As you saw in Chapter 5, giving an element the declaration `display: none;` doesn't just hide that element; it tells the browser not to even render it so that no box is generated at all and the layout is treated as though this element doesn't exist—even though it's still present in the HTML.

If you would like to hide an element but still have it affect layout, see the `opacity` and `visibility` properties, which were covered in Chapter 5.

position, top, right, bottom, and left

Initial value: static | Inherited: No | Applies to: All | CSS2.1

Browser support: IE 4+, Firefox 1+, Chrome 1+, Opera 4+, Safari 1+

position is another property that affects the flow of a document. The values that can be used are static and relative, which affect the normal flow, and fixed and absolute, which take elements out of flow.

The CSS3 Positioned layout module found at www.w3.org/TR/css3-positioning/ introduces two new values, center and page, but unfortunately they are yet to be implemented into any browsers, so it is too early to cover them.

You can use the position declaration in conjunction with the properties top, right, bottom, and left (except for when using position: static;), which allow you to change the position of an element. How these properties relate to the position of an element is determined based on the value of the position declaration.

You can give top, right, bottom, and left any type of value such as percentages, pixels, or ems.

static

Elements are position: static; by default. A static element is a normal box laid out in the normal flow. Static elements aren't affected by the top, right, bottom, and left properties.

relative

When you make an element position: relative;, it too is laid out in the normal flow of a document—known as the "normal position." From its normal position, you can then offset the position of an element relative to its normal position using the top, right, bottom, and left properties. The elements following a relative element are affected based on the normal position of that element; its relative position doesn't affect layout.

Assume you would like to change the position of the <h1> page title on the Cool Shoes & Socks page. In Figure 9-10, you can see the page title is static and in flow, meaning the <p> elements and <img> below it are placed below it.

If you give <h1> the declaration position: relative;, the page appears exactly the same as when that element is position: static;. However, a relative element can be manipulated with top, right, bottom, and left.

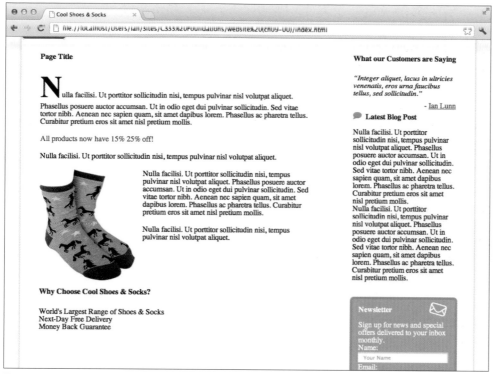

FIGURE 9-10 The page title in its default static position.

In Figure 9-11, I gave the `<h1>` a `top` value of `30px`. This value moved the page title 30px, relative to the top of its normal position.

Note the only difference between Figure 9-10 and Figure 9-11 is the position of the text—the area taken up by the `<h1>` element doesn't change. The flow of the document isn't affected because the page title's normal position remains in flow and in the same position, so although the text is offset, the contents below aren't affected in any way.

When an element is `position: relative;`, `top`, `left`, `right`, and `bottom` offset that element relative to the top, left, right, and bottom of the normal position, respectively.

FIGURE 9-11 The page title with the declarations position: relative; top: 30px;.

absolute

When you make an element position: absolute;, it is taken out of the document's flow and ignores the layout of elements surrounding it.

Now use position: absolute; to finally move that pesky More Information button:

1. In styles.css, add the following declarations to the .showcase .button rule set:

```
position: absolute;
top: 0;
```

2. Save styles.css.

   When you make the button absolute, it is taken out of flow (see Figure 9-12), and the main container finally touches the bottom of the product showcase. This effect was always intended, but because the button was in flow and sat between the two, they were separated.

FIGURE 9-12 The More Information button no longer affects the flow of the page.

Note that after this change, the button touches the top of the page, which isn't the intended final position. This happens because the position of an absolute element is relative to the next containing element with a defined position other than `static`. Because you haven't declared any other element as being `absolute, relative, or fixed` yet, the browser treats the `<html>` element as the containing element, and as such, the button is positioned relative to the overall page. So, as you can see, `top: 0;` makes the button touch the top of the page.

3. In styles.css, add the following declaration to the `.showcase` rule set:

```
position: relative;
```

4. Save styles.css.

Now that you've made the `<div class="showcase">` element relative, the button contained within it is positioned relative to it, as shown in Figure 9-13. It touches the top of the showcase, but it would look better if it were placed over to the right and vertically centered.

FIGURE 9-13 The More Information button is now positioned relative to its containing the <div class="showcase"> element.

Unfortunately, vertically centering an element via CSS isn't as straightforward as it could be. There *is* a vertical-align property, but it doesn't work in a way you may initially expect—it caught me out to begin with. Continue with the position property for now and come back to the vertical-align property later in this chapter along with a hack to make the showcase button vertically centered.

Make the footer stretch across the entire page (regardless of the page size and disrespecting the containing <body> element):

1. In styles.css, add the following declarations to the #footer rule set:

   ```
   left: 0;
   position: absolute;
   width: 100%;
   ```

2. Save styles.css.

Although the footer is contained with the `<body>` element, because the footer has no containing element with a `position` declaration, it is positioned relative to the `<html>` element.

fixed

The final value for the `position` property is `fixed`. As with absolute elements, a fixed element is taken out of a document's flow and does not affect the layout of elements around it. Unlike absolute, however, a fixed element is positioned relative to the viewport (the browser window) and does not move when the page is scrolled.

For this example, add a banner image to the bottom of the page:

1. In index.html, below the closing `</footer>` and above the closing `</body>` elements, add the following HTML:

   ```
   <img class="banner-ad" src="images/banner-25percent.png"
     alt="25% Off All Purchases" />
   ```

2. Save index.html

3. In styles.css, add the following declaration:

   ```
   .banner-ad {
       bottom: 0;
       position: fixed;
       right: 0;
   }
   ```

4. Save styles.css.

As shown in Figure 9-14, the 25% off banner remains fixed to the bottom right of the browser window. No matter whether or not the user scrolls, that element remains fixed in that position, so it's always on display—sort of like you had the power to glue an element to the inside of the user's screen!

Unfortunately, Internet Explorer 6 doesn't support `position: fixed;`, and furthermore, very few browsers on mobile devices support `position: fixed;` due to technical performance issues. Fixed elements tend to be used for noncritical aspects of a page, such as notices and adverts, so for browsers that don't support fixed elements, they can be hidden or modified to be displayed in a different way using styles specific to those nonsupporting browsers; this topic is covered in Chapter 15. Because the 25% banner used for Cool Shoes & Socks is an image—that can only be square in proportion—the transparent section of the image prevents a user from clicking anything below that invisible area, so for smaller screen sizes where that area may cover any part of the page that may be interacted with, it is necessary to hide that banner anyway.

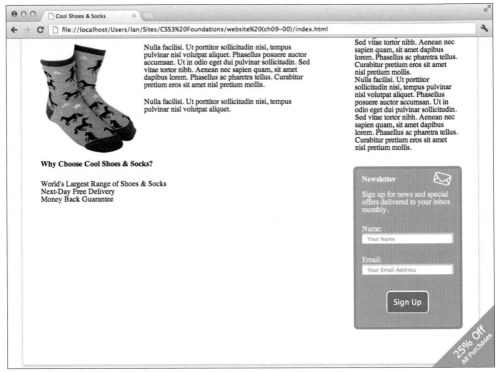

FIGURE 9-14 The banner ad fixed to the bottom and right of the viewport.

Code Challenge: Change the Position of the Quotes Around the Customer Testimonials Without Affecting the Flow

In styles.css, do the following:

1. Add a new rule set for `blockquote` with the declaration `position: relative;`.

2. Add the declarations `position: absolute; left: -20px; top: -10px;` to the `blockquote p:before` rule set.

3. Add the declarations `position: absolute; right: 0; bottom: -20px;` to the `blockquote p:after` rule set.

Project files update (ch09-01): If you haven't followed the previous instructions and are comfortable working from here onward or would like to reference the project files up to this point, you can download them from `www.wiley.com/go/treehouse/css3foundations`.

Using display, position, and z-index to Create a Drop-Down Menu

Now that you have the power of `display` and `property` tucked into your CSS utility belt, you can flex this knowledge and create a drop-down menu.

1. In index.html, below this HTML:

```
<a href="#" title="Visit our shop">Shop</a>
```

Add the following HTML:

```
<ul>
    <li><a href="#" title="">Trainers</a>
        <ul>
            <li><a href="#" title="">Womens</a></li>
            <li><a href="#" title="">Mens</a></li>
        </ul>
    </li>
    <li><a href="#" title="">Shoes</a>
        <ul>
            <li><a href="#" title="">Womens</a></li>
            <li><a href="#" title="">Mens</a></li>
        </ul>
    </li>
    <li><a href="#" title="">Slippers</a></li>
    <li><a href="#" title="">Socks</a></li>
</ul>
```

2. Save index.html

    This HTML will add a submenu to the Shop link. Now to style it:

3. In styles.css, below the `#header nav > ul > li` rule set, add the following rule sets:

```
#header nav ul > li:hover {
    background: #f5f5f5;
}
#header nav ul ul > li:hover {
    background: white;
}
```

These rules make each navigation link of the top-level list a gray color and any link from second-level lists onward white whenever hovered over.

4. Below the `#header nav ul ul > li:hover` rule set, add the following rule set:

```
#header nav ul li a {
    color: black;
    display: block;
    padding: 10px 20px;
}
```

Here, you make the links within the list items `display: block;`. When you make the <a> elements block (remembering they're inline by default), they can now take on dimensional properties and, as such, become bigger than if they were left as inline.

Take a breather here for a minute. As shown in Figure 9-15, you now have a partially styled submenu but it's more of a drop-up list at the moment! This is caused because the child lists of the top-level lists are in flow and affecting the elements around them. The answer is to take them out of flow.

FIGURE 9-15 The second-level unordered lists, which need to be positioned differently.

5. Add the following rule set below the `#header nav ul li a` rule set:

```
#header nav ul ul {
    /*style all lists below the top-level list*/
    background: #f5f5f5;
    border: 1px solid #ccc;
    border-bottom-left-radius: 8px;
    border-bottom-right-radius: 8px;
    border-top: none;
    padding: 20px 0;
    position: absolute;
    min-width: 140px;
}
```

This rule set styles any unordered list below the top-level list, and because the drop-down menu consists of quite a few rule sets, a comment is added in this rule set to remind you or anyone else in the future what this rule set selects—a good practice, particularly when selectors start to get complex.

Along with the borders, padding, and a minimum width, you also give the drop-down menus an absolute position, moving them out of flow so they no longer affect the elements around them. However, as shown in Figure 9-16, although the drop-down menu kind of looks as though it's in the right position, it's hidden behind the product showcase.

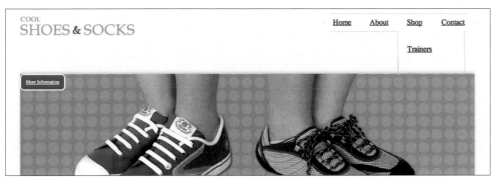

FIGURE 9-16 The drop-down menu out of flow but hidden behind the product showcase.

For now, fix this and then come back to the explanation after the drop-down menu is working.

6. In the same rule set, add the following declaration:

```
z-index: 10;
```

The drop-down menu now appears above the product showcase, although the third level of links isn't quite styled correctly.

7. Below the #header nav ul ul rule set, add a new rule set:

```
#header nav ul ul ul {
    /*style all lists below the second-level list*/
    border: 1px solid #ccc;
    border-right: none;
    border-bottom-left-radius: 0;
    border-bottom-right-radius: 0;
    padding: 0;
}
```

The links Trainers and Shoes both have their own drop-down menus (a third-level list of links). As shown in Figure 9-17, these menus appear over their parent menu at present; ideally, it would be good to have those menus appear to the left of their respective parent links.

Third-level list of links belonging to Shoes

Third-level list of links belonging to Trainers

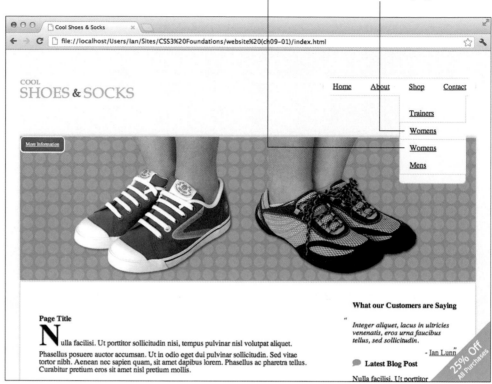

FIGURE 9-17 The third-level menus appear over their second-level parents.

8. Add the following declarations to the `#header nav ul ul ul` rule set:

```
left: -100%;
top: -1px;
```

Now the menus appear to the left perfectly, *but* each menu sits in the same position at the top. These third-level lists inherit the declaration `position: absolute;` from their parent lists. Remember that the position of an absolute element is relative to its parent, so at the moment, the declaration `top: -1px;` places *all* third-level lists 1 pixel above the place where the second-level list is positioned. Having each third-level list start in the same vertical position as the second-level link it belongs to would make more sense.

9. Below the rule set `#header nav ul ul`, add a new rule set:

```
#header nav ul ul li {
    position: relative;
}
```

Now the third-level menus are positioned relative to their respective second-level link instead of the overall second-level list. The `top` value of –1px accounts for the 1 pixel border.

This wouldn't be much of a drop-down menu if it constantly sat there with every link showing; after all, the point of a drop-down menu is to make better use of space, hiding links until the user needs to use them.

10. Add a declaration to the `#header nav ul ul` rule set:

    ```
    visibility: hidden;
    ```

11. Below the rule set `#header nav ul ul ul`, add a new rule set:

    ```
    #header nav li:hover > ul{
        /*show the menu of the list item being hovered over*/
        visibility: visible;
    }
    ```

    Here, you hide any list of links below the top level and allow them to become visible only when the user hovers over their respective parent link.

    Finally, for the drop-down menu, make the corners of the top-level list rounded.

12. Below the rule set `#header nav > ul > li`, add two new rule sets:

    ```
    #header nav > ul > li:first-child {
        border-top-left-radius: 20px;
        border-bottom-left-radius: 20px;
    }

    #header nav > ul > li:last-child {
        border-top-right-radius: 20px;
        border-bottom-right-radius: 20px;
    }
    ```

13. Save styles.css.

Congratulations! The drop-down menu is now fully functional, as was shown in Figure 9-2. Before you move on, though, you need to understand what that `z-index` declaration does.

z-index

Initial value: `auto` | Inherited: No | Applies to: Positioned elements | CSS2.1
Browser support: IE 4+, Firefox 1+, Chrome 1+, Opera 4+, Safari 1+

When giving elements a position declaration, you might find that sometimes elements overlap one another. The problem you saw in Figure 9-16, where the drop-down menu appears behind the product showcase, is that both of these elements have a defined position and neither one is in flow, making them visually clash—meaning one sits behind the other. When elements are taken out of flow, a page becomes three-dimensional, and by using z-index, you can control the stacking order of those elements.

The z-index, by default, is auto, meaning the stacking order is 0. By giving the z-index property a number as a value, you determine how high up the stack an element is.

Before you gave the drop-down menu a z-index, it and the product showcase had a default stack order of 0. If two elements are both at the same position in the stack order, their positioned is determined by the order of the HTML; elements that appear later in the HTML are given precedence. By giving the drop-down menu a z-index of 10, you move it above the product showcase.

Why 10? The navigation is the most important part of the website that has a position declaration, so at no point should it be hidden below another element. There aren't 10 positioned elements on the page, so 10 can be assumed as being the highest level. If you want to be extra safe though, you can give it a z-index of 10000 or even 1000000. The CSS specification doesn't determine a maximum number for z-index but some very dedicated people have done tests to determine this number for each browser. You'll be pleased to know that every browser in use today can support stack orders higher than 2 billion (for more information, visit www.softwareas.com/whats-the-maximum-z-index). I hope that's enough for you! Of course, if you want to make your CSS maintainable now and in the future, it's best to be sensible with z-index values.

Code Challenge: Apply z-index to Other Elements

In styles.css, do the following:

1. Add the declaration z-index: 5; to the .showcase .button rule set.

2. Add the declaration z-index: 9; to the .banner-ad rule set.

Project files update (ch09-02): If you haven't followed the previous instructions and are comfortable working from here onward or would like to reference the project files up to this point, you can download them from www.wiley.com/go/treehouse/css3foundations.

vertical-align and Vertical Centering Techniques

As explained early in this chapter, achieving vertical alignment via CSS is unfortunately not as straightforward as you might expect. Although the `vertical-align` property seems like a perfect fit for the job, it works only for inline-level and table-cell elements. Let's look at the `vertical-align` property and then use some "hacks" to make block-level elements vertically center.

vertical-align

Initial value: `baseline` | Inherited: No | Applies to: inline-level and table-cell elements | CSS2.1
Browser support: IE 4+, Firefox 1+, Chrome 1+, Opera 4+, Safari 1+

The small speech bubble image that is included in the "Latest Blog Post" title is inline-level (remember images are inline by default):

```
<h3><img src="images/bg-blog.png" alt="Latest Blog Post" />Latest
  Blog Post</h3>
```

The initial value for `vertical-align` is `baseline`, meaning the bottom of the speech bubble image vertically aligns with the baseline of the title, as shown in Figure 9-18.

Latest Blog Post

Nulla facilisi. Ut porttitor sollicitudin nisi, tempus pulvinar nisl volutpat aliquet. Phasellus posuere auctor accumsan. Ut in odio eget dui pulvinar sollicitudin. Sed vitae tortor nibh. Aenean nec sapien quam, sit amet dapibus lorem. Phasellus ac pharetra tellus. Curabitur pretium eros sit amet nisl pretium mollis.

FIGURE 9-18 The speech bubble vertically aligned to the baseline of the text.

`vertical-align` also accepts the following values, as demonstrated in Figure 9-19:

- `middle`—Aligns the vertical midpoint of the inline element with the baseline and half of the x-height (the height of the lowercase *x* character). In Figure 9-19, note that because the speech bubble image is 15 px tall, the browser doesn't quite perfectly center the image.

- `sub`—Lowers the baseline of the inline element to meet the position for subscripts `<sub>`.

- super—Raises the baseline of the inline element to meet the position for superscripts `<sup>`.

- `text-top`—Aligns the top of the inline element with the top of the text.

- `text-bottom`—Aligns the bottom of the inline element with the bottom of the text.

CSS3 Foundations: Styling the Modern Web (Baseline)

CSS3 Foundations: Styling the Modern Web (Middle)

CSS3 Foundations: Styling the Modern Web (Sub)

CSS3 Foundations: Styling the Modern Web (Super)

CSS3 Foundations: Styling the Modern Web (Text-Top)

CSS3 Foundations: Styling the Modern Web (Text-Bottom)

FIGURE 9-19 The speech bubble when vertically aligned to the baseline, subscript, superscript, text-top, and text-bottom positions.

 This vertical alignment demonstration page can be found in the project files ch09-02, named vertical-align-property-demo.html

You can give two other values to `vertical-align`: `top` and `bottom`. Where `text-top` and `text-bottom` align an inline-level element relative to text, `top` and `bottom` align an inline-level element with the top or bottom of the parent's content area.

In Figure 9-20, I demonstrated this technique by adding an inline image of those awesome horse socks with a `vertical-alignment` of `text-bottom` (aligning its bottom with the bottom of the text). In the first example, I gave the speech bubble image a vertical align of `text-top`, which aligns its top with the top of the text. However, because the image of the socks is much taller than the rest of the contents, the parent's content area is bigger too. If you want to position the speech bubble relative to the top of the content area instead of the text, you can specify a vertical alignment of `top`.

If none of those values take your fancy and you want a little more control, you can also specify a unit of length or a percentage where 0 represents the same as `baseline`. A positive number raises the inline-level or table-cell element above the baseline, and a negative number lowers it.

FIGURE 9-20 The difference between vertically aligning the speech bubble to the text-top and top.

Vertical Centering Techniques

It's both disappointing and initially misleading that the vertical-align property can be used only on inline-level and table-cell elements. The position: center; declaration introduced in the CSS Level 3 Positioned layout module found at www.w3.org/TR/css3-positioning/ will, I hope, see the light of day and make vertical alignment easier in the future. For now, though, let's go back to positioning the showcase button and cover a few different techniques for making it vertically centered.

The following techniques all have their own pros and cons, and unfortunately, there isn't a perfect solution. Therefore, when you are vertically aligning elements in the future, use your best judgment.

To give you an understanding of each technique, steps are provided that ask you to make changes to the project files, then undo those changes to try the next technique. If you want to follow along, please do. However, if you just want to understand the technique that the Cool Shoes & Socks page will use, please follow the instructions for the third technique only.

The Fake Table Cells Technique

If you can't go to the party, you can bring the party to you. You can use vertical-align only on inline-level and table-cell elements, so cheat and use display: table-cell; as follows:

1. In styles.css, add the declaration `display: table` to the `.showcase` rule set:

   ```
   display: table;
   ```

2. Remove the following declarations from the `.showcase .button` rule set:

   ```
   position: absolute;
   top: 0;
   ```

3. Add a `width` declaration to the `.showcase img` rule set:

   ```
   width: 100%;
   ```

4. Add a new rule set below the `.showcase .button` rule set:

   ```
   .button-cell {
       display: table-cell;
       vertical-align: middle;
       width: 148px;
   }
   ```

5. Save styles.css.

   When you use `display: table-cell;` on an element, that element must be contained in a table (or an element mimicking a table with the declaration `display: table;`). Because the showcase `<div class="showcase">` contains the showcase button, *that* is given the declaration `display: table;`. If the `.showcase .button` rule set were to be given the declaration `display: table-cell;`, the button would become 100% tall because cells stretch to fill the entirety of the containing table. This is the downfall to using fake table cells. Although this approach emulates vertical alignment beautifully, it requires an additional element to be wrapped around the one you want to vertically align to prevent that element from becoming 100% tall.

6. In index.html, modify:

   ```
   <a class="button purchase" href="#" title="Purchase product">
       More Information
   </a>
   ```

   Make sure it is contained in a `<div>` with the class `button-cell`:

   ```
   <div class="button-cell">
       <a class="button purchase" href="#" title="Purchase
     product">
           More Information
   </a>
   </div>
   ```

7. Save index.html.

The other problem, as shown in Figure 9-21, is that elements within a table can only sit aside each other, meaning the button isn't visually over the top of the showcase images

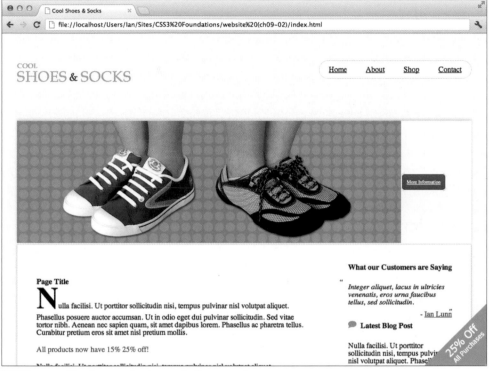

FIGURE 9-21 The showcase button vertically centered.

Using fake table cells offers the most robust vertical alignment. When you are increasing text size in browsers such as Mozilla Firefox, the element stays vertically centered, but it means using more HTML and, in the showcase example, prevents elements from appearing on top of each other. Furthermore, `display: table-cell;` doesn't work in Internet Explorer versions 6 and 7.

The Stretched Element Technique

Stretching an element positions the element absolutely in relation to its containing parent and allows for both vertical and horizontal alignment.

1. Undo the changes made for the Fake Table Cells technique both in index.html and styles.css.

2. In styles.css, add the following declarations to the `.showcase` `.button` rule set:

```
bottom: 0;
left: 0;
```

```
right: 0;
height: 16px;
margin: auto;
width: 148px;
```

As shown in Figure 9-22, this technique is much easier than the Fake Table Cells technique and works in a way more desirable for the product showcase.

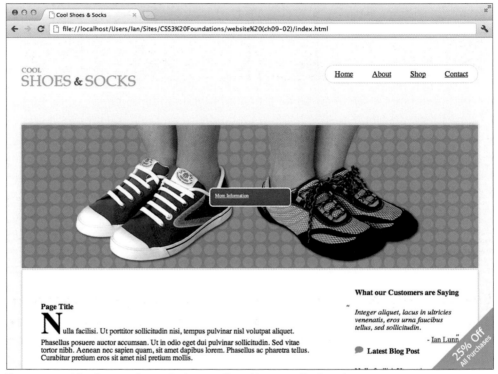

FIGURE 9-22 The showcase button both vertically and horizontally aligned.

3. Because the button should be positioned over to the right, you can remove the `left` declaration and modify the `right` declaration:

```
right: 2.1875em;
```

4. Save styles.css.

The Stretched Element technique is another useful method, particularly because it's so easy and can horizontally center an element, too. However, when you are increasing the size of text in a browser such as Firefox, as shown in Figure 9-23, although the button always stays vertically centered, the text breaks out of the button. Because the purpose of resizing text is to make a page more readable, the user may be annoyed to find this happens to the text at a larger size.

FIGURE 9-23 The showcase button vertically centered but with a larger font size in Mozilla Firefox.

The 50% Top Minus Half the Elements Height Technique

Another solution, and the final solution used for the Cool Shoes & Socks page, is to set the top position of the showcase button to 50% and then pull up the button by half of its own height to make it vertically centered:

1. Undo the changes made for the Stretched Element technique.

2. In styles.css, change the top declaration in the `.showcase` `.button` rule set:

   ```
   top: 50%;
   ```

3. In the same rule set, add the following declarations:

   ```
   font-size: 1.6em;
   right: 2.1875em;
   margin-top: -26px;
   ```

4. Save styles.css.

As shown in Figure 9-24, the button is now vertically aligned. When you give the button a top position of 50%, the top of the button is placed in the vertical center of the product showcase. However, this isn't a true vertical alignment. For it to be perfectly centered, the vertical center of the button needs to be in the vertical center of the showcase. To achieve this result, you specify a `margin-top` of `-26px`, half of the element's overall height, which pulls up the button by 50%.

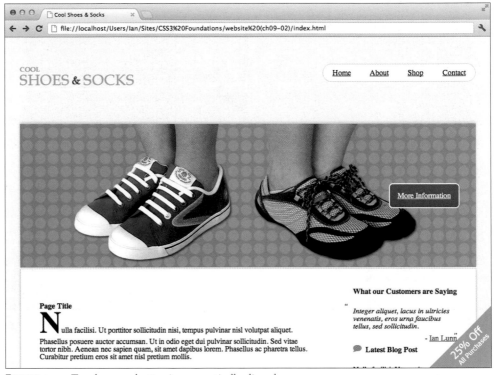

FIGURE 9-24 The showcase button is now vertically aligned.

Yes, this breaks the rule I've mentioned several times already: You should try not to declare or expect an element to be a specific height because in some browsers, users can change the font size to their liking.

Because the showcase button doesn't have a specified height, though, it stretches with the size of the text. So with this technique, unlike the Stretched Element technique, the text doesn't break out of its containing box.

This does mean, however, that the button loses its vertical alignment if the text *is* resized, as shown in Figure 9-25, but it means the text is more readable—better serving the purpose of a browser's text resizing feature. Putting readability before aesthetics is a good priority.

Although the Cool Shoes & Socks page uses the 50% Top Minus Half the Elements Height technique, all three vertical alignment techniques have their uses. Which technique you use really depends on the scenario. On the web, you can find other vertical alignment techniques, such as at `www.css-tricks.com/centering-in-the-unknown/`, which also have their own pros and cons.

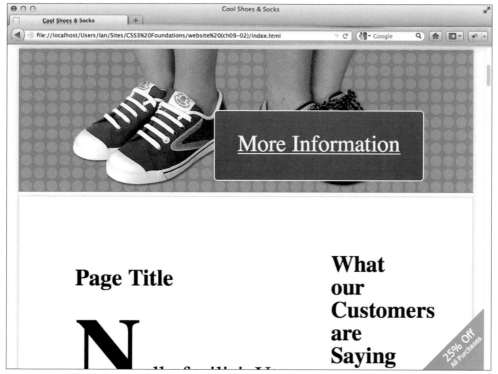

FIGURE 9-25 The web page in Firefox with the default text size increased.

overflow

Initial value: `visible` | Inherited: No | Applies to: block elements | CSS2.1
Browser support: IE4+, Firefox 1+, Chrome 1+, Opera 7+, Safari 1+

When creating a web page, sometimes you find that content you want to place in a containing element is bigger than its container. Throughout *CSS3 Foundations*, I have mentioned that you shouldn't restrict an element to a specific height because in some browsers, a user can control the size of text and content may grow bigger than the height of that element. If you do have content bigger than its containing element or you absolutely have to give an element a specific height (clients and bosses can be pushy!), you can use the `overflow` property to better control how that overflowing content is displayed—or not displayed, as the case may be.

Go ahead and restrict the height of the "Latest Blog Post" element:

1. In styles.css, add a new rule set for the `.post` element, under the `.testimonials` rule set:

```
.post {
    height: 200px;
}
```

In Figure 9-26, I also gave the `<aside class="post">` element a red border along with its height of 200px to demonstrate the boundaries of that element. As you can see, with no specified `overflow` declaration, the overflowing content is visible. Note that the containing element affects the document flow, but the overflowing content does not. It all looks a bit messy and unreadable.

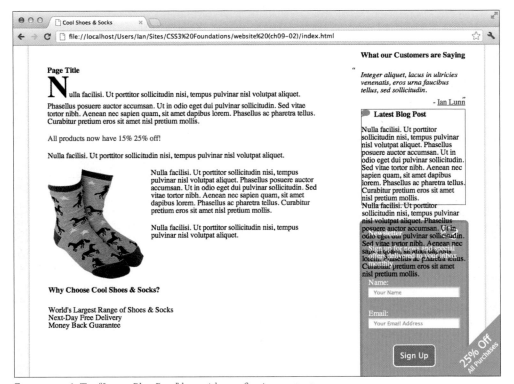

FIGURE 9-26 The "Latest Blog Post" box with overflowing content.

If you feel that the content isn't very important, you can simply hide the overflow by giving it an overflow declaration of `hidden`.

2. Add an `overflow` declaration:

`overflow: hidden;`

As shown in Figure 9-27, the overflowing content is now hidden, *but* the line of text at the bottom is cut off. Because it's text being cut off and not something less forgiving, such as an image, hiding text in this way isn't ideal. It may lead the users to becoming frustrated because they know they are missing out on some content they can't get to

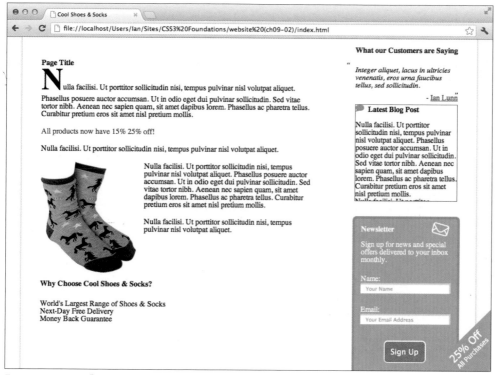

FIGURE 9-27 The "Latest Blog Post" with its overflowing content hidden.

This is where `scroll` value for `overflow` comes in handy.

3. Change the hidden value of the `overflow` declaration to `scroll`:

```
overflow: scroll;
```

Figure 9-28 shows how the "Latest Blog Post" box is displayed in Mozilla Firefox on an Apple Mac and a Windows PC; now the box has a scroll bar of its own. Firefox, Opera, and Internet Explorer show both vertical and horizontal scroll bars for an `overflow: scroll;` element, even if the content of that element overflows only on one axis. Chrome and Safari are a little more intelligent and show a scroll bar only when it is needed. To work around this and make the experience more consistent across browsers, you can use the properties `overflow-x` and `overflow-y`.

Because the `.post` element has a specified height with the default width `auto`, it never overflows horizontally, only vertically. So, to make Firefox, Opera, and Internet Explorer show only a vertical scroll bar, you can move on to step 4.

Horizontal scroll bars

FIGURE 9-28 The "Latest Blog Post" with a scroll bar to allow the user to see overflowing content. Viewed in Firefox on an Apple Mac to the left and Firefox on a Windows PC to the right.

4. Change the property `overflow` to `overflow-y`:

   ```
   overflow-y: scroll;
   ```

5. Save styles.css.

Now, as you can see in Figure 9-29, all browsers show only the vertical scroll bar.

FIGURE 9-29 The "Latest Blog Post" with a vertical scroll bar only. Viewed in Firefox on an Apple Mac to the left and Firefox on a Windows PC to the right.

Summary

You've finished the main layout of the Cool Shoes & Socks page. Looks pretty cool, don't you think? Of course, it functions well, too. The page now has quite a lot of navigation links, but they're all tucked away nicely in a drop-down menu, which means users can find where they want to navigate quickly without being overwhelmed by choice.

If you view the page in a browser other than the one you're using to create Cool Shoes & Socks, almost certainly you will find inconsistencies and broken bits. Breathe a sigh of relief—that's to be expected. In Chapters 15 and 16, you learn to make Cool Shoes & Socks cross browser compatible and modify its layout for when it is viewed on mobile devices.

In the next chapter, you learn to change the font and font styles, characteristics that can really make Cool Shoes & Socks unique.

part 4

Typography

chapter ten
Changing the Font

FONTS ARE AN important part of the design aesthetic. Although text—whether on the web or in print—conveys a particular message, the choice of font can greatly reinforce that message, representing voice, authority, friendliness, competence, and so on.

Until recently, the range of fonts available for web design was rather lacking. Although a quick search on the web shows hundreds of thousands of fonts are available to download and use, in reality, not every device has the font you want to use for your web page. In fact, only a handful of fonts that you can use are shared across the majority of devices. These fonts are known as "web safe" because you can use them safe in the knowledge that almost everyone can see them.

When features of CSS3 were first implemented into browsers, however, the technology became available to allow for displaying a font that wasn't installed on a computer. This means you can now choose from a much larger selection of fonts for your web page.

In this chapter, you learn how to apply different fonts to the Cool Shoes & Socks page, using third-party services such as Google Web Fonts to access a wider range of fonts.

Choosing a Web Safe Font Using font-family and Font Stacks

Web safe fonts are those fonts that are likely to be installed on the majority of devices accessing the web. Between computers with varying operating systems, you can find around 50 web safe fonts, but with mobile devices now accessing the web too, the number of web safe fonts drops to just a handful. Thankfully, to work around this number, you can specify which font you would ideally like a user to see a web page presented in and then add more fonts after that in a comma-separated list—known as a font stack—to act as fallbacks in case your chosen font is not present.

If a device has no fonts whatsoever—which is unlikely unless somebody decided to just delete them all—the CSS specification defines five generic font names to act as fallbacks: serif, sans-serif, cursive, fantasy, and monospace, as shown in Figure 10-1. These fallbacks don't necessarily represent a specific font but should express particular characteristics.

- **Serif**—Characters tend to have finishing strokes, flared or tapering ends, or actual serifed endings.
- **Sans-serif**—Characters tend to have stroke endings that are plain.
- **Cursive**—Characters have either joining strokes or other cursive characteristics, resulting in a handwritten look.
- **Fantasy**—Characters are primarily decorative but still contain representations of characters.
- **Monospace**—All characters have the same fixed width, similar to a manual typewriter and often used to set samples of computer code.

- serif
- sans-serif
- cursive
- fantasy
- monospace

FIGURE 10-1 The five generic fonts when viewed in Google Chrome.

> This generic font demonstration page can be found in the project files ch10-00, named generic-fonts-demo.html.

font-family

Initial value: browser dependent | Inherited: Yes | Applies to: All | CSS2.1
Browser support: IE 3+, Firefox 1+, Chrome 1+, Opera 3.5+, Safari 1+

The `font-family` property enables you to specify a font or list of fonts to be applied to an element.

1. In styles.css, find the rule set for `body` and add the following:

   ```
   font-family: serif;
   ```

   The initial value for `font-family` is dependent on the browser, but for all desktop browsers, each has chosen serif as its default. As a result, you don't yet see a difference to the page, but nonetheless you have specified a fallback font for the entire page, which is always wise. Wise...but kind of boring, right? So you can change this font declaration into a font stack.

2. Change the `font-family` declaration to the following:

   ```
   font-family: Georgia, serif;
   ```

3. Save styles.css.

As shown in Figure 10-2, the Cool Shoes & Socks page is now entirely set in Georgia. When a browser comes to render this declaration, it first tries to set the font as Georgia, but if the device doesn't have it, the browser then falls back to serif. This is known as a *font stack*. A font stack can consist of a long list of fonts, starting with your most desired, working down through fonts that are closer to being web safe, finally reaching one of the generic fonts that best represents the characteristics of your desired font. Georgia, however, is web safe, so it is almost certainly installed on all devices.

Of course, web safe fonts have been used time and time again, so try using the CSS3 `@font-face` rule to use a font that can be displayed without users initially having it on their device.

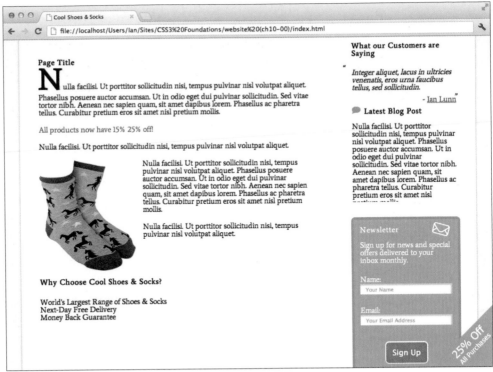

FIGURE 10-2 The Cool Shoes & Socks page with a font-family of Georgia.

Applying Fonts Using @font-face

Browser support: IE 4+, Firefox 3.5+, Chrome 4+, Opera 10+, Safari 3.1+

`@font-face` is a rule set of its own rather than a property, which allows you to specify a font to be downloaded from a particular source. Although `@font-face` appears only in the CSS3 Fonts module (`www.w3.org/TR/css3-fonts/`), it was actually a feature first implemented by Microsoft in Internet Explorer 4—yes, another one of those situations in which Microsoft did as it pleased. This is good news, though; it means every browser in use today supports `@font-face`, *but* it isn't without its caveats.

Fonts come in the following formats:

- .ttf (TrueType Font)

- .otf (OpenType Font)

- .eot (Embedded OpenType)

- .woff (Web Open Font Format)

- .svg (Scalable Vector Graphics)

When Internet Explorer 4 implemented @font-face, it supported only the .eot format, and the situation remained that way up to Internet Explorer 8. Because the .eot format is proprietary, belonging to Microsoft, no other browser supports it. The only format to be supported by all other browsers (including Internet Explorer 9) is .woff. So, when using @font-face, you should aim to have .eot and .woff formats of the same font.

If you have only one font type, numerous tools available online take that one format and convert it into the rest for you. My personal recommendation is Font Squirrel's @font-face Generator, found at www.fontsquirrel.com/fontface/generator.

Converting fonts to a different format may be against the license for a font, so you should always be certain a font license allows for this behavior before going ahead. More on font licenses in a moment.

The Cool Shoes & Socks project files contain an .eot and .woff font called Average. Tell the browser to download this font for later use:

1. In styles.css, above the body rule set, add the following:

    ```
    @font-face {
        font-family: Average;
        src: url("../fonts/Average-Regular.eot");
        src: local("Average"),
            url("../fonts/Average-Regular.woff");
    }
    ```

    Because this rule set doesn't have a selector, it only lets the browser know the name of the font and where it is located, via the src declaration. Due to Internet Explorer 6, 7, and 8 supporting only .eot font formats; you specify two src properties. Internet Explorer 6, 7, and 8 read and apply the first property, but because they don't understand the syntax of the second, they ignore it.

    The second src property consists of two functions: local() and url(). By placing the local() function first, you tell the browser (those which aren't Internet Explorer versions below 9) to check to see whether the device already has the font saved locally, and if not, to download it from the source specified in the url().

    At a minimum, the @font-face rule must include font-family and src declarations; otherwise, it is ignored.

    Now to use this font, do the following:

2. In the body rule set, modify the font-family declaration:

    ```
    font-family: Average, Georgia, serif;
    ```

3. Save styles.css.

When a browser reads the Average font as the first font in the list, it renders the text in that font. However, if that font isn't available (you've made a good job of making sure it is via the @font-face rule, so it should be), the browser moves onto the next font Georgia and tries to render the text using that font.

Along with the font-family and src that are included in a @font-face rule set, you can also give the font default styles using properties such as font-size and font-weight, which are covered in the next chapter.

To specify multiple fonts per stylesheet, you simply add another @font-face rule. The Cool Shoes & Socks page uses two different fonts using the @font-face rule, but instead of getting the browser to download these fonts from the server, you actually use a third-party font service instead.

Font Licenses and Third-Party Font Services

Although @font-face offers a way to use fonts that may not be installed on a user's computer, that doesn't mean you can start using every font you have on your own computer. When you use @font-face, a user's computer has to download a copy of that font, meaning *you* are distributing that font. Why does that distinction matter? Often fonts aren't licensed to allow for distribution. By distributing a font, you are essentially giving it away free. You should be cautious when using @font-face and always make sure a font's license allows for distribution.

You can find the license information for the Average and Belgrano fonts in text files distributed with the *CSS3 Foundations* project files.

A growing number of third-party services offer fonts to be used on web pages, some free and some paid. Some of these services use the @font-face technique, whereas others use JavaScript to display a font in a way that means a user doesn't have to download it—working around the licensing issue somewhat.

The Average font was downloaded free from Google Web Fonts (www.google.com/webfonts), which is becoming one of the web's most popular font services. What's more, all its fonts are completely free and licensed for web page usage, meaning it's one of if not *the* easiest and most carefree font delivery services.

Google Web Fonts

Although Google Web Fonts makes all its fonts available to download free, you're best to use the stylesheet it provides. This stylesheet references the font on its web server, meaning you don't need to save the font on your own server. In doing this, you save yourself some bandwidth usage, and fonts tend to load faster when hosted by Google. Go ahead and remove the @font-face rule from the Cool Shoes & Socks stylesheet so Google can host the font instead:

1. In styles.css, find the `@font-face` rule set and delete it (keep the `font-family` declaration in the `body` rule set, however).

2. In your web browser, navigate to Google Web Fonts (`www.google.com/webfonts`) and search for "Average." When the Average font is displayed, as in Figure 10-3, click Add to Collection.

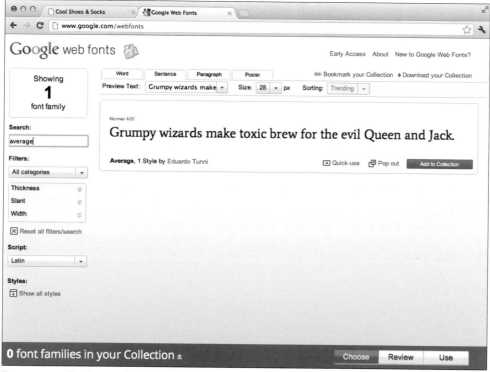

FIGURE 10-3 The Average font selected on the Google Web Fonts page.

The blue box at the bottom of the page shows the fonts you have in your collection. Google Web Fonts allows you to add as many fonts to your page as you like, so find another font, too.

3. Search for the font "Belgrano," and when it appears, click Add to Collection.

4. Now you have two fonts, click Use in the blue collection box.

   - Step 1 of this page shows that these fonts have a "Normal 400" style. This means the fonts come in only a normal style, nonbold, nonitalic, and so on. However, when learning to change the styles of fonts in the next chapter, you see that the browser can change a font's style without there being a specific variant of that font. In this step, you also see a speed dial that shows these fonts will be quick to load. Great! If a font comes with more styles and you know you're never going to use them, you can uncheck those styles to speed up the delivery of fonts.

- Step 2 shows the character set to be used. More often that not, you will use only the Latin set, so you don't need to change anything in this step.

- Step 3 provides the code you must use to have your chosen fonts working on your web page. You're presented with three different methods of adding the fonts to a page. For this example, use the Standard method.

5. Copy the HTML under the Standard tab:

```
<link
    href='http://fonts.googleapis.com/
  css?family=Average|Belgrano'
    rel='stylesheet' type='text/css'>
```

6. In index.html, paste this HTML above the link to the styles.css stylesheet, like so:

```
<link
    href='http://fonts.googleapis.com/
  css?family=Average|Belgrano'
    rel='stylesheet' type='text/css'>
<link rel="stylesheet" href="css/styles.css" type="text/css" />
```

7. Save index.html.

- If you're curious about what this step is doing, you can actually navigate to the external stylesheet by visiting fonts.googleapis.com/css?family=Average|Belgrano, and as you will see, Google uses the @font-face rule to tell the browser you will be using the Average and Belgrano fonts:

```
@font-face {
    font-family: 'Belgrano';
    font-style: normal;
    font-weight: 400;
    src: local('Belgrano'), local('Belgrano-Regular'),
    url('http://themes.googleusercontent.com/static/fonts/
  belgrano/v3/9nICvxZmkDv7_ninPVYjoXYhjbSpvc47ee6xR_80Hnw.
  woff')
    format('woff');
}

@font-face {
    font-family: 'Average';
    font-style: normal;
    font-weight: 400;
    src: local('Average'), local('Average-Regular'),
    url('http://themes.googleusercontent.com/static/fonts/
  average/v1/4iG3r29DvHyol7Yxf3Wz2wLUuEpTyoUstqEm5AMlJo4.woff')
    format('woff');
}
```

- Note that Google Web Fonts doesn't use two `src` declarations as you did to get the font working in versions of Internet Explorer below version 9. Does this matter? Because the fonts Average and Belgrano aren't displayed for these older versions of Internet Explorer (unless users have them installed on their device), the browser moves down the font stack you created to apply the Georgia font instead. Because the font is such a close match, it doesn't particularly matter.

The final step explains how to make use of these fonts by adding a `font-family` declaration to the stylesheet. You gave the `body` rule set a `font-family` declaration earlier, so the Average font is already applied. Now apply the Belgrano font.

8. In styles.css, find the `h1, h2, h3, h4` rule set and add the following:

   ```
   font-family: Belgrano, Georgia, serif;
   ```

9. Save styles.css.

Now, as illustrated in Figure 10-4, all the text on the Cool Shoes & Socks page is styled in the Average font, except for the titles that are styled in Belgrano—all generously hosted and provided free by Google Web Fonts.

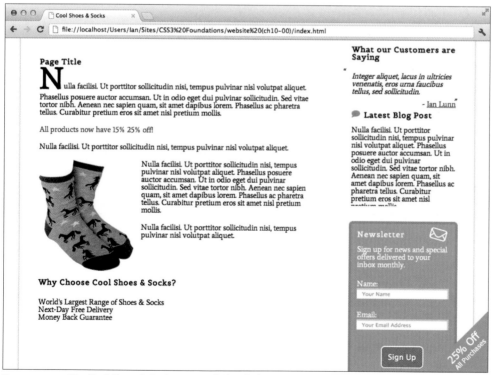

FIGURE 10-4 The Cool Shoes & Socks page styled with the Average and Belgrano fonts.

Other Font Services

Of course, other font services are available, too.

- `www.fontdeck.com`—Fontdeck has a wide selection of fonts and a great pricing structure that means you pay only for the exact font you need. Prices per font start at $2.50 per year, which includes 1 million page views a month. You can also try every font free for as long as you like.

- `www.typekit.com`—Typekit also has a great selection of fonts. Pricing is based on subscription plans that offer varying features. The free plan offers 25,000 page views per month with access to fonts in the Trial Library. The personal plan offers 50,000 page views per month with access to the Personal Library at a cost of $24.99 a year. A portfolio plan offers 100,000 page views with access to the entire library of fonts, at a cost of $49.99 a year. Typekit also offers performance and business plans if you need more than 1 million page views per month.

You may also like to try the following:

- **Font Squirrel**—`www.fontsquirrel.com/`
- **Webtype**—www.webtype.com/
- **FontsLive**—www.fontslive.com/
- **TypeFront**—www.typefront.com/

Summary

In this chapter, you added fonts to the Cool Shoes & Socks page that users may not necessarily have installed on their device. If you use the `@font-face` rule along with the Google Web Font service, the user can still see those fonts.

Now that you've added some fonts to the page, in the next chapter, you learn to style those fonts to give certain text weight and emphasis.

chapter eleven
Styling Fonts and Text

IN THE PRECEDING chapter you gave the Cool Shoes & Socks page some unique fonts via Google Web Fonts. With a knowledge of `@font-face` and third-party font services, you have access to tens of, if not hundreds of thousands of, fonts to give web pages a unique style of their own. Why stop there, though? CSS offers many ways to style fonts and text to make a page even more useful and unique.

Project files update (ch11-00): If you haven't followed the previous instructions and are comfortable working from here onward or would like to reference the project files up to this point, you can download them from www.wiley.com/go/treehouse/css3foundations.

Styling Fonts

Changing the appearance of text doesn't end at changing the font face. If all text on a page were the same style, no matter how fancy the font, the page would look dull and wouldn't direct the users eye particularly well. By changing attributes relating to the font, such as size, variant, weight, and so on, you can help the user determine which text is more important than other text, allowing them to scan the page quicker.

font-style

Initial value: `normal` | Inherited: Yes | Applies to: All | CSS2.1
Browser support: IE 4+, Firefox 1+, Chrome 1+, Opera 7+, Safari 1+

By using the `font-style` property, you can change the style of a font between `normal`, `italic`, and `oblique`. In the preceding chapter, I mentioned that the two fonts chosen from Google Web Fonts are only available in a normal style. Fonts often have various styles, such as oblique and italic. Both of these styles are slanted; oblique is a distorted version of the normal style, and italic is a style of its own, generally cursive in nature. The default `font-style` is `normal`, so at present all fonts on the Cool Shoes & Socks page have a normal style.

Because the fonts you used from Google Web Fonts come only in a normal style, does that mean you can't use italic and oblique styles? No. Assuming you declare a `font-style` of `italic`, a browser looks to see whether an italic version of a font is available. If not, it looks for an oblique version, and if that doesn't exist either, the browser renders the normal style of font with a sloping transformation applied—making an oblique style.

1. In styles.css, in the `p + .offer` rule set, add the following:

   ```
   font-style: italic;
   ```

2. Save styles.css.

Here, you declare an italic `font-style` for the offer text "All products now have 15% 25% off!" (later in this chapter you will learn how to put a strike through 15%, showing the discount has increased), but because the font doesn't have an italic or oblique variant to fall back to, the browser renders an oblique style of its own, as shown in Figure 11-1.

All products now have 15% 25% off!

FIGURE 11-1 The offer text set in oblique.

font-variant

Initial value: `normal` | Inherited: Yes | Applies to: All | CSS2.1
Browser support: IE 4+, Firefox 1+, Chrome 1+, Opera 3.5+, Safari 1+

The `font-variant` property simply takes the values `normal` or `small-caps`. By default, the `font-variant` is `normal`. When you set the value to `small-caps`, the font is changed to a variant that uses `small-caps`, meaning the lowercase letters look similar to the uppercase letters but with smaller proportions.

font-weight

Initial value: `normal` | Inherited: Yes | Applies to: All | CSS2.1
Browser support: IE 3+, Firefox 1+, Chrome 2+, Opera 3.5+, Safari 1.3+

You use `font-weight` to change the weight of characters in a font, their degree of blackness, or stroke thickness. You briefly used this property in Chapter 3 by giving some elements the declaration `font-weight: bold;`.

You can use these four keyword values: `normal`, `bold`, `bolder`, and `lighter`. You can also use the values 100 to 900 in 100-point increments that commonly correspond to these weight names:

- 100—Thin
- 200—Extra Light (Ultra Light)
- 300—Light
- 400—Normal (equivalent of the `normal` keyword)
- 500—Medium
- 600—Semi Bold (Demi Bold)
- 700—Bold (equivalent of the `bold` keyword)
- 800—Extra Bold (Ultra Bold)
- 900—Black (Heavy)

By using the `bolder` and `lighter` keywords, you declare the weight of the font should be bolder or lighter than the inherited value.

You will find that very few fonts support the complete range of weights; in this case, the browser uses the nearest weight to the one you specified.

Because both of the Google Web Fonts used for Cool Shoes & Socks are available only in "Normal 400," much like how a browser can render an oblique font style using the normal font, a browser can also render bolder and lighter fonts if an alternative weight of font is not present.

1. In styles.css, add a declaration to the `.button` rule set to make its text bold:

   `font-weight: bolder;`

2. Save styles.css.

The More Information button `<a class="button purchase" href="#" title="Purchase product">` and Sign Up button `<input class="button" id="submit-newsletter" type="submit" value="Sign Up" />` inherit a default `font-weight` of `normal`. By changing the `font-weight` to `bolder`, you tell the browser to make the font of those buttons heavier than `normal`. The "Average" font has no weight variants, so the browser takes the normal font and renders it as bold (or 700).

3. Add a declaration to the `label` rule set to change the weight of the input labels in the Newsletter box:

   `font-weight: 900;`

4. Save styles.css.

Although this declaration for the `label` rule set is different from that of the `.button` rule set, the same effect is achieved because the "Average" font doesn't have a 900 variant. The browser again takes its own action and renders the font bold.

Obviously, it's better to be consistent with `font-weight`. Although the "Average" font doesn't have any styles other than "Normal 400," fallback fonts (the ones specified in the font stack) may have, in which case `font-weight: bolder;` and `font-weight: 900;` *may* be rendered differently. If you like, change the previously added declarations to `font-weight: bold;` or `font-weight: 700;` to keep them consistent.

font-size

Initial value: `medium` | Inherited: Yes | Applies to: All | CSS2.1
Browser support: IE 5.5+, Firefox 1+, Chrome 1+, Opera 7+, Safari 1+

The `font-size` property controls the layout of the text on a web page. You can change `font-size` in many ways, each with advantages and disadvantages. As already established, Cool Shoes & Socks uses the em unit for not just font sizes but also other properties such as `padding` and `margin`.

Let's come back to using the em unit for `font-size` in a moment, but first see what other methods you can use to change the font size.

Keywords

Similar to `font-weight`, `font-size` can be changed using a series of keywords: `xx-small`, `x-small`, `small`, `medium`, `large`, `x-large`, and `xx-large`. Likewise, you can use the keywords `larger` and `smaller` to increase or decrease the font size relative to an element's inherited `font-size`.

Using these keywords makes changing font sizes easy; however, you may feel slightly limited by them. What's more, the CSS specification provides a guideline to browser vendors that suggests what size of font these keywords should relate to. Although browsers do a good job of adhering to the guidelines, you may find inconsistencies between browsers.

Percentages

When you use a percentage value, the font size is relative to the parent element's font size—that which is inherited. Assuming the inherited `font-size` of an element is 16px, if you declare that element's `font-size` should be 50%, the calculated `font-size` is 8px.

Using percentages offers a wide range of control over the size of a font and also allows a font to be resized easily. However, because percentages relate to different factors depending on the property they are used on, they don't allow for a consistent workflow during the creation of a website. More on this topic when comparing percentages and ems in a moment.

Absolute Length Units

Absolute length units are those such as pixels (px), centimeters (cm), inches (in), and so on. Pixels are the most common absolute length unit and allow for very specific control over the size of a font. Absolute length units are fixed, however, and should be used only when the output environment is known. Because many types of devices access the web nowadays, it is wise to avoid absolute length units because although a font size of 16px on a desktop may look perfectly readable, on a much smaller device, it may be too small. By using absolute length units, you also prevent users from being able to increase the size of text via their browser's built-in functionality.

Relative Units

Relative units are those such as em and ex. On the modern web, ems are the suggested unit for `font-size`. Much like percentages, font sizes that use relative units are calculated relative to the parent element's font size and can easily be scaled where necessary.

To help you better understand why relative units are important—and in the long run save you time—Figure 11-2 shows Cool Shoes & Socks in Opera's Mobile Emulator. On a small device, notice how small the font is? Although the Cool Shoes & Socks page is sized well for reading on a desktop computer, it's difficult to read on a mobile device.

In Figure 11-3, I modified the `body` rule set to increase the `font-size` from `62.5%` to `1.2em`. Because all the fonts relate to that `font-size`, they are all scaled up, too, making the entire page much more readable on smaller devices.

FIGURE 11-2 The current Cool Shoes & Socks page viewed in Opera Mobile Emulator.

I'm jumping ahead a little though. You work on improving the readability on mobile devices in Chapter 15.

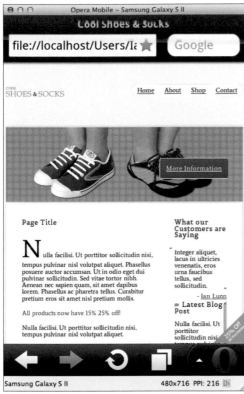

FIGURE 11-3 A version of the Cool Shoes & Socks page viewed in Opera Mobile Emulator with the body font increased to 1.2 em.

Percentages Versus Ems

If relative units, such as ems, work in the same way as percentages, why choose ems?

When you specify a `font-size` using percentages or ems, 1 em is the equivalent of 100%, 0.5 em is the equivalent of 50%, and so on. Ems and percentages work in the exact same way when applied to `font-size`. However, when used on other properties such as `padding` and `margin`, they differ.

Ems are always relative to an element's `font-size`, whereas percentages are relative to another value, such as the `height` and `width` dimensions of an element. Consider the following CSS as an example:

```
div {
    font-size: 16px;
    padding-left: 1em;
    width: 200px;
}
```

The calculated `padding-left` is 16 px because 1 em is relative to the `font-size` multiplied by one, which is 16 px. A `padding-left` of 2 em creates a calculated `padding-left` of 32 px and so on.

```
div {
    font-size: 16px;
    padding-left: 100%;
    width: 200px;
}
```

In this example, the `padding-left` is changed to a percentage, so it relates to the `width` of the element instead, and the calculated `padding-left` is therefore 200px.

Because properties such as `padding` and `margin` better relate to the size of text, it is best to use ems for `font-size`. When I scaled up the font size between Figure 11-2 and Figure 11-3, the padding and margins scaled also, aiding the readability of the page.

When working with relative units and calculated values, rather than doing all of the calculations yourself, you can use your browser's web developer tools to find the calculated value of any element. Please refer to the sidebar "Working with Relative Units" in Chapter 4.

You may also like to refer to Chapter 4's description of the Rem unit, which always inherits `font-size` from the <html> element, making dealing with inheritance easier. Unfortunately, at the time of writing, Rem doesn't have enough browser support to make it useful in a real-world website. It will almost certainly be the unit used for `font-size` in the future though.

line-height

Initial value: `normal` | Inherited: Yes | Applies to: All Elements | CSS2.1
Browser support: IE 4+, Firefox 1+, Chrome 1+, Opera 7+, Safari 1+

`line-height` specifies the minimal height of a line of text within an element. The initial value of `normal` means the `line-height` is the same value as the `font-size`. You also can specify a unit of length, percentage, or number. A number value is a multiplication of an element's font size.

1. In styles.css, find the `#content p, #content ul` rule set and add the following declaration:

   ```
   line-height: 1.4em;
   ```

2. Save styles.css.

As shown in Figure 11-4, the main content now has an increased `line-height` (the space between lines of text has increased). You can achieve the same effect by using the declarations `line-height: 140%;` or `line-height: 1.4;`.

Before:
Nulla facilisi. Ut porttitor sollicitudin nisi, tempus
pulvinar nisl volutpat aliquet. Phasellus posuere
auctor accumsan. Ut in odio eget dui pulvinar
sollicitudin. Sed vitae tortor nibh. Aenean nec sapien
quam, sit amet dapibus lorem. Phasellus ac pharetra
tellus. Curabitur pretium eros sit amet nisl pretium
mollis.

After:
Nulla facilisi. Ut porttitor sollicitudin nisi, tempus
pulvinar nisl volutpat aliquet. Phasellus posuere
auctor accumsan. Ut in odio eget dui pulvinar
sollicitudin. Sed vitae tortor nibh. Aenean nec sapien
quam, sit amet dapibus lorem. Phasellus ac pharetra
tellus. Curabitur pretium eros sit amet nisl pretium
mollis.

FIGURE 11-4 The line-height of the main content is increased.

font (Shorthand)

Browser support: IE 4+, Firefox 1+, Chrome 1+, Opera 3.5+, Safari 1+

As you've seen, styling and changing the font consist of quite a lot of properties. To make life easier, you can use the `font` property, which is a shorthand consisting of the properties `font-style`, `font-variant`, `font-weight`, `font-size`, `line-height`, and `font-family`. Use the following syntax when using the `font` property:

```
font: font-style font-variant font-weight font-size/line-height
font-family;
```

At a minimum, `font-size` and `font-family` must be present. When specifying `font-size` and `line-height`, you separate the two with a forward slash (`/`).

1. In styles.css, find the `body` rule set and delete the following declarations:

   ```
   font-family: Average, Georgia, serif;
   font-size: 62.5%;
   ```

2. In their place, add this shorthand `font` declaration:

   ```
   font: 62.5% Average, Georgia, serif;
   ```

3. Save styles.css.

When you use the shorthand `font` declaration, all font-related properties are first reset to their initial values, so in the declaration you just added, `font-style`, `font-variant`, and `font-weight` are absent and will be set to their initial value of `normal`. `font-size` will be set to `62.5%`, `line-height` is also absent so will be set to `normal`, and finally, `font-family` will be set to `Average, Georgia, serif`.

Now, you might want to go through the rest of the font-related properties in the Cool Shoes & Socks stylesheet to make them shorthand, but doing so wouldn't be efficient. Consider the following rule set:

```
h1, h2, h3, h4 {
    font-weight: bold;
    font-family: Belgrano, serif;
}
```

Because the `font` declaration resets all font-related properties to their initial value, when you use the `font` property in this rule set, the `font-size` is reset to `medium`, overriding the more desirable font size that is inherited. Of course, you could specify the `font-size` as well, like so:

```
h1, h2, h3, h4 {
    font: bold 1em Belgrano, serif;
}
```

By doing this though, you're making a little extra work for yourself because these elements will inherit a `font-size` anyway. Using shorthand properties where possible is a good idea, but in this case—and with all other font-related declarations in the Cool Shoes & Socks stylesheet—it's more efficient to use the longhand properties instead, allowing inheritance to work its magic.

Code Challenge: Change the Style of More Fonts

In styles.css, do the following:

1. In the rule set `#header nav ul li a`, add the declaration `font-weight: bold;`.

2. In the rule set `input[type="submit"][class="button"]`, add the declaration `font-size: 1em;`.

3. In the rule sets `blockquote p:before` and `blockquote p:after`, add the declaration `font-size: 2em;`.

4. In the rule set `label` and `input[type="text"], input[type="email"]`, add the declaration `font-size: .8em;`.

Styling Text

The previously described properties manipulate the font face but properties of the text can also be changed, such as color, decoration, alignment, and so on.

color

Initial value: browser dependent | Inherited: Yes | Applies to: All | CSS2.1
Browser support: IE 3+, Firefox 1+, Chrome 1+, Opera 3.5+, Safari 1+

The initial value for the color of text is browser dependent although all browsers in use today use black text, except for links, which are blue when unvisited, purple when visited, and red when active.

1. In styles.css, below the `.benefits` rule set, add a new rule set:

   ```
   .benefits ul {
       color: #38AEDB;
   }
   ```

2. Save styles.css.

The text under "Why Choose Cool Shoes & Socks?" is now blue, helping draw the users eye to it. Shortly you'll add images to these points to make them stand out even more.

Color values such as keywords, hex values, and `rgb()` can be used to apply color to text, as explained in Chapter 3.

text-decoration

Initial value: `none` | Inherited: No | Applies to: All | CSS2.1
Browser support: IE 3+, Firefox 1+, Chrome 1+, Opera 3.5+, Safari 1+

The `text-decoration` property allows you to change the line decoration applied to text. You can use the values `underline`, `overline`, and `line-through`. The CSS2.1 specification also describes the value `blink`, but due to the accessibility concerns blinking text raises, the CSS3 Text module no longer lists this value and browsers do not support it.

The CSS3 Text module (www.w3.org/TR/css3-text/) shows that the text-decoration property will eventually become a shorthand for the properties text-decoration-line, which takes the same values as the current text-decoration (underline, overline, and line-through); text-decoration-color, which lets you change the color of the line; and text-decoration-style, which lets you change the style of the line to either solid, double, dotted, dashed, or wavy. However, only Mozilla Firefox version 6 and onward support these properties by adding the –moz prefix to each property. Until these properties get better support in browsers, you can only safely use text-decoration, which decorates text with a solid line the same color as the text.

The offer text that you made italic, shows that the price of the products is now marked down by a percentage, but there are two percentage values. To strike out one of those values, do the following:

1. In styles.css, below the p + .offer rule set, add a new rule set:

```
.strike {
    text-decoration: line-through;
}
```

2. Save styles.css.

The 15% is wrapped with span tags with a class of strike. As shown in Figure 11-5, the 15% discount now has a line through it so the user can see the discount has been increased to 25%. Maybe this company should have been called *Cheap Shoes & Socks*!

All products now have ~~15%~~ 25% off!

FIGURE 11-5 The 15% discount with a line through it.

If you would like an element to have multiple text decorations, you can specify multiple values, each separated by a space, such as text-decoration: line-through underline overline;.

text-transform

Initial value: none | Inherited: No | Applies to: All | CSS2.1
Browser support: IE 4+, Firefox 1+, Chrome 1+, Opera 7+, Safari 1+

Sometimes you might want to change text case. Rather than go in to the HTML and make those changes, you can tell the browser to automatically change that case for you, using the text-transform property.

`text-transform` takes the following values:

- `none`—Do not transform the text.
- `uppercase`—Change all the text to uppercase (capital letters).
- `lowercase`—Change all the text to lowercase.
- `capitalize`—Change the first letter of each word to uppercase.

Because the discount in the body text of the Cool Shoes & Socks page may persuade a user to make a purchase, you can make that text stand out a little more by making it uppercase:

1. In styles.css, add the following declaration to the `p + .offer` rule set:

   ```
   text-transform: uppercase;
   ```

2. Save styles.css.

text-shadow

Initial value: none | Inherited: Yes | Applies to: All | CSS3
Browser support: IE 10+, Firefox 3.5+, Chrome 2.1+, Opera 9.5+, Safari 1.1+

Much like how you give a box a shadow using the `box-shadow` property, which was covered in Chapter 5, you can also give text a shadow using the `text-shadow` property (see Figure 11-6). `text-shadow` works in all browsers without a prefix except for Internet Explorer versions 6, 7, 8, and 9. Because a text shadow is only a visual style, the fact it isn't shown in these versions of Internet Explorer doesn't matter.

1. In styles.css, add the following declaration to the `p + .offer` rule set:

   ```
   text-shadow: 2px 2px 1px rgba(0, 0, 0, 0.2);
   ```

2. Save styles.css.

ALL PRODUCTS NOW HAVE 15% 25% OFF!

FIGURE 11-6 The text-shadow applied to the offer text.

The `text-shadow` syntax works in a similar way to `box-shadow` but takes a maximum of three values, rather than four, which modify the shadow as follows:

- The first value represents the horizontal offset—how far the shadow is to the right of the text, a negative value to its left. The shadow you added is offset 2 pixels to the right.

- The second value represents the vertical offset—how far the shadow is to the bottom of the text, a negative value to the top. Again, you gave the offer text shadow a 2-pixel offset to the bottom.

- The third value is the blur of the shadow. This value is optional, and in its absence, the shadow would have no blur. When you declare a blur of 1 px, the shadow applied to the offer text has a very mild blur.

Following from the shadow values is an optional color. By default, a shadow is black, but the shadow you added uses the `rgba()` color function to apply black with an alpha opacity of `0.2`, making it more of a gray color.

As with `box-shadow`, you can use multiple shadows on text by separating each shadow with a comma:

1. In styles.css, modify the `text-shadow` declaration to include two text shadows on the offer text:

   ```
   text-shadow: 2px 2px 1px rgba(0, 0, 0, 0.2),
                4px 4px 2px rgba(0, 0, 0, 0.1);
   ```

2. Save styles.css.

A shadow that follows another is placed behind it. The second text shadow applied is even subtler than the first, but both work together to help the text stand out a little more.

letter-spacing

Initial value: `normal` | Inherited: Yes | Applies to: All Elements | CSS2.1
Browser support: IE 4+, Firefox 1+, Chrome 1+, Opera 3.5+, Safari 1+

The `letter-spacing` property allows you to control the amount of space between each individual character with the initial value of `normal` being the default amount.

By giving this property a length value, you can increase the space between characters in addition to the default space.

1. In styles.css, find the `.showcase .button` rule set and add the following declaration:

   ```
   letter-spacing: 2px;
   ```

2. Save styles.css.

As you can see in Figure 11-7, when you give the More Information button a `letter-spacing` of 2px, the space between characters is slightly increased.

Before:

After:

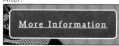

FIGURE 11-7 The difference between the "More Information" button before and after having its letter-spacing modified.

word-spacing

Initial value: `normal` | Inherited: Yes | Applies to: All Elements | CSS2.1
Browser support: IE 6+, Firefox 1+, Chrome 1+, Opera 3.5+, Safari 1+

Just like `letter-spacing`, the `word-spacing` property enables you to change the spacing between words. The initial value of `normal` represents the default space between words, and you can specify a length value to adjust this space as you see fit.

direction

Initial value: `ltr` | Inherited: Yes | Applies to: All Elements | CSS2.1
Browser support: IE 5.5+, Firefox 1+, Chrome 2+, Opera 9.2+, Safari 1.3+

The `direction` property determines the direction of text. The initial value `ltr` means left to right. The value `rtl` (right to left) can be used for Hebrew and Arabic text. Note however, that specifying the direction of text is normally done in the HTML using the `dir` attribute.

text-align

Initial value: `start` | Inherited: Yes | Applies to: Block Containers | CSS2.1
Browser support: IE 3+, Firefox 1+, Chrome 1+, Opera 3.5+, Safari 1+

By using `text-align`, you can align content to the left, right, or center of its parent; in addition, you can make that content justified, meaning flush to both sides of the parent. The CSS2.1 specification describes the values `left`, `right`, `center`, and `justify` to be used with `text-align` and an initial "nameless" value that acts as `left` if the direction of text is left to right or `right` if the text direction is right to left (for languages such as Arabic and Hebrew).

For the sake of completeness CSS Level 3 introduces two new values, `start` and `end`, with `start` replacing the "nameless" initial value of `text-align`. `start` and `end` achieve the exact same results as `left` and `right` but make more sense when used in conjunction with differing directions of text, `start` being whatever side the text starts from and `end` being the opposite. However, `start` and `end` are currently supported only in Firefox, Chrome, and Safari. Until support improves, it's best just to work with the CSS2.1 values: `left`, `right`, `center`, and `justify`.

1. In styles.css, add a declaration to the `p + .offer` rule set to make the text centered:

    ```
    text-align: center;
    ```

2. Add a declaration to the `blockquote` rule set to make the text justified:

    ```
    text-align: justify;
    ```

3. Save styles.css.

As shown in Figure 11-8, the offer text is now centered relative to its containing parent element, and the customer testimonial is justified, spaced out to touch the edges of its containing parent.

text-align: center;   text-align: justify;

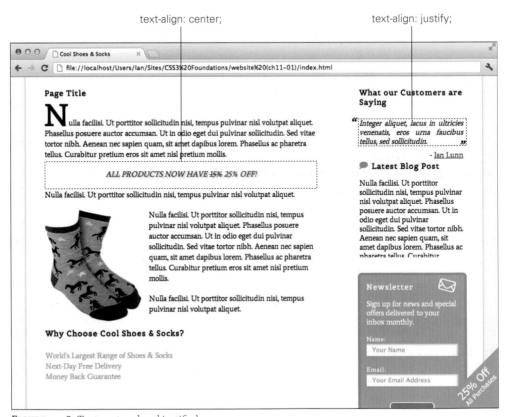

FIGURE 11-8 Text centered and justified.

text-indent

Initial value: 0 | Inherited: Yes | Applies to: Block Containers | CSS2.1
Browser support: IE 3+, Firefox 1+, Chrome 1+, Opera 3.5+, Safari 1+

You can use text-indent to apply an indentation to the first line of text in a block container, using either a unit of length such as pixels and ems, or a percentage that is relative to the width of the containing block.

If, like me, you were taught at school to always indent a new paragraph—which seems to be old-fashioned now—you could use the following rule set to indent all <p> elements:

```
p {
    text-indent: 1.25em;
}
```

white-space

Initial value: normal | Inherited: Yes | Applies to: All Elements | CSS2.1
Browser support: IE 5.5+, Firefox 1+, Chrome 1+, Opera 4+, Safari 1+

The white-space property determines how white space inside an element is handled. Consider the first paragraph of the Cool Shoes & Socks page as an example:

```
<p>Nulla facilisi. Ut porttitor sollicitudin nisi, tempus pulvinar
nisl volutpat aliquet. Phasellus posuere auctor accumsan. Ut in odio
eget dui pulvinar sollicitudin. Sed vitae tortor nibh. Aenean nec
sapien quam, sit amet dapibus lorem. Phasellus ac pharetra tellus.
Curabitur pretium eros sit amet nisl pretium mollis.</p>
```

With white-space set to its initial value of normal, white space is collapsed (meaning any space within this HTML does not take effect), and lines are wrapped (broken and pushed onto a new line) where necessary to fill the containing element. So the following achieves the same visual representation as the preceding example:

```
<p>Nulla facilisi. Ut porttitor sollicitudin nisi, tempus pulvinar
nisl volutpat aliquet. Phasellus posuere auctor accumsan.

Ut in odio eget dui pulvinar    sollicitudin. Sed vitae tortor nibh.
Aenean nec sapien quam, sit amet dapibus lorem. Phasellus ac pharetra
tellus. Curabitur pretium eros sit amet nisl pretium mollis.</p>
```

You also can use the following values with `white-space`:

- `pre`—White space isn't collapsed, and lines are broken only when they are broken in the HTML.

- `nowrap`—White space is collapsed as per `normal`, but lines of text are never wrapped.

- `pre-wrap`—White space isn't collapsed, but lines are wrapped where necessary or when broken in the HTML.

- `pre-line`—White space is collapsed, and lines are wrapped where necessary or when broken in the HTML

overflow-wrap and word-wrap

Initial value: `normal` | Inherited: Yes | Applies to: All Elements | CSS3
Browser support: IE 5.5+, Firefox 3.5+, Chrome 1+, Opera 10.5+, Safari 1+

`word-wrap` is another of those properties that was introduced by Microsoft and was later added to the CSS3 specification. It has undergone a little bit of a makeover in the CSS3 Text module (`www.w3.org/TR/css3-text/#overflow-wrap`) and now has the new name `overflow-wrap`. However, because only CSS3 supporting browsers recognize `overflow-wrap`, you should use `word-wrap`, which both modern browsers and Internet Explorer versions 6, 7, and 8 support.

The initial value of `normal` means lines of text may break only between words. Usually, this is fine, but if a word is longer than the element it is contained within, it will overflow rather than break, as shown in Figure 11-9. Where this effect is undesirable, you can use the value `break-word` to force a word to break and wrap onto a new line instead, also shown in Figure 11.9.

FIGURE 11-9 The difference between word-wrap: normal; and word-wrap: break-word.

Code Challenge: Change the Style of Various Text Elements

In styles.css, do the following:

1. Add a new rule set for `a.button:link` below the `.button` rule set with the declarations `text-transform: uppercase; text-decoration: none;`.

2. Add the declarations `text-transform: uppercase; text-decoration: none;` to the `#header nav ul li a` rule set.

> Project files update (ch11-02): If you haven't followed the previous instructions and are comfortable working from here onward or would like to reference the project files up to this point, you can download them from www.wiley.com/go/treehouse/css3foundations.

Styling Lists

A list, such as the unordered list of benefits under "Why Choose Cool Shoes & Socks?", is made up of text as well as a marker such as a bullet point. Using CSS, you can change the type of marker used and change its position.

list-style-type

> Initial value: `disc` | Inherited: Yes | Applies to: Elements with `display: list-item` | CSS2.1
> Browser support: IE 4+, Firefox 1+, Chrome 1+, Opera 3.5+, Safari 1+

The `list-style-type` property specifies the appearance of list item markers. When you declare none, a list has no markers.

You can use the following values to mark list items with glyphs:

- `disc`
- `circle`
- `square`

The following values can be used to mark list items with numbers:

- `decimal`—Decimal numbers, beginning with 1
- `decimal-leading-zero`—Decimal numbers padded by initial zeros

- `lower-roman`—Lowercase Roman numerals
- `upper-roman`—Uppercase Roman numerals
- `georgian`—Traditional Georgian numbering
- `armenian`—Traditional uppercase Armenian numbering

The following values can be used to mark list items with alphabetic systems:

- `lower-latin` or `lower-alpha`—Lowercase ASCII letters
- `upper-latin` or `upper-alpha`—Uppercase ASCII letters
- `lower-greek`—Lowercase classical Greek alphabet

Figure 11-10 shows each `list-style-type`.

- disc
- circle
1. decimal
01. decimal-leading-zero
i. lower-roman
I. upper-roman
ჰ. georgian
Ա. armenian
a. lower-latin
A. upper-latin
a. lower-alpha
A. upper-alpha
α. lower-greek

FIGURE 11-10 Examples of each list-style-type.

 This demonstration page can be found in the project files ch11-02, named list-style-demo.html.

Note that although the initial value for `list-style-type` is `disc`, the CSS Reset you applied in Chapter 2 changed all list items to have a `list-style-type` of `none`. Now give the "Why Choose Cool Shoes & Socks" disc markers:

1. In styles.css, find the `.benefits ul,` rule set, and add the following:

   ```
   list-style-type: disc;
   ```

2. Save styles.css.

list-style-image

Initial value: none | Inherited: Yes | Applies to: Elements with `display: list-item` | CSS2.1
Browser support: IE 4+, Firefox 1+, Chrome 1+, Opera 7+, Safari 1+

If none of the `list-style-type` markers takes your fancy, you can use your own image as a marker using the `list-style-image` property and declaring a `url()` function as its value:

1. In the `.benefits ul` rule set, add this new declaration:

   ```
   list-style-image: url("../images/check.png");
   ```

2. Save styles.css.

Although a marker image takes the place of a basic marker determined by the `list-style-type`, it's wise to specify a `list-style-type` along with a `list-style-image` just in case the browser can't get the image.

list-style-position

Initial value: `outside` | Inherited: Yes | Applies to: Elements with `display: list-item` | CSS2.1
Browser support: IE 4+, Chrome 1+, Opera 3.5+, Safari 1+

As shown in Figure 11-11, the list of benefits now uses images in place of the browser-rendered markers. Note that the markers sit outside the principal block of content. `outside` is the initial value for `list-style-position`, a property that changes the position of list markers.

Why Choose Cool Shoes & Socks?
✔ World's Largest Range of Shoes & Socks
✔ Next-Day Free Delivery
✔ Money Back Guarantee

FIGURE 11-11 The "Why Choose Cool Shoes & Socks" list now with images used for the markers.

1. In the `.benefits ul` rule set, add the following declaration:

   ```
   list-style-position: inside;
   ```

2. Save styles.css.

As you can see in Figure 11-12, by declaring a `list-style-position` of `inside`, you can position list markers inside the principal block.

FIGURE 11-12 The list markers are now positioned inside the principal block.

list-style (Shorthand)

You are able to combine `list-style-type`, `list-style-image`, and `list-style-position` into one handy shorthand declaration, `list-style` with the following syntax:

```
list-style: list-style-type list-style-position list-style-image
```

1. Remove the three declarations from the `.benefits ul` rule set and replace them with the `list-style` shorthand declaration:

   ```
   list-style: disc inside url("../images/check.png");
   ```

2. Save styles.css.

Summary

In this chapter, you added the finishing touches to the fonts and text on the Cool Shoes & Socks page. Any text that needs to stand out and grab the users' eyes does so, and the main text is well laid out and easy to read.

In the next chapter, you jump deep into the modern web, learning some of CSS3's most unique features: 2D transforms!

part 5

Taking It to the Next Level with Transforms and Animations

chapter twelve
Adding 2D Transforms

IN THIS CHAPTER, you leave behind older browsers and make use of one of CSS3's most exciting features, transforms, which let you move, rotate, and scale elements, among other manipulations.

Project files update (ch12-00): If you haven't followed the previous instructions and are comfortable working from here onward or would like to reference the project files up to this point, you can download them from www.wiley.com/go/treehouse/css3foundations.

Safely Using Experimental CSS3 Properties

Because all the CSS features explained in this chapter are from the CSS3 specification, they are unsupported in Internet Explorer 6, 7, and 8. Likewise, 3D transforms, transitions, and animations described in Chapters 13 and 14 are also unsupported in these browsers, as well as Internet Explorer 9. They do however have good support in Internet Explorer 10 and other major browsers.

Although these CSS3 properties are "experimental" and a part of Working Draft modules, they have been implemented in modern browsers for some time, and are actually close to being safe enough to use without prefixes. At the time of writing though, these properties should be used with prefixes, so you'll learn to do just that—the most future proof way to use the latest CSS3 features.

Because I am creating the Cool Shoes & Socks page in Google Chrome, I use the `-webkit-` prefix. If you are using a different browser, replace the `-webkit-` prefix with your browser's prefix:

- `-webkit-` for Google Chrome and Apple Safari
- `-moz-` for Mozilla Firefox
- `-o-` for Opera
- `-ms-` for Microsoft Internet Explorer

In Chapter 15, you use a tool that adds the missing prefixes to your stylesheet so that the Cool Shoes & Socks page works across all browsers.

transform and 2D Transform Functions

Initial value: none | Inherited: No | Applies to: All elements with a `display` declaration relating to block, inline or table | CSS3

Unprefixed browser support: IE 10+, Firefox 16+, Opera 12.5+

Prefixed browser support: IE 9+, Firefox 3.5+, Chrome 12+, Opera 10.5+, Safari 3.1+

The `transform` property allows you to manipulate the position, size, rotation, and skew of an element. When prefixed, the property itself looks like this:

```
-webkit-transform
-moz-transform
-ms-transform
-o-transform
```

The values to be used with `transform` are all functions: `translate()`, `translateX()`, `translateY()`, `scale()`, `scaleX()`, `scaleY()`, `rotate()`, `skewX()`, and `skewY()`. They all affect an element in 2D. The next chapter covers 3D functions to be used with the `transform` property.

translate(), translateX(), and translateY()

The translate functions allow you to move elements around on a web page. That capability may not seem very exciting because you've already seen this happen lots with properties such as position, top, left, right, and bottom, but translate() is an easier way to move elements around without affecting the rest of the document. Ideally, you use translate functions when you want to animate the position of elements, creating movement.

Remember that "25% Off" banner image you fixed to the bottom of the Cool Shoes & Socks page in Chapter 9? I mentioned that the image is square and has a transparent section, which may prevent users from interacting with elements below it. By using the transform property, you can make that banner without using an image and work around that problem of the image taking up an area it doesn't need to.

1. In index.html, find the following HTML and delete it:

   ```
   <img class="banner-ad" src="images/banner-25percent.png"
     alt="25% Off All Purchases" />
   ```

2. In its place, add the following:

   ```
   <div class="banner-ad"><span>25% Off</span>All Purchases</div>
   ```

3. Save index.html.

   Now that you've replaced the image, add some CSS to make the <div> look like the image.

4. In styles.css, add the following declarations to the .banner-ad rule set below the existing declarations:

   ```
   background: #00B0DC;
   color: white;
   text-align: center;
   font-family: Tahoma, Verdana, sans-serif;
   font-size: 1.1em;
   font-weight: bold;
   min-height: 50px;
   width: 200px;
   ```

5. Below the .banner-ad rule set, add a new rule set:

   ```
   .banner-ad span {
       clear: both;
       display: block;
       font-size: 2.2em;
   }
   ```

6. Save styles.css.

As shown in Figure 12-1, the banner advertisement image is replaced with text and CSS. At the moment, the banner sits square on the page, but you can change that position using the transform property.

FIGURE 12-1 The banner advertisement now made using CSS rather than an image.

7. In the .banner-ad rule set, add the following declaration:

```
-webkit-transform: translate(50px, -25px);
```

8. Save styles.css.

The banner now sits partially off-screen, outside the viewport, as shown in Figure 12-2. This change is all part of the master plan and puts the banner in a place where you can rotate it in a moment.

FIGURE 12-2 The banner advertisement moved 50px on the X axis and −25px on the Y axis.

By giving the translate() function two values (the X and Y positions), you tell the browser to move the banner 50px horizontally to the right and move it vertically upward 25px on the Y axis. Negative values on the X axis move an element horizontally to the left and vertically upward on the Y axis.

Putting the banner in this position may seem strange, but it makes more sense when you consider the origin of the element. Each element has an origin, which is the position used to calculate transforms. As shown in Figure 12-3, an element's origin (represented by a cross) is its center by default, which you can change via the transform-origin property that is covered shortly.

By using the translate() function to position the center of the banner here, you can then rotate it to be perfectly positioned in the way the image was.

Before:

After:

−25px

50px

FIGURE 12-3 The origin of the banner advertisement and how it is used to calculate the banner's new position.

You can give the `translate()` function any unit of length or a percentage as its values. If the second value, representing the Y axis, is absent, it is assumed to be 0.

`translate()` is the shorthand function for `translateX()` and `translateY()`, which change the X and Y axis, respectively.

rotate()

If you're itching to get to it, you can rotate that banner straight away and then take a closer look at the `rotate()` function:

1. In styles.css, change the `transform` declaration in the `.banner-ad` rule set to include a `rotate()` function:

   `-webkit-transform: translate(50px, -25px) rotate(-45deg);`

2. Save styles.css.

As shown in Figure 12-4, the banner is now rotated and appears in the same way that the image did. Why go to that effort? Although the element is still square after you rotate it, the diagonal top of the banner is now the top of the element, so there is no invisible space, as there was with the image. What's more, in Chapter 14, you take this process further and animate the banner when it's hovered over.

FIGURE 12-4 The banner advertisement rotated to sit at −45 degrees in the corner of the viewport.

Now look at that code you added:

```
-webkit-transform: translate(50px, -25px) rotate(-45deg);
```

Because the banner is to be both translated and rotated, you add two functions to the `transform` declaration, separated by a space. You can give a `transform` declaration as many functions as required.

You can give the rotate function a value either in degrees, gradians, radians, or turns:

- **Degrees (**`deg`**)**—There are 360 degrees in a full circle.

- **Gradians (**`grad`**)**—There are 400 gradians in a full circle.

- **Radians (**`rad`**)**—There are 2π radians in a full circle (meaning 3.1415 is the equivalent of 180 degrees).

- **Turn (**`turn`**)**—There is 1 turn in a full circle.

When you specify a `rotate()` value of `-45deg`, the banner is rotated counterclockwise by 45 degrees. A positive number rotates an element clockwise.

scale(), scaleX(), and scaleY()

The `scale()` function increases or decreases an element in size. As with `translate()`, `scale()` takes two arguments: the X and Y axes. If the second value is absent in `scale()`, however, unlike `translate()`, that one value is applied to both the X and Y axes. If you want to transform only one axis, you can use the functions `scaleX()` and `scaleY()`.

1. In styles.css, change the `transform` declaration in the `.banner-ad` rule set to include a `scale()` function:

   ```
   -webkit-transform: translate(50px, -25px) rotate(-45deg)
     scale(1.1);
   ```

2. Save styles.css.

When you specify a `scale()` value of `1.1`, the banner element and its contents are scaled by 110% of its original size. You can give `scale()` only a number, which is a multiplication of its calculated size.

skewX() and skewY()

Skewing an element makes that element appear slanted or twisted.

You may be wondering why there's no skew() function to go with skewX() and skewY(). An early version of the CSS3 Transforms module (www.w3.org/TR/css3-transforms/) *did* include skew(), and you may find browsers still render the function, but it has been removed from the specification. This was due to concerns about its name being misleading. For this reason, you should only use skewX() and skewY().

skewX() and skewY() skew an element around its X and Y axis, respectively.

I'll use the More Information button to demonstrate skew transforms but not actually keep the effect:

```
-webkit-transform: skewX(10deg);
```

As shown in Figure 12-5, when you give the rule set .showcase .button a transform of skewX(10deg), the More Information button is skewed 10 degrees counterclockwise from the Y axis.

FIGURE 12-5 The More Information button with a 10-degree skew applied to the X axis.

When skewX(10deg) is replaced with skewY(10deg), like so:

```
-webkit-transform: skewY(10deg);
```

The button is skewed 10 degrees clockwise from the X axis, as shown in Figure 12-6.

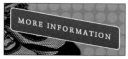

FIGURE 12-6 The More Information link with a 10-degree skew applied to the Y axis.

If you want to skew both axes, rather than use the no-longer standard skew() function, simply use both skewX() and skewY() separated by a space:

```
-webkit-transform: skewX(10deg) skewY(10deg);
```

Skew functions accept degrees, radians, or gradians as arguments.

matrix()

The `transform` property also accepts the `matrix()` function, which allows for complex transformations. Because this is an advanced feature, it is not demonstrated in *CSS3 Foundations*, but if you want to learn more, I recommend reading Opera's article, "Understanding the CSS Transforms Matrix," available at `http://dev.opera.com/articles/view/understanding-the-css-transforms-matrix/`.

transform-origin

Initial value: `50% 50%` | Inherited: No | Applies to: All elements with a `display` declaration relating to block, inline or table | CSS3

Unprefixed browser support: IE 10+, Firefox 16+, Opera 12.5+

Prefixed browser support: IE 9+, Firefox 3.5+, Chrome 12+, Opera 10.5+, Safari 3.1+

When you are transforming an element, that element has a transform origin, which, by default, is `50% 50%` (on both the X and Y axes)—the center of the element.

As shown in Figure 12-7, the top element has the default origin of `50% 50%`, which places the origin in the center (represented by a cross). When you apply a rotate transform of 45 degrees, that element is rotated around its origin.

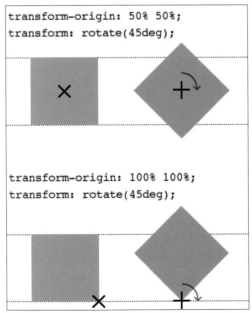

FIGURE 12-7 An element being rotated 45 degrees around an origin of 50% 50% and 100% 100%.

In Figure 12-7, the element at the bottom has an origin that is placed 100% on the X axis and 100% on the Y axis (the bottom-right corner). When you rotate the element 45 degrees around *this* origin, the transformation creates a different effect.

Let's go back to the "25% Off" banner advertisement to make use of `transform-origin`.

Although the banner is in the desired position, as shown in Figure 12-8, when the text size is scaled in a browser such as Firefox, the banner goes a bit crooked, and not all the text can be seen! This happens because the Y axis in the `translate()` function is -25px, which is supposed to be half the height of the element. When text is resized, the height of the element grows, and that -25px value may no longer be half the height of the banner, causing its position to go off center.

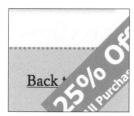

FIGURE 12-8 The banner advertisement goes crooked when text is resized.

You can fix this problem by changing the origin of the banner:

1. In styles.css, add the following declaration to the `.banner-ad` rule set:

   ```
   -webkit-transform-origin: 50% 100%;
   ```

2. Modify the `transform` declaration, as follows:

   ```
   -webkit-transform: translate(75px, -25px) rotate(-45deg)
      scale(1.1);
   ```

3. Save styles.css.

As shown in Figure 12-9, the origin is still placed on the center of the X axis but at the bottom of the Y axis. The `translate()` value for the X axis is 75px = 100 px (half of the banner's width) − 25px (to place the X origin 25px inside the viewport), and the Y axis is -25px to also place it 25 px inside the viewport. Because the banner has a specified width of 200px, the X origin is always a constant, and now that the origin on the Y axis is changed to the bottom of the element, it too is a constant, allowing the banner to grow as tall as it needs and always remain anchored 25px inside the viewport.

FIGURE 12-9 The origin of the banner element now placed on the center of the X axis and the bottom of the Y axis.

Summary

In this chapter, you scratched the surface of 2D transforms. Making the banner advertisement out of text and CSS instead of an image doesn't prevent users from interacting with elements below it like the image did. Although not all browsers support 2D transforms, those that don't still see the banner, just without the transforms applied to it (as it was in Figure 12-1). In Chapter 14, you learn to animate that banner to make it move in and out of the page when interacted with.

In the next chapter, you make some elements jump off the page using 3D transforms!

chapter thirteen

Going Beyond with 3D Transforms

IN THE PRECEDING chapter, you used the transform property to create 2D visual effects, but you can also use it for 3D effects. As with the 2D effects, the 3D effects are great for adding visual flair to a site, especially when used in conjunction with the transitions and animations covered in the next chapter.

At the time of writing, Internet Explorer 10 and Firefox 16 do not require vendor prefixes for properties relating to 3D transforms. Like 2D transforms though, for the safest possible implementation, use vendor prefixed properties followed by the official unprefixed property.

In this chapter, you make the Cool Shoes & Socks sidebar rotate in a 3D space.

Project files update (ch13-00): If you haven't followed the previous instructions and are comfortable working from here onward or would like to reference the project files up to this point, you can download them from www.wiley.com/go/treehouse/css3foundations.

perspective

Initial value: none | Inherited: No | Applies to: All elements with a `display` declaration relating to block, inline or table | CSS3

Unprefixed browser support: IE 10+, Firefox 16+

Prefixed browser support: Firefox 10+, Chrome 12+, Safari 4+

Before you can begin making elements 3D, you need to create a 3D space using the `perspective` property.

1. In styles.css, find the #main rule set and add the following declaration:

   ```
   -webkit-perspective: 1000px;
   ```

2. Save styles.css.

This declaration doesn't create any visual effect on the page; it just tells the browser to make the main content container `<div id="main" class="group">` 3D.

Think of the perspective as being how far the viewer is from an object.

Figure 13-1 shows that if `perspective` is 50px and an element is moved toward the viewer by 25px, the element is 50% closer to the viewer. If `perspective` is 500px and the element is again moved toward the viewer by 25px, the element is only 5% closer. A lower number of pixels applied to the `perspective` creates a greater visual impact because the viewer appears to be closer to the elements onscreen.

FIGURE 13-1 A low number applied to perspective has a greater visual impact.

You can give `perspective` any unit of length as a value.

perspective-origin

Initial value: 50% 50% | Inherited: No | Applies to: All elements with a `display` declaration relating to block, inline or table | CSS3

Unprefixed browser support: IE 10+, Firefox 16+

Prefixed browser support: Firefox 10+, Chrome 12+, Safari 4+

Whereas `perspective` determines how far the viewer appears to be looking at a 3D element, `perspective-origin` determines the appearance of the viewer's position. The initial value of 50% 50% means the viewer will see a 3D element as if that viewer is looking at it straight on. The X and Y position will be in the middle.

Again, `perspective-origin` just sets up the 3D space for the elements within it, so alone it doesn't create any visual representation. I demonstrate how it does affect elements in a moment when using the `transform` function, `translateZ()`.

`perspective-origin` takes two values, the X and Y positions, and can be given any length value; a percentage; or the keywords `left`, `center`, `right`, `top`, and `bottom`. A percentage value of 0% 0% is the equivalent of `left top`, 100% 100% is `right bottom`, and so on. If only one value is given, the second is assumed to be `center`.

transform and 3D Transform Functions

Initial value: `none` | Inherited: No | Applies to: All elements with a `display` declaration relating to block, inline or table | CSS3

Unprefixed browser support: IE 10+, Firefox 16+

Prefixed browser support: Firefox 10+, Chrome 12+, Safari 4+

In the preceding chapter, you used 2D transform functions such as `translateX()`, `translateY()`, `scaleX()`, `scaleY()`, and so on. When creating 3D transforms, you can use functions that control the Z axis along with the X and Y axes.

translateZ() and translate3d()

Whereas the functions `translateX()` and `translateY()` move an element left and right and up and down, the `translateZ()` function moves forward and back (toward and away from the viewer).

The following instructions are temporary, used to demonstrate `translateZ()`. If you'd like to follow them to experiment in your own browser, note that the additional HTML and CSS will be removed afterward.

Place an empty `<div class="temp"></div>` element immediately inside the main container `<div id="main" class="group">` and give it the following rule set:

```
.temp {
    border: black solid 5px;
    box-sizing: border-box;
    position: absolute;
    height: 100%;
    width: 100%;
}
```

Temporarily remove the `padding` declarations from the `#main` rule set and make it `position: relative;` so that the empty `<div class="temp">` becomes the same width and height, as shown in Figure 13-2.

FIGURE 13-2 Google Chrome zoomed out to show the empty div with a black border around it.

With the main content container `<div id="main" class="group">` set to have a perspective of 1000px, its direct child elements can be moved in that 3D space, which is what you can do with the empty `<div class="temp">`:

```
-webkit-transform: translateZ(-500px);
```

After you transform the empty `<div class="temp">` and move it back 500 pixels on the Z axis, it appears to move away from the viewer, as shown in Figure 13-3.

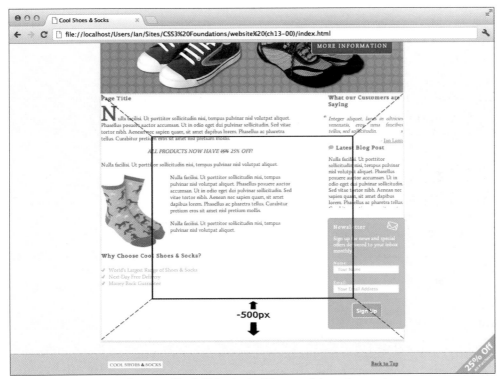

FIGURE 13-3 The empty div, moved back 500px in the 3D space of the main container.

Now look at how `perspective-origin` can affect this 3D effect by applying the following declaration to the `#main` rule set:

```
-webkit-perspective-origin: 30% 30%;
```

As Figure 13-4 shows, when you change the `perspective-origin`, the element is no longer viewed straight on. The viewer now sees the element as if looking at it from an angle.

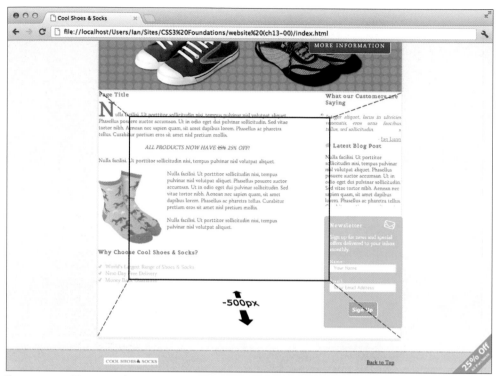

FIGURE 13-4 The empty div, now viewed from a different perspective origin.

Of course, this is just a visual demonstration to better show how 3D space works on a 2D screen.

To add a real-world 3D effect, remove the previous modifications if you chose to follow them, then go ahead and apply `translateZ()`, like so:

1. In styles.css, below the `.sidebar` rule set, add a new rule set:

```
.sidebar:hover {
    -webkit-transform: translateZ(100px);
}
```

2. Save styles.css.

Now, when the sidebar is hovered over, it appears to move toward the viewer by 100px, as shown in Figure 13-5. You may think this effect seems excessive, and I agree! At the moment, the entire sidebar moves forward, which may get annoying for the user. Shortly, you change this effect so it applies only to the newsletter box, and I explain why you can't do that just yet.

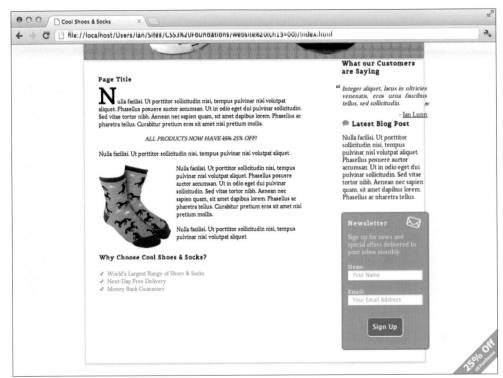

FIGURE 13-5 The Cool Shoes & Socks page zoomed out to show the sidebar moves toward the viewer when hovered over.

When creating 3D effects, if you are declaring more than one translate function, instead of specifying `translateX()`, `translateY()`, and `translateZ()`, you can use the shorthand function `translate3d()`, which takes three arguments: the X axis, Y axis, and Z axis, in that order.

rotateX(), rotateY(), rotateZ(), and rotate3d()

In the preceding chapter where you manipulated elements in two dimensions, you rotated the "25% Off" banner using the `rotate()` function.

When rotating in 2D, elements can be rotated only clockwise or counterclockwise. Now that the main content container is a 3D space, any elements within it can be rotated not just in 2D but in 3D too, either rotated on the X, Y, or Z axis, or a combination.

Now rotate the sidebar of the Cool Shoes & Socks page.

1. In styles.css, find the `.sidebar` rule set and add the following declaration:

   ```
   -webkit-transform: rotateX(10deg);
   ```

2. Save styles.css.

`rotateX()` rotates an element on the X axis. Rotated on a positive angle, the `.sidebar` is rotated away from the viewer at the top and toward the viewer at the bottom, as shown in Figure 13-6; it kind of looks like the *Star Wars* opening crawl text! A 180-degree rotation on the X axis would flip an element vertically.

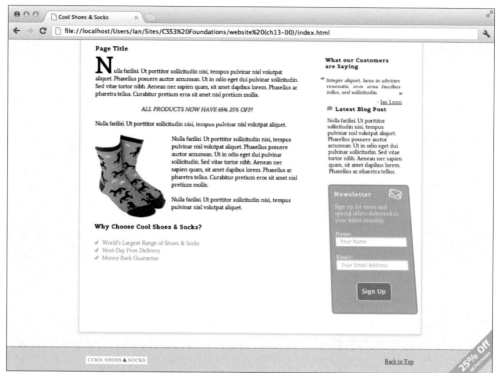

FIGURE 13-6 The Cool Shoes & Socks page zoomed out to show the sidebar rotated on the X axis by 10 degrees.

Because the X axis rotation is unsuitable for the page, change it to a Y axis rotation instead.

3. In the `.sidebar` rule set, modify the `transform` declaration as follows:

```
-webkit-transform: rotateY(-40deg);
```

4. Save styles.css.

Rotating on the Y axis by a positive angle rotates an element's left side toward the viewer and right side away. The opposite occurs when rotating by a negative angle, which is what you do by modifying the `transform` declaration, as shown in Figure 13-7. A 180-degree rotation on the Y axis would flip an element horizontally.

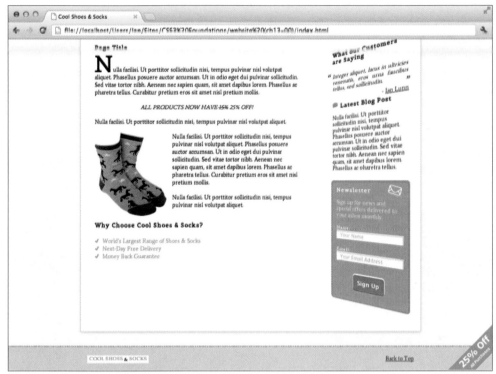

FIGURE 13-7 The Cool Shoes & Socks page zoomed out to show the sidebar rotated on the Y axis by −40 degrees.

Finally, using `rotateZ()` to rotate on the Z axis achieves the same effect as the `rotate()` function in a 2D space. A positive angle rotates an element clockwise; and a negative angle, counterclockwise.

If rotating more than one axis, you may consider using the shorter `rotate3d()` function, which should be given the X, Y, and Z values in that order.

scaleZ() and scale3d()

If you can translate and rotate in 3D, you won't be surprised to read you can scale, too. A quick recap: `scaleX()` scales an element horizontally, and `scaleY()` scales an element vertically. So what about `scaleZ()`?

`scaleZ()` controls depth but, of course, not the depth of the element because an element doesn't have a thickness; it can only be flat. `scaleZ()` works in conjunction with `translateZ()` to scale an element along the Z axis, affecting its visual size (although not its actual dimensions) as if it were moved toward or away from the viewer.

At the moment, when the sidebar is hovered over, it's moved forward 100px by this declaration:

```
-webkit-transform: translateZ(100px);
```

You can increase this visual effect by scaling on the Z axis:

1. In styles.css, find the `.sidebar:hover` rule set and modify the `transform` declaration:

   ```
   -webkit-transform: scaleZ(2) translateZ(100px);
   ```

2. Save styles.css.

This modification scales the sidebar on the Z axis by 2, meaning the size of the element is the same size as if it were sitting on the Z axis at 200px, as shown in Figure 13-8. Again, this effect is over the top, but you can make it a little more sophisticated as you go on.

FIGURE 13-8 The sidebar scaled on the Z axis by 2.

A transform such as

```
transform: scaleZ(2) translateZ(100px);
```

creates the same visual effect as

```
transform: translateZ(200px);
```

`scaleZ()` can be given only a number as its argument, which is a multiplication of an element's position on the Z axis.

If you need to scale all three axes, rather than specify three separate functions, `scaleX()`, `scaleY()`, and `scaleZ()`, you can use the function `scale3d()`, which takes three arguments: the X, Y, and Z values.

Multiple 3D Transform Functions

As with 2D `transform` functions, you can use as many as necessary by separating functions with a space, such as

```
transform: rotateY(-40deg) scaleZ(2) translateZ(100px);
```

Note that when you list `transform` functions in this way, a browser treats each as if it is specified separately in the order listed. This effect is particularly important when you're using `scaleZ()`. The Z axis must be scaled prior to an element being translated on that axis. Therefore,

```
transform: rotateY(-40deg) scaleZ(2) translateZ(100px);
```

scales on the Z axis, whereas

```
transform: rotateY(-40deg) translateZ(100px) scaleZ(2);
```

doesn't scale on the Z axis.

transform-style

Initial value: `flat` | Inherited: No | Applies to: All elements with a `display` declaration relating to block, inline or table | CSS3

Unprefixed browser support: IE 10+, Firefox 16+

Prefixed browser support: Firefox 10+, Chrome 12+, Safari 4+

When an element is given a `perspective` declaration—making it a 3D space—only its direct child elements can be manipulated in 3D. The sidebar, which is currently rotated in 3D, is the direct child of the main content container `<div id="main" class="group">`.

Child elements of that sidebar are treated as having a `transform-style` of `flat`. This is the reason you couldn't apply the `translateZ()` and `scaleZ()` functions only to the newsletter box previously. With a `transform-style` of `flat`, the newsletter box wouldn't have been affected by those transforms because it doesn't exist in a 3D space yet.

Now tell the browser that the sidebar should pass down its 3D space to its child elements (each `<aside>` element):

1. In the `.sidebar` rule set, add the following declaration:

   ```
   -webkit-transform-style: preserve-3d;
   ```

2. Save styles.css.

   By doing this, you can now manipulate the child elements of the sidebar in the same 3D space, something you couldn't do before, and this is the reason you applied the 3D effects to the whole sidebar instead of just the newsletter box.

   Make it so that the "What Our Customers Are Saying" and "Latest Blog Post" sections rotate only when hovered over and the newsletter box moves toward the viewer.

3. Change the `.sidebar:hover` selector to `.sidebar aside:nth-child(3):hover`.

4. Modify the `transform` declaration in the `aside:nth-child(3):hover` rule set to include `rotateY()` and `translateX()` functions:

   ```
   -webkit-transform: rotateY(40deg) translateX(-50px) scaleZ(2)
      translateZ(100px);
   ```

5. Below the `.sidebar` rule set, add a new rule set:

   ```
   .sidebar aside:hover {
       -webkit-transform: rotateY(40deg);
   }
   ```

6. Save styles.css.

Now, when the individual sections of the sidebar are hovered over, they rotate 40 degrees, back to a flat position so the user can read the contents in 2D. The newsletter box also rotates, but it moves toward the user in a 3D space. By making the newsletter box "pop" off the screen, you can hope that it will persuade the user to consider signing up for the Cool Shoes & Socks newsletter.

In the next chapter, you apply smooth animations to these transforms.

backface-visibility

Initial value: `visible` | Inherited: No | Applies to: All elements with a `display` declaration relating to block, inline or table | CSS3

Unprefixed browser support: IE 10+, Firefox 16+

Prefixed browser support: Firefox 10+, Chrome 12+, Safari 4+

As mentioned previously, a 180-degree rotation on the X and Y axes would "flip" an element—as if somebody picked it up and turned it over. Try this on the `.sidebar` rule set, for example:

```
-webkit-transform: rotateY(180deg);
```

You can see the sidebar from the back, as shown in Figure 13-9.

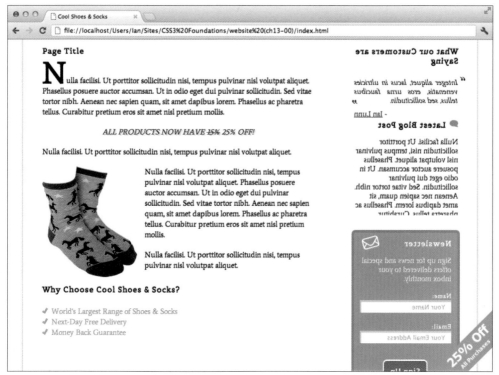

FIGURE 13-9 The sidebar "flipped" 180 degrees, so it displays in reverse.

You have control over whether the contents of an element are shown when they're viewed from the back like this, via the `backface-visibility` property. By default, all transformable elements have a visible backface; however, if you want to hide an element when it is showing its backface, you can use the following:

```
-webkit-backface-visibility: hidden;
```

Summary

In this chapter, you learned how to go beyond the traditional 2D layout of a web page and move elements in a 3D space. The `transform` property has a huge amount of potential with all the 2D and 3D functions it offers. Because this is a reasonably new CSS feature, the web is only beginning to see what creative possibilities can be made with the power of 3D transforms.

Not all browsers support transforms, but that's not a problem; the visual effects you added in this chapter simply don't show in nonsupporting browsers, and the content still appears perfectly readable and accessible, as it did prior to adding these transforms.

The fun with transforms doesn't stop here. Possibly the best thing about them is that they can be animated, too! You do just that in the next chapter.

Bringing Your Website to Life with Transitions and Animations

POSSIBLY CSS3'S MOST exciting features are transitions and animations. Transitions allow the values of properties to change smoothly over a specific duration, meaning the color of an element can fade from red to blue, slide from one area of the page to another, shrink and grow when hovered over, and so on. The possibilities are endless.

Whereas transitions change an element from a start to end state, animations allow you to have more control over those states, specifying keyframes, the exact moments when a property should change.

Project files update (ch14-00): If you haven't followed the previous instructions and are comfortable working from here onward or would like to reference the project files up to this point, you can download them from www.wiley.com/go/treehouse/css3foundations.

Animating Elements from A to B Using Transitions

To demonstrate transitions, make the "25% Off" banner transition in size when it's hovered over. Before you add transitions to the element though, first set up the start and end states of the transition:

1. In styles.css, find the `.banner-ad` rule set and modify the `transform` declaration to reduce the `scale()` function, as follows:

```
-webkit-transform: translate(75px, -25px) rotate(-45deg)
  scale(.8);
```

2. Below the `.banner-ad` rule set, add a new rule set:

```
.banner-ad:hover {
    cursor: default;
    -webkit-transform: translate(75px, -25px) rotate(-45deg)
  scale(1.1);
}
```

3. Save styles.css.

As yet, these changes haven't added a transition to the banner. In the first step, you make the banner scale down to 80%. Then by adding the `.banner-ad:hover` rule set, you make it so that the banner will scale up to 110% when hovered over. Think of the first rule set as the start state and the `:hover` rule set as the end state of a transition. You are telling the browser how the banner should look at the start and end. Now you need to tell it how to transition between those two states using several `transition` properties.

transition-property

Initial value: `all` | Inherited: No | Applies to: all elements | CSS3
Unprefixed browser support: IE 10+, Firefox 16+, Opera 12.5+
Prefixed browser support: Firefox 4+, Chrome 4+, Opera 10.5+, Safari 3.1+

Because an element can have many different CSS properties applied to it, when making it transition, you might need to be specific about which property is transitioned. For example, say an element has the following properties:

```
color: blue;
height: 100px;
```

The initial value for `transition-property` is `all`, meaning all animatable properties are animated. You might want only the `color` property to transition, though. The `transition-property` allows you to specify that.

1. In styles.css, in the `.banner-ad:hover` rule set, add the following declaration:

```
-webkit-transition-property: -webkit-transform;
```

2. Save styles.css.

The -webkit-transform value refers to the property in the same rule set, which you added a moment ago:

```
-webkit-transform: translate(75px, -25px) rotate(-45deg)
  scale(1.1);
```

Although you've now told the browser you only want the `transform` declaration to animate, it won't animate until a duration is also specified, which you'll do in a moment.

The only other property in this rule set is `cursor:  default;`, which is a property that can't be animated anyway. Technically, you could get away with not including this declaration in the rule set because the initial value of `all` selects only the `transform` property anyway. Of course, for maintainable CSS, it's better practice to specify exactly which properties you want to animate in case you add more properties in the future that you may not want to have animated.

If you want to specify more than one property, separate each with a comma, like so:

```
transition-property: transform, color;
```

For a list of properties that can be animated, see the list of animatable properties at www.w3.org/TR/css3-transitions/#animatable-properties.

transition-duration

Initial value: 0s | Inherited: No | Applies to: all elements | CSS3
Unprefixed browser support: IE 10+, Firefox 16+, Opera 12.5+
Prefixed browser support: Firefox 4+, Chrome 1+, Opera 11.6+, Safari 3+

Now that the browser knows you want to have the `transform` property transition, you need to tell it how long that transition should take—the time between going from the start to end states.

1. In the `.banner-ad:hover` rule set, add the following declaration:

    ```
    -webkit-transition-duration: 1s;
    ```

2. Save styles.css.

Here, you specify a one-second duration between the start and end states. Hover over the banner in your browser, and you see this happen (see Figure 14-1). Cool, right? The banner now transitions from an 80% scale to 110% over a one-second period.

Before:

After:

FIGURE 14-1 The start and end states of the banner.

The `transition-duration` is specified in seconds although if you want a millisecond value, you can place a decimal point before the value; that is, `.1s` is the equivalent of 100 milliseconds.

transition-timing-function

Initial value: `ease` | Inherited: No | Applies to: all elements | CSS3

Unprefixed browser support: IE 10+, Firefox 16+, Opera 12.5+

Prefixed browser support: Firefox 4+, Chrome 1+, Opera 11.6+, Safari 3+

Although you've now achieved the transition on the banner, you can use a few more properties to have even more control over the effect. The `transition-timing-function` property describes how the intermediate values used during a transition are calculated—in other words, how the bit between the start and end acts.

The initial value for `transition-timing-function` is ease, and there are a lot of other keyword values you can use with it, too:

- `ease`—This timing function starts gently (not quite slow), speeds up in the intermediate, and then ends slow.

- `linear`—Start, intermediate, and end are all at the same constant speed.

- `ease-in`— This timing function starts slow, speeds up in the intermediate, and continues until end.

- `ease-out`—Start and intermediate are the same speed, then it slows down at the end.

- `ease in-out`— This timing function starts slow, speeds up in the intermediate. and slows down at the end.

- `step-start`— This timing function jumps immediately to the end and stays there.

- `step-end`— This timing function stays in its start state until the end and then jumps immediately to the end state.

There are also some advanced functions you can use to *really* have complete control over the transition: `steps()` and `cubic-bezier()`.

These functions aren't covered in *CSS3 Foundations* because they are a little too advanced, but if you want to know more, visit www.w3.org/TR/css3-transitions/#transition-timing-function-property. If you want to experiment with `cubic-bezier()`, which essentially allows you to create the keyword values and everything in between, I recommend visiting http://cubic-bezier.com/, which allows you to easily create your own timing functions.

transition-delay

> Initial value: `0s` | Inherited: No | Applies to: all elements | CSS3
> Unprefixed browser support: IE 10+, Firefox 16+, Opera 12.5+
> Prefixed browser support: Firefox 4+, Chrome 1+, Opera 11.6+, Safari 3+

The final `transition` property is `transition-delay`, which allows you to specify a delay that occurs prior to the transition starting. Its initial value of `0s` means a transition will start immediately. A `transition-delay` of `1s`, for example, causes the browser to wait one second prior to starting a transition. As with `transition-duration`, if you would like to use an amount less than one second, you can place a decimal point before the value to specify milliseconds.

With `transition-delay`, you also are able to specify a negative value. Assuming you give the banner a `transition-delay` of `-.5s`, the transition does not occur for half a second and then appears to begin partway through—from half a second onward.

transition (Shorthand)

> Unprefixed browser support: IE 10+, Firefox 16+, Opera 12.5+
> Prefixed browser support: Firefox 4+, Chrome 1+, Opera 11.6+, Safari 3+

To make working with transitions easier, you can combine the transition-related properties into one easy-to-use declaration using the `transition` property.

1. In styles.css, in the `.banner-ad:hover` rule set, remove the following declarations:

   ```
   -webkit-transition-property: -webkit-transform;
   -webkit-transition-duration: 1s;
   ```

2. In their place, add the shorthand declaration:

   ```
   -webkit-transition: -webkit-transform 1s;
   ```

3. Save styles.css.

The shorthand property should take the following syntax:

```
transition: transition-property transition-duration transition-
   timing-function transition-delay;
```

Because you don't use `transition-timing-function` and `transition-delay` properties here, you can omit them from the shorthand declaration. Note that because `transition-duration` and `transition-delay` can be given the same type of value, the order in which they are specified is important. The first value is treated as the duration; and the second, the delay.

When applying the transition to more than one property, you should separate values of the transition shorthand property with a comma. For example,

```
transition: transform 1s ease 0s, color 2s linear 0s;
```

This declaration causes the `transform` property in a rule set to transition for one second with an ease and the `color` property to transition for two seconds with a linear timing function. Neither property has a delay.

Making the Banner Transition Back to Its Normal State

Now that the banner is transitioning just the way you like when it's hovered over, you may notice it snaps back to its start state when the cursor is moved away from it. How to make it transition back? All you need to do is apply the same `transition` declaration to the `.banner-ad` rule set:

1. In the `.banner-ad` rule set, add the following declaration:

   ```
   -webkit-transition: -webkit-transform 1s;
   ```

2. Save styles.css.

Code Challenge: Make the Sidebar Sections Transition

In styles.css, do the following:

1. In the `.sidebar aside:hover` rule set, add the declaration `-webkit-transition: -webkit-transform .5s;`.

2. Add a new rule set for `.sidebar aside` below the `.sidebar` rule set with the declaration `-webkit-transition: -webkit-transform .5s;`.

> Project files update (ch14-01): If you haven't followed the previous instructions and are comfortable working from here onward or would like to reference the project files up to this point, you can download them from `www.wiley.com/go/treehouse/css3foundations`.

Animating Elements from A to Z Using Keyframes

The transitions you just added to the page make an element smoothly change from one property value to another over a specific period of time. These transitions occur when an event is triggered, such as a user hovering over an element.

Animations also make an element smoothly change between different property values, but unlike transitions, they don't have to just consist of a start and end state. Using keyframes, you can create points that an animation should reach before changing again, allowing much more control over the effect onscreen. If an animation is 10 seconds long, you can specify exactly what happens over that period of time, maybe changing an element's color to blue at 2 seconds, green at 6 seconds, and black at 10 seconds. Animations can also be triggered by events or can be started when the page is loaded, with options to allow you to decide how many times an animation should repeat.

To demonstrate animations, you turn the product showcase (the section with the image of some trainers and a More Information button) into a set of images that cycle from one to the other.

Set up the basics first:

1. In index.html, find the following code:

```
<div class="showcase">
    <img src="images/banner-trainers.jpg"
alt="Some of our cool trainers" />
    <a class="button purchase" href="#" title="Purchase
  product">
        More Information
```

```
    </a>
</div>
```

2. Replace it with the following:

```
<div class="showcase">
    <ul>
        <li>
            <img src="images/banner-trainers.jpg"
alt="Some of our cool trainers" />
        </li>
        <li>
            <img src="images/banner-shoes.jpg"
alt="Some of our cool shoes" />
        </li>
    </ul>
    <a class="button purchase" href="#" title="Purchase
  product">
        More Information
    </a>
</div>
```

3. Save index.html.

This HTML adds two product images to the product showcase (you add a third later), each in its own list item `<li>`, as shown in Figure 14-2. Using CSS, you place one image over the other so only one can be seen at a time. You then use CSS3 animation properties to make the images cycle between one another.

4. In styles.css, find the `.showcase .button` rule set and increase the z-index from 5 to 9.

5. Find the `.showcase .button:hover` rule set, and below it, add these rule sets:

```
.showcase ul {
    background: #009CC8;
    position: relative;
    z-index: 9;
}

.showcase li {
    position: absolute;
    top: 0;
    width: 100%;
}
.showcase li:first-child {
    z-index: 3;
    position: relative;
}
```

```
showcase li:nth-child(2) {
    z-index: 2;
}
```

6. Save styles.css.

FIGURE 14-2 The Cool Shoes & Socks page zoomed out to show two product images in the showcase, which will be eventually be positioned one over the other.

When you add this CSS, the Cool Shoes & Socks page appears the way it did prior to your adding the new showcase HTML. However, the second product image now sits behind the first. When you make `.showcase ul` a `relative` position, its child elements (the list items `<li>`) can be positioned absolutely. The `z-index` of 9 makes it appear above all positioned elements, apart from the drop-down menu.

Each list item `<li>` is positioned `absolute` so that it doesn't affect the flow of the document and is placed at the top of the showcase (making all list items added to the showcase stack on top of each other).

By using the pseudo-selector `:first-child`, you select the first list item that contains a product image. Because this is the first product image to be displayed, it's given a `z-index` of 3 (you eventually make the product image consist of three images). In the preceding paragraph,

I said that each list item is positioned `absolute` so it doesn't affect the document flow and the items can be stacked on top of each other. If the list items were all left like this, the showcase would disappear because it has no contents affecting it, and its height would become 0 px. To stop this from happening, you position the first list item only as `relative`. This way, it still affects the document's flow, and because it's the first image in the showcase anyway, it is always at the top. Another way to work around this situation is make the position of all list items `absolute` and then specify a height for `.showcase ul`. If you do this, though, the product showcase is always a set height and doesn't shrink with the images when the browser window is resized.

Finally, you use another pseudo-selector, `.showcase li:nth-child(2)`, to select the second list item and place that below the first, using `z-index`.

With this code added, you're good to go! Now to animate the showcase images...

@keyframes

Unprefixed browser support: IE 10+, Firefox 16+, Opera 12.5+
Prefixed browser support: Firefox 5+, Chrome 1+, Opera 12+, Safari 4+

When creating CSS animations, you must declare the states of an animation in a `@keyframes` rule. Because animations are still experimental, you should prefix the `@keyframes` rule, such as `@-webkit-keyframes`.

1. In styles.css, below the `.showcase .button:hover` rule set, add a `@keyframes` rule:

```
@-webkit-keyframes fadeOut {

}
```

This rule consists of the prefixed `@-webkit-keyframes` keyword and an identifier `fadeOut`, which is the name of the animation you will create; you're free to use whatever identifier you like. The name of the `@keyframes` rule is referenced using the `animation-name` property, which links the animation you're going to create to the element you want it to apply to.

Within this `@keyframes` rule, you can now place rule sets that act as the states of the animation:

2. In the `@-webkit-keyframes fadeOut` rule, add the following rule sets:

```
from {
    opacity: 1;
}

to {
```

```
    opacity: 0;
    }
```

3. Save styles.css.

The first rule set, `from`, tells the browser an element should begin with an `opacity` of 1 (opaque) and then animate `to` an `opacity` of 0 (transparent). Because the `fadeOut` animation is not yet linked to an element, no elements fade yet.

The `from` keyword represents 0% of an animation (the start), and the `to` keyword represents 100% (the end). An animation that goes from 0% to 100% works in the same way as a transition (changing from one style to another), but within animations, unlike transitions, you can add keyframes anywhere, using percentage values. Later, you use this rule to complete the cycling product showcase:

```
@-webkit-keyframes fadeOut {
    from {
        opacity: 1;
        z-index: 4;
    }

    16.666% {
        opacity: 0;
        z-index: 4;
    }

    50% {
        opacity: 0;
        z-index: -1;
    }

    51%{
        opacity: 1;
    }
}
```

This animation makes an element start with a `z-index` of 4, and then 16.666% (I explain this percentage later) into the animation, change its `opacity` to 0 (fading out the element). At 50% in, the `z-index` changes to -1 (moving the element behind other elements in the product showcase), and then at 51% in, the `opacity` changes back to 1 to make the element visible again, ready for the animation to be cycled.

Don't worry if this description goes over your head. For now, stay with the simple `from` - `to` animation to learn how to apply it to an element and then come back to this more complex animation later.

animation-name

Initial value: none | Inherited: No | Applies to: all elements | CSS3
Unprefixed browser support: IE 10+, Firefox 16+, Opera 12.5+
Prefixed browser support: Firefox 5+, Chrome 1+, Opera 12+, Safari 4+

The animation-name property links an element to a @keyframes rule. The animation you added to styles.css is called fadeOut, so reference that now:

1. In styles.css, in the .showcase li:first-child rule set, add the following declaration:

   -webkit-animation-name: fadeOut;

2. Save styles.css.

That's all there is to it. The first list item now has the fadeOut animation applied to it, but the element doesn't animate just yet because it doesn't know how long to animate.

You can also give the animation-name the value none, in case you need to stop an element from inheriting an animation.

animation-duration

Initial value: 0s | Inherited: No | Applies to: all elements | CSS3
Unprefixed browser support: IE 10+, Firefox 16+, Opera 12.5+
Prefixed browser support: Firefox 5+, Chrome 3+, Opera 12+, Safari 4+

animation-duration works in the exact same way as transition-duration. You give it a value in seconds, like so:

1. In .showcase li:first-child add the following declaration:

   -webkit-animation-duration: 5s;

2. Save styles.css.

With the animation-duration added to the first list item, when the page loads, the animation runs, causing the image to go from an opacity of 1 to 0 over a five-second period. As the first image fades out, the second that sits behind it is shown, as shown in Figure 14-3.

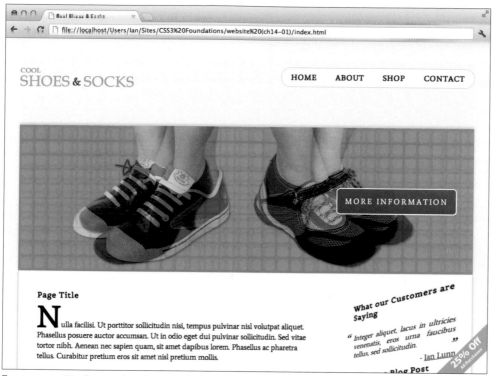

FIGURE 14-3 The first product image midway through fading out, revealing the second product image.

animation-timing-function

Initial value: ease | Inherited: No | Applies to: all elements | CSS3

Unprefixed browser support: IE 10+, Firefox 16+, Opera 12.5+

Prefixed browser support: Firefox 5+, Chrome 3+, Opera 12+, Safari 4+

`animation-timing-function` does exactly the same as the `transition-timing-function` property. It describes how the intermediate values used during a transition are calculated. Because animations can repeat multiple times, the `animation-timing-function` describes these intermediate values over each cycle of an animation.

1. In `.showcase li:first-child,` add the following declaration:

   `-webkit-animation-timing-function: ease-in-out;`

2. Save styles.css.

For the full list of timing functions you can use, see the `transition-timing-function` property description earlier in this chapter.

animation-delay

Initial value: 0s | Inherited: No | Applies to: all elements | CSS3
Unprefixed browser support: IE 10+, Firefox 16+, Opera 12.5+
Prefixed browser support: Firefox 5+, Chrome 3+, Opera 12+, Safari 4+

Just like transitions, animations can also be given a delay, which works in the exact same way.

1. In `.showcase li:first-child`, add the following declaration:

   ```
   -webkit-animation-delay: 5s;
   ```

2. Save styles.css.

Now, when the page is first loaded, the first product image doesn't start fading out until after a five-second delay.

As with `transition-delay`, you can also specify a negative delay that causes an animation to wait for *x* number of seconds and then start *x* number of seconds into that animation.

animation-iteration-count

Initial value: 1 | Inherited: No | Applies to: all elements | CSS3
Unprefixed browser support: IE 10+, Firefox 16+, Opera 12.5+
Prefixed browser support: Firefox 5+, Chrome 3+, Opera 12+, Safari 4+

`animation-iteration-count` determines how many times an animation should occur. You can give it a number or the keyword `infinite` to make an animation cycle with no end. By default, `animation-iteration-count` is 1.

1. In `.showcase li:first-child`, add the following declaration:

   ```
   -webkit-animation-iteration-count: infinite;
   ```

2. Save styles.css.

When you make the iteration count `infinite`, the animation constantly cycles with no end.

animation-direction

Initial value: normal | Inherited: No | Applies to: all elements | CSS3
Unprefixed browser support: IE 10+, Firefox 16+, Opera 12.5+
Prefixed browser support: Firefox 5+, Chrome 3+, Opera 12+, Safari 4+

At the moment, the `opacity` of the product image is animated to make it fade out, but when the animation cycles back to its start, the image instantly snaps back to opaque, which doesn't look quite right. Using the `animation-direction` property, you can make the animation reverse when it reaches its end.

1. In `.showcase li:first-child` add the following declaration:

   `-webkit-animation-direction: alternate;`

2. Save styles.css.

When you alternate the animation direction, odd iterations of the animation cause the product image to fade out, and each even iteration reverses the animation, making the product image fade in, achieving a much more subtle effect.

You can use the following keywords with `animation-direction`:

- `normal` (initial value)—All iterations of the animation are played as specified.

- `reverse`—All iterations of the animation are played in the reverse direction from the way they were specified.

- `alternate`—The animation cycle iterations that are odd counts are played in the normal direction, and the animation cycle iterations that are even counts are played in reverse.

- `alternate-reverse`—The animation cycle iterations that are odd counts are played in reverse, and the animation cycle iterations that are even counts are played in a normal direction.

> The `reverse` and `alternate-reverse` keywords are currently only supported in Internet Explorer 10+, Firefox 16+, and Chrome 19+.

Note that when an animation is reversed, the timing functions are also reversed. So, when played in reverse, an `ease-in` animation appears to be an `ease-out` animation.

animation-play-state

> Initial value: `running` | Inherited: No | Applies to: all elements | CSS3
> Unprefixed browser support: IE 10+, Firefox 16+, Opera 12.5+
> Prefixed browser support: Firefox 5+, Chrome 3+, Opera 12+, Safari 4+

The `animation-play-state` property determines whether or not an animation is paused. By default, all animations have the value `running`, but you can also use `paused` to pause an animation.

Dealing with a WebKit Bug

Due to a bug in WebKit browsers (Google Chrome and Apple Safari), it is recommended that you comment out or do not use the `animation-play-state` property because it doesn't work as expected when used with `animation-delay`. The purpose of vendor prefixes shows their worth here; although the WebKit property doesn't work, you can still use the property for browsers that do, like so:

Example:

```
.showcase ul:hover li {
    /* -webkit-animation-play-state: paused;
  */
    -moz-animation-play-state: paused;
    -ms-animation-play-state: paused;
    -o-animation-play-state: paused;
    animation-play-state: paused;
}
```

1. In styles.css, below the `.showcase li` rule set, add the following rule set:

```
.showcase ul:hover li {
    -webkit-animation-play-state: paused;
}
```

2. Save styles.css.

With this rule set, whenever the product showcase `.showcase ul` is hovered over, each list item that contains an image is paused.

animation-fill-mode

Initial value: none | Inherited: No | Applies to: all elements | CSS3

Unprefixed browser support: IE 10+, Firefox 16+, Opera 12.5+

Prefixed browser support: Firefox 5+, Chrome 3+, Opera 12+, Safari 4+

The last property to be used with animations is `animation-fill-mode`, which defines what values are applied by the animation outside the time it is executing.

The initial value for `animation-fill-mode` is none, meaning properties defined in a `@keyframes` rule apply only to an element while it is being animated.

Before you added the `animation-direction` property with a value of `alternate`, the animation just snapped back to the beginning when it reached its end, which looked a little messy. Sometimes you just want an animation to run on an element and then stay that way after the animation finishes. You can achieve this effect by using the `animation-fill-mode` value `forwards`. This value tells the browser that after an animation ends, the final styles applied to the element in that animation should continue forward, outside the animation's execution time.

Likewise, you can use an `animation-fill-mode` value of `backwards` to have the first values of an animation applied to an element before the animation begins, or a value of `both`, which combines the `forwards` and `backwards` values.

Because the `fadeOut` animation you currently have set up is infinite (it has no end), changing the `animation-fill-mode` doesn't make a difference, but you use it later to make the cycling image showcase better.

animation (Shorthand)

Unprefixed browser support: IE 10+, Firefox 16+, Opera 12.5+

Prefixed browser support: Firefox 5+, Chrome 3+, Opera 12+, Safari 4+

In total, eight properties relate to animations, and for this reason, they can be combined into the shorthand property `animation`—all except `animation-play-state` because, as you saw, that tends to get added to a different rule set, such as `:hover`.

The shorthand property should take the following syntax:

```
animation: animation-name animation-duration animation-timing-
   function animation-delay animation-iteration-count
   animation-direction animation-fill-mode
```

Just like the `transition` shorthand, because some values can be the same (such as `animation-duration` and `animation-delay`), the order in which the `animation` property is formed is important.

1. In styles.css, remove the six animation properties from `.showcase li:first-child` and replace with the following shorthand `animation` declaration:

   ```
   -webkit-animation: fadeOut 5s ease-in-out 5s infinite
      alternate;
   ```

2. Save styles.css.

Using this shorthand doesn't change the page visually in any way; it's just a nicer and more maintainable way to write animations.

Creating a Cycling Image Showcase

You've learned how to use the animation properties, but the cycling image showcase consists of only two images and doesn't particularly look that great yet. Now take a look at a slightly more advanced animation technique.

Start by adding a third image to the product showcase:

1. In index.html, look for the following HTML:

```
<li>
    <img src="images/banner-shoes.jpg"
alt="Some of our cool shoes" />
</li>
```

2. Below that HTML, add another list item:

```
<li>
    <img src="images/banner-socks.jpg"
alt="Some of our cool socks" />
</li>
```

3. Save index.html.

Because the current fadeOut animation only hides and shows the top image over a five-second period, this newly added third image won't ever be shown with the animation as it is.

1. In styles.css, below the .showcase li:nth-child(2) rule set, add a new rule set for the third product:

```
.showcase li:nth-child(3) {
    z-index: 1;
}
```

2. Remove the following declaration from .showcase li:first-child:

```
-webkit-animation: fadeOut 5s ease-in-out 5s infinite
    alternate;
```

Here, you remove the animation from the first product so that you can apply an animation to all the images; that way, they each fade out.

3. In the .showcase li rule set, add the following declaration:

```
-webkit-animation: fadeOut 15s ease-in-out 5s infinite
    forwards;
```

4. Save styles.css.

   This animation is modified somewhat. It still refers to the `fadeOut` @keyframes animation but now spans over a 15 second period and no longer alternates (goes in reverse when it reaches the end). The animation also has a 5-second delay. Because this animation applies to all the products in the showcase, they all fade out at the same time. Now make it so that they fade out at different times.

5. In the `.showcase li:nth-child(2)` rule set, add the following declaration:

   ```
   -webkit-animation-delay: 10s;
   ```

6. In the `.showcase li:nth-child(3)` rule set, add the following declaration:

   ```
   -webkit-animation-delay: 15s;
   ```

7. Save styles.css.

   A useful feature of CSS is that you can apply the shorthand `animation` property to multiple elements but then overwrite individual values of `animation`, as you do here—overwriting the `animation-delay`. The second product image now has a 10-second delay, and the third has a 15-second delay.

   Finally, you need to adjust the animation itself to get the product images fading out one at a time.

8. In the `@-webkit-keyframes fadeOut` rule, replace the `from` and `to` rule sets with the following:

   ```
   from {
       opacity: 1;
       z-index: 4;
   }

   16.666% { /*2.5s*/
       opacity: 0;
       z-index: 4;
   }

   50% { /*7.5s*/
       opacity: 0;
       z-index: -1;
   }

   51%{
       opacity: 1;
   }
   ```

9. Save styles.css.

With this animation now added to the stylesheet, each product image is visible for 5 seconds and then takes 2.5 seconds to fade out (revealing the next image).

I added comments to the 16.666% and 50% rule sets to show that they are active at 2.5 seconds and 7.5 seconds into the animation, but because there's quite a lot going on here, let's take a closer look at what's happening (see Figure 14-4).

After the initial 5-second delay on the first product (which occurs only once, when the page loads), the from rule set is activated, and the first product is placed on top of the others and made opaque. From the start of the animation, the first product image begins to fade until it is completely transparent at 16.666% into the animation (16.666% of 15 seconds is roughly 2.5 seconds).

FIGURE 14-4 The events of the animation over a 15-second period.

So, at 2.5 seconds into the animation, the first product is now transparent, which means the second is showing. For another 2.5 seconds, the second image is displayed until it too begins to fade.

At 50% into the animation (7.5 seconds), the third image is displayed because the second product image is transparent, and the first image is moved behind them both.

Just after the first image is moved to the back, at 51%, is it then made opaque, ready and waiting for the third image to fade and reveal it, completing one cycle of the animation.

Summary

CSS3's transitions and animations are great additions to the technology you have for creating web pages. The most exciting aspect is that because they're so new, there are many cool things to be done with them yet to be discovered; you just need some imagination!

Unfortunately, transitions and animations aren't supported in all browsers, but because they only add an extra edge to the page, the fact that some browsers don't understand them doesn't matter. You can safely use them in the knowledge that in their absence they don't cause a page to look broken.

In the next chapter, you look at the Cool Shoes & Socks page you created using other web browsers and begin fixing their inconsistencies to make the page cross browser compatible.

part 6

Preparing for Multiple Browsers and Devices

chapter fifteen
Testing Across Multiple Browsers

THE FIRST THING to do to make your website cross browser compatible is to get yourself a glass of water (to drink, not to throw over the computer) and take a deep breath. You've spent countless hours trying to make your website perfect. You've used best practices and been extra careful to use the latest CSS3 features safely. But when you open a browser you haven't developed in—especially older browsers such as Internet Explorer versions 6 and 7—you're going to see broken bits, sometimes just a few broken bits, other times lots. Fear not, this happens to everyone and is just the nature of creating web pages. Usually, a broken page looks worse than it actually is, and you can fix it in no time.

Obviously, every web page is different, so how you go about achieving cross browser compatibility is unique to each page. The most universal approach is to follow best practices— keeping your code clean and semantic, which you've done throughout *CSS3 Foundations*.

In this chapter, you start by making sure the Cool Shoes & Socks page works in modern browsers, add the CSS3 properties that need to be prefixed for other browsers, and then move on to add fixes for Internet Explorer versions 6, 7, and 8.

Project files update (ch15-00): If you haven't followed the previous instructions and are comfortable working from here onward or want to reference the project files up to this point, you can download them from www.wiley.com/go/treehouse/ css3foundations.

Vendor Prefixing the Easy Way

Until now, you've used vendor prefixes only on CSS3's experimental properties to save having to write out the same property multiple times.

I developed the Cool Shoes & Socks page in Google Chrome, and now that it's complete, I want to take a look at it in Mozilla Firefox. If you used Firefox to create Cool Shoes & Socks, take a look at it in another modern browser, such as Chrome, Safari, or Opera.

Pleasingly, Cool Shoes & Socks doesn't look too bad at all in Firefox. Figure 15-1 shows that the page has a few issues, but they all relate to the fact that the stylesheet uses experimental CSS3 properties, which is yet to include those properties with a -moz- prefix—or any other vendor prefix for that matter. Without the full set of vendor prefixes, the showcase doesn't animate, the input fields in the newsletter box are too wide (because of no prefixed box-sizing property), and the "25% Off" banner isn't rotated.

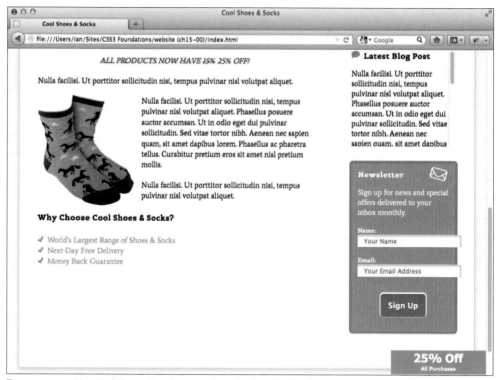

FIGURE 15-1 The Cool Shoes & Socks page viewed in Mozilla Firefox.

In Chapter 3, I mentioned the free tools available to speed up writing prefixed properties. My personal recommendation is www.prefixr.com/.

Using Prefixr, you can have the prefixed properties you wrote for the Cool Shoes & Socks page converted into those that you purposely did not write to save yourself some time.

1. In styles.css, highlight and copy all the text from the body rule set onward.

2. Visit www.prefixr.com/ in your browser.

3. Click the text area on the Prefixr website and delete any content within it.

4. Paste your copied stylesheet into the empty text area, as shown in Figure 15-2.

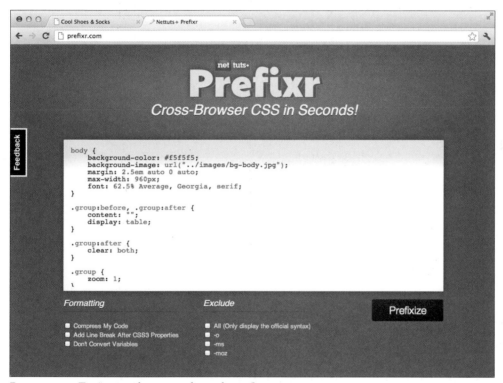

FIGURE 15-2 The #main rule set copied into the prefixr.com text area.

5. Uncheck the Add Line Breaks After CSS3 Properties option (all options should be unchecked).

6. Click the Prefixize button.

   Prefixr then returns the stylesheet with any necessary prefixed properties included.

7. Highlight and copy this modified stylesheet from the Prefixr text area.

8. Paste the modified stylesheet in place of the existing one.

9. Save styles.css.

Prefixr—or any other automatic CSS prefixer tool for that matter—doesn't quite do 100% of the job, so you need to make a few changes manually. Making these manual changes, however, is much less work than having to write all the vendor prefixes yourself. Let's look at what Prefixr *does* and *doesn't* do:

1. In styles.css, find the #main rule set:

```
#main {
    background: white;
    background: rgba(255, 255, 255, 0.6);
    border: #ccc solid 1px;
    -webkit-box-shadow: 0 3px 8px 0 #ccc;
    box-shadow: 0 3px 8px 0 #ccc;
    padding: 2.5em;
    -webkit-perspective: 1000px;
}
```

In Chapter 5, you added the box-shadow declaration to this #main rule set. As you can see, Prefixr automatically adds the prefixed -webkit-box-shadow declaration for you. You can use the box-shadow property in all modern browsers without a prefix, but some mobile browsers that use the WebKit layout engine still require the prefixed property, so Prefixr adds it.

Prefixr unfortunately doesn't automatically prefix the perspective property, so you can do that manually.

2. After the -webkit-perspective: 1000px; declaration, add the following:

```
-moz-perspective: 1000px;
-ms-perspective: 1000px;
-o-perspective: 1000px;
perspective: 1000px;
```

3. Save styles.css.

Note that just as Prefixr does, you should always place the official, nonprefixed property below the prefixed versions; that way, the official property will be used over the unofficial properties as soon as a browser supports it.

The next rule set that Prefixr works its magic on is .showcase .button. As you can see, this tool takes the work out of having to write the gradient applied to the showcase button:

```
background: -webkit-linear-gradient(top, #FB3876 0%, #d4326d
    100%);
background: -moz-linear-gradient(top, #FB3876 0%, #d4326d
    100%);
background: -o-linear-gradient(top, #FB3876 0%, #d4326d 100%);
background: -ms-linear-gradient(top, #FB3876 0%, #d4326d 100%);
background: linear-gradient(top, #FB3876 0%, #d4326d 100%);
```

No action is required here, but I'm sure you'll agree, not having to write out all these properties with the heavy syntax of `linear-gradient()` is a timesaver.

Just below the `.showcase .button` rule set, you see the `@keyframes` rules. Prefixr takes the `@-webkit-keyframes` rule and makes one for each browser, including a nonprefixed `@keyframes` rule. Unlike other rule sets, the keyframes rules are only referenced, so their position within a stylesheet isn't essential. Prefixr chooses to place the official `@keyframes` rule above the prefixed versions, which isn't a problem.

As mentioned in Chapter 5, when you use the `opacity` property—which isn't supported by Internet Explorer versions 6, 7, and 8—Prefixr automatically adds the `filter` property, which emulates `opacity`. You used `opacity` in the `@keyframes` rules, but because old versions of Internet Explorer don't understand `@keyframes` anyway, the `filter` property can safely be removed. The `filter` properties don't actually cause any harm if they remain in the stylesheet, so this step is optional, but always trying to keep your stylesheets as clean as possible is good practice.

4. Remove any instance of the `filter` and `-ms-filter` properties from styles.css.

   As you make your way through the stylesheet, you see that Prefixr prefixes many more properties too:

   - The `.showcase li` animations from the preceding chapter

   - The `box-sizing` property in `input[type="text"]`, `input[type="email"]`

   - The `transform` property added to several of the `.sidebar` elements

   - The `transform`, `transform-origin`, and `transition` properties added to the `.banner-ad` rule set

   None of these modifications require your action. However, Prefixr slightly tampers with the content declarations in the `blockquote p:before` and `blockquote p:after` rule sets. The `content` properties originally have the values `"\201C"` and `"\201D"`, but Prefixr strips out the backslashes, so you need to add them back in.

5. In `blockquote p:before`, add a backslash inside the quotation marks:

   ```
   content: "\201C";
   ```

6. In `blockquote p:after`, add a backslash inside the quotation marks:

   ```
   content: "\201D";
   ```

   Finally, because Prefixr also strips out some of the prefixed `border-image` properties in the `#footer` rule set, add those back in.

7. In the `#footer` rule set, below the `-moz-border-image` declaration, add the following:

   ```
   -ms-border-image: url("../images/bdr-footer.png") 4 repeat;
   -o-border-image: url("../images/bdr-footer.png") 4 repeat;
   ```

8. Save styles.css.

All in all, when you run a stylesheet through Prefixr, you need to do a little work to tidy things up afterward, but overall you save some time and, most importantly, your sanity. Writing those prefixed properties isn't fun!

Testing Modern Browsers

Now that you've prefixed all the necessary CSS3 properties, how do those changes help with the cross browser compatibility of Cool Shoes & Socks?

When testing cross browser compatibility, look for visual issues, but also test the functionality of the page. Hover over the drop-down menus and other elements with :hover rules, make sure the showcase animation runs correctly, and also resize your browser to make sure everything scales correctly.

Firefox 13 and Safari 5

Now the stylesheet contains the necessary prefixed properties, and due to modern browsers all closely supporting the CSS specifications, achieving browser consistency isn't particularly hard. In Figure 15-3, you can see that Firefox now displays the page just as Chrome does. Safari 5 also renders the page just as Chrome and Firefox do.

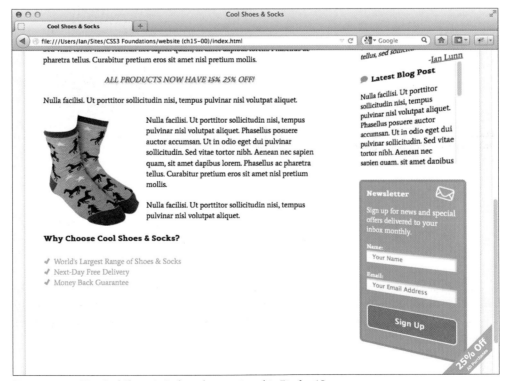

FIGURE 15-3 The Cool Shoes & Socks web page viewed in Firefox 13.

Opera 11 and 12

When viewed in Opera 11 and 12, Cool Shoes & Socks doesn't provide quite the same experience as the other browsers, due to Opera 11 and 12 not supporting @keyframes or 3D transforms, as shown in Figure 15-4. This is not a problem, though; Opera still displays the web page perfectly well, and the code exists in the stylesheet for the time when Opera *does* decide to support 3D transforms, making the page future proof.

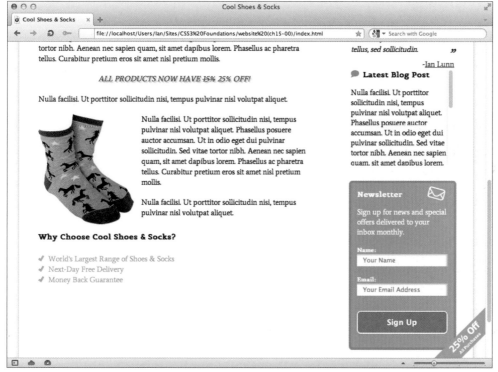

FIGURE 15-4 The Cool Shoes & Socks web page viewed in Opera 12.

Internet Explorer 10

At the time of writing, Microsoft Internet Explorer 10 has not been officially released but has been made available for testing. Visually, Internet Explorer 10 has no issues, but there is an issue with the 3D transform applied to the sidebar when hovered over, as shown in Figure 15-5.

Internet Explorer 10 unfortunately doesn't support `transform-style: preserve-3d` yet, which, as shown in Figure 15-5, is why the newsletter box appears to be positioned strangely when hovered over, causing horizontal scroll bars to appear—something you've tried to avoid up until now.

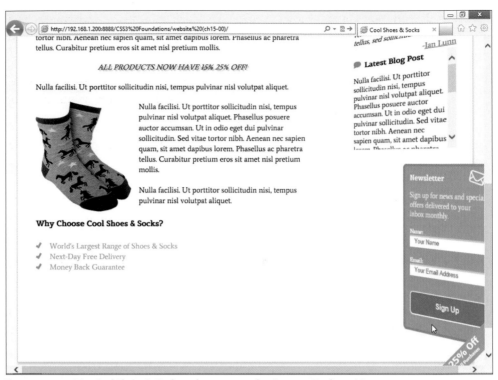

FIGURE 15-5 The Cool Shoes & Socks web page viewed in Internet Explorer 10.

You can find the CSS that affects the sidebar within the `.sidebar` rule set:

```css
.sidebar {
    float: right;
    width: 25%;
    -webkit-transform: rotateY(-40deg);
    -moz-transform: rotateY(-40deg);
    -ms-transform: rotateY(-40deg);
    -o-transform: rotateY(-40deg);
    transform: rotateY(-40deg);
    -webkit-transform-style: preserve-3d;
    -moz-transform-style: preserve-3d;
    -ms-transform-style: preserve-3d;
    -o-transform-style: preserve-3d;
    transform-style: preserve-3d;
}
```

Unfortunately, Microsoft chose to support the nonprefixed `transform` property despite not yet supporting `transform-style: preserve-3d`. This means that you can't simply remove the prefixed `-ms-transform` property to fall back to a 2D sidebar because the nonprefixed `transform` property is still applied. You could remove the `transform` property too, but then all other browsers that *do* support `transform-style: preserve-3d` would also lose out on the 3D sidebar.

This situation is somewhat frustrating. Microsoft shouldn't really have decided to support the nonprefixed `transform` property until the prefixed `-ms-transform` property worked fully. You can work around this issue, however:

1. In styles.css, find the `.sidebar` rule set and delete the following declaration:

    ```
    -ms-transform: rotateY(-40deg);
    ```

2. In the same rule set, below the `transform: rotateY(-40deg);` declaration, add the following:

    ```
    -ms-transform: none;
    ```

3. In the `.sidebar .aside:hover` rule set, delete the following declaration:

    ```
    -ms-transform: rotateY(-40deg);
    ```

4. In the same rule set, below the `transform: rotateY(-40deg);` declaration, add the following:

    ```
    -ms-transform: none;
    ```

5. In the `.sidebar .aside:nth-child(3):hover` rule set, delete the following declaration:

    ```
    -ms-transform: rotateY(40deg) translateX(-50px) scaleZ(2)
      translateZ(100px);
    ```

6. In the same rule set, below the `transform: rotateY(40deg) translateX(-50px) scaleZ(2) translateZ(100px);` declaration, add the following:

    ```
    -ms-transform: none;
    ```

7. Save styles.css.

The `.sidebar` rule set now looks like this:

```
.sidebar {
    float: right;
    width: 25%;
    -webkit-transform: rotateY(-40deg);
    -moz-transform: rotateY(-40deg);
    -o-transform: rotateY(-40deg);
    transform: rotateY(-40deg);
    -ms-transform: none;
    -webkit-transform-style: preserve-3d;
    -moz-transform-style: preserve-3d;
    -ms-transform-style: preserve-3d;
```

```
    -o-transform-style: preserve-3d;
    transform-style: preserve-3d;
}
```

What you do here is break the rules a little—by placing a prefixed property below the non-prefixed property—but only to fix the issue caused by Microsoft breaking the rules—supporting the nonprefixed `transform` property before it fully supported the nonprefixed `-ms-transform` property.

Because you place the `-ms-transform:  none;` declaration below the `transform: rotateY(-40deg);` declaration, Internet Explorer 10 does not have a transform applied to it. The sidebar just falls back to 2D. This is the safest way to deal with Microsoft's shortcomings. If—and it's always a big *if* with Internet Explorer—Microsoft does follow the advice set out in the CSS specifications, it will eventually drop support for prefixed properties such as `-ms-transform`, so your declaration of `-ms-transform:  none;` will be ignored and the `transform:  rotateY(-40deg);` declaration will be used in its place. This result is what is desired for Cool Shoes & Socks anyway; you just have to take these measures temporarily while Internet Explorer 10 doesn't fully support 3D transforms.

Internet Explorer 9

Internet Explorer 9 offers a similar experience to Opera 12. `@keyframes` and 3D transforms aren't supported. Neither are transitions, so when you hover over the "25% banner," the banner just snaps between sizes. The rounded corners on elements are also unsupported. Again, this lack of support isn't a problem. The users will never know anything is wrong because the page still appears and functions perfectly for them; they just miss out on a few visual treats.

Firefox 3.6

In Chapter 1, I mentioned that Firefox 3.6 is still in use today—despite the latest Firefox being version 13 at the time of writing! Firefox 3.6 provides a similar experience to Internet Explorer 9, and thanks to the best practices you've adhered to throughout *CSS3 Foundations*, it doesn't require any additional attention; it displays and functions to the level the browser is capable of.

Testing Older Versions of Internet Explorer

So far, the browser-testing ride has been pretty smooth. Cool Shoes & Socks works in the latest versions of modern browsers used today. It's a certainty that older versions of Internet Explorer will require some extra attention though.

Internet Explorer 8

From the outset, Cool Shoes & Socks doesn't look too bad in Internet Explorer 8, although a few issues arise as you move down the page, as shown in Figure 15-6.

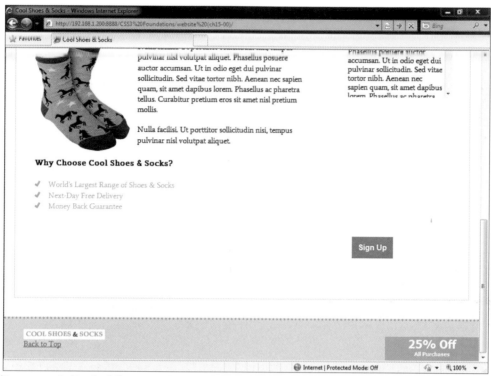

FIGURE 15-6 The Cool Shoes & Socks web page viewed in Internet Explorer 8.

First of all, the newsletter box disappeared! This isn't actually a browser bug, though. When adding multiple backgrounds to the newsletter box in Chapter 5, I didn't include an instruction to provide a fallback for older browsers that don't support multiple backgrounds. If you forget to add fallbacks—we all do from time to time—you can pick up these omissions during browser testing and fix them:

1. In styles.css, find the #newsletter rule set:

    ```
    #newsletter {
        color: white;
        border-radius: 8px;
        border: rgba(0,0,0,0.1) solid 5px;
        background: url("../images/icon-newsletter.png") no-repeat
        91% 2%, url("../images/bg-newsletter.png") repeat 0 #00ACDF;
        padding: 6%;
        margin-left: -4px;
        width: 88%;
    }
    ```

2. Above the background declaration, add another background declaration:

    ```
    background: url("../images/bg-newsletter.png") repeat 0 #00ACDF;
    ```

3. Save styles.css.

   With two `background` declarations, browsers that don't understand the second multiple image declaration simply ignore it and apply the first.

   Now that the background image is in place, it also becomes apparent that the `border` declaration isn't being applied either. The reason is that Internet Explorer 9 doesn't understand the `rgba()` function used to style the border. Add another fallback property.

4. In the `#newsletter` rule set, above the `border` declaration, add the following:

   ```
   border: #009CC8 solid 5px;
   ```

5. Save styles.css.

This procedure provides browsers that don't support the `rgba()` function a value that they do understand.

With the border fixed, you may notice the Sign Up button in the newsletter box isn't centered as it is in other browsers. This is a bug in Internet Explorer 8, and to work around it, you need to give the Sign Up button a `width`.

1. In styles.css, find the `input[type="submit"][class="button"]` rule set and add the following declaration:

   ```
   width: 100%;
   ```

2. Save styles.css.

Finally, for Internet Explorer 8, the Cool Shoes & Socks logo and Back to Top link in the footer aren't floated to the left and right of the page. The reason is that the rule sets for these elements use the `:nth-child()` selector, which isn't supported in versions 6, 7, and 8 of Internet Explorer.

The Cool Shoes & Socks page uses the `:nth-child()` selector five times, but three of those are to apply transforms and animations to the product showcase and sidebar, which older versions of Internet Explorer don't support anyway. Because only two of the `:nth-child()` selectors affect Internet Explorer 6, 7, and 8, the simplest solution is just to give the elements a class name and change the rule set to use a class selector instead of `:nth-child()`.

1. In index.html, find the two `<li>` elements within `<div class="nav container">`.

2. Change the first `<li>` to give it the class `small-logo`, like so:

   ```
   <li class="small-logo">
   ```

3. Change the second `<li>` to give it the class `back-to-top`, like so:

   ```
   <li class="back-to-top">
   ```

4. Save index.html.

5. In styles.css, find the rule set `#footer li:nth-child(1)` and change the selector to `#footer .small-logo`.

6. In styles.css, find the rule set `#footer li:nth-child(2)` and change the selector to `#footer .back-to-top`.

7. Save styles.css.

Although this is a sensible option for the Cool Shoes & Socks page, you might not always want to have to change all your advanced selectors to simpler ones that older browsers can understand; otherwise, there would be no point in using them. One solution for this problem is to use JavaScript to help older browsers understand advanced selectors. Rather than write your own JavaScript to give them this capability, though, you can use a free utility to do this job for you. Called Selectivizr, it is located at `www.selectivizr.com/`.

When you download and place a `<script>` reference in the `<head>` of the page—just as you did with live.js in Chapter 2—along with a JavaScript library such as jQuery, many advanced CSS selectors work in older browsers. Visit the Selectivizr website at `www.selectivizr.com/` for complete instructions on how to add this reference if you need to.

Conditional Comments for Internet Explorer 6, 7, and 8

Internet Explorer versions 6 and 7 never made much of an effort to adhere to standards—with Internet Explorer 8 doing a little better but still not great—and because of that, whenever you check a web page in them, you certainly find issues, in particular in Internet Explorer 6. Sometimes you need to make fundamental changes to a page to get it working in these older versions of Internet Explorer, but that is at the detriment to the other browsers that *do* work. Thankfully, you can use conditional comments to apply styles to specific versions of Internet Explorer.

Let's look at some of the issues in Internet Explorer 7 and then use conditional comments to add fixes.

As shown in Figure 15-7, the first issue with Internet Explorer 7 is the layout of the navigation links; they appear vertically one after the other rather than side by side.

In Chapter 9, I mentioned that Internet Explorer 6 and 7 don't support `display: inline-block;`, which is what is applied to these navigation links. Luckily, these browsers treat `display: inline;` as if it were `display: inline-block;` anyway.

If you go into styles.css and change the `#header .nav > ul > li` rule set so that the `display` property has a value of `inline`, this change fixes Internet Explorer 6 and 7 but breaks modern browsers. Instead, create a conditional stylesheet:

FIGURE 15-7 The Cool Shoes & Socks web page viewed in Internet Explorer 7.

1. In index.html, below the `<link>` reference to `css/styles.css`, add the following:

   ```
   <!--[if lt IE 8]><link rel="stylesheet" href="css/styles-ie7.
     css" type="text/css" /><![endif]-->
   ```

2. Save index.html.

   This code adds a stylesheet to the page that is to be applied only when a specific condition is met. The condition `if lt IE 8` means "if less than Internet Explorer 8." So, when the Cool Shoes & Socks page is viewed in any version of Internet Explorer below version 8, the styles-ie7.css stylesheet is applied.

   Following are a few examples of conditional comments you might like to use:

   - `if IE`—If any version of Internet Explorer

   - `if IE 6`—If the browser is specifically Internet Explorer version 6

   - `if gt IE 8`—If the browser is greater than version 8 of Internet Explorer

   - `if gte IE 8`—If the browser is greater than or equal to version 8 of Internet Explorer

- `if lt IE 9`—If the browser is less than version 9 of Internet Explorer

- `if ltc IE 8`—If the browser is less than or equal to version 8 of Internet Explorer

You can also use an exclamation mark (`!`) to apply to anything that does not match a condition; for example, `if !IE` applies to anything that isn't Internet Explorer. For more information about conditional comments, see `www.quirksmode.org/css/condcom.html`.

Now that you have a conditional comment set up, add a new stylesheet to be applied to Internet Explorer 7.

3. Create a new file called styles-ie7.css and save it in the css folder.

4. In styles-ie7.css, add the following rule set:

```
#header .nav > ul > li {
    display: inline;
    vertical-align: top;
}
```

5. Save styles-ie7.css.

Because you add the conditional stylesheet below the main stylesheet, any styles added to it overwrite the main styles. This rule set overwrites the navigation links' `display: inline-block;` declaration from the main stylesheet and makes them `display: inline;` instead. You also include `vertical-align: top;` to make each link align to the top.

Also shown in Figure 15-7 is that the page has a horizontal scroll bar. Sometimes, older versions of Internet Explorer have inexplicable bugs such as this, and the best way to find a fix is through trial and error. By commenting out sections of HTML in index.html, I found that it was either the sidebar `<div class="sidebar" role="complementary">` or an element within the sidebar that was causing the page to be wider than necessary. By then commenting out sections within the sidebar, I found that it was the `<cite>` tag within the `<blockquote>`. With this knowledge, I then went into styles.css and commented out each declaration in the `blockquote cite` rule set until I found the culprit: `float: right;`.

The `<cite>` element appears to be acting bigger than it is (causing the page to become wider), so my natural reaction was to specify a `width`. As with the Send button issue you saw in Internet Explorer 8, this issue appears to be similar. To fix it, add an Internet Explorer 7–specific style:

1. In styles-ie7.css, add the following rule set:

```
blockquote cite {
    width: 100%;
```

```
    text-align: right;
}
```

2. Save styles-ie7.css

Just one visual issue is left in Internet Explorer 7. The input fields in the newsletter box are too wide for the box. The reason is that you used `box-sizing: border-box;` on these elements, which isn't supported in Internet Explorer 6 or 7. Internet Explorer 6 and 7 only treat `box-sizing` as the default `padding-box`. For more information on this issue, see Chapter 7.

1. In styles-ie7.css, add the following rule set:

```
input[type="text"],input[type="email"] {
    width: 88%;
}
```

2. Save styles-ie7.css.

Because the newsletter box has a `padding` of `6%` both on the left and right sides, when you make the width of the input fields `88%`, they perfectly fit in the box again. Note that this effect is true only when the width of the browser is 960px or greater—which leads to the next Internet Explorer fix.

In the next chapter, you use media queries to make the Cool Shoes & Socks page adapt based on the width of the page. Internet Explorer 6, 7, and 8 don't support media queries, though, so you can add a conditional style sheet for them that prevents the web page shrinking below 960px.

1. In index.html, above the previously added conditional stylesheet, add the following:

```
<!--[if lt IE 9]><link rel="stylesheet" href="css/styles-ie.
  css" type="text/css" /><![endif]-->
```

2. Save index.html.

3. Create a new file called styles-ie.css and save it in the css folder.

4. In styles-ie.css, add the following declaration:

```
body {
    width: 960px;
}
```

When you add this conditional stylesheet that applies to all versions of Internet Explorer below version 9, Cool Shoes & Socks viewed in those browsers isn't able to shrink below a width of 960px. This workaround ensures the layout doesn't shrink down to the point where content becomes unreadable.

Universal Internet Explorer 6 Stylesheet

Now comes the gut-wrenching moment...when viewing Cool Shoes & Socks in Internet Explorer 6, it isn't going to be pretty. Thankfully, the days of supporting Internet Explorer 6 are close to over—if not already over.

If you absolutely have to support Internet Explorer 6 and make it appear close to how other browsers do, you can add fixes in the same way as with Internet Explorer 7 and 8: Create a conditional stylesheet that applies styles to Internet Explorer 6 only. Cool Shoes & Socks takes more of a radical approach, though.

As shown in Figure 15-8, Cool Shoes & Socks viewed in Internet Explorer 6 isn't pretty. Rather than spend x number of hours fixing it with a conditional stylesheet, you can simply remove all styles, leaving just the bare content—all that's really important on the page.

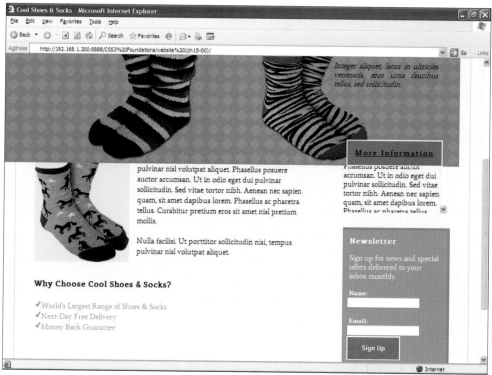

FIGURE 15-8   The Cool Shoes & Socks web page viewed in Internet Explorer 6.

Using Andy Clarke's (www.stuffandnonsense.co.uk/) Universal Internet Explorer 6 Stylesheet code.google.com/p/universal-ie6-css/, you can achieve this result easily.

1. In index.html, modify the <link> reference to styles.css so it is wrapped in a conditional comment, like so:

```
<!--[if ! lte IE 6]><!--><link rel="stylesheet" href="css/
    styles.css" type="text/css" /><![endif]-->
```

This lines hides the main stylesheet from Internet Explorer versions 6 and below but still allows it to apply to everything else.

2. Below the `<link>` reference to styles-ie7.css, add the following line:

```
<!--[if lte IE 6]><link rel="stylesheet" href="http://
    universal-ie6-css.googlecode.com/files/ie6.1.1.css"
    media="screen, projection"><![endif]-->
```

3. Save index.html.

With this last line you add, versions of Internet Explorer less than or equal to version 6 are given a basic stylesheet that removes all but the necessary styles from Cool Shoes & Socks and any other page you care to add it to in the future.

Summary

In this chapter, you made the Cool Shoes & Socks web page cross browser compatible for desktop browsers—not the easiest of tasks but one that is essential. Each browser now displays Cool Shoes & Socks without issues and at a level it is capable of.

The steps you took to provide a basic experience for Internet Explorer 6 may seem radical, but with Internet Explorer 6 having a very small market share now—and not even Microsoft supports it anymore—that experience still provides any remaining users of Internet Explorer 6 with all the content the page has to offer. They just don't get the bells and whistles.

In the next chapter, you use media queries to make the page change based on the attributes of the device it is being viewed on, making mobile experiences in particular richer.

chapter sixteen

Making Your Website Look Great Across Multiple Devices

WITH SO MANY different types of devices able to access the web today, how a web page is displayed on those devices needs to change to best suit the device it is being viewed on. At the moment, the Cool Shoes & Socks page is suited for desktop browsers, but cramming all of that page into the small screen of a mobile device, for example, makes the content very small and difficult to read.

As you saw in Chapter 2, CSS2 offers media types (www.w3.org/TR/CSS2/media.html), which allow you to apply styles to specific conditions such as screen, print, and handheld. Of course, these media types were rather short-sighted. What is handheld? A mobile phone? A tablet device, such as an iPad? A Nintendo DS? All these devices could be considered as "handheld," but they still differ greatly—in size, in features, and the environment in which they are used.

The CSS3 media queries module (www.w3.org/TR/css3-mediaqueries/) adds many new ways for you to query attributes of a device on which a page is being viewed and to set up styles specific to those conditions.

In this chapter, you use the free Opera Mobile Emulator (www.opera.com/developer/tools/mobile/) to build and test a Cool Shoes & Socks page that is capable of adapting to varying device conditions.

Using Opera Mobile Emulator

Before you begin adding media queries to the Cool Shoes & Socks stylesheet, first take a look at the page in Opera Mobile Emulator.

1. Download and install Opera Mobile Emulator from `www.opera.com/developer/tools/mobile/`.

2. After it is installed, open Opera Mobile Emulator.

   When you open Opera Mobile Emulator, you are presented with the options for the device you want to emulate, as shown in Figure 16-1. By changing these settings, you can set up an environment similar to many Android devices such as Samsung Galaxy S, HTC Desire, Motorola Xoom, and so on.

FIGURE 16-1 The initial window of Opera Mobile Emulator.

   Opera Mobile Emulator conveniently has a list of profiles for many devices, which saves you from having to change options such as Resolution and Pixel Density.

   Ideally, you should test in as many devices as possible, but as you did with desktop browsers, choose one profile to develop with, and when you're done, test in other profiles.

3. From the Profile list, select Samsung Galaxy S II and click Launch.

   When a profile launches, you are presented with a window that has the same dimensions as the Samsung Galaxy S II, and you can start using the Opera Mobile browser as if you were using it on that device.

4. With the Cool Shoes & Socks page open in your desktop browser, copy the URL of the page from the address bar.

5. Return to Opera Mobile Emulator, click the address bar, and paste the URL. Then press Return on your keyboard or click the Go button in the bottom right.

You now see the Cool Shoes & Socks page in the same way it would be viewed on a Samsung Galaxy S II, as shown in Figure 16-2. Cool stuff, right? You can view your pages in a whole range of mobile devices.

FIGURE 16-2 The Cool Shoes & Socks page viewed in a Samsung Galaxy S II profile using Opera Mobile Emulator.

In the bottom-right corner of the Opera Mobile Emulator window is a small rotate symbol, as shown in Figure 16-3. Click this symbol to rotate the device, as if it is in your hands and you are changing it from portrait to landscape view and vice versa.

As you can see, Cool Shoes & Socks is difficult to read on such a small device. If this were the real device in your hand, you would probably zoom in to read the content. Using media queries, you can make it so that users don't need to zoom in and swipe around the page to be able to read it, while generally improving their experience of Cool Shoes & Socks when viewing it on a mobile device.

Rotate button

FIGURE 16-3 The rotate button in Opera Mobile Emulator that allows you to change the emulated device between portrait and landscape views.

Scaling the Viewport on Mobile Devices

When you view a web page on a mobile device, many mobile browsers scale the viewport so the page fits on the screen without the need for horizontal scroll bars. The reason Cool Shoes & Socks is so small when viewed in Opera Mobile Emulator—and you'll find the same happens across many devices—is that the page is scaled down to fit.

Because media queries are a new technology, many websites don't use them. Therefore, a mobile browser scaling down the viewport in this way provides a solution that makes the majority of web pages display reasonably well on a smaller screen. Text can often be hard to read at this size, but users can get a quick overview of the page and zoom in to the sections they want to see or read—a better approach than being able to show only a small part of a web page at a higher zoom level.

Because you're working on the Cool Shoes & Socks page now, though—with the media queries module in a Recommendation status—you get the privilege of choosing how your web page looks on a mobile device. Letting a mobile browser scale the viewport is a quick fix but not a perfect one, which is where media queries step in.

As yet, there isn't a way to change the scaling of the viewport via CSS, although the feature is on its way in the CSS Device Adaption module (dev.w3.org/csswg/css-device-adapt/#the-viewport-rule). However, you can scale the viewport using HTML.

1. In index.html, below `<meta charset="utf-8" />`, add the following:

   ```
   <meta name="viewport"
   content="width=device-width, initial-scale=1, maximum-scale=1">
   ```

2. Save index.html.

When you specify the `width` as `device-width`, the viewport is set to the same width as the device. The `initial-scale` is the zoom applied to the page when it first loads, 1 being the equivalent of 100%. When `maximum-scale` is set to 1, the page can't be zoomed in more than 100%. The CSS Device Adaption module explains that the `initial-scale` property will actually be called `zoom`; likewise, similar properties such as `minimum-scale` and `maximum-scale` (which determine how far in and out the user is allowed to zoom) will be translated to `min-zoom` and `max-zoom`.

Because the CSS Device Adaption module is an Editor's draft at the time of writing, *CSS3 Foundations* doesn't cover that module. If you would like more information about `<meta name="viewport">`, see the Mobile Web Application Best Practices at www.w3.org/TR/mwabp/#bp-viewport.

So what does this change do to Cool Shoes & Socks? As shown in Figure 16-4, the page now zooms right in. Everything is bigger but crammed into a smaller place, so whether the page is more readable is arguable. Likewise, some elements look a little broken and/or could do with being positioned differently. Using media queries, you can address all these issues and only for the mobile experience—the desktop experience isn't changed.

FIGURE 16-4 The Cool Shoes & Socks page viewed in Opera Mobile Emulator with an `initial-scale` of 1 and the viewport width set to be the same as the device's width.

Using Media Queries

Browser support: IE 9+, Firefox 3.5+, Chrome 4+, Opera 9.5+, Safari 4+

Although the media queries module is a part of the CSS3 specification, these queries are in a Recommendation status, meaning they are no longer experimental and can be used safely. Unfortunately, Internet Explorer 6, 7, and 8 don't support media queries, but you already took steps in the preceding chapter to work around that issue. What's more, mobile devices and tablets don't use these older browsers, so media queries and older versions of Internet Explorer don't pose much of a problem.

As you saw in Chapter 2, you add media types to a stylesheet using the `@media` rule, for example:

```
@media screen {
    /* styles to be applied to screen devices here */
}
```

Any rule sets placed with this `@media` rule apply only to the screen. Media queries use the same syntax and build on media types. Whereas the previous media type applied to the screen, the following media query applies to a *color* screen:

```
@media screen and (color){
    /* styles to be applied to color screen devices here */
}
```

You can use the same query with the `media` attribute in a `<link>` element, like so:

```
<link rel="stylesheet" media="screen and (color)"
href="styles.css" />
```

You place media queries in parentheses `()`; they are logical expressions that can either be true or false. Here, if the media is a color screen, the query is true and the necessary styles are applied; otherwise, the query is false and the styles are ignored.

Color is just one of the many media features that you can use to compose a media query, which you look at after learning how to use logical operators.

Using Logical Operators

Logical operators allow you to create complex `@media` rules—stringing media queries together.

And

The `and` keyword enables you to combine features of a query. For example:

```
@media screen and (color)
```

In this query, the media must be a screen *and* a color one at that. If the media is a screen but can display only black and white, the `@media` rule is false and the styles don't apply.

Or

To specify a logical OR expression, you can list queries, separated by a comma. For example:

```
@media screen and (color), projection and (color)
```

This query applies to color screens *or* color projectors. Only one of the queries in the list needs to be true for the `@media` rule to be true.

Not

When you use the `not` keyword, the result of a media query is negated. The following `@media` rule is true on a color screen:

```
@media screen and (color)
```

The following is false for a color screen but true for everything else:

```
@media not screen and (color)
```

This means anything that isn't a color screen has the specified styles applied to it.

Only

Because older browsers can read `@media` rules but not media queries, older browsers may ignore the query and still apply a stylesheet regardless of whether the query is true or false. To prevent that from happening, you can place the `only` keyword at the start of an `@media` rule to make older browsers ignore the entire rule, like so:

```
@media only screen and (color)
```

Modern browsers know that the `only` keyword is just present to throw off older browsers, and they continue reading everything after it. The `only` keyword is used with every Cool Shoes & Socks `@media` rule.

Applying Styles to Specific Media Features

Media features, such as `color` shown previously, are used in media queries to describe the requirements of the environment you want to apply styles to.

Many features accept optional `min-` or `max-` prefixes to express "greater than or equal to" and "less than or equal to." For example, `min-width: 100px` is true for anything with a width of 100px or more.

In this section, below the name of each media feature, you see which media type a media feature applies to and whether it supports `min-` and `max-` prefixes.

Let's look at what each media feature describes and then implement some of them into the Cool Shoes & Socks stylesheet.

width

Applies to: all visual and tactile (a device that allows for being touched) media types | Accepts min/max prefixes: yes `width` describes the width of the viewport on a targeted display, that is, the width of the browser's viewing area.

Assuming you want to apply styles to a viewport with a width equal to or less than 960px, such as the 700px wide browser window shown in Figure 16-5, you can use the `max-width` media feature:

```
@media only screen and (max-width: 960px) {
    /* styles to be applied to screen devices when the viewport has
 a width equal to or less than 960px */
}
```

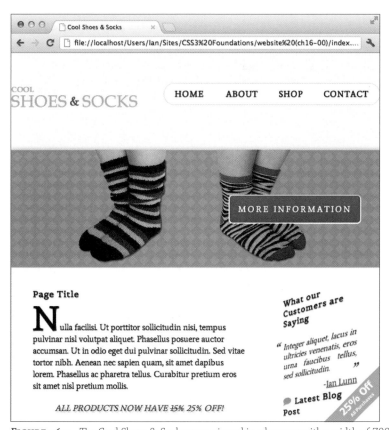

FIGURE 16-5 The Cool Shoes & Socks page viewed in a browser with a width of 700px.

Using the query `@media only screen and (width: 960px)` applies only to viewports with an exact width of 960px.

height

Applies to: all visual and tactile media types | Accepts min/max prefixes: yes

`height` describes the height of the viewport on a targeted display, that is, the height of the browser's viewing area.

Media queries tend to use the `width` media feature more than `height`, but this feature still has its uses.

For example, you could query the height of the browser to move important elements—ones that you want the users to see as soon as they visit the page—further up the page when their viewport has a small height. You may decide that the "25% Off" banner on the Cool Shoes & Socks page would get in the way of more important content when the browser height is smaller than usual and therefore use a media query to hide it below a certain height.

```
@media only screen and (max-height: 500px) {
    /* styles to be applied to screen devices when the viewport has
a height equal to or less than 500px */
}
```

device-width

Applies to: all visual and tactile media types | Accepts min/max prefixes: yes

Whereas the media feature `width` is the width of the viewport, `device-width` is the width of the screen.

`device-width` is often used to target devices such as mobiles and tablets. Consider the following example:

```
@media only screen and (min-device-width: 320px)
```

```
and (max-device-width: 480px)
```

With this query, all screen devices with a screen width ranging between 320px and 480px have the specified styles applied to them. This range of widths applies to many mobile devices both in portrait and landscape orientations, but not bigger devices such as tablets and desktop computers.

Unlike the viewport, the size of a screen obviously can't be changed.

device-height

Applies to: all visual and tactile media types | Accepts min/max prefixes: yes

device-height describes the height of a screen. As with the height media feature, it is not as commonly used as width or device-width but shares similar purposes as those described for height.

orientation

Applies to: bitmap (devices that output an image, such as screen or print) media types | Accepts min/max prefixes: no

The orientation media feature takes two values, portrait and landscape, and is written as follows:

```
@media only screen and (orientation: portrait)
@media only screen and (orientation: landscape)
```

orientation is portrait when the value of the height media feature is greater than or equal to the value of the width media feature; otherwise, orientation is landscape.

aspect-ratio

Applies to: bitmap media types | Accepts min/max prefixes: yes

aspect-ratio is the ratio between the width and height media features (the width and height of the viewport). As with many of the media features, aspect-ratio tends to be used with a min- or max- prefix.

This media query describes a viewport with a width that is equal to or greater than its height:

```
@media only screen and (min-aspect-ratio: 1/1)
```

device-aspect-ratio

Applies to: bitmap media types | Accepts min/max prefixes: yes

device-aspect-ratio is the ratio between the device-width and device-height (the width and height of a screen).

The following media query describes a device's screen with an aspect ratio of 16/9:

```
@media only screen and (device-aspect-ratio: 16/9)
```

color, color-index, monochrome, resolution, scan, and grid

The following media features are used for more specialized pages and applications:

- `color`—Describes the number of bits per color component of the output device
- `color-index`—Describes the number of entries in the color lookup table of the output device
- `monochrome`—Describes the number of bits per pixel in a monochrome frame buffer
- `resolution`—Describes the resolution of the output device
- `scan`—Describes the scanning process of `tv` output devices
- `grid`—Queries whether the output device is grid or bitmap

For more information on these media features, see the Media Queries module at `www.w3.org/TR/css3-mediaqueries/#device-aspect-ratio`.

Adding Media Queries to Cool Shoes & Socks

Now that you know what media features are available, you can modify the layout of Cool Shoes & Socks specifically for mobile devices and then move on to adjusting the tablet experience and desktop experience when the browser window is narrower than 960px.

Media Queries for Mobile Devices

As you saw in Figure 16-4, Cool Shoes & Socks when viewed on a smaller device gets messy, so let's tidy it up and make the experience better for smaller devices.

1. At the bottom of styles.css, add the following `@media` rule:

```
/* Mobile (portrait and landscape)*/
@media only screen and (max-device-width: 480px) {

}
```

This rule applies to devices that have a screen width up to 480px—many mobile devices. It's a good idea to include a comment above the `@media` rule to remind you and/or your colleagues what exactly a media query is targeting.

2. Inside the @media rule, add the following declarations:

```
#header .logo {
    display: block;
    float: none;
    margin: 0 auto;
}

#header {
    padding: 0 10px;
}

#header nav, .sidebar, #content{
    float: none;
    width: 100%;
}

.banner-ad {
    display: none;
}
```

The first two rule sets, #header .logo and #header, center the logo and add padding to either side of the header.

The third rule set, #header nav, .sidebar, #content, is one you will see a lot for mobile layouts (the selectors may be different but the declarations the same). Because the desktop version of Cool Shoes & Socks has multiple columns, when the width of the page is much smaller on devices such as mobile, there isn't enough room for two columns. When you set the header navigation, sidebar, and content area to float: none; and width: 100%;, those elements all stretch out into one column, giving them the space they need to become more readable.

The fourth rule set, .banner-ad, hides the "25% Off" banner, which, as mentioned previously, may get in the way of content. What's more, fixed position elements don't work well on mobile devices, so it's a good idea to avoid them where possible.

The mobile layout isn't quite right yet, so add a few more rule sets to the same @media rule.

3. Inside the @media rule and below the other rule sets you just added, add the following:

```
#header nav > ul {
    border: none;
}

#header nav li {
    border-radius: 20px;
    border: #ccc solid 1px;
```

```
    margin: 0 0 5px 0;
    width: 100%;
}

#header nav ul ul {
    display: none;
}

.sidebar {
    border-top: 3px dotted #ccc;
    clear: both;
    margin: 60px 0 0 0;
    padding: 20px 0 0 0;
}

.sidebar, .sidebar aside:hover,
.sidebar aside:nth-child(3):hover {
-webkit-transform: none;
    -moz-transform: none;
    -o-transform: none;
    -ms-transform: none;
    transform: none;
}

#footer li {
    display: block;
    float: none;
    line-height: 200%;
}
```

The first rule, #header nav > ul, removes the border around the navigation, and the second rule, #header nav li, adds borders around each navigation link instead. Because mobile devices often have touch capabilities now, it is good practice to make sure any link on a page has a wide target area so the users can easily press it without having to concern themselves about being too accurate.

The third rule set, #header nav ul ul, hides the drop-down menus. It's a good idea to hide complex drop-down menus on touch devices. Just remember to make sure the top-level pages have links to their child pages or provide an alternative navigation.

The fourth rule set, .sidebar, changes the layout of the sidebar somewhat. Now that the sidebar sits below the content (rather than to its side as in the desktop version), it's given a top border to visually separate it and some margin and padding on top to push it a little further away from the bottom of the content area.

The fifth rule set, `.sidebar, .sidebar aside:hover, .sidebar aside:nth-child(3):hover`, overrides the transforms when the sidebar elements are hovered over. Because the mobile layout is a smaller space, it's better to hide these animated transforms.

The last rule set, `#footer li`, tidies up the links in the footer.

Finally, modify the product showcase for mobile devices.

4. Still inside the `@media` rule and below the other rule sets you just added, add the following:

```
.showcase {
    height: 200px;
    overflow: hidden;
}

.showcase li {
    -webkit-animation: none;
    -moz-animation: none;
     -ms-animation: none;
    -o-animation: none;
    animation: none;
}

.showcase img {
    height: auto;
    margin-left: -50%;
    max-width: 200%;
    width: 200%;
}
```

5. Save styles.css.

Because the product showcase shrinks a little too small on mobile devices, the first rule set, `.showcase`, increases its height and also hides any overflowing content, which works well with the changes made in the third rule set.

The second rule set, `.showcase li`, removes the cycling animation from the product showcase. Note that in Opera Mobile Emulator, the browser doesn't support animations, so the users don't see them anyway. Other browsers that do support them, such as Safari on the iPhone, don't support the animation particularly well, so that has been removed from the mobile experience.

The last rule set, `.showcase img`, makes the product images twice as wide (and thus twice as tall). It also overwrites the inhertied `max-width: 100%;` declaration, because in this case, having the image bigger than its container is desired. To keep the product image in the center, you give it a `margin-left` of –50%.

With all these styles applied that are specific to mobile devices, the mobile experience is much improved. Figure 16-6 shows how Cool Shoes & Socks looks in Opera Mobile Emulator; the logo is centered, and the navigation is much more suited to a touch device.

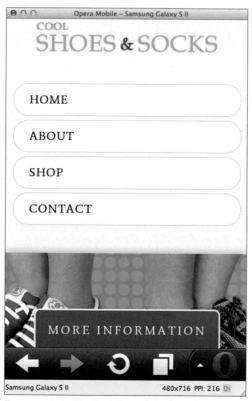

FIGURE 16-6 The Cool Shoes & Socks web page viewed in Opera Mobile Emulator with styles applied to it that are specific to mobile devices.

Figure 16-7 shows that the product showcase has been slightly modified for the mobile experience, and the content is all in one easier-to-read column.

If you rotate the device into landscape, you see the same rules still apply, but thanks to the fluid layout you built, the page stretches out to make use of the extra width, as shown in Figure 16-8.

FIGURE 16-7 The product showcase and content area.

FIGURE 16-8 The same Cool Shoes & Socks web page viewed in landscape view.

You may feel the product showcase when viewed in landscape needs tweaking, to bring the product image up a small amount, as shown in Figure 16-9.

FIGURE 16-9 The product showcase when viewed in landscape.

I personally like the slightly abstract nature of the image in this way and am happy to have it stay like that. If you want to change it, you could add another media query that targets mobile devices only when in landscape orientation, like so:

```
/* Mobile (landscape)*/
@media only screen and (max-device-width: 480px) and (orientation:
  landscape) {
    .showcase img {
       margin-left: -25%;
       width: 150%;
    }
}
```

 Project files update (ch16-01): If you haven't followed the previous instructions and are comfortable working from here onward or would like to reference the project files up to this point, you can download them from `www.wiley.com/go/treehouse/css3foundations`.

Media Queries for Tablets and Narrow-Size Desktop Browsers

Cool Shoes & Socks now provides a much better experience for mobile devices with a width up to 480px. The desktop experience looks great at 960px and higher, but there's still a gap between 480px and 960px that may need some additional styles. This gap covers tablet devices in addition to desktop experience when the browser is narrower than 960px.

Let's start with the desktop browser below 960px. In Figure 16-10, the browser window has been reduced to a width of 800px.

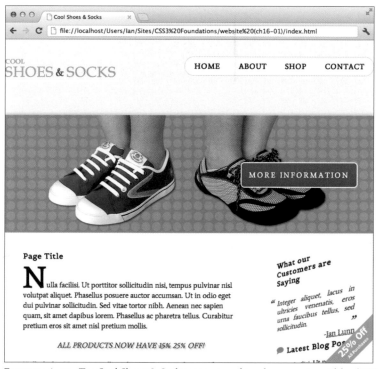

FIGURE 16-10 The Cool Shoes & Socks page viewed in a browser at a width of 800px.

For the most part, the normal desktop experience is sufficient, although notice that the logo and navigation in the header touch the sides of the browser window. You can change that:

1. At the bottom of styles.css, add the following @media rule:

```
/*viewport 960px and below*/
@media only screen and (max-width: 960px) {
    #header {
        padding: 0 40px;
    }
}
```

2. Save styles.css.

This media query applies to screen devices where the viewport width is 960px or less. Because the maximum width of the website is 960px, whenever the browser window is equal to or less than that, the header has some space on either side of it.

Now, what if the width of the browser window is reduced even more? Figure 16-11 shows that at a width of 700px, the navigation and logo no longer have enough space to sit aside each other. The content and sidebar sitting side by side are also starting to look a little cramped.

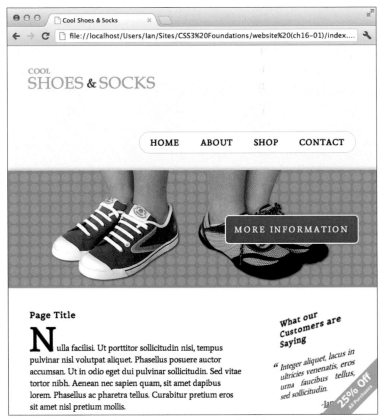

FIGURE 16-11 The Cool Shoes & Socks page viewed in a browser at a width of 700px.

The point where the navigation moves down below the logo is at about 710px; this point can be determined by resizing the window slowly or by using a tool such as responsivepx (www.responsivepx.com). This is known as a breakpoint. You could add a few styles to change the layout of the navigation at 710px or below, but because the content area starts to get too squashed as this point, a better approach would be to adopt a similar layout to the mobile layout.

Rather than write another @media rule and lots more styles, adapt the @media rule that was written for mobile devices.

3. In styles.css, find the following @media rule:

```
/* Mobile (portrait and landscape)*/
@media only screen and (max-device-width: 480px)
```

4. Change that @media rule and the comment that describes its purpose to the following:

```
/* Mobile (portrait and landscape) and viewports up to
a 735px width */
@media only screen and (max-width: 735px) {
```

When you change the last query to max-width: 735px, the mobile layout applies to mobile devices and viewports equal to or below a width of 735px. Although it was determined that the breakpoint of the navigation was at 710px, the navigation got a bit too close to the logo, so it's been increased to 735px.

The mobile layout disabled the animation on the product showcase, which is undesired, so make another @media rule specific to mobile devices only and move the showcase rule sets into that.

5. From the @media rule @media only screen and (max-width: 735px), remove the following:

```
.showcase {
    height: 200px;
    overflow: hidden;
}

.showcase li {
    -webkit-animation: none;
    -moz-animation: none;
    -ms-animation: none;
    -o-animation: none;
    animation: none;
}

.showcase img {
    height: auto;
    margin-left: -50%;
    max-width: 200%;
    width: 200%;
}
```

6. Above @media only screen and (max-width: 735px), add the following:

```
/* Mobile (portrait and landscape) */
@media only screen and (max-device-width: 480px) {
```

```
.showcase {
    height: 200px;
    overflow: hidden;
}

.showcase li {
    -webkit-animation: none;
    -moz-animation: none;
    -ms-animation: none;
    -o-animation: none;
    animation: none;
}

.showcase img {
    height: auto;
    margin-left: -50%;
    max-width: 200%;
    width: 200%;
}
}
```

7. Save styles.css.

When you move the showcase rule sets out of the @media rule that applies to mobile devices and viewports up to a width of 735px, the slideshow begins animating again in desktop browsers (where browsers support CSS3 animations). To keep it from working on mobile devices, you then add an @media rule specific to mobile again.

With the desktop experience below a viewport width of 735px now taking on the mobile layout, the newsletter box looks a little stretched, as shown in Figure 16-12, so you can change that.

8. At the bottom of styles.css, add the following:

```
/* viewport between 480px and 735px */
@media only screen and (min-width: 480px) and (max-width:
  735px) {
    #newsletter {
        margin: 0 auto;
        width: 50%;
    }
}
```

This rule causes the newsletter box to be 50% wide when the viewport is between a width of 480px and 735px.

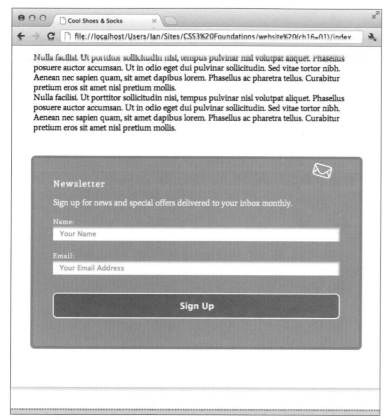

FIGURE 16-12 The newsletter box is a little too stretched when viewed in a browser window at 700px.

Summary

In this chapter, you made the final changes to Cool Shoes & Socks, and you now have a web page that is responsive and adapts to present itself in the best possible way for the particular device it is being viewed on!

At times, you may question why media queries are necessary when mobile browsers attempt to automatically scale web pages for better user experience, but as time goes on and many more differing devices are released, media queries will truly show their strength. Implementing them now doesn't just future proof a web page; it offers a superior experience for your users, too.

chapter seventeen
Final Steps and Conclusion

COOL SHOES & SOCKS is now a truly modern web page. It looks and functions great both on mobile and desktop devices and, with the approach you've taken, should stand the test of time, continuing to be a great page as technology and devices advance. Of course, because it is only one page, you will almost certainly want to create more. The page you created throughout *CSS3 Foundations* makes for a great template that you can easily duplicate and modify for existing pages.

Project files update (ch17-00): If you haven't followed the previous instructions and are comfortable working from here onward or would like to reference the project files up to this point, you can download them from www.wiley.com/go/treehouse/css3foundations.

Final Steps

When you're happy with the site, what's next? The page will need some final adjustments to get it ready to show the world!

Removing Production Code and Preparing to Go Live

In Chapter 2, I mentioned that all styles should be placed in one stylesheet where possible. This step is optional but one that can improve the performance of a web page. Cool Shoes & Socks consists of four stylesheets: reset.css, styles-ie.css, styles-ie7.css, and styles.css. Because styles-ie.css and styles-ie7.css are conditional stylesheets, they have to stay separate, but you can combine reset.css and styles.css.

1. In styles.css, find the following @import rule and delete it:

   ```
   @import url("reset.css");
   ```

2. Open reset.css, highlight all the styles, and copy them.

3. In styles.css, paste the copied reset.css styles where the @import rule was located.

4. Save styles.css.

   Now that the reset styles are included in styles.css, you can minify them. Minifying is also optional but good for performance. Minifying a stylesheet causes all spaces to be removed from that file, reducing the file size—so it can be downloaded faster—and making it easier for a browser to read.

   Many minifying tools are available, but my personal recommendation is www.cssminify.net, which is one of the easiest and quickest to use.

5. Create a new file, call it styles.min.css, and save it in the css folder.

6. In styles.css, highlight all the styles and copy them.

7. In your browser, navigate to www.cssminify.net.

8. In the text area on the www.cssminify.net site, paste the styles from styles.css.

9. From the Compression drop-down menu, select Highest and click Minify.

   When you click Minify, spaces and returns are stripped out of the styles in the text area.

10. Highlight and copy all the minified styles from the text area.

11. Return to styles.min.css and paste the minified styles.

12. Save styles.min.css.

    Now that you have a minified version of styles.css, index.html needs to reference it.

13. In index.html, find the reference to styles.css and change it to reference styles.min.css:

    ```
    <!--[if ! lte IE 6]><!--><link rel="stylesheet"
    href="css/styles.min.css" type="text/css" /><![endif]-->
    ```

14. Save index.html.

Cool Shoes & Socks now uses the minified styles from styles.min.css instead of the production styles found in styles.css.

Testing, Testing, Testing

In Chapter 15, you prepared Cool Shoes & Socks to begin modifying it with media queries. Having modified the site in this chapter and Chapter 16, you should test it again to be doubly sure it is cross browser compatible. Although testing can sometimes be tiresome, it is a very important step and should be your last step before making a page live for everybody to see.

Going Live! Uploading to a Web Server

When you're satisfied that a web page is cross browser compatible, to make it live, you need to upload it to a web server, most commonly done using FTP software.

Many text editors nowadays come with built-in FTP software, and if this is the case, consult the instructions provided with your text editor to set it up. Alternatively, dedicated FTP programs are available, some free and some paid.

My recommendations are Cyberduck (`www.cyberduck.ch`) and FileZilla (`www.filezilla-project.org`), both free and both available on Mac and Windows.

If you choose to use one of these FTP clients, see the documentation made available on its website for instructions on how to use it.

The Future Web

With Cool Shoes & Socks, you created a page suited not just to the modern web but also the future web. Its robust, responsive layout will make it appear and function great across many different types of devices now and in the future. Will CSS offer anything more for the future, though? Of course!

Because the CSS3 specification is still being modified, you will be able to use many new technologies in the near future. Here are a couple:

- Filter Effects (`http://dvcs.w3.org/hg/FXTF/raw-file/tip/filters/index.html`), which changes the style of an image similar to what you can do in photo-editing applications such as Adobe Photoshop.

- Flexible Box Layout (`www.w3.org/TR/css3-flexbox/`) and Regions (`http://dev.w3.org/csswg/css3-regions/`), which make laying out a page easier and more robust.

What's more, work has already started on new CSS modules, which propose new selectors and media features, with no doubt lots more exciting goodies on the way, too!

The web is a fascinating technology to be a part of. And now styling beautiful content is easier than ever. If you can dream it, you can create it.

Index

box model
    applying borders to make elements visible, 129
    box-sizing property for, 136–139
    developer tools for understanding, 129–130
    invisible nature of, 128
    padding affecting, 127–128
    relationship between content, padding,
        borders, and margins, 128–129
    width calculations complicated by, 134–136
box-shadow property, 91–93, 274
box-sizing property
    border-box value of, 137–139
    content-box value of, 136–137, 139
    key information for, 136
browsers. See also testing across multiple
    browsers; vendor prefixes; specific kinds
    advanced selector compatibility issues for, 48
    author's preferences, 10–11
    CSS3 support among, 10
    desktop usage statistics for, 12
    developer tools for, 11, 15–17
    handling older versions, 14–15
    layout engines for, 11
    major ones available now, 10
    market share by version number, 13
    mobile/tablet usage statistics for, 12
    narrow, media queries for, 307–311
    older versions on the web, 12–15
    property compatibility issues for, 78
    user agent stylesheets applied by, 33–34
button class, 47, 51

C

call to action (CTA), 27, 47
Candidate Recommendation stage of modules, 9
capitalize value of text-transform
    property, 211
cascade
    defined, 61
    !important rule overriding, 61–62
    points system for, 60–61
Cascading Style Sheets. See CSS
center value
    background-position property, 97
    position property (not yet implemented),
        162, 177
    text-align property, 213, 214
centering
    background images, 97
    fixed-width layouts, 119

position: center property (not yet
    implemented), 162, 177
text-align property for, 213–214
vertical, Fake Table Cells technique for,
    177–179
vertical, 50% Top Minus Half the Elements
    Height technique for, 181–183
vertical, Stretched Element technique for,
    179–181
vertical-align property for, 175–177
.cf class, .group class versus, 149
:checked( ) pseudo-class, 57
child combinators, 49
child elements
    defined, 45
    in drop-down menus, 154–155
    inheritance by, 44
    taking out of flow, 154–155
China, old browsers in, 13
Chrome browser
    animation-play-state property bug
        in, 262
    author's preference for, 10–11
    color picker for, 66
    desktop market share of, 12
    developer tools for, 16, 129–130
    download site for, 10
    market share by version number, 13
    user agent stylesheet of, 33
    Webkit engine used by, 11
Clark, Andy, 287
class naming conventions, 47
class selectors
    attribute selectors versus, 50
    ID selectors versus, 47
    replacing :nth-child( ) pseudo-class,
        282–283
    specificity of, 47
    using, 47
clear property
    adjusting multicolumns using, 147–150
    with float property, 143–144
    key information for, 143
    micro clearfix hack, 149–150
.clearfix class, .group class versus, 149
colon (:)
    for pseudo-classes, 52
    for pseudo-elements (:: or :), 58
color keywords, 47, 63–64
color media feature, 300
color pickers, 66

cycling image animation *(continued)*
   `animation-iteration-count` property for, 260
   `animation-name` property for, 258
   `animation-play-state` property for, 262
   `animation-timing-function` property for, 259
   creating, 264–266
   `fadeOut` rule for, 257, 258, 263, 264, 265
   `@keyframes` rule for, 256–257
   pausing on hover, 262
   removing on mobile devices, 303, 310
   setup for, 253–256, 264

D

`dashed` border style, 82
declarations
   multiple per rule set, 42–43
   in rule sets, 41, 42
   semicolon ending, 42
dependent files, separating from main HTML files, 21
descendant combinators, 48–49
descendant elements, 44–45. *See also* child elements
design. *See also* structure
   adaptive, 123–124
   fixed-width layouts, 117–119
   fluid-width layouts, 117, 118
   hybrid layouts, 120–123
   mobile first, 125
   responsive, 123, 125
developer tools
   for adding vendor prefixes, 80
   box model aids, 129–130
   Element Inspector, 72
   for linear gradients, 102
   similarity among browsers, 11
   summary of desktop tools, 15–17
   text editors, 17–18
Device Adaptation module, 293
`device-aspect-ratio` media feature, 299–300
`device-height` media feature, 299
devices. *See also* Media Queries module; media types; mobile devices; `@media` rules
   CSS2 allowing for differences in, 9
   Device Adaptation module, 293
   displaying fonts not installed on, 192–194
   variety accessing the web, 5
`device-width` media feature, 298

`direction` property, 213
directory structure, 20–22
`:disabled( )` pseudo-class, 56, 57
`display` property
   `block` value of, 155–156, 170
   `inline` value of, 157–158, 159, 161
   `inline-block` value of, 159–161
   key information for, 155
   `list-item` value of, 158, 161
   `none` value of, 110, 161
   overview, 155–161
   `table` value of, 161, 178
   `table-cell` value of, 178
`<!DOCTYPE html>` declaration, 25, 30
document, defined, 153
document flow
   `display` property's affect on, 155–161
   normal, 153–154
   `position` property's affect on, 162–168
   taking an element out of flow, 154–155, 164
   `z-index` property for elements out of flow, 171, 174
dot (.)
   classes represented by, 47
   two dots in relative URIs, 95
`dotted` border style, 82
`double` border style, 82
downloading
   browsers, 11
   Firebug add-on for Firefox, 17
   Opera Mobile Emulator, 290
   project files, 20
drop shadows
   `box-shadow` property for, 91–93, 274
   `text-shadow` property for, 211–212
drop-down menu
   borders for, 170, 171, 173
   hiding on mobile devices, 302
   hover settings for, 169
   HTML for, 169
   padding for, 170, 171
   `position: absolute` property for, 154, 170, 171
   `position: relative` property for, 172–173
   taking child elements out of flow for, 154–155
   unordered list styles for, 170–171
   `visibility` properties for, 173
   `z-index` setting for, 171, 174
dynamic pseudo-classes, 52–53

horizontal scroll bars, avoiding, 118–119

hot linking, avoiding, 95

hover
    banner ad size change on, 247–248, 249–250, 252
    cursor appearance change on, 111
    drop-down menu settings, 169, 173
    element appearance change on, 52
    pausing cycling image animation on, 262
    sidebar movement toward viewer on, 238
    visibility change on, 173

`:hover( )` pseudo-class, 52, 169

`href` link values, hash symbol for, 22

HSL and HSLA color values, 68, 69

HTML (Hypertext Markup Language)
    for drop-down menu, 169
    empty element as multicolumn fix, 148
    `<footer>` listing, 28
    `<head>` listing, 26
    `<header>` listing, 26–27
    inline styles using, 32
    knowledge required for this book, 1
    list of elements inline by default, 157
    product showcase listing, 27
    sidebar listing, 27–28
    web page template (index.html) listing, 22–29

hybrid layouts, 121–123

hyphen, adding with `:before( )` pseudo-element, 112–113

I

ID selectors, 46–47

IDs, 47

`if` condition for comments, 284–285, 286

images. *See also* background images; cycling image animation
    `background-image` property for, 43, 44, 98–99
    border, 86–91
    floating, 142–143
    hot linking, avoiding, 95
    moving in 2D, 225–227
    moving in 3D, 235–239
    naming conventions for, 22
    replacing text with, 107–108
    rotating in 2D, 227–228, 230
    rotating in 3D, 239–241
    scaling in 2D, 228
    scaling in 3D, 241–243
    skewing, 228–229

`@import` rules
    for CSS Reset, 35, 314
    performance impact of, 31
    stylesheets referenced by, 30–31

`!important` rule, 61–62

indenting text, 215

index.html. *See* web page template

inheritance
    by descendant elements, 44–45
    element relationships in, 44–45
    em units affected by, 72–73
    `none` keyword for removing styles, 82
    of properties, 44, 78

initial value of properties, 78

inline styles, 32

`inline` value of `display` property
    changing navigation links to, 158
    elements inline by default, 157
    `inline-block` value compared to, 159, 161
    properties affecting layout not usable with, 157
    size of element with, 157

`inline-block` value of `display` property
    browser support issues for, 161
    changing navigation links to, 159–160
    dimensional properties usable with, 159
    `inline` value compared to, 159, 161
    white space separating elements, 159, 160

`inset` border style, 82

Inspect Element feature. *See* Element Inspector

installing
    Firebug add-on for Firefox, 17
    Opera Mobile Emulator, 290

Internet Explorer browser. *See also specific versions*
    avoiding for web page creation, 11
    color picker for, 66
    desktop market share of, 12
    developer tools for, 17
    download site for, 10
    `filter` property, 99, 275
    `@font-face` first implemented by, 192, 193
    market share by version number, 13
    Trident engine used by, 11
    vendor prefix for, 80

Internet Explorer 6
    Asian market share of, 13
    attribute selectors not supported in, 50
    border images not supported by, 86
    `box-sizing` property not supported by, 138
    conditional comments for, 283–286
    CSS gradients not supported by, 99

Internet Explorer 6 *(continued)*
    CSS implementation in, 13
    CSS3 properties not safe for, 78
    deprecation of, 13
    desktop market share of, 13
    `display: inline-block` not
      supported by, 161
    general sibling combinators not supported
      in, 50
    handling compatibility for, 15
    language pseudo-class not supported by, 57
    negation pseudo-class not supported by, 58
    as old browser, 13
    `position: fixed` not supported by, 167
    structural pseudo-classes not supported by,
      55, 56
    UI element states pseudo-classes not
      supported by, 57
    Universal Internet Explorer 6 Stylesheet,
      287–288
Internet Explorer 7
    border images not supported by, 86
    `box-sizing` property not supported by, 138
    conditional comments for, 283–286
    CSS gradients not supported by, 99
    CSS implementation in, 13
    CSS3 properties not safe for, 78
    desktop market share of, 13
    `display: inline-block` not
      supported by, 161
    language pseudo-class not supported by, 57
    negation pseudo-class not supported by, 58
    as old browser, 13
    structural pseudo-classes not supported by,
      55, 56
    UI element states pseudo-classes not
      supported by, 57
Internet Explorer 8
    border images not supported by, 86
    conditional comments for, 283–286
    CSS gradients not supported by, 99
    CSS implementation in, 13
    CSS3 properties not safe for, 78
    desktop market share of, 13
    as old browser, 13
    Select element by click feature, 130
    structural pseudo-classes not supported by,
      55, 56
    testing in, 280–283
    UI element states pseudo-classes not
      supported by, 57
    Windows XP restricted to, 13

Internet Explorer 9
    availability of, 13
    border images not supported by, 86
    CSS gradients not supported by, 99
    desktop market share of, 13
    testing in, 280
    user agent stylesheet of, 33–34
Internet Explorer 10
    availability of, 11
    testing in, 277–280
`italic` value of `font-style` property, 200

J

JavaScript
    Selectivizr tool for advanced selectors, 283
    for third-party font display, 194
`justify` value of `text-align` property,
    213, 214

K

keyframe animations
    `animation` property (shorthand), 263,
      264, 265
    `animation-delay` property, 260, 265
    `animation-direction` property,
      260–261
    `animation-duration` property,
      258–259
    `animation-fill-mode` property,
      262–263
    `animation-iteration-count`
      property, 260
    `animation-name` property, 258
    `animation-play-state` property,
      261–262
    `animation-timing-function`
      property, 259
    `fadeOut` rule, 257, 258, 263, 264, 265
    `@keyframes` rule, 256–257
    setup for examples, 253–256, 264
    transitions compared to, 247, 253
`@keyframes` rule, 256–257

L

landscape orientation in mobile devices, 306
language pseudo-class (`:lang( )`), 57–58
Last Call stage of modules, 9
`:last-child( )` pseudo-class, 55
`:last-of-type( )` pseudo-class, 56
"Latest Blog Post" element overflow, 183–186

@media rules, *(continued)*
  monochrome media feature, 300
  orientation media feature, 299
  for print stylesheets, 32
  resolution media feature, 300
  scan media feature, 300
  for screen devices, 294–295
  for tablets and narrow-size desktop browsers, 307–311
  width media feature, 296–297
media types
  further information, 289
  introduction in CSS2, 9
  Media Queries module building on, 8, 9
  stylesheets applied to, 31–32
medium border width, 83
menu, drop-down. *See* drop-down menu
Meyer, Eric (CSS Reset creator), 34, 35
micro clearfix hack, 149–150
Microsoft Internet Explorer. *See* Internet Explorer browser
middle value of vertical-align property, 175, 176
minifying styles.css, 314
mobile devices. *See also* Media Queries module; media types; @media rules
  browser usage statistics for, 12
  designing first for, 125
  font-size property values for, 204–205
  hiding drop-down menu on, 302
  landscape orientation in, 306
  Opera Mobile Emulator for, 289–292
  position: fixed not generally supported by, 167
  removing multicolumn layout for, 301, 302
  scaling the viewport on, 292–294
mobile first design, 125
Mobile Web Application Best Practices, 293
modularity, as purpose of classes, 47
monochrome media feature, 300
monospace generic font name, 190
More Information button
  Fake Table Cells vertical-centering technique, 177–179
  50% Top Minus Half the Elements Height vertical-centering technique, 181–183
  font-weight: bolder property for, 201–202
  as inline element, 158
  letter-spacing property for, 212–213
  linear gradient for, 100–101, 102

position: absolute property for, 164–165
positioning relative to showcase image, 165–166
Stretched Element vertical-centering technique, 179–181
taking out of flow, 163–164
transform: skewX( ) property for, 229
move cursor style, 111
-moz- vendor prefix. *See also* vendor prefixes
  browsers applicable for, 80
  for linear gradients, 100, 101
  for transform and 2D transform functions, 224
Mozilla Firefox. *See* Firefox browser
-ms- vendor prefix. *See also* vendor prefixes
  browsers applicable for, 80
  for transform and 2D transform functions, 224
multicolumn layout
  clear property for, 143–144, 147–150
  creating, 145–151
  empty HTML element as fix for, 148
  Flexbox and Regions modules for (Working Draft), 141, 315
  float property for, 141, 142–143, 145–146, 151
  .group class for, 149–150
  hacks needed for, 141, 146
  for logo and navigation links in header, 151
  micro clearfix hack for, 149–150
  removing on mobile devices, 301, 302
  specifying main container height for, 147

N

naming conventions
  for classes, 47
  for images, 22
  for project files, 20, 22
navigation links
  changing display property from inline to inline-block, 159–160
  changing display property from list-item to inline, 158
  floating header links to the right, 151
  in <footer> section, 28
  hash symbol href values for, 22
  in <header> section, 27
negation pseudo-class [:not( )], 57–58
ne-resize cursor style, 111
newsletter box
  background image for, 96, 97
  background-clip property for, 103–104

text-shadow property, 211–212
text-top value of vertical-align property, 176, 177
text-transform property, 210–211
thick border width, 83
thin border width, 83
third-party font services
    display techniques for, 194
    Fontdeck, 198
    Google Web Fonts, 194–197
    Typekit, 198
3D transforms
    backface-visibility property for, 245–246
    Internet Explorer 10 issues for, 278–280
    overriding on mobile devices, 303
    perspective property for 3D space, 234, 274
    perspective-origin property for 3D space, 235
    rotateX( ), rotateY( ), rotateZ( ), and rotate3d( ) functions for, 239–241, 244, 245
    scaleZ( ) and scale3d( ) functions for, 241–243
    transform-style property for, 243–244
    translateZ( ) and translate3d( ) functions for, 235–239
    using multiple functions for, 243
top value
    background-position property, 97
    position property, 162, 163
    vertical-align property, 176, 177
transform property
    2D transform functions, 225–230
    3D transform functions, 235–243
    key information for, 224
    matrix( ) function with, 230
    overriding transforms on mobile devices, 303
    rotate( ) function with, 227–228
    rotateX( ), rotateY( ), rotateZ( ), and rotate3d( ) functions with, 239–241, 244, 245
    scale( ), scaleX( ), and scaleY( ) functions with, 228
    scaleZ( ) and scale3d( ) functions with, 241–243
    skewX( ), and skewY( ) functions with, 228–229
    transition-property property with, 248–249

translate( ), translateX( ), and translateY( ) functions with, 225–227, 231, 243, 244
    translateZ( ) and translate3d( ) functions with, 235–239
    using multiple functions with, 243
    vendor prefixes for, 224
transform-origin property
    for banner ad, 231–232
    key information for, 230
    rotate transform example, 230
transform-style property, 243–244
transition property (shorthand), 251–252
transition-delay property, 251
transition-duration property, 249–250
transition-property property, 248–249
transitions
    banner ad size change on hover, 247–248, 249–250, 252
    keyframe animations compared to, 247, 253
    properties for, 248–252
    properties that can be animated by, 249
transition-timing-function property, 250–251
translate( ) functions with transform property
    transition-property property with, 248–249
    translate( ), translateX( ), and translateY( ), 225–227, 231, 243, 244
    translateZ( ) and translate3d( ), 235–239
transparency
    alpha, in HSLA color values, 68–69
    alpha, in RGBA color values, 67
    properties for, 94, 108–109
transparency value of background-color property, 94
Treehouse, 2
Trident browser engine, 11
TrueType Font (.ttf) format, 192
2D transforms
    matrix( ) function for, 230
    overriding on mobile devices, 303
    rotate( ) function for, 227–228
    scale( ), scaleX( ), and scaleY( ) functions for, 228
    skewX( ), and skewY( ) functions for, 228–229

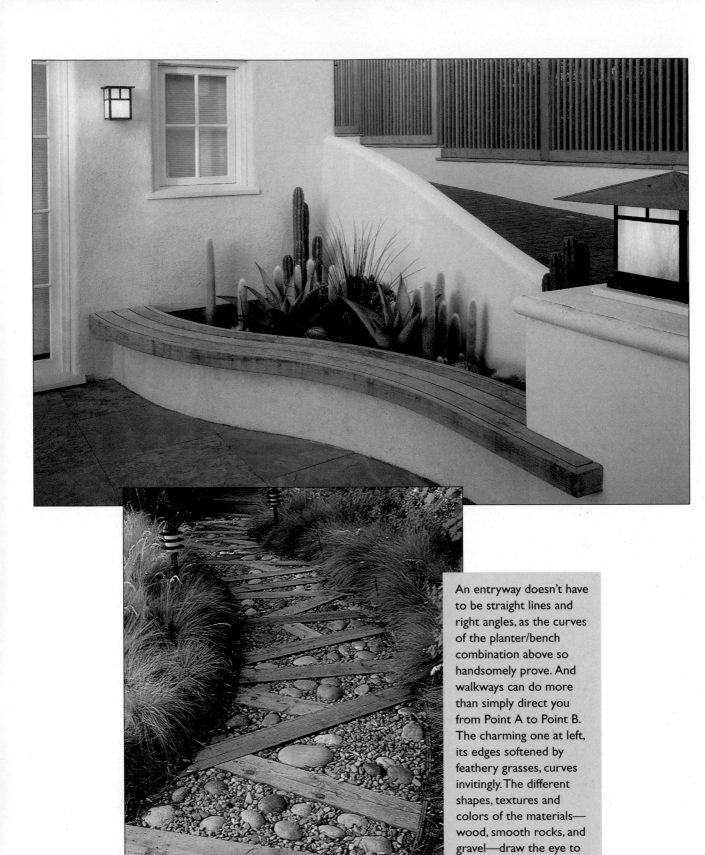

An entryway doesn't have to be straight lines and right angles, as the curves of the planter/bench combination above so handsomely prove. And walkways can do more than simply direct you from Point A to Point B. The charming one at left, its edges softened by feathery grasses, curves invitingly. The different shapes, textures and colors of the materials—wood, smooth rocks, and gravel—draw the eye to follow wherever the path may lead.

What Should Your Backyard Be?

Just outside your door is the backyard you've always dreamed of—a place where you can relax in the shade of a flowering tree or challenge the youngsters to a game of touch football. Or perhaps your ideal backyard is an intricately laid out garden where you can lose yourself in the pleasure of coaxing flowers to bloom.

All you need do is look at your backyard with fresh eyes, maybe making a few changes to your existing layout. The photos below and on the following pages are meant to inspire you with visions of the different worlds a backyard can create, and to get you thinking about how to make the yard of your dreams a living reality.

Even a sloping lot can provide a spot for outdoor dining. Here, a flagstone patio and stepped wall turn a slope into an elegant eating area, surrounded by a profusion of spring blooms. Plants on the steps help bring the garden down to the patio.
Design: Christian Kiillkkaa and Alan Counihan

Enjoying BACKYARD LIFE

Today's backyard is more than just a place where the lawn needs mowing—it is a dynamic living space, an extension of your home, where you can indulge in your favorite pastimes. Whether you prefer quiet dinner parties, friendly sports, or just whiling away the evening in a garden gazebo, your backyard can be designed for your leisure activities. The pages to come will give you a wide range of ideas for creating the environment that suits your needs, taste, and budget. You'll also discover suggestions for backyard activities, such as planning and cooking a festive summer meal with your family, or tracking the changing position of the constellations. Some backyard building projects are included, so you can experience the pleasure of shaping your environment with your own hands. It's all about enjoying your backyard to the fullest.

Built over a sparkling pool amidst tulips and magnolias, this freestanding gazebo helps create the charm of a country garden in an urban setting. Privacy is assured by a picket fence high enough to block sight lines, but not so high as to create a claustrophobic feeling.

Table of Contents

MAKING THE MOST OF
Your Own Backyard

SUNSET BOOKS

SUNSET BOOKS

President and Publisher: Susan J. Maruyama
Director, Sales & Marketing: Richard A. Smeby
Editorial Director: Bob Doyle
Production Director: Lory Day
Retail Sales Development Manager: Becky Ellis
Art Director: Vasken Guiragossian

SUNSET PUBLISHING CORPORATION

Chairman: Jim Nelson
President/Chief Executive Officer: Stephen J. Seabolt
Chief Financial Officer: James E. Mitchell
Publisher, Sunset Magazine: Anthony P. Glaves
Circulation Director: Robert I. Gursha
Director of Finance: Larry Diamond
Vice President, Manufacturing: Lorinda B. Reichert
Editor, Sunset Magazine: Rosalie Muller Wright

Making the Most of Your Own Backyard
was produced in conjunction with

ST. REMY MULTIMEDIA

President/Chief Executive Officer: Fernand Lecoq
President/Chief Operating Officer: Pierre Léveillé
Vice President, Finance: Natalie Watanabe
Managing Editor: Carolyn Jackson
Managing Art Director: Diane Denoncourt
Production Manager: Michelle Turbide

Staff for this Book:
Senior Editors: Jim McRae, Pierre Home-Douglas
Assistant Editor: Jennifer Ormston
Writers: Adam Van Sertima, Stacey Berman
Art Directors: Michel Giguère, Odette Sévigny
Designer: François Daxhelet
Picture Editor: Sonia Di Maulo
Contributing Illustrators: Gilles Beauchemin, François Longpré,
    Mark Pechenik, Jacques Perrault
Production Coordinator: Dominique Gagné
System Coordinator: Eric Beaulieu
Scanner Operators: Martin Francoeur, Sara Grynspan
Technical Support: Jean Sirois
Proofreader: Judy Yelon
Indexer: Christine M. Jacobs

Book Consultants:
Don Vandervort
Roberta Conlan
Richard Day
Normand Fleury

Cover:
Photography: Chris Shorten
Prop Stylist: Liz Ross

Note to Readers

Sunset Publishing Corporation provides no warranties of any kind, express or implied, regarding the construction and use of any of the ideas, plans, or designs discussed or illustrated in this book and shall not be responsible or liable for any injuries or damages incurred during the construction and/or use of those ideas, plans, or designs. Before building any projects from this book, check with your local building department regarding soil conditions, local codes, and required permits.

First printing July 1996
Copyright © 1996
Published by Sunset Publishing Corporation,
    Menlo Park, CA 94025.
First edition. All rights reserved, including the right
    of reproduction in whole or in part in any form.

ISBN 0-376-03077-1 (Hardcover)
ISBN 0-376-03078-X (Paperback)
Library of Congress Catalog Card Number: 96-067825
Printed in the United States

For additional copies of *Making the Most of Your Own Backyard* or any other Sunset book, call 1-800-634-3095.

MAKING THE MOST OF
Your Own Backyard

Mature apple trees frame a brick walk-way, lending their fragrance and bountiful harvest to the extensive terraced yard at left. The symmetry of the walkway's herringbone pattern sets off the clipped hedges of the formal garden at the base of the slope. A freestanding gazebo like the one below offers a quiet retreat from the world, inviting you to take a moment to relax and enjoy the view.

Taking full advantage of a sloping hillside, this multilevel red-wood deck makes the most of a riverside view, with ample room for entertaining, dining, or just soaking up the sun. Built-in benches offer plenty of seating, and planters bring a touch of garden color to the deck.

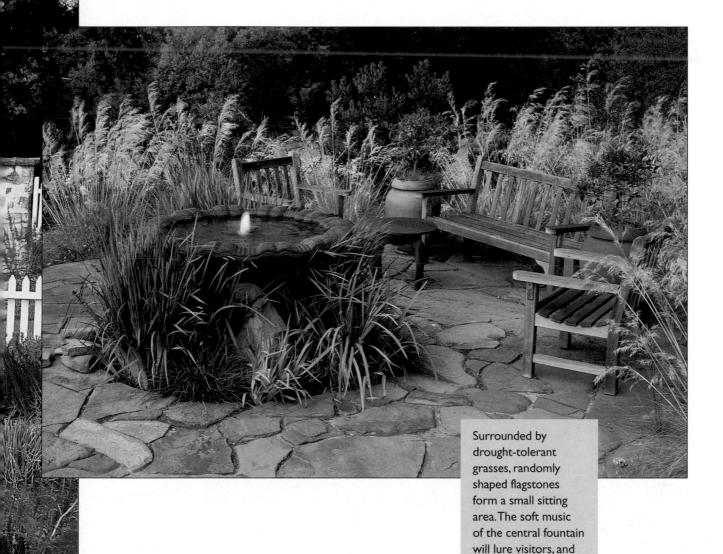

Surrounded by drought-tolerant grasses, randomly shaped flagstones form a small sitting area. The soft music of the central fountain will lure visitors, and the comfortable, weathered outdoor furniture entices them to stay.
Landscape architect: Katzmaier Newell Kehr

Flowering plants and culinary herbs grow together in a profusion of color and fragrance in this cottage garden. The structure provided by the central sundial and paved paths complement the soft, natural plantings and keep the garden from looking unkempt.

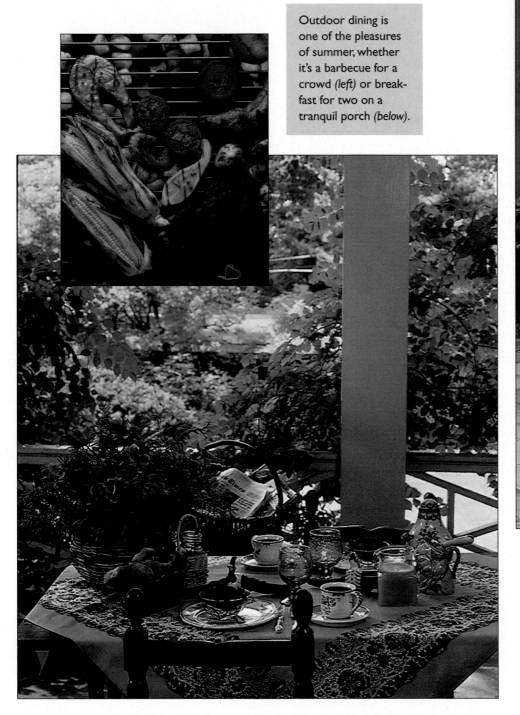

Outdoor dining is
one of the pleasures
of summer, whether
it's a barbecue for a
crowd *(left)* or break-
fast for two on a
tranquil porch *(below)*.

A patio or deck
next to the
house can help
make the transi-
tion from indoors
to outdoors. Tiled
in earthy tones to
match the house,
the patio above
is a welcoming
space where col-
orful squash and
potted plants add
a fall touch.

14

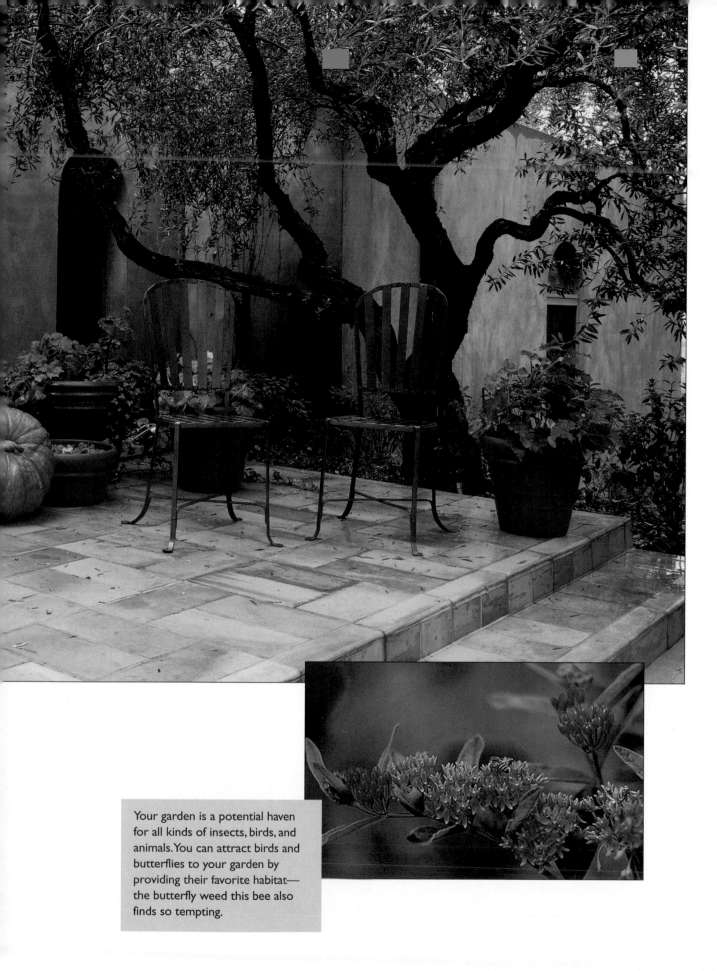

Your garden is a potential haven for all kinds of insects, birds, and animals. You can attract birds and butterflies to your garden by providing their favorite habitat—the butterfly weed this bee also finds so tempting.

This curving brick wall appears to both hold back the lawn and enclose the wood deck. Built of a combination of used bricks and flashed bricks (a process that adds color tones) with occasional stones thrown in, the wall gains informal charm from the mixed vertical and horizontal placement of the bricks.
Landscape architect: Woodward Dike

What could be more inviting after a long, hot day than a dip in a cool, blue pool? The stepped edge of the patio and the angled corner of the pool above add interest to an otherwise square yard. Youngsters who love to climb and swing will spend hours on a play structure such as the one at left. A small dedicated area of the yard adapts well to either a build-it-yourself or a manufactured set.

Elements of Today's Backyard

For many, the backyard has come to symbolize peace and quiet—a family-centered space that is a haven from the outside world. But the backyard can also be a place to entertain dinner guests, to play games and sports, and to welcome your neighbors and friends.

To enjoy all these aspects of backyard life, you'll have to juggle a variety of needs that may seem, at first glance, to be in conflict with each other. This problem can often be solved by designating areas of your yard for different functions, and then separating them from each other physically or visually—or both.

On the opposite page, you'll find a sample yard illustrating one possible arrangement of some common backyard features. Of course, the elements you choose will depend on the size and shape of your lot, and what you want to do in it.

A central element of many backyards is a patio or a deck—either attached to the house or a freestanding structure. A gazebo or overhead can provide shade, and a pool or garden pond brings charm and sparkle. Shrubs and trees, raised planting beds, and vegetable gardens can all be integrated into your yard, whether as a focal point or tucked inconspicuously into a corner.

Whatever your particulars, the four principles on page 20 will help you create a satisfying design and, for ideas for how to handle an oddly shaped lot, turn to page 22.

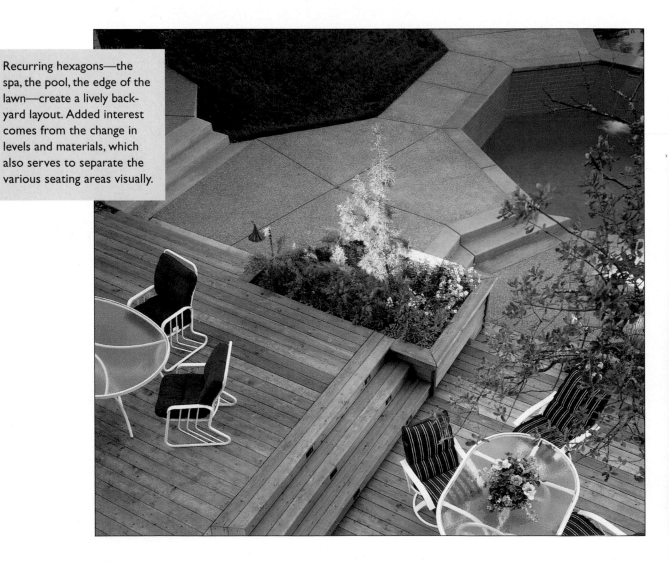

Recurring hexagons—the spa, the pool, the edge of the lawn—create a lively backyard layout. Added interest comes from the change in levels and materials, which also serves to separate the various seating areas visually.

A SAMPLE BACKYARD

Illustrated here are some of the structural and planting elements you might want in your backyard. This plan is just one possible arrangement, designed for a specific site. What you include in your backyard, and how you organize it, depends on your own circumstances. For more information on any of the elements shown, turn to the pages listed.

Centrally located on the patio, close to both the deck and the more private leisure area in the back corner, this barbecue pit does double duty: When it's not in use, it can be covered with a low table that's ideal for games or buffet-style dining. For more barbecuing ideas, including grilling tips and recipes, turn to page 24.

A backyard pool provides the perfect haven for swimming and escaping the heat. See page 108 for more pool ideas.

A shaded, secluded leisure area is created by well-maintained hedges and a tall deciduous tree. For information on trees and shrubs, turn to page 181.

The extensive paving unifies the area and requires a minimum of maintenance. To install pavers or other patio materials, turn to page 238.

Even an open overhead like this one can provide welcome shade. For more overhead options, turn to page 298.

Small, manageable patches of lawn provide cushioned play areas, and soften the edges of the lot. For tips on lawn choices and maintenance, see page 174.

This freestanding deck offers space away from the house for dining and relaxing. Instructions for building a low-level deck begin on page 268.

Shade-loving plantings thrive under trees. To choose the right plants for your situation, turn to page 210.

Privacy is ensured with fences that enclose the lot. If you need a fence or screen, turn to page 288.

Planting the vegetable garden close to the house means it's easily accessed for maintenance and harvesting, and doesn't interfere with the main yard area. You'll find gardening information on page 198.

Designing Like a Professional

A well-designed yard is an irresistible lure: you stroll out into it, relax in the shade of its trees, or play in its open expanses. The design that's right for you will not only provide spaces for the outdoor activities that you enjoy—quiet relaxation, family games, or dining and entertaining—but also combine these spaces in an appealing way. The following design principles will help you achieve a pleasing layout.

Order: The design should provide a framework or structure to the physical space, organizing it in a logical way to accommodate a range of activities. Visual order also plays a role; the views, lines, property configuration and circulation patterns must work together.

Dominance: To create dominance in a landscape, you can introduce focal points or specimens–an interesting tree, a bench, or a sculpture.

ILLUSTRATED PRINCIPLES

These illustrations show the four design principles in action–and what the yard might look like if these principles are not considered.

Designs: Timothy N. Thoelecke Jr., APLD, ASLA
Garden Concepts, Inc.

Order
In the design at left, there's a logic to the layout. The patio's two distinct areas could be used for multiple activities (perhaps an eating area and a sunning area), and the substantial lawn is available for games or other activities. By contrast, in the same-size lot at right, the plants have been located haphazardly, breaking the lawn up into unusable pockets.

House

Dominance
The specimen tree at the end of the view from the patio (upper right) creates a focal point and links the yard to the house. The specimen is framed by the plantings next to the patio, helping to draw the eye and keeping the viewer's gaze from going beyond the yard.

view

Focal points can be used to create links between different activity areas, and to lead the eye from one part of the yard to another, creating a feeling of movement. More than one dominant feature is possible, but each should dominate a different space or view.

Unity: In a unified landscape, all the elements work together. Strong, observable lines and the repetition of geometric shapes contribute to a sense of unity, as does simplicity—for example, using just a few harmonizing colors in the structural elements and the plantings.

Balance: The design doesn't need to be symmetrical, but the elements should provide the same visual weight on either side of a center of interest. For example, you can balance a mature tree on one side of your pool with perimeter benches on the other.

Unity
The repetition of elements and shapes, and the reduction of competing elements, creates a unified design; geometric shapes are easier to work with than free-form patterns. In the lot at left, plantings are grouped in masses and placed to emphasize the zigzag border of the yard. Below, where the plantings are randomly scattered, there is no sense of connectedness between the planted elements, and even the geometric shapes of the lawn and patio seem less related to each other.

Balance
Asymmetrical balance is the goal of most landscape design. Balance can be achieved with symmetry, but it may look static and contrived. In the lot above, the plantings, although not symmetrical, provide equal visual weight on each side of the yard. The lot at right, by contrast, is severely unbalanced.

Making Your Space Work for You

One of the secrets of landscaping is knowing how to change a liability into an asset. This is especially useful in designing for a lot that is small, or unpromisingly shaped. Even in the most awkward situation, artful landscaping can do wonders. It can create outdoor areas that, besides being functional, offer strong visual appeal, a sense of increased space, and pleasing elements of surprise.

Below and opposite are examples of how to make the best use of space on four typically shaped lots. Thoughtfully landscaped with both structural and planting elements, the designs work with the space, emphasizing some features and downplaying others. Using a combination of basic geometric shapes, such as circles, squares, and rectangles, allows the designer to soften and modify the overall shape of the lot, and to draw the eye toward areas of interest. The arrows on the drawings indicate the way a viewer's attention is directed around the yard by various features.

Landscape designs: Roy Rydell

SOLUTIONS FOR CHALLENGING SPACES

Pie-shaped lot
The challenge of this lot, which offers maximum privacy at the back and sides, is how best to use the generous but irregularly shaped space. In the backyard, three separate areas have been established around the living room wing, which projects into the main garden; two circular lawns, ringed by trees, and a semicircular paved patio off the living room that leads to a gazebo. In one corner near the house there is space for a small vegetable garden.

Square lot
On a square lot, the roughly rectangular space often remaining for outside use can be pleasantly modified by group plantings and structures with contrasting configurations. An oval-shaped lawn artfully varies the angular lines of the lot and house. For variety, two areas of interest are faced off at either end of the yard. Toward the left on leaving the house, a circle of "trees" with high-pruned trunks conceals a private glade. The trees are actually deciduous shrubs of vertical growth habit, planted closely enough together to encourage them to reach up for light. At the opposite end is a small greenhouse.

Greenhouse

Long, narrow lot

One way to minimize the narrowness of this type of lot is to divide the space into two distinct offset areas, as shown here. Closest to the rear terrace of the house (below) is a circular expanse of lawn, framed by a partial square of trees backed against the lot lines. The eye follows the S-curved stepping-stone path from the first backyard area to the somewhat separated second area, complete with swimming pool, covered poolside shelter, and a fairly large vegetable plot in the far corner. Off the master bedroom (top), a small terrace, screened by high shrubs, offers a private retreat.

Small terrace

"Court"

Front entrance

Extremely shallow lot

To use this kind of lot to best advantage, manipulate space visually by placing the outdoor living areas at either end. In this plan, the entryway is expansive and welcoming: Low walls, hedges, and small trees surrounding small paved terraces beside the front entrance create areas for family use in the front of the house, and balance the more open areas in the backyard. An atrium-like court serves as a green core for the entire yard because of its small, tree-ringed circular lawn. From here, the eye is drawn to a gazebo at the far right corner, and to an arbor-covered, built-in bench at the left. A vegetable garden occupies the south-facing side of the house.

Outdoor Cooking and Dining

Dining outdoors seems to sharpen the appetite and add spice to even the simplest of meals. While dinner served in the backyard can also feature quite elaborate dishes, the informal mood of an outdoor party eases the burden on the hosts. But make no mistake about it—a formal dinner gains extra cachet when served beneath a garden marquee or under a summer night's starry sky. The center of most outdoor dining is the barbecue grill. Barbecuing exists in all cultures in some form, since it is just one step from cooking over a simple, open fire. Mediterranean cooking, for example, with its kebabs and seafood dishes, adds an accessibly exotic approach to backyard menus.

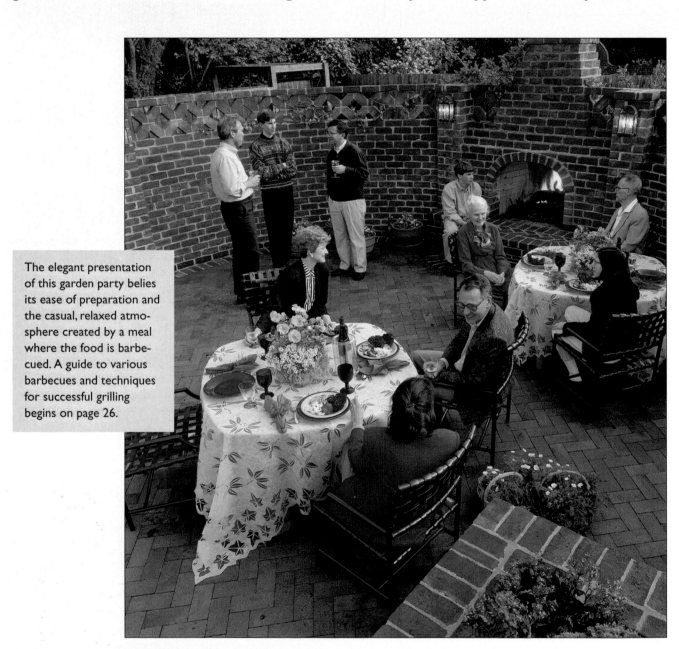

The elegant presentation of this garden party belies its ease of preparation and the casual, relaxed atmosphere created by a meal where the food is barbecued. A guide to various barbecues and techniques for successful grilling begins on page 26.

Even the standard fare of hamburgers, always reliable, is easily "gussied up." A Texas-style barbecue is a genre unto itself, featuring hearty meals of chicken and ribs, prepared with western panache. On the pages to come, you will learn to master the techniques of grilling outdoors, providing you with an amazing range of cooking possibilities.

And with a variety of recipes and menus to choose from, it becomes a pleasure to sit down to a meal with family and friends, especially for festive occasions such as birthday suppers, or holidays such as the Fourth of July. With a little planning, you can set a relaxed party around a tantalizing menu and happily serve four—or forty.

The varied menu of an outdoor buffet lunch satisfies almost any appetite. Tasty, no-wilt dishes, fresh breads, and a choice of grilled meats free up the chefs to socialize with guests. Recipes begin on page 34.

The Art of the Barbecue

Barbecues can be charcoal-fired, gas, or electric. Your choice will depend on where you'll use the barbecue, the number of people you'll usually be serving, and the kinds of food you're most likely to be preparing for your family and guests *(see page 28)*.

Charcoal-fired barbecues: The most popular models are open braziers, covered kettles, and boxes with lids. Open braziers vary from tabletop portables to large, free-standing models. Covered kettles and boxes with hinged lids can be used either covered over for cooking by indirect heat, or open or covered for direct heat grilling.

THE ULTIMATE BARBECUE

The defining feature of a barbecue is its grill, suspended above a burning source of heat. But some modern barbecues can do more than just grill—their various features can often rival an indoor range top. The barbecue at right has the elements for virtually any approach to cooking.

Hood
Shapes and hinging action vary.

Rotisserie
Clip-on electrical motor and skewer rest on fixed brackets.

Shelf
Handy swing-up or fixed shelves are available on most units.

Side burner
One or two are available for most grills. These high-output, commercial-grade burners are particularly good outdoors, where wind can dissipate heat.

Controls
Sturdy knobs control brass valve within. Each burner has its own spark igniter.

Grates
Heavy steel racks retain heat; porcelain coating makes cleanup easy.

Smoker
Pull-out drawer holds wood chips. This grill has a long, narrow burner just for the smoker drawer, so foods like salmon and cheese can be "cold smoked".

Burners
Cast-iron burners rest in double wall, stainless steel enclosures.

Radiant shields
Ported stainless steel trays support rocks in some grills, and keep drippings off burner outlets.

Rock layer
Rocks absorb heat from burners and radiate it to food. This unit uses lava rock, favored by professional chefs. Other units use ceramic disks or squares.

Cart
Heavy-duty, coated steel. Also available in stainless steel.

Gas and electric barbecues: All gas and some electric models use a briquet-shaped material such as lava rock above the burner. Features such as smokers, auxiliary burners, and rotisseries allow extra flexibility. Smokers, for example, can merely add smoke flavoring to grilled food, or can be designed to cold smoke food. Gas barbecues often have the same capabilities as gas ranges, allowing you to prepare sauces, and other dishes outside. Rotisseries allow the slow roasting of large cuts of meat. Instant-on grills, and other built-in conveniences make the barbecue as easy to use as a kitchen stove.

GRILL INSTALLATION

This barbecue features heat-proofing, allowing it to be installed in a wood enclosure. The rolltop doesn't interfere with the rotisserie.

The gas grill above, which fits in a prefab synthetic stone enclosure,. has a twin rotisserie burner and a large cooking surface.

This grill is designed for permanent installation, bolted to a patio. The unit's shelves swing up for use.

Basic Barbecue Techniques

Direct- or indirect-heat cooking techniques differ in how the coals are arranged and in whether or not the grill is covered. For direct-heat grilling, any barbecue is satisfactory; to cook by indirect heat, you'll need a model with a lid.

By direct heat: Open the bottom dampers if your barbecue has them; for a covered barbecue, remove or open lid. Spread briquets on the fire grate in a solid layer that's 1 to 2 inches bigger than the grill area required for the food.

Then mound the charcoal and ignite it. When the coals reach the fire temperature specified in the recipe, spread them out into a single layer again. Set the grill at the recommended height above the coals. Grease the grill. To maintain

WHAT KIND OF HEAT?

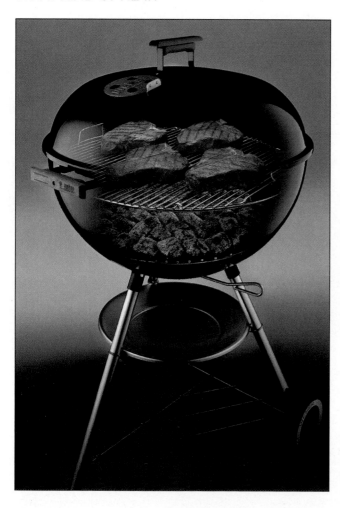

Direct heat
Backyard chefs should choose direct heat when searing steaks, hamburgers, and chops. This method works by cooking the food with the direct heat of the flame beneath it.

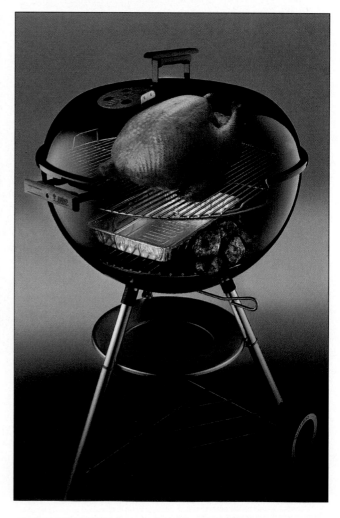

Indirect heat
Choose indirect heat for larger cuts of meat such as roasts or turkeys. This method cooks by warming the enclosed space of the barbecue—creating, in effect, an outdoor oven.

an even heat, scatter new briquets over the fire bed every hour.

By indirect heat: Remove or open the lid of covered barbecues and open the dampers if you have them. Mound and light briquets as for the direct-heat method. When coals are the right temperature, bank them on either side of a drip pan. Place the grill 4 to 6 inches over the drip pan and put the food on the grill directly over the drip pan. Add the briquets to each side of the fire grate at 30- to 40-minute intervals to keep the temperature constant *(see page 30)*.

When you are using a covered barbecue grill, wood chips or chunks placed beneath the cooking grate can add a delicate smoked flavor *(see page 37)*.

BARBECUING OPTIONS

Rotisserie cooking
With this technique, sometimes called spit roasting, the diameter of the meat and its distance from the heat determine cooking time. Bone-in roasts, boneless roasts, and poultry are all suitable for spit roasting. For a delicious recipe, see page 54.

Smoke cooking
Very slow, even cooking in a smoker produces succulent, smoky-flavored meats, fish, and poultry that taste as good or better than high-priced commercial products. For more on smoking food, see page 37 and 51.

Grilling on the barbecue
This is the most commonly used approach to barbecuing. Choose direct or indirect heat (opposite page). You'll find a recipe for succulent grilled chicken on page 42.

Firing Up Your Barbecue

Charcoal refers to 2-inch pressed briquets, which may differ somewhat in density and composition. For best results, choose long-burning briquets, and ignite them using one of the following techniques.

Fire Chimney: Place wadded sheets inside a chimney starter, add briquets, then light. In about 30 minutes, the coals will be ready. Lift off the chimney and arrange the coals on the grate.

Electric starter: This is one of the easiest and cleanest charcoal starters you can buy. Set the device on a few briquets, pile more briquets on top, then plug it in. After 10 minutes, remove the starter

BARBECUE FUELS AND FIRE STARTERS

Chimney starter

Solid starter cubes

Electric starter

Propane starter
Used instead of a match for lighting a propane barbecue

THE RIGHT AMOUNT OF CHARCOAL

The quantity of charcoal you will need for indirect cooking depends on how large your grill is, and the length of cooking time. The quality of the briquets you use can also affect how many you'll need to add each hour; cheaper briquets tend to burn out faster than denser briquets.

On average, a 26¾" grill requires 30 briquets for the first hour, then 9 briquets for each additional hour of cooking. A 22½" grill requires 25 briquets to start, then an additional 8 briquets per hour. Start with 16 briquets in an 18½" grill, then top up with 5 briquets for each additional hour.

from the pile; in about another 20 minutes, the coals should be ready. (If you leave an electric starter in too long, the heating element will burn out.)

Solid starter: These small, compressed, blocks or sticks light easily with a match and continue to burn until the coals are ready (about 30 minutes).

Liquid propane or natural gas: Gas barbecues use either liquid propane or natural gas as fuel. Liquid propane is stored in a refillable tank mounted on the grill. Expect 20 to 30 hours of use from each tank fill-up. Natural gas is piped through a permanent hookup to a gas line. *Note:* Never use one kind of fuel in a barbecue that is designed for the other.

A built-in gas supply is convenient, but installation is best left to a plumber. Make sure the outlet has an exterior shutoff valve as shown in the photo above. Your gas barbecue may require a regulator, depending on the pressure of your gas supply.

Barbecue Safety Tips

Follow the manufacturer's instructions carefully and heed the rules below to ensure safety while you grill.

• Never leave a hot grill unattended. Keep children and pets at a safe distance.

• Never use a charcoal or gas grill indoors or in a closed garage or enclosed patio.

• Do not use gasoline or other highly volatile fluids as charcoal lighters.

• Do not add any liquid starter to hot—or even warm—coals.

• Place your grill in an open, level area away from the house, wood railings, trees, bushes, or other combustible surfaces.

• Do not attempt to barbecue in high winds.

• Wear an insulated, fire retardant barbecue mitt and use long-handled tools designed for grilling.

• Do not wear clothing with loose, flowing sleeves that might catch fire.

• Be sure that the ashes are completely cold (sparks can linger for hours) before you dump them into a paper or plastic container.

Is It Done Yet?

Direct-heat grilling is best for relatively thin pieces of food that will be cooked in less than 25 minutes: many steaks, chops, and burgers fall into this category. The direct cooking method is also used for bone-less chicken breasts, turkey tenderloins, turkey breast slices, fish fillets and steaks, and shellfish.

Indirect-heat cooking should be used for thicker-cut pork chops, steaks, and cut up pieces of poultry that need to cook for more than 25 minutes at lower temperatures. This technique is also used for roasts, ribs, whole fish, turkeys, chickens, and other whole birds. The food is not turned, and the grill must be

GRILLING GUIDE FOR MEAT AND POULTRY

	CUT OF MEAT	THICKNESS OR WEIGHT	APPROXIMATE COOKING TIME
BEEF			
Place steaks on cooking grate using Direct Method for a charcoal grill, Indirect/Medium heat for a gas grill. Sear, if desired, then cook for the time listed on the chart, based on medium-rare (145°F), or until desired doneness; turn once halfway through cooking time.	**Steaks**	1 inch	10-12 minutes
		1½ inches	14-16 minutes
		2 inches	20-25 minutes
	Flank steak	1-2 lbs	12-15 minutes
	Skirt steak	¼ -½ inch	7-9 minutes
POULTRY			
Place food on cooking grate, using Indirect Method for both charcoal or gas grills. Cook bone-in pieces bone side down. Cook whole birds breast side up. Use thermometer, inserted in thickest part of thigh (not touching bone). The food is done when it registers 180°F.	**Chicken & duck (whole)**	3½-4 lbs	1-1½ hours
	halves	1½-1¾ lbs	50-60 minutes
	breast halves	About 8 oz each	30-35 minutes
	wings	About 3 oz each	30 minutes
	Turkey (whole)	10-13 lbs	1½-2¼ hours
		14-23 lbs	2½-3½ hours
	breast halves	3-3½ lbs	1-1½ hours
	thighs	1-1½ lbs each	55-65 minutes
PORK			
On a charcoal grill, use Direct Method for ¾- to 1-inch thickness, and the Indirect Method/Medium heat for thicker chops. On a gas grill use Indirect Method/Medium heat for all chops. Use times in chart, based on medium (160°F), or until meat near bone is no longer pink; turn once halfway through cooking time. Sear, if desired.	**Chops (rib, loin, shoulder)**	¾ inch	10-12 minutes
		1 inch	12-14 minutes
		1¼-1½	25-35 minutes
BURGERS & SAUSAGES			
Place patties or sausages on cooking grate, using Direct Method for a charcoal grill, Indirect Method/Medium heat for a gas grill. Cook for time given in chart, or until no longer pink in the center and juices run clear; turn once halfway through cooking time.	**Lean ground beef, lamb, or pork**	¾ inch	160°F for medium; about 10 minutes
	Sausages (uncooked), Italian, bratwurst, or other gourmet-type meat combination	About 1 inch diameter	18-20 minutes

kept covered: Opening the lid increases the cooking time.

Use the fire temperature recommended in the recipe. With gas and electric grills, this is adjusted with the appropriate controls. The following trick is useful for gauging the temperature of charcoal grills. **Hot:** You can hold your hand close to the grill for only 2 to 3 seconds. Coals are barely covered with ash. **Medium:** You can hold your hand at grill level for 4 to 5 seconds. Coals glow red through a layer of gray ash. **Low:** You can hold your hand at the grill level for at least 6 to 7 seconds. The coals are covered with a thick layer of ash.

GRILLING GUIDE FOR FISH AND SEAFOOD

	TYPE OF SEAFOOD	THICKNESS OR WEIGHT	APPROXIMATE COOKING TIME
FILLETS, STEAKS & BONELESS CUBES FOR KEBABS			
Place fish on cooking grate (support less-firm fillets on heavy-duty foil), using Direct Method for a charcoal grill, Indirect Method/Medium heat for a gas grill. Cook for time given in chart or until fish is opaque but still moist in thickest part; turn once halfway through cooking time (unless fish is on foil).	**Fillets**	½ inch	6-8 minutes
		¾ inch	8-10 minutes
	Fillets and steak	1 inch	10 minutes
	Boneless cubes for kebabs	1 inch	8-10 minutes
WHOLE FILLETS & WHOLE FISH			
Place whole fillets and whole fish, skin side down, on cooking grate (support less-firm fish on heavy-duty foil), using Indirect Method for charcoal grill, Indirect Method/Medium heat for gas grill. Cook time as per chart or until fish is opaque but still moist in thickest part.	**Whole fish fillets**	1½ inches	20 minutes
	Whole fish	1-1½ inches	10-15 minutes
		2-2½ inches	30-35 minutes
		3 inches	45 minutes
SHELLFISH			
Place shellfish on cooking grate, using Direct Method for a charcoal grill, Indirect Method/Medium heat for a gas grill. Cook crab, lobster, shrimp, and scallops for time given in chart or until opaque in thickest part; turn once halfway through cooking time. Scrub and rinse live clams, mussels, and oysters; cook them until shells open; discard any that do not open.	**Crab, whole (precook 5 minutes)**	About 2½ lbs	10-12 minutes
	Lobster, whole (precook 5 minutes)	About 2 lbs	8-10 minutes
	Lobster tails	8-10 oz	8 minutes
	Shrimp (also called prawns)		
	large	Under 30 per lb	4-5 minutes
	colossal	10-15 per lb	6-8 minutes
	extra-colossal	Under 10 per lb	8-10 minutes
	Scallops	1-2 inches	5-8 minutes
	Clams	Medium size	5-8 minutes
	Mussels	Under 12 per lb	4-5 minutes
	Oysters	Small	8 minutes

Grilling Classics

The aroma of steaks or hamburgers on a barbecue evokes memories of summer for most North Americans, and for good reason: These two foods are the most commonly prepared on grills. The ubiquitous hot dog rounds out the trio of grilled dishes favored by all ages. The classic American hamburger is shown below, this version picked up with a spicy jerk sauce. Steak takes on a whole new dimension when marinated in tequila and a Latin-style hot dog provides a new take on an old standby.

The Great American Hamburger

4 large (about 12 inches)
    ears of corn
Jerk Sauce (recipe
    follows)
1 to 1½ pounds of lean
    ground beef
4 hamburger buns
Rinsed and crisped
    lettuce leaves
Mayonnaise and salt

- Pull husks down from corn, but leave attached to cob. Remove and discard silk. Rinse corn and pat dry. Smear about 1 tablespoon jerk sauce over each ear. Lay husks back around corn; tie with cotton string.
- Shape beef into 4 equal patties, each ¾ inch thick. If convenient, cover and chill corn and beef up to two hours.
- Place corn on a grill 4 to 6 inches above a solid bed of *hot* coals. Turn corn as needed to keep husks from burning; grill until kernels are very hot, 15 to 20 minutes.
- Place beef patties on grill. Allow about 8 minutes for rare, 10 minutes for medium and 15 minutes for well done.
- Serve beef on buns with lettuce; add jerk sauce, mayonnaise, and salt to taste. Husk corn and season to taste with more jerk sauce and salt.
Serves 4.

JERK SAUCE
In a blender, mince 1 cup chopped green onions; ¼ cup lime juice; 2 tablespoons each dark molasses, soy sauce, and chopped fresh ginger; 2 cloves garlic; 2 fresh jalapeno chilies, stemmed and seeded; ½ teaspoon ground cinnamon; and ¼ teaspoon each ground allspice and ground nutmeg.
Makes ¾ cup.

Cooking Safely Outdoors

- Our recipes were all tested with the grill 4 to 6 inches above coals. Cooking times will be shorter if the grill is closer.
- Salting food after cooking will keep it moist.
- The USDA recommends that ground meat be cooked to 160°F (71°C) in the center of patties or until no longer pink and the juices run clear. Ground poultry should be cooked to 165°F (74C°).
- Always thaw poultry in the refrigerator.
- Wash hands, utensils, and work surfaces with hot, soapy water after handling raw poultry.
- Sanitize surfaces and utensils with dilute chlorine bleach (2 to 3 teaspoons per quart of water) and rinse well.

Tequila Beefsteak

4 New York strip steaks (each 8 to 10 oz.,
    cut 1 to 1½ inches thick), fat trimmed
½ cup tequila
2 tablespoons olive oil
1 tablespoon pepper
2 teaspoons grated lemon peel
1 clove garlic, pressed or minced
Salt

• With a damp paper towel, wipe steaks; put meat
in a 1-gallon plastic food bag. Add tequila, oil,
pepper, lemon peel, and garlic; seal bag and turn
to mix seasonings. Set bag in a bowl; chill at least
1 hour or up to a day; turn bag over occasionally.
• Drain the steaks and place on a grill 4 to 6 inches
above a solid bed of hot coals.
• Turn steaks to brown evenly; for medium-rare
cook 12 to 14 minutes (cut to test). Transfer meat
to plates; season to taste with salt.
Serves 4.

Spiced-Up Hot Dogs

Hot Black Beans (recipe follows)
Pickled Cabbage (recipe follows)
Fresh tomato Relish
Guacamole
18 large (12-inch diameter) or 24 small
    (about 8-inch diameter) flour tortillas
2 to 4 lbs. (¼ to ½ lb. per person) fully
    cooked sausages, such as old-fash-
    ioned frankfurters or knackwurst
About 4 cups shredded cheddar cheese
Purchased salsa or taco sauce

• Prepare Hot Black Beans and
Pickled Cabbage.
• Sprinkle each tortilla with a few
drops of water. Stack them, wrap in
heavy-duty foil, and bake at 350° until
warm (about 15 minutes). Keep warm.
• Let guests cook their own sausages
by placing them on a lightly greased

grill above a solid bed of medium coals.
Cook, turning often, until well browned
and hot throughout (5 to 10 minutes
depending on the diameter of the
sausage). Wrap each sausage in a warm
tortilla and add spoonfuls of black
beans, cabbage, tomato relish, guacamole, cheese, and salsa.
Makes 8 to 10 servings.

Hot Black Beans: Sort 1 pound dried
black beans and remove any debris.
Rinse beans and drain. Place beans in a
4- to 5-quart pan and add 9 cups water;
1 large onion, cut into chunks; and ½
cup lightly packed fresh cilantro leaves.
Bring to a boil over high heat; then
reduce heat, cover, and simmer until
beans mash easily with a fork (2½ to 3
hours). Pour about half the bean mix-

ture at a time into a food processor
and whirl until pureed. Season to taste
with salt and cayenne pepper. May be
made up to a day ahead, covered and
refrigerated. To reheat, cover beans
and bake in a 350° oven until hot
throughout (35 to 45 minutes).
Makes about 3 cups.

Pickled Cabbage: Using a food processor or sharp knife, coarsely shred
about 1 pound (about 4 cups) cabbage.
Place in a bowl and add ½ cup each
chopped onion and shredded carrot,
⅓ cup white wine vinegar, and ½ teaspoon oregano leaves. Mix well; season
with salt. Cover and refrigerate for at
least 4 hours or up to one day. Stir
before serving.
Makes 5 cups.

Texas Barbecue

At the heart of most debates about which barbecue tastes best is the kind of wood used to smoke it. Most Texan barbecue masters favor mesquite or hickory, which home cooks anywhere can buy in chip form.

Here Texas author and former caterer Sam Higgins provides his mixed grill of beef brisket, chicken and spareribs, adapted for a covered kettle barbecue. The meats are first rubbed with a blend of salt, pepper, paprika and chilies, then seared briefly over hot coals before wood chips are added for flavorful low-temperature cooking (*see opposite*). The brisket is finished off in a foil package in the oven.

Texas Two-Step Mixed Grill Barbecue

4 to 6 cups hickory or mesquite wood chips
1 broiler-fryer chicken (about 3½ lbs.)
1 beef brisket (4 to 5 lbs.)
1 rack pork spareribs (3 to 4 lbs.)

For Pepper Rub:

3 tablespoons New Mexico or California ground chilies
3 tablespoons paprika
1½ tablespoons salt
1½ tablespoons pepper

• In a bowl, pour water over chips to cover; soak them at least 30 minutes.
• Split chicken in half lengthwise, rinse and pat dry. Rub chicken, beef, and ribs with pepper rub, using all.

• When a full layer of barbecue coals are well dotted with gray ash, place grill 4 to 6 inches above them and cook meats until browned (*3 to 5 minutes per side*).
• Lift off grill; mound coals against one side of fire grate. Scatter 2 cups drained wood chips on coals. Replace grill and set all meats on grill, but not over any coals. Cover barbecue and adjust vents to maintain temperature between 200° and 225°F for 1 hour.
• After 1 hour, remove lid, tilt up grill and add a few more briquets and 1 to 2 cups more wood chips. Replace grill and lid and continue smoking for another hour. Repeat this step and cook until meat at thigh bone of chicken is no longer dark pink and meat pulls easily from sparerib bones (*1 to 1½ hours longer*). *Note: Smoke causes meat just under skin or at surface to turn bright pink.*

• Remove meat from grill; chicken and ribs will be ready to eat, but brisket takes more cooking. Seal beef in foil and set in a pan. Bake in a 200°F oven until very tender when pierced (*about 2½ to 3 hours*). About 30 minutes before beef is done, seal chicken and ribs separately in foil and put in oven.
• Drain and save beef juices; skim and discard fat. Reserve juices for sauce recipe (*below*).
• Slice beef across the grain, cut ribs between bones, and cut chicken into pieces. Add barbecue sauce to taste. *Serves 20 to 24.*

Two-day method Day 1: Cook beef; finish in oven. Let cool; chill overnight. Day 2: Smoke chicken and ribs; at same time heat beef packet in pan on grill.

SAM HIGGINS' BARBECUE SAUCE

In a 1½- to 2-quart pan, combine 1½ cups catsup, the reserved beef juices (from beef brisket) and enough water (or regular-strength beef broth) to make ¾ cup, ¾ cup Worcestershire sauce, ½ cup lemon juice, 6 tablespoons firmly packed brown sugar, ½ cup chopped onion, and 2 teaspoons liquid hot pepper seasoning.
• Simmer, uncovered, until reduced to 3 cups, 35 to 40 minutes. Serve warm or cool; add more liquid pepper to taste. If making ahead, cover and chill up to 2 weeks. Makes 3 cups.

Cooling Off with Iced Tea

Tea Concentrate

This extra-strong concentrate can be used alone—diluted with water—or as a base for a variety of drinks. Combine ¼ cup loose tea leaves or 12 tea bags (any flavor or variety) with 5 cups water in a 3- to 4-quart pan. Boil over high heat, uncovered, until liquid reduces to 4 cups *(about 6 minutes)*. Pour liquid through a fine strainer into a container; discard residue. Cover and chill concentrate until cold, at least 3 hours or up to 2 weeks.
Makes 12 servings when diluted.

Cinnamon Citrus Tea Sparkler

1⅓ cups tea concentrate
Thinly pared zest of 1 small orange
1 cinnamon stick, about 2 inches long
2⅔ cups chilled sparkling water
Ice cubes
¼ to ½ cup thawed frozen orange or tangerine juice concentrate

• In a 1- to 1½-quart pan, combine tea concentrate, orange peel, and cinnamon stick; bring to boiling. Cover and chill until cold, up to 2 days. Discard zest and cinnamon stick. Combine juice concentrate with water.
• Fill 4 tall glasses with ice cubes. To make liquid layers, pour thawed orange juice concentrate equally into each glass, then gently pour tea mixture into glasses. Stir before sipping.
Makes 4 servings.

Lemon Ginger Sparkler

1⅓ cups tea concentrate
1 lemon, thinly sliced

¼ cup finely chopped crystallized ginger
2⅔ cups chilled ginger ale
Ice cubes

In a 1- to 1½-quart pan, combine tea concentrate, half the lemon slices, and ginger; bring to boiling. Cover and chill up to 2 days. Pour through a fine strainer into a pitcher and add ginger ale; discard used lemon slices and ginger. Pour tea into tall ice-filled glasses. Drop remaining lemon slices into tea, or use to garnish glasses.
Makes 4 servings.

Cranberry Cherry Tea Sparkler

1⅓ cups tea concentrate
⅓ cup dried cranberries
1⅓ cups chilled canned cherry cider or juice
1⅓ cups chilled sparkling water
Ice cubes

In a 1- to 1½-quart pan, combine tea concentrate and cranberries; bring to boiling. Cover and chill up to 2 days. Pour mixture through fine strainer into large pitcher, discarding cranberries. Add cider and sparkling water; mix. Pour into 4 tall ice-filled glasses.
Makes 4 servings.

Kebabs

Grilled food on a skewer can be found in the national cuisines of Greece, Indonesia, and Thailand, among others. Each has its own particular style and characteristic flavors, both bold and subtle. In the Middle East, *shish kebab* (literally, meat on a stick) describes any skewered, grilled meat. But to the majority of American cooks, shish kebab means the traditional Greek-style version: cubes of lamb marinated in lemon juice, olive oil, and herbs, then skewered with vegetables and grilled over hot coals.

Greek Shish Kebab

⅓ cup olive oil or salad oil

3 tablespoons lemon juice

1 large onion, finely chopped

2 bay leaves

2 teaspoons oregano leaves

½ teaspoon black pepper

2 lbs. lean boneless lamb (leg or shoulder cut into 1½-inch cubes)

1 large mild red onion, cut into 1-inch pieces

1 large red or green pepper, seeded and cut into 1½-inch squares

½ lb. medium-size mushrooms

1 cup cherry tomatoes

• In a large nonmetallic bowl, stir together oil, lemon juice, chopped onion, bay leaves, oregano, and black pepper. Reserve ¼ cup of marinade. Add lamb; stir to coat. Cover and refrigerate for at least 4 hours or up to one day, stirring several times.

• Lift meat from marinade and drain briefly. Add red onion, bell pepper, and mushrooms to marinade; turn to coat, then lift out (reserve marinade). On 6 sturdy metal skewers, thread meat alternately with vegetables.

• Place skewers on lightly greased grill above a solid bed of coals.

• Cook, turning and basting often with marinade, until meat is well browned but still pink in center *(10 to 15 minutes)*; cut to test. Garnish with the cherry tomatoes.

Makes 6 servings.

Robust lamb chunks, scented with lemon and garlic, alternate on skewers with onions, mushrooms, and bell peppers to make Greek Shish Kebab. Dry red wine makes a perfect complement to the meal.

SKEWERS

Kebab rack and skewers

Thin metal skewers

Bamboo skewers

Decorative metal skewers

Grilling fruits and vegetables

Both vegetables and fruit benefit from a marinade or baste to give them flavor and keep them moist. Grilling them is much the same as with meats, but cooking time is less and fruits and vegetables need turning frequently.

- Vegetables require much the same preparation, in terms of cleaning and peeling, as if they were to be roasted. Root vegetables, such as potatoes and carrots should be boiled then grilled.

Leafy vegetable such as broccoli, should be blanched.

- Generally the precooked vegetables and more delicate vegetables cook in 5 to 10 minutes. More substantial veggies, such as squash, eggplants, and onions require between 10 and 20 minutes to cook on the grill.
- Vegetables such as bell peppers and squash can be grilled without additional preparation.

- Suitable fruits include apples and apricots cut in half, bananas (unpeeled, cut in half lengthwise), figs, nectarines, unpeeled oranges and tangerines (halved crosswise, or cut into ¾-inch slices), papayas (peeled and sliced), peaches, and pears (halved). Remove cores and large pits; halve or cut into smaller pieces as necessary. Small pieces need 4 to 6 minutes; larger pieces need 10 to 12 minutes.

Family Dining Outdoors

The beauty of the barbecue is that you don't have to be an experienced and accomplished cook to create a meal that you and your family will enjoy. On the contrary, even a novice backyard chef is capable of turning mealtime into something special. With that in mind, there's practically no end to what you can do.

The following pages present a tasty assortment of grilling ideas, from the unconventional pizza on the grill on the opposite page to the more commonplace chicken with barbecue sauce featured on page 42. Homemade lemonade and ice cream add a sweet twist to the section, while a Fourth of July feast adds some pop.

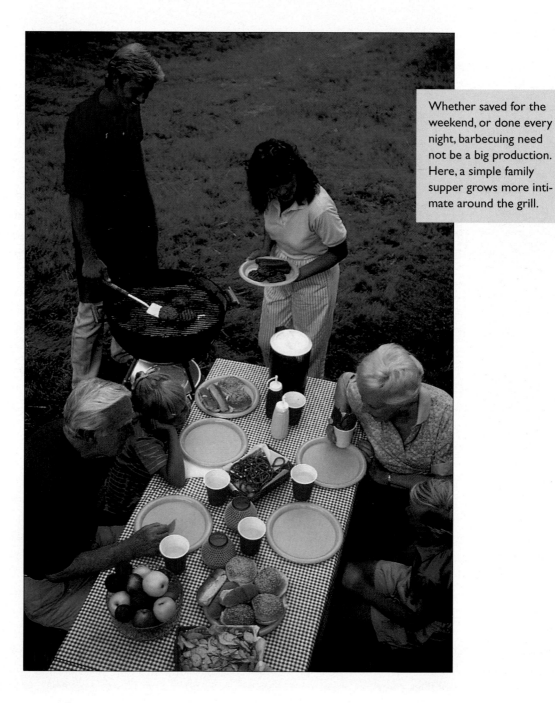

Whether saved for the weekend, or done every night, barbecuing need not be a big production. Here, a simple family supper grows more intimate around the grill.

Quick & Easy Cooking

No wonder that barbecuing is so popular with today's busy families. It's one of the easiest and speediest methods of cooking, saving time and trouble in the kitchen for both preparation and cleanup.

A few helpful tips can make life even simpler grill-side. Plan a menu for each night of the week and shop for several meals at a time. Take advantage of meals that can be cooked in advance and reheated on the grill; marinate the day before. When grilling a whole meal, the foods that take the longest should be started first. Of course, this sort of planning will work with any meal—those that follow are just a few examples.

Grilled Tomato and Pesto Pizza

1 loaf frozen whole-wheat or
*   white bread dough, thawed*
2 tablespoons olive oil
4 large Roma-type tomatoes, cut length-
*   wise into ½-inch slices*
8 tablespoons prepared pesto sauce
2 cups shredded mozzarella cheese
Salt and pepper

• On a floured board, divide and shape dough into 4 equal balls. Roll each into a 5- to 6-inch-wide round. Brush tops and bottoms with oil, set on foil, and flatten to ⅛ inch. Let rise, uncovered, at room temperature until slightly puffy (15 to 25 minutes). Meanwhile, place tomatoes on grill above a solid bed of hot coals. Brown on both sides (about 5 minutes).
• Flip dough onto the grill over medium coals; peel off and discard foil. Cook until golden brown on the bottom (2 to 3 minutes). With a spatula, transfer dough to 12-by-15-inch baking sheet, browned side up. Spread 2 tablespoons of pesto sauce on each bread round, and top with grilled tomato slices and mozzarella cheese.
• Remove pizza from baking sheet and return to grill. Cover barbecue, open vents, and cook until topping is hot and bottom of bread is crisp and flecked with brown (3 to 4 minutes). Remove from grill; add salt and pepper to taste.
Makes 4 servings.

Chili-Mint Lemonade

¾ cup sugar
1½ cups coarsely chopped fresh mint
4 to 8 small dried hot red chilies
1 cup lemon juice
Fresh mint sprigs
Ice cubes

• In a 3- to 4-quart pan over high heat, boil 2 cups water, sugar, chopped mint, and chilies, uncovered, until reduced to 1 cup, 12 to 14 minutes; stir occasionally. Let cool; pour mint- and chili-flavored mixture through a strainer into a pitcher, pressing to extract liquid. Discard mint; rinse chilies and add to pitcher along with lemon juice and 1 quart of water.
• Cover and chill the lemonade until cold, at least 1 hour or up to 1 week. Serve in pitcher or a tall decorative bottle, adding mint sprigs. Pour into ice-filled glasses and garnish each portion with more mint sprigs.
Makes 6 cups; serves 4 to 6.

Chicken for a Hungry Dozen

3 frying chickens (3 to 3½ lbs. each), quartered
Barbecue Sauce (recipe follows)

• Prepare barbecue sauce; set aside.
• Rinse chicken under running water, pat dry, and place on a lightly greased grill over medium coals.
• Cook, turning occasionally, for 20 minutes; then brush generously with barbecue sauce. Continue to cook, turning and basting several times, until meat near thigh-

bone is no longer pink; cut to test (20 or 30 more minutes). Heat any remaining barbecue sauce and pass at the table to spoon over individual servings.
Makes 12 servings.

Skewered Beef and Corn

Pineapple-Wine Marinade (see below)
4 pounds boneless chuck roast, trimmed of fat, cut into about 1½-inch cubes
¼ cup melted butter or margarine
¼ cup salad oil
5 medium-size ears of corn, husked and cut into about 2-inch lengths
3 medium-size green peppers, cut into about 1½-inch squares
2 large red onions, cut into about 1½-inch chunks
1 medium-size pineapple, peeled, cored, and cut into about 1½-inch cubes

Pineapple-Wine Marinade
1½ cups each pineapple juice and dry red wine

1½ tablespoons minced onion
1½ teaspoons each Worcestershire and dried thyme
¾ teaspoon dried mustard
¼ cup firmly packed brown sugar
¼ teaspoon pepper
2 cloves garlic, minced or pressed

• In a large bowl, combine ingredients for Pineapple-Wine Marinade. Set aside ⅓ cup of the marinade; pour remaining marinade into a large heavy-duty plastic food bag or non-reactive bowl. Add meat and seal bag (or cover bowl). Rotate bag to distribute marinade and place in a shallow pan. Refrigerate for at least 6 hours or until next day, turning meat occasionally.

• In a small bowl, combine butter, oil, and reserved marinade; set aside. Remove meat from bag and drain, discarding marinade in bag. On 8 long metal skewers, thread meat with corn (through cob), bell peppers, onions, and pineapple. Brush all over with butter mixture.
• Arrange skewers on cooking grate. Place lid on grill. Cook, turning once and brushing with remaining butter mixture halfway through cooking time, until meat is done to your liking (about 15 minutes for medium rare; cut to test). Transfer skewers to individual plates.
Makes 8 servings.

Fajita Nachos

¼ cup lime juice
¼ cup olive oil
½ cup beer
2 cloves pressed garlic
1 teaspoon each ground coriander
and ground cumin
1 fresh jalapeno chili, stemmed,
seeded, and minced
Seasoned Beans (recipe follows)
1 pound beef skirt or flank steak
1 pound chopped onions
1 cup shredded cheddar cheese
Guacamole, purchased or home made
Lime Salsa (recipe follows)
Corn tortilla chips, purchased

• In a large plastic bag, mix lime juice, oil, beer, garlic, coriander, cumin, and chili; remove 3 tablespoons marinade and set it aside for the beans. Place steak in bag and seal. Rotate bag and set it in a pan. Chill for at least 2 hours or up to one day, turning occasionally.
• Place meat on a grill over a bed of hot coals. Grill until brown and cooked to your liking (3 to 5 minutes for rare); cut to test. Meanwhile, fry the onions in a pan with 1 tablespoon olive oil. Set aside. Thinly slice meat crosswise, then cut each slice in half.

• Spread hot beans into a 10-inch round on a large ovenproof platter (protect dish by setting it on a metal pan or platter if heating on the barbecue). Top evenly with onions and steak; sprinkle with cheese. Set on the grill over medium coals and cover barbecue until cheese melts, 4 to 6 minutes.
• Remove from barbecue and top with guacamole and salsa. Tuck about ⅓ of the tortilla chips around edges. Accompany with remaining chips and salsa. Scoop layered mixture onto chips to eat. Makes 6 servings.

Seasoned Beans
In a 2- to 3-quart heavy pan on medium heat, combine reserved marinade, two 15-oz cans drained pinto beans, and ½ cup beer. Stir often, using back of spoon or potato masher to coarsely mash beans, until mixture thickens slightly (15 to 20

minutes); add salt to taste. Use hot. If made ahead, cool, cover, and chill up to one day. To reheat, stir over low heat or medium-hot coals.

Lime Salsa
Mix 1 large (about ½ lb.) ripe yellow or red tomato, cored and finely diced; 2 large (about ½ lb. total) tomatillos, husks removed, chopped; ¼ cup minced red bell pepper; 2 tablespoons minced red onion; 1 teaspoon grated lime peel; and 1 tablespoon lime juice. Serve, or let stand, covered, up to 2 hours. *Makes about 2½ cups.*

Homemade Ice Cream

1 cup milk
1 cup heavy cream
½ cup sugar
1 egg
1 teaspoon vanilla extract

Accessories needed:
1 one-pound-size coffee can with cover
1 larger container with cover
(container should be able to hold the

coffee can plus ice cubes)
2 gallons ice cubes
1 bag rock salt
1 mixing bowl
1 egg beater
1 roll of heavy-duty tape

• Mix all the ingredients with egg beater. Pour mixture into small can; tape lid shut. Place small can into container; add

layer of ice and rock salt until container is full; tape lid shut.
• Roll container across flat surface for 10 to 15 minutes, then refill with salt and ice as necessary. Add favorite fruit, if desired, then continue rolling for another 10 to 15 minutes.

Feasting on the Fourth

There is no other summer celebration quite like the Fourth of July. In backyards all across America, families and friends come together to celebrate the red, white, and blue with generous portions of national pride and equal helpings of scrumptious food. Menus vary from region to region and family to family, but the theme to dining on the Fourth remains the same: Do it big, do it your way, and have fun!

The suggestions offered here, from the easy main course to the decorations and the pretty dessert, are designed to help with your preparations—and to spark your own festive imagination.

PATRIOTIC POTLUCK FOR A HUNGRY DOZEN

Potlucks and the Fourth have a proven track record as good partners. Foods that can be made in advance, and shared contributions from visitors, produce the easily paced meal starring grilled hot dogs and sausages and Firecracker Rice Salad shown at left. (See the opposite page for details.)

Begin preparations the day before, if you like. The salad keeps well in the refrigerator for up to two days. A berry- and cream-filled cake (see recipe opposite) offers the perfect finish.

To please all appetites, invite guests to bring a condiment they like; expect variety from salsa to chutneys, cheeses to mustards. Have plenty of buns on hand; leftovers can always be frozen.

A trio of Star-Spangled Banners provides the perfect centerpiece to this Fourth of July spread. Put together with the help of guests, the meal is sure to please the palate of all comers.

Firecracker Rice Salad with Avocados and Tomatoes

9 cups regular-strength
*   chicken broth*
5 cups long-grain white rice
1 cup lime juice
½ cup minced cilantro (fresh)
2 small (about 1 oz. total) jalapeno
*   chilies, stemmed, seeded, and*
*   minced*
¾ pound jack cheese, shredded
2 large (about 1¾ lb. total) firm-
*   ripe avocados*
6 medium-size (about 3 lbs. total) firm-
*   ripe tomatoes, cored and sliced*

• In a 3- to 4-quart pan over high heat, bring 8 cups broth to a boil. Add rice, cover, and simmer until rice is just tender to bite *(about 15 minutes)*. Drain rice, reserving any liquid. Pour rice into a large bowl and let cool to room temperature.
• Mix rice with reserved broth, remaining 1 cup broth, ¾ cup lime juice, cilantro, and chilies. If making ahead of time, cover and chill for up to 2 days.
• Spoon salad onto a large platter; sprinkle cheese over and around entire salad.
• Pit, peel, and slice the avocados lengthwise; moisten slices with the remaining lime juice. Arrange avocado and tomato slices on platter around rice.
Makes 12 to 16 servings.

Star-Spangled Banner Cake

If you want to decorate dessert plates, rinse, drain, and purée separately 1 to 1½ cups each of blueberries and hulled strawberries. Sweeten purées to taste and dribble onto plates shortly before serving.

1 angel food cake (9-inch size)
3 cups rinsed and drained strawberries
3 cups whipping cream
⅓ cup sugar
1 teaspoon vanilla
1 cup rinsed and drained blueberries
*   (or frozen unsweetened blueberries)*

• Cut a 1-inch-thick horizontal slice from the top of the cake. Hollow out a trench in the cake, leaving ½-inch-thick walls and bottom. Reserve cake pieces and top.
• Hull 1½ cups of the strawberries; reserve remaining berries. Purée hulled berries in a blender or food processor; pour into a bowl.
• In a large, deep bowl, whip cream until it holds soft peaks; mix in sugar and vanilla. Spoon 2 cups of the whipped cream into the strawberry purée. Tear reserved cake pieces into about ½-inch chunks and drop into the strawberry mixture. Gently fold mix together and spoon into the hollowed trench in the cake; use all the filling, pressing down gently to fill corners.
• Set cake top in place; frost top and sides with remaining cream. Cover cake (under a large inverted bowl) and chill at least 4 hours or up to 1 day. Decorate with remaining strawberries or blueberries.
Serves 12 to 16.

An all-American dessert
Berry-cream cake, served on white plates drizzled with purée of blueberries and strawberries, offers a cool and creamy finish to this Fourth of July feast.

A collage of condiments
Guests will provide the variety at the condiment bar if you invite them to bring their favorite toppings for hot dogs and sausages. Set the condiments out to share.

Stars and streamers
Trim your table with red, white, and blue ribbons and a smattering of star confetti. They're inexpensive and add just the right touch for the spirit of the day.

Outdoor Entertaining

The Gershwins' song pegged summer perfectly as a time when "the livin' is easy." And summer is also a time when entertaining is easy. As warm weather adds the patio, the garden, and perhaps the pool to your options for home entertaining, it invites a laid-back approach.

Grilled salmon or roast game hens are just as at home on an outdoor grill as in a formal dining room. Your barbecue offers you a quick and easy way to have an elegant soiree with little effort.

The following party ideas rely on foods that hold up well on hot days and have many make-ahead steps. We've also included fresh and festive outdoor decorations and handsome table accessories you can create. As you plan your summer parties, use the tips below to ensure success.

Dinner Party Tips

The most important part of planning is to make a list of what you want to serve at your party, along with what you have, what you'll need to obtain, and when you'll need it. Dishes such as appetizers and salads can often be prepared before the day of the party.

Lighting, such as votive candles in decorative glass containers, will help provide soft illumination when dinners extend beyond dusk.

Weather can't be counted on to cooperate, so plan for eventualities. A marquee provides shelter from sun as well as a sudden shower. Planning a rain date, or a meal that can be prepared indoors are sensible options if a gazebo or marquee is unavailable.

If your party is likely to include children as well as adults, consider preparing a simplified menu for them. Miniature hamburgers can please young tastes, and double as appetizers for parents.

A variety of beverages to suit all your guests is a must. Soft drinks, fruit juices, beer, and wine can be kept on ice in a large container, such as a handsome ice chest. Together with appetizers this kind of self-serve hospitality ensures your guests a relaxed atmosphere. Be sure to place baskets or bags for litter in several locations, especially near a bar. Baskets or pans in which to deposit used utensils, plates, and glasses are also useful: This way, cleanup is easier, and the entertaining area stays clear for other activities.

A well-planned dinner party affords you the time to enjoy playing host, as well as chef. Even midweek, a dinner party in your backyard makes a relaxing break, perfect for socializing.

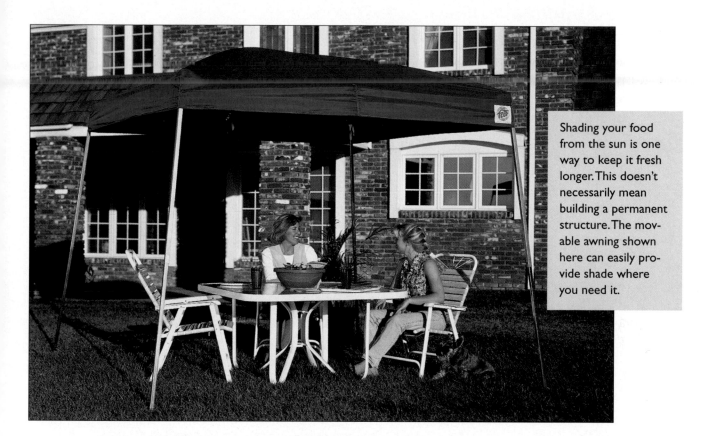

Shading your food from the sun is one way to keep it fresh longer. This doesn't necessarily mean building a permanent structure. The movable awning shown here can easily provide shade where you need it.

KEEPING FOOD FRESH

The same temperatures that keep you comfortable provide the ideal environment for bacterial growth, which can cause at least discomfort and at worst serious illness.

Three hours at temperatures of between 75° to 80°F is a safe period if the foods are well chilled and come directly from the refrigerator or out of ice.

It is the combination of time and temperature that permits bacteria to multiply to dangerous levels. Most bacteria that might be present on food surfaces (fruits and vegetables as well as meats) are destroyed at 160°F. But even cooked foods can be recontaminated, enabling bacteria to flourish again: This might happen if you stir raw foods, then use the same spoon, unwashed, to stir cooling cooked foods.

The simplest precaution is to assume that bacteria is always present. Thoroughly rinse fruits and vegetables in cold water, and drain on a clean surface. To peel or trim, use a clean knife. Clean, dry fruits and vegetables aren't likely to harbor harmful bacteria, but can pick them up from surfaces,

hands, and utensils. High-acid foods, such as salads with tart dressings and fruit in wine, resist bacterial growth.

Not only do you want foods to be safe, but you want them to stay fresh and appealing, too. The easiest tactic is to provide shade. Make use of umbrellas, roof overhangs, marquees, the shadow of a building, or trees and shrubs. But avoid placing food where debris can drop on it.

Some foods—roasted vegetables, sliced tomatoes, and cucumbers, for example—are naturally long-lasting. In addition, large pieces of food stay fresh longer than small ones; opt for chunks of meat or cheese and whole loaves of bread or rolls. Some foods should be kept on ice: leafy greens and other foods that go limp in heat, creamy dressings and sauces, sliced meats, cold beverages, and other things that simply taste best cool.

You can easily improvise an ice-chilled container by resting a rimmed food container on the lip of a larger, deeper unit filled with crushed ice.

Alluring Appetizers

For relaxed entertaining, flavorful mixtures to scoop up and eat are among the most easily managed appetizers. They can be ready on call and require no last-minute assembly or individual touches. Each of these appetizers is so simple to make you can whip it up in minutes. All can wait for a day in the refrigerator. If served chilled, they stay fresh at least 3 hours. They may all be served in bowls, but the Red Bell Cheese is firm enough to swirl into mounds and present on a handsome platter, surrounded by its accompaniments.

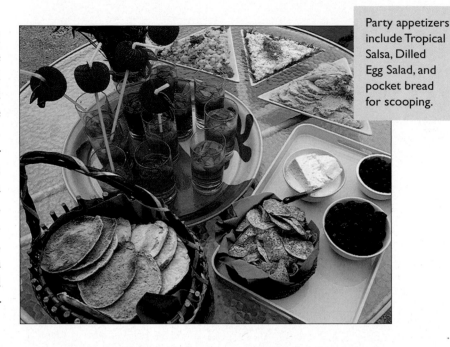

Party appetizers include Tropical Salsa, Dilled Egg Salad, and pocket bread for scooping.

Tropical Salsa

2 medium-size (about 2¼ lbs. total) firm-ripe papayas
1 medium-size (about ¾ lb.) mango
1 large (about 10 oz.) firm-ripe avocado
2 small fresh serrano chilies (or 1 jalapeno), stemmed, seeded, and finely chopped
½ teaspoon grated lime peel
¼ cup lime juice
¼ cup chopped fresh cilantro (coriander)
Salt

• Peel and seed papayas.
• Peel and pit mango.
• Peel and pit avocado.
• Cut all fruit into about ¼-inch cubes.
• Mix gently in bowl with chilies, lime peel, lime juice, cilantro, and salt to taste.
• Serve with chips. If made ahead, cover and chill up to a day.
Makes 5 cups, 20 servings.

Red Bell Cheese

1 jar (about 7 oz., or ¾ cup) roasted red bell peppers or pimientos, drained and patted dry
3 packages (about 4 oz. each) herb-seasoned cheese such as boursin or rondelé
About 1 pound Belgian endive
2 tablespoons minced parsley

• In a food processor or blender, purée the peppers. Whirl or stir in the cheese.
• Cover and chill up to 2 days or, if ready to serve, mound on platter.
• Rinse endive; trim off discolored leaves and stem ends. If prepared ahead, wrap in towels, enclose in a plastic bag, and chill up to 2 days. Cut stem ends to release leaves, separating endive; arrange leaves, pointed ends out, on a platter beside cheese. Sprinkle with parsley.
Makes 1¾ cups cheese, 10 servings.

Dilled Egg Salad

10 hard-cooked large eggs, shelled and mashed
½ cup unflavored, non-fat yogurt, light sour cream, or sour cream
2 tablespoons lemon juice
2 tablespoons chopped fresh dill or 2 teaspoons dried dill weed
2 teaspoons prepared horseradish
½ teaspoon Worcestershire
Salt
Fresh dill sprigs
Toasted pocket bread

• In a bowl, stir together eggs, yogurt, lemon juice, dill, horseradish, Worcestershire, and salt to taste.
• Serve, or chill airtight up to a day. Mound in a bowl and garnish with dill sprigs. Scoop onto toasted pocket bread.
Makes about 2½ cups, 20 servings

Food is the star of most meals, while decoration plays a background role. But homemade tablecloths and floral centerpieces deserve best supporting actor status because they help set the tone for a party.

Festive tablecloths can be made by cutting out patterns, adding stick-on flowers from art supply stores, or merely spattering brightly colored paint on sheets of fabric. Arrangements of seasonal flowers and plants give the fresh-from-the-garden look that adds just the right note to picnic tables and outdoor buffets.

Intricate as a giant doily, the cover above reveals solid color cloth through cutout leaf designs. To make the cover you'll need 5 yards of a sheer but sturdy non-woven interfacing (sold in 45-inch widths), a sewing machine, sheets of thin cardboard, a fine-blade craft knife, and a pencil. Place two 2½-yard lengths of interfacing right sides together, then pin and stitch them together ¼ inch from one long edge. Press seam flat. Fold the fabric square in half (right sides together) to make a rectangle, then in quarters, then finally into a triangle. Make the stencil by drawing a ribbed leaf shape onto a square of cardboard, then cut out the interior of the shape. Lay the stencil on the fabric triangle and trace the leaf shapes onto the fabric; space the shapes at least 4 inches apart. Cut out the shapes with the craft knife then unfold the cloth. This material is delicate, and should be cleaned with a sponge.

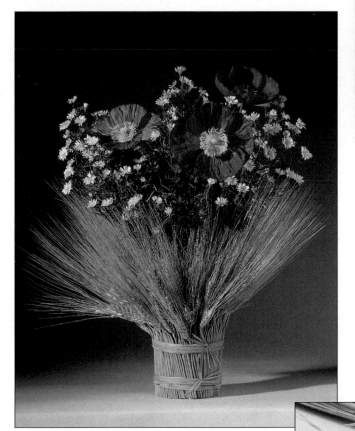

This colorful splay of meadow flowers is set off by a spray of wild grasses. The grasses can be picked from the roadside or purchased at a florist's, along with strips of florist's clay. Press the clay around a glass jar (right), then lay the grasses a few at a time around the jar, the seed heads lined up at top. Secure with raffia ties; use scissors to trim bottom stalks flush. Weight the jar with pebbles in the bottom before filling with water and flowers.

Turkey on the Grill

A whole roasted turkey is the traditional centerpiece for many a holiday meal, but for a no-fuss treat try it on the barbecue or in a smoker (*opposite*). Glazes add sizzle.

Turkeys are grilled using the Indirect Method (*page 29*) and the lid of your barbecue. First remove and discard the leg truss and any lumps of fat. Remove giblets. Rinse the bird inside and out and pat dry, then insert a meat thermometer straight down to the bone through the thickest part of the breast. Rub the bird lightly with oil and set it breast side up on grill over a drip pan. Cover with the lid (open vents on charcoal barbecue) and cook according to times in the chart below, covering with foil if the bird is getting too dark before it is done.

Gourmet Glazes

Brown Sugar Crackle Glaze

2 cups firmly packed brown sugar
5 tablespoons Dijon mustard
2 teaspoons coarse-ground pepper

• Mix sugar, mustard and pepper. (*If making ahead, cover and chill up to 3 days.*) During the last 45 minutes the turkey cooks (the thermometer should read about 135°F for birds up to 18 lbs., about 145°F for heavier birds), brush turkey with half the glaze. Cook 20 minutes more; brush with rest of glaze. Continue to cook until the thermometer registers 180°F. If sections of the glaze start to darken too much, drape with foil. *Makes enough glaze for a 12- to 24-lb. bird.*

Sage Butter Baste

¼ cup (⅛ lb.) butter or margarine, melted
¼ tablespoon. minced fresh or 1 tablespoon crumbled dried sage
2 tablespoons lemon juice

• Mix butter, sage, and lemon juice. Baste often with mixture during the last 45 minutes the turkey cooks (or when thermometer reaches 135° to 145°F). Continue to cook until thermometer reaches 180°F.
Makes enough for a 12- to 24-lb. turkey.

Chili-Orange Glaze

3 tablespoons ground dried New Mexico or California chilies, or
3 tablespoons chili powder
1 large container (12 oz., or 1½ cups) frozen orange juice concentrate, thawed
2 tablespoons grated orange peel (zest only, not white pith)
1 teaspoon ground cumin

• Mix the ground chilies (or chili powder), orange juice concentrate, orange peel, and cumin. (If making ahead, cover and chill up to 3 days.) When the turkey thermometer reaches about 150°F, brush glaze on turkey generously. Continue to cook until thermometer registers 180°F; if the glaze starts to get very dark or burn, drape dark areas with foil.
Makes enough to glaze a 12- to 24-lb. turkey.

BARBECUED TURKEY			
TURKEY WEIGHT WITH GIBLETS	**OVEN TEMPERATURE**	**INTERNAL TEMPERATURE**	**COOKING TIME**
10 to 13 lbs.	350°F	180°F	1½ to 2¼ hours
14 to 23 lbs.	325°F	180°F	2 to 3 hours
24 to 26 lbs.	325°F	180°F	3 to 3¾ hours
28 to 30 lbs.	325°F	180°F	3½ to 4½ hours

Smoker

Drip pans

Thermometer

Fuel holder

ACCESSORIES

Items such as thermometers and drip pans are virtual necessities for all but the simplest grilling recipes. This is just as true of smoke cooking, whether in a dedicated smoke cooker (*above, left*) or in a barbecue equipped with one. Some accessories, such as fuel holders, are useful conveniences; they hold charcoal briquets properly for the Indirect Heat method of barbecuing.

SUCCULENT SMOKED TURKEY

Very slow, even cooking in a smoker produces a succulent, smoky-flavored bird. Many types of smokers are sold in hardware, department, and outdoor supply stores; outdoor equipment catalogues also offer them by mail order.

One of the most popular units is the water smoker, which uses steam to keep the inside temperature low and even. Thanks to the long, slow cooking, foods remain moist and have plenty of time to absorb the swirling fragrant smoke.

To prepare foods for smoking, you can brush them with olive oil or salad oil, or soak them in a spicy sweet brine. Brining has marked advantages—not only do foods stay moister, but the salty-sweet brine also complements the smoky flavor and triples the shelf life of the food.

Cooking time varies with the type of smoker; refer to the manufacturer's instructions.

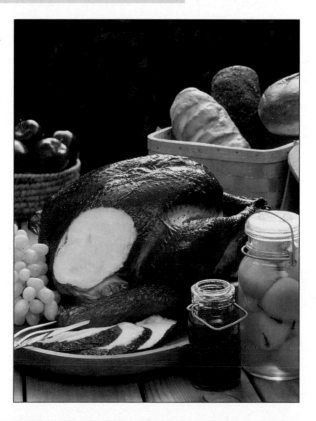

Fish on the Grill

Fish that are both full-flavored and at least moderately oily—such as salmon, trout, halibut, sea bass, swordfish, and tuna—benefit most from barbecuing because smoke enhances their flavor. Lean, delicate fish do not grill as well.

Shrimps and and scallops are easily barbecued on skewers. And for delicious appetizers, you can place live oysters, clams, and mussels directly on the hot grill and cook until their shells open. Use Direct Heat to barbecue fish steaks, fillets, small whole fish, kebabs, and certain kinds of shellfish. Use the Indirect Heat method to grill whole fillets of large fish, such as salmon, and for chunks and steaks more than 1½ inches thick, as well as for large whole fish.

Salmon with Potato and Watercress Salad

3 pounds small (about 2 inches wide)
    red thin-skinned potatoes
1 cup thinly sliced red onion
1 cup seasoned rice vinegar
½ pound watercress, rinsed
    and crisped
1 salmon fillet (about 2 lbs.)
1 tablespoon soy sauce
1 tablespoon firmly packed
    brown sugar
2 cups alder or mesquite wood chips,
    soaked in water
Salt

and immerse in cold water. When potatoes are cool, drain well. If making ahead, cover and chill up to 1 day.

• Soak onions about 15 minutes in cold water to cover. Drain and mix onions with rice vinegar. Cut potatoes into quarters; add to onions.

• Trim tender watercress sprigs from stems, then finely chop enough of the coarse stems to make ½ cup. Mix chopped stems with potato salad. Mound watercress sprigs on a large oval platter with potato salad alongside. Cover and cool.

• Rinse the salmon and pat dry. Place, skin side down, on a piece of heavy foil. Cut foil to follow outlines of fish, leaving a 1-inch border. Crimp edges of foil to fit up against edge of fish. Mix soy sauce with brown sugar and brush onto the salmon filet.

• **On a charcoal barbecue:** Use the Indirect Method at medium heat. Drain the wood chips and sprinkle them

• In a 5- to 6-quart pan, bring about 2 quarts water to a boil over high heat; add potatoes. Cover and simmer over low heat until potatoes are tender when pierced (15 to 20 minutes). Drain

---

TIPS FOR GRILLING SEAFOOD TO PERFECTION

• Firm-textured fish fillets and steaks can be place directly on the grill. Less sturdy pieces require a sheet of foil for support.

• Bastes add moisture and flavor.

• For kebabs, choose non-flaky fish, or fish with firm flesh, such as halibut, swordfish, or tuna. You can skewer large scallops or shelled, deveined shrimp.

---

evenly onto mounds of hot coals.

• **On gas barbecue:** Turn gas on high. Place the drained wood chips in barbecue's metal smoking box or in a small shallow foil pan, and set directly on the heat in the corner. Close lid until barbecue is hot (about 10 minutes). Adjust gas for Indirect Heat cooking method.

• Lay the fish on center of grill, not over coals or flame. Cover with barbecue lid (open vents for charcoal) and cook until fish is barely opaque in its thickest part (15 to 20 minutes). Cut to test. Transfer fish to the platter with potato salad. Add salt to taste. Serve hot or cool.
Makes 6 servings.

When you want a low-fat side dish to serve with naturally lean fish or shellfish, try one of these. They are easy-to-prepare recipes for 6 that can be made quickly.

Grilled Zucchini Ribbons with Thyme

1½ tablespoons minced fresh thyme
1 tablespoon olive oil
1½ teaspoons lemon juice
1 clove garlic
4 medium-size zucchini

• In a small bowl, combine thyme, oil, lemon juice, and garlic; set aside. With a sharp knife, slice zucchini lengthwise into ¼-inch strips. Sprinkle lightly with salt. Arrange zucchini on grill. Cover with lid. Cook, turning once halfway through cooking time *(7 or 8 minutes)*. Transfer zucchini to a platter. Drizzle with thyme mixture.

Marinated Vegetable Grill

3 onions, about 3 inches in diameter, unpeeled,
    cut in half crosswise
3 each large red and green bell peppers
3 or 4 medium-size tomatoes
½ cup red wine vinegar
¼ cup olive oil
2 cloves garlic, minced or pressed
2 tablespoons drained capers
¼ teaspoon pepper

• Arrange onions, cut side down, on cooking grate. Place lid on grill. Cook for 10 minutes. Add bell peppers and tomatoes. Cook, turning bell peppers and tomatoes occasionally, until charred in spots and soft when pressed *(about 30 more minutes)*. Let cool briefly. Meanwhile, combine vinegar, oil, garlic, capers, pepper, and ¼ cup water in a small bowl; set aside. Peel, core, and seed bell peppers. Core tomatoes. Cut off ends and slip skin from onions. Arrange vegetables in a shallow dish and stir in caper mixture. Cover and let stand for at least 1 hour, or up to 6 hours.

Corn Salad with Three-Herb Dressing

½ cup white wine vinegar
¼ cup salad oil
4 teaspoons Dijon mustard
2 teaspoons sugar
4 cups corn kernels cut from steamed corn (6 or 7 ears)
½ cup each finely chopped fresh mint and cilantro
¼ cup finely chopped fresh dill
Salt and pepper
1 large avocado, cut into 12 wedges
1 large tomato, cut into 12 wedges
Mint, cilantro, or dill sprigs

• In a large bowl, whisk vinegar, oil, mustard, and sugar until blended. Stir in corn and chopped mint, cilantro, and dill. Season to taste with salt and pepper. Mound corn salad on a platter. Arrange avocado and tomato wedges around salad. Garnish with mint sprigs.

Thai Noodle Salad

8 oz. dried capellini or thin rice noodles
1 medium-size cucumber, seeded and thinly sliced
1 medium-size red bell pepper thinly sliced
⅓ cup each thinly sliced green onions, chopped cilantro,
    and chopped fresh basil

Chile Dressing

½ cup rice vinegar or wine vinegar
¼ cup soy sauce
1 tablespoon each sugar, minced fresh ginger, sesame oil
½ to 1 teaspoon crushed red pepper flakes
1 clove garlic, minced or pressed

• In a small bowl, combine salad ingredients; set aside. In a 4- to 5- quart pan, bring 2 quarts water to a boil over high heat. Stir in pasta, reduce heat to medium-high, and cook until just tender *(about 4 minutes for capellini, 2 to 3 minutes for rice noodles)*. Drain. Rinse with cold water; drain again. Pour into a wide bowl. Top with the vegetables. Add dressing and lift with forks to mix.

Roasting and Rotisseries

Slow roasting on a spit helps ensure that food remains moist while also being properly cooked. This method is especially suited to large cuts of meat, and whole chickens and other poultry. The most ambitious backyard roast is a whole suckling pig. This is not for the faint of heart, and best attempted after you have gained a fair amount of experience.

In spit-roasting, the diameter of the meat and its distance from the heat determine cooking time. Use the Indirect Method as described on page 29 for charcoal or gas barbecues. The heat required depends on the size and type of food.

Bone-in roasts, boneless roasts, and poultry are all suitable for spit roasting. In every case, it's important to load and balance the meat on the spit, as explained on the opposite page.

Additional attachments can aid rotisserie cooking. A kebab wheel allows you to roast several kebab skewers at the same time, and does make the job easier than manually turning the kebabs on a grill. This device is also useful for cooking sausages. A chicken cage saves tying the chicken so the wings and legs won't hang and burn. You can still baste easily.

HOLDERS

Various types of holders ease the handling of roasts on the grill. The cage above holds poultry on the rotisserie. The roast holder at left has a built-in drip pan. The one below is open.

Italian-Style Spit-Roasted Chicken

1 chicken, 3½ to 4 pounds
Salt and pepper
¾ cup ricotta cheese
¼ cup grated parmesan cheese

1 clove garlic,
    chopped
Parsley, chopped
Dried hot red chili
    flakes
2 tablespoons olive oil
3 tablespoons lemon
    juice
1½ teaspoons Italian
    herb seasonings or ¼
    teaspoon each dried
    basil, dried marjoram,
    dried oregano, and
    dried thyme

• Remove neck and giblets from chicken; reserve for other uses. Remove and discard any extra fat. Rinse chicken

inside and out and pat dry. Season inside and out with salt and pepper.
• Combine cheeses, garlic, chopped parsley and chili flakes to taste. Stuff mixture under breast skin. Secure skin over cavities with small metal skewers. Tie legs together and twist wing tips under back.
• In a small bowl, combine oil, lemon juice, and Italian seasoning. Brush over chicken.
• Secure chicken on spit and cook using Indirect Method. Baste occasionally with remaining herb mixture. Chicken is done when meat thermometer in thickest part of thigh reaches 180°F (1 to 1½ hours). Let stand 10 minutes before carving.
Serves 4.

Sesame Beef Roast

⅓ cup sesame seeds
½ cup each salad oil and soy sauce
⅓ cup lemon juice
2 tablespoons white wine vinegar
1 tablespoon sugar
2 cloves garlic, minced or pressed
1 medium-size onion, sliced
4-pound crossrib or sirloin tip roast

• Toast sesame seeds in a wide frying pan over medium heat until golden *(about 3 minutes)*, shaking pan often. Remove from heat and add oil, soy, lemon juice, vinegar, sugar, garlic, and onion. Place meat in a close-fitting bowl; pour marinade over meat, cover, and refrigerate for at least 8 hours or up to one day, turning meat occasionally.

• Barbecue meat by indirect heat *(see page 29)*. Lift meat from marinade and drain briefly (reserve marinade); then place on a lightly greased grill, directly above drip pan. Cover barbecue and adjust dampers as necessary to maintain an even heat. Cook, basting occasionally with marinade, until a meat thermometer inserted in thickest part registers 135° to 140°F for rare *(1½ to 1¾ hours)*. Let meat stand for 10 minutes, then cut across the grain into thin slices.
Makes 6 to 8 servings.

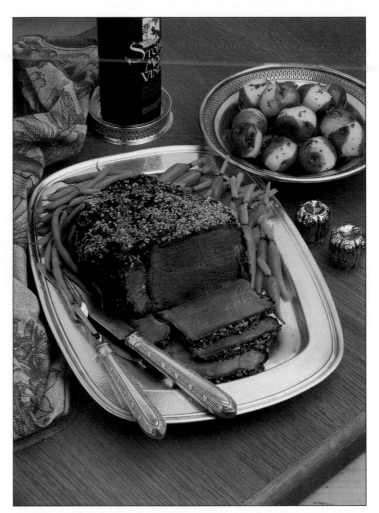

LOADING THE SPIT

Boned, rolled, and tied roasts are very easy to balance on a spit; so is poultry. Just run the spit through the center of the meat or through the neck and body opening of a bird. You can rotisserie cook a pair of chickens or a quartet of squab or game hens together. For best browning, place them end to end, securing each with spit forks. The length of the barbecue and spit capacity determine the number. Most spits can manage up to 12 pounds of meat at a time.

The basic technique is simple: Push a spit fork onto the spit with sharp ends pointed toward the oncoming meat. Center the meat on the fork. Slip another spit fork onto the spit; push pointed ends of forks against the meat. With cotton string, tie up any loose sections such as flaps of meat, skin, drumsticks, or wings. Snip off string close to knots.

To test the balance of a loaded spit, support the ends of the spit in your palms and roll it. The meats should turn all the way over with relative smoothness. The real test is when the motor is running. Properly balanced, it should turn without straining; if it is improperly balanced, the meat will flop over with each rotation and the motor will whine.

Irregularly shaped bone-in cuts present a real challenge. Attach a counterweight to the spit; several inexpensive kinds are available. Adjust according to design and test with several turns of the spit.

The Comfort Zone

Your backyard is your own private sanctuary, away from the stress and noise of the outside world, and the pressures of everyday living. So, whether you plan to use your backyard for playing sports, swimming in your pool, lounging on the patio, or swinging in a hammock, you'll need to put some thought into designing your space.

By following the four basic landscaping principles, you can achieve a beautiful backyard. The principles are unity (elements shouldn't look out of place), variety (to avoid monotony), proportion (all elements should be in scale with your house and garden), and balance, (so that your eye isn't drawn to only one area of interest).

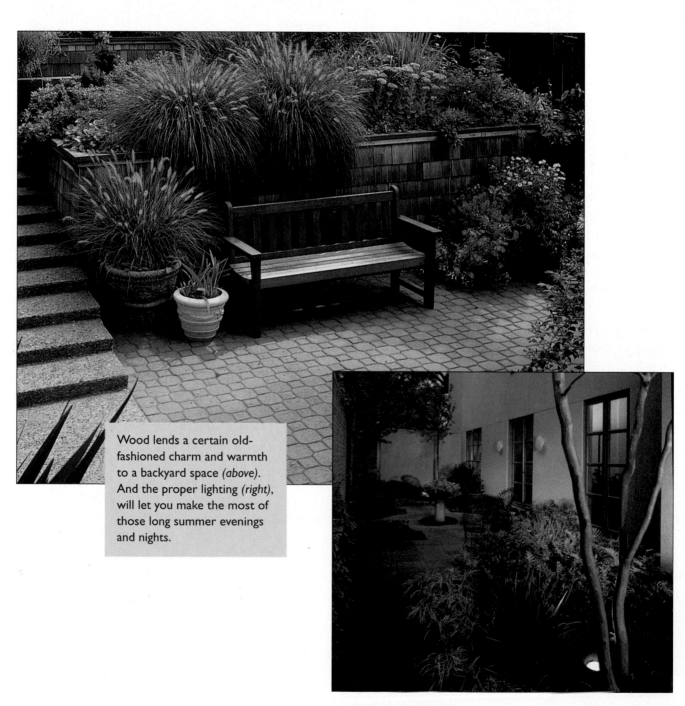

Wood lends a certain old-fashioned charm and warmth to a backyard space *(above)*. And the proper lighting *(right)*, will let you make the most of those long summer evenings and nights.

If you want to sit, read, or eat outside, you'll need patio chairs, tables, and benches. Wood furniture can be elegant, sturdy, and—best of all—it is relatively easy to make yourself, as you'll discover in the following pages. You can also buy wooden furniture, of course, along with plastic and other types of furniture. Just make sure that you consider outdoor wear and tear when you are buying or building—durability is important in the outdoor setting.

And when you just feel like whiling away those warm summer days in peace and serenity, try a hammock—nothing beats it for old-fashioned comfort and style.

Hammock Styles

One version of summertime Utopia might well include a comfortable hammock, a glass of lemonade, and a warm breeze.

Today's hammocks have evolved beyond the classic versions that were made of cotton rope or string, and suspended between two trees. There are now wide-ranging styles, colors, and materials from which to choose. Check synthetic materials carefully; some are softer, more comfortable, and more durable than cotton, but others may be harder on the skin. And hammocks now even come in sizes large enough to rock you and the kids to a peaceful sleep. As for trees: If your yard doesn't have two that are strong or close enough, the hammock can be mounted on a frame. The pictures below show some styles and hammock materials that you may want to try out yourself.

Synthetic mesh
This hammock style has woven-leaf patterns and hefty spreader bars to provide broad, smooth, breathable support for lounging.

Nylon net
The weave is softer and tighter than rope hammocks. The mesh at the ends can even be used to hold your books or cast-off shoes.

Multicolored Mayan
This exotic style weaves almost two miles of nylon string into a sturdy, vibrant, graceful form.

Quilted and reversible
This hammock has batting sandwiched between striped and solid-color sides.

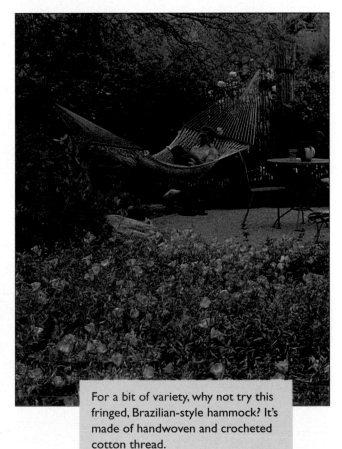

For a bit of variety, why not try this fringed, Brazilian-style hammock? It's made of handwoven and crocheted cotton thread.

Patio Furniture

When you choose patio furniture, remember that you'll be spending a lot of time using it, so make sure, first and foremost, that it is comfortable. Consider its durability as well, since you don't want to keep replacing outdoor pieces because they become weathered or weak. Most standard garden furniture is made of aluminum, wrought iron, plastic or resin composites, or wood. Folding furniture stores easily, but it's not as durable. Wood furniture, though weighty, has a timeless appeal; it's also long-lasting, provided it has been weatherproofed and is made of durable wood. Built-in perimeter benches are useful for year-round seating space. The photos here show functional yet beautiful patio furniture.

The furniture for your patio is an important design element that should tie in with the look of your yard. The white-webbed furniture at right creates an airy counterpoint to all the wood of the deck and gazebo. The modern metal furniture below suits the sleek look of the stone patio.

58

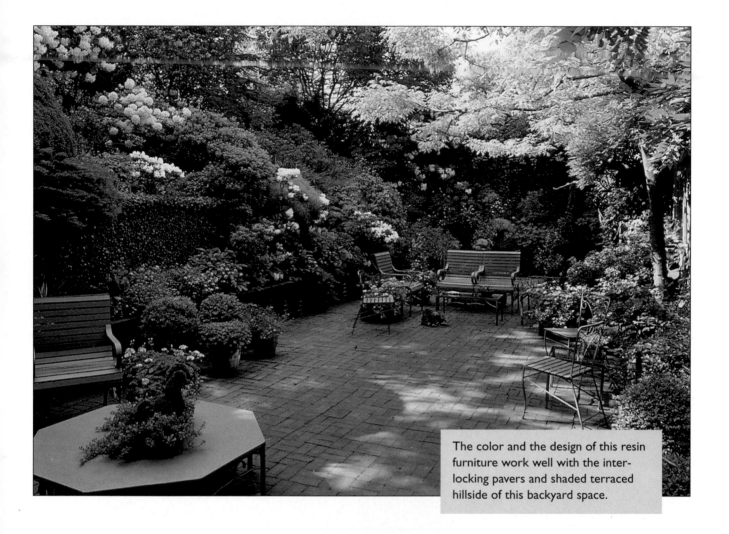

The color and the design of this resin furniture work well with the interlocking pavers and shaded terraced hillside of this backyard space.

Whatever your choice for patio style, furniture material, or planting arrangement, you'll need to figure out how best to use your available space. Outdoor furniture generally takes up more space than indoor furniture, and container plants take up their share of room. And don't forget traffic patterns: You'll need to leave enough space for people to maneuver around tables and other furniture. The illustration at right shows one example of how to calculate clearances around furniture.

Clearance for table with chairs

18"

*Side passage 22"
(32" for handicapped)*

Rising space 32"

Wooden Furniture

There's an enduring graciousness to outdoor wood furniture that can't be matched by its more practical cast resin or metal counterparts. But if you choose wood furniture for your backyard, it must be more than simply inviting to relax in; it must be rugged enough to survive outside. Outdoor pieces are typically subjected to harsher conditions than the average indoor piece, but with appropriate materials, design, joinery, hardware, and finishing, you can purchase or fashion outdoor furniture that will be long-lasting, and attractive. Start by choosing the appropriate wood species.

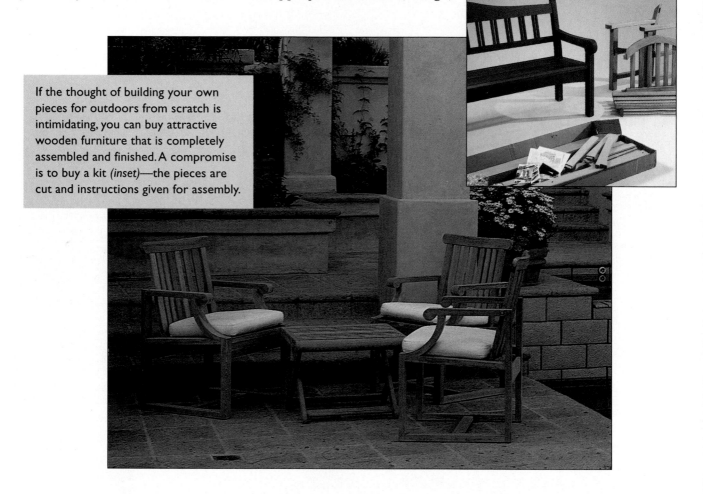

If the thought of building your own pieces for outdoors from scratch is intimidating, you can buy attractive wooden furniture that is completely assembled and finished. A compromise is to buy a kit *(inset)*—the pieces are cut and instructions given for assembly.

Outdoor Woods

If you wanted to, you could make all your outdoor furniture of wood and no two pieces need look alike. Different woods give different feels, looks, and textures. Some combine strength and resistance, but are expensive and too difficult to work with for most people. Other types cost less and are easy to work with, but are relatively weak and prone to decay. Good compromises include cedar and white oak, which are relatively long-lasting, but not too expensive. Start by selecting wood that's straight and flat, not bowed, twisted, or warped in any way. For the best quality, look for the highest grade lumber you can afford. If you plan to finish your pieces, your lumber needn't be perfect—you can use construction grades. The samples opposite show woods you can use for your own outdoor furniture. Keep in mind when you are building any of the projects shown in this book that the cutting and material lists quote nominal, rather than actual size. So, for example, a 1-by-6 is actually ¾ inches by 5½ inches.

Bald Cypress
This inexpensive softwood is naturally light yellow to brown, with a straight grain and oily texture. It's both water- and decay-resistant, making it ideal for outdoor use.

American Beech
This heavy, moderately priced wood is fairly decay-resistant, and has average strength and durability. Its color ranges from reddish-brown to light brown heartwood with off-white sapwood. The straight-grain gives it an even texture. It can shrink, bind on saws, and burn when drilled.

Western Red Cedar
This is one of the most durable, decay-resistant, and light softwoods, making it a good choice for outdoor use. It's straight-grained and coarse-textured—easy to work and not too expensive.

Jatoba
Although moderately priced, this hardwood is difficult to work and fairly tight-grained. Also named courbaril, it varies in color from rust to red-brown. It is occasionally used as a cheaper substitute for teak. Stronger and denser than white oak.

Mahogany
This straight-to-interlocked-grained wood is slightly coarse and reddish-brown. Its moderate price is coupled with durability, workability, and resistance to fungus—good for the outdoors.

White Oak
Moderately priced, this strong, very decay- and wear-resistant wood is also naturally watertight. It's not too hard to work with and bends fairly easily. Lght tan with a yellowish tint, it has a straight grain that gives it a bit of a coarse feel.

White Pine
This highly versatile and workable straight-grained wood has an even texture and is inexpensive. It's fairly decay-resistant, but can be too soft for some furniture. Its color varies from light yellow to reddish-brown.

California Redwood
Well known for traditional outdoor furniture and outdoor living, this softwood is strong and decay-resistant.. It has a straight grain and even texture, and is deep reddish-brown.

Willow
Light and tough with a straight grain, it has a fine texture and is grayish-brown with reddish-brown streaks. It's fine for temperate climates, but needs a yearly coat of water sealer.

Common Joinery Methods

The quickest and easiest way to join pieces of wood is with metal fasteners *(see opposite)*. A more elegant and time-honored technique, however, is to use a joint cut in the wood. Wood joinery dates back to the days of the ancient pharaohs, when sarcophagi were assembled with the help of the venerable mortise-and-tenon joint.

Today, outdoor furniture makers use a variety of joints, including the more common ones shown below.

Most joints require the use of adhesive to bind the two pieces of wood together. Choose your glues carefully because you will need one that is weatherproof. A chart of suitable adhesives is shown on the following page.

Mortise-and-tenon joints
This chair connects two right-angle units, and locks them in place using dowels. This sturdy bond is hardly noticeable to the casual observer.

FURNITURE JOINTS

Dado joint
A U-shaped recess cut across the grain on the face of a board. Strong and easy to make; often used to install shelves.

Rabbet joint
An L-shaped recess cut along the edge of a board to accommodate another piece. Reinforced with fasteners. Generally, the width of the joint is equal to the thickness of stock, and the depth is one-half the thickness. Easy to cut and assemble.

Through mortise-and-tenon
Among the strongest of the joints, it is used to build everything from doors and furniture to wooden ships. A projecting tenon in one board fits into a rectangular, round, or oval hole in another—the mortise. Can be reinforced with dowels. Often used to join chair parts.

T half-lap joint
Also called mid-half-lap, it's formed with a combination of a dado and a rabbet.

End half-lap joint
Formed from rabbets cut in two boards, this joint is frequently used to make frames

Angled T half-lap joint
Like the T half-lap joint, this is a combination of two joints, the dado and the rabbet.. In this case, the joints are angled. Harder to make than regular half-lap, but sheds water better.

Metal Fasteners

Screws, nails, bolts, and adhesives come in handy when you want to fasten and reinforce your outdoor wood furniture. Since nailing is the fastest way to join pieces, this is the most popular fastener, combined with glue. Use rust-free stainless steel, aluminum, or galvanized nails. But if you need extra strength and a finer look, screws are best. They're more expensive and time-consuming to use, but they create stronger joints—especially when combined with glue. The most common are shown below. When reinforcement is all you need, oversize lag screws or bolts are the answer. Again, use fasteners made from weather-resistant materials.

See the chart below for comparisons of the different types of glues.

Brass hardware
This wood chair's arms are joined to the frame using hexagonal-head bolts and barrel nuts. These serve to reinforce the joints, providing a stable, yet esthetically pleasing final product.. Brass hardware is naturally corrosion-resistant; so, too, is stainless steel.

COMMON SCREWS

Lag screw
Use a flat washer with this sturdy, oversize screw, which has a square or hexagonal head.

Flat washer

Lock washer

Machine bolt
Hexagonal head, driven with wrench.

Flathead screw
The most common type, its head sits flush with the wood surface. A brass screw with a finishing washer adds a decorative touch.

Finishing washer

Carriage bolt
Self-anchoring head digs into the wood as nut is tightened.

Screwdriver slots
From left to right, they are straight, Phillips, and square drive. The latter two keep the screwdriver from slipping.

Panhead sheet metal screw
This thick, sturdy fastener has excellent holding ability.

Nuts
From left to right: wing-nut, acorn-nut, and T-nut.

Flathead   **Oval head**   **Round head**

Screw length   Root diameter   Body diameter

WOODWORKING ADHESIVES		
TYPE	**CHARACTERISTICS**	**USES**
Resorcinol glue	Extremely strong, permanent, and toxic; must mix it; waterproof; dries a dark color	Bonds wood when moisture is high; fills gaps; must be clamped
Yellow carpenter's glue (weatherproof)	Extremely strong, heat-resistant; weatherproof; dries clear	Good gap-filler; must be clamped; best for general woodworking
Epoxy resin	Extremely strong; weatherproof; toxic if uncured	Bonds unlike materials; fills gaps
Urethane glue	Strong; waterproof; moisture cures the bond	General repairs; clamp; fills gaps
Contact cement	Water-resistant; apply to both surfaces	Bonds thin materials to a base
Plastic resin	Strong; must mix; water-resistant; potentially toxic	Fills small gaps; coat for protection
Instant/super glue	Water-resistant; sets quickly; moisture-curing	Needs clamping; bonds woods

Wood Finishing

If you have built your outdoor furniture from naturally decay-resistant woods you may choose not to finish it. Cedar, for example, will turn a silvery-gray color eventually and require little maintenance other than scrubbing away dirt and mildew occasionally. This will save you time in the future, because once you have applied a finish, you will need to renew it periodically.

If, on the other hand, you selected a less decay-resistant wood, finishing is your best choice to protect the wood and beautify it too.

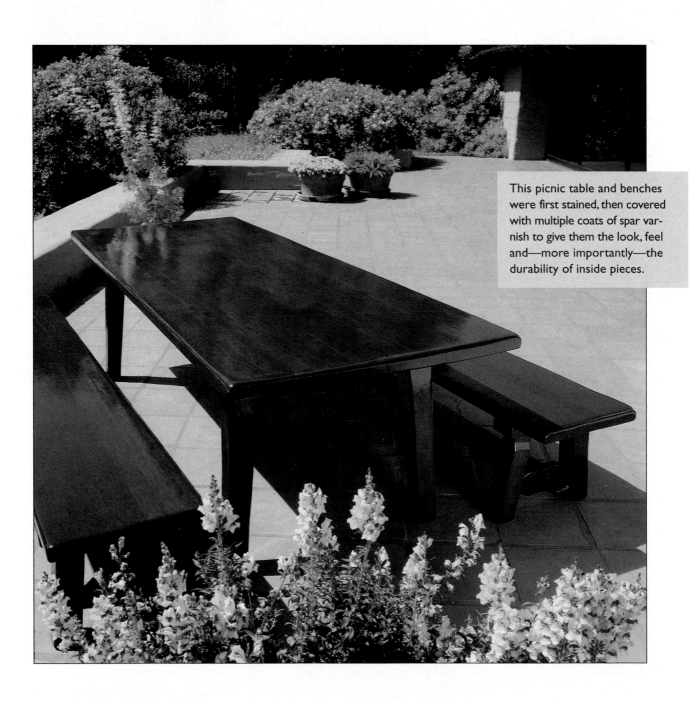

This picnic table and benches were first stained, then covered with multiple coats of spar varnish to give them the look, feel and—more importantly—the durability of inside pieces.

Finishing keeps insects from eating through your furniture. And a colored topcoat will also conceal any mismatched grain.

Water and sunlight are your furniture's worst enemies. Penetrating oils, varnishes, and paints are the finishes most commonly chosen to eliminate water damage. Use paint to protect pieces from sun. Generally, the higher the gloss, the better the sun protection. Some finishes, such as spar varnish, contain ultraviolet (UV) filters, which protect the wood from the damaging effects of the sun's radiation.

The most common choices in finishes are given in the chart below, along with information that can help you decide how best to protect your furniture.

CHARACTERISTICS OF COMMON OUTDOOR FINISHES

TYPE	ADVANTAGES	DISADVANTAGES	GENERAL TRAITS
CLEAR FINISHES			
Penetrating resin	Easiest to apply. Gives a natural, no-finish look.	Provides little surface protection.	Soaks into wood pores and darkens the wood grain.
Polyurethane	Simple to brush on. It's tough, alcohol-, heat-, and water-resistant.	Slow-drying. You can't coat other finishes with it.	Protects with a thick coating, and enhances the grain with a slight darkening effect.
Varnish	Seals and protects with 4 to 5 coats	Tends to yellow with age.	Shaking it creates bubbles, which may mar the finish.
STAINS			
Pigmented oil stain	Simple to wipe on and off with a rag, it's useful for changing and matching wood colors.	Often obscures pores and grain.	Colors don't fade or bleed, and are available ready-mixed in a wide variety of hues.
Penetrating oil stain	Similar to a penetrating resin, but with color; pores and grains show.	Penetrates irregularly on softwoods and plywoods; not good for matching colors.	Soaks into wood, and colors by means of dyes, not pigments.
Water stain	Bright, clear, and permanent. Thins easily and cleans off with water.	Water swells the fibers, so you need to resand; slow drying, hard to apply.	Comes in a powdered-mix form, dyeing the wood.
PAINTS			
Oil-base enamel	Durable, washable; good adhesion and coverage.	Slow-drying.	All gloss, semigloss, and flat colors totally conceal the grain.
Latex enamel	Use water to thin and clean it; quick-drying.	Has less durability and coverage than oil-based.	All semigloss and flat colors are available. Completely conceals grain.

Lawn Chair

If you're looking for comfort as well as classic styling in a piece of outdoor furniture, this classic Adirondack chair has both. With a tilted backrest and a reclining seat, it offers an inviting and relaxing place to sit, while its wide armrests provide enough surface for a few magazines or a refreshing drink.

CUT OUT THE PATTERNS

Use the grid patterns on the opposite page as a guide to cut out arm pieces (A and B) and seat legs (D) from 1-by-6s. The cutting list, also shown opposite, gives the dimensions of the arms and legs as well as the other pieces of the chair. For the tapering outside back slats (G), rip and sand a 32-inch 1-by-3 into two identical pieces, with ends measuring ½ and 1⅞ inches wide.

START AT THE FRONT

Cut a ¾-inch-deep by 3½-inch-long dado in each front leg (E), starting 10½ inches up from the bottom. Attach the arm supports (B) so

FINISHING UP

Once the chair has been assembled, it can be painted, stained, or left to its natural wood color. If you choose not to paint it, protect the wood against the elements with a nontoxic water-repellent preservative.
Design: William Crosby.

The chair is held together with waterproof glue and galvanized screws. Predrill and countersink all screw holes before assembling the chair. Here, the maneuverability of a cordless drill makes the job easier.

they're flush with the top and front edges of the legs, then attach support blocks (C) flush with the tops of the legs behind the arm supports. Attach the front stretcher (F) between the front legs; the stretcher should sit flush in the dado. Secure the seat legs (D) to the front legs so they butt against the back of stretcher F and are flush with the top edge.

SEAT AND BACK

Mount the center back slat (H) on the wide side of the 1-by-3 bottom cross brace (I), making sure the bottoms are flush. Attach two inside full slats (J) ⅝ inch from each side of H, then attach the outside full slats (K) ⅜ inch from the J pieces. Screw the ½-inch end of each of the G slats to the brace, spacing them ¼ inch from the adjacent slats. Center and screw in the upper cross brace (L) so its bottom is 27½ inches up from the

bottom of the back slats. Rip a 30° bevel along the top edge of the middle cross brace (M), then mount M 15½ inches up from the bottom of the back slats. Use a string extending to 14 inches below the top of the H slat to trace an arc in the chair back, then cut out the arc.

ATTACHING THE UNITS

Attach the 1-by-3 back brace (N) on the seat legs. Tuck the seat back's brace (I) under N, then screw the legs to the brace. Position the arms so they overhang the front of the supports (B) by 3 inches and the inner edges of the front legs by ¼ inch, then screw the support blocks (C) to the arms. Use single screws to attach the arms to the end of the brace (M), making sure they're even with one another. Screw the seat legs (D) into the brace (I); then attach the N brace to the I

brace with four screws. Finally, attach the six 1-by-3 slats (O) ½ inch apart so the front edge of the first one is flush with the front of the stretcher.

CUTTING AND MATERIALS LIST		
A	Arm	Two 1x6s @ 28½"
B	Arm support	Two 1x6s @ 10½"
C	Support block	Two 1x3s @ 3½"
D	Seat leg	Two 1x6s @ 31½"
E	Front leg	Two 1x4s @ 21"
F	Front stretcher	One 1x4 @ 23"
G	Tapering black slat	Two 1x3s @ 32"
H	Center back slat	One 1x6 @ 35"
I	Bottom cross brace	One 1x3 @ 20"
J	Inside full slat	Two 1x3s @ 35"
K	Outside full slat	Two 1x3s @ 34"
L	Upper cross brace	One 1x2 @ 21"
M	Middle cross brace	One 1x2 @ 24"
N	Back and leg brace	One 1x3 @ 21½"
O	Seat slats	Six 1x3s @ 21½"
	Galvanized flathead wood screws	1¼" x #8 (1 box)
	Waterproof glue	
	Finishing materials	

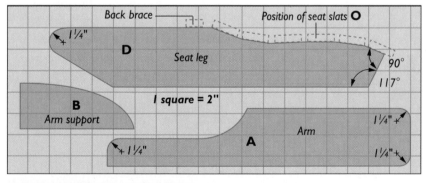

Scale drawings for arms and seat legs
In the scale drawing above, 1 square equals 2 inches. Simply enlarge the grid to produce the right-size patterns for cutting out the arms and seat legs.

Deck Chair

This folding deck chair is not only sturdy and comfortable—perfect for poolside or under a shady tree—it also stores so compactly, you'll want more than one. The simple instructions on these pages show you how to make a few of your own.

The curved rails that serve as legs, as well as supports for the seat and back, are a little tricky to cut. But with a bit of patience and a saber saw, you should have no real problem. You can expect to take a weekend to make your first chair, but as you become familiar with the design each subsequent chair should take less time. Use clear all-heart redwood for a richly colored chair that will weather well.

STARTING OUT

Follow the materials list on the opposite page to gather the items you'll need. When you're ready to begin cut the 2-by-8 lumber into 3-foot pieces. Then enlarge the grid drawing below to help you outline the curves of the back rail (upper piece) and seat rail (lower piece). Transfer these patterns to the 2-by-8s, then use a saber saw to cut them out. Alternately, you can use a compass to measure the curves, keeping in mind that the inside edge has a 63-inch radius.

CUTTING AND ASSEMBLING

The back rail is 2½ inches wide, and the seat rail is ⅛ inch narrower; the

COMFORT IN STYLE

These attractive and comfortable deck chairs can either be stained or left natural, as shown in the photos on the opposite page. Their practical design means that they take up very little space when stored. Design: Phoebe Brunner and Steve Hausz.

Scale drawing for back and seat rails
In the scale drawing at right, 1 square equals 2 inches. Each 3' length of 2x8 lumber yields one back and one seat rail. To provide sturdy stops for the seat rails, the two 1x4 boards attach to the back rails.

Position of seat slats **B**   Position of back slats **C**

Back rail   **A**

Seat rail

Position of 1x4s   63" radius

seat rails thus slip easily inside the
other rail assembly for storage.
Cut both pairs of rails, making sure
the seat rails are slightly narrower
than the back rails. Sand the rail
surfaces smooth.

Cut the 1-by-2s and the 1-by-4 to
19¾-inch lengths, and position the
slats on the rails as shown in the
scale drawing opposite. You
should have 13 1-by-2 slats and
two 1-by-4 slats on the rails. (The
1-by-4s are attached to the back
rails to provide stops for the seat
rails.) Slats on the seat rails
should hang 2½ inches over the
outside of the seat rails; slats on
the back rails should extend ⅞
inches from the inside edges of
the back rails so the back and
seat fit together easily for storage.

Glue all the connecting surfaces, then put one deck screw
into each end of each 1-by-2 and
two into each end of each 1-by-4.

MATERIALS LIST		
A	**Rails**	Two 2x8s @ 6'
B	**Seat Slats**	One 1x2 @ 10'
C	**Back slats**	One 1x2 @ 12'
D	**Stops**	One 1x4 @ 4'
Self-tapping deck screws		34 @ 2"
Waterproof glue		
Exterior stain, or paint, if desired		

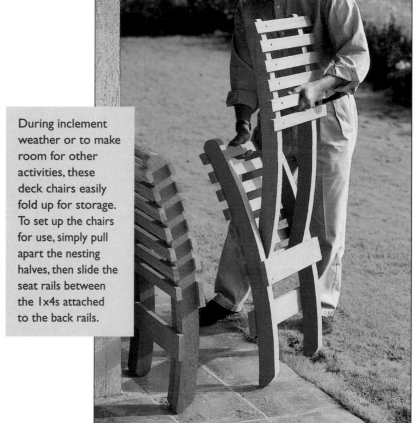

During inclement
weather or to make
room for other
activities, these
deck chairs easily
fold up for storage.
To set up the chairs
for use, simply pull
apart the nesting
halves, then slide the
seat rails between
the 1x4s attached
to the back rails.

Garden Planter/Bench

Nothing brings a garden closer to you than a planter/bench. With the simple design featured on these two pages, you can build your own and sit in the shade of small planter trees or relax amid the beauty of your favorite plants.

BUYING THE RIGHT LUMBER

Use weatherproof clear redwood or cedar lumber. The list on the opposite page tells you how much wood to buy and how to cut it; the illustrations below show the assembly.

GETTING STARTED

To make each container base, butt two front and back pieces (B) between two side pieces (A) and nail them in place with 3¼-inch finishing nails. Nail a plywood bottom (I) to the base, using 2¾-inch nails Then drill five ¾-inch drain holes through the bottom piece.

Mark each side piece (E) end with the locations of the ¼-inch rods and ¼-inch lag screws *(see Diagram 2)*. Next, counterbore ¾-inch-wide, 5/16-inch-deep holes for the washers, nuts, and bolt heads. Continue drilling ¼-inch

holes for the bolts and rods. Lay four D and four E pieces flat. Measure 2 inches from the lower edge and mark a line along the length of each board at that measurement. Build each container as shown in Diagram 1, aligning the top edge of the base with the marked lines on each of the two D and two E pieces. Nail a support (C), with the mitered edge up, into each container, using 2¾-inch nails.

Diagram 2

Counterbore ¾"-wide, 5/16"-deep holes Drill ¼" through

3/4"
1 1/4"
3 5/8"
6"
2 1/4
E

Diagram 1

C
20"   24"
E
D
E
See Diagram 2
48"
G
D
14½"
H
2¾"x 3/8" lag screw with washer
F
G
C
D
I
1½"
B
21"
¾" drainage hole (cut 5)
¼" threaded rods with washers & nuts
¼"x3" lag screw with washer
E
23¼"
A
17"

BUILDING PLANS

Diagram 1 shows how all the pieces of the planter/bench come together. Diagram 2 offers a side view of a container, showing the location of the drill holes for the rods and lag screws. Design: Don Vandervort

FINISHING THE CONTAINERS

Clamp four E pieces to the container supports (C). Use the ¼-inch holes in all the E pieces as guides to drill through the supports. Position four D pieces between the sides (E). Clamp them in place by inserting the rods, adding washers, and tightening the nuts. Then secure each D piece by inserting ¼-inch lag screws through the remaining holes in the E pieces. Nail the supports (C) to the upper four side pieces (E) with 2¾-inch nails.

Drill three ⅜-inch holes in each bench support H and then bolt it to the containers with ⅜-inch lag screws and washers. Place containers in position before attaching the bench.

Set the bench slats F on the supports H, spacing each slat evenly; nail it in position with 3¼-inch finishing nails. Place the bench faces (G) against the front and back slat edges, keeping the top edges flush; nail in place with 3¼-inch nails. Finally, set all the visible nail heads, fill the holes with wood putty, and sand all the exposed surfaces.

BASIC BENCHES

If instead of a planter/bench you would rather build a regular bench, follow these simple steps. For a straight bench, saw shoulders in 4-by-4 posts (A) and set in place; then bolt 2-by-4 braces (B) to the posts and nail on the planks (C). For a corner bench, mark posts (D), saw shoulders and add braces(E), and then nail on the mitered planks (F).

Straight bench

1"
3½"
A
4x4 post set 18" deep in concrete

⁵⁄₁₆"x6" bolts
B

Three 2x6s
C
15"-18"
Countersunk nails or lag screws

Corner bench

3¼"
45°
1½"
D

bolts
E
2x4

2x6s
F
Cut ends at 45°

CUTTING LIST		
A	Container base sides	Four 2x4s @ 17"
B	Container base fronts and backs	Four 2x4s @ 18"
C	Container supports	Eight 2x4s @ 18"
D	Container fronts and backs	Twelve 2x8s @ 21"
E	Container sides	Twelve 2x8s @ 20"
F	Bench splats	Three 2x6s @ 48"
G	Bench faces	Two 2x8s @ 48"
H	Bench supports	Two 2x6s @ 17"
I	Container bottoms	Two pieces ¾" plywood @ 17"x21"
Threaded rods with washers and nuts	12 @ ¼"x2"	
Lag screws	48 @ ¼"x3"	
Lag screws with washers	6 @ ⅜"x2¾"	
Galvanized finishing nails	12d @ 3¼"	
Galvanized common finishing nails	9d @ 2¾"	
Wood putty		
Water-repellent wood preservative		

Picnic Table and Benches

Picnic tables and backyards go together like America and apple pie. The design shown below, complete with matching benches, is sturdy, practical, durable, and simple to make. And by following the instructions on these two pages, there's no reason why you can't build one in time for your next cookout.

GETTING STARTED

The table and benches are made entirely of clear redwood. Begin by cutting pieces A through H according to the cutting list on the opposite page. Then lay the top pieces (A) best side down on a clean, flat surface, in groups of two for the benches and five for the table. Space them side by side, 1/8" apart (2½" box nails work well as spacers), keeping all ends flush.

JOINING THE TOPS

Set the table cleats (B) across the table top pieces, and bench cleats

Diagram 2

F
¼"x3" lag screw
H
6"
C
D
5/16"x4½" carriage bolt
60"
7"
10½"
A
¼"x3½" lag screw

Diagram 1

E
¼"x3½" lag screw
G
B
B
G
E
5/16"x4½" carriage bolt
¼"x3½" lag screw
60"
7"
1"
26"
28"
A
1¾"x No. 10 screws
1"

TABLE AND BENCHES

In Diagram 1, the picnic table is upside down, showing how the leg assemblies are attached to the top. Diagram 2 shows the same for one of the benches. Note that the top for table is equal in length to the tops of the benches, achieving a unifying effect. The finished project is illustrated above left

(C) and (D) across the bench top pieces, positioning them as shown in Drawings 1 and 2. Drill countersunk holes for 1¾" No. 10 screws through the cleats and into the top. Remove the B, C and D pieces, remembering where they go, then spread glue along their undersides and screw them in place.

PREPARING THE LEGS

You will need to cut grooves for the interlocking joints in the table and bench legs at the points where they cross. To locate these, first drill ⁵⁄₁₆" holes through the legs as indicated in Drawings 1 and 2. Join pairs of legs by pushing carriage bolts through them. Spread them in an X shape until

the distance between their bottom measures 26½" for the table legs and 15½" for the bench legs. Mark along their edges where they intersect.

JOINING THE LEGS

Remove the carriage bolts and cut the grooves for the interlocking joints by making a series of parallel cuts ¾" deep between the marks; then chisel out the waste wood. Next, counterbore and drill pilot holes for the lag screws and then attach the table legs (E) to their braces (G), and bench legs (F) to their braces (H).

INSTALLING THE TOPS

With the table top upside down,

set the leg assemblies upside down on the cleats (B) and fasten the leg assemblies to the table top with 3½" lag bolts with washers. Follow the same procedure for the bench tops, using 3" lag screws to fasten the braces (H) to the cleats (D). Turn the table and benches right side up on a flat surface. If any of the legs tend to rock, trim them slightly. Sand all corners, edges, and surfaces, then apply two or three coats of polyurethane penetrating oil-sealer.

Cutting details for legs and braces
The drawings above show the cutting details for the table legs (E), bench legs (F), table leg braces (G), and bench leg braces (H) and will help you cut the proper angles at the ends of each piece, as well as position the lag screws and carriage bolts.

	CUTTING AND MATERIALS LIST	
A	Tabletop and benchtops	Nine 2x6s @ 60"
B	Table cleats	Three 1x4s @ 26"
C	Bench cleats	Six 1x4s @ 10½"
D	Bench cleats	Four 1x4s @ 6"
E	Table legs	Four 2x4s @ 36"
F	Bench legs	Eight 2x4s @ 19"
G	Table leg braces	Two 2x4s @ 20"
H	Bench leg braces	Four 2x3s @ 10½"
	Carriage bolts	Six ⁵⁄₁₆" x4½"
	Lag screws	Fourteen ¼"x3½" Four ¼" x3"
	Flathead screws	Seventy 1¾"x No. 10
	Nuts and washers	
	Waterproof glue	
	Penetrating oil sealer	

Serving Cart

When it comes to entertaining outdoors, there's nothing like an extra set of helping hands to carry food and drink. This serving cart is the perfect candidate for the job. Attractive and simple to build, it makes life a lot easier around the pool, patio, or gazebo.

MAKING THE FIRST CUTS

Begin by cutting the pieces to length according to the cutting list on the opposite page. Then, use a table saw to rip each leg (A) and top frame piece (B) so that they are exactly 2⅜ inches wide. At the edge opposite the ripped side of the B pieces, and along one edge of the bottom frame pieces (C), rabbet a one-inch by one-inch

groove, as shown in Drawing 3. Then cut a ¾-inch wide by ½-inch-deep dado in each leg, 1½ inches from the end. The bottom end slats (G) should fit into the dadoes *(see Diagram 2).*

THE LEGS AND FRAME ASSEMBLY

Counterbore ¾ inch-diameter holes ⅜ inch deep in A and B, as shown in Drawing 1, for the lag screws. Center a ¼-inch bit in these holes and drill clearance

Diagram 1

Mount H to F with glue & four 2" x No. 8 screws.

Counterbore and drill for 3" lag screws through B into the top ends of all As.

Fasten with glue and 1½" finishing nails.

Diagram 3

Cut rabbet

Rip

Glue and nail two 1½" finishing nails at each end of each F

Counterbore and drill for 3½" lag screws through all A pieces into both C pieces.

Diagram 2

Dado a ½"-deep groove in A for G

BUILDING PLANS

The main pieces of the serving cart are shown in Diagram 1. Diagram 2 shows the detail of the dado cut that joins the the two bottom end slats to the legs. Diagram 3 shows how the main slats fir into the rabbet cut in the top frame piece.

holes through B into A and through A into C. Finish drilling pilot holes in the ends of A and C with a 5/32-inch bit. Glue and screw the pieces together, slipping a washer onto each lag screw. Let the glue dry, then sand the frames. Stand them up and fit the G pieces into the dadoes in the legs. Space the main slats (F) evenly, about 1/2 inch apart, along the rabbeted

CUTTING AND MATERIALS LIST

A	Legs	Four 2x3s @ 20"
B	Top side frame	Two 2x3s @ 29½"
C	Bottom side frame	Two 2x3s @ 24¾"
D	Handles	Two 2x3s @ 9"
E	Bottom leg	Two 2x3s @ 6¾"
F	Main slats	Eighteen 1x3s @ 20"
G	Bottom end slats	Two 1x3s @ 19"
H	End frames	Four 1x3s @ 21"
Lag screws		Four @ 2"x No.8 Four @ ¼"x3" Four @ ¼"x3½"
Flathead screws		Four @ 2¾"x No.14 Four @ 2¼"x No.14
1½" finishing nails		½ pound
Rubber wheels		Two @ 12" diameter
Steel rod		30"-long @ 7/16"
Waterproof glue		
Wood filler		
Polyurethane penetrating oil-sealer finish		

edges of B and C. Glue and nail them in place with 1½-inch finishing nails, then set the nails. Cut the end frame pieces (H) to match the widths of B and C (see Diagram 1).

CUTTING THE HANDLES

Use a saber saw to rough-cut the handles to the shape shown in the drawing below; smooth them with a rasp, then sand. Glue and screw the handles flush to each end of one of the H pieces, first drilling pilot holes for countersinking 2¾-inch No. 14 screws. Glue and screw that H piece to one end of the top of the cart, first drilling pilot holes for countersinking 2-inch No. 8 screws into the edge of the slat (F). Glue and nail the remaining H pieces, using 1½-inch finishing nails. Sand all the surfaces and fill any holes with wood filler. Sand again and seal with one coat of polyurethane penetrating oil-sealer finish.

MOUNTING THE WHEELS

Drill 7/16-inch holes for the axle in both C pieces, as shown in Drawing 1. Push the axle through both holes in the cart. On one side, slip two washers on the axle, then a wheel, another washer, and a hub nut. Measure the distance from C to the end of the hub nut. On the other side, mark the axle at that distance plus ⅛ inch, use a hacksaw to cut off any excess axle, then attach the other wheel.

ATTACHING THE BOTTOM LEGS

With the cart level, measure from the bottom of C to the ground; add 1½ inches (the total should be 6¾ inches). Round the corners at one end of each bottom leg (E). Drill pilot holes through the bottom end slats and the end frames into E for 2¼ inch No. 14 screws. Screw through G from the top and through H from one end to attach the legs.

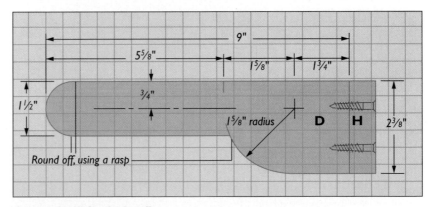

Cutting detail for the handles
The drawing above shows the cutting detail for the serving cart handles. Follow the measurements closely to shape a pair of handles for your project. Remember that the initial cutting doesn't have to be precise, a wood rasp and sand paper will take care of any imperfections.

Lounge Chair

CUTTING AND MATERIALS LIST

A	**Back supports**	Two 2x2s @ 24"
B	**Back braces**	Two 1x2s @ 12"
C	**Crossbrace**	One 1x2 @ 19"
D	**Back adjuster cleats**	Two 1x2s @ 10"
E	**Front and back stretchers**	Two 1x6s @ 19¼"
F	**Rear stretcher supports**	Two 1x2s @ 5½"
G	**Top slats**	30 1x2s @ 23⅞"
H	**Front legs**	Four 1x6s @ 13¼"
I	**Seat rails**	Two 2x6s @ 6'
J	**Back legs**	One 2x6s @ 3'
K	**Threaded rod**	2' @ ⁵⁄₁₆"
L	**Copper plumbing pipe**	2' @ ½"
M	**Plastic spoke wheels**	Two @ 6"-diameter
	Brass pivot hinges	Two @ No. 3½
	Lag screws	Two @ ¼"x2" with 4 washers Four @ ⅜"x6" with 4 washers
	Exterior self-tapping deck screws	82 @ 1⅜" No. 8
	Exterior glue	

No outdoor furniture collection is complete without the ultimate relaxation piece: a lounge chair.

GETTING STARTED

Cut your wood to length. Then, with a saber saw, cut notches and rounded corners for 12-inch back braces (B), as shown in Diagram 2. Drill a ⁵⁄₁₆-inch hole centered ¼ inch in from the rounded ends. Then saw the back adjuster cleats (D), using Diagram 3 and 4 as a guide. For each seat rail (I), use a circular saw to make the two angled cuts shown in Diagram 5. The back legs (J) are made by sawing the 2x6 diagonally so each piece has a 24-inch long side and a 12-inch short side (see Diagram 6).

CHAIR BACK & SEAT ASSEMBLY

Use a screw pilot where called for, and a good exterior glue to bond all the screwed surfaces.

Separate each hinge assembly into its two parts. Mount one of the parts so it's centered and flush with one end of a back support (A); its other part attached to a seat rail (I). To determine where the hinge goes on the rail, align A with I's top and back edges (see Diagram 7). Then separate the hinge pieces. Mount the notched ends of back braces (B) to the crossbrace (C). The back braces attach 2⅛ inch in from the ends of the crossbrace.

This support assembly then attaches to the back supports (A). Measuring 8 inches back from the hinged ends of each A, predrill a centered hole for a ¼- by 2-inch lag screw, then mount the support assembly with a washer on both sides of each back brace (B). Set the lags snug, but loose enough for the brace to swing freely. Using a screw pilot and 1⅜ inch No. 8 screws, mount the back adjuster

BUILDING PLANS

Diagram 2   *Diagram 3*

Diagram 1

cleats (D) to the inside faces of the seat rails (I), 5 inches in from the back end and 2⅜ inches down from the top edge. Then slip the hinges together to join B and I. Screw four slats (G) to the top surface: two on each side of the hinges and spaced ⅞ inch apart; the slats should overhang the outside of I by ¾ inch.

BACK LEG ASSEMBLY

The wheels slide onto a threaded rod secured to the back legs (J);

Diagram 4

the copper pipe keeps the wheels apart. On the inside faces of the back legs, drill a ⁵⁄₁₆-inch-diameter hole 1 inch deep; center the hole ¾ inch in from the 6-inch side. With a hacksaw, cut the threaded rod to 21 inches and the copper pipe to 17 inches, then thread a wheel onto the rod with the circular hub facing inward. Slide the copper pipe onto the rod so it fits into the wheel's hub. Then slide the other wheel on the other side so its hub fits over the pipe. Push the rod ends into the holes in the back legs until the wheels bump. Flip the seat-frame assembly upside down, glue the back leg assembly in position, then clamp it in place and drill a ¼-inch countersunk hole and a ⁵⁄₁₆-inch pilot hole as shown in Diagram 8. Attach the four long lag screws with washers. Mount one rear stretcher (E) to the ¾-inch edges of the rear stretcher supports (F). Attach E so

it butts against the angled edge of the back adjuster cleat (D).

FRONT LEG ASSEMBLY

Cut one notched and one unnotched piece to form each front leg (H), using Diagram 9 as a guide. Then, for each leg, hold one unnotched angled piece against the inside face of the seat rail (I) 6 inches from the front end. The top of H should be flush with the top edge of I. Mark a line on H along the angled lower edge of I, then cut along this line.

Now pair each of these H pieces with a longer notched board, and screw them together through the longer board. Mount the front stretcher (E) in the notches. Slide the front rail assembly against I 6 inches from the front end and screw it in place. Then screw the slats (G) in position, leaving a gap of ⅞ inch between each one.

Diagram 5

Diagram 6

Diagram 7

Diagram 8

Diagram 9

Lighting Up the Night

There's no need to leave your patio in the evening just because it's getting too dark to keep an eye on the kids or whip up a barbecue dinner. With the proper lights you can enjoy your backyard as late into the night as you want.

Good outdoor lighting is both functional and esthetic. On the practical side, it will give you the right kind of light when you need it for entertaining, outdoor cooking, or a lively evening volleyball game. And it can add to the beauty of your outdoor space by highlighting architectural elements and garden plantings.

Thoughtful planning is the key to effective lighting. First, decide how much light you need. If you want casual evening conversation,

Pathway marker

Well light

Fluorescent floodlight

Sensor-controlled "security light"

Uplight

Hanging light

Bollard light

Spread light

Downlight

Wall fixture

OUTDOOR FIXTURES

Outdoor lighting fixtures come in many variations, some depicted above. Regardless of what you choose, you'll want to avoid glare. An opaque covering on a fixture will create a warm glow rather than a hot spot of light. You can also use lower light levels. At night, a little light goes a long way: 20 watts is considered "strong."

soft and indirect illumination will give you enough light to see without robbing the evening of its mood. If you're an outdoor chef, you will need a bright light for the barbecue area. And if you want an area lighted for outdoor games, you will need high-intensity illumination. Include your garden in your lighting scheme. Day or night, your patio or deck serves as a transition from the house to the garden, so lights used to highlight trees or groups of plants will sustain your visual interest before the sun goes down.

Downlighting
Use this technique to gently light up your porches, patios and walkways. It's also good for accenting trees, shrubs and flowers, while letting you see where you're going at night.

OUTDOOR LIGHTING TECHNIQUES
You can use the fixtures shown on the previous page to light up your surroundings in various imaginative ways. Some standard lighting techniques are illustrated here. You can also combine techniques for interesting results. For example, a moonlight effect can be achieved by placing both uplights and downlights in a large tree. And don't forget, in food and cooking areas, you'll need stronger lights than you may want just for lounging.

Diffused lighting
A low level of lighting is often enough for low-traffic areas. Light railings and fences indirectly from underneath or behind to outline the edges of the structures.

Path lighting
Low or slightly raised fixtures that spread soft pools of light can define a walkway and highlight elements of your garden.

Spread lighting
You can light up your shrubbery with spread lights in the planting beds themselves. Try different colored bulbs for different effects.

Silhouetting
To silhouette a tree, shrub, or bed of flowers, try aiming a spotlight or wall washer at a fence or wall from close behind the plant.

Wiring the Outdoors

Though the principles are the same for both indoor and outdoor wiring, some materials used outdoors are specially designed to resist the weather. Driptight subpanel boxes and watertight switch boxes, for example, remain safe in damp and wet locations. Underground electrical cable has a thick solid plastic covering that makes it watertight when buried directly in the ground. Typically, however, outdoor wiring is routed through rigid metallic and rigid nonmetallic conduit, which protect it from the weather and acci-

Adding a 12-Volt System

To install a low-voltage system for outdoor use, you'll need a transformer, usually housed in a waterproof box, to step the household current of 120 volts down to 12 volts. Mount the transformer near the watertight switch or receptacle and then run a cable a few inches below the ground from the low-voltage side of the transformer to the desired locations for your lights. Some fixtures simply clip onto the wire, while others must be wired into the system. Some low-voltage lights come in a kit with a transformer. Be sure to use the right-sized wire given in the instructions. If you don't already have an outlet to plug the transformer into, have an electrician install a GFCI-protected outlet *(below)*.

Circuit breaker GFCI

GFCI receptacle
According to present electrical codes, any new outside receptacle must be protected by a ground fault circuit interrupter (GFCI, or GFI). Whenever the amounts of incoming and outgoing current are not equal—indicating current leakage (a "ground fault")—the GFCI opens the circuit instantly, cutting off the power.

Receptacle GFCI

A typical 12-volt installation
Since a 12-volt system uses a greatly reduced voltage, special conduit and boxes of other outdoor wiring are not required. Most transformers are rated for home use from 100 to 300 watts. The higher the rating, the more lengths of 100-foot cable—and consequently the more light fixtures—can be connected to the transformer. Most transformers are encased in watertight boxes; to be safe, though, plan to install yours at least a foot off the ground in a sheltered location.

Watertight switch
Turns low-voltage lights on and off.

Transformer
Converts 120-volt current to the low voltage required by the lighting fixtures.

Walkway
Protect cable by running it under or alongside a walkway.

Low-voltage light
May be an individual fixture or installed in a series.

UF direct burial cable
Connects transformer to lighting fixture.

dental damage. You can bring electricity outdoors by having an electrician extend an inside 120-volt power source by tapping into an existing switch, lighting, or receptacle outlet box. A simpler alternative is low-voltage lighting. Operating on only 12 volts, low-voltage wiring is easy to install yourself and doesn't present the dangers of 120 volts.

Whatever the system, use the protection of ground fault circuit interrupters (GFCIs) on all outdoor circuits. Make sure you consult an electrician before you start work.

Setting Up a 120-Volt System

A 120-volt outdoor lighting system offers several advantages. For starters, a light from a single fixture can illuminate a larger area—especially useful for security and for lighting trees from the ground. In addition, a 120-volt system offers flexibility: not only light fixtures, but also power tools, patio heaters, and electric garden tools can be plugged into 120-volt outdoor outlets.

A 120-volt outdoor system consists of a set of fixtures, of course, and some underground 120-volt cable (if allowed by local code) or conduit; the length used depends on the size of the wire. Your electrician will probably connect the system through an indoor switch and timer to an existing electrical source or circuit, as shown below. This will allow you to turn lights on and off by hand or let the timer do it for you.

The diagrams shown here will help you understand the basics of installing a 120-volt system. But unless you are well versed in all aspects of electricity you should leave the job to a professional. If you decide to do the installation yourself, remember to shut off the power to the circuit before beginning work.

Switch bypass timer

Hot wire

Hot white wire (should be painted black near switch and splice)

Timer

Neutral wires

Hot wires

Hot wire

Grounding wires

From existing power source

To 120-volt outdoor fixtures

120-volt wiring at a glance
The illustration below depicts a standard outdoor wiring set-up, using a 120-volt system. The outdoor fixture, housed in the watertight box, is attached by a rigid steel conduit to the existing indoor circuit structure. You can place the cable and wiring up to two or so feet underground. To wire an indoor switch and timer for 120-volt outdoor fixtures, see the illustration at right.

Existing indoor box
NM cable
New watertight box
Locknut
Rigid steel conduit
Conduit-to-cable adapter

From source
Existing outdoor box
Watertight extender ring
Locknut
Rigid steel conduit
UF cable

Outdoor fixture
Redwood board (Protects cable where it is not under slab)
Ridgid steel conduit

Lighting a Patio & Garden Path

Showcasing your plants and flowers, guiding you through your garden, and turning your patio into a nighttime as well as a daytime entertainment area—all this can be accomplished by effectively lighting your patios and garden paths. If the patio leads directly off a room in the house, strive to balance light levels on both sides of a window or sliding doors to avoid a "black hole" effect. Ideally, you are trying to create as seamless a transition as possible from indoors to outdoors. If your house has deep eaves or an overhang extending the length of your walk, you might consider installing weatherpoof downlights to illuminate your walk and plantings without any visible fixtures.

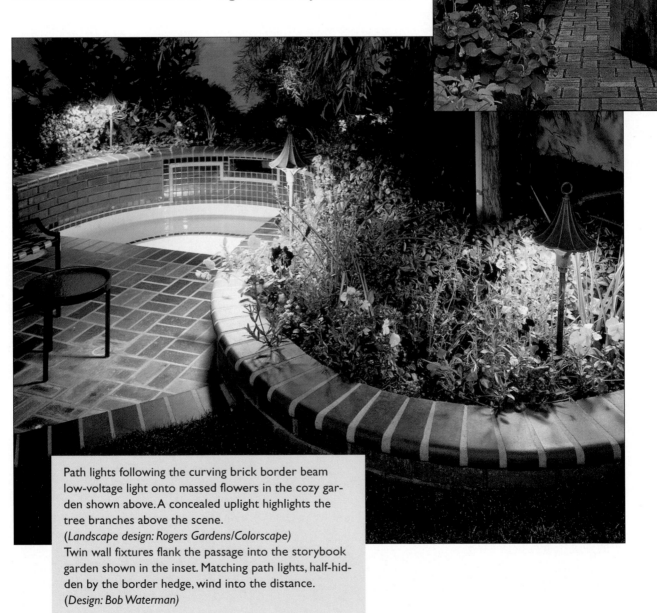

Path lights following the curving brick border beam low-voltage light onto massed flowers in the cozy garden shown above. A concealed uplight highlights the tree branches above the scene.
(*Landscape design: Rogers Gardens/Colorscape*)
Twin wall fixtures flank the passage into the storybook garden shown in the inset. Matching path lights, half-hidden by the border hedge, wind into the distance.
(*Design: Bob Waterman*)

Lighting a Deck

On a deck, a low level of light is often perfectly adequate for quiet conversation or alfresco dining. By lighting steps, railings, or benches indirectly from underneath—or directly with strings of mini-lights—you can outline the edge of your structure. This is especially important for safety's sake if your deck is elevated.

Don't forget to add stronger light wherever you plan to do your serving or barbecuing. Downlighting is a popular choice *(see page 79)*, but indirect lighting—diffused through plastic or another translucent material—may also prove useful. As with any wiring projects, you may want to consult with a professional before you start, especially if you have chosen a 120-volt system. But once you finish you can enjoy your extended "daylight" hours and relax the summer away.

LOW-VOLTAGE DECK LIGHTING

Home improvement centers and hardware stores offer low-voltage deck-lighting kits, including post-style lights, a transformer, and cable. Installation is easy, following manufacturer's instructions, but you'll need an outlet equipped with a GFCI *(page 80)*. The illustration below shows what's involved in adding a 12-volt lighting system to a deck. The low-voltage cable connecting the lighting fixtures to the transformer can be clamped unobtrusively to the bottom side of the deck floor. Decide on the fixture you'll use according to taste or the lighting effect you want.

Transformer and timer
In weatherproof box

Low-voltage deck lights

Low-voltage cable

GFCI-protect outlet

Clamp connector

Outdoor Heating

A patio or deck that receives too much sun or wind can have its climate modified in many ways. Overheads and trees, for example, can serve to protect the structure from sun, while screens can moderate the effects of gusty winds. But to get the most out of your outdoor resting areas, you may want to consider adding some type of heating device to take the edge off the weather and lengthen the hours and days you can spend outdoors.

Patio heaters and fire pits allow you to turn your patio or deck into a pleasant place to spend a brisk morning or evening. You can buy freestanding heaters, or can mount

Gas heaters
Gas-fired directional heaters mount to a house's eaves, allowing them to throw their heat efficiently without being obtrusive. They're usually quite expensive, ranging from $500 to $700 for the complete installation and hookup of two heaters. And you'll need to check them periodically for bugs and other maintenance considerations.

Different heaters are available for different needs. Mushroom heaters *(right)*, for example, are freestanding and moveable. Other types, like the directional heater shown attached to the roof of the gazebo in the photo at left, are more permanent installations. Though their output is usually substantially less than mushroom heaters, directional heaters are much less affected by wind, and waste less heat. They also require smaller clearances, so they can mount unobtrusively to walls or other part of a structure.

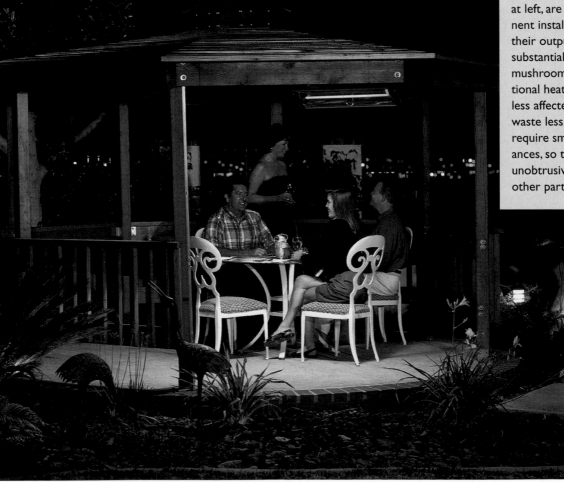

a more permanent gas or electric unit; these are often less visible and more effective.

For heating units to perform well, they will need the right location. Shelter your heaters from the wind. Pick a spot that's intimate and comfortable. If you heat near a wall or other solid structure, the heat will radiate back into your space and warm the area. The ideal location contains a combination of walls, fences, and overhead structures that will prevent the wind from blowing directly through your selected area. Pay particular attention to stopping the breeze at ground level—because feet get cold quickly, you'll appreciate it if this area is supplied with a warm, still pocket of air.

Mushroom heater

This stainless-steel heater, also known as an umbrella, radiates its warming rays from the top cylinder. It provides a comfort zone of about 12 to 15 feet in diameter. The base hides a propane tank. Though this model sells for roughly $800, you can buy less expensive, painted models. Mushrooms may be the most powerful heaters in terms of energy output, but much of the heat radiates horizontally, above the desired area. Of all outdoor heaters, these are the most wind-sensitive. It's best to put these units away when not in use, as bugs, moisture, chlorine, and salt can affect their performance.

FIRE PITS

Fire pits, or rings that often double as barbecues, are good sources of heat. If you want to be able to move the fire around, try a low, round metal brazier—or more than one to help distribute the heat evenly. If your patio or other space can accommodate it, consider using a full-scale fireplace.

Portable pottery fire pits generate generous amounts of heat from only a small fire. But use them cautiously: they're lightweight and reasonably fragile, and they may break if the fire inside is too hot. You'll get the best results by burning kindling-size wood.

Remember that any open fire is a potential hazard. Be sure your fire is away from the tree branches or patio overheads that could be ignited by flying sparks. In some areas, a permit is needed for any outdoor fire, so call your fire department first to check local regulations.

The photograph below shows how you can incorporate a fire pit into your own backyard patio or deck.

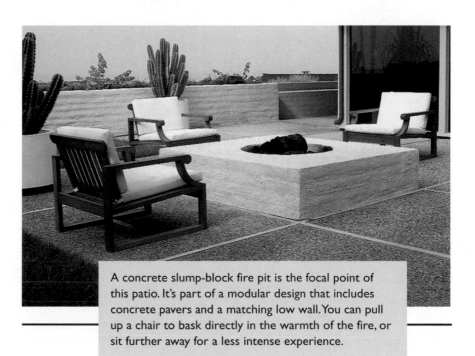

A concrete slump-block fire pit is the focal point of this patio. It's part of a modular design that includes concrete pavers and a matching low wall. You can pull up a chair to bask directly in the warmth of the fire, or sit further away for a less intense experience.

The Wild Backyard

Make your yard a more enchanting place by encouraging wildlife to visit it. Birds, bees, bats, and butterflies can all be made welcome with a little thoughtful planting and organization. You'll attract more birds, for example, if you opt for an overgrown garden style approximating their natural habitat, rather than a lawn.

If you want aquatic life, of course, you'll have to create the right environment for it, including installing a garden pond *(page 102)*. For colorful examples of two popular fish you can choose from, see pages 100 and 101. And if you need to deal with some uninvited natural visitors to your yard, turn to pages 104 and 105.

Attracting Birds

Birds share our daily lives—roosting on roofs, warbling in a treetop, or splashing in a birdbath. Whether they show up singly, in pairs, or in flocks, their activities and song help us to feel more alive, in tune with the natural world.

Chances are that some birds are already finding their way to your garden, even if they are only the briefest of guests. You can encourage them to linger by providing the essentials of life–food, water, protective cover, and a safe place to raise their young.

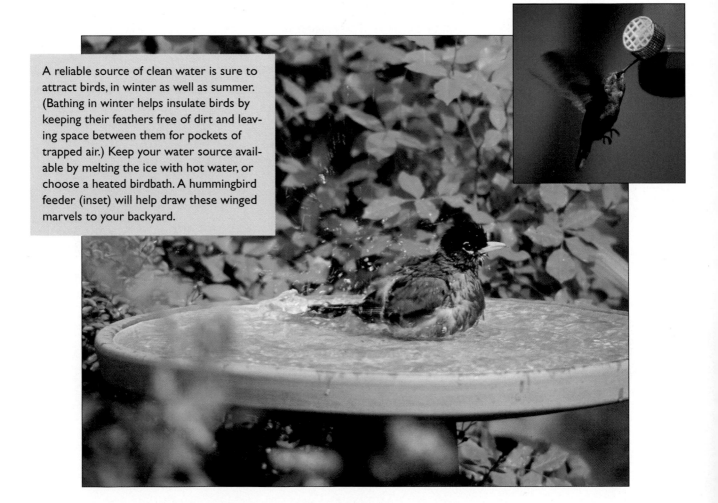

A reliable source of clean water is sure to attract birds, in winter as well as summer. (Bathing in winter helps insulate birds by keeping their feathers free of dirt and leaving space between them for pockets of trapped air.) Keep your water source available by melting the ice with hot water, or choose a heated birdbath. A hummingbird feeder (inset) will help draw these winged marvels to your backyard.

In nature, birds are accustomed to the mingling of diverse plants, so variety is the key to planting an appealing bird-scape. These tips will help you create an arrangement of plants similar to what occurs where a woodland and a meadow or grassland meet.

• Plant the birdscape's border with varied trees and shrubs; large shade trees for a canopy and shorter trees to create an understory. Plant shrubbery near the trees to form a bridge into open spaces.

• Limit lawns to small areas, placing mass plantings of graduated trees and shrubs around the lawn's perimeters. Shrubs directly bordering the lawn should branch low to the ground.

• In cold-winter regions, a stand of dense evergreen trees is ideal for winter shelter. A hedge of hemlock (*Tsuga*) can serve the same purpose.

• If you can spare a corner just for the use of birds, turn it into a wild area. Let grasses grow high to produce seeds, and allow a dense thorny shrub (such as *Rosa multiflora*) grow into a tangled thicket for nesting and refuge. If a tree dies or drops a limb, leave it to decay naturally; birds will savor its insects and may use it for nesting.

• Include a garden oasis, however small, where water is available for drinking and bathing. Keep the water clean, and locate it within quick reach of cover.

This East Coast garden offers many inducements for birds in early autumn. From left to right, fading gloriosa daisies attract a pine siskin, while purple finches dip in the bird-bath. Evening grosbeaks snack at a sunflower seed feeder hung from a red oak tree, and a downy woodpecker clings to a suet feeder. Viburnum below the tree and Euonymus alata in the background offer more food; blue spruce branches provide refuge, if necessary.

Bird Feeders

Adding a bird feeder increases your garden's powers of attraction. Birds often remember where they had a good meal months before, and will return to the same spot for more.

Many people provide feeders in the fall, winter, and early spring. During spring and summer, feeders are less popular, probably because birds are more territorial and chase rivals away, and because naturally available food is more appetizing than supplemental foods. Don't expect instant success—it may be weeks before birds use a feeder.

Squirrel-proof (weighted perch) feeder

Oriole fruit feeder

Gazebo feeder

Dome covered feeder

Suet basket

A RANGE OF STORE-BOUGHT FEEDERS

You can choose from sleek acrylic, lightweight metal, or classic wood designs. Certain feeders are designed for certain birds. A fruit holder will attract tanagers, orioles, and warblers. To attract goldfinches, put out a feeder designed for their favorite food—niger (thistle) seed. Suet is a great treat for insectivores, such as woodpeckers and mockingbirds.

Tube-style feeder

Seed tray

Seed tray

Redwood hopper feeder

Feeder post

Straight-arm bracket

Thistle feeder

Hummingbird feeder

Squirrel-proof pole

Squirrel baffle

A Shop-built Bird Feeder

You can design a bird feeder to go with your garden's style, and add your own personal decorative touches. Home-built feeders don't have to involve difficult carpentry; most can be built with a few standard homeowner's tools, such as a saw, a measuring tape, and a hammer. Decay-resistant woods, such as redwood and cedar heartwood, will last longest, but any scraps you have on hand will do.

A feline-foiling feeder tray
Hanging from a slippery 7' pipe system, this feeder design helps keep cats and scavenging squirrels at bay. Build the inner frame of 1x1s, then nail on seven slats to make the feeding platform. You may have to rip a slat lengthwise for an accurate fit. Add the four eyebolts, and nail the ½"x½" strips for the food trap to the platform's top. Miter the 1x4s for the outer frame and nail them in place. Assemble the post and pipe system, and suspend the feeder from eyebolts with S-hooks and chain.

1" galvanized pipe, 3' long

Eyebolt

½" brass chain

1" couplings

1" sweep elbow

1" galvanized pipe, 7' long

½"x½" strips

Food trap

14¼"   14¼"

4x4 post, set 2' in concrete

Floor

Eyebolt

Eyebolts   24"   24"

½x4 slats

Drain holes

Outer frame

1x4

1x1s

Inner frame, 24"x24"

Mitered corner

25½"   25½"

Pipe clamp to attach pipe to post

Birdhouses

By putting birdhouses in the right places, you can sharply increase the number of birds in your garden. Whether your birdhouse attracts the birds you intend it for depends to some extent on whether its dimensions, entrance hole, and mounting height are to the birds' liking. For example, a wren might not use a house with a 2-inch hole, because larger birds could enter and threaten the occupants. It's an inexact science, but some basic dimensions and mounting heights are given below. Mount the birdhouse atop a metal pole to keep it safe from cats and raccoons. Face the entrance away from prevailing weather, and don't put the house near a feeder (the activity makes nesting birds nervous).

Robin shelf

Wren house

Screech owl house

Chickadee house

Purple martin apartment

Bluebird house

Wren house

BIRD-SIZE ACCOMMODATIONS

Wood is the traditional birdhouse material, and birds seem to accept wood houses well—the rougher the better. Bird experts caution against paint. Lead-base paint and some clear finishes may be toxic, and bright colors seem to discourage birds.

One exception: Aluminum purple martin apartments are popular, and much easier to hoist into place than their wooden counterparts.

BASIC BIRDHOUSE DIMENSIONS

	SPECIES				
	BLACK-CAPPED CHICKADEE	**BLUEBIRD**	**ROBIN**	**PURPLE MARTIN**	**SCREECH OWL**
Floor size	4"x4"	5"x5"	6"x8"	6"x6"	8"x8"
Height	8"-10"	8"	8"	6"	12"-15"
Entrance above floor	6"-8"	6"	*	1"	9"-12"
Diameter of entrance hole	1⅛"	1½"	*	2½"	3"
Height above ground	6'-15'	5'-10'	6'-15'	15'-20'	10'-30'

*One or more sides open.

Birdbaths

Birds love a dip in a cool pool on a hot day as much as people do. They'll happily use a streambed or a puddle, but a reliable source of clean water in your garden can be a powerful attraction.

A birdbath can take many forms, from the traditional bowl on a pedestal to the more whimsical shapes shown below. Most birds bathe by wading into shallow water that's no deeper than their legs are long, so a couple of inches is deep enough. If the sides slope gradually, birds can wade in to a comfortable depth. To attract several birds at a time, choose a bath at least 24 to 36 inches in diameter.

Looking like the real thing, but weighing only about 60 pounds, this fiberglass boulder was molded from a real rock.

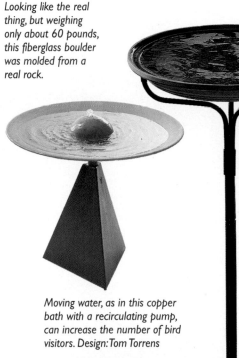

Set on a slim metal rod that sticks into the ground, this glazed terra-cotta saucer birdbath uses new materials but keeps the traditional pedestal shape.

SPARKLING BATHS

Birdbaths can be made from a variety of materials, including concrete, glazed ceramic, metal, plastic, and terra-cotta. The surface texture should be rough enough to offer traction; you can add gravel to slippery baths, but that will make cleaning more difficult.

Moving water, as in this copper bath with a recirculating pump, can increase the number of bird visitors. Design: Tom Torrens

Bring birds to your eye level with a hanging or post-mounted bath. The bath above can dangle from a tree limb or the house eaves.

The 3/4 circle terra-cotta bath above can be attached directly to a deck post. The plastic saucer shown below, called Deck Oasis, can be attached with its steel ring to a deck post or a house wall.

The simplicity of this traditional white pedestal birdbath is a pleasing contrast to the colorful plantings that surround it.

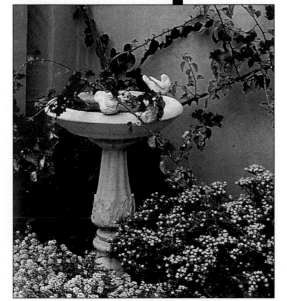

Beautiful Butterflies

Attracting butterflies to your garden is much easier than you may think. You can start small, with just a few of the right plants, or smaller—some butterfly gardens are no bigger than a single pot.

The plants that attract adult butterflies are not always the same as those that support caterpillars (larvae). Butterflies lay their eggs on a plant the larvae need for food. Some larvae can consume a vari- ety of plants, and others need one specific plant. The larvae of the monarch butterfly, for example, feed only on milkweed.

Old-fashioned, fragrant flowers that have retained their nectar are

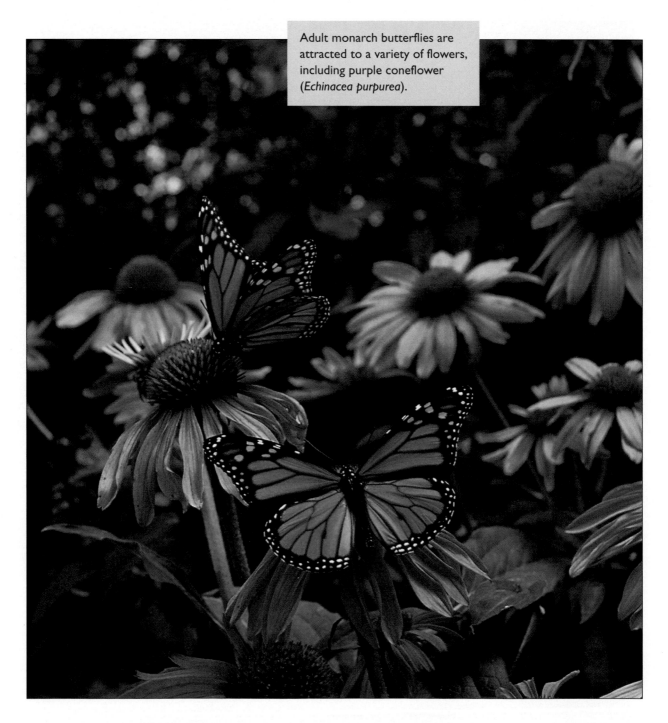

Adult monarch butterflies are attracted to a variety of flowers, including purple coneflower (*Echinacea purpurea*).

good choices to attract adult butterflies. Hybrids are usually not as successful; they may have had their nectar bred out of them or the flower shape may make it difficult for the butterflies to get at the nectar. Tubular or upright blooms, such as those of lantana or dandelion, are best; hanging flowers are less attractive.

Butterflies seem to prefer yellow and red blooms, but any bright flower in full sun will attract them; they rarely go to flowers in shade or wind. In general, perennials prove more popular than annuals. Ideally, choose plants native to your region.

Butterflies tend to like old-fashioned fragrant flowers like this wild rose, shown here attracting a pale swallowtail.

The flowers of the butterfly weed attract a variety of butterflies, including the tiger swallowtail, seen here.

A bright cosmos has drawn an eastern black swallowtail to sip its nectar. Cosmos are a favorite for adult butterflies.

California Dutchman's pipe (also called pipevine) is the food plant of the pipevine swallowtail caterpillar, which will turn into a coal black butterfly.

A BUTTERFLY GARDEN

An ideal butterfly garden that will allow you to observe all the stages of a butterfly's life should include both nectar plants for adult butterflies and food plants for larvae. It is sheltered from the wind, and may include a moist or damp area and some boulders or a rocky area.

Locate your butterfly-attracting plants where they'll be in sun between 11 A.M. and 3 P.M., which is the time when most butterflies tend to be active.

Use plants that grow to different heights to create a sheltered atmosphere. Place taller, longer-lived shrubs and small trees, such as abelia, buddleia, and ceanothus in the background to provide a windscreen as well as food and nectar. Low-growing plants such as blue salvia and marigolds can then be planted in front, with bright annuals and perennials in the middle at the visual focal point to attract the butterflies.

Nectar plants for adult butterflies: butterfly bush *(Buddleia davidii)*, especially varieties with pink flowers; butterfly weed *(Asclepias tuberosa)*; California buckwheat *(Eriogonum fascinculatum)*; cosmos, lantana *(L. camara, L. montevidensis*, and hybrids*)*; Shasta daisy *(Chrysanthemum maximum)*; and zinnias.

Food plants for larvae: butterfly weed *(Asclepias tuberosa)* and other milkweeds (other *Asclepias* varieties); passion vine *(Passiflora*, especially *P. caerulea* and *P. incarnata)*; California Dutchman's pipe *(Aristolochia californica)*; and senna *(Cassia*, especially *C. didymobotria*, and *C. armata)*.

Beekeeping in the Backyard

Beekeeping is a time-honored activity that can be at once educational, profitable, and entertaining. With sufficient nectar available from flowering trees, shrubs, and other plants, an average hive can produce upwards of 100 pounds of honey in a single season.

Of course, bees are delicate creatures that require a good deal of care and consideration when handling. It's best to learn as much about them as you can before you begin keeping. The information on the following pages—from the starter kit on the opposite page to the tips below on locating your hive—will point you in the right direction.

Before you install a hive, check your local ordinances; some municipalities restrict or ban beekeeping in inhabited areas. Also, try to acknowledge any concerns that your neighbors may have about your new hobby. Talk to them before beginning. Contact your local county extension office or beekeeping association for further advice.

Bees work together very efficiently, building the wax honeycomb *(as shown at left)*, caring for immature members, and cleaning and defending the hive. They also use a fascinating series of "dances" to communicate the location of nectar-bearing flowers to each other.

LOCATING YOUR HIVE

Although bees are not naturally aggressive, they will resort to stinging to defend the hive. With this in mind, position your hive so that the the bees' flight path keeps them away from human traffic areas as much as possible as shown at right. Try surrounding the hive with flowering hedges to limit the size of the defensive zone in which they feel threatened. And because bees require a lot of water, making fresh water available close to the hive encourages them not to roam into your neighbor's pool or a pet's dish.

Beehives

Bee flight path

Hedge

Getting Ready for Your Bees

For a novice, the best way to start a beekeeping hobby is to buy a beginner's kit *(below)* from a supplier. It will come with all the equipment you need to set up your first hive. You'll have to buy your bees as well; try ordering up to four months in advance so they arrive just as fruit trees start to bloom in your area.

Be prepared for your bee's arrival. Have sugar syrup on hand, as well as a beekeeper's veil and smoker. Make sugar syrup by combining equal amounts of hot water and white sugar; allow to cool before using.

When the bees arrive, maintain them in a dark room at about 60°F. Spray the cage with sugar syrup just before hiving the bees.

The queen is shipped inside the package in a cage. Take out the cage, then remove the cork that covers the end of the cage that has a candy plug. Place a cup of bees in the hive, next to the queen cage; they will gradually free the new queen. Gently tap the package so the remaining bees are dumped outside and can walk into their new home.

Once the bees are installed in the hive, feed them more syrup, but don't disturb them for at least five days. After that, you should see eggs in the bottom of the cells. After an additional five days, capped larvae should be present. Once there is sufficient nectar available, the bees will stop eating the sugar syrup.

Cover
Removable, it allows the beekeeper access.

Frames
These slide in and out of the hive and support the comb.

Hive body
The main structure of the hive.

Bottom board
This removable bottom allows space for ventilation and the bees to fly in and out.

Feeder
Provides sugar syrup, when needed.

Inner cover
Present on some hives, it improves ventilation and adds insulation from extremes of heat or cold.

Wax foundation
Provides bees with material to start building combs.

Veil
Protective headgear.

Smoker
Produces smoke for pacifying bees (used in small quantities).

Hive tool
Used for opening hives and removing frames.

Gloves
Lightweight work gloves with gauntlets

HONEY-APPLE FREEZE

This simple dessert uses honey for a tasty summer confection.

1 cup applesauce
¼ cup honey
3 tablespoons lemon juice
1 teaspoon grated lemon rind
1 cup evaporated milk

• Combine all ingredients and mix well (honey must be dissolved).
• Freeze as you would ice cream, *(see page 43).*

Bats: Denizens of the Nighttime Garden

If you notice bats flying around your garden, consider yourself fortunate. Bats feed on plant-damaging insects and are much more likely to be useful than harmful.

To attract bats, you can set up a commercially available bat house, or build your own like the model shown on the opposite page.

A bat house must be sufficiently warm, but not too hot. Choosing the right paint color and properly locating the house will help achieve the right temperature. Paint the house black if the average high July temperature is 80°-85°F or less; a dark color (dark brown, gray, or green) if it's 85°-95°F; a medium or light color if it's 95°-100°F; and white if it's 100°F or higher. In cooler climates, the house should get 10 hours of sunlight daily; even in areas where the average July temperature is up to 100°F, 6 hours of daily sun exposure are required.

Vent slots at the bottom of the house will make the box cooler below and warmer above, allowing the bats to move around inside to find their preferred temperature over daily and seasonal fluctuations. Making the vents slots only ½ inch wide offers good ventilation without allowing in too much light.

Mount the house about 15-20 feet above ground on a pole or against a house to offer protection from predators. Bat houses usually work best in areas of diverse habitat, such as where there's a mixture of agricultural and natural vegetation.

A variety of species of bats can be attracted to nest in home-made boxes, including the pallid bat, shown above eating a scorpion. The box at right is basically a multilevel version of the house featured on the following page.

A Bat House for the Backyard

Built of plywood sandwiched around 1x2 furring strips, this bat house is easy to construct. The strip creates a ¾-inch-wide chamber—the ideal size for most bats, while discouraging wasps from using the house. The back of the house extends about 4½ inches lower than the front to act as a landing platform.

Cut three pieces of ½-inch exterior grade plywood to the dimensions shown below for the back and the two parts of the front. Then cut three lengths of 1x2: one 24-inch-long top piece, and two 20¼-inch-long side pieces.

Caulk along one side of the 24-inch-long 1x2, align it with the top of the plywood back, then screw through the plywood into the 1x2 with 1⅝-inch screws. Apply caulking compound to the side pieces of 1x2, butt them against the top 1x2, and screw them in place.

Cut a 20x22½-inch piece of ⅛-inch mesh plastic netting and staple it to the inside of the back panel, starting at the bottom and making sure it lies flat. The netting roughens the surface, making it easier for the bats to grip.

Apply caulk to the fronts of the furring strips, then screw the top front piece of plywood in place, aligning it with the top and sides. Fasten the bottom front piece in place, leaving a ½-inch gap between it and the top front piece for ventilation.

Caulk around the outside joints, if necessary, to seal the chamber, then apply at least two coats of exterior paint.

Mount a single-chambered house like this on the wall of a wood or masonry building to help stabilize the internal temperature. Or build two houses and mount them back to back, with a ¾-inch space between them. Attach netting to the backs of the houses, and add ¾-inch horizontal access slots across the backs about 10 inches from the bottom. (Don't cover the slots with the netting.) This will create a three-chambered house, which is more likely to provide an appropriate range of temperatures. You can cover the two houses with a tin roof, if you wish.

Front view — 24" ; Top front 16½" ; Bottom front 5" ; 26½" ; Back ; Side view

Plastic netting ; 1x2 ; ½" plywood ; Side view

Bat house plans and related information from The Bat House Builder's Handbook are reprinted with permission from Bat Conservation International (BCI). For a donation in any amount, BCI will send you the handbook. For more information about membership in BCI or in the North American Bat House Research Project, please write or call: Bat Conservation International, P.O. Box 162603, Austin, Texas 78716. (Tel: 512-327-9721)

Fish in the Garden

A school of shimmering fish can transform a garden pond into a major attraction. Goldfish and koi, two common pond fish, are described on pages 100 and 101; both require the same basic care: a well-designed pond, well-balanced water, and proper feeding.

In fish ponds, shape is unimportant, but the depth is crucial.

Minimum depth for a pond is 18 inches, but depths of more than 24 inches will protect the fish from animal predators, such as raccoons. Fish can survive winter outside if the pond doesn't freeze solid; depths of about 2½ feet should suffice if the water is kept moving.

Fish need oxygen, so the pond's surface should be as broad as possible; a fountain, waterfall, or submersible pump is recommended. Toxic chemicals to look out for include ammonia, chlorine, and chloramines. Ammonia, produced by fish waste, and other wastes can be controlled by plant filtration, mechanical filtration, or chemicals, or by bacteria that break the toxins down into a harmless nitrogen gas.

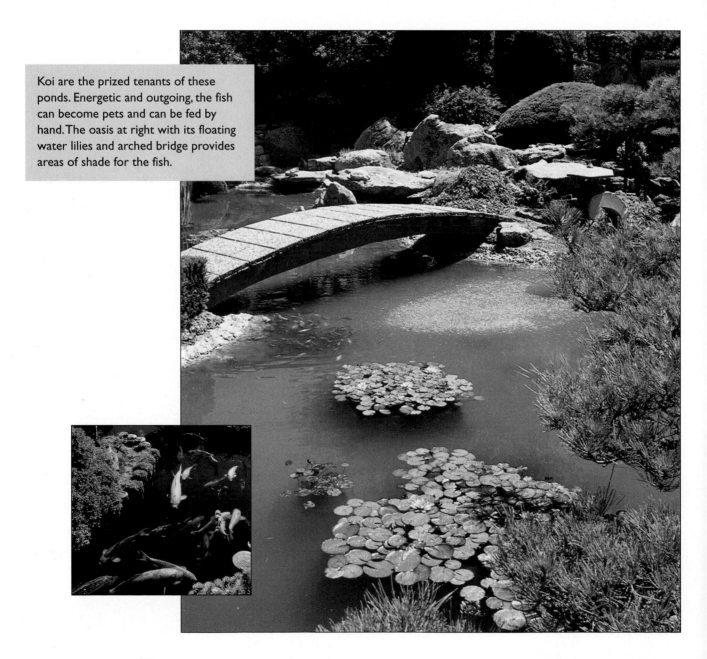

Koi are the prized tenants of these ponds. Energetic and outgoing, the fish can become pets and can be fed by hand. The oasis at right with its floating water lilies and arched bridge provides areas of shade for the fish.

Chlorine, which may be in your tap water, is bad for fish, and chloramines—combinations of chlorine and ammonia that may be added to municipal water supplies—are very toxic to fish. Both will dissipate in a few days if the waste is kept moving with a pump. Or you can use chemicals to break them down.

The water's pH, or acidity, is also important. A level between 6.5 and 7.5 is best for fish ponds. A balanced pond environment will maintain this level naturally.

Don't overfeed. Fish can only eat a small amount at a time, and any excess just fouls the water. Feed them only what they will eat raven-ously; when they seem uninterested, they've had enough. Commercial fish foods contain a balance of protein, carbohydrates, and vitamins. Try the floating kinds; any uneaten food can be skimmed off. Pet stores carry live food supplements. Worms, brine shrimp, ant eggs, and daphnia are a treat for fish.

FISH IN A WATER GARDEN

Fish are the beautiful visual showstoppers of a garden pond. But they can also be useful in creating ecological balance in a water garden.

Garden pools are often plagued by excessive algae growth, which makes the water look green. But there are several ways to control algae naturally.

First, because algae thrives on sunlight; a key step is to deprive them of it. Floating-leafed plants that cover some of the surface of the water will compete with the algae for this commodity. Fish help with the algae problem because they feed on it. As an added bonus, they also devour insect larvae, which helps to minimize the mosquito problem around your aquatic garden. Water snails also feed on algae, but can overregulate your pond. Finally, oxygenating plants, such as anacharis take up carbon dioxide and release oxygen, both to other plants and to fish. For a 6-by-8 foot pond, try two bunches of oxygenating grasses (six stems to a bunch), floating-leafed aquatic plants to cover about 60 percent of the surface, 6 water snails, and two 3- to 5-inch fish.

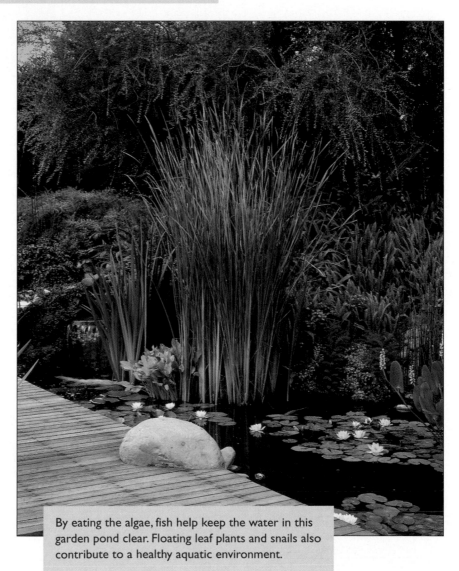

By eating the algae, fish help keep the water in this garden pond clear. Floating leaf plants and snails also contribute to a healthy aquatic environment.

A Guide to Goldfish and Koi

Goldfish are a good choice for a small pool. They're normally quite docile, and can be mixed with other fish. Young goldfish are much less expensive than their larger kin. Buy them at least 2 to 3 inches long; smaller fish have a fairly high mortality rate. Avoid buying fish with red streaks in the fins or tail; they are physically stressed and likely will die before very long. Outdoors, some varieties of goldfish may grow up to 10 inches in length. Goldfish live about three or four years under favorable conditions.

GOLDFISH VARIETIES

Goldfish have clearly discernible types, and vary in color, fin size and shape, body shape, and even eyes. They also come in different scale patterns: matte (without luster) and metallic.

Veiltail
The fins and tail of this type are even longer than those of the fantail and drape down; they should not be ragged. The body is rounded. The calico, a popular type, is colored like the shubunkin shown below. The telescope veiltail has protruding eyes and poor eyesight.

Common Goldfish
The "original model" from which the fancy varieties were developed, it has short fins all around, is an excellent swimmer, and is very hardy. Though color is normally orange-gold, the common sometimes has other markings: silver types are called Pearl; yellow types are called Canaries.

Japanese Black Moor
Velvety black, with a small, chunky body and protruding eyes, the Japanese black moor has a profile shape similar to the fantail. The Chinese black moor is similar, with less-protruding eyes and flatter body. They're the only truly black goldfish.

Fantail
This type has a heavy, egg-shaped body and swims at a deliberate, leisurely pace. Its double tail and fins are much longer than those of the common goldfish; they should not be ragged. Two popular types are the calico, which is scaleless and colored like the shubunkin, and the Japanese, which has common goldfish coloring.

Shubunkin
Similar to the common goldfish in shape, the London or calico type has matte scales, and beautiful colors—a pale-blue background flecked with red, blue, and black. The Bristol shubunkin has larger fins.

Comet
Similar to the common goldfish, and often sold under that name, the comet has a longer body, larger fins all around, and a more deeply forked tail. The fastest of the fancy goldfish varieties, the comet does very well in outdoor pools.

100

Japanese koi, or *nishikigoi*, can become family pets, coming when called, following owners around the pool, and even allowing themselves to be petted. Koi are carp—not goldfish—with two pairs of whiskers, called barbels, on their upper lips, which goldfish lack. Koi can reach lengths of 3 feet and live as long as 60 years. Prize koi specimens command great prices, but it's best for beginners to start with inexpensive fish (about $10) and move up as they become more experienced caring for them.

Ohgon
One of the most popular koi types in North America, the ohgon is a single-color variety, metallic gold or orange gold in color.

Inazuma Kohaku
The kohaku type is all red on a white background, although there are many subcategories within this popular type. The exact pattern determines the subcategory. So, for example, inazuma kohaku have a "lightning" pattern, and nidan kohaku have two red patches.

Gin Matsuba
A metallic silver fish with a pinecone scale pattern, the gin matsuba is a variety of shiro ohgon, a popular single-color variety that is a platinum metallic color.

Shusui
This type of koi is similar to the agasi type, which have light blue on the top (dorsal) part of the body, and some red on the head and below. They may have a pinecone pattern, normal scales, or be armored (doitsu type). The shusui type always have doitsu scales and have prominent dark blue scales down the middle of the back.

Tancho Sanke
This type is predominantly white with one red spot—or "rising sun"—on the head only and small black patches behind. It's a variation of the taisho sanke, a popular three-color koi variety with red and black markings on a white background.

JAPANESE KOI

Color, pattern, and scale type differentiate koi. There are single-, two-, three-, and multicolor varieties. Scales may be *muji* (matte), or *ohgon* (metallic); in addition, a German variety of armored koi has been interbred with Japanese koi to produce *doitsu*, which can be either heavily scaled ("armored") or scaleless ("leather skin"). Pattern distinctions include *matsuba* (pinecone pattern), *bekko* (tortoise shell), as well as eye color. If there's a koi club in your area, you might consider joining it. More knowledgeable members help beginners with their purchases and the clubs sponsor shows, where you can learn more about these remarkable fish.

Building a Garden Pond

One of the easiest ways for a do-it-yourselfer to build a garden pond is with a flexible liner; you should be able to complete the project in just a few days.

Flexible liners may be made from polyolefin, polyvinyl chloride (PVC), or synthetic rubber (EPDM). You can buy a precut rectangle of the size you need, or you can order a liner sized to fit your pool. To protect the liner from punctures, add a layer of sand to the hole; you can also install liner protection fabric under the liner.

For an ornamental pond, a depth of about 24 inches is good. But for fish, a deeper pond is better, because it is more difficult

1 Lay out the pond

Outline the shape of the pond, then dig around the outline. If you're cutting into a lawn, keep the sod in a shady spot; use it later for patching around the border. Dig a shelf around the pond for an edging—rocks, bricks, or flagstones that hold down the edges of the liner. For the most natural look, the top of the edging should be level with the ground. Next, dig out any plant shelves you've planned; 10" to 12" wide is common. Continue digging out the main area, measuring the depth as you go (or use a marked stake to check depth). If you're planning to use a sand bed, dig an extra 2". It's important to level the pond's rim. Once the pond is full, the water will level, leaving the liner exposed at high points of the rim, vulnerable to abrasion and deterioration. To reduce the chances of exposed liner, submerge the edging. Check for level with a long, straight 2x4 and a carpenter's level, or use a line level or a water level.

Finished depth, +2" for sand layer, if any

Shallow shelf for edging

Plant shelf, 10" to 12" deep

Pleats and wrinkles in liner

3 Fill the liner

As the pond fills, let the liner slip into the hole. Lift the weights on the liner if you need to, so it can conform to the shape of the hole without stretching. Smooth the liner to the shape of the pond, folding or pleating it as needed; you may have to stand in the hole to do this.

for predators, such as raccoons and skunks to raid. If your pond is going to be primarily for fish, place it where it will get at least some shade. This is good for the fish—their colors tend to be richer and deeper—and helps reduce algae formation. Aquatic plants need sunshine, however, so you may have to compromise.

To determine the size of liner you need, outline the shape of the pond using a flexible hose or a line of flour. Then draw an imaginary rectangle around it and measure maximum length and width. To each of these measurements, add twice the pond's maximum depth plus two feet to give you the necessary surplus of material

to extend beyond the edge of the excavated area.

Safety is a concern with ponds. Check with your local building department for regulations for fencing, electrical circuits for pumps and lights, and pond depth. For ponds less than 24 inches deep, you probably won't need a building permit.

2 Position the liner

Remove all rough edges–rocks, roots, and debris–from the excavated hole; use a pick, pruning shears, and a broom. If you're adding a sand bed, lay a 2" layer of fine, damp sand over all surfaces, spreading it evenly and packing it into place. Smooth the surface with a board or a concrete float. Or, install a sheet of liner protection fabric. If you lay the liner out in the sun it will be more pliable and easier to install. With helpers, spread the liner loosely over the hole. A quick up-down motion with your arms will force air under the liner to help float it into place. Make sure the liner overlaps the edges evenly; sharp corners may require folded pleats. Weight down the edges with heavy stones or bricks and slowly begin filling the pond.

Weights for edges

Flexible liner

Garden hose for slow filling

Edge of liner

Rocks for edging

4 Add an edging

Once the pond is nearly full, you can begin to set the edging in place. If you choose rocks, as shown here, use broad, flat-bottomed rocks that butt tightly together. Lay the rocks on the shallow shelf and trim off the excess liner behind the rocks level with the ground. Mask the excess liner and spaces between rocks with gravel. For a natural effect, add a ground cover or other plants around the edges.

Keeping Birds at Bay

Some gardeners coexist happily with birds by planting more vegetables and fruit than they need and expecting a certain percentage of their crop to be consumed. Others—often those with smaller lots—feel a more pressing need to protect their crops.

Two main methods of dissuading birds are barriers and scare devices. You can be sure of protecting vegetable seedlings and fruit by covering them with flexible plastic bird netting, or aviary wire. For plastic netting to be successful, it must completely cover the plant. Drape netting over the plant and secure it to the ground or, for a tree, gather it around the trunk. Netting is easiest to use on blueberries, cane berries, and small bushes; covering a tree is difficult.

Row crops, such as strawberries, can be covered with aviary wire or plastic netting secured to wooden or plastic pipe frames. They're easy to make, mobile, and reusable.

Scare devices, such as inflatable owls and reflective tape, are not as reliable as barrier methods of protection, since they don't physically cover the crop but are meant only to frighten birds away.

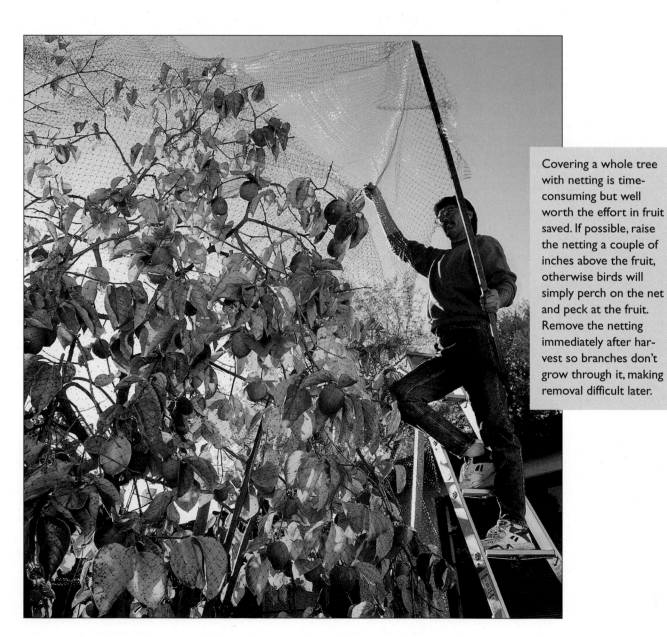

Covering a whole tree with netting is time-consuming but well worth the effort in fruit saved. If possible, raise the netting a couple of inches above the fruit, otherwise birds will simply perch on the net and peck at the fruit. Remove the netting immediately after harvest so branches don't grow through it, making removal difficult later.

Living with Deer

If you live in an area where deer are plentiful, you may find their foraging in your garden a source of frustration. But rather than trying to keep them out with expensive perimeter fences or cages for individual plants, you can adapt your garden so it's less desirable to the deer. All it takes is some experimentation and a little patience.

Deer's diet differs from place to place—what they don't eat in one garden they may devastate in gardens only a few miles away. To create a deer-resistant garden, first set out a selection of small plants in containers and take note of what is left untouched. Then simply create a garden as you normally would with the plants the deer left alone; use them in pleasing combinations of form, texture, and color to make a garden that you'll enjoy, but the deer won't.

This garden is planted with a variety of deer-resistant plants. In spring, yellow yarrow, lime green euphorbia and purple *Erysimum linifolium* 'Bowles Mauve' provide bright color. Other successful plants include dusty miller, guara, penstemon, helianthemum, nierembergia, various salvias, Santa Barbara daisy, snow-in-summer, and herbal plants with a pungent odor, such as catmint, curry plant, lavenders, and ornamental and edible oreganos and thymes.

DEALING WITH RACCOONS

Raccoons can climb well, open gate latches, and even spring traps. They have a varied diet, including small animals, fruit, nuts, and possibly your garden plants. They may dig up the ground in search of grubs, and if you have a fish pond, they're likely to be quite interested in its occupants. You may be able to keep them out of the yard with a poultry-wire fence. Make it at least 4 feet high and bend the last foot or so out away from the garden. Other options are to cover individual beds or plants with bird netting or to try to repel them by leaving human-scented clothes or dog droppings spread around in the garden.

If raccoons are a significant problem, trapping and relocation is an option, but it's best to hire a professional; raccoons can be mean when caught.

All Fun and Games

For the ideal place to enjoy outdoor activities and games, you probably need look no further than your own backyard. Not only is it private and adaptable, it's also remarkably convenient.

The next few pages will provide just a sampling of the many things you and your family can enjoy, starting with a relaxing dip in the pool or soak in a spa. You'll find helpful information on all the popular standbys, such as horseshoes, basketball, and badminton, as well as some surprises. Why not try out an aqua fitness program in your pool, for instance, or invite the neighbors over for a game of bocce on your lawn? Whatever your choice of recreation, consider planning it in your backyard—it's an arena that's literally yours to command.

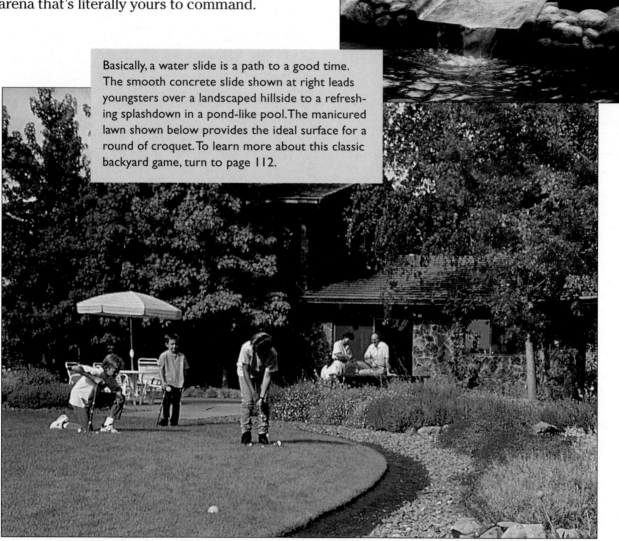

Basically, a water slide is a path to a good time. The smooth concrete slide shown at right leads youngsters over a landscaped hillside to a refreshing splashdown in a pond-like pool. The manicured lawn shown below provides the ideal surface for a round of croquet. To learn more about this classic backyard game, turn to page 112.

106

Spas—Your Bit of Backyard Therapy

Its easy to understand why people love spas. Hot hydromassage can soothe away tension and stress in minutes. Whether taken as a morning ritual or after a day's work, a soak gently replenishes the body and mind like no other tonic.

Spas massage bathers with a froth of hot, moving water and tiny, bursting bubbles. Contemporary spas come in a wide array of styles ranging from plastic portables to tiled and landscaped installations of splendid proportions. Hot tubs boast a rustic wooden charm that hasn't changed in decades. While they each have their advantages—spas are generally easier to clean and hot tubs usually have a greater gallon capacity—it's clear that both are good for what ails you.

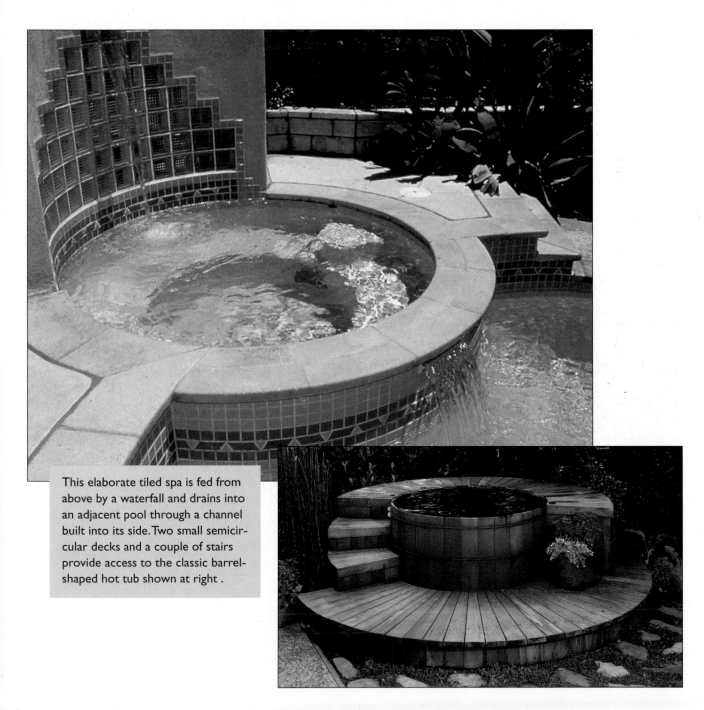

This elaborate tiled spa is fed from above by a waterfall and drains into an adjacent pool through a channel built into its side. Two small semicircular decks and a couple of stairs provide access to the classic barrel-shaped hot tub shown at right .

A Splashing Good Time

What more versatile element in a backyard setting than a pool? That refreshing body of water can be a private exercise area for your early morning laps, a playground for splash-happy kids on a sunny afternoon, or a tranquil gathering spot for evening cocktail or dinner parties. And, with the right amount of attention given to landscaping, the pool area can add sparkling aesthetic appeal to the yard.

Basically, you have two ways to go when it comes to selecting a pool: aboveground, which is more affordable, or inground, which adds more value to a property. Both versions are shown here, and the following pages will give you a few ideas for keeping yourself and your family fit in your backyard watering hole. Some maintenance tips and important safety considerations are offered opposite.

This aboveground pool has a deck built on one side for access. The path leading to the deck's stairs is blocked with a children's security gate when the pool is not in use. The entire pool area in enclosed by a series of fences.

These two pools are a study in contrast. With its clean lines and formal setting, the inground model above is well suited to quiet lap-swimming sessions and poolside gatherings. The kidney-shaped pool at right has as much vibrancy as the garden that surrounds it. The springboard is a perfect launching pad to hours of fun for the young or the young at heart.

TIPS FOR MAINTAINING YOUR POOL

These are some general reminders for pool mainte-nance. Talk to a professional at a pool supply store for more detailed information.

• Use a leaf skimmer to collect debris floating on the water's surface or lying on the bottom of the pool.

• Clean the strainer baskets in the skimmer and pump daily during swimming season.

• Scrub the tile and walls of the pool weekly.

• Vacuum the pool at least once a week.

• Backwash (reverse the water flow) and service the fil-ter regularly.

• Regularly test the water for proper chemical balance. Test kits are available at pool supply stores.

• Add appropriate chemicals for filtration cleaning and water treatment. Always read the labels for instructions on proper usage and handling of pool chemicals.

• Hose down the pool's coping and deck to prevent swimmers from tracking dirt into the pool.

Pool Safety

Listed here are just a few of the many rules that you can follow to provide a safe environment around the pool. Contact your local branch of the Red Cross for a more complete list.

• Enclose the pool area with a fence or dense hedge to keep unsupervised children and pets out. (Check your local government for guidelines on height and construction.)

• Always have an adult who knows how to swim on hand when others are in the pool. No one swims alone—adult or child.

• Be sure nobody uses the pool without the owner's knowledge and permission.

• Keep anyone who doesn't know how to swim a safe distance away from the edge of the pool.

• Never swim unless the pool cover has been taken off completely.

• Do not swim during electrical storms.

• Do not allow nighttime swimming unless the pool is equipped with appropriate lighting.

• Do not permit any running, pushing, or horse-play around or in the pool.

• If you have a diving board, allow only one per-son at a time to jump or dive off the front of the board.

• If you don't have a diving board, permit diving only into the deep end and then only if the pool is more than 6 feet deep.

• If you have a water slide, allow only one per-son at a time—and always feet first in a seated position—to use it.

• Swimmers in the water have the right-of-way over sliders or divers.

• Keep refreshments away from the pool.

• Clean all debris from pool decks and remove any slippery spots.

Water Games and Exercises

Most people immediately think of swimming when they think of recreation in the pool. But that's only a drop in the bucket, so to speak. While it is true that swimming—apart from being a quick way to cool off on a hot day—is the most popular pool activity, other forms of recreation are equally suited to the water.

When it comes to games, there seems to be no limit as to what can be played in the pool. The games don't have to be complicated—the water itself is enough of an attraction to satisfy most people. But always try to keep in mind the age of the players. Though small children might enjoy a balloon race

across the width of the pool, older kids demand more vigorous challenges, like water polo, water basketball, tag, or water volleyball *(shown below)*. You can even add a basketball net to your pool by bolting a standard backboard to a 1½-inch angle-iron frame that clamps onto the end of the diving board

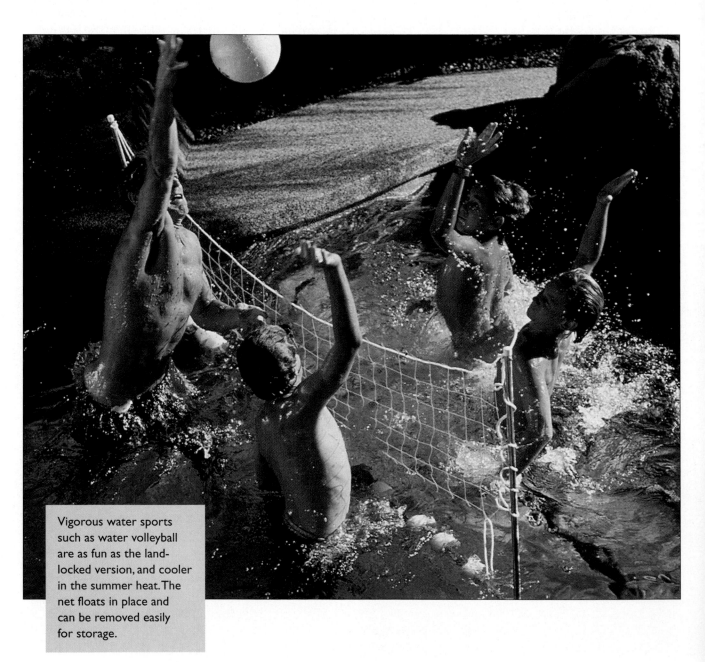

Vigorous water sports such as water volleyball are as fun as the land-locked version, and cooler in the summer heat. The net floats in place and can be removed easily for storage.

with C-clamps. (Just be sure it locks on so it won't fall.)

Manufactured games that float are popular because they can be removed at the end of the day. Some are variations on standard games, such as volleyball and horse shoes; others are floating boards for check-ers and other less-active games. You can also purchase underwater rings for youngsters to swim through or grab and bring to the surface.

Activities that normally have been relegated to the gymnasium floor are now finding their way into the pool, too. For example, since exercising in water diminishes the impact on joints, walking, march-ing, or jogging in waist-deep water are all popular ways to provide a stimulating workout without caus-ing stress to joints. For a primer on aqua fitness, see the simple pro-gram outlined below.

AQUA FITNESS

The beauty of exercising in water is that you can shape up and slim down without breaking a sweat. Pools and spas lend themselves to a low-impact exercise program that can keep your body toned, fit, and limber. The program offered below is a very basic starting point. To learn more about water fitness, enroll in a program at your local recreation department or health club. Fitness pro-fessionals at these institutions will show you how to do the exercises properly. Then, it's just a mat-ter of transferring what you've learned to your backyard pool. Before starting any new exercise routine, be sure to check with your doctor. Once you have the go ahead, follow the guidelines recommended at right.

Water fitness program
• 5- to 10-minute warmup:
Walking and bobbing in the water followed by some stretching
• 20-minute workout:
Pushups on the side of the pool to give the upper body a workout
Leg lifts and kicks in the pool to give the lower body a workout
Combination exercises such as jumping jacks in the pool to work both the upper and lower body
• 5- to 10-minute cooldown:
Walking and bobbing in the water

If you're looking for a dif-ferent and enjoyable way to get in shape, a water exercise routine in your spa or pool may be just the ticket.

Exercise guidelines
• Start slowly. Relax and enjoy the water before exercising.
• Submerge the body parts you're targeting, so they work more effectively.
• Move slowly and gently as you concentrate on the muscles you are working on.
• Breathe rhythmically.
• Make the water work for you—it offers a constant gentle resistance.
• Follow through a complete joint range of motion but don't force it. Stop if you feel sudden or increased pain.
• Begin by doing three to eight repetitions. Build up slowly to longer workouts.
• Work different parts of the body on alternating days to ensure a complete workout.

A Quiet Game of Croquet

Croquet has been enjoyed worldwide for more than a century, in part because it is well-suited to almost any backyard setting. All that's required is some simple equipment, a reasonably level, well-clipped lawn, and a few friends.

Although croquet is played at the professional level on a six-wicket format, the nine-wicket game is the most popular backyard version.

Croquet can be played by two, four, or six people. The object of the game is to race your opponent(s) around a course of wickets and be the first to hit the finishing stake.

These pages will give you illustrations of croquet equipment, an outline of the field of play, and some basic rules of the game.

A steady aim and a deft touch with the mallet are two important qualities for success in a round of croquet. In the photo above, a player lines up a wicket shot under the watchful eye of his partner.

BASIC CROQUET RULES

These are a brief set of rules for amateur, nine-wicket croquet, as outlined by the United States Croquet Association.

• The game is played in teams of two, blue and black vs. red and yellow, with the order of play being blue, red, black, then yellow.

• The toss of a coin (or drawn lots) determines the team's order of play.

• Each ball begins halfway between the starting stake and the first wicket.

• A player may hold any part of the mallet handle with one or both hands and must hit the ball (not shove or push it) with the striking end of the mallet.

• It shall be counted as a stroke if the mallet hits the wicket or the ground but not the ball or misses the ball completely.

• A player earns one extra stroke for each wicket made.

• A player earns two extra strokes for striking (roqueting) another ball. The first of these is played from where the roqueted ball stops, with the balls placed in contact.

• The first team to score all 14 wicket points and hit the finishing stake with both balls is the winner.

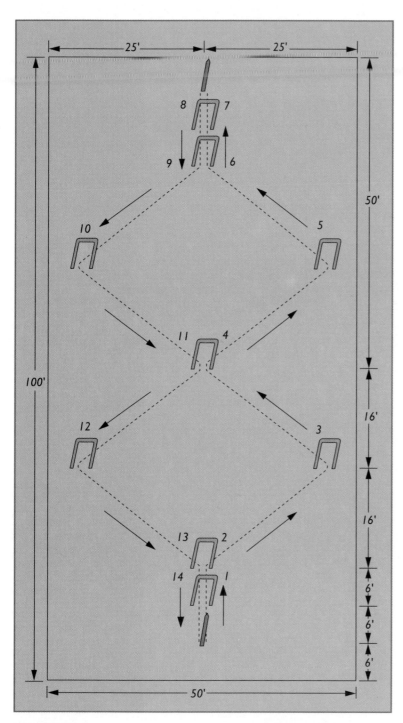

Diagram labels: 25', 25', 8, 7, 9, 6, 10, 5, 50', 11, 4, 16', 100', 12, 3, 16', 13, 2, 14, 1, 6', 6', 6', 50'

THE TOOLS OF THE GAME

Although aficionados often have mallets custom made for themselves, croquet equipment is relatively simple. The balls are made of wood and are painted blue, black, red, yellow, and for larger sets, green and orange. Nine U-shaped wickets, usually made of metal, and two wooden stakes are used to lay out the field of play. Many sets come with a cart to carry and store the equipment.

The field of play
The croquet field illustrated above is the traditional nine-wicket, double diamond, in which 14 wicket points are scored. (Balls pass through some wickets twice.) Beyond the layout, there need be no particular boundary. It is acceptable to lay out the wickets in a smaller pattern if the size of the playing area is small.

Hoop Dreaming

Probably the quickest way to turn a quiet spot in your backyard into a hotbed of athletic activity is to install a basketball hoop. Whether it's used for pickup games by the children and their neighborhood friends, determined teenagers who want to improve their jump shots, or parents looking for a way to stay in shape, a backyard basket is a sure way to attract athletes of all ages.

The following pages will give you all the information you need to introduce hoops to the home front. Practical dimensions for a backyard court and rules for some shooting games are featured on the opposite page. Step-by-step information on installing a backboard and hoop, whether it's supported from the ground or attached to the house or garage, begins on page 116.

The budding NBAers at left go head to head on a court with a permanent post and backboard setup *(see page 116)*. Above is an interesting alternative—the portable hoop. Apart from its mobility and easy storage, the backboard on these modern baskets can be adjusted to accommodate the height of the participants.

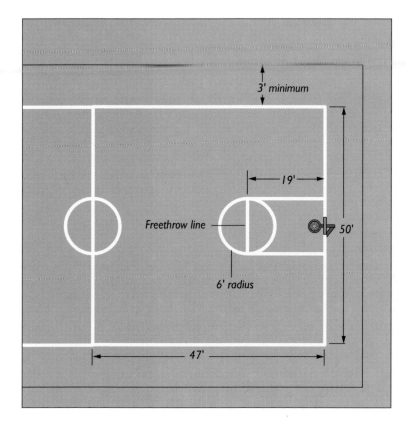

3' minimum

19'

Freethrow line

50'

6' radius

47'

Basketball on a half court

It would take an enormous backyard to install a regulation size court, so you'll need a smaller playing surface for your home-grown basketball games. The drawing at left shows a half-court layout. If this is still too big for your area, consider installing just the key with a surrounding area for ball handling and dribbling. While it's unlikely that you'll be able to stage full games of five-on-five on this type of court, you could easily enjoy spirited games of three or two on a side, and of course, one-on-one. No matter what size court you choose, the dimension of the key should remain the same. Plan to make it 19 feet from free throw line to baseline. The backboard should be installed in the middle of the baseline. The free throw line is 15 feet from the backboard. Draw a circle 6 feet in radius at the top of the key. Position the rim an even 10 feet above the playing surface; this should be adjusted lower for really young players.

SHOOTING GAMES

Even the most basic rules of basketball are too numerous to cover here. Instead, try these shooting games for fun.

Basic rules of 21

• Two players stand at the free throw line and take turns trying to sink a basket.

• A player opens the scoring and earns 1 point when he makes a basket.

• Each successive basket made from the line is worth 2 points.

• When a player misses a shot, the other player collects the rebound and shoots from wherever he stands. Baskets made from the key (not the free throw line) are worth 1 point.

• After scoring from the key, the player returns to the free throw line to shoot.

• If a player misses the hoop entirely (doesn't touch the rim) his opponent can shoot from anywhere in the key.

• The first player to score 21 points wins.

Basic rules of S.P.O.T.

• The first player takes the ball and tries a tough shot—whether it's a long-distance jump shot or a flashy reverse layup—that the next player might have trouble duplicating.

• If the first player makes the shot, the second player has to match it.

• If the first player misses the shot, the second player can then create a shot of his own that the first player has to match.

• A player is given one letter from the word spot—beginning with the S—each time he can't duplicate his opponent's shot.

• The first player to force his opponent to spell out S.P.O.T. wins.

Three ways to install backboard

1 A roof-mounted backboard

Backboard mounting brackets—available at sporting goods stores—support backboards in various ways. *(NOTE: In all cases, you'll need to work from a ladder; follow the safety instructions on the ladder's label.)* For a slanted roof *(left)*, assemble the brackets according to the manufacturer's instructions. Place the brackets on the roof so their front edges clear the rain gutter. (Install wood spacers to raise the brackets if necessary.) Use lag screws to fasten the brackets through roofing and sheathing into the rafters. Seal holes with roofing cement. Attach backboard to the brackets with carriage bolts and install hoop.

2 A pole-mounted backboard

To install the pole, see instructions on the opposite page. Assemble the bracket according to the manufacturer's instructions and, with the aid of a helper, position it on the pole at the desired height. As with a wall-mounted backboard, you'll want to ensure the bracket is level. Then, secure the bracket at the top and bottom *(as shown at right)* with two U-bolts and nuts. Attach the backboard to the bracket with carriage bolts and install the hoop.

3 A wall-mounted backboard

Assemble the support bracket according to the manufacturer's instructions. With the aid of a helper, place the bracket on the wall a couple of inches below the roof's soffit, as shown. The front edge of the bracket should extend out past the rain gutter. (Install wood spacers under the bracket if necessary). With the helper, use a level to ensure that the bracket is level and secure it to wall studs with long lag screws. Attach backboard to the bracket with carriage bolts and install the hoop.

Setting a backboard pole in cement

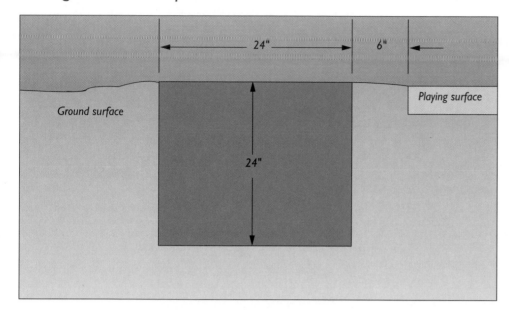

Ground surface

24"   6"

Playing surface

24"

1 Dig the hole
As with the backboard support brackets, poles for supporting backboards are available at sporting goods stores. To install the pole, begin by digging the hole. In mild winter regions, dig down 24". In colder climates, you'll need to dig below the frost line, in some cases as much as 4'. The hole should be 24" in diameter and positioned so that its edge is no more than 6" from the playing surface.

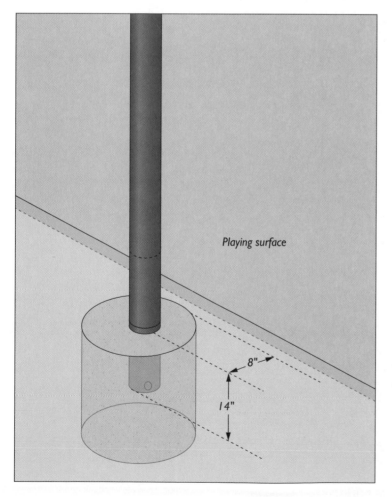

Playing surface

8"

14"

2 Place the concrete and pole
Mix enough concrete to fill the hole *(see page 247 for mixing instructions)*. Place the concrete, leaving the top slightly mounded so that water runs off. As shown in the illustration at left, the minimum distance from the center of the pole to the edge of the hole should be 8". Insert the pole to a depth of 14", using a level to make sure it's straight. (For added stability, some manufacturers suggest filling the bottom half of a hollow pole with concrete.) Allow approximately one week of curing time before installing the backboard.

Lively Volleyball

Although volleyball has grown from an informal game to an Olympic sport, it still has all the fun, excitement, and simplicity that makes it suitable for backyard recreation.

The beauty of volleyball is that it can be adapted to suit almost any size of group or level of play. As few as four players (two on either side) might regularly meet for a vigorous match, or as many as 18 people (nine on a side) can fill the evening hours after a barbecue with a boisterous round.

The object of the game is for each team to send the ball over the net, trying to ground it on the other side. The first to reach a certain number of points, 15 for example, wins. Information on rules, equipment, and court layout is on the opposite page.

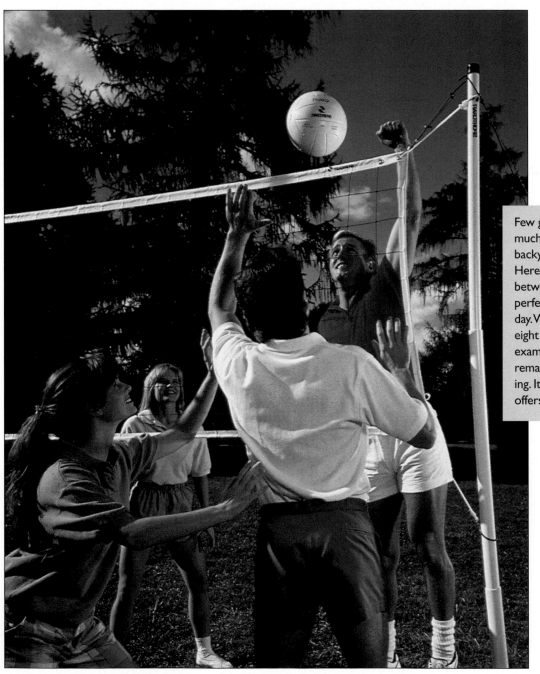

Few games provide as much enjoyment in the backyard as volleyball. Here, a low-key game between couples is the perfect activity on a sunny day. With larger groups, eight or nine a side, for example, have everyone remain seated while playing. It's a fun twist that offers a lot of laughs.

BASIC VOLLEYBALL RULES

Here are the basic rules for beach volleyball, the version most common to the backyard. A game is won by two points.

• The ball is put into play by the right back-row player who may serve from anywhere behind the endline. (Rotation ensures that everyone plays both at net and the back court.)

• A player is not allowed to hit the ball twice consecutively, except when attempting a block.

• The ball must be contacted cleanly, not held, lifted, pushed, caught, carried or thrown.

• A player must not touch the net while the ball is in play.

• The ball is in play until it touches the ground, goes "out," or a team fails to return it.

• Only the serving team may score a point, except in the deciding game when rally-point scoring is used.

THE TOOLS OF THE GAME

The only equipment required for volleyball is a regulation ball and net. Nets are held in place with lightweight metal poles. These assemblies are usually quite portable, so your game can travel with you to backyards of friends and relatives. The ball is lighter than a basketball and slightly smaller in size.

A volleyball court
The court illustrated at right shows the dimensions of a regulation outdoor court as outlined by USA Volleyball. Use it as a guideline, keeping in mind that you might need to alter the dimensions to fit your space. An outdoor court is best set up on flat grass or sand. When playing on sand, the sand should be at least 18" deep. A flat, grassy surround is best for safety around the court. Make sure the net posts are rounded to avoid injury from sharp edges. Net height should be 7'11⅝" for men's and coed play and 7'4¼" for women's play.

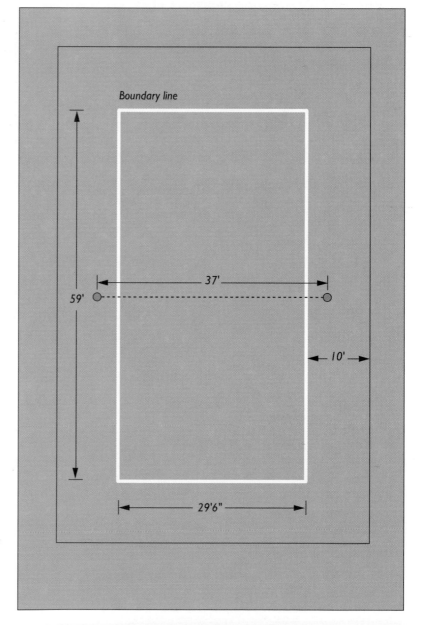

Boundary line

59'

37'

10'

29'6"

Badminton Anyone?

Badminton is one of today's most popular forms of recreation—and it's easy to see why. While other sports call for lightning speed or brute strength, badminton requires good reflexes, quickness, and finesse. And those who like to play at a leisurely pace can enjoy simply rallying the shuttle back and forth across the net; they'll still get their exercise and have fun, too.

Badminton can be played either in singles or doubles format. The object of the game is to send the shuttle over the net, trying to ground it on your opponent's side. It's important to keep the racket head high and—unlike tennis—use plenty of wrist action in your stroke when making contact. As a rule of thumb, try to make a swishing sound with your racket each time you make a shot.

Some basic badminton rules, along with a layout of the court and a photo of the necessary equipment are shown opposite.

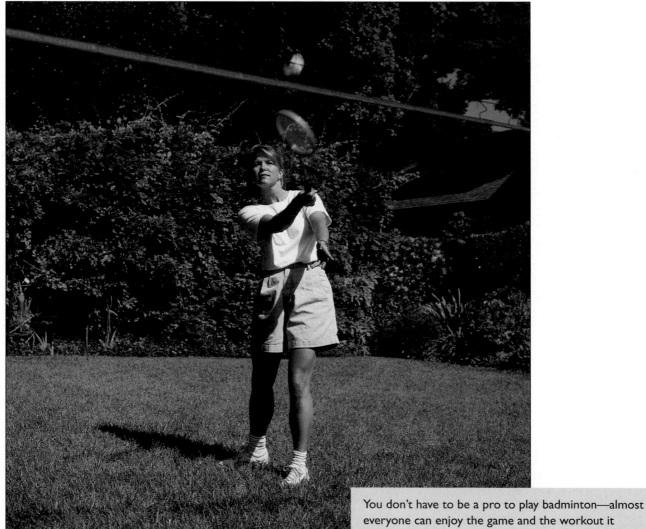

You don't have to be a pro to play badminton—almost everyone can enjoy the game and the workout it brings. Children can master the game, as well, since the rackets and shuttles are so light, making this the perfect game for family play in the yard. With practice, you'll learn to use wrist action to perfect your shots.

BASIC BADMINTON RULES

These are some of the basic rules as outlined by the United States Badminton Association.

• The server stands inside the service court *(see court layout below)* on the right side. The receiver stands on the opposite right side. (Partners stand on either side.)

• In singles play, the server stands on the right side if the score is even (0, 2, 4, etc.), and on the left if odd. In doubles play, when a team's score is even, the team is in the starting positions, when odd, reverse the positions.

• The server on the right side serves to the receiver on the opposite right side.

• The receiver remains still until the serve is hit.

• The server must: keep both feet on the ground; hit the base of the shuttle; hit the shuttle while it's below his waist; hit the shuttle with the racket's head below the racket hand; move the racket continuously forward.

• Points are scored on the serve.

• Games are played to 15 points; 11 for women's singles.

THE TOOLS OF THE GAME

Badminton equipment is relatively simple and inexpensive. There are many rackets and shuttles from which to choose— from professional to novice. Easy-to-install nets are also easily purchased. When set up, the net should stand 5' feet high at center court, and 5'1" where it crosses the sidelines.

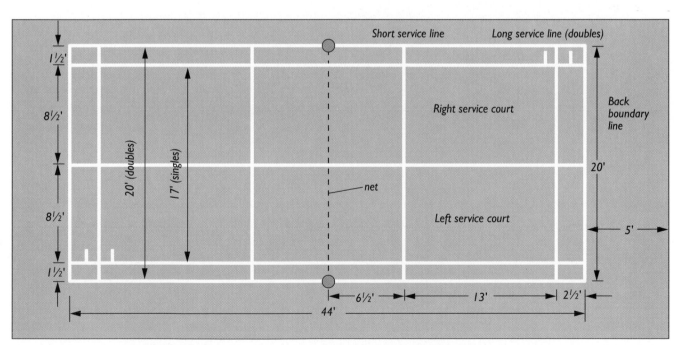

A badminton court
Although you may choose to have an unofficial badminton court in your backyard, the above illustration outlines the dimensions of the regulation version. Plan to locate your court on flat, even ground, preferably with a grass surface.

Letting Fly with Horseshoes

Pitching horseshoes is a game that predates the American Civil War. At that time, it's said, blacksmiths and farriers (specialists in shoeing horses) were the first to pitch the shoes. Today, millions of people from all walks of life pursue the game across North America. Probably an equal number enjoy the pastime in their own backyard.

The object of the game is to pitch the shoes closer to the stake than your opponent. The closest shoe to the stake (within 6 inches) scores points *(see the basic rules listed below)*. The first player to 21 wins.

Setting up your own court is a pretty simple matter. Providing you have the room, all it takes is some sand, or a mixture of sand and sawdust, for the pits, wood for the backstops, and metal rods for the stakes. Refer to the illustration below for the dimensions of an official court.

BASIC HORSESHOE PITCHING RULES

Apart from following these general rules, keep safety in mind when playing horseshoes. Spectators should be kept at a safe distance, and players should stand to the rear or behind the pitching area when an opponent is playing.

• The stakes should be 40 feet apart, with 15 inches showing above the ground, and leaning toward each other by 3 inches.

• Men pitch from behind 40-foot foul line; women from behind 30-foot line.

• Players are not allowed to walk to the opposite pit until all the shoes have been played. (When playing in teams, half the team throws from one stake and half throws from the other.) WARNING: The non-throwing players should always stand well back from the pit during play.

• A shoe must be within 6 inches of the stake to be considred for points. The closest shoe to the stake scores 1 point; 2 shoes closer than an opponent's scores 2 points; one ringer and closest shoe of the same player scores 4 points; one ringer scores 3 points. A ringer atop an opponent's ringer cancels both out.

• Leaners (shoes leaning on a stake) score 2 points and are considered closer than any other shoe except a ringer. (Official rules don't recognize leaners.)

• Casual games are played to 21; for a shorter game, you can stop at 15. Games must be won by 2 points, so games may go longer.

THE TOOLS OF THE GAME

Horseshoe pitchers don't pitch actual horseshoes anymore. The real shoes are too light. These days, they throw shoes specially made for the sport *(see above)*. Two shoes are required for each pitcher. The only other pieces of equipment needed are two metal stakes, positioned as in the illustration at right.

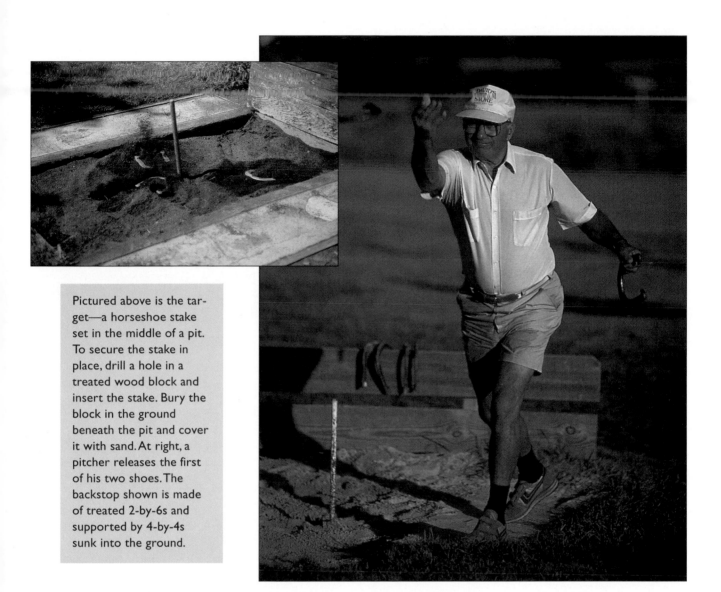

Pictured above is the target—a horseshoe stake set in the middle of a pit. To secure the stake in place, drill a hole in a treated wood block and insert the stake. Bury the block in the ground beneath the pit and cover it with sand. At right, a pitcher releases the first of his two shoes. The backstop shown is made of treated 2-by-6s and supported by 4-by-4s sunk into the ground.

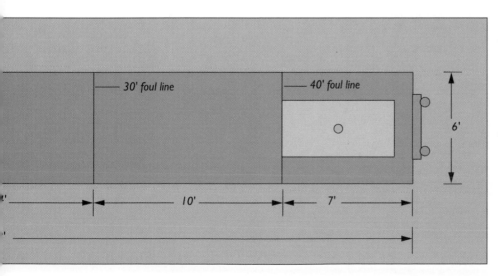

— 30' foul line

— 40' foul line

6'

10'

7'

Horseshoe pitching court
Although the actual court is 48' long and 6' wide, it should be set on a parcel of land 60' by 12' to allow enough room for mis-thrown shoes that go out of bounds. The diagram at left, provided by the National Horseshoe Pitchers' Association, shows the position of the pits on a regulation court. The metal stakes are positioned in the center of each pit. Wooden backstops are built one foot behind each pit.

Scoring Big with Bocce

Like its cousins pétanque and lawn bowling, bocce (pronounced *bah-chee*) is a relaxed game that requires strategy and control. And although it is often played on regulation courts, as shown on the opposite page, bocce can be enjoyed wherever there's an open plot of land, such as a backyard.

The game is played by two teams of one to four players each. Each team has its own set of four large colored balls—red or green, for example—called bocce. The object of the game is to roll or toss your bocce closer to the object ball, or pallino, than your opponent. The more effectively one team can do this, the more points it scores.

Some basic rules of bocce, along with the dimensions of a regulation court, are featured on these pages. Shown in the photo below are the large bocce balls and the pallino, basically all the equipment you'll need for the game.

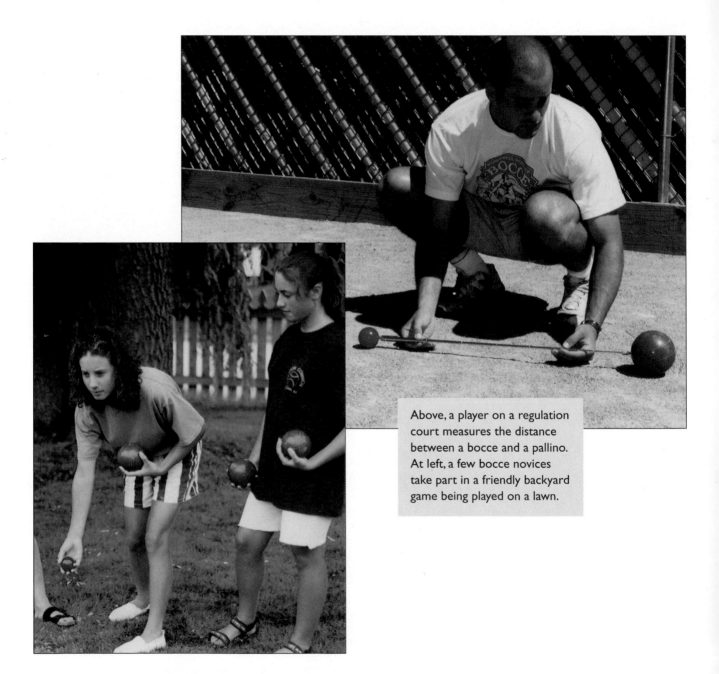

Above, a player on a regulation court measures the distance between a bocce and a pallino. At left, a few bocce novices take part in a friendly backyard game being played on a lawn.

124

THE TOOLS OF THE GAME

There are nine pieces to a bocce set, eight large bocce balls—four of one color, four of another—and one smaller pallino of a different and lighter color. The bocce are about 4¼ inches in diameter and weigh close to 2 pounds. The pallino is about 2¼ inches in diameter and weighs approximately ½ pound.

BASIC BOCCE RULES

Although there are official international rules to bocce, the following guidelines are sufficient for a backyard game.

• The first player of one team throws the pallino onto the court.

• The player then tries to position a bocce as close to the pallino as possible, bowling overhand or underhand so the ball travels through the air or rolls along the ground.

• The first player on the opposing team then tries to position a bocce closer to the pallino.

• The opposing team continues to play until it places a ball closer to the pallino or uses up all of its bocce.

• If the opposing team places a ball closer to the pallino, the first team must better the shot.

• The round continues until all the bocce have been played.

• A point is awarded for each bocce closer to the pallino than the closest bocce of the opponent. Four points can be scored per round.

• A player may use a fast rolling shot (raffa), or a toss (volo), to knock an opponent's ball out of scoring position. The pallino can also be knocked away in this manner.

• Games are played to 11, 12, 15, 16, or 21 points.

Point from which to roll the bocce or shoot the "raffa"

Point from which to toss the "volo"

The pallino must be tossed beyond this point

Backwall

10'   13'

87'

Bocce court
Illustrated at left is an official bocce court and its dimensions. The court's surface is usually clay laid over a base of crushed stone on top of sand. The surface will harden over time, allowing for faster play. Wooden backboards and sideboards, as seen in the photo opposite, aren't strictly necessary, but they do help to contain the balls.

Backyard Shuffleboard

Shuffleboard dates back to the 15th century, when it was a popular game among English aristocrats. In the earlier part of the 20th century, it was adapted for play on cruise ships. Today, the game is played by countless people in clubs across the country, and is popping up more and more in backyard settings.

The trickiest part of setting up a shuffleboard site at home is installing the court. The concrete surface needs to be level and ultra smooth—a job best left to a professional. Call a shuffleboard club in your area for information on who they might recommend to install your court.

As for the game itself, the object is quite simple: players use cues to propel disks onto a scoring pattern, trying either to score or to prevent an opponent from scoring.

Some basic rules of the game, information about the equipment, and dimensions of a shuffleboard court, are listed on the opposite page.

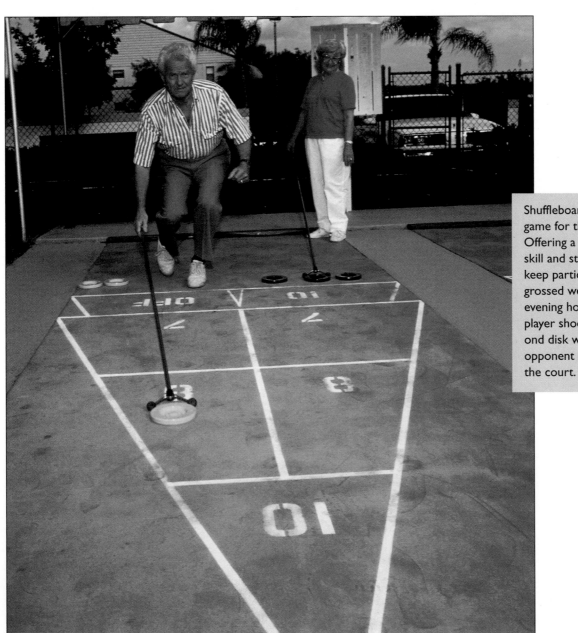

Shuffleboard is an ideal game for the backyard. Offering a mixture of skill and strategy, it can keep participants engrossed well into the evening hours. Here, a player shoots his second disk while his opponent sizes up the court.

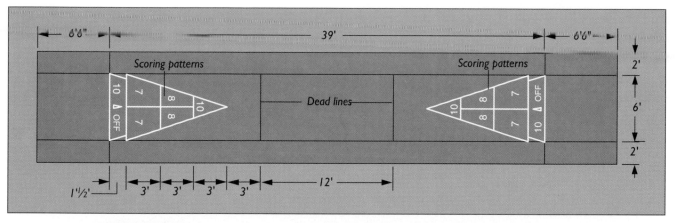

Shuffleboard court

An official shuffleboard court with dimensions is illustrated above. If your space is limited, maintain the width of the court, even if you shorten its length. Smooth portland cement is considered the only suitable material for an outdoor surface. A coating of shuffleboard wax will help the disks slide smoothly.

BASIC SHUFFLEBOARD RULES

Here are some of the basic rules as outlined by the Florida Shuffleboard Association.

• The game is played by two players (singles), or teams of two (doubles).

• The player with the yellow disks starts. (Players switch colors after each game.)

• Players must stand behind the scoring pattern when shooting (shuffling) their disks.

• The first player shoots the disk, trying to place it within the scoring pattern on the other end of the court.

• The second player also tries to place his or her disk in the scoring pattern, or tries to knock the first player's disk out of the pattern.

• Disks that fall between the deadlines are not in play and should be removed from the court.

• The round ends after eight disks, four each, are shot.

• Disks remaining on the scoring pattern at the end of the round earn points according to where on the pattern they've landed.

• In singles play, players change ends after each round. In doubles play, partners play the same color from opposite ends of the court.

• Games can be played to 50, 75, or 100 points.

THE TOOLS OF THE GAME

Shuffleboard equipment is pretty simple. The disks, shown in their carriers in the photo above, are 1" thick and 6" in diameter. The game is played with yellow and black or white disks. The cues, shown between the disks, are not more than 6'3" in length. They are designed so that no metal parts come into contact with the playing surface.

Out Gazing at Stars

The night sky has always inspired wonder and curiosity in earthbound humans, who long ago learned to track the movement of stars and planets. All you really need to take part in this timeless activity is a clear night, a quiet spot, and some simple tools.

While the best place for viewing the cosmos may be the clear, dark conditions of a countryside setting, astronomers who live in towns or cities can get rewarding views of the major constellations from their own backyard. Keep in mind, however, that it is always best to stay away from direct lighting, if possible, when star searching.

A few things to help you get started—binoculars, telescopes, and charts of the night sky—are featured on the opposite page. For more information, contact a local astronomy club.

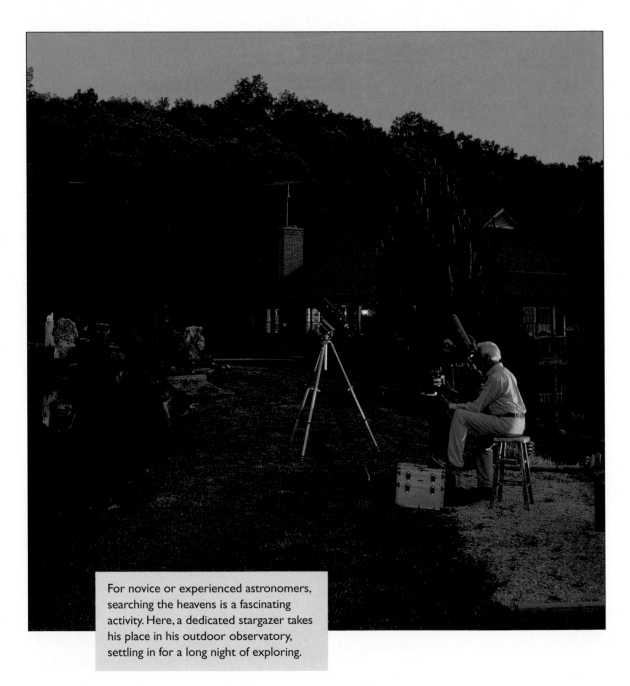

For novice or experienced astronomers, searching the heavens is a fascinating activity. Here, a dedicated stargazer takes his place in his outdoor observatory, settling in for a long night of exploring.

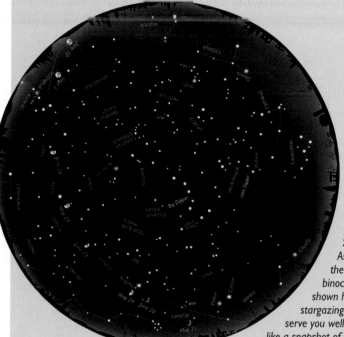

Perpetual star finder

Like a sky chart, a perpetual star finder offers a glimpse of the night sky for a given latitude—in this case, 40° North. But unlike a static chart, the finder allows the user to adjust for the time of year and the time of day by aligning the points on the edges of two revolving disks (above). The image of the sky that then appears in the window corresponds to the actual star alignment at that time.

Sky charts

As with every activity, it's best to start astronomy at the beginning by getting to know the night sky. While binoculars, telescopes, and perpetual star finders, all shown here, will undoubtedly be handy tools for future stargazing, a simple sky chart (left) and the naked eye will serve you well as you get familiar with the cosmos. Sky charts are like a snapshot of the night sky at a point in time for a given latitude. The one at left, shows the May-June 1996 sky for the northern United States, and includes all the major stars, constellations, and planets. By using it to identify the formations—such as the Big Dipper and the Little Dipper—you'll get to know the placement of the stars. From there, you can graduate to some of the more sophisticated tools. The charts are commonly available in astronomy magazines or at astronomy supply stores.

Binoculars

To put it simply, owning a set of binoculars is like having two low-strength telescopes attached together—one for each eye. The most common type of binoculars are called Porro prism. They gather and magnify light through a series of prisms. Common strengths range from 7x35 magnification to 8x24, with the most popular being 7x50. The 11x80 binoculars shown at right offer greater magnification and light gathering capabilities. They are equipped with a bracket for tripod mounting so they can be steadied during use. Binoculars should be purchased at an established optical equipment store.

Telescopes

The two most common types of telescopes are refractors and reflectors. A refractor uses a pair of lenses to gather and magnify light. A reflector uses a mirror instead of a lens to collect and focus light. The 80 mm refracting telescope shown here on a tripod is sure to provide bright, sharp images of stars. Telescopes of this type and size are popular with beginners, especially youngsters. To purchase a good quality telescope, shop at an established optical equipment store.

For the Kids

Kids love the outdoors. As they explore it through endless kinds of play, their delight is obvious. You can hear it in the giggles rippling from the sandbox and see it in the antics on any school playground. And what better place is there for them to take advantage of fresh air and sunshine than your own backyard? Many of the features found in a playground, such as slides and swings, can be built by the do-it-yourselfer with a modicum of ability.

Whether your children are toddlers or school age, you can add outdoor fun to their backyard play area with the ideas in this section. From a simple rope swing *(page 132)* to an elaborate jungle gym *(page 142)*, from a tree fort *(page 150)* to a lemonade stand *(page 154)*, you'll discover enough inspiration in this section to turn any backyard into a child's heaven. There's even advice on setting up your own skating rink *(page 156)*.

A final word of caution: While all the ideas shown here have been tested by parent-builders, there is still a certain element of risk in any playground-type activity, especially one involving heights, such as a jungle gym. Check the safety tips on page 131, but remember that children need to be supervised by an adult at all times.

Planning the Area

Before you put in a swing set or other play structures you'll need to take a few things into consideration, Check whether your designated play area gets too much sun throughout the day. You may need to construct a simple canopy over at least a portion of the play yard to create a shaded area. Make sure the size of the area is adequate for the type of play and number of children involved. And always ensure there's adequate clearance—at least six feet—between structures that will be used for active play and any buildings or fences in your yard.

Once you've planned your play area, you'll want to choose the right play equipment. Keep the following tips in mind:

Age and skill level: Remember that not all games and structures are appropriate to all ages. Buy sets that allow you to add or change components as your youngster grows.

Size: Your structures should not crowd your play areas, but should fit nicely within their boundaries. Measure before building or buying equipment.

Material: Metal is more durable, but wood is warmer and friendlier, and should last at least as long as your children will be using the equipment.

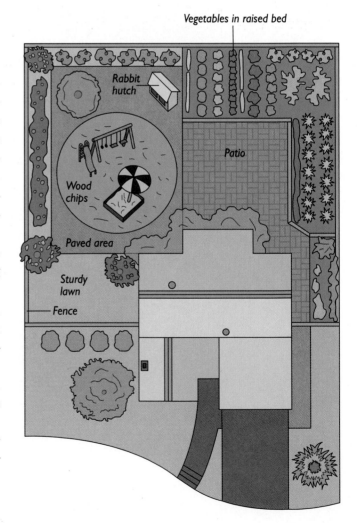

Vegetables in raised bed

Rabbit hutch

Patio

Wood chips

Paved area

Sturdy lawn

Fence

A home-built swing and play set, like the one shown at right, can provide hours of active fun for both you and your children. Remember to surround the play area with soft wood chips, sand, or sturdy grass to cushion the unavoidable falls *(see page 133).*

Outdoor Play

Play is important to help kids develop, both physically and mentally. In good weather and under safe conditions, the outdoors makes prime play territory, as sun, breeze, grass, leaves, sand, and dirt inspire their imagination and kindle their energy.

Make sure the structures you choose offer plenty of safe, imaginative play, while encouraging varied physical exercise. Swing sets and sand aren't the only things that delight young kids. Here are some other ideas to consider.

Garden pets: Alongside the ever-popular family dog or cat, you may want to raise a rabbit, or duck. Check your local zoning laws before you bring in exotic animals.

Outdoor artwork: Because of the mess they make inside, painting and ceramics can be more fun to pursue outdoors. Set up an old table or easel, sheltered from wind and direct sun, with a nearby cupboard for supplies.

Gardening: Children love to dig in dirt, so planting is a natural pleasure. Give them each a plant or two to care for over the summer, and watch their nurturing nature grow along with their gardens. And why not involve them in some of your gardening jobs, like pulling weeds, or harvesting fresh vegetables before dinner?

Whatever you choose, the play area should be able to keep the kids entertained and busy for as long as they play in the backyard.

Play yard safety

You can't prevent the occasional scrape, but it's important to protect your kids from serious harm. Here are some safety guidelines and tips to consider when planning a play area.

Clean and clear: Make sure the site is well drained and clear of debris. Remove harmful plants and those that have burrs, as well as sharp garden tools. And make sure your fences and gates are free of splinters, nails, or other sharp edges.

First aid: List emergency numbers near your phone, and learn first-aid techniques. Get a handbook and first-aid kit from the Red Cross, or from a drugstore.

A Swingin' Time

Children's swings never go out of style and, compared to other toys, they haven't changed much over the years. The tire suspended from a tree by a sturdy rope is still the do-it-yourselfer's simplest and most commonly used option. In order to ensure that your children are swinging freely and safely, consider the following tips.

Choosing a tree: The kind of tree is not as important as the fact that it should be tall, and strong enough to support each swinger, plus the occasional child who will try to scale the tree itself. If you attach the rope 8 to 10 feet from the trunk for a seat swing, the limb's diameter should be 3 to 4 inches. The branch must be well attached to

the trunk; look for one not larger than half the diameter of the tree's trunk, so that the tree is growing around it. The branch should look like a doweled-in chair leg.

Tire maintenance: For a tire swing, you'll need to clean an old tire with soap, water and a scrub brush, then coat it with vinyl or rubber protectant-

SECURING YOUR TIRE SWING

Although you can attach your tree-swing using chains and mounting hardware, the simplest method is to use soft, sturdy rope. This will also prevent little hands from getting caught in hard metal links. The illustration above shows one of the simplest methods of attaching a tire swing to a tree limb—the bowline knot. Starting at point (1), make a loop (2), wind the rope around the tire twice (3), then thread the end back up and around (4), and down again.

132

sealant for a shiny, finished look and protection from the elements. But make sure the coating dries before you sit on the tire.

Tying techniques: One way to secure a tire swing is to drape a rope over a limb, then make an eye splice instead of tying a knot. For those not up to the technical demands of this approach, a simpler alternative is to wrap the rope around the limb a few times, then tie it with a bowline. Next loop the rope around the tire several times, and tie another bowline there, as shown in the illustration on the opposite page.

Ropes: Rock-climbing rope is the strongest and most sturdy, but also the most expensive. There is really no need for rope that has a breaking point of thousands of pounds. Instead, try Philippine hemp with a minimum diameter of ¾ inch as an inexpensive alternative.

Swinging safely: No one should ever cross the path of a moving swing. And to minimize injury, use swing seats made of soft materials, such as canvas or rubber.

SOFT LANDINGS

For your child's safety, as well as your own peace of mind, prepare for the inevitable playtime tumbles. Cover the play area with one of an assortment of cushioning ground covers, taking into account the maintenance requirements and resilience of the material before you decide. By building a low wall around a play yard, you can help to contain the material, so the cushion stays thick and your replenishing costs are minimal.

Wood chips and sand: Wood chips are soft and giving, but can lose their cushioning effect when exposed to dirt, and rainy or humid weather. You'll need to re-level the area from time to time, as is also the case wth sand. Layer the chips and sand up to six inches and 12 inches deep, respectively.

Hardy grass: Consider this for a visually appealing surface. It's not as spongy as other materials, but provides an effective cushioning when grown two inches high.

Pea gravel: For use by those who don't want to be bothered with mess and upkeep. The only drawback of a three-inch-deep bed of gravel is that young children may have trouble running on the smooth stones.

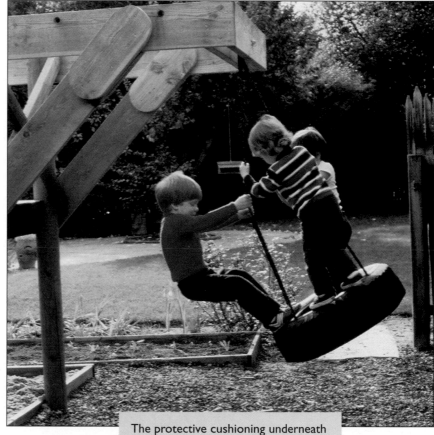

The protective cushioning underneath this tire swing (above) ensures that accidents won't come between your youngsters and their summer fun.

Flying Horse Swing

Whoosing through the air on a swing is one of life's great delights. And what could be simpler to make? All you need are a few pieces of wood, some rope, a place to hang it, and best of all, just a few hours' time.

BUILDING THE BODY

Cut the pieces to size. Clamp head (D) and spacer block (C) between legs (A), and drill the holes as shown opposite; all are ¾ inch, except the holes for the hand rest (G), which should be 1 inch. Insert the dowels for the foot rest (H) and supports (I) in the proper holes in one leg, and add washers to them. Next, put on the head (D), body (B), and spacer (C), then fit the remaining washers in place. Finally, position the other leg. Make sure the body pivots freely, then lock the supports (I) into position with glue and finish-ing nails in the dowels through each leg. Nail the hand rest (G) and foot rest (H) in place.

ADDING THE SEAT

Glue and screw saddle (E) in place; you may want to omit the glue if you feel you'll need to adjust the height as your child grows. Reinforce the seat with tri-angular support blocks (F).

FINAL TOUCHES

Coat the wood with several layers of sealant. Thread the rope through the holes in the handles and body, and hang the swing.

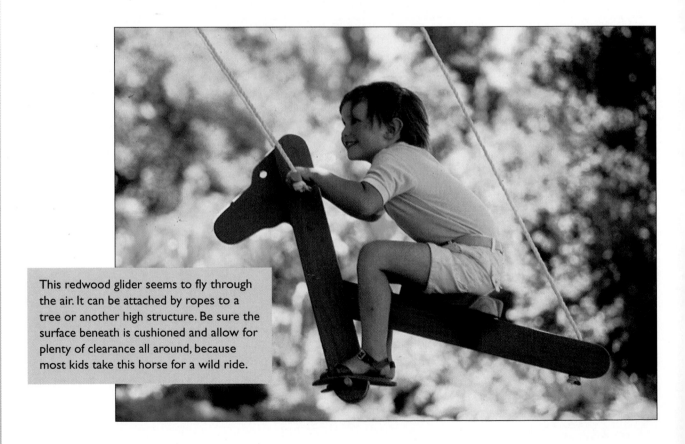

This redwood glider seems to fly through the air. It can be attached by ropes to a tree or another high structure. Be sure the surface beneath is cushioned and allow for plenty of clearance all around, because most kids take this horse for a wild ride.

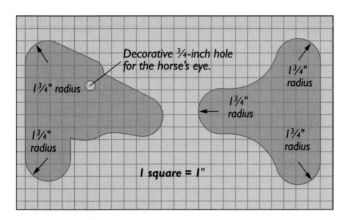

Decorative ¾-inch hole for the horse's eye.

1¾" radius

1¾" radius

1¾" radius

1¾" radius

1¾" radius

1 square = 1"

Head and saddle templates
Use the templates above to cut out the horse's head (D) and its saddle (E). Each square is equal to 1 inch.

CUTTING AND MATERIALS LIST

A	**Legs**	Two 2x4s @ 27"
B	**Body**	One 2x4 @ 30"
C	**Spacer block**	One 2x4 @ 3½" diameter
D	**Head**	One 2x12 @ 11" long, shaped as shown
E	**Saddle**	One 2x12 @ 10" long, shaped as shown
F	**Triangular seat support**	Two 2x4s @ 3½"x 3½"
G	**Hand rest**	One 1"-diameter hard wood dowel @ 18"
H	**Footrest**	One ¾" dowel @ 12"
I	**Supports**	Three ¾" dowels @ 6"
	Rope	⅜"-diameter, length optional
	Washers	Eight @ 1" inner diameter
	Finishing nails	Ten @ 6d
	Flathead woodscrews	Two @ 3" x #12
	Waterproof glue	
	Clear, nontoxic wood preservative	

3" x #12 flathead woodscrews

1¾"

3½"

3½"

3½"

Washers, 1" inner diameter

⅜" hole, 1" from both ends, for rope

D

G

I

A

E

F

B

A

Pivot point, a 1" hole

⅜" hole for rope

Nail braces to body and saddle

9¼"

1¾"

C

H

RIDE 'EM, COWBOY!

This flying horse swing is an updated version of an old playground standard: the three-rope, push-pull animal. You can build it from redwood, or, to save money, from construction-grade Douglas fir.
Design: Peter O. Whiteley

Redwood Play Structure

Slide, swing set, sandbox, balance beam, chinning bar—this sturdy redwood structure is all this and more. The rustic wood requires little maintenance and takes on a character of its own over time. Once you've completed the layout and installed the post, you can build the structure easily with an assistant's help.

Platform

E

L

F K J D

Drill for swing hardware

½"x10" machine bolt

pipe flange

⅜"x6" lag screw

E Y D

W

N

X

H

V

B 1" galvanized pipe

I

A

P M

O

L

C

⅜"x6" machine bolts

⅜"x6" lag screw

⅝" polypropylene rope

AA

Z

U

J

F

Q

G

⅜"x3½" lag screw

26-gauge galvanized sheet metal

S

BUILDING PLANS

Consult the overall view on this page of the play structure for a general idea of how it is constructed. The posthole layout on page 137 will help you situate the posts that form the backbone of the structure. Detailed views of specific elements are shown on pages 138-39.

CUTTING AND MATERIALS LIST

A	**Post**	One 4x6 @ 8'
B	**Post**	Two 4x4s @ 10'
C	**Post**	Two 4x4s @ 30"
D	**Post**	Two 4x4s @ 10'
E	**Post**	Two 4x4s @ 10'
F	**Post**	One 4x4 @ 10'
G	**Post**	Two 4x4s @ 30"
H	**Swing beam**	One 4x6 @ 10'
I	**Balance beam**	One 4x6 @ 10'
J	**Platform joist**	Two 2x6s @ 46¼"
K	**Platform joist**	Three 2x6s @ 53"
L	**Platform board**	Ten 2x6s @ 39¼"
M	**Ramp board**	Twelve 2x6s @ 46¼"
N	**Platform beam**	One 4x4 @ 55"
O	**Ramp support**	Two 4x4s trimmed to length
P	**Ramp cleat**	Three 2x6s @ 24"
Q	**Outside slide rail**	Two 2x12s trimmed to length
R	**Slide cleat**	Two 2x4s @ 8'
S	**Slide cleat**	Two 2x4s @ 12'
T	**Slide crosspiece**	Six 2xX6s @ 36"
U	**Inside slide rail**	Two 2x6s trimmed to size
V	**Railing upright**	Thirteen 2x4s @ 37½"

W	**Railing**	Four 2x6s @ 53"
X	**Railing cap**	One 2x4 @ 46"
Y	**Railing cap**	One 2x4 @ 39"
Z	**Sandbox end**	Four 2x6s @ 46"
AA	**Sandbox side**	Four 2x6s @ 101"
BB	**Toe guard**	One 2x6 @ 39¼"
CC	**Slide core pieces**	¾"–4x8' sheet
Galvanized sheet metal (26-gauge)		One @ 3'x10'
Galvanized pipe		1"-diameter
Pipe flanges		Two @ 1"
Lag screws		Two @ 2½", Thirty-one @ ⅜"x3½", Three @ ⅜"x6"
Common nails		5lbs 16d, 1lb 10d
Machine bolts		Three @ ½"x10", Four @ ⅜"x6"
Polypropylene rope		12' @ ⅝"diameter
Ready-mix concrete		Ten sacks
2 swing sets with hardware		
Clear or tinted wood preservative		
Washers & locknuts for bolts/screws		
(Details of ramp, railings, and sides shown on pages 138-39)		

Posthole layout
Refer to the diagram at left before you sink the first posthole for the play structure. It's best to mark each post location with a stake or some chalk before you dig the holes. And don't forget to tamp down the cement with a bar or stick once you've set the posts. If the frostline in your region is deeper than the depth of the postholes shown here, you will have to buy longer posts.

Redwood play structure continued ▶

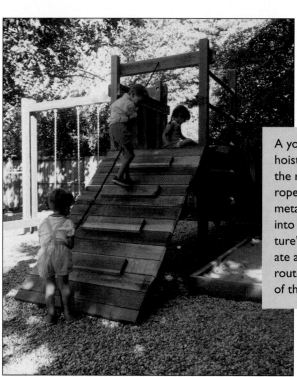

A young climber hoists his way up the ramp by a rope. Traditional metal bars, built into the structure's side, create an alternative route to the top of the structure.

Trim ends

$\frac{3}{8}$"x$3\frac{1}{2}$" lag screw

J   M   **Ramp**   P

Bevel

X   W   O   **Railing**

16d nails

V

4"   K

1"

GETTING STARTED

Cut all the pieces following the diagrams and the cutting and materials list on page 137. Before beginning assembly, bore all screw holes and bolt holes, and add decorative dadoes and bevels, if desired.

SETTING UP THE SWING

Assemble posts B and D, and swing beam (H) using $\frac{1}{2}$-by-10-inch machine bolts. To keep the pairs of posts parallel, nail one-foot scraps of 4-by-4 between them, flush with their bases. With a helper, position the swing assembly in the holes, Install all posts, and pour cement into each hole.

BUILDING THE PLATFORM

Install two outside joists (K) first, 52 inches above the ground, using $\frac{3}{8}$-by-$3\frac{1}{2}$-inch lag screws, then add joists (J). Secure center joist K with $3\frac{1}{2}$-inch nails, then nail platform boards (L) to the joists with $3\frac{1}{2}$-inch nails. Cut and bevel platform beam (N) and fasten it to posts E with two $\frac{3}{8}$-by-6-inch lag screws.

THE RAMP AND SLIDE

Set one ramp support (O) against the platform at the desired angle, scribe the angle onto the face of O, then cut along this line. Saw a matching angle in the other O piece. Then attach the supports

to the platform from behind with $\frac{3}{8}$-by-$3\frac{1}{2}$-inch lag screws. Nail ramp boards (M) to the supports, then attach ramp cleats (P).

For the slide, place the slide plywood pieces on top of the sheet metal so that two 6-inch strips of metal are exposed on each end. Bend the metal over the plywood ends, forming a curved edge.

CLEATS AND RAILS

To make the slide cradle, fasten side cleats (R) to outside slide rails (Q), then add slide cleats (S) as shown in the illustration on the opposite page. Next, position the rails parallel to each other and

Slide cradle

24"

24"

Q

R

16d nails

S T 6" 3¼"

BB

Slide

3" nails

Q

CC

U

26-gauge galvanized
sheet metal

3'x8' plywood

Plumb cut

1'x3' plywood

A CLOSEUP LOOK AT THE RAMP, RAILINGS, AND SLIDE

The diagrams above show how the ramp, railings, and slide are assembled.
As long as the wood is secure, the connections are strong, and the kids are
willing, this unit will provide hours of safe, easily supervised fun. Make sure
to sand all surfaces to prevent splinters.

add the slide crosspiece (T). With
a helper, hoist the cradle into position atop the platform, adjust for
the desired angle, and mark the
rails along the back of outside
posts D and post F. If desired, mark
decorative plumb cuts at the bottom of rails Q. Remove the cradle,
make the cuts, and rehang the
assembly using countersunk ⅜-by-
6 inch machine bolts. Then add
the toe guard (BB) where the slide
meets the platform.

SECURING THE SLIDE

Place the slide in its cradle and
secure it along the edges with 3½-
inch nails driven through cross-
pieces T and into cleats R and S;
begin nailing at the top, smoothing

out the metal as you go. Finally,
cut slide rails (U) to conform to
the lower bend in the slide and nail
them to Q with 3-inch nails.

TAPERED RAILINGS

Install the railings (W), then add
the uprights (V), spacing them
evenly, and nail them onto the railing caps X and Y with 3½-inch nails.

BALANCE BEAM AND
CHINNING BAR

Fasten one end of the balance
beam (I) to posts C with a countersunk ½-by-10-inch machine
bolt. Level the beam, then fasten
the opposite end to post B with a
countersunk ⅜-by-6-inch lag screw.
Thread the pipe flanges onto the 1-

inch pipe, then secure the flanges
to the posts A and B at the desired
height, using 2½-inch lag screws.

ROPE AND SANDBOX

Attach the rope, knotted for hand-
pulling, to platform beam (N)
through the hole drilled for it.
Attach sandbox ends (Z) and
sides (AA) to the outside of posts
G and the inside of posts D, E, and
F, one row at a time with ⅜-by-3½-
inch lag screws.

FINISHING TOUCHES

Smooth any remaining sharp
edges with a sander, then treat
the redwood with cedar or cedar-
tinted wood preservative.

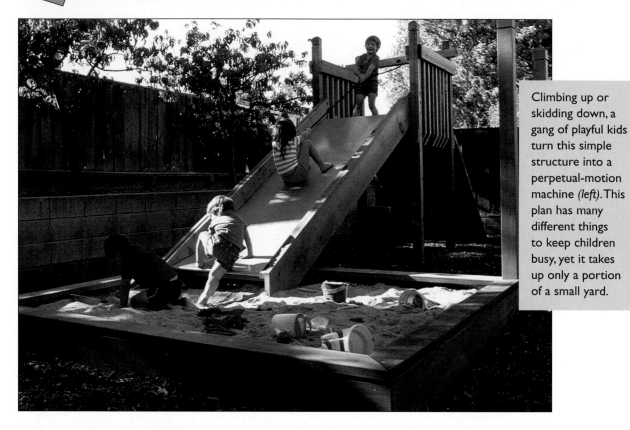

Climbing up or skidding down, a gang of playful kids turn this simple structure into a perpetual-motion machine *(left)*. This plan has many different things to keep children busy, yet it takes up only a portion of a small yard.

Backyard Gym

If you don't have the space for the larger redwood play structure featured on pages 136-139, this project offers a scaled-down alternative. Most of its features are almost identical to the larger project, but it is very compact.

POSTS

Cut the seven sandbox posts (B), then bevel and dado the tops of the six remaining tall posts (A), if desired. Dig each post hole at least 8 inches wide; refer to the illustrations on page 141. You'll need a helper to position the posts, making sure they're plumb and aligned, Then pour cement into each hole.

PLATFORM, RAMP, SLIDE, AND RAILINGS

Follow the same methods given for the redwood play structure to assemble the platform, ramp, and railings. Then assemble the slide. Note that, unlike the larger project, the railing caps are the same on both sides of the platform. Finally, attach the rope.

SANDBOX

Fasten the sides to the posts with countersunk ⅜-by-2½-inch lag screws, then add the mitered caps (F and G) as shown on the next page. At the corner where the caps meet the chinning bar post, add 2-by-4 cleats *(see Diagram 2)*.

FINISHING UP

Attach the chinning bar, then sand any sharp edges smooth. Finish the whole structure with preservative.

Design: Playscapes by Kelly.

140

MATERIALS LIST

J-Y Pieces		Same as in Redwood play structure (p.136-139).
A	**Platform posts**	Four 4x4s @ 10'
B	**Sandbox posts**	Seven 4x4s @21¼"
C	**Chin bar posts**	Two 4x4s @ 8'
D	**Sandbox sides**	Two 1x8s @ 10'
E	**Sandbox sides**	Two 1x8s @ 8'
F	**Cap material**	Two 2x6s @ 10'
G	**Cap material**	Two 2x6s @ 8'
Lag screws		Two @ ⅜x6" & Eleven @ ⅜x3½" & 24@ ⅜x2½"
Machine bolts		Four @ ⅜x6"

Metal, pipe, flange, nails, rope, concrete, preservative—as in the Redwood structure on pages 136-139

Posthole layout
Like with the larger redwood play structure shown on pages 136-139, the placement of the posts is critical to the building of the backyard gym. Consult the diagram at left to plot where your posts should go.

46 ¼"   53"
70"   48"
2"
7' 6"
8' 6"

⅝" polypropylene rope

N

X

A 4x4 posts, 10' long, 25" deep

W

Diagram 1

26-gauge galvanized sheet metal

L

J

O

V

U

Q

Pipe flange

1" galvanized pipe

C 4x4 posts, 8' long, 25" deep

Diagram 2

2x6 cap

4x4 post

2x4 cleats

1x8 side

COMPACT FUN

The central platform, rope-pull, ramp, and slide are virtually the same as for the larger play structure shown on pages 136-139. This version has a chinning bar attached to the roomy sandbox.

Miter ends

D 1x8x10'

E 1x8x8' sides

7' 6"

8' 7½"

B 14" deep

F 2x6 cap

G 2x6 cap

Ultimate Playground

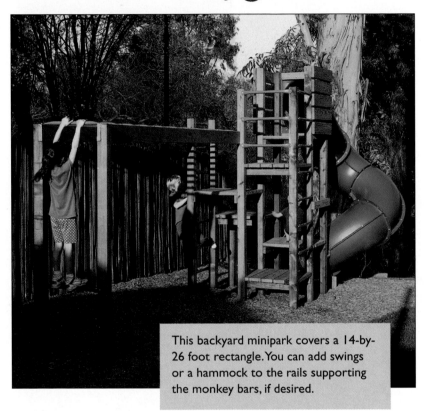

This backyard minipark covers a 14-by-26 foot rectangle. You can add swings or a hammock to the rails supporting the monkey bars, if desired.

	CUTTING AND MATERIALS LIST	
A	Support posts	Six 4x4s @ 12'
B	Platform post	One 4x4 @ 8'
C	Monkey bar remote post	Two 4x4s @ 10'
D	Monkey bar posts	Two 4x4s @ 10'
E	Platform supports	Twelve 2x4s @ 29"
F	Platforms/ steps (6)	Thirty 2x6s @ $29\frac{7}{8}$" (trimmed to 29")
G	Monkey bar rails	Two 2x6s @ 12'
H	Top platform sides	10 2x6s @ $29\frac{7}{8}$"
I	Ladder rungs	Thirty metal bars @ 22" (Store bought)
J	Steering wheel support	One 2x4 @ $29\frac{7}{8}$"
K	Steering wheels	Two @ 12" diameter
L	Slide assembly	One (Store bought)
Underlay		Grass, wood chips, etc.
Cement post concrete		Eleven bags
Deck screws		One 10 lb box @ $2\frac{1}{2}$"
Lag screws & washers		Twenty-two @ $\frac{5}{16}$" x $1\frac{1}{2}$"
Lag screws & washers		Thirty-eight @ $\frac{5}{16}$" x $2\frac{1}{2}$"

Almost any safe play area design can create a wonderland of possibilities if it's planned with imagination and care. When enough space is available, as in public playgrounds, a wide range of games becomes possible, but much the same quality can be brought into many backyards as well, even on a limited budget. The playground shown above combines a variety of favorite childhood activities into one structure. It should take about three weeks of work to get the ultimate playground ready for your kids.

GETTING STARTED
Buy the materials and cut the parts as listed in the cutting and materials list on this page. You can use a pressure-treated hemfir called sunwood if redwood seems too expensive.

SETTING THE POSTS
The distance between the inside faces of each pair of posts is 22 inches, and each posthole

should be about two feet deep. Set the two support posts (A) in concrete. Once these are solid, place the remaining posts in position and add cement.

INSTALLING THE SLIDE

You'll need one helper to put the slide together, and two to position and install it. Assemble and hang the slide (L) to get a quick idea of the distance from the ground to the top platform. Sit the bottom of the slide on temporary scrap blocks if you need to make up for the depth of the fill before the slide's permanent support bracket is put in place.

BUILDING THE PLATFORMS

The entrance to the slide should be roughly 78 inches off the ground, so this should be the height of the topmost of six platforms (F). Space the remaining five platforms about 13 inches apart, so that kids can climb easily from the ground to the top of the slide. Beginning with the bottom platform, position the platform supports (E) on the posts so they run from front to back. If posts are slightly off-kilter—which

BUILDING PLANS

These plans were dictated by the height of the slide, the width of the rungs, and an 8-inch allowance below for the fill. The spacings between the rungs, platforms, and activity area are based on guidelines published by the U.S. Consumer Product Safety Commission. If the frost line in your area is deeper than two feet—the depth the posts are sunk for this plan—adjust the length of the posts you buy accordingly.

Mount seven ladder rungs on the front side, three on the adjacent side, and seven on the back. (Note that the ones on the back start lower.) The top rungs are 32" above the adjacent platform; the post tops rise 2" higher.

Allow a 6' setback from the fence.

Follow the slide manufacturer's assembly and mounting directions.

29⅞"

H

L

H

Position all rungs 1' apart.

D

G

10'

22"
gap

A
4x4 posts

F
assembly

I

⅜" gap

All posts
buried 2'
deep

K

1" gap

A

J

F

E
29" 2x4s

C

22"

Ground-covering material should be at least 8" deep.

Note how platform slats run at right angles to the slats of the platform below.

I

B

A

To create a jumping-off platform, cut the 8-foot post flush to top of the 2-by-4 platform support so the outer slat sits on top of it.

Ultimate Playground continued ▶

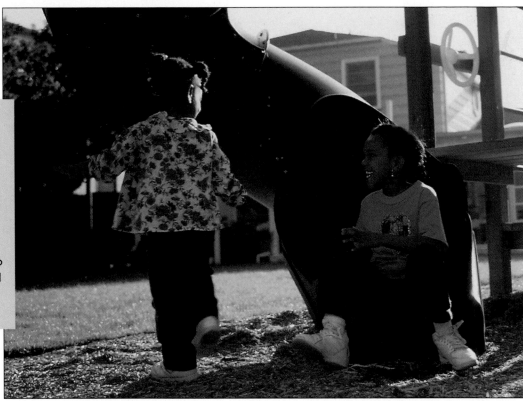

Your backyard playground can have elements such as a steering wheel—which lets your children pretend that they are at the controls of anything from a race car to a space ship—and a slide for hours of slippery fun.

happens more often than not in the real world—the gaps between the posts may be more or less than 22 inches. Posts can be a little less than 22 inches apart, but they can't be more or else the screws that hold the ladder rungs won't have enough wood to grab. If you encounter this problem, pull the tops of the posts toward each other until the gap at each platform level is 22 inches. You can use anything from a pipe or bar clamp to a rope tourniquet to do this.

SUPPORTING THE POSTS

If your posts are aligned, mount the E supports to the posts, trim the F slats to 29 inches, and mount them to the supports, leaving ⅜ inch between them, as shown in the illustration on page 143. Cut 3½-inch-square notches in the ends of the outer slats to fit around the posts. Use deck screws for all wood-to-wood connections.

If the posts aren't aligned, position the slats before you cut them to their finished lengths. Put a measuring stick across the outsides of the posts and mark the cutoff lines at both ends. Remove the boards, trim them, and then mount them in position.

BUILDING THE PLATFORMS

Build one platform (F) at a time, working from the bottom up so there's plenty of room to run your drill and/or your screwdriver from above. Orient the 2-by-4 supports (E) so they always point toward you as you go from one level to the next. That's so little fingers can grab onto the slats as kids boost themselves up the structure.

SETTING UP THE MONKEY BARS

The four posts supporting the monkey bars require tricky notch cuts to accept the 12-foot rails

(G). To do this, clamp the rails in position with the bottom edge 72 inches off the ground, making sure they're both level—by themselves and to each other.

Mark their positions on the posts, then remove the rails. Set your circular saw to form 1½-inch-deep cuts, then make multiple passes with the saw so you leave a bunch of roughly ¼-inch horizontal fins between the two marked lines. When you've finished each section, snap the fins out and clean the notch with a chisel.

MOUNTING THE MONKEY BARS

Once all the notches are cut, mount the 2-by-6 G rails to the posts, then cut off the excess at all four rail ends. Also saw the tops of the two remote posts flush with the top edges of the 2-by-6s. Position the 11 ladder rungs (I) that you will use for the monkey bars one foot apart before you attach any of them, adjusting them if necessary for even spacing. If you have set the posts correctly, the spacing should be right. Use the shorter lag screws to attach the horizontal bars.

ATTACHING LADDERS AND SIDES OF TOP PLATFORM

Using the longer lag screws, attach two ladder rungs (I) one and two feet up from the final play surface on the remote posts. Also mount the climber rungs on the sides of the posts, as shown on page 143. Attach the 2-by-6s top platform sides (H), spacing them one-inch apart. Chisel out the ends of the two 2-by-6s that overlap the climber rungs so the 2-by-6s can be mounted flush to the post. Cut the posts around the top platform flush with the tops of H, then saw the remaining posts to two inches above the top climbing rungs.

ATTACHING THE STEERING WHEELS

Mount a 2-by-4 steering wheel support (J) 20 inches above the second platform to support one of the steering wheels (K), then center the other in the top 2-by-6 on the top platform.

INSTALLING BASE MATERIAL

Choose a ground cover, such as wood chips, grass, or an engineered wood fiber, such as Fibar. Make sure you consider price, durability, attractiveness, and cleanliness. See page 133 for more on choosing an appropriate ground cover for the play area.

Design: Bill Crosby

Monkey bars allow your kids test their strength as well as their agility. Kids can swing freely, or climb along the bars from the top. You can cut the bars yourself, or buy ready-made ones.

Storybook Cottage

Roof framing

Roof sheathing

1x8 fascia

2½"nails

Y

Support cleat

Z

W

E

Corner construction

⁵⁄₁₆"x2½" lag screw

V

Q

1x3 trim

⁵⁄₁₆"x3½" lag screw

Front **B**

O

K

Floor **G**

Side **E**

2"

¾" galvanized pipe

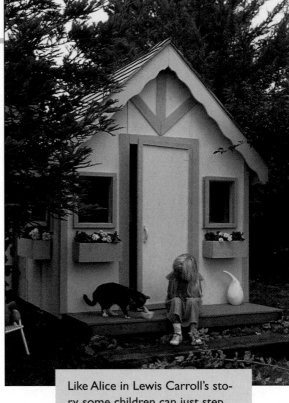

Like Alice in Lewis Carroll's story, some children can just step outside the house to enter wonderlands of their own. The storybook cottage shown here takes just a few weekends to build, and will help transport your children into the world of make-believe.

BUILDING PLANS

The illustrations here and on the following pages provide various views of the cottage construction details, from flooring to rafter construction.

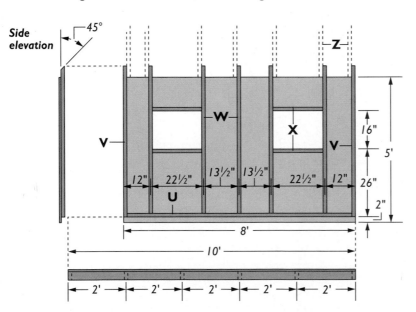

Side elevation

45°

Z

W

X

V

V

16"

5'

12" 22½" 13½" 13½" 22½" 12"

26"

U

2"

8'

10'

2' 2' 2' 2' 2'

4'

2'

Y

3'

Q **T**

P

2'

16"

S

Cut out door (front only) and windows

R

5'

12"

6"

26"

O

2¼"

6'

Front elevation

70½"

PARTS AND MATERIALS LIST

A, B	**Front pieces**	One each $^5/_8$" plywood 4x8, as shown
C, D	**Back pieces**	One each $^5/_8$" plywood 4x8, as shown
E	**Side pieces**	Four $^5/_8$" plywood @ 48"x5"
F	**Floor pieces**	Four $^5/_8$" plywood @ 45"x35$^1/_4$"
G	**Floor pieces**	One $^5/_8$" plywood @ 24"x70$^1/_2$"
H	**Roof pieces**	Two $^5/_8$" plywood @ 12"x96"
I	**Roof pieces**	Two $^5/_8$" plywood @ 18"x60"
J	**Roof pieces**	Two $^5/_8$" plywood @ 48"x96"
K	**Floor pieces**	Two 2x4s @ 10'
L	**Floor pieces**	Six 2x4s @ 67$^1/_2$"
M	**Floor pieces**	Three 2x4s @ 22$^1/_2$"
N	**Floor pieces**	Two 2x4s @ 21$^3/_4$"
O, U	**Sole plates**	Two 2x2s each @ 64$^1/_2$" & 93"
P, Q	**Wall studs**	Four 2x2s each, cut to length
R, S	**Framing pieces**	Eight 2x2s each @19$^1/_2$" & 16"
T	**Door header**	One 2x4 @ 22$^1/_2$"
V	**Outside studs**	Four 2x2s @ 62$^1/_4$"
W	**Inside studs**	Ten 2x2s @ 60$^3/_4$"
X	**Framing pieces**	Eight 2x2s @ 21"
Y	**Ridgeboard**	One 2x4 @ 8'
Z	**Rafters**	Fourteen 2x2s @ 58$^1/_2$"
Fascia boards		Two 1x8s @ 10' Four 1x6s @ 12'
Slide, door, and window trim		Five 1x4s @ 10' Eight 1x4s @ 8'
Door frame		Six 1x3s @ 8'
8 Corner trim boards & window frames		Twelve 1x3s @ 6' Two 1x2s @ 8'
Vertical battens (front & back walls)		One 1x2 @ 6'
Acrylic sheets		$^3/_{16}$", to fit windows
Nails, hardware, and finish as required		

A playhouse—a room of one's own—can be the ticket to a world of fun and fantasy. This model is built from 2-by-2 and 2-by-4 framing and plywood—either AC exterior for all surfaces, or rough-sawn, prestained plywood for the walls. Floor framing should be made from redwood or another rot-resistant species. Use construction grade douglas fir for pieces O-Z, and grade 2 or better for the fascia boards, trim, door and window frames, and vertical battens. The details and finishing trouches can be as fancy or as plain as you like. For instance, you can omit the rear windows if you will be placing the cottage against a row of trees at the border of your yard.

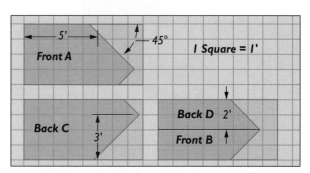

Detail of floor and plywood sheathing
The diagrams above show how to construct the floor platform (top), and how to make the angle cuts in the plywood pieces for the front and back of the cottage (below). The side pieces of plywood sheathing are rectangular and need no angle cuts.

Storybook Cottage continued ▶

Wavy-cut
1x6 fascia

1x2
battens

1x4
trim

1x3
corner
trim

Window boxes

Flashing

Overlapping
ridge shingles

Wood
shingles

Y

Z

Q

J

H

I

Wavy-cut
1x8 fascia

Window
box

1x4
trim

Colorful flowers growing in the sunny window boxes of the cottage add a nice touch. Your children can plant and care for the flowers themselves and use them to decorate a table set for a tea party.

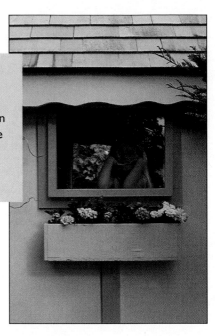

ADDING TRIM

Once the basic structure of the cottage is completed you need to add the door and windows *(opposite)*, and the trim *(above)* to provide the final decorative touches

CONSTRUCTING THE FLOOR

Nail the floor framing pieces K, L, M, and N together with 3½-inch nails. Add the plywood flooring pieces F and G, centering the pan-el edges over the framing pieces, then nail every 6 inches around the perimeter, and every 12 inch-es along intermediate supports with 2-inch nails.

To keep the cottage from shift-ing, stake the corners with ¾-inch pipe and lag screws, as shown in the detail on page 146. If your yard slopes, you could substitute 2-by-6 floor framing members for the floor and level the structure as required on posts and con-crete piers.

RAISING THE WALLS

Mark the positions of wall fram-ing pieces O through X on the inside surfaces of the plywood walls. Cut the framing pieces and nail them together at the various connections, using 3½-inch nails. Temporarily tack the framework to the plywood; turn the assem-bly over and nail through the ply-wood into the framing with 2-inch nails spaced every 12 inches.

CUTTING DOOR AND WINDOW OPENINGS

Use a portable saber saw, circular saw, or keyhole saw to cut the door and window openings. Set the door panel aside.

ATTACHING WALLS TO FLOOR

With a helper, position one side wall on the floor. Hold the wall plumb, then drill pilot holes in the sole plate about every 32 inches and attach the wall to the floor with ⁵⁄₁₆-by-3½-inch lag screws. Then position the back wall, drill pilot holes in the corner studs, and secure the studs together with ⁵⁄₁₆-by-2½-inch lag screws. Now add the remaining walls.

FRAMING THE ROOF

Add support cleats for the ridge-board (Y) at the roof peak, as shown on page 146 *(top)*. Then nail Y to the front and back walls with 3½-inch nails. Cut both ends of rafters (Z) at a 45° angle, then face-nail each to the stud on the ridgeboard. Add roof sheathing H, I, and J, using 2-inch nails every 6 inches along the edges, every 12 inches everywhere else.

SHINGLING THE ROOF

Use nails that are short enough not to poke through the underside. Begin at the eaves and work upward. Allow a 5-inch exposure for asphalt shingles, and a 3¾-inch exposure for 16-inch wood shingles. Offset the joints.

ADDING TRIM AND EXTRAS

Add flashing at the ridge, then install the overlapping ridge shingles, as shown in the illustrations on the opposite page.

Cut the wavy-edged fascia boards for the roof and trim them to length. Nail the 1-by-8 boards to the rafter ends and drive 2-inch screws through the sheathing to secure them. At the front and back, clamp the 1-by-6s in place and screw down through the roof. Where they meet in the center, add a nailing cleat. Then nail the pieces together at the corners.

DOORS AND WINDOWS

Use the reserved plywood panel to build the doors and windows. The design is entirely up to you. Some ideas are shown below. Hang the doors and windows with brass or galvanized butt hinges.

FINISHING TOUCHES

Caulk all the seams carefully, and allow the caulk to dry before proceeding. You can then paint or stain the walls. Paint the trim pieces to match the cottage and attach them to the structure. Make the window boxes from plywood scraps, then secure them with carriage bolts.

Design: Don Vandervort

Door

Brass butt hinge

Nail to plywood cutout

1x3 trim

Window options

³⁄₁₆" acrylic

1x3 trim

³⁄₁₆"-wide dado

Plywood spacer

Window box

⅝" plywood

¼"x2½" carriage bolt

Tree Houses

Tree houses give kids their own piece of real estate unmatched by anything built for adults. Perched high above their ordinary existence of homework, television, chores, and family life, kids can chat and giggle with each other or read a book in leafy seclusion—far away from the adult world, but still within view for parents to keep a watchful eye on their offspring and any visiting kids. If a tree house has any drawback at all, it's that most pets can't climb up, too. Otherwise, it's a child's dream come true.

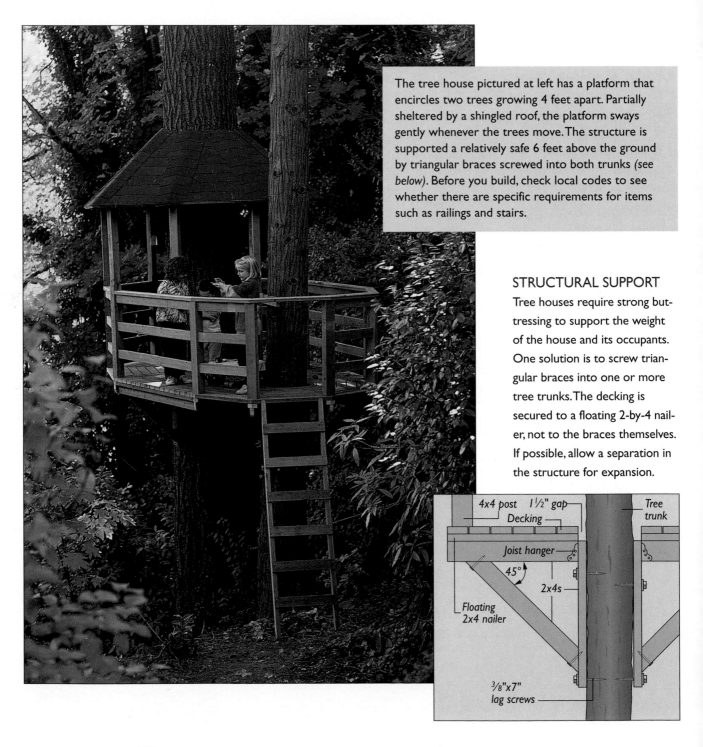

The tree house pictured at left has a platform that encircles two trees growing 4 feet apart. Partially sheltered by a shingled roof, the platform sways gently whenever the trees move. The structure is supported a relatively safe 6 feet above the ground by triangular braces screwed into both trunks (see below). Before you build, check local codes to see whether there are specific requirements for items such as railings and stairs.

STRUCTURAL SUPPORT

Tree houses require strong buttressing to support the weight of the house and its occupants. One solution is to screw triangular braces into one or more tree trunks. The decking is secured to a floating 2-by-4 nailer, not to the braces themselves. If possible, allow a separation in the structure for expansion.

4x4 post 1½" gap
Decking
Tree trunk
Joist hanger
45°
2x4s
Floating 2x4 nailer
⅜"x7" lag screws

150

Many parents might hesitate to build a tree house in their yard. To start with, the project requires a strong tree with sturdy branches; if you have any doubt after trying your own weight, find a stronger tree. Another solution is to build the structure around, not on, a tree.

Some parents object to driving lag screws into a healthy tree trunk. Again, if you decide to build the platform around a tree and support the platform from the ground, there's no need to disturb the trunk or the branches. Of course, with this method, you will have to make allowance for the fact that the tree will sway and increase its girth with age. Be sure to allow for extra space in your tree house base.

No matter what you decide, your children's tree house is sure to become their favorite home-away-from-home.

If you are including a porch in the design of your children's home up in the treetops, remember to install a railing that is high enough and sturdy enough to prevent any accidental falls.

One of the challenges of building a tree house is figuring out a way to use an existing tree to support the structure. Here, the builders have straddled two branches with a strong board that supports the floor of the house.

Backyard Hideaways

2x6 ridge beam

2x4 rafters

2x4 flanked by ½" plywood

7'

¼" plywood

⅝" plywood

¾" plywood

⅜" plywood

2x6 joist

2x3 stud

8'

10'

SKELETON VIEW
The straightforward use of joints, studs, and rafters is apparent with this bare-bones view of the bungalow. The dimensions are geared for 7- to 10-year-old children.

Everyone loves to have a place to call their own—and that includes kids. Here are a couple of ideas that you can adapt to your own backyard. Each offers a private child-scale refuge and play space.

The playhouse shown on this page is a cozy miniature dwelling where lunch, tea, a card game, or a meeting of a secret club can take place. It also has enough space for a bunk bed and even a desk at the back, making it ideal for occasional "camping out."

The structure rests on 2-by-6 joists. The walls are framed by 2-by-3 studs, covered with ⅜-inch plywood. The roof is a scaled-down version of a regular house roof, with 2-by-4 rafters and a 2-by-6 ridge beam, topped by sheets of

Complete with windows and French doors, this playhouse is a bright, open dwelling with plenty of space for friends and siblings to join in the fun.
Design: Marc Appleton

¾-inch plywood. You can finish the roof with shingles or any other common roofing material.

The playhouse shown below rises from a triangular sandbox on 6-by-6 posts anchored in concrete footings. Two sets of 2-by-4s bolted to the posts make reinforcing rim joists that support the floor and the roof. The floor is more than 7 feet above the sand, leaving ample headroom below and even providing some shade for hot summer days.

The structure has 2-by-6 decking for the floor, a plywood and asphalt roof, complete with flashing, a skylight, and walls made from alternating 2-by-4s and 2-by-6s screwed to the rim joists. By closing the front door and shuttered side windows, children can escape into a world that's above it all and scaled just for them.

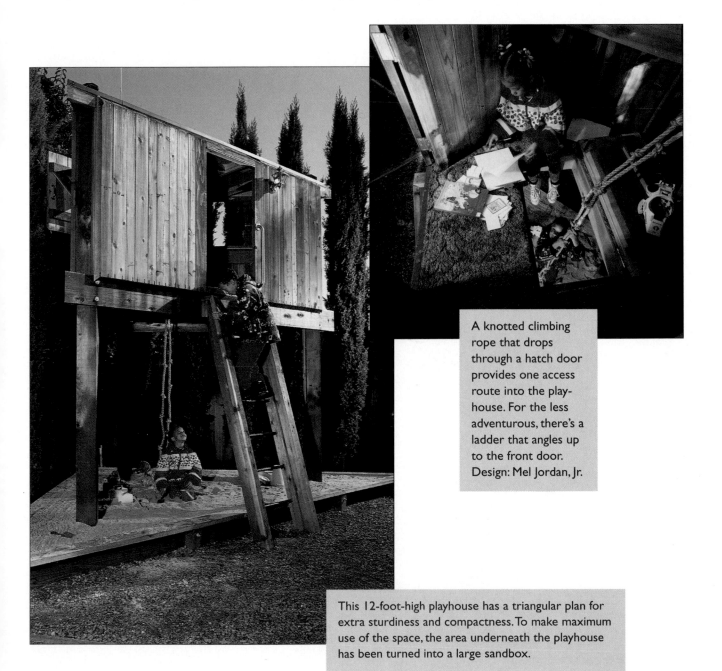

A knotted climbing rope that drops through a hatch door provides one access route into the playhouse. For the less adventurous, there's a ladder that angles up to the front door. Design: Mel Jordan, Jr.

This 12-foot-high playhouse has a triangular plan for extra sturdiness and compactness. To make maximum use of the space, the area underneath the playhouse has been turned into a large sandbox.

Lemonade Stand & Puppet Theater

Whether your child is an aspiring entrepreneur or showman, this dual purpose lemonade stand and puppet theater offers the perfect outlet. The project can be built in a day; it disassembles in minutes and stores flat. To build it, just follow these easy steps and diagrams.

BUILDING THE FRONT PANEL
Cut the pieces to size *(see below)*. Secure the front pieces (E) to the

Whether they're serving up lemonade (left), or laughter (above), children will have a great time entertaining their friends with this lemonade stand/puppet theater. It can be converted from one to the other in minutes and stores easily.
Design: Jim Vanides

CUTTING AND MATERIALS LIST

A	**Front panel**	One ¹/₂-inch plywood 24"x30"
B	**Roof top piece**	One ¹/₂-inch plywood 24"x30"
C	**Roof top piece**	One ¹/₂-inch 6"x30"
D	**Side panels**	Two ¹/₂-inch plywood 30"x42"
E	**Front pieces**	Two 1x2s @ 23¹/₄"
F	**Front lip**	One 1x3 @ 29"
G	**Roof side pieces**	Two 1x2s @ 30"
H	**Roof side piece**	One 1x3 @ 30"
I	**Curtain rods**	Three 1x1s @ 27¹/₂"
J	**Signposts**	Two 1x2s @ 42"
K	**Serving shelf**	One 1x12 @ 28¹/₂"
L	**Shelf piece**	One 1x1 @ 28¹/₂"
M	**Shelf piece**	One 1x12 @ 28¹/₂"
Machine bolts with T-nuts		Two @ ⁵/₁₆"x⁵/₈" Two @ ⁵/₁₆" x 1"
Carriage bolts		10 @ ⁵/₁₆"x1¹/₂"
Nuts & washers		10 (for carriage bolts)
Flathead woodscrews		40 @ 1¹/₄" x No. 6
Finish washers		34
Finishing nails		6d (as needed)
Exterior enamel and clear finish		
Curtain material and blackboard		
Hardboard for sign		

front panel (A), ½ inch in from each 24-inch-long side and ¾ inch down from the top. Use three woodscrews and finish washers for each E board. Then, using two woodscrews and washers, mount the front lip (F) on top of the E pieces so it's on edge and flush with A. Finally, nail F to E.

MAKING THE ROOF
Join side pieces (G and H) to top pieces (B and C). The two G pieces run along the sides of the roof ½ inch in from the top edge. Piece H is flush with the top edge of B. Use three screws and washers per board. Then nail H to both G pieces. Use three screws and washers to attach a curtain rod (I) next to H. Attach a second rod 9 inches

back from the first, and a third along the rear edge.

SIDE PANELS
Attach each side panel (D) to the E pieces with carriage bolts. Drill bolt holes through D into E about 3 inches from the top and bottom of the front (A). Repeat steps to attach the D pieces to the G pieces of the roof.

INSTALLING THE SIGNPOSTS
Mount the signposts (J) to the inside faces of the D panels with carriage bolts 2 and 7 inches from one end of each signpost.

SECURING THE SHELF
Serving shelf (K) slips snugly over F on the front panel. From the

underside, join shelf piece L to K with three screws and glue. Use more screws and glue to secure shelf piece M to L. Run 2 machine bolts through M into T-nuts in the underside of F to clamp the shelf in place *(see Diagram 2)*.

THE FINISHING TOUCHES
Decorate the lemonade stand with colorful lemon slices and a sign *(see the scale drawing below)*. Mount the blackboard, if desired, with woodscrews and washers. Staple the curtain material to the rods on the roof's underside.

BUILDING PLANS
Diagram 1 shows the general construction of the project. Use birch or lauan plywood for pieces A-D and pine for pieces E-M. Diagram 2 offers a closeup of the serving shelf assembly.

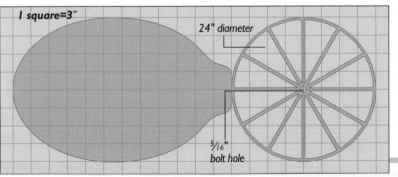

Diagram 2 (serving shelf)

**Cutting layout
(lemonade sign and lemon slices)**
The scale drawings at left show the pattern for the decorative lemon slices and the lemonade sign. Use tempered hardboard for the cutouts. Secure the slices to the sides (D) with machine bolts and T-nuts. Mount the sign to the signposts (J) with four woodscrews.

Diagram 1

I square=3"

24" diameter

5/16" bolt hole

Your Own Skating Rink

In many regions of the country, the onset of winter generally means cold, snow, and the beginning of indoor play season for the kids. But with a little effort and some help from Mother Nature, there's one sure-fire way to help the children beat the boredom of a long winter season: Lay down a backyard skating rink and watch them go!

Providing you have the space, you can begin laying the rink when the temperature dips below 25° for three to five consecutive days. The rink should be at least 20-by-30 feet so there's enough room for a handful of hockey players or aspiring figure skaters.

As shown in the steps on the opposite page, a garden hose and some snow shovels are all the tools you'll need. Plan to make your finished ice approximately three inches thick. It should take about a week of consistent watering to achieve this, providing the weather cooperates. As a general rule, water in the early morning or late evening hours, when the temperature is cooler and the sun is less likely to melt your efforts. (Keep in mind that the ice will retard grass growth, or may even kill it. Don't locate the rink in a prominent area).

Beginner skaters should wear helmets and elbow pads to help protect against falls. Skate blades should be kept sharp and clean; wipe them down after each use.

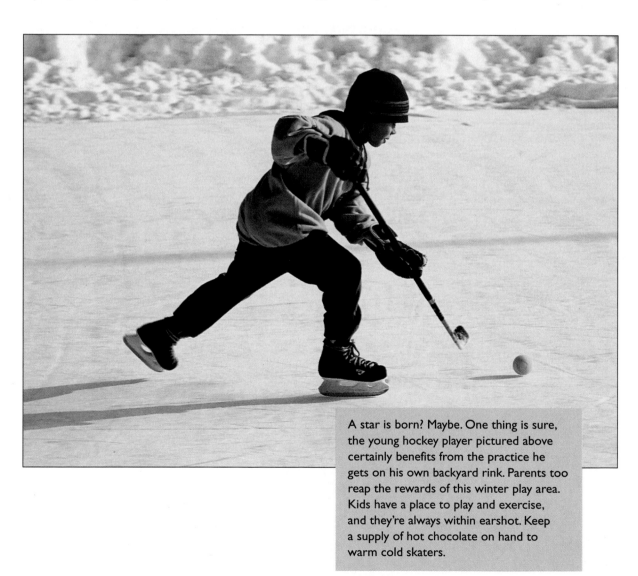

A star is born? Maybe. One thing is sure, the young hockey player pictured above certainly benefits from the practice he gets on his own backyard rink. Parents too reap the rewards of this winter play area. Kids have a place to play and exercise, and they're always within earshot. Keep a supply of hot chocolate on hand to warm cold skaters.

Making an ice rink

1 Lay out the rink

Remove a shovel-wide swath of snow to outline the perimeter of the rink; clear all the snow from the center. Then, frame the outlined area by building up a snowbank border. This will ensure that the water you spray won't be lost to seepage into surrounding areas. The border also serves to more clearly define the skating area. Pile the snow and pack it tightly with the back of a shovel *(left)*. Smooth the surface of the bank by removing any chunks of hard snow or ice, and fill the gaps they leave with loose snow. Sweep the uncovered grass lightly with a broom to remove any lumps of snow.

2 Apply the base

Use a fine mist from a garden hose to spray water inside the perimeter of the shoveled-out area. Be sure to spray the snowbank border as well *(right)*, this will make it solid and help keep it intact throughout the winter. Take care not to drag the hose over the areas that have just been sprayed.

3 Layer the surface

Once the base is completely frozen, add more water. Spray at an upward angle so that it gently "rains" down onto the surface *(left)*. To ensure complete and even coverage, make long, slightly overlapping passes from one side of the rink to the other. Wait at least two hours between sprayings. Continue adding water until the ice is approximately 3 inches thick. To resurface the rink after heavy use, scrape it gently with a snow shovel, then add a new, thin layer of water.

Gardening For PLEASURE

Have you always yearned for a colorful cottage garden? Does the idea of garden-fresh produce make your mouth water? Or would you prefer the peaceful expanse of a welcoming green lawn? Whether it be large, small, or something in between, your backyard can be a place to enjoy the pleasures and rewards of gardening. This chapter will show you how to grow just about anything you fancy, from herbs and vegetables to bulbs and perennials. You'll also learn how to water and fertilize your soil to get the best results from whatever you plant.

Few pastimes are as rewarding as gardening. All you need to get started are a few tools, a piece of ground to call your own, and some basic knowledge.

Planning Your Backyard

There are probably just as many ways to create a rewarding garden as there are people approaching the task, but successful gardens all have something in common: they are the end result of a lot of careful planning. For the back-yard gardener, the planning process is doubly important. This section offers some helpful insight—dealing with style, design, and working with the elements—that will help you create just the right garden for your space.

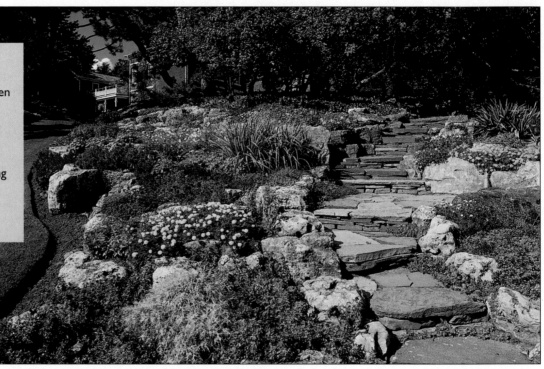

Gracefully hugging a gentle slope, this charming rock garden adds a delightful splash of color that contrasts with the lawn and eliminates the need for mowing along the irregular edges of the mean-dering stone steps.

Planning Basics

Planning your garden—deciding on a style and then choosing the plants that will flesh out a design—begins with knowing what your aim is.

Defining your goals: What do you want out of your garden? This may seem like an obvious question, but it is one you should ask yourself before you begin to plant. Your aim may be to create a private, restful retreat, a place to entertain friends, a children's play area, or a source of cut flowers or vegetables. If you have several goals, make a list and prioritize your needs.

Level of maintenance: Consider how much time you want to spend maintaining your yard. Will you enjoy spending your leisure time keeping your garden looking its best? Or would you prefer a yard that requires minimal care? Certain garden features require more up-keep than others. Some common elements—listed in order of main-tenance demands from the *least* amount of care needed to the *most*—include: paving and struc-tures, trees and large shrubs, shrub borders and screens, ground cov-ers, lawn, and perennial and annu-al flowers.

Choosing a style: Although you don't have to decide in advance what every plant will be and where it will go, having a general design or theme will help you select plants and set them out in harmonious arrangements. And when you're choosing and placing plants—either for remodeling an existing land-scape or starting from scratch—keep in mind that structural elements (paths, pools, etc.) also influence style.

Formal or informal? You can design your garden to be formal or informal. A formal garden is typically symmetrical, with straight lines; it usually has a clear focal point and may include plants trained to grow in unnatural forms (sheared hedges and topiary, for example). An informal garden is characterized by a lack of symmetry and by flowing lines, curves, and plant forms that look natural. Many themes can be interpreted either formally or informally—an oblong pool flanked by two square planting beds would be a formal water garden, but an irregularly shaped pool in a relaxed woodland setting would be an informal interpretation of the same theme.

Sometimes a combination of formal and informal elements is called for. If the style of your house or the decor of a room opening onto the garden is formal but your taste in landscaping is informal, you may want to temper the garden's natural look with a few formal touches.

Illustrated below are some of the garden styles you have to choose from, ranging from formal to the informal profusion of the cottage.

Endless variations are possible; sometimes changing the plant selection will alter the look of a garden.

Dealing with climate: A major factor influencing plant selection is climate. In general, plants thrive in specific climatic zones and not in others. And although it is possible to grow many plants under less than ideal conditions, it's best to choose plants that are well adapted to your climate. The map on page 162 and the plant selection charts at the end of this chapter will help you make the right choice for your garden.

GARDEN STYLES

Formal
Small, flat, rectangular plots are well suited to the formality of the medieval knot garden. Clipped hedges are used to enclose flower beds. Gravel walkways and a central sundial continue the geometry that brings order and tranquillity.

Cottage
For centuries the English have excelled at packing an astonishing variety of annuals and perennials into a small space with great effect. Various flowers can be chosen based on harmonizing colors and then set off against the deep green of a curving hedge.

Oriental
Restraint and simplicity result in the desired serenity of this style of garden. A naturalistic arrangement of rocks and gravel and a few plants of varying size and texture achieve the effect.

Spanish
The courtyard of a Spanish-style house, with its central fountain, adobe walls, and wrought-iron grillwork, becomes a cool, formal oasis with a few careful plantings of shrubs and dwarf trees.

CLIMATE ZONES

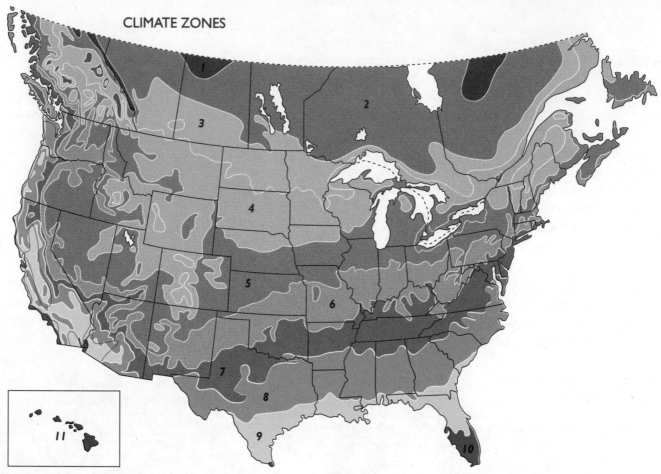

This map will help you determine the plants that will grow in your area. The zones are based on average expected low temperatures. To use the map, locate the zone in which you live, then consult the plant listings beginning on page 210, noting the zone number or range given for the particular plant you're considering. That zone listing indicates the range of hardiness zones for which each plant is adapted. If your zone falls within the given range, the plant should grow in your region.

	Zone	Temperature
	Zone 1	Below -50°F/-46°C
	Zone 2	-50°F/-46°C to -40°F/-40°C
	Zone 3	-40°F/-40°C to -30°F/-34°C
	Zone 4	-30°F/-34°C to -20°F/-29°C
	Zone 5	-20°F/-29°C to -10°F/-23°C
	Zone 6	-10°F/-23°C to 0°F/-18°C
	Zone 7	0°F/-18°C to 10°F/-12°C
	Zone 8	10°F/-12°C to 20°F/-7°C
	Zone 9	20°F/-7°C to 30°F/-1°C
	Zone 10	30°F/-1°C to 40°F/4°C
	Zone 11	Above 40°F/4°C

GARDEN MICROCLIMATES

In addition to your geographical region, you'll need to take into account that there may be major variations, called microclimates, even on a single piece of property—the extra heat on a south-facing wall of the house, for example, or the dark, cool area under a stand of evergreens. During your garden planning, try to match your selection of plantings with the specific conditions in various places in your backyard.

162

Knowing what to look for under the surface of the soil when shopping for container-grown plants can help you pick a winner. A plant should be potted just long enough to have developed a root ball that will hold together when it is removed. The root system should be unencumbered—not tangled or constricted. If you notice roots protruding above the soil or growing through the pot's drainage holes, the plant is rootbound.

Sometimes a plant's roots may not be developed enough for transplanting. A plant that has just been put into its container, for instance, will not have a developed root system to hold the soil ball together. And a plant that is undersized for its container may have been transplanted very recently.

You should also be suspicious of plants that are extremely leggy, or unusually large for their containers, or that have dead twigs or branches.

The plant on the right has a well-developed root system and is more likely to be successfully transplanted than the one on the left.

Of course, it's often easier to judge the condition of a plant by how it looks above the soil. In general, plants with an overall healthy, vigorous appearance and good foliage are a safe bet. Buds are not necessarily an asset for a container plant. The plant on the left has several buds, but is spindly, with poor structure; the plant on the right has no buds, but it's a much better choice—its low branching means that good structure will follow.

And don't be swayed by a plant's size. Smaller plants usually cost less, and often catch up to their bigger counterparts within one season.

Although the plant at right isn't budding, it is actually a better choice than the one on the left.

Waterwise Gardening

In areas that experience long, dry summers, or periods of drought—or both—gardeners are always searching for ways to conserve water.

Know your plants: If you're planting a new garden or extensively revising an existing one in a water-poor area, you can help reduce your water consumption by choosing plants that don't need continual watering—once they have become well established—in order to survive the hot, dry months.

As for trees and shrubs, try extending the time between waterings for as long as the plants look presentable. You can usually tell by a plant's leaves when it really needs water. Most leaves will exhibit a dullness, loss of reflective quality, or curling edges just before they wilt. But be alert: a wilted plant is seriously dry, and must be watered immediately if it is to survive at all.

Efficient irrigation: Hydrozoning—grouping plants with similar watering needs so they can be irrigated together—ensures that no plant will receive too much or too little water. A low-pressure drip irrigation system (see page 173) is usually the most efficient method (except for watering a lawn, where a sprinkler system is better). You can strategically position emitters so that water is delivered directly to the plants that need it. And since the water is applied slowly on or near the ground, there is no runoff and little or no loss to evaporation. Electronic timers attached to an automatic watering system can be programmed to deliver water at predetermined intervals. If you're watering by sprinkler, the best time is when it's windless and cool, such as in the early morning, so water is not lost to evaporation.

CONSERVING WATER ON A SLOPE

Plants on slopes can be a challenge to irrigate, since water may run downhill faster than it seeps into a plant's root zone. Terracing (below) or basins (right), help direct water to a plant's roots, preventing wasteful runoff.

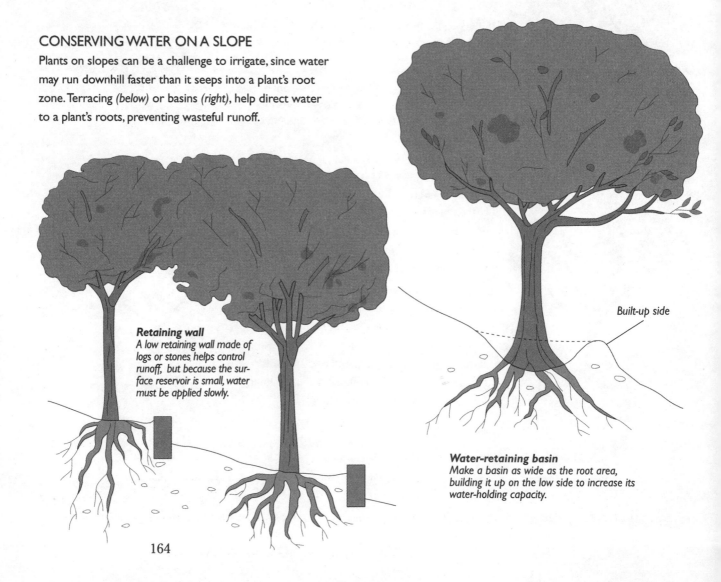

Retaining wall
A low retaining wall made of logs or stones helps control runoff, but because the surface reservoir is small, water must be applied slowly.

Built-up side

Water-retaining basin
Make a basin as wide as the root area, building it up on the low side to increase its water-holding capacity.

164

Mulching is one of the easiest and most effective methods for conserving water in the garden. Placing mulch over the ground occupied by a plant's roots will protect the soil from sun and wind, keeping it cool and moist. Mulches also have the added benefit of suppressing unwanted weeds; any that appear are easily pulled.

Many materials can be used as mulch—anything from crushed rock, layered newspapers, and plastic sheeting to various organic materials such as grass clippings, straw, manure, leaves, and compost. If you use plastic sheeting, you can cover it with a thin layer of more attractive material: bark chips *(right)* or small rocks or gravel, for instance.

Designing with Plants

When choosing plants for your garden, keep in mind their forms, textures, and colors, and choose complementary combinations.

Think about what already is growing in your yard, and consider the year-round appeal of your garden. Try to choose plants that provide some sort of interest all year long: pleasing shape, attractive branching habit, color, beautiful flower form, fragrance, or unusual fruit, for example.

The right form: A plant's form refers to its shape and its growth habit—vining or upright-growing, pyramidal, roundheaded, vase-shaped, sprawling, weeping, spiky, or irregular.

A pleasing garden design has enough different plant forms to make it visually interesting, but not so many that it looks jumbled. You can create a feeling of depth by double-planting—placing one row of plants in front of another—using different forms in each row.

Different textures: Leaf size is the major determinant of a plant's texture: Large-leafed plants tend to have a coarse appearance; plants with smaller leaves look more finely textured. As a rule, glossiness shifts a plant toward coarse texture, while a dull surface gives it a finer appearance. Remember that glossy surfaces will reflect light, bringing a shiny leaf forward to the eye; dull surfaces will absorb light, causing the leaf to recede visually.

You can manipulate fine, medium, and coarse textures to make a space seem larger. You might, for example, use fine texture in the background and then a coarse-textured plant close up as an accent.

What about color?: When planning color, think beyond just the usual annual and perennial flowers.

Many trees, shrubs, vines, and ground covers also have showy blossoms, and some offer bright berries or other fruit as appealing accents in the garden palette. Foliage itself may add colorful interest. Some plants have striking colored or variegated foliage all year long, and many deciduous trees and shrubs exhibit brilliant foliage in autumn. Fall color is usually more spectacular in cold climates, but some plants put on a show even in mild-winter areas. Check with your local nursery for shrubs and trees with reliable fall foliage color in your area.

Don't overlook the fact that bark can also contribute color to the garden. The bare branches of the red-twig dogwood *(Cornus stolonifera)* are scarlet in winter; the gray or light brown outer bark of crape myrtle *(Lagerstroemia indica)* flakes off to reveal smooth pink inner bark.

Maintaining and Improving Your Soil

In a perfect world, garden soil would always be moist, dark, deep, and rich—an earthworm's heaven. But like anything else, gardening is often an imperfect endeavor. You'll eventually come across soil conditions that are less than favorable for growing your favorite fruits, vegetables, or flowers. However, there's no reason to let an uncooperative soil discourage your itchy green thumb. As you will discover in the following pages, there are a number of ways to deal with virtually any growing condition and to improve the soil in your garden.

Soil Types

All soil is basically a mass of mineral particles mixed with living and dead organic matter, and different quantities of air and water. The size and arrangement of the particles are the factors that influence a soil's ability to hold water and nutrients, the amount of air present, and its workability. Knowing the characteristics of your soil will help you decide what to grow, and how. You'll also be better able to decide whether or not you need amendments, such as fertilizer or compost, to make the garden more hospitable to your plants.

At one extreme of the soil spectrum is clay–the gardener's nightmare. Squeeze a handful and you'll get a gummy mass that holds its shape. It dries as a solid clump that is difficult to work with and tends to crack.

Sandy soil, by contrast, has a loose consistency and doesn't retain water or fertilizer very well. No matter how often you water it, it quickly dries up.

The happy compromise is loam, a soft, crumbly soil that holds water and nutrients well.

Clay soil
Plant roots refuse to grow in clay soil because the mineral particles are so small and fit so closely together that air has a hard time circulating through it. Plants will often drown because clay soil drains poorly. And because it's so thick, clay is the slowest soil to warm in spring. It's also called adobe, gumbo, or heavy soil.

Sandy soil
The large, squarish particles in sandy soil don't fit together well, so there is too much room for air to circulate. This makes it difficult to keep plant roots wet. It's even harder to keep your plants well-nourished with fertilizer, which just runs right through sand with the water. And sandy soil gets hotter more quickly in the warm summer months.

Loam
It contains a mixture of small, medium, and large mineral particles. Loam is generally considered the ideal gardening soil. It drains well, is well-supplied with organic matter, and contains enough air for a healthy root growth.

PARTICLE SIZES

Apart from being names of soil types, clay and sand are also terms used to distinguish the size of mineral components in soil. Clay particles are the smallest, usually less than $1/12{,}500$ inch. Silt is made of particles of intermediate size between clay and sand, and is usually up to $1/500$ inch in size. Sand is made up of the largest mineral particles in soil. Particle sizes can range from about $1/250$ inch for fine sand, to about $1/12$ inch for the largest sand particles.

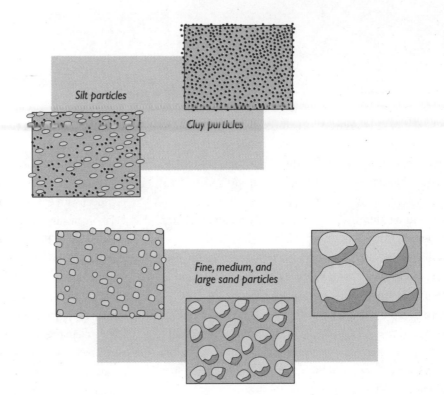

Silt particles

Clay particles

Fine, medium, and large sand particles

Working the Soil

Working the soil—turning it by hand or with a tiller—is one of the basic activities of gardening. Turning soil will help break up and aerate the soil in your garden, making it fit for planting. If your spade or shovel goes into the ground easily, you're ready to go. If not, use a square, sharp spade for deep digging and cutting through roots and hard chunks of soil. Push it into the ground with your foot to maximize force and minimize effort. Don't flip each spadeful all the way over, since the debris on the surface would then form a barrier to air and water circulation below. A pointed, scoop-shaped shovel is best for mixing and turning.

If you have a big job, consider using a power tiller. Spread amendments with a rake first before cultivating in one direction, then another, tilling the top 8 or 9 inches of soil.

Amendments

Soil amendments, or conditioners, are either organic or inorganic. The first may be almost anything that comes originally from an animal or plant (bonemeal, peat moss, or manure). Some organic materials are a source of nutrients and are used in small quantities as fertilizer. Bonemeal, for example, is rich in phosphorus. Others—sawdust or ground bark—may have few nutrients but help fluff up heavy soil and then rot to produce humus. Because all organic materials are continuously being decomposed by soil organisms, even good soils will benefit from periodic application of organic amendments.

Inorganic amendments include such things as sand, perlite, pumice, and vermiculite. Added to fine, heavy soil, they stay in place more or less permanently.

Inorganic amendments provide no nourishment for the soil but are useful for regulating the pH level. Lime, for example, is commonly used to cure overly acidic soil.

One technique often used to add amendments is called double digging *(page 169)*. This process involves digging down two spade depths into the soil to break up the lower-level soil and to add amendments. Double digging is labor-intensive, but it is a good way to improve your soil, or to prepare earth that has never been worked for a garden.

One of the best sources of organic soil amendment *(page 167)* is compost—a soft, crumbly, brownish or blackish substance resulting from the decomposition of organic material. Composting takes time, effort, and space. But if you have a ready supply of plant waste or a small garden that could be supplied by a continually maintained compost pile, the time and effort will be well spent.

The simplest way to compost is to toss your grass trimmings, fallen leaves, and spent plants onto a pile and leave them pretty much alone for up to two years, or until they're completely decomposed. If you have the time and some spare wood, however, you might consider building a compost bin like the one shown below, which will allow you to stack the material for composting and keep it in a contained area.

Turn the piled-up material at least once a week to aerate the mass and to relocate pieces in various stages of decompo-sition. (Compost decomposes more rapidly in the heat and moisture of the pile's interior than on the outside.) Thoroughly moisten the pile as needed; it should be about as wet as a squeezed-out sponge. Adding a few shovelfuls of soil to the compost with every sizable load of raw material will add beneficial organisms and hasten the decomposition.

A few other things to keep in mind: Don't toss other food scraps onto the compost, such as meat or bones, which will attract animals and flies. Weeds that have come to seed and diseased plants should not be added either, as weeds will eventually sprout from the compost and disease organisms from sick plants will remain active in the material. And make sure any big pieces are chopped up, since these take longer to decompose. A compost grinder can help make this part of the chore even simpler. Depending on the temperature, moisture, and size of materials, your compost can be ready to apply in the garden in as little as six weeks.

Garden debris

Partly decomposed material

Finished compost

1x6

1x1

1x2 spacer

4x4 post

Composting receptacles vary from simple to sophisticated. The one shown above is a classic three-sectioned composting container that is easy to build. The bin on the left holds new material; the one in the center contains partly decomposed material; the bin on the right holds finished compost. Material is forked from bin to bin as composting progresses. Side boards are spaced for air penetration and slide out for easy turning and removal of compost.

Double digging

Soil removed from trench

Amendments

Spade

1 Dig a trench
Begin by digging a trench 12" to 18" wide, 8" or 9" deep (or one spade depth), running the length of the planting bed *(left)*.

Added amendments

2 Add amendments
Break up the soil at the bottom to a depth of another 8" or 9". Add compost or other amendments *(right)*, and mix thoroughly.

3 Dig a second trench
Dig another trench alongside the first one, one spade deep. Mix in soil amendments and fill in the first trench with the amended soil from the second trench *(left)*. Then, continue digging up the bottom level of the second trench, mixing in the amendments as you did in the first trench.

Soil from first trench fills up last trench

4 Complete the task
Continue digging and mixing until you have added amendments to the entire planting area. Use the soil removed from the first trench and amendments to fill the last one *(right)*.

A Soil Sifter

A quick way to get rid of any big clumps of earth, or debris such as twigs and rocks, is to use a soil sifter, which can also be used to separate compost. The sifter shown here is easily assembled from standard-dimensioned lumber.

The sifter is made of ¾-inch pine cut to the dimensions shown in the illustrations. First, saw two ends for the sifter box. Cut out hand slots, which you'll use to hold the sifter when you shake it back and forth. Cut pieces for the sides, then nail them to the ends and attach a ¼-inch galvanized hardware-cloth or mesh screen to the bottom of the box. You can set finer screens on top of the fixed one when needed. Cut four

legs, clamping each to the corners of the box so their ends line up with the top of the box and the edges are flush with its sides. Use round-headed 2-inch bolts to attach the legs. Secure the bolts with wing nuts and washers. For extra support, install a cross beam on each pair of legs. A coat of paint will give your sifter a finished look.

Set up the unit over a tarpaulin to catch the sifted earth and fill the box with soil or compost *(below, left)*. Then back off the wing nuts a bit and move the legs together *(below, right)*, rocking the sifter back and forth until all the soil or compost has passed through the screen. Finally, discard any debris.

1"

1½"

5½"

4" Hand slot

30" Leg

14" Cross beam

24" Side

14" End piece

2½"

Tarpaulin to catch sifted matter

Watering Systems

In addition to offering basic sustenance, water keeps roots moist and allows them to expand downward and outward in the soil. In general, plants, flowers, and grasses need to be watered often, but not too much at one time. Remember that the hotter the weather and the more roots in an area, the more you'll need to water. But this doesn't mean you have to spend hours outside with a hose. As shown over the next few pages, modern watering systems deliver water efficiently to their targets. Choose a system that suits your needs, then let it do the work for you.

Planning a Watering System

Water is essential to the growth of any plant, even one that is drought tolerant. For home gardens, there are two main methods of watering. **Stationary water systems:** A stationary system can either be an underground sprinkler system using rigid pipes and fixed-position watering heads, or a drip-irrigation system, which features flexible plastic tubing laid on or just beneath the soil surface. Drip irrigation is very efficient since there is scarcely any runoff or evaporation. And because the foliage never gets wet, there is no risk of water-related diseases such as rust. Turn to page 173 for instructions on installing a drip irrigator. **Portable water systems:** A portable system is the more traditional watering method. Using a sprinkler head attached to the end of a garden hose, the sprinkler is placed in a specific area every time watering is needed. An assortment of sprinkler head attachments is shown below. Like sprinklers, soil soaker hoses are portable and easy to use. Made of canvas or perforated plastic tubing, they are simply attached to a hose and placed beside the target plantings. Long and narrow in design, they are best used in gardens where plants are growing in rows.

SPRINKLERS

Illustrated at right are a few of the most common and easy-to-install sprinklers on the market today. Whether you need to water a single potted plant or an entire lawn, there is a sprinkler head for the job. Apart from watering, they can be effective in washing bugs off plants.

But sprinklers do have certain drawbacks you should consider. Quite often water is lost to the wind or runs off nearby pavement and into the gutter. By dampening foliage, they can also encourage such plant diseases as black spot and rust, and can damage fragile plant leaves and stems.

Oscillator, which sweeps back and forth, is excellent for spot coverage.

Fan head gives a wide, coarse spray for watering beds.

Impulse (impact or machine gun) can send out a strong jet of water or a gentle mist.

Bubbler head, with a low-intensity water flow, is best for container plants.

A lawn audit lets you know how much water your lawn is getting and how evenly it's distributed. Place a grid of equal-sized containers around your lawn. Then run your watering system for 15 minutes. With the water turned off, measure the depth of water that has accumulated in each container, keeping track on a piece of paper. If there is more than a ¼-inch difference between containers, you may want to make some changes in your system, whether it's adjusting or changing sprinkler heads or experimenting with the positioning of hose-end sprinklers. Once you've achieved a more consistent pattern, rerun the test.

Deep Watering

Roots develop in the presence of water, air, and nutrients. To ensure strong, healthy roots, you should water deeply. Although water tends to seep downward in soil, it can move laterally, especially in clay. So run the water long enough to allow it to reach the root zones, but don't let it pool on the surface. (This chart shows ideal root depths, but any roots reaching at least two-thirds of this depth are doing well.) A good rule of thumb for monitoring deep watering is to squeeze a handful of soil. If it's moist and holds together, you've applied the right amount of water. If it's muddy or pasty, you've watered too much. Get out the hose or watering can if the soil feels crumbly.

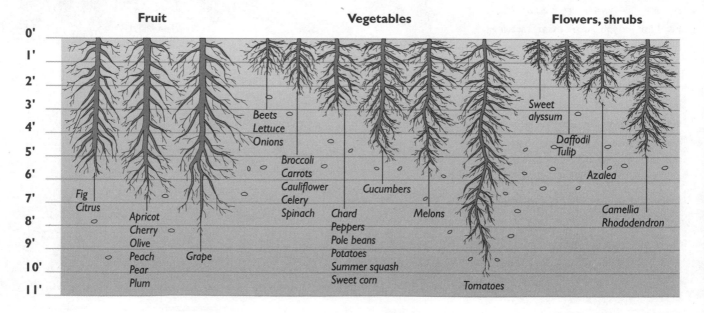

Fruit	Vegetables	Flowers, shrubs

0' 1' 2' 3' 4' 5' 6' 7' 8' 9' 10' 11'

Fig
Citrus

Apricot
Cherry
Olive
Peach
Pear
Plum

Grape

Beets
Lettuce
Onions

Broccoli
Carrots
Cauliflower
Celery
Spinach

Chard
Peppers
Pole beans
Potatoes
Summer squash
Sweet corn

Cucumbers

Melons

Tomatoes

Sweet
alyssum

Daffodil
Tulip

Azalea

Camellia
Rhododendron

Installing a drip system

1 Hook up to the pressure regulator
A drip irrigation system can be attached to your home's main water line. For the conventional type shown, attach the anti-siphon valve assembly to the pressure regulator and filter unit. Then connect the ½" polyethylene hose to the filter unit. Tighten any threaded connections with a pipe wrench.

Anti-siphon valve

Shutoff valve

Pressure regulator

Main water line

Filter

2 Lay out the tubing
Measure the amount of tubing you need and lay lateral lines in rows between the plants. Connect lateral lines to each other using tees and 90° elbow fittings. Use a tee to connect the hose to the lateral water supply. Flush dirt from the system by running water through the lines after they've all been assembled. Attach end caps.

Lateral lines

Rigid plastic tubing

Tee fitting

Elbow fitting

½-inch polyethylene hose

Microtubing

Emitter

3 Attach the emitters
Drill holes in the plastic tubing according to manufacturer's instructions. Connect the emitter to the plastic tubing using microtubing, as shown. Flush the lines again, making sure the system is clean and that all of the emitters work. Protect the lines with a few inches of mulch, if desired, leaving any free microtubing above ground. Place the emitters near the base of the plants and open the shutoff valve. It's a good idea to check the emitters and microtubing for dirt about once a month. Flush the lines every four to six months.

A Lush Carpet of Grass

Whether it acts as a cushiony play surface for the kids or a green showpiece for formal display, a lush lawn is a homeowner's pride. Cultivating such a lawn requires that you first choose the type of grass most suitable for the region where you live. Very often you will decide you want a mixture or blend of grasses. Then you need to know how to plant, water, and fertilize the grass to ensure that it grows and remains healthy and green.

The following section will show you how to do precisely that.

Understanding Grasses

Of the many hundreds of grasses that grow in the Northern Hemisphere, only about 40 types are usually cultivated as lawns. Many of these have varieties, developed to give you a wide selection. Grasses differ widely in their performance, appearance, watering needs, and maintenance requirements. Cultivating a lawn your neighbors will envy means paying attention to all these factors.

There are two basic grass types. Cool-season grasses withstand cold winters, but most varieties wane in the hot summer weather. They're used mainly in northern latitudes. Warm-season grasses love summer sun, growing vigorously in hot temperatures. They become dormant and turn brown, though, when the temperature dips below freezing. Grasses from the same group may act differently in various climates.

A grass's root depth may be an important factor in your choice of type. Generally, shallow-rooted grasses, such as Kentucky bluegrass, need to be watered more often for shorter periods of time than deep-rooted grasses like Bermuda grass. Of all the types listed in the chart, only Kentucky bluegrass, rough-stalk bluegrass, annual ryegrass, and perennial ryegrass have shallow roots, up to 8 inches deep. All others range between intermediate, from 8 to 36 inches, and deep, greater than 36 inches.

To choose the best grass for your region, consult the map below and the chart on the opposite page.

CLIMATE ZONES

The map at right is divided into seven climate zones, each of which is characterized by particular climate conditions. The chart on the opposite page offers a range of grasses for each zone. Combining cool- and warm-season grasses will keep a lawn green year-round.

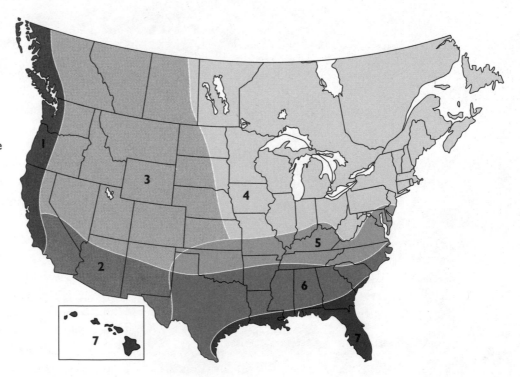

Secrets of a Great-Looking Lawn

Should you go for a sweeping expanse of green carpeting for your yard or be content with a smaller patch of healthy grass? Keep in mind that most activities require only about 600 square feet of lawn. A smaller lawn is easier to maintain and a simple, geometric shape is easier to water and mow. In temperate zones, watering your lawn twice a week is sufficient; you'll have to water more in warmer climates. As a rule, it's best to water deeply rather than frequently. Not only does this conserve water, but it develops a stronger lawn by encouraging deep, firm rooting.

Use nitrogen fertilizer to nourish your lawn regularly. Cool-season lawns require feeding throughout the fall and spring. Feed warm-season lawns in late spring and summer. If you cut back on watering, hold back on fertilizing, too.

Mow your lawn when the grass is about a third taller than its optimum height; grass weakens if it is allowed to grow too long. Clippings left on the lawn add nitrogen to the soil as they decompose.

GRASS TOLERANCE

This chart shows the tolerance of popular grasses to adverse conditions. Use it in conjunction with the map on the opposite page to choose the best grass for your environment. Although using a single type of grass will emphasize a particular characteristic, it also may leave the lawn susceptible to a particular disease. Blends and mixtures have a less pronounced texture, but are hardier.

	ZONE	COLD	HEAT	DROUGHT	SHADE	DISEASE	PEST
COOL-SEASON GRASSES							
Colonial bent grass	1,4,7	H	M	M	M	L	L
Creeping bent grass	1,3,4,7	H	M	L	L	L	L
Kentucky bluegrass	1,3,4,5,6	H	M	M	M	L	M
Rough-stalk bluegrass	4,5	H	L	L	H	L	L
Chewing fescue	3,4,7	H	M	H	H	M	M
Creeping red fescue	3,4,7	H	M	H	H	M	M
Hard fescue	3,4,7	H	M	H	H	H	M
Tall fescue	3,6	L	M	H	M	H	H
Annual ryegrass	4,5,7	L	L	L	L	L	M
Perennial ryegrass	1,2,4,5,7	M	M	M	M	M	M
WARM-SEASON GRASSES							
Bahia grass	7	L	H	M	M	M	M
Common Bermuda grass	2,6,7	L	H	H	L	H	H
Hybrid Bermuda grass	2,6,7	M	H	H	L	H	H
Centipede grass	6,7	L	H	M	M	H	H
Seashore paspalum	2	L	H	H	M	M	H
St. Augustine grass	2,6,7	L	H	L	H	M	M
Zoysia grass	2.6,7	L	H	H	M	H	H

L Low **M** Moderate **H** High

Ground Covers: An Easy Alternative to Grass

Wherever you want a carpet of green but don't want to cope with keeping a lawn healthy, consider ground covers. They usually require far less maintenance, fertilizing, and watering than lawn grasses.

Ground covers are the obvious solution to such less-than-perfect situations as deep shade, poor soil, hot and dry expanses, steep slopes, and soil infiltrated by competing tree roots. And where water conservation is essential, certain ground covers are the only viable means of achieving an expanse of low verdure.

Choosing the right cover: Knowing what you want your ground cover to do will help you choose your plants. For example, flowering gaza-nias can add color alongside a stone path, and chamomile can eliminate the need for frequent mowing on an awkward slope. Your local nursery should be able to help you select plants appropriate to the conditions in your backyard.

How the plants grow: Ground covers spread in three ways: by suckers that run below ground, then send up new plants; by runners that stay above ground; or by simply growing horizontally. For covers to grow properly, they should be adequately spaced. This may vary from a few inches to a couple of feet, depending on the size of the mature plant. As a rule, it's best to be patient, waiting a year or two for the plants to fill in rather than try-ing to cover your area quickly by adding more plants.

Sun and shade: Ground covers may thrive in sunny or shady conditions, or somewhere between the two extremes. The term "partial shade" indicates that the plant will do well in both sun or shade, while "light shade" refers to a need for filtered light throughout the day.

Planting: For the most part, ground covers require the same planting methods as other plants. However, when planting ground covers on slopes—and especially when using them to prevent erosion—individual terraces will help the plants take hold and thrive. The illustration below shows how to seat the plants on an incline.

Planting ground cover on a steep slope

Sloping ground frequently is prime territory for ground-cover planting: it is too steep to mow or to cultivate easily, and it is prone to erosion in the rainy season. For successful planting, create a terrace for each plant and set the plant on it, making sure the crown of the plant is fairly high. Mound earth so that there is a watering basin on the uphill side of the plant, as shown. The high planting keeps the crown of the plant from becoming saturated during waterings or buried if soil gradually washes down-slope into the basin.

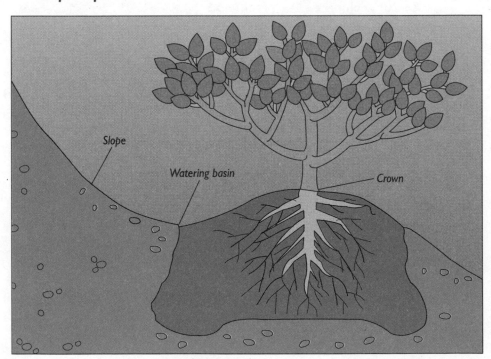

Slope

Watering basin

Crown

Planting a Lawn

Before you begin planting you will have to decide whether you are going to start your lawn from seed or sod. The pros and cons of each are dealt with below. Your choice will then determine the finished grade of the lawn area. For a seed lawn, the finished grade should be about ½ inch above the level of the surrounding ground or paving to allow for settling. For sod, make the grade level with or ½ inch lower than the surrounding area.

When seeding, buy the highest quality seed you can. Remember, it will be the foundation of your lawn for years to come. The amount of seed you need varies according to the type of grass you choose and your local environment.

Read the label carefully, as it will often have information about how much area the seeds will cover on either a new or an established lawn. Or it may tell you—usually in pounds of seed per 1,000 square feet of lawn—how many pounds of seed are required. The number of seeds per pound in various mixes and blends can vary considerably.

The best time to spread seed is in the fall, early enough so that the grass can get established before facing the rigors of winter. Before you plant, be sure to finish grading the site and ensure that proper drainage and soil preparation are completed. Install a sprinkler system and edgings, if so desired.

SEED vs. SOD

Sod or seed? Each method has its pros and cons. Consider these: Seeded lawns require more work to install, and a lot of care to establish, but they are much less expensive than sod. Seed has another advantage in that you can choose any suitable grass type for your lawn, or a custom blend or mixture to meet your needs. Also, seeded lawns often have deeper root systems, allowing for heavy use.

Sod is both easy to install and to establish. It must be well watered, but will not be ravaged by weeds, seedling diseases, washouts, or birds. It is also less messy. The bare earth associated with a seeded lawn can mean weeks of tracking dirt into your house while the lawn grows in.

Sod also simplifies growing a lawn around trees, as it will not compete with the tree's roots for nutrients the way sprouting seeds do. But sod is expensive, and doesn't offer a wide variety of grasses. And since it's grown on a layer of foreign soil, it may not bind well to its new soil.

Whether you use seed or sod, you'll need to roll the lawn to press newly sown seed into the earth. Rolling brings sod layers into contact with the soil and flattens out seams.

Planting from seed

1 Sow the seeds
After preparing the soil and compressing the seed bed lightly with a roller, sow the seeds with a broadcast spreader *(below)* or by hand. Sow half the seed by making passes across the area. Then sow the remaining seed by making passes perpendicular to the first ones. Lightly rake the soil to cover the seeds for germination.

2 Add peat moss
Add ¼"-deep layer of peat moss to the soil *(above)* and spread it out with a rake to help prevent the top layer of soil from drying out. Spread fertilizer on top *(opposite page)*, then lightly water the entire area with a fine spray. Keep the soil moist until the seedlings appear. Then water at least once a day until the lawn is well established.

Planting sod

After preparing the soil and leveling the surface with a roller, unfurl the strips of sod in parallel rows; stagger the ends and keep the seams between the strips tight and level. Trim off any excess with a sharp knife. Once all the sod is laid, go over the entire surface with a roller again to smooth the seams and any uneven spots and to bond the layer of sod to the soil below.

Fertilizing

No matter what kind of grass seed or sod you use or how carefully you plant it, a lawn must be fertilized regularly if it is to thrive.

When to fertilize: Your lawn's fertilizing needs will vary with grass type, climate, and the type of fertilizer used. Learn to read your lawn. Loss of color or vigor are signs that it needs fertilizing. Timing is important. Fertilizing in the spring will ensure a strong, healthy lawn before the hot weather. In mild climates, a second feeding in the fall allows grass to thrive through the winter months. Controlled release fertilizers give off nutrients slowly over periods of three to eight months.

What kind to use: Fertilizers can be purchased in granular form, packaged in sacks or cartons, or bottled as liquid. Read the labels to choose the right one for your lawn. If you're not sure which one is best, ask a nursery professional for help. Your local county extension office can suggest a private lab that will test your soil and tell you which kind of fertilizer your lawn needs.

Instructions on the package will tell you how to apply the product properly. But don't think of these directions as the only answer as far as timing is concerned. Learn to time applications so that *your* grass, in *your* soil and climate, receives a fertilizing whenever it begins to show the need.

The three basic components of all fertilizers are nitrogen, phosphorus, and potassium. Your lawn will need any one or all of these depending on its condition. Every package of fertilizer—whether organic or inorganic—will display three large numbers indicating what percentage of each nutrient the fertilizer contains.

Nearly all fertilizers require a thorough watering after being applied. If you leave any dry particles sitting on the grass, you may end up with brown, burned, or even dead areas.

Using a hopper spreader

A hopper-style spreader drops fertilizer onto the turf through a hopper instead of throwing it out in broadcast fashion. It may take longer to fertilize your lawn using this type of spreader, but it is the most accurate of all applicators. Start by making two passes at each long edge of your lawn. This ensures complete coverage and provides sufficient room to turn around as you make passes over the center of the lawn. Make parallel passes in the center, closing the hopper at the end of each one. (Attempting to turn with the hopper open will leave both gaps and overlaps.) Turn and start the next run, running one wheel of the hopper onto the previous pass *(left)*. Maintain a steady pace to distribute the fertilizer evenly. Leave no gaps, but don't overlap; a buildup of fertilizer will damage the lawn.

Mowing

The rewards for mowing your lawn can extend beyond the nostalgic smell, look, and feel of newly cut grass. Mowing it at the proper height and at the right time can also help the lawn fend off pests and diseases. Adjusting the height of the lawn helps it survive periods of drought or severe heat, while timely mowing can protect fragile crowns, or tips, from exposure.

Mowing frequency: When it comes to following an established schedule for mowing your lawn the best advice is: don't. During their res-pective growing seasons, cool-season and warm-season grasses may require mowing every two or three days. However, off-season cutting may only be needed every two weeks or even once a month. A good rule of thumb is to pay attention to your grass height and mow your lawn as it needs it.

Grass height: Let your grass grow about one-third above its recommended height before mowing. If it grows too tall, you'll be forced to cut deeply into the crowns. This weakens the plants, giving weed seeds a better chance to germinate. Cutting it when it's too short will shock the roots, killing the plants or making them vulnerable to disease and other adverse conditions.

Cutting: Always cut the grass when it's dry. Water after cutting if your lawn is newly established. It's best to change mowing directions every other time you cut. The mower's wheels can create ruts, and the grass may grow darker or lighter in the rutted areas. Leave the clippings on the lawn; they're an excellent fertilizer.

MOWING STRIPS

You may want to consider making a mowing strip edging to separate your lawn from adjoining surfaces. The strip neatly contains the turf and also provides a surface for mower wheels so the blades can easily trim the edge of the grass. Mowing strips can be made from brick, poured concrete, or masonry blocks.

Wood is a popular and easy-to-use material, although it can be easily damaged by the mower's blades. Construction Heart redwood or Select cedar are woods of choice, but remember that these labels don't always guarantee quality. Be sure to avoid cedar containing large knots or redwood with streaks of sapwood. A long-lasting alternative is pressure-treated lumber, as long as the boards have been commercially treated.

Masonry—either brick or concrete—makes a strong, permanent edging. Concrete edgings are excellent for areas where your lawn butts up against a paved patio or driveway. Brick is attractive, but requires very firm earth to hold the edgings in place.

Regardless of your choice of edging, it should be installed after you've prepared the soil and re-established the rough grade. For more information on installing edgings, see pages 239 and 240.

180

Trees and Shrubs

Imagine your landscape without its trees and shrubs and you'll quickly grasp the importance of these plants in our daily lives. Trees and shrubs can define the overall character of your backyard, while providing shade, privacy, protection from the wind, or a place to hang a swing.

The simplest way to differentiate trees from shrubs is that you walk under one and around the other. More technical definitions exist, but applying them can be complicated since some plants can be classified as either tree or shrub, depending on how they are pruned.

As with any plant, trees and shrubs must be chosen with an eye to climate. Also consider the suitability of the soil and the availability of water. The plant's growth rate and size are also important. Beginning below and continuing over the next few pages, we'll show you some common shapes of trees and shrubs and give you a few tips on how to plant and prune them.

COMMON SHAPES

Study the different shapes shown here to help you decide on the most attractive trees and shrubs for your backyard. Contrasting shapes tend to set each other off, creating a casual, natural feel to your landscape. Choosing similar shapes creates a more unified look, and provides a dignified and elegant effect.

Spreading

Vase-shaped

Pyramidal or conical

Oval

Round

Columnar

Dome-shaped

Weeping

Irregular

Tree and Shrub Planting Strategy

For a young tree or shrub to take root successfully you must choose the best time of year to plant it. This will vary, depending on where you live and the type of plant you have selected. Another critical factor is soil. It is your plant's food, so you need to pay particular attention to whether it will provide the right nourishment.

Climate: For the best first-year growth with the least amount of stress on the new tree or shrub, plant in advance of the spring growing season, while the soil is cool. This encourages root growth before the plant has to support foliage. In milder climates, where soil freezes seldom or not at all, autumn through winter is the preferred planting period. In colder regions, late winter to late spring will get most new plants off to a good start.

Some cold-climate gardeners prefer to set out deciduous plants in the fall, allowing for some root growth before winter. Needle-leafed evergreens should only be planted in the spring, however, otherwise they can die over winter because their roots cannot draw enough moisture to support foliage.

Soil: When it comes to planting, the object is to match the soil around the roots as closely as possible to that of your garden. For bare-root planting, this normally isn't a problem. Simply refill the planting hole with the backfill soil you dug up from the hole. With balled-and-burlapped plants, however, you'll need to take extra care. B-and-B plants have a ball of soil around the roots covered with burlap (or other sturdy material); they are useful because certain plants have roots that won't survive bare-root transplanting. But you can end up with two soils of different texture—the soil in the burlap and the soil in the planting hole, which may affect uniform water penetration to the roots.

The texture of the soil in the ball is often medium to heavy. If the soil in your backyard is similar, you can plant without amending it. But when the balled-and-burlapped soil is denser than your soil, you will need to supplement the soil. Make a mixture of one shovelful of organic amendment—peat moss, ground bark, or nitrogen-fortified sawdust, for example—to every three shovelfuls of backfill.

Digging the hole

The central part of the hole you dig should be a bit shallower than the root ball or root system of the plant it will receive. Dig deeper around the edges of the hole and roughly taper the sides outward as you dig down; this lets roots penetrate more easily into the surrounding soil. The firm plateau of undug soil in the middle will support the plant at the proper depth and minimize settling after planting and watering.

Planting balled-and-burlapped plants

1 Position the plant
Set the plant into its hole, placing the root ball on the firm plateau in the center. The top of the root ball should be about 2" above the surrounding soil.

2 Peel back the burlap
Untie the burlap and spread it out to uncover about half of the root ball. Drive a stake into the soil alongside the root ball before filling the hole with backfill. (The burlap will eventually decay.)

3 Secure and water the plant
After lightly tamping down the backfill, make a berm of soil to form a watering moat around the plant. Water gently, then loosely tie the plant to the stake.

Wooden wheelbarrow

For moving heavy loads around the garden, wheelbarrows are indispensable. Of course, there are many commercial models to choose from at the hardware, but for time-less appeal and overall handiness, consider making the wooden classic shown below. Charming and easy to construct, it's sturdy enough to transport a half yard of soil.

Use the measurements in the plans as a general guide. The dimensions will vary a little depending on the size of wheel you use. The steel-rimmed wheel shown was recycled from a 30-year-old wheelbarrow. Ball-bearing wheels with pneumatic tires lack rustic charm, but they are easier to find and roll better over rough ground.

Assemble the frame to fit your wheel, using ¾-inch plywood, screws and 5/16-inch carriage bolts; glue all joints. Fashion the two axle supports from short pieces of heavy channel iron or angle iron.

Round off the handles with a coarse wood rasp, sand the wood, and apply a protective finish.

Design:
Ralph P. Olsson

Removing the sides of the wheelbar-row allows you to shift large objects in and out easily *(left).* The plywood sides are held in place by stiles that fit into mortises cut in the bed of the wheel-barrow—also made of plywood.

Planting bare-root shrubs and trees

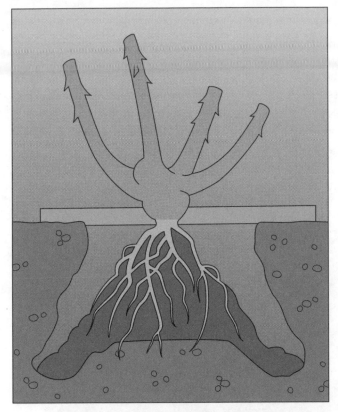

1 Set up the roots
Dig a hole like the one shown on page 182, with a firm cone of soil in the bottom. Spread the roots over the cone, positioning the plant at the same depth as—or slightly higher than—it was in the growing field. Use a straightedge to judge the depth.

2 Position the plant
Backfill the soil nearly to the top, firming it with your fingers as you go. Add water, pumping the plant up and down if it settles. When the soil is saturated, raise the plant to proper level.

3 Top off the soil
With the plant at its correct height, fill in any remaining soil. When the growing season begins, make a berm of soil around the hole to form a watering basin.

Pruning Trees and Shrubs

Although not all trees and shrubs require pruning, in many cases it is the key to strong and attractive plants. Pruning is done on damaged, diseased, or dead parts of the plant, with the aim being to make cuts that callus and seal off healthy wood. In addition, pruning is used to control and direct a plant's growth *(pages 187 and 188)*, ensuring a compact and shapely form. In some cases, it will even increase the quality or yield of fruits and flowers.

As illustrated below, there are two ways to prune: Thinning preserves the natural shape of the tree or shrub. Heading, which includes pinching and shearing, is done to fruit trees to establish main framework branches and to hedges to keep them compact. In general, thinning is a preferable form of pruning, since it does not alter the natural shape of a plant.

Proper pruning technique

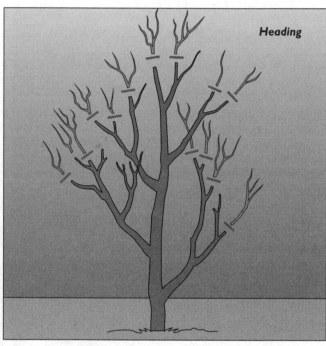

Thinning *(above, left)* is the preferred pruning method. It involves removing lateral branches at their points of origin, or shortening branches to create smaller lateral branches. This opens a plant to sun and reduces its size, while accentuating its natural form. Heading *(above, right)* involves cutting branches back to a stub or tiny twig. There are a few cases where it is warranted *(see above)*, but it tends to encourage new growth that is weakly attached and prone to breaking.

A correct pruning cut is slanted upward at about a 45-degree angle with its lower point even with the top of a growth bud.

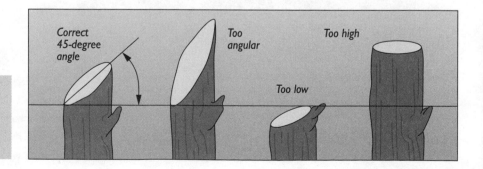

Shaping a Hedge

A hedge is a living barrier or fence made up of many plants, usually of one species. When planted close enough together, and after several years of growth, the individual plants will appear to be one unit. Developing a hedge takes considerable planning and care in the first couple of seasons. After that, you can concentrate chiefly on routine maintenance.

There are two basic styles of hedges: Formal hedges are pruned so that the sides are perfectly straight, creating a solid, smooth appearance. Informal hedges are pruned selectively, allowing the plants to achieve a more natural shape, with a soft and feathery look.

Space the individual plants 1 to 3 feet apart, depending on how large they will grow. After planting, cut the plants back to a height of 6 to 12 inches. This forces them to branch out close to the ground, preventing an unsightly framework of bare, lower trunks. Don't prune plants during the first season, unless a strong stem grows much higher than the rest. In that case, snip it back level with the rest of the

hedge. Keep the hedge tapered, with the top narrower than the bottom *(bottom, left)*. Tapering helps light reach the lower branches, which keeps them healthy and leafy. Cutting back hedges will create a dense and mature look. If your hedge consists of extra vigorous plants, you may need to prune it more than once a season to create the optimum density.

1st Year   **2nd Year**   **3rd Year**

Right
Taper allows sunlight to reach entire plant.

Wrong
Sunlight can't reach bottom of plant.

Formal

Informal

An espalier is a tree or shrub trained against the flat plane of a trellis, fence, screen, or other support so that its trunk and branches create an artistic pattern, adding interest to an otherwise bare surface.

Along with growing well in narrow planting spaces, espaliers can be cultivated in containers. Whatever their location, they require careful pruning, done with an eye for detail and artistic balance, and it may take several seasons of training before the plant conforms exactly to the shape you want it to take. Many nurseries sell espaliers that have already been started, saving you the trouble of training and the wait for results.

To espalier against a fence, you must provide support; wire or wood lath, spaced 4 to 6 inches in front of the fence is most often used. The space between the fence and the support allows air circulation around the plant. Use soft materials—strips of cloth or plastic ties—to hold the plants in place.

Although it began in Europe as a method to save space when growing fruit trees, espaliering is most commonly done today for decorative purposes. Espaliers can be trained into a wide variety of shapes. Here are some of the more popular designs.

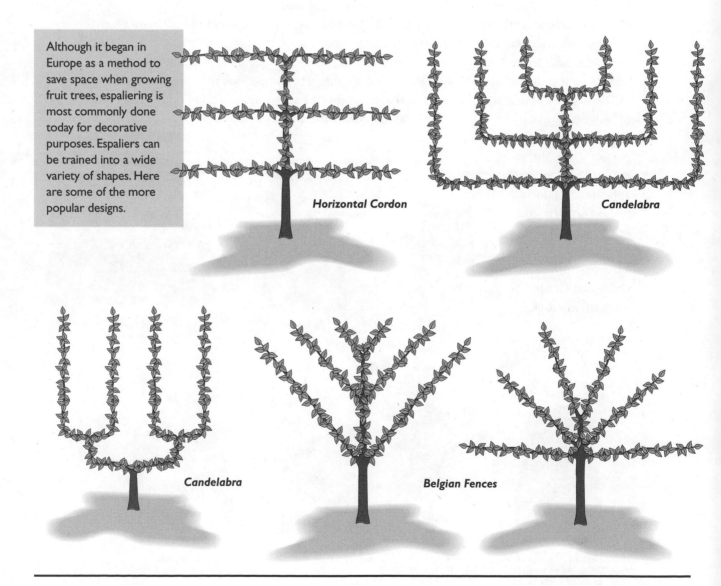

Horizontal Cordon

Candelabra

Candelabra

Belgian Fences

188

Fertilizing Trees and Shrubs

In nature, whatever comes from the soil usually returns to it. This natural cycle is disturbed, however, if nutrients taken from the ground in the form of fruit, flowers, and spent plants, are not returned. By adding fertilizer to soil, you'll provide your trees and shrubs with all the elements they need to grow.

Chemical fertilizers are available in dry, liquid, and tablet form, and can contain all three needed food elements—nitrogen, phosphorus, and potassium. The label will show what percentages of these primary nutrients the fertilizer contains. Your plants may not always require all three, so fertilizers containing only one element are available. Organic fertilizers such as cottonseed meal, bonemeal, or guano use the same system of labeling to indicate their fertilizer content. Manure and compost are not fertilizers in the true sense. Rather, they promote the growth of soil bacteria, which then help your plants take nourishment from the soil.

Some plants benefit from a customized schedule of fertilizing. Generally, however, most should be fertilized in the spring, when the leaf growth begins, and again three months later, except in cold climates, where one application in spring is the usual course of action.

Options for fertilizing

In regions with sandy soil or a wet climate, spread granular fertilizer on the surface inside a tree's drip line; you can do this by hand or use a broadcast spreader, as shown. Soak the fertilized area thoroughly with a garden hose.

In mild areas with moderate rainfall, root plug fertilizing is best. With a soil-sampling tube or pipe, make 6- to 12-inch-deep holes 2 to 3 feet apart inside a tree's drip line. Mix granular fertilizer with an equal amount of sand and pour it into the holes. Fill the holes with soil and water well.

Gardening with Flowers

Flowers can make any space come alive with their range of colors. But color alone is not the only consideration; how you arrange different types of flowers will also help to define the character of the space. You can make a small area seem cozy or wide open, depending on the color and texture of the plants you choose and where you site them.

As a general rule of thumb, choose flowers that have different bloom times and life cycles, and envision how they will change the look of your garden from one season to the next. Annuals are fast-growing plants that thrive for one season then die. Biennials develop foliage the first year, then bloom and die the second, and perennials flower for more than two summers. Bulbs, which

Planting container flowers

1 Remove the plant
Press on the bottom of the individual cell or pot *(left)*. If the soil is too tightly packed, loosen the plant by running a knife along the inside edge of the container.

2 Prepare the roots
Lightly separate matted roots. Cut off any pads of coiled-up white roots at the bottom so the roots will grow outward into the soil. (Don't buy flowers with roots protruding out the top or bottom, or those with dead leaves or stems.)

3 Plant and water
Dig a generous planting hole for each specimen. Place the flower inside, spreading the roots out into the soil, then fill up the hole with unamended earth. Form a basin around each plant, watering each separately with a gentle flow so as not to disturb the delicate soil and roots *(left)*.

190

store food in swollen underground parts, sprout roots, leaves, and flowers each spring.

But don't build your garden around flowers alone. Carefully selected foliage plants can provide a contrasting backdrop to set off colorful blooms. The shapes and textures of plants are equally important features to consider. Most avid gardeners will tell you that gardening is an art, with your garden as your canvas and the plants as the paints on your palette.

Ultimately, plant selection comes down to individual taste, and you'll choose plants that appeal to you for your garden. But for a few tips on harmonizing colors, turn to the color wheel section on page 192. With a little imagination, there's no limit to what you can create.

Sowing seeds

If you need to plant large flower beds you can sow seeds directly in the area where you want them. Prepare the soil, then outline the area with gypsum, flour, or stakes and string. Spread the seeds evenly *(right)*, pressing them into the soil with the back of a spade, then cover them with a thin layer of peat moss. Keep the soil barely damp until seeds sprout, about a week or two later. Don't let water pool over the area.

Transplant or thin out the beds *(left)* when seedlings have two sets of true leaves. Remove weeds and protect the seedlings from snails, insects, birds, and strong sunlight. Water older plants with a bubbler hose; let the top 2 inches of soil dry before watering again. Fertilize your plants only when watering them.

COLOR WHEEL

Yellow-orange
Yellow
Yellow-green
Orange
Green
Red-orange
Blue-green
Red
Blue
Red-violet
Blue-violet
Violet

A color wheel tells you which colors go well together and should help you choose flowers as you plan your garden—as well as help you select the right colors for such garden accessories as furniture. Red, yellow, and blue are known as primary colors. Colors between any two primaries are graduated mixtures of the two and harmonize. Gardens planted with harmonious colors can bring unity to a landscape. Complementary colors are directly opposite each other, such as red and green. Thoughtful use of the contrast can be used to direct the eye to a certain area; usually it's best to highlight one color with just a touch of its complement.

The wheel divides into cool colors, centered on blue, and warm colors, centered on orange. The wheel also ranges from light to dark shades. No matter what the shade, colors retain the same contrasting and harmonious relationships. Lighter shades harmonize with white, while darker shades provide contrast.

WALL FLOWERS

Even retaining walls can be brought to life with a few well-placed flowers. Simply plant hardy, firm-rooted flowers in any good planting space on the wall, such as between stones as shown in the illustration at right. On pre-existing walls, it may be necessary to add soft and easily worked soil over joints composed of masonry or sand, for example.

Flowers mounted in walls are just as thirsty as those planted in the ground and need appropriate watering. So whether your wall is made of logs, unsurfaced lumber, or stone, make sure there's a route for water drainage. Surface water from light rain and spraying can flow into a shallow ditch behind the top of the wall. Deeper water can be drained from a gravel backfill through weep holes in the wall.

Flowers and plants soften the look of stone walls. A structure with a slight slope and the overall weight of the wall give the plantings stability.

Container Gardening and Hanging Baskets

Gardening on a small scale—in containers and hanging baskets—is not only popular, but also a great way to bring your flowers closer to eye level, where you can better appreciate them. Areas such as patios and entryways that would otherwise be bereft of color can be brought to life with a few well-placed baskets.

Choose a lightweight, sterile potting soil designed for container gardening, never ordinary garden soil. You can buy potting soil at nurseries, garden centers, or from companies that sell topsoil.

Tips for watering and fertilizing: Container soil dries out quickly, so you might have to water more than once a day in very hot or windy weather. If your containers feel light, or if the top 2 inches of the soil are dry, it's time to water. You know you've watered enough when water drips out of the holes in the bottom of the pot.

If water runs down between the edges of the container and the earth, your root ball is probably too dry, and has shrunk away from the edges of the pot. To correct this, partially submerge the container in a tub so that moisture can be absorbed into the roots.

To stretch the intervals between watering, mix super-absorbent soil polymers into your soil. These are available at most nurseries.

You can also use a drip-irrigation system to water container plants. Check out your local nursery or irrigation supply store for suggestions on the best system for you.

Container-grown plants lose most of their nitrogen when water runs through the soil. Potting soils contain very few nutrients, so it's best to add liquid fertilizer right after planting and at least every two weeks after that.

Decorative ideas: Consider placing hanging basket containers right in your garden. Moss-lined hanging baskets are particularly pretty, and you can easily set them up yourself, as illustrated at right. They're available at most nurseries, along with a variety of wood, plastic, or clay hanging baskets. But remember that plants in these containers get extra exposure, so they dry out faster. You'll have to water more often—about twice a day in hot weather.

To set up hanging baskets, line a metal frame with moist sphagnum moss, pushing it firmly between the wires (top). With your finger, make holes in the sides of the basket, then insert each annual so that the plant leaves and flowers are facing out (middle). Add container soil, then plant more annuals on the top (bottom), leaving enough space for plants to fill out.

Bulbs, the Garden Surprises

Bulbs store food in swollen underground parts during dormant seasons. When their growth season begins, roots, leaves, and flowers sprout from this natural storehouse. **When to plant:** As with all living things, bulbs go through different periods during their growth cycle. The dormant period, or just prior to it, is the time that most bulbs should be planted. Generally, retailers will make bulbs available during their optimum planting period. Be wary of bulbs that have been on the shelf for a while, however, as those sold late in the season may have deteriorated. Try to buy and plant bulbs as soon as they're available. The length of the dormancy and the appearance of the bulbs during this stage vary. Daffodils and tulips, for example, have no leaves and roots, while bearded irises and daylilies do.

How to plant: Ask a nursery professional where you should plant your bulbs. Some thrive in sunshine, others in shade. Water the area thoroughly before you plant, and when the soil is easy to work, dig the planting holes a few inches deep. If you will be planting many bulbs in one bed, it may be easier to dig a trench or to excavate the bed to the desired planting depth than to dig individual holes. Mix a tablespoon of bonemeal into the bottom of each hole and then add an inch of sand. Set a bulb in each hole and cover it with soil. Bulbs vary in the depth they should be planted. Tulips and hyacinths, for example, should be planted 6 inches deep, while daffodils and other narcissus bulbs should be set 4 to 5 inches deep. Water thoroughly after planting so the roots take. Apply fertilizer once the blooms have faded.

A NATURAL LOOK FOR PLANTING BULBS

In nature, flowers often grow in drifts, or informal clumps that spread naturally. You can have this same wildflower look in your backyard. For the best annual display, choose bulbs that adapt to naturalizing and that thrive in your climate and location.

To plant in drifts, toss handfuls of bulbs over the planting area, mixing up varieties if you wish *(left)*. Take into account the sun, shade, and water requirements of the bulbs. You want to choose those bulbs that need the least amount of effort to maintain.

Plant each bulb where it falls—some in clusters, others farther apart. Bury each at the proper depth for its species *(below, middle)*. Your nursery professional can tell you what this is. Loosen the base of each hole so that the bulbs rest on fine soil, not above an air pocket *(below, right)*.

Spreading bulbs

Planting bulbs

Right   **Wrong**

Bulb resting on fine soil   Bulb resting above an air pocket

GLADIOLUS

Basal plate

Cormels

Roots

Corm

A corm is a swollen underground stem base—solid tissue (in contrast to bulb scales) but with a basal plate from which roots grow. A growth point is on the corm's top; many corms have tunics that consist of dried bases of the previous season's leaves. An individual corm lasts just one year. New corms form from buds on the top of an old corm as it completes its growth cycle. Fingernail-size cormels will take 2 to 3 years to flower; larger corms should bloom the following year.

Basal plate

Offset

**NARCISSUS
(daffodil)**

True bulb

A true bulb is a short underground stem (on a solid basal plate) surrounded by modified fleshy leaves, or scales, that protect and store food for use by the plant. The new bulb (often called an offset) is formed from a bud on the basal plate; the old bulb may die or, like daffodils, keep coming back each year. Bulblets can be separated from the mother bulb and then replanted to increase the stock of the original plant.

TYPES OF BULBS

Horticulturists and the general public use "bulb" as a generic term for plants that grow from five distinct types of underground structures: true bulbs, corms, tubers, rhizomes, and tuberous roots. The differences among them are explained on this page.

Certain aspects of basic culture differ from type to type but one trait is common to all: function. They all hold a reserve of nutrients in a thickened underground storage organ that will keep the plant alive from one growing season to the next, through drought, cold, or other climatic adversities.

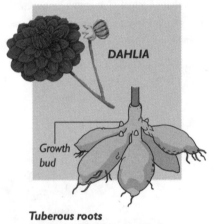

DAHLIA

Growth bud

Tuberous roots

Of the five "bulb" types, only the tuberous root is a true root, thickened to store nutrients, rather than a specialized stem. In a full-grown dahlia, daylily, or other tuberous-rooted plant, the roots grow in a cluster, with the swollen tuberous portions radiating out from a central point. Growth buds are at the bases of old stems rather than on the tuberous roots. To divide, cut apart so that each division contains both roots and part of the stem's base with one or more growth buds.

Leaves

Rhizome

A rhizome is a thickened stem that grows partially or entirely beneath the ground. Roots generally grow from the underside; the principal growing point is at the tip, although additional growing points will form along the rhizome's length. To divide, cut into section that have visible growing points. Because growth proceeds horizontally and because additional growth points give rise to full-fledged new plants, a planting that began with an individual rhizome will grow larger each year, as more and more rhizomes reach out into surrounding soil.

**BEGONIA
(tuberous)**

Roots

Tuber

Like corms, tubers are swollen stem bases. But while a corm has a fairly clearly organized structure, a tuber does not. There is no basal plate, so roots can grow from all sides; multiple growth points are distributed over the upper surface. An individual tuber can last for many years. Some (cyclamen, for example), continually enlarge, but never produce offsets; others (such as caladium) form protuberances that can be removed and planted separately. Divide tubers by cutting into sections that have growth buds.

Raised Flower Beds

Raised beds are useful if you need to make maximum use of a small planting area or if you are searching for a simple way to add a design element to your garden.

Design: Building a sturdy raised bed isn't difficult, but if you plan to go higher than 3 feet or build on sloping or unstable ground, consult your local building code first.

Raised beds are either box type or of the low, stepped-bed variety. You can vary the design and materials to get the form you want. Box-type beds range in size from 3 to more than 10 feet long, and from less than 1 foot to more than 3 feet high. They can be made of almost any material you'd use for a wall, such as brick, concrete, stone or wood—decay-resistant redwood, cedar, cypress, or pressure-treated lumber at least 2 inches thick.

Raised beds can harmonize with an existing garden design. You can work around irregular or difficult slopes in the lawn, for example, with a series of beds, providing a neat transition from one level to the next. By adding a wide top cap, a raised bed can provide extra room for potted plants or a comfortable place for a gardener to sit while weeding.

For a finished look, you can stain plank boxes and add detailing to tie the beds into the overall landscape design. To fit into a more rustic landscape, box-type beds can be built of railroad ties or logs—whole or cut in half.

Soil: As with hanging baskets, it's a good idea to use a good potting soil in raised bed gardening. Watering schedules will vary with the climate, but as a rule, if you stick a finger into the soil and it feels dry an inch below the surface, it's time to water.

For raised beds with open bottoms, replace the earth below the boxes with amended soil that will improve the growing conditions. If the box has a solid bottom, drill drain holes. Before planting, soak the soil so that it settles to a natural level. Keep the soil surface in raised beds about an inch or two below the top border of the container.

Trellis

SPACE-SAVERS

An efficient way to use wooden box beds is to stack them "ziggurat-style." This type of raised bed can hold more than 20 different kinds of flowers and fits into a 4-by-4-foot space. A trellis adds a vertical element and extra growing space.

1x4s

24"

34"

1x6

4'

Looking After Your Flowers

Choosing the right flowers for your garden is just the prelude to the real pleasure of planting and growing your selections. But to ensure that your time has been well spent and that your plants flower brightly, you'll have to look after them.

Improving the soil: Soil doesn't always contain enough of the nutrients necessary for plant growth, so use fertilizers to make up for any shortfalls. These are most needed between the first growth of the year and the flowering period, usually from late winter to mid-spring.

Watering: For best plant performance, the soil should be moistened deeply. Roots are reluctant to extend into dry soil; deep watering will encourage deeper rooting.

This, in turn, makes plants less vulnerable to moisture fluctuations close to the surface.

Weeding: Keep weeds pulled or hoed from the very beginning. They rob desirable plants of water and nutrients while making your flower bed look unkempt.

Staking: If a plant starts to fall over or becomes too leggy when in bloom, it needs to be staked. Staking is usually necessary only with the tallest plants, or ones that are not getting enough sun. Different types of stakes and cylinders are available at nurseries or garden centers. The important thing is to support the flowers while concealing the stakes.

Separating bulbs: If you have planted bulbs, remember that as their roots grow outward, new bulbs form and sprout plants of their own, leading to overcrowding. With limited room for outward growth, the roots eventually begin to grow downward, into less fertile soil. When this occurs, usually after the first two years or so, bulbs will stop growing and flowering.

To get the most out of each bulb, pull up the plants during the dormant season and remove the bulblets. Replant the smaller, newer bulbs in different areas.

Additional care: To keep your plants looking neat, cut back old and new stems, and prune and deadhead flowers, as in the illustration below. Not only does this keep the garden tidy, it may prolong flowering and fruiting.

PROPER PRUNING

To maintain your plants, pinch out tips of new growth to induce branching lower on the stem (*above*). Cut spent flowers to curtail seed production, and to divert energy to the production of more flowers (*right*).

Vegetables and Herbs

Planting a vegetable or herb garden is a good idea for many reasons: Not only will you experience the satisfaction of growing your own produce from the ground up, you'll also benefit from having the freshest possible food to put on your table. Moreover, you'll have the opportunity of growing a diverse range of vegetables that may be unavailable at your local store. Whether your backyard is large or small, you can probably find the room to grow some of your favorite produce. This section will tell you how to get started—from laying out the plot to storing the harvest. Then, it's just a matter of investing a little time and energy before you can enjoy Mother Nature's bounty.

Laying Out Your Plot

Good planning is the secret to good gardening. Before you turn your first shovelful of soil, there are some decisions to make. Where's the best place in your backyard to grow vegetables? How big a plot do you want? How much time are you willing to spend in the garden? And what vegetables do you and your family like to eat?

Picking the site: The site you select should get at least six hours of full sun daily, and be protected from wind. But don't plant too close to trees or shrubs, which can compete with crops for water and nutrients. Choose level ground, if possible, to make watering and care a lot easier. If you have only sloping ground to choose from, look for an area that slopes toward the south or southeast, to take full advantage of the sun. Finally, try to place the garden near a convenient water source, such as a hose bib.

If you're a beginning gardener, it's probably a good idea to start with a small plot, say 100 square feet. However, even 30 square feet, planted with only one or two plants of

Cane Berries —
Spinach
Chard
— Corn

Cabbage —
Tomatoes
Bush Cucumbers

Green Onions —
Bush Peas
— Eggplant

Zucchini
Lettuce
— Peppers

Carrots —
Beets

Summer Squash
— Bush Beans

Parsley —
Radishes

Left side Plant in early spring, then replant with second crop (facing page)

Right side Plant in late spring

1 square = 1 foot

If you don't want to set aside space for a strictly utilitarian food garden, or if your backyard is the only sunny spot for the lettuce or strawberries you want to grow, try mixing crops with your ornamental plantings. Many vegetables, berries, and herbs display a diverse array of showy "fruits" as well as foliage textures and colors. You can also add annuals and perennials.

If you interplant your garden, leave yourself access for harvesting your crops, and be sure to read fertilizer and pesticide labels carefully—some products that are fine for ornamentals may not be safe for use on edibles.

try things that often aren't available in supermarkets. You'll be surprised at all the varieties there are of your favorite vegetables—tomatoes, carrots, and even onions, for example.

How to plant: Plan the plot on graph paper, as shown opposite and below, to ensure that the plants will have ample room to grow. Transfer the plan to your plot with a tape measure and string. On level ground, lay out the rows north to south; on a slope, they should follow the contour of the hill. Locate tall plants on the north side of the garden, so they won't cast shadows on shorter plants. Put perennials (asparagus, rhubarb, etc.) in one section so you won't have to disturb their roots each year at planting time.

each of your favorite varieties, can be enough to supply plenty of vegetables for a family of two.

Time commitments: With any garden, the biggest time outlay is the initial preparation of the plot and planting. After that, short, regular periods of time are required; an average of about four hours a week is typical.

Choosing vegetables: You can plant most of your plot with vegetables and herbs you already know and like. But save some room for a bit of diversity. One of the joys of growing your own vegetables is that you can

MAKING THE MOST OF YOUR SPACE

Vegetables are divided into warm-season and cool-season categories. Warm-season vegetables need both soil warmth and long days of high temperatures; cool-season vegetables grow best at average temperatures 10° to 15° lower, and many will even withstand some frost. You can take advantage of this fact to lay out a garden that will produce a continuous supply of crops from spring all the way through autumn/winter. The left side of the 22x16-foot plot shown on the opposite page can be planted in early spring with cool-season vegetables, and then re-worked and replanted in mid- to late summer with a new crop *(left)* after the initial one has been harvested. The right side is planted with warm-season vegetables in late spring.

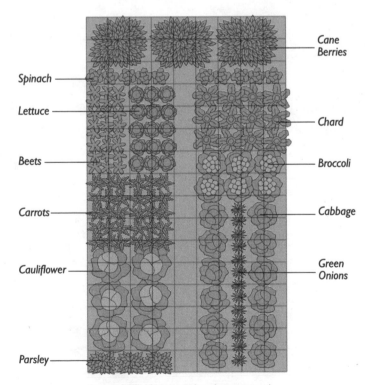

Spinach

Lettuce

Beets

Carrots

Cauliflower

Parsley

Cane Berries

Chard

Broccoli

Cabbage

Green Onions

Left side (replant in mid- to late summer)

Planting Your Garden

Once you have your garden plot located and laid out, it's time to prepare the soil and plant your vegetables. You can choose from seeds, transplants, sets (small bulbs), or crowns (growth buds with roots attached), depending, in part, on the type of plant. Crops that are tricky for home gardeners to start from seed can be purchased as transplants. Transplants are also a good idea if you're planting only one or two of each kind of plant.

Preparing the soil: Prepare the soil by adding fertilizers and necessary amendments as described on page 205. Rake and level the soil to form beds for planting, breaking up large clods and removing stones and other materials. Use a hoe, rake, or piece of wood to form the planting furrows, laying the furrows in straight and even lines *(below)*.

Sowing seeds: Seeds come in packets, and may be pelletized—coated like a small pill—to make handling and spacing easier. Tear off one corner of the packet and gently tap the seeds out as you move the packet along the furrow or seed bed, or pour a small quantity into your palm and scatter pinches of seeds as evenly as possible. Seed tape—seeds appropriately spaced and embedded in strips of biodegradable plastic—can be placed in straight lines in the furrow.

With all seeds, follow the packet instructions for optimum planting depth and row spacing. When the seedlings begin to appear, thin them to the spacing recommended on the packet. To sow seeds indoors, fill flats, trays, or pots with moistened potting mix; punch holes in the bottom of the container, if necessary for drainage. Scatter the seeds over the mix, or sow larger ones in furrows dug with a small stake. Water the mix lightly and set the container under a bright light in an area that is protected from cold and drafts.

When the new seedlings have developed their second set of true leaves, either thin them to about two inches apart—snip them off with scissors or pinch them off with your fingers—or transplant them to individual pots or cups. A few weeks after the initial thinning or transplanting, seedlings should be ready to go into the garden.

STAYING ON THE STRAIGHT AND NARROW

To make sure your rows of plants are straight, lay a board on the ground and use it as a guide along which to dig the furrow or plant along its edge *(below, left)*. An alternative method is to stretch a string between two stakes and set your plants in the earth beneath the string *(below, right)*.

Plants grown indoors from seeds should be hardened off—adjusted gradually to outdoor conditions—before they are transplanted to the garden. Move them outdoors for increasing intervals of time over a period of a week or more; at that point they should be able to stay out overnight. Alternatively, place them in a cold frame (below).

Planting sets or crowns: Sets and crowns are planted in furrows, just like seeds. Spacing and planting depth depend on the crop.

Plants of the onion family are often grown from sets, but can be grown from seeds as well. Perennial vegetables, such as asparagus and rhubarb, can be grown from crowns—sometimes also referred to as roots or divisions—to shorten the length of time between planting and first harvest. Starting perennials from seeds requires patience: It could be three years until the first harvest.

Planting transplants: Whether you've grown them yourself or bought them at a nursery, transplants are set out the same way: Dig a hole twice as wide and deep as the root ball, create a mound of soft soil at the bottom of the planting hole, and set the plant in place. Fill in soil around the root ball and water the plant thoroughly right away.

Cold frames

For many gardeners, a well-built, well-tended cold frame is nearly as useful as a small greenhouse. It certainly is more manageable and less expensive. A low-profile structure with a transparent, usually sloping roof, a cold frame functions as a passive solar energy collector and reservoir: During the day, the sun's radiation comes in through the transparent lid or roof, warming the air and soil inside the frame. At night, heat stored in the soil radiates out and keeps plants warm. Nighttime temperatures inside a cold frame can be 10° to 20° warmer than the air outside.

A cold frame is especially useful for early planting of summer annuals and seeds. It protects tender plants in winter, helps cuttings to root faster, and raises many kinds of delicate, hard-to-start plants that would otherwise be impossible to grow.

In reading gardening literature, you may encounter the term "hill," which can cause some misunderstanding since it's not necessarily a hill at all. A hill in gardening refers to the grouping of seeds or plants in clusters, not necessarily on mounds. A hill of squash or corn can consist of two or three plants growing together, on the same level ground as the rest of the garden. Hills, or clusters, are usually contrasted with rows, in which plants are spaced equal distances apart.

With a frame of rot-resistant wood, such as cedar or redwood heartwood, and an old window sash for a roof, this cold frame is easy and economical to make. Lath can replace the sash in the summer; or on warm days, prop open the roof.

Staking Your Vegetables

Climbing vegetables, such as pole beans, and sprawling vegetables, such as tomatoes and cucumbers, benefit from vertical support. Not only will you save space by propping up these crops, you'll also help prevent them from rotting by keeping them off the ground.

The best time to put up stakes, poles, trellises, and other supports is when planting. Since roots haven't formed yet, there is little risk of disturbing them. As the plants grow, train or tie them to the supports, making sure the ties are not too tight. In hot climates, don't use metal frames, chickenwire, or galvanized clothesline wire: Plant leaves can be burned when the metal becomes too hot.

Green-painted bamboo and wood stakes are easily found at most garden centers. Also available are green plastic or metal stakes. Ties hold more securely on rough wood than on smooth surfaces; use soft ties, such as strips of cloth. A selection of vegetable supports is illustrated below. For a fun alternative, see the tepee on the opposite page.

VEGETABLE SUPPORTS

A variety of props, from simple stakes to cylinders and tents, can help your climbing and sprawling plants to thrive. For a single tomato plant, tie the stalk to a stake with strips of cloth (near right). To minimize tying, try surrounding the plant with a cylinder of welded wire fencing (far right); reach through the mesh to harvest. For a row of plants, use crossed pairs of bamboo poles tied together at a crosspole (below, left). To support cucumbers, squash, pole beans, and peas, drive in a row of metal fencing stakes 4 to 6 feet apart and attach broad-mesh plastic netting to hooks in the posts (below, right).

Stake

Wire cylinder

Bamboo poles

Plastic netting

Kids love to play in tents, and this cool, leafy hideout is the perfect place for their make-believe games or quiet time. Best of all, they can grow it themselves—with just a little help from you.

Begin with eight bamboo or other thin poles about 6 to 8 feet long, some heavy twine, and a package of scarlet runner or other pole bean seeds.

To make the frame, draw a 5-foot-wide circle in the soil in a sunny part of your garden. Prepare the soil around the mark as described on page 169, or use a spot at the edge of your garden where the soil has already been prepared. Push the ends of the poles into the ground, evenly

spaced around the circle, leave a little extra space on one side for an entrance. Lean the poles together at the top, like a tepee, and tie them securely with the twine.

To ensure that the beans have plenty of climbing surface, make twine "poles" between the bamboo poles: First tie twine securely to one side of the entranceway near the bottom of the frame, then pull it tightly around the frame, wrapping it around each pole. Fasten the twine to the pole on the other side of the entranceway. Tie pieces of twine between every two poles, from

the top of the frame to the twine circle at the bottom.

Plant the bean seeds in holes 1 to 2 inches deep, about every 3 to 6 inches apart, all around the frame, cover them with soil, and gently water. When the seedlings are about 2 inches tall, thin them to 6 inches apart, keeping the sturdiest specimens. Weed, water, and fertilize the plants regularly, and they'll cover the frame quickly—in as little as two months. Flowers will follow in another month, and shortly after your first beans should appear.

Twine "poles"
create extra
climbing surface

Bamboo
poles

Watering Vegetables

Proper watering is something of an art. Just how often and how much to water tends to be a matter of learning by experience. Food crops need a steady supply of water from the time of planting until they are harvested. Overwatering can drown the roots, but too little watering is just as damaging and can cause plants to die of thirst.

Moisture level: Ideally, you want to keep the moisture level as even as possible to below the depth of the roots; don't allow the soil to dry out enough to cause the plants to wilt.

The proportion of clay, sand, and silt in the planting soil determines the rate and depth of water penetration. Turn to page 166 for a discussion of soil density and its effect on water retention. Ultimately, the best way to determine whether water is reaching plant roots is to dig down and see.

Crops: Different crops need different amounts of water. Leafy crops require more water than root crops, and young vegetable seedlings with small, shallow roots need to be watered frequently—sometimes as often as two or three times a day—to keep the roots moist.

Weather: Naturally, watering schedules are also affected by weather. Cool, cloudy days allow the soil to stay moist longer than it will in hot, dry weather. In some areas, rainfall during the growing season supplies all the water necessary for a successful harvest.

Two methods for watering are shown below. Other options include drip irrigation (*page 173*) and hand watering from a can or with a hose and sprinkler nozzle.

Two Watering Options

A soaker hose (*above*) delivers thin jets of water from pinprick-size holes. This system works well if you want to provide slow soaking with no runoff.

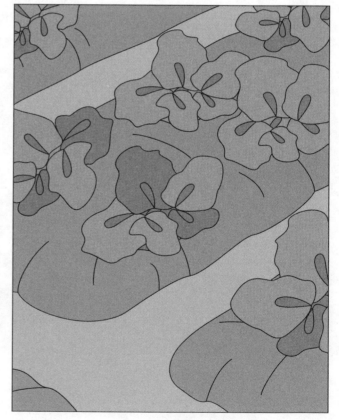

Furrow irrigation (*above*) is good on level ground for leafy crops that could be damaged by overhead watering.

Fertilizing Vegetables

Plants, like other living things, must have nourishment to thrive. Soil contains the elements necessary for plant growth, but the supply gradually diminishes as plants use up the available nutrients. Fertilizing your plants replenishes and maintains the supply of vital elements, and adding organic material to the soil creates a healthy environment for the growth of soil organisms that help to keep the natural cycle going.

When to fertilize: You can add fertilizer before you plant. For many vegetables, this initial fertilizing will be enough to meet their nutrient needs throughout the growing season. But some crops benefit from periodic follow-up feedings, also called side dressings, during the growing season.

Soil needs: A complete fertilizer contains all three of the major nutrients—nitrogen, phosphorus, and potassium. A simple fertilizer contains just one. Your soil may contain enough phosphorus and potassium, but you'll almost certainly have to add nitrogen; you can have your soil tested if you want to be sure.

What to apply: Organic fertilizers, such as cottonseed meal, bonemeal, and blood meal, release nutrients as they decompose, so they're slower-acting than inorganic fertilizers but they often last longer. Dig the fertilizer into the soil before planting.

With inorganic fertilizers, sometimes called chemical fertilizers, nutrients are available to plants quickly, because they're released when the fertilizer dissolves in water. Available in various forms, including dry, liquid, and slow-release form, they can be dug into the soil before planting or used as a side dressing.

Fertilizers recommended for vegetables (sometimes labeled "vegetable food") can be considered a fairly good choice to meet your plants' nutrient needs; follow package specifications for the amounts to apply.

Two Fertilizing Options

Dry fertilizer can be applied before or during the growing season. Spread a narrow band of fertilizer about 4 to 6 inches away from the plants, scratch it into the soil lightly, then water thoroughly.

Liquid fertilizer can be applied during the growing season. Make a solution of fertilizer and water, as recommended on the package, then use a watering can to apply it to the plant's watering basin.

Growing Herbs

When you plant an herb garden, you become part of a tradition that harks back to the Middle Ages. Both charming and practical, herb gardens can be adapted to any space, large or small, providing the area gets sufficient sun.

Choosing the style: Your herb garden can be formal or informal, depending on your tastes. Formal herb gardens have their origins in the walled courtyards of the Middle Ages and the Renaissance, where plants grew in orderly, geometrically shaped beds, bordered by low, clipped hedges and separated by paths *(below)*. Sometimes benches were present, from which to sit and appreciate the garden's fragrances. A sundial, birdbath, or fountain provided a central accent. If you like the formal layout, but want a less rigid look, you can trim the herbs in soft curves so that they retain their natural mounding shapes. An idea for a practical informal garden on a small scale is featured on the opposite page.

Choosing the plants: The plant group known as herbs includes a

THREE FORMAL HERB GARDEN PLANS

The classic herb garden is formal in style, with symmetrical planting beds and paths bordered by clipped hedges. There are as many attractive layouts as there are gardeners. Three possibilities are shown here, but let your garden space and your own imagination be your guide.

206

wide variety of annuals, biennials, perennials, and a few shrubs that have at some time in history been valued as sources of seasonings, medicines, or fragrances. The traditional plant for clipped borders in formal herb gardens is the boxwood, although it's not an herb. Unless you're planting strictly for culinary purposes, you'll probably choose plants for both their ornamental and their culinary properties. This means that you'll need to consider the growth habits, shape, foliage colors, textures, and flowers of each herb, in addition to the tastes and aromas they offer.

For general culinary and ornamental purposes, 12 herbs are considered classic: basil, chives, lovage, dill, oregano, sweet marjoram, parsley, rosemary, sage, spearmint, French tarragon, and thyme.

For fragrance and interesting flowers, add borage, burnet, lavender, lemon verbena, nasturtium, and santolina. Nasturtium and borage blossoms are edible, as well, and add a distinctive and decorative touch to salads.

A COOK'S GARDEN

Imagine your favorite herbs growing with colorful annual flowers just outside your kitchen window. This easy-to-build window box makes it all possible. See diagram *(far right)* for design details.

Place loose, lightweight potting soil in the box, keeping it at least 1 inch below its top edge, and spacing the plants closely. Or, fill the box with coarse vermiculite and sink containers (6 inches or more in diameter) into it. The vermiculite helps keep plants from drying out. Frequent and thorough watering is essential for keeping window box plants alive and well.

Planted with culinary herbs and geraniums, this kitchen window box sits behind a false front, sheathed in siding to match the house; it's topped off with redwood trim. A length of plastic tubing drains water away from the house wall.
Design: *Karl G. Smith, Margaret Simon*

Storing Your Harvest

Unless you've limited yourself to a patch of ground only a few feet square, you'll probably end up with more produce from your backyard garden than you can can possibly eat at one time. Knowing how to store the excess will assure you of mouth-watering vegetables for months to come.

The aging process: The objective of storage is to keep vegetables aging slowly. Because the process of aging involves the vegetables' own stored "food," the faster it's used up, the more quickly the quality of the vegetables' flavor and texture declines. Eventually this results in rotting. Vegetables differ in the storage conditions they require: The shortest-lived crops must be refrigerated and used promptly, others can last for many months, under proper conditions.

Cool and dry storage: The two most widely grown bulb crops—onions and garlic—require cool and dry storage. Both crops require an initial curing period in a shady, dry spot at room temperature—about 10 days for garlic, up to three weeks for onions. Then store them where it's cool, about 35° to 50°F (2° to 10°C), dry, and well-ventilated.

Warm and dry storage: Pumpkins and hard-skinned winter squash require warm and dry storage. First cure these crops at a fairly high temperature 80° to 85°F (27 to 29°C) for about 10 days—in a small room heated for this purpose— then place them in an upstairs storage room or warm garage, with a temperature of 55° to 60°F (13° to 16°C.) Leave space between them.

Cool and damp storage: Vegetables that have a high moisture content and fairly thin skins lose moisture quickly and thus require cool and damp storage. The optimum temperature for this environment is between 32° and 34°F (0° to 4°C). Some vegetables in this category must be eaten within a few days, while others can last for months. Those with the shortest life, such as asparagus, broccoli, and eggplant, should be kept in the refrigerator. Longer-lived vegetables, such as carrots, beets, and rutabagas, can be stored in a root cellar.

FREEZE HERBS FOR FRESHNESS

Herbs keep their flavor well when frozen: in cooked dishes, you may not even be able to tell the difference between garden fresh and those from your freezer.

Rinse the herbs and drain or pat until dry, then spread them out in a single layer on baking sheets. Freeze them until rigid (about one hour), then seal them in a freezer bag with the air removed and put in the freezer. To use, simply remove what's needed, reseal the bag, and return it to the freezer.

Tender-leaf herbs, such as basil, may darken when thawed. Blanching them for two or three seconds before freezing will preserve their color: Plunge them into ice water until cold, spread them on towels, and pat them dry, then freeze and bag them.

Canning

You can enjoy the produce of your garden throughout the year by canning it. The canning process is a relatively simple one: You prepare enough vegetables for one canner-load at a time, place them in canning jars, and heat them at a specific amount of pressure for a specific time. Let them cool in the canner, then lift them out to cool at room temperature for 12 to 24 hours.

Two packing methods can be used: hot-pack, in which you cook the vegetables briefly before canning and pack them in their cooking liquid; and raw-pack, in which you place raw vegetables in the canning jars and cover them with boiling water. Different vegetables require different preparation and different amounts of canning time. For example, the quart jars of hot-packed green beans shown below should be processed at 10 pounds pressure in a weighted gauge canner for 25 minutes. Typically, canners feature a lid that can be secured tightly in place and a pressure gauge. Adjusting the heat increases or decreases the pressure as required.

Consult the manual that came with your canner for specific information regarding the kind of vegetables you want to can, or contact your county cooperative extension service office for details.

Before canning, slide a narrow nonmetallic spatula between the vegetables and the sides of the jar to release air bubbles *(above, left)*. Space the jars in the canner so they're not touching each other or the sides of the canner *(above, right)*. Always use a jar lifter to place jars in the canner or on the counter *(left)*.

A Gallery of Plantings

The most important question to ask when you choose a garden plant is whether it will thrive in your region. Some plants cannot survive sub-freezing temperatures; others actually need winter frost to bloom properly the following spring.

Refer to the zone map on page 162, which divides North America into 11 zones based on average minimum temperature. Then, check the zone reference in the upcoming pages to see whether the climate in your region is suitable for the perennials, bulbs, shrubs, or trees you have selected. Some plant varieties are hardier than others; a nursery professional can advise you.

For vegetables, annuals and biennials, and herbs that aren't perennials, you will have to gear your planting to the date of the last frost in your region. Talk to a nursery professional to see whether your growing season is long enough.

Common trees

Trees can fulfill a variety of roles, from screening an unwanted view to acting as a windbreak. If you are looking primarily for summer shade, think of choosing a tree that loses its leaves in winter to let through sunlight on cold days. If you need to block the wind, an evergreen will offer protection year-round.

Illustrated here are just a few trees to consider for your yard. Each entry includes the tree's Latin name, a reference to the zone range where it will thrive, its growth rate, and the average height for each type. If a tree is not available in your area, a nursery professional can suggest one with similar attributes.

(D) Deciduous **(E)** Evergreen

Dogwood (D)
Cornus florida
Zones 5-8
Slow to moderate
Up to 30 feet

Eastern redbud (D)
Cercis canadensis
Zones 5-9
Moderate
25-35 feet

Flowering crabapple (D)
Malus 'Katherine'
Zones 5-8
Moderate to fast
Up to 20 feet

Flowering plum (D)
Prunus blireiana
Zones 5-8
Moderate
Up to 25 feet

Japanese maple (D)
Acer palmatum
Zones 5-8
Slow to moderate
Up to 20 feet

Japanese tree lilac (D)
Syringa reticulata
Zones 4-7
Moderate
Up to 25 feet

Loquat (E)
Eriobotrya japonica
Zones 8-10
Moderate
15-30 feet

Russian olive (D)
Elaeagnus angustifolia
Zones 2-9
Fast
Up to 20 feet

Saucer magnolia (D)
Magnolia soulangiana
Zones 5-9
Slow
Up to 25 feet

Shadblow (D)
Amelanchier laevis
Zones 4-7
Slow
30-35 feet

210

Silver bell (D)
Halesia carolina
Zones 5-8
Moderate
20-50 feet

Washington hawthorn (D)
Crataegus phaenopyrum
Zones 4-8
Moderate
Up to 25 feet

Bradford pear (D)
Pyrus calleryana 'Bradford'
Zones 5-8
Moderate
Up to 30 feet

Flowering cherry (D)
Prunus serrulata
Zones 6-9
Moderate to fast
Up to 30 feet

Glossy privet (E)
Ligustrum lucidum
Zones 7-10
Fast
35-40 feet

Jacaranda (D-E)
Jacaranda mimosifolia
Zone 10
Moderate
25-40 feet

Japanese snowdrop (D)
Styrax japonicus
Zones 5-9
Slow to moderate
Up to 30 feet

Katsura (D)
Cercidiphyllum japonicum
Zones 5-9
Slow
40 feet or more

Kentucky coffee tree (D)
Gymnocladus dioica
Zones 5-9
Fast
Up to 50 feet

Little-leaf linden (D)
Tilia cordata
Zones 4-8
Slow to moderate
Up to 30-50 feet

Mountain ash (D)
Sorbus aucuparia
Zones 4-7
Moderate to fast
20-30 feet or more

Pagoda tree (D)
Sophora japonica
Zones 5-9
Moderate
Up to 40 feet

Persian parrotia (D)
Parrotia persica
Zones 6-9
Slow
30 feet or more

Persimmon (D)
Diospyros kaki
Zones 7-10
Moderate
30 feet or more

Red horse chestnut (D)
Aesculus carnea
Zones 5-8
Moderate
Up to 40 feet

Silk tree (D)
Albizia julibrissin
Zones 7-10
Fast
Up to 40 feet

Silver dollar gum (E)
Eucalyptus polyanthemos
Zones 9-10
Fast
20-60 feet

Sour gum (D)
Nyssa sylvatica
Zones 4-9
Slow to moderate
30-50 feet

Sweet gum (D)
Liquidambar styraciflua
Zones 6-9
Moderate
60 feet or more

White birch (D)
Betula pendula
Zones 3-8
Fast
30-40 feet

Annuals and Biennials

Annuals are fast-growing plants that bring color to your garden for one season, then die. Biennials complete their life cycle in two years. Also included here are a few tender perennials—plants that thrive for several seasons—usually grown as annuals.

Plant spring-blooming annuals in early spring; summer-blooming annuals should be planted after the last frost. For winter and early-spring bloom in areas that have mild winters, set out the plants in late summer or early autumn while days are warm enough for good growth but nights are lengthening. In hot, dry climates, annuals planted in autumn will bloom during the winter and spring, but then will be killed by the summer heat.

Whatever the climate, plant all your annuals in full sun unless you know they will tolerate shade. Newcomers to seed gardening might start with marigolds, nasturtiums, and zinnias—all easy and fast growing.

Ageratum
Ageratum houstonianum
Tiny lavender-blue, white or pink flowers in dense clusters. Dwarf varieties make excellent edgings or pattern plantings.

Balsam
Impatiens balsamina
Long, sharply pointed, deeply toothed leaves. White, pink, rose, lilac, or red flowers. Needs ample water.

Calendula
Calendula officinalis
Orange, yellow, cream, apricot daisylike flowers on 1'-2' plants. Blooms in winter in warm climates. Effective in masses.

California poppy
Eschscholtzia californica
Orange, red, or white flowers on feathery plants. Plant in informal groups. Poppies may reseed themselves in warm areas.

Calliopsis
Coreopsis tinctoria
Yellow, orange, reddish flowers on 1½'-3' plants with wiry stems. Much like cosmos in growth habits. Dwarf and double.

Chinese pink
Dianthus chinensis
Erect, 6"-30" high; stems branching at top; rose-lilac flowers. Compact varieties covered in bright pink, red, white flowers.

Cineraria
Senecio hybridus
Clusters of daisylike flowers in blue, violet, pink, white. Lush foliage. Grows best in cool shade. Will reseed itself.

Cosmos
Cosmos bipinnatus
Daisylike flowers in white, lavender, pink, rose, purple, crimson on plants 36"-48" tall. Feathery foliage.

Forget-me-not
Myosotis sylvatica
Sprays of tiny blue flowers 6"-12" tall. Plant in shaded areas—good under flowering shrubs. Will reseed itself.

Foxglove
Digitalis purpurea
Erect plant to 4' or more with tubular flowers in purple, yellow, white, pastels. Leaves clump at base. Plant in shade.

Gaillardia
Gaillardia pulchella
Red, yellow, gold flowers on stems to 2'. Sun-loving plants thrive in heat. Plant in warm soil after frost danger is past.

Hollyhock
Alcea rosea
Single or double flowers in rose, red, pinks, yellow, white, apricot. Stems to 9' tall; best used as background. Biennial. Will reseed itself.

Impatiens
Impatiens walleriana
White, pink, rose, orange, or red flowers on bushy plants. Set out plants after frost in full sun (light shade in heat).

Lobelia
Lobelia erinus
Tiny white or blue flowers on low-growing plants. Compact and trailing types. Good in containers and as borders.

Madagascar periwinkle
Catharanthus roseus
Phloxlike flowers in pure white with red, pink, or rose eye. Excellent in hot climates. Often called Vinca rosea.

Marigold
Tagetes
Yellow, orange, rust single or pompomlike flowers on stems from a few inches to 4' tall. Easy to grow.

Nasturtium
Tropaeoleum majus
Trailing or bushy plant 8"-18" tall; can climb to 6'. Maroon, orange, yellow, red flowers. Grows in sun or partial shade.

Nicotiana
Nicotiana
Fragrant flowers in white, red, greenish yellow, mauve on 1'-3' stems. Flowers open at night or on cloudy days; some stay open.

Pansy
Viola
Two types: Pansies have large variegated blooms; violas have smaller solid-colored flowers. Both prefer semishade

Petunia
Petunia hybrida
Flowers in many colors; single, ruffled, or double. Plant in containers or group together in beds. Grows well in sun or light shade.

Phlox
Phlox drummondii
Numerous, showy bright and pastel flowers in clusters at tops of 6"-18" stems. Good mass effect in full sun.

Portulaca
Portulaca grandiflora
Small, roselike flowers in many brilliant colors on trailing, succulent stems. Flowers open fully only in sun.

Scarlet sage
Salvia splendens
Tall, thin flower spikes (in red, rose, lavender, or white) 8"-30" on dark green plants. Use as a border or background plant.

Snapdragon
Antirrhinum majus
Perennial, usually treated as annual. Many colors, forms. Well-suited for sunny borders and cutting.

Spider flower
Cleome spinosa
Shrubby, branching plant 4'-6' tall with many open clusters of pink or white flowers. Especially vigorous in warm areas.

Stock
Matthiola incana
Strongly scented flowers in white, red, pink, cream, lavender, or purple on 1'-3' plants. Valued for fragrance.

Sweet alyssum
Lobularia maritima
Masses of tiny flowers in white, red, or violet. Use for quick cover in a bulb bed or as a low border. A prolific reseeder.

Zinnia
Zinnia
Plants come in many sizes, bright colors. Likes hot summer. Subject to mildew in foggy areas or when sprinkled.

Perennials

Perennials are the perennial favorites of gardeners everywhere, flowering year after year, and often forming the backbone of a flower garden. As a group, perennials are a hardy lot, with a fortunate affinity for cold climates. In milder areas, they may even hold their foliage year-round.

If you mass perennials, choose them carefully so that they will work together in a harmonious pattern of color, form, size, and texture. Study blooming times to avoid having all your plants flower at the same time. A carefully planned border or bed will have two crescendos of special glory—early summer and early autumn—but you should try to plan it so that there is some color at other times. Adding a few bulbs and annuals to the bed will ensure that you have something colorful in bloom from spring to fall.

Astilbe
Astilbe
Zones 4-8
Pink, red, or white feathery blooms on stems up to 3' or more. Takes sun, light shade.

Balloon flower
Platycodon grandiflorus
Zones 4-9
Balloonlike buds open into star-shaped flowers in blue, white, violet or pink. Light shade in warm areas.

Bergenia
Bergenia
Zones 3-8
Pink, rose, or white flowers on stalks 12"-18" high; rounded, glossy-leafed foliage. Plant in shade. Blooms early.

Bleeding heart
Dicentra spectabilis
Zones 4-8
Pink and white heart-shaped flowers hang from 2'-3' arching stems. Best in shade garden. Blooms in spring.

Campanula
Campanula
Zones 4-7
Blue, white, or pink bell-shaped flowers. Many kinds from a few inches to several feet tall. Blooms in spring and summer.

Candytuft
Iberis sempervirens
Zones 4-9
White flowers in clusters on spreading plants 4"-18" high. Showy bloom in spring, sporadic bloom where mild.

Columbine
Aquilegia
Zones 4-9
Spurred flowers in red, yellow, blue, or purple on 1'-4' plants. Good in woodland gardens. Blooms early in year.

Coral bells
Heuchera sanguinea
Zones 4-8
Pink, red, or white flowers on stalks to 2' tall above low rosettes of dark green summer leaves. Blooms spring, summer.

Coreopsis
Coreopsis
Zones 4-9
Yellow, orange, maroon, or reddish flowers on long stems. Blooms spring to autumn if faded flowers are removed.

Daylily
Hemerocallis
Zones 3-9
Many shades of yellow, red, orange, or cream lilylike flowers on stems to 4'. Blooms spring to autumn.

Delphinium
Delphinium
Zones 3-10
Tall blue, white, lavender, or pink flower spikes reach 6'. Stems need staking. Blooms in summer.

Dianthus
Dianthus plumarius
Zones 3-9
Single or double rose, pink, or white flowers. Excellent edging for borders. Spicy carnation scent. Blooms summer, autumn.

English daisy
Bellis perennis
Zone 4-8
White, red, or pink blooms on low rosettes of rounded leaves. Needs shade in hot areas.

Gaillardia
Gaillardia grandiflora
Zones 3-9
Yellow, bronze, or red daisylike flowers on 2'-3' plants. Gray-green foliage. Blooms summer, autumn.

Gazania
Gazania
Zones 8-10
Yellow, white, pink daisylike flowers on clumping or trailing gray foliage to 10" tall.

Geranium
Pelargonium hortorum
Zones 8-10 (As annual, 3-8)
Enormous variety of form and color in flowers and leaves. Blooms summer, autumn. Prefers sun.

Gloriosa daisy
Rudbeckia hirta
Zones 3-9
Big yellow, orange, or brownish daisies to 7" across. Plants grow to 4' tall. Blooms summer, autumn. Tough, easy plants.

Lily of the valley
Convallaria majalis
Zones 4-9
Clusters of tiny, bell-shaped flowers above broad leaves. Needs cold winter. Blooms in spring. Prefers shade.

Lupine
Lupinus hybrids
Zones 1-8
Great color variety in flowers in dense clusters on 1½'-4' plants. Blooms in summer. Needs cool weather.

Michaelmas daisy
Aster novae-angliae, A. novi-belgii
Zones 5-8
Graceful, branching plants to 4' tall. Many varieties. Flowers in white, pink, rose red, purple. Long bloom period.

Oriental poppy
Papaver orientale
Zones 4-9
Brilliant and pastel flowers (reds, pinks, white) on showy 4' plants. Blooms in spring; foliage dies back in summer.

Pelargonium
Pelargonium domesticum
Zones 8-10 (As annual, 3-8)
Showy flowers in white and shades of pink, lavender, red. Blooms in spring, summer. Hardy to about 15°F/-9°C.

Peony
Paeonia
Zones 4-8
Spectacular red, white, pink, or cream flowers. Plants 2'-4' tall, wider spread; large, handsome leaves. Needs cold, frosty winter.

Phlox
Phlox
Zones 4-8
Many flower colors. Different varieties range from 6" to 5' tall. Uses vary. Blooms in summer.

Plantain lily
Hosta
Zones 4-9
White or lilac flowers on thin spikes above massed clumps of handsome foliage up to 3' high. Needs shade. Summer.

Sedum
Sedum spectabile
Zones 4-9
Many varieties with red to pink flowers. Succulent leaves, clumps of erect stems. Blooms summer, autumn.

Shasta daisy
Chrysanthemum maximum
Zones 4-8
Big, white single or double daisies 3" to 4" wide, 2' to 4' tall, above dark, coarse foliage to 18" high. Blooms in summer.

Yarrow
Achillea
Zones 3-8
Yellow, white, rose, or red flowers in flat clusters on plants from 8" to several feet tall. Blooms in summer and autumn.

Bulbs

The term "bulb" is often loosely applied to a number of unrelated kinds of plants, all of which store food in swollen underground parts during dormant seasons. When the plant's growth season comes around, roots and leaves sprout from this natural storehouse. Hardy bulbs will survive cold winters, while half-hardy ones may suffer in such weather. Tender bulbs have low tolerance for freezing temperatures. Pick off dead blooms, but leave the foliage, which is needed to make food for the next season's growth and bloom.

Canna
Canna
Zones 7-10
Many colors.
Plant in May or June; needs sun.
Blooms in summer. Half-hardy.

Crocus
Crocus
Zones 3-8
Yellow, orange, lavender, purple, or white flowers. Plant in autumn; sun, light shade. Needs winter chill.

Daffodil
Narcissus
Zones 3-9
Yellow, orange, white, or bicolored flowers. Plant in autumn; sun, light shade. Blooms in spring. Hardy.

Dahlia
Dahlia
Zones 7-11
Many colors. Plant in spring; sun. Blooms late summer, autumn. Lift tubers in cold winters.

Gladiolus
Gladiolus
Zones 7-11
Many colors and shades. Plant in spring (winter in desert regions); sun. Tender.

Grape hyacinth
Muscari
Zones 2-9
Blue or white flowers. Plant in autumn; sun, light shade. Blooms in spring. Half-hardy.

Hyacinth
Hyacinthus
Zones 5-9
Red, pink, blue, purple, white, or yellow flowers. Plant September-November; sun, light shade. Needs winter chilling.

Iris
Iris
Zones 3-10
Many colors, species. Plant July to October; sun. Blooms in spring; some varieties repeat bloom. Many species hardy.

Lily
Lilium
Zones 4-8
Many colors. Plant in autumn; sun or part shade. Blooms in summer. Hardy.

Ranunculus
Ranunculus
Zone 11
Many colors. Plant in autumn; sun. Blooms in spring. Half-hardy.

Snowdrop
Galanthus
Zones 3-9
White flowers. Plant in autumn; sun, part shade. Blooms in early spring, even in snow.

Tuberous begonia
Begonia tuberhybrida
Zone 11
Many colors. Plant in winter, early spring; filtered sun. Blooms summer to fall. Tender; used as bedding, potted plant.

Tulip
Tulipa
Zones 4-11
Many colors. Plant in autumn; sun, light shade. Blooms in spring. Hardy. Needs winter chilling.

Windflower
Anemone
Zones 6-8
Blue, red, pink, or white flowers. Plant October-November; sun, light shade. Blooms in spring. Hardy.

Herbs

The fragrance, flavor, and healing qualities of herbs are woven into the rich tapestry of biblical stories, quaint herbals, and scientific works. Yet herbs are remarkably up-to-date, and are vigorous, undemanding plants that require only average soil and moisture. Most are sun lovers, but some will take part shade. Herbs make attractive and serviceable ground covers, edgings, and shrub or pot plants, as well as adding rich and subtle flavors to your meals.

Basil
Ocimum basilicum
Zone 11
Annual. Grows readily from seed sown in spring. Sun or part shade.

Caraway
Carum carvi
Zones 3-9
Seeds develop in second year, then plant dies. Harvest in midsummer when seeds are ripe but before they drop.

Chamomile
Chamaemelum nobile
Zones 6-9
Roman or English is the variety most often planted. Good ground cover around garden paths. Sow in early spring or late autumn.

Chives
Allium schoenoprasum
Zones 2-11
Usually bought as small plants but can be grown from seed. Plants can be divided.

Dill
Anethum graveolens
Zones 3-10
Annual. Plant in full sun in well-drained, good garden soil.

Fennel
Foeniculum vulgare
Zones 4-9
Propagate by seeds sown in spring. Likes full sun and light, well-drained garden soil.

Marjoram
Origanum majorana
Zones 4-10
Sow seeds early in spring or propagate from cuttings or divisions. Can be grown indoors in sunny window boxes.

Mint
Mentha
Zones 3-9
Perennial. Most varieties grow almost anywhere and spread rapidly by underground stems and runners. Best contained in pots or boxes.

Oregano
Origanum vulgare
Zones 4-8
A good container plant, but replace about every three years. Grow new plants from seed or divisions. Annual in cold climates.

Parsley
Petroselinum crispum
Zones 3-10
Biennial, treated as annual. Grow from nursery plants or sow seeds in spring. Soak seeds in warm water for 24 hours before planting. Part shade or sun.

Rosemary
Rosmarinus officinalis
Zones 7-9
Will tolerate poor soil if it's well drained; likes hot sun. Perennial shrub in mild climates. Good in containers or indoors.

Sage
Salvia officinalis
Zones 5-9
Tolerates poor but well-drained soil, full sun; fairly drought resistant. Annual in cold climates; grow from seed or cuttings.

Savory
Satureja
Zone 11
Start summer savory (annual) from seed, winter savory (perennial) from cuttings or divisions.

Thyme
Thymus
Zones 4-10
Many species and varieties. Perennial; start from seeds or cuttings.

Vegetables

It's surprising how many vegetables you can raise in a small garden plot. Some are decorative plants that can be interspersed with flowers and small shrubs. Vegetables need all the sunlight you can give them, and just the right amounts of water and nutrients. Plant seeds and care for them according to the package. If you are using seedlings from a nursery, ask for advice on cultivation and the best combination of water and fertilizer to get the best harvest from your crop.

Artichokes
Can spread to 8 feet in width; needs long mild winter and cool summer. Harvest period is late winter through midsummer.

Asparagus
Perennial; requires winter dormancy period. Start from roots, available in late winter at nurseries.

Beans
Many varieties available. Require warm soil (65°F/18°C) to sprout reliably. Low growing (bush types) and tall growing (pole types) available; growing season varies.

Beets
Biennial planted as annual. Plant seeds at monthly intervals as soon as spring soil is workable. Thin plants to 2" apart. Harvest when 1-3" in diameter.

Broccoli
Easy to grow. Plant to mature in cool weather. After central head is removed, side shoots will produce additional heads.

Brussels sprouts
Require long cool growing period. In cool climates, buy young plants and set out in early spring for fall harvest; in mild climates plant in autumn for spring harvest.

Cabbage
Early varieties mature in 7 to 8 weeks; late varieties in 3 to 4 months. Plant to mature during cold weather.

Carrots
Sow seeds thickly, 20 to 30 per foot in rows at least 12" apart. When seedlings are 2" high, thin them to leave 1½" between each one. Avoid sowing during excessively hot or cold months.

Cauliflower
Grows best in a cool, moist climate. Set out plants in late summer for autumn harvest. Sprinkle daily, especially during hot, dry periods.

Celery
Difficult to grow. Requires very mild climate, much water and fertilizer. Start indoors then plant out in early spring.

Corn
Plant corn after soil has warmed and frosts are past. It must be planted in rows so the wind distributes pollen effectively. Likes hot sun and needs a lot of water.

Cucumbers
To save space, train cucumbers to grow up trellises. Plant 18" apart. Once plant has grown to top of trellis, pinch off tops to encourage lateral growth.

Eggplant
Heat-loving, frost tender. Grows slowly; start from nursery plants. Space 3' apart in rows 3' to 4' apart.

Garlic
Grow from "mother" bulbs. Break bulb into cloves, and plant cloves with bases downward, 1" to 2" deep and 2" to 3" apart in rows 12" apart.

Leeks

Sow seeds in early spring. As plants grow, mound soil around the fat, round stems to make the bottoms white and mild-tasting. Autumn harvest.

Lettuce

Butterhead varieties are loosely folded with smooth yellow center leaves. Loose-leaf lettuces are best grown in hot climates. Romaine stands heat moderately well.

Melons

Need 2½ to 4 months of heat to ripen to full sweetness. Cantaloupes are easiest to grow because they ripen fastest.

Onions

All onions are especially easy to grow as long as they have fairly rich soil and regular watering.

Parsnips

Need deep, loose soil; in cold-winter areas, sow seeds in late spring. In milder climes sow in autumn for spring harvest.

Peas

Peas are a cool-weather crop; plant them in autumn, winter, or early spring.

Peppers

Sweet peppers will grow in all but the coolest climates; hot peppers prefer longer, warmer seasons.

Potatoes

Plant white potatoes early in spring or in midwinter in sandy, well-drained soil. Dig new potatoes when tops begin to flower, mature ones after tops die back.

Pumpkins

Require a lot of space. Sow on mounds of earth in early summer. Spacing varies from 4' to 10', depending on variety.

Radishes

Fast growth and relatively easy culture make this vegetable popular. Sow seeds as soon as soil is workable and then at 2-week intervals.

Rhubarb

Perennial. Requires cold weather for dormant period. Stalks are edible, but the leaves are poisonous.

Spinach

Sow from July to September so plants mature either in autumn, winter, or spring, depending on your climate. Thin seedlings after they get a good start.

Squash

Summer squash grows in about 2 months; winter squash requires 3 or 4 months.

Swiss chard

Ideal for any vegetable garden. Plant seed outdoors as soon as soil can be worked. Harvest outer leaves as needed.

Tomatoes

Nurseries sell best varieties for your local climate. Plant seedlings 3 feet apart. Set plants deeply, supply stake or wire cylinder supports, and water well.

Turnips and rutabagas

Both spring and autumn crops are possible; usually plant in midsummer for autumn harvest. Space plants to allow full root growth.

Ground Covers

Wherever you want a carpet of green—but don't want to cope with keeping a lawn healthy—you'd do well to consider an appropriate ground cover. While ground covers usually require less maintenance, water, and fertilizer, they aren't suitable for heavy traffic areas.

Before you choose a ground cover for your garden, consider a few things. Does it need sun or shade? How fast does it grow, and how far apart should the plants be spaced? A few popular ground covers, suitable for different growing zones, are shown below.

Ajuga
Ajuga reptans
Zones 3-8
Fast growing; thick carpet of dark hairy leaves. Blue flowers in spring and early summer. Sun or part shade.

Cotoneaster
Cotoneaster
Zones 4-9
Several varieties of good, fast-growing ground covers. Deciduous, semideciduous, evergreen varieties. Sun, part shade.

Creeping St. Johnswort
Hypericum calycinum
Zones 7-9
Evergreen; semideciduous where winters are cold. Short-stalked leaves, bright yellow flowers. Sun or shade.

Dwarf periwinkle
Vinca minor
Zones 4-8
Trailing stems root as they spread. Lavender-blue flowers; some forms with white, double blue, deeper blue flowers.

Dwarf plumbago
Ceratostigma plumbaginoides
Zones 5-8
Wiry-stemmed perennial. Bronzy green to dark green leaves. Blue flowers from July until frost. Cut back in winter.

English ivy
Hedera helix
Zones 5-9
Evergreen, woody ground cover or climbing vine. Dark, dull green leaves with paler veins. Sun or shade in most climates.

Ice plant
Lampranthus
Zone 10
Succulent. Brilliant flowers winter-spring. Full sun; little water. Cut back after bloom. Hardy to 20° to 30°F/-7° to -1° C.

Japanese spurge
Pachysandra terminalis
Zones 4-8
Rich, dark green leaves. Small, fluffy spikes of white flowers in summer. Plant in shade. Spreads by runners.

Juniper
Juniperus
Zones 3-9
Ground cover varieties range from a few inches to 2'-3' high. Prostrate and creeping junipers often used in rock gardens.

Mondo grass
Ophiopogon japonicus
Zones 7-10
Dark green leaves; light lilac flowers in summer. Slow to establish as ground cover. Needs shade in hot, dry areas.

Snow-in-summer
Cerastium tomentosum
Zones 3-7
Good in mild or cold climates, coastal or desert areas. Silvery gray foliage; masses of white flowers in early summer.

Winter creeper
Euonymus fortunei
Zones 5-9
Good ground cover where temperatures drop below 0°F/-18°C. In desert climates, takes full sun better than ivy.

Shrubs

Along with trees, shrubs form the basic framework of many gardens. Once you plant shrubs, you can look forward to enjoying them year after year.

You'll find shrubs available for any use in your garden. Most will do well in sun or part shade. The best shrubs for permanent landscaping are generally those that grow slowly but, once established, maintain their character. And don't judge a shrub strictly by its flowers. Look for form and foliage—let perennials, annuals, and bulbs add the color.

Boxwood
Buxus
Zones 5-9
Many species. Widely used for low or medium hedges, edgings. Hardy to 0°F/-18°C, depending on species. Evergreen.

Euonymus
Euonymus
Zones 4-9
Slow to medium growth, 7'-10'. Hardy to 0° to -10°F/-18° to -12°C or more depending on species. Evergreen kinds valued for texture, form. Evergreen and deciduous.

Firethorn
Pyracantha
Zones 6-11
Fast, vigorous growth. Glossy green leaves, thorny branches, red or orange berries in fall. Most types hardy to 0° to -10°F/-18° to -23°C. Evergreen.

Forsythia
Forsythia
Zones 4-9
Somewhat fountain-shaped; bare branches covered with yellow flowers February-April. Hardy to 0° to -20°F/-18° to -29°C. Deciduous.

Hydrangea
Hydrangea
Zones 5-9
Big leaves; large clusters of long-lasting flowers in white, pink, red, or blue, summer and fall. Most hardy to 0° to -10°F/-18° to -23°C. Deciduous.

Japanese privet
Ligustrum japonicum
Zones 7-9
Dense, compact growth to 10'-12'. Excellent for hedges, screens, small standards. Hardy to 0° to 10°F/-18° to -12°C. Evergreen.

Juniper
Juniperus
Zones 3-11
Needled evergreen with fleshy, berry-like fruits. Many forms, from shrubs to tall, slender types. Hardy to -10° to -20°F/-23° to -29°C. Evergreen.

Lilac
Syringa
Zones 3-8
Best where winter brings definite chill. Can reach 20'. Clustered, fragrant lavender or white flowers in May or June. Hardy to -10°F/-23°C. Deciduous.

Mock orange
Philadelphus
Zones 5-9
Large, vigorous plant with medium green foliage. White, fragrant flowers. Hardy to 0° to -10°F/-18° to -23°C. Deciduous.

Rhododendron
Rhododendron
Zones 5-9
Many species and hybrids. Mostly spring-blooming. Most hardy to 0° to 10°F/-18° to -12°C; some tender. Evergreen.

Spiraea
Spiraea vanhouttei
Zones 4-8
Fountain-shaped growth to 6'. Blue-green leaves on arching branches. Showy snow-white clusters, June-July. Hardy to -10° to -20°F/-23° to -29°C. Deciduous.

Weigela
Weigela
Zones 5-9
Voluminous flower display in late spring. Coarse-leafed, stiff plant; prune to prevent ranginess. Hardy to 0° to -10°F/-18° to -23°C. Deciduous.

Building In Your BACKYARD

The ideal backyard is many things to many people. For some, a simple low deck may be enough to bridge the transition from house to garden. Or you may choose to add a brick patio and a Victorian-style gazebo with a meandering path joining the two. Whatever your vision, this chapter will show you how to design back-yard structures that will complement your house and yard, creating your own private sanctuary from the hurly-burly of everyday life. If you enjoy the satisfaction of building it yourself, the step-by-step information will make your job straightforward. But even if you prefer to hire a professional to do some—or all—of the work, these helpful ideas will ensure that you make the most of your backyard space.

In the leafy shade of an ancient oak, a redwood deck offers an inviting place to relax and enjoy this backyard's woodsy appeal.

Coming Up With a Plan

You have a vision of how you want to transform your backyard: a shady patio, perhaps, or a flagstone path meandering through the garden to a charming gazebo. But before you pick up your tools, some careful planning is in order.

Here you'll learn how to evaluate your site to take advantage of some of its features and minimize the effects of others. A base map of your site *(page 226)* will help you see how all your yard's elements can work together to create a pleasing design. Finally, you'll find architect-designed plans for two lots—one small, one large—illustrating ways to turn your own space into the backyard of your dreams.

One goal of good planning is to harmonize various elements. This is achieved in the backyard above, where a concrete patio frames a garden pool. The pavers are softened by lush plantings.

SUN AND SHADE

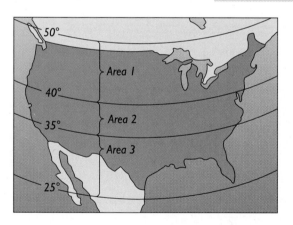

How much sun a site receives depends on its orientation. A site that faces north tends to receive little sun, while a south-facing site is warmed by the sun all day. An east-facing site receives only morning sun; a west-facing one gets the full force of the afternoon sun. The seasonal path of the sun also affects your site. The sun crosses the sky in an arc that changes slightly every day, becoming lower in winter and higher in summer; changes in this path also alter shade patterns in a yard. You can determine where the sun will fall on different areas of your yard at various times of the year by finding your location on the map *(left)*, then referring to the chart below for sun angles.

THE SUN IN YOUR YARD

SEASONAL SUN ANGLES	SUN'S POSITION/HOURS OF DAYLIGHT (SEE MAP ABOVE)		
Season	Area 1	Area 2	Area 3
A) 12/21, Noon	21°/8 hrs.	29°/9 hrs.	37°/10 hrs.
B) 3/21 and 9/21, Noon	45°/12 hrs.	53°/12 hrs.	60°/12 hrs.
C) 6/21, Noon	69°/16 hrs.	76°/15 hrs.	83°/14 hrs.

Understanding Weather

While no one has yet learned how to change the weather, there are ways to moderate its influence. This is especially important when you are designing your backyard in order to make the best use of it throughout the year.

Wind, rain, and snow: Having too much wind on a cool day can be just as unpleasant as no breeze at all on a hot day. You can locate patios and decks in sheltered areas, as shown at right *(top)*. Or you can encourage or control wind with fences, screens, or plants.

Rain and snow can also be neutralized by careful planning. For example, if you know that winter storms generally blow in from the north or east, you can choose to locate your patio or deck on the south side of the house, where it will take less of a beating. Or if you live in an area of frequent summer cloudbursts, you can build a covered structure where you can sit outside during summer rains.

Identifying microclimates: Weather pockets created by very localized conditions—also known as microclimates—can exert their own influence on your backyard. A recorded temperature of 68° in the shade, for example, can feel like 62° if it is accompanied by a 15-mile-an-hour wind. Although sun and wind exposure are the major factors of these microclimates, they're not the only ones. Several potential microclimate considerations are shown at right.

DEALING WITH WIND

Prevailing wind

An open fence
A lattice screen or fence can break up a strong wind into a series of more pleasant breezes.

Prevailing wind

House-protected site
Your house can act as a barrier to the prevailing winds.

MICROCLIMATES

Light materials at noon
Light surfaces spread sun and heat.

Downhill air movement
Cold air flows downhill like water, forming "puddles" in basins, which can be dammed by walls or solid fences. If you build a sunken patio, you may find yourself shivering at sunset, while higher surroundings are quite balmy.

Cold air

Dark surfaces at night
Masonry releases absorbed heat.

Deciduous plantings (winter)
Skeletal branches let the sun warm the patio.

Deciduous plantings (summer)
Summer foliage shades the patio.

Developing a Backyard Plan

This section will cover the factors you should consider when planning the location of various backyard elements. Once you've taken these into account, draw a site plan like the one shown below. Some helpful tools for this are illustrated on page 228. The following information should appear on your site plan:

Boundary lines, dimensions, and structures: Outline your property accurately and to scale, mark the dimensions, and indicate any required setback allowances *(see opposite page)* from your lot lines. Show your house (and other structures) precisely and to scale. Note all overhangs, exterior doors and the direction that they open.

Exposure: With a compass, mark North on your plan. Indicate the direction of the prevailing winds, any windy spots you want to shield, and the shaded and sunlit areas of your landscape.

Utilities and easements: Map the location of outdoor faucets and all underground lines, including the sewer or septic system. If you're contemplating a tall structure, mark any overhead lines; note any easements *(see opposite)* and check local regulations that may limit development of those areas.

Downspouts and drainage: Mark the locations of all downspouts and drainage tiles, drainpipes, or catch basins. Note the direction of drainage, any point where drainage is impeded (leaving soggy soil) and any place where runoff from a steep hillside could cause erosion.

Existing plantings and views: If you're remodeling an old landscape, note any established plantings that you want to retain. Also indicate all views—attractive or unattractive—from every side of your property and consider views into your yard from neighboring houses or streets.

SAMPLE BACKYARD SITE PLAN DRAWN TO SCALE

Local Regulations

Before you go too far in planning your backyard landscape, consult your local building department for specific regulations. For many structural projects, such as a deck, you will need to file for a building permit and comply with all the appropriate code requirements. Also be aware of local zoning ordinances, which can determine what and where you can build.

Code requirements vary from region to region, setting minimum safety standards for materials and construction techniques, helping to ensure that any structures you build will be safe for you and any future owners of your property.

These municipal regulations restrict the height of residential buildings, limit lot coverage, specify setbacks, and may stipulate architectural design standards you need to follow.

Be sure to get the required permits before you begin construc-tion: Officials can fine you as well as require you to bring an improperly built structure up to standard, or even to dismantle it.

Where can I build?

Lot coverage limits
The allowable percentage of the lot that all structures can cover. Any structure you build (a deck or patio, for example) increases your overall lot coverage—an important consideration since it might limit future additions to your home.

Easements
Areas that must be left accessible to someone other than the property owner, such as utility workers. Often specified on the deed.

Height limit
The maximum height for structures.

Setback
The minimum distance between a building or other structure and the property lines.

WORKING WITH PROFESSIONALS

Whatever your needs, professionals are available at every stage of the design and installation process.

Landscape and building architects: These state-licensed professionals can help you set objectives, analyze the site, and produce detailed working plans. Landscape architects specialize in outdoor structures, but if your project poses particular engineering problems, you can consult a building architect.

Landscape designers: Landscape designers often have a landscape architect's education and training, but not a state license. They can generally offer the same services as a landscape architect, and are often more experienced in residential projects.

Structural and soils engineers: Your town may require that your plans be approved by a structural or soils engineer. An engineer's stamp may be required if the structure will be on an unstable or a steep lot, or if strong winds or heavy loads are a factor.

Landscape contractors: Trained to install landscapes: plantings, pavings, structures, and irrigation systems, landscape contractors may also offer design services. On a large project, the contractor assumes the responsibility of hiring and supervising the subcontractors, if any are required.

Landscaping Basics

When you're planning your land-scape, you need to consider more than just what structural elements you require. You also need to consider how they'll work together to create a pleasing whole, and how foot-traffic will move through it. Keep in mind the landscaping principles discussed on page 20—unity, variety, proportion, and balance. Designing with these principles in mind should ensure a pleasing result.

Think about the relation of structural elements to both the garden and the house. If, for instance, you're planning a covered sitting area off the living room, consider whether the overhead will make the room too dark. If your design looks too blocky, try varying the shapes of some elements—change a square patio to a polygon, or add a curve to the edge of a deck to lead the eye toward an interesting garden feature. Try to think in three dimensions; ideally, you want variety from the horizontal plane.

You'll want the colors of your landscape to complement each other, so keep color in mind as you choose structural materials. Don't forget to consider your house: since it's the most prominent feature of your landscape, the materials for other structures in your yard should harmonize with it.

Visualize foot-traffic to and from the house and the various areas you're considering, and through the garden. Will too much traffic be channeled through areas meant for relaxation? Can guests move easily from the entertainment area into the rest of the backyard?

These are the basic elements of good design that you should consider as you're drawing your balloon sketches *(opposite)*.

TOOLS OF THE TRADE

It doesn't take an artist to design an outdoor environment—just a few basic drawing tools. Even if you don't have all the tools shown here, you can make do with graph paper and a ruler. You'll need tracing paper to sketch your design ideas on top of your base map. Note: If you own a computer, there are programs on the market that deal with landscape design.

Drafting brush
Keeps board and drawings clean.

Drawing board
Any flat surface with one true, straight edge and with a vinyl cover to keep the surface smooth. Can be homemade from a vinyl sheet (available at art supply stores) fastened to a board with double-faced tape.

Protractor
Measures and marks angles.

Compass
For drawing circles and arcs.

Templates
Patterns for most common sizes of circles, arcs, and other geometrical figures; found at art or drafting supply stores.

Architect's scale
Flat or triangular scale rule. Flat type is easier to read, but triangular models have more scales.

Triangles
Laid on top of T-square or rule to draw vertical and angled lines. Buy a 45° and a 30°/60° model. Can be combined to mark 15°, 75°, or 105°.

Parallel rule
Used to draw horizontal lines; rides on wires attached to the drawing board.

Eraser
Type intended for pencil.

Pencils
Wood or mechanical type. Choose medium lead between HB and 3H; have several different leads on hand for different weights of line or lettering.

Erasing shield
Exposes line to be erased, protecting lines to be saved.

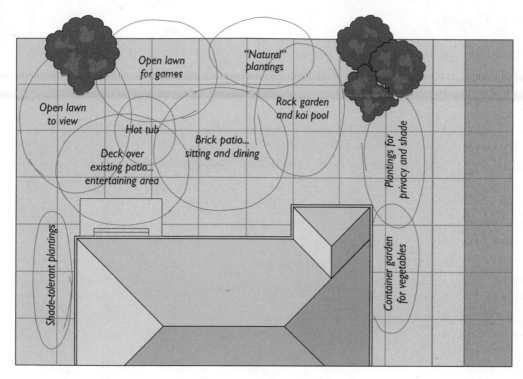

Open lawn
for games

"Natural"
plantings

Open lawn
to view

Rock garden
and koi pool

Hot tub

Brick patio...
sitting and dining

Deck over
existing patio...
entertaining area

Plantings for
privacy and shade

Shade-tolerant plantings

Container garden
for vegetables

CREATING A BALLOON SKETCH

Review and establish your priorities. How do you want to use your backyard? Do you need space for entertaining, recreation, relaxation, storage, or some combination of these? Make a list, and keep it in front of you as you draw, but remember that your project may end up requiring some trade-offs. Place tracing paper over your base map (page 226) and sketch "balloons"—rough circles or ovals—to indicate use areas and other features. Use a different sheet of paper for each design, and draw as many as you need to clarify your ideas. At this stage, changes cost nothing.

As you draw, concentrate on logical placement and juxtaposition. Are you locating a children's play area in full view of your living area? Is the small, private space you envision easily accessible from the master bedroom? Do you really want a patio designed for entertaining guests located next to your trash bins?

Plan generously—you can always cut back later if the plan becomes too costly. Creating a strong design now will help you distinguish the elements you care most about from those you are willing to forgo.

SELECTING STRUCTURES

What structures do you need to include to create your own ideal outdoor environment? Which materials will work best? As you begin to firm up your design, keep these elements in mind:

- Retaining walls for hilly or sloping areas
- Walls, fences, or screens for privacy or noise control
- Patio roof or gazebo
- Decking or paving materials
- Steps or formal stairs for changes in level
- Walks and footpaths linking use areas
- Edgings where appropriate

CHOOSING AMENITIES

Of course you can add finishing touches to your yard at any time on an on-going basis, but now is the best time to think about the amenities you want and to sketch them on your design. Here are some items you might want to consider:

- Garden pool, fountain, waterfall, or stream
- Spa or hot tub
- Outdoor heater or fire pit
- Barbecue area or kitchen facilities
- Storage shed
- Built-in benches or other furniture
- Outdoor lighting (120-volt or low-voltage)
- Raised beds for plants or built-in planters
- Outdoor water faucet

Design Ideas for a Small Lot

Suppose you have a flat, rectangular backyard that's nondescript and very small. What could you do with the space?

That was the challenge faced by three architects from different regions of the country who were each given the plan shown below, and the following information about the hypothetical owners: The owners are professionals in their early forties, with two teenagers and no pets. They do not wish to make any structural changes to the house, but want a relaxing, beautiful retreat with plants that are in keeping with their climate and water resources.

The three solutions illustrate that, for just about any situation, there are likely to be a number of successful treatments.

THE BASIC LOT

Not only is this lot flat and empty, but there are no special features or plants on the neighboring properties worth including visually. In fact, there are some undesirable elements: a second-story deck on the house next door, a shed abutting the back corner of the property, wood side fences that are in poor condition, and a neighbor's swing set and tetherball pole that are visible above an unattractive back wall.

New England Appeal
An expansive light red brick patio off the family room looks right at home in this design; header courses of darker bricks echo the line of the lattice trellis enclosure. Azaleas and hydrangeas on one side of the door and a kitchen herb garden on the other add color. On the garden side, stepping-stones lead to a small stone pool and fountain. Two rhododendrons, a vernal witch hazel, and a kousa dogwood hide the shed; a sour gum tree anchors the opposite (southwest) corner. A bench with built-in uplights is tucked below the trellis along the back wall.

Landscape architect: Carol R. Johnson & Associates, Inc., Cambridge, Massachusetts.

Northwest Cedar Deck

The availability of wood in the Pacific Northwest and the popularity of the outdoors result in this low-level deck solution. New French doors flanked by colorful pots open to a decking of 2x4s laid on edge in a semicircular pattern. Steps stretch out as patio seating. A pop-out window off the kitchen is filled with herbs; below is a garden storage area. A stepping-stone pathway, with river rock in between, skirts the moss garden, which functions like grass but needs no mowing. Three vine maples hide the shed, a fourth screens out the neighbor's deck. A fountain in the southwest corner has three basalt columns with the lowest drilled for a recirculating bubbler. A vine-covered trellis provides enclosure.

Landscape architect: Harvard and Associates, Seattle, Washington

Stepping-stone pathway

Vine maple

Pop-out window

Moss garden

Vine maples

Fountain

Trellis

Trellis

Bougainvilleas

Concrete landing

Trumpet vine

Pool

The California Solution

Local flagstone paving, natural boulders, and waterwise plantings distinguish this design from Southern California. Cut-stone pavers set 18 inches below floor level are reached by a cast concrete landing and steps softened by a large planter. In the south corner, the pavers give way to an angular garden pool with waterfall. Native boulders retain planting beds. Privacy is ensured by new stucco walls clad with trumpet vine; by a two-story, bougainvillea-covered trellis that screens the eastern view; and by Leyland cypress trees that block both the shed and the neighbors' second-story deck.

Landscape architect: Eriksson, Peters, Thoms, San Juan Capistrano, California.

Stucco wall

Leyland cypress

BUILDING IN YOUR BACKYARD   231

Design Ideas for a Large Lot

As with the small lot shown on the preceding pages, the designs shown here are landscape architects' suggestions for how to handle the sample lot below. This time, the lot is larger, with room for a few amenities, and with a sloping grade that opens up a number of options.

It's now empty except for a tree and a small concrete slab, neither of which the owners feel has to be preserved. A door from the living room leads out to the existing concrete slab patio. The bedrooms, several feet above grade in this split-level house, offer a view of the backyard.

Again, the hypothetical owners are professionals with two teenage children. They enjoy outdoor entertaining, but would also like space for private relaxation. They are willing to make a few structural changes, such as installing a masonry patio, a wooden deck, or a spa or swimming pool, in order to realize their goals. As well, the owners want to screen out the view of their neighbor's backyard on one side of their property.

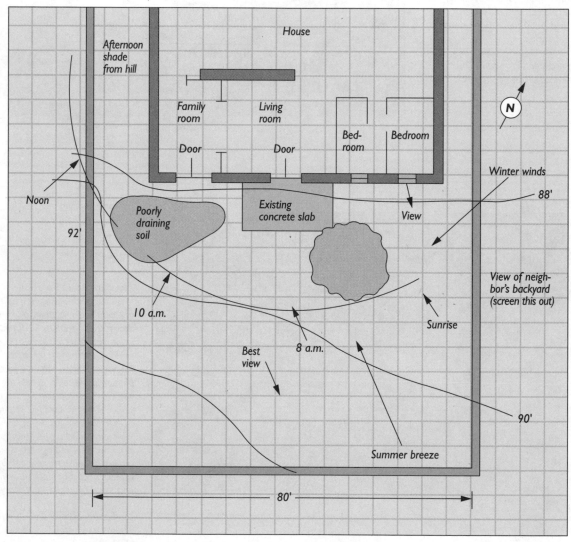

The Basic Lot
Bare except for a tree and a small concrete slab, the lot slopes several feet to the house. Doors from both the family room and living room lead outside.

Bluestone pavement cut pattern

Bluestone pavement irregular pattern

Spa

Stone wall

Lap pool

Sculpture

Evergreen edge

Neat and Orderly

Formal and precise, this plan has bluestone pavement in an irregular but highly crafted version off the living room and a 2-foot cut pattern for the main patio area. The large lawn and 12x40-foot lap pool with integral spa are major activity areas; here, the lot has been graded flat, and drainage provided. The lap pool reflects the sky; the sculpture at the end of the pool is an important focal point and can be viewed from the bedrooms. The hillside garden in the south corner, visible from the house and patio, provides texture and color, as does the perennial garden at the corner of the patio. A high evergreen hedge screens the adjacent property and establishes a visually protected environment. Stone walls set off the geometric patio area from the softer plantings.

Landscape architect: Stephenson & Good, Washington, D.C.

Many Spaces in One

This multispace, multilevel solution artfully combines a variety of materials and use areas. The principal patio surface is flagstone, accessed from the house by sliding glass doors. Beyond is an expanse of lawn—a possible future pool site—along with a private sitting alcove fitted with a built-in bench, and partially shaded by tall trees. Flagstones laid in sand provide the paving underfoot.

Opposite, steps climb up to a wood deck equipped with a barbecue, a tiled serving counter, and built-in seating. The deck opens at the back to a boulder-edged natural pool and small waterfall. Behind is a second, more private deck, complete with a spa and an arbor with built-in towel racks and lights. Drought-tolerant plantings line fences and property lines; thirstier plants are near the house.

Landscape architect: Ransohoff, Blanchfield, Jones, Inc., Redwood City, California.

Flagstone

Flagstones laid in sand

Bench

Tiled serving counter

Pool

Tall trees

Spa

Arbor

Dealing with Drainage

Good drainage is critical to any well conceived backyard. Without it, prized pavings and precious plants can be ruined by puddles or ponds. Worse still, runoff can leave scars on unprotected slopes and even undermine the house.

Most drainage problems can be avoided by proper grading. The key is to keep water flowing away from your house and other structures. If problems arise, try solving them with one or more of the methods covered on the following pages.

A Few Drainage Solutions

Before you make changes to improve drainage, it's a good idea to contact your building department for any permits you might need. Also, make sure that your runoff finds its way to a sewer or storm drain and not your neighbor's property.

Grading: All horizontal backyard surfaces, with the exception of decks, should be sloped away from the house at a minimum grade of ⅛ inch per foot, so that water runs off before it forms puddles.

In difficult cases, grading will require the services of a landscape contractor. In general though, you can take some fairly simple action of your own to deal with the majority of grading problems. For many homeowners, this may mean nothing more than leveling humps, filling depressions, and smoothing out the ground to provide a gentle slope and a swale to carry the water away. If you need to improve grading in one specific location, such as the site for a new patio, there are a few quick and easy steps you can follow (see opposite page).

Drainage systems: Along with grading, it's smart to provide added drainage to direct water away from patios, walkways, and other pavings. You'll find a couple of easy-to-install drainage systems, along with a dry well for collecting water, on page 236.

Retaining walls: If your backyard slopes, you may need to build a retaining wall to hold the earth in place during times of heavy runoff. The average do-it-yourselfer can handle small walls, although those over two feet high require a permit in most municipalities, and anything over four feet needs to be designed by an engineer. You'll find different types of retaining walls illustrated on page 237.

GRADING OVERVIEW
This illustration shows how a properly graded site improves overall drainage. The land slopes away from structures so that runoff is directed toward the street or a swale (low-lying stretch of land).

Slope

Swale

Deck

House

Swale

Street

Slope

Swale

Grading for a Patio

1 Measure the grade

Before grading, outline your site with stakes driven into the ground. *(To learn how to make square corners, turn to page 262.)* Mark your preferred level for the patio on the corner stake against the house. Attach a length of string at the mark and stretch it toward the outside corner stake; level the string with a line level placed at the center of the span *(inset)*. Mark the outside corner stake where the line crosses it. Repeat for each stake. Calculate the amount you need to drop the marks downward to achieve a standard grade of 1 inch in 8 and mark it on each outside stake below the level mark. Add a few more stakes along the sides of the outlined site and attach reference lines to them *(right)*. This will form a grid that will guide the excavation.

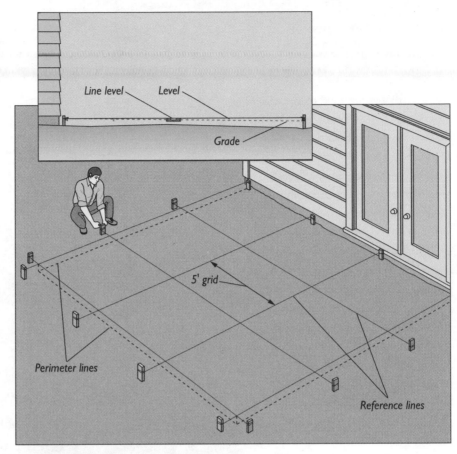

Line level Level

Grade

5' grid

Perimeter lines

Reference lines

2 Excavate the site

Measure down from the grid lines and use a square-sided shovel to excavate below the lines to a depth equal to the paving thickness plus the thickness of the setting bed. Take shallow scoops, working parallel to the ground to remove the minimum amount of soil needed for the correct depth. If you need to even out a low spot, use sand, spreading it evenly with a rake; moisten it, then tamp it several times with a hand tamper or a rented power vibrator.

DRAINAGE SYSTEMS

Whenever you pave an area, its drainage is affected, since water tends to run off even the most porous paving. A site with a natural slope, or one that has been graded to create a slope (page 234), will handle the surface runoff effectively. Often, the bed below the paving, whether it's sand or a thicker layer of gravel, will provide adequate drainage. But sometimes, additional provisions are necessary. Shown here are different ways to handle runoff around a paved site. Note: If your backyard needs one of these systems, and you plan to do the work yourself, remember that both the surface drain box and perforated drainpipe setup require placing concrete. For tips on working with concrete, turn to page 247.

Dry well
To build a dry well, dig a 2- to 4-foot-wide hole at least 3 feet deep (keep the bottom above the water table). Next, dig trenches for the drainpipes that will carry water into the dry well from other areas. Fill the dry well with coarse gravel or small rocks, then cover it with impervious material, such as heavy roofing felt, and conceal it with topsoil.

Perforated drainpipe
Perforated drainpipes drain water from under pavings. Place pipe, perforated side down, in a trench dug 12 inches deep (deeper in frost areas) under the center or around the edge of the site. Pack in 6 inches of gravel and replace with soil. To route a drainage trench through a mortared patio, as shown, first form a concrete channel; then leave open (ungrouted) joints between units bridging the trench.

Surface drain box
To drain water from a low-lying area, install a surface drain box, digging the hole for it at the lowest point. Set a ready-made concrete box (available at building supply stores) into the hole or place the concrete yourself. Set a grate on top and dig a sloping trench from the hole for a drainpipe to direct water toward a dry well or storm drain (if permitted).

RETAINING WALLS

The safest way to build a retaining wall is to locate it at the bottom of a gentle slope and fill in behind it with soil. The hill can also be held with a series of low, terraced walls, or with a single high wall. Notice that each of the walls illustrated here rests on cut or undisturbed ground, never on fill. Retaining walls must have adequate drainage to prevent water from building up behind them. Subsurface water can be collected in a gravel backfill and channeled away either through a drainpipe behind the wall or through weep holes spaced along the wall at ground level.

Dry stone
This stone wall can be laid without mortar and is a good choice for a low, fairly stable slope. The stones' uneven surfaces will help hold them in place. Soil-filled pockets between the rocks are ideal for colorful plantings.

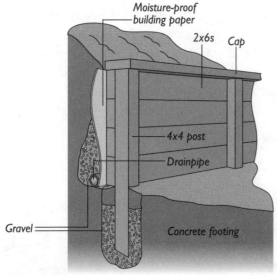

Dimension lumber
This wooden wall can be made of decay-resistant dimension lumber (such as redwood or treated lumber) set vertically or horizontally. Moisture-proof building paper helps preserve the wood. Anchor the posts in concrete and use a 2-by-6 cap to strengthen the wall and provide a garden seat.

Railway ties
Railway ties offer a bold, rugged look for this wall. The ties are stacked in a shallow trench with their joints staggered; pipes add strength. Runoff seeps through joints.

Concrete blocks
Concrete blocks are ideal for a high wall. The blocks rest on a reinforced footing; horizontal reinforcing can be added as needed. A ¾-inch coat of mortar, or parge coat, troweled onto the back of the wall will help to control dampness on the face. Consult your building department before attempting such a complex job.

Patios and Walkways

Virtually every modern backyard has either a patio or a walkway—often both—as a key element. Patios provide a perfect location for dining and entertaining, and walkways can lead visitors through a garden or to a swimming pool. Here and on the following pages you'll find a few of the material choices you can make for your patio finish—whether it be pavers that you can easily lay yourself, or a cast-in-place decorative concrete slab, a job that is best left to a professional *(see page 246)*. You'll also learn how to lay a simple concrete walkway. And whatever your paved area, the edgings shown on the opposite page will help you define it.

Choosing a Patio Paving

Before selecting your paving material, consider cost, upkeep, and durability. Then think about how you want to use your patio. Smooth surfaces are great for dancing, for example, but are slippery when wet—not good near a pool. Rough surfaces, with more traction, are best if the area will be used for games, but are too absorbent to be practical near a barbecue. In hot, sunny areas, consider non-reflective materials. Below are the characteristics of six choices. Cast concrete interlocking pavers are the most common.

Brick
A traditional surface. Needs to be reworked after severe freezes.

Interlocking pavers
Very durable. Special edging pieces make finishing easy.

Adobe
Its rounded, massive form looks good with crevice planting.

Tile
Creates a more formal effect and a smoother, more reflective surface.

Mexican pavers
Octagonal units have a grainy, hand-crafted look. Small squares complete the pattern.

Stone
Rugged finish resists scratches and stains; gives a rough-hewn effect.

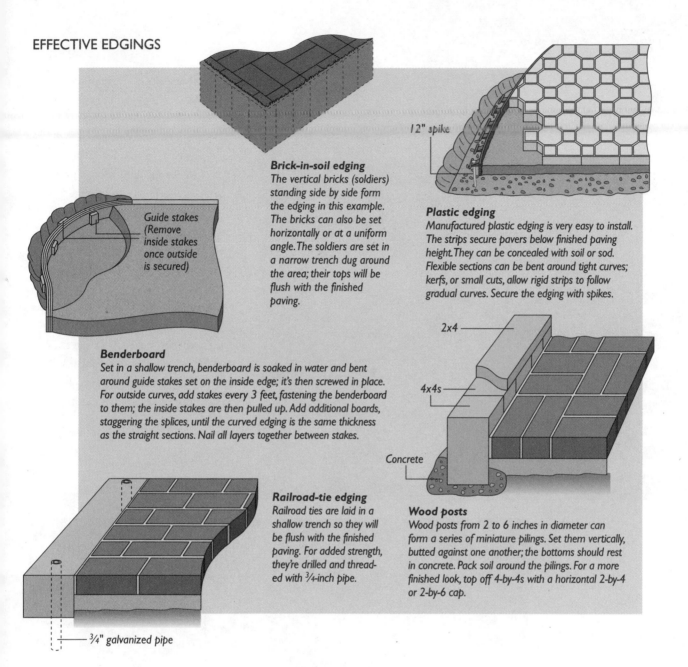

Brick-in-soil edging
The vertical bricks (soldiers) standing side by side form the edging in this example. The bricks can also be set horizontally or at a uniform angle. The soldiers are set in a narrow trench dug around the area; their tops will be flush with the finished paving.

Guide stakes (Remove inside stakes once outside is secured)

12" spike

Plastic edging
Manufactured plastic edging is very easy to install. The strips secure pavers below finished paving height. They can be concealed with soil or sod. Flexible sections can be bent around tight curves; kerfs, or small cuts, allow rigid strips to follow gradual curves. Secure the edging with spikes.

Benderboard
Set in a shallow trench, benderboard is soaked in water and bent around guide stakes set on the inside edge; it's then screwed in place. For outside curves, add stakes every 3 feet, fastening the benderboard to them; the inside stakes are then pulled up. Add additional boards, staggering the splices, until the curved edging is the same thickness as the straight sections. Nail all layers together between stakes.

2x4

4x4s

Concrete

Railroad-tie edging
Railroad ties are laid in a shallow trench so they will be flush with the finished paving. For added strength, they're drilled and threaded with ¾-inch pipe.

Wood posts
Wood posts from 2 to 6 inches in diameter can form a series of miniature pilings. Set them vertically, butted against one another; the bottoms should rest in concrete. Pack soil around the pilings. For a more finished look, top off 4-by-4s with a horizontal 2-by-4 or 2-by-6 cap.

¾" galvanized pipe

Defining the Area with Edging

Almost any patio or walkway will require some form of edging. In addition to outlining the space, edgings confine the surfacing material within a desired area, an important function when you're using loose materials, casting concrete or setting pavers in sand. When used to curb paved areas, edgings are usually installed after the base has been prepared, but before the paving is laid. Edgings are very often made of wood, but other materials also can provide the same defining and containing functions with attractive results, as illustrated above. Invisible brick and concrete curb edgings are featured on page 240.

If you are planning to use a wood edging, choose a wood that is highly resistant to rot and termites, such as pressure-treated lumber or the heartwood of cedar, redwood, or certain types of cypress. Redwood is a good choice for benderboard.

Plastic and brick-in-soil edgings are the easiest to make, but you must have firm soil to hold bricks. Invisible brick edges are strong and are good for brick-in-sand paving.

Two kinds of brick edging

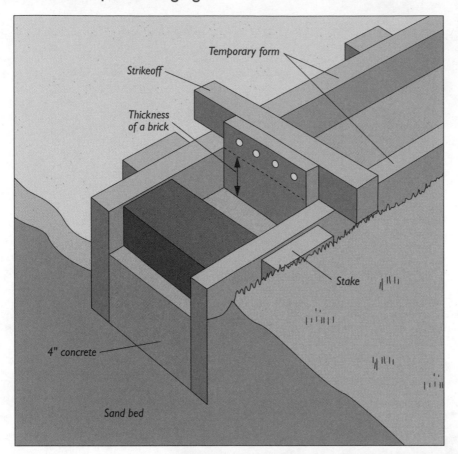

Temporary form

Strikeoff

Thickness of a brick

Stake

4" concrete

Sand bed

Build an "invisible" brick edging

So-called invisible edging secures paving units without any obvious support. Set temporary form boards made of 2x8 lumber next to the sand bed that will support the paving units for the walkway or patio. The forms should be one brick length apart, and nailed to 2x2 or 1x4 stakes. Place concrete between the boards to a depth of about 4", then use a strikeoff to level the concrete one brick thickness below the top of the form. As you move the strikeoff along, place bricks in the concrete and set them with a few taps of a rubber mallet. After the concrete has cured, remove the form. Use the brick edging as a guide to strike off the sand, then add the paving units.

Create a curb

Concrete edgings are done in a manner similar to invisible edgings, except that the concrete is placed higher, to be level with the masonry units. Use 2x4 lumber for the temporary form and strike the concrete off flush with the top of the form as you would for a concrete walkway (page 250), creating a curb for the paving units.

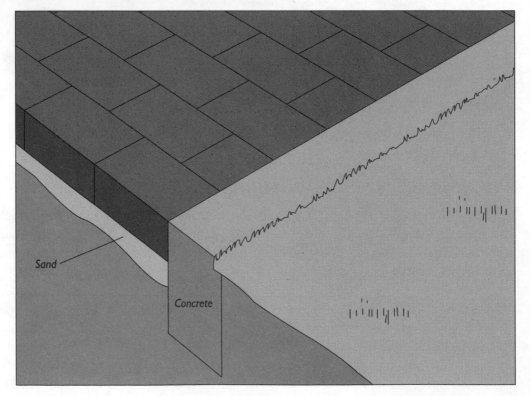

Sand

Concrete

240

Laying Down Your Pavers

The method for laying unit paving depends on the material you have decided to use. Bricks, for example, may be set in sand, or in wet or dry mortar. (A few of the most popular brick patterns are illustrated below).

Concrete pavers are set in sand and most align almost automatically. Non-interlocking concrete pavers can be set in either sand or in dry mortar. If you have to cut a few pavers, you can probably do the job with a brickset, scoring the paver on all four sides and then making the cut with one sharp blow. But for numerous or complex cuts, rent a machine called a tub saw, fitted with a diamond blade. Wear safety goggles for the job.

Adobe pavers are laid in sand with 1-inch sand or dirt-filled joints. The large joints help accommodate size irregularities in the individual adobe blocks, improve drainage, and allow for crevice planting. Adobe is cut the same way as brick.

Tiles can be dry mortared, but are best mortared over concrete slabs and wood decks. They are cut with a tile cutter or a tile nipper.

Flagstone is heavy enough that it can be laid directly on stable soil, or in sand or mortar. It's cut with a hand-drilling hammer and brickset or stonemason's chisel.

Pick a Pattern

Building with brick is pleasant work. The units are easy to lift with one hand and require only the most basic tools and technique. Moreover, a brick path or patio can be graceful as well as sturdy. This traditional and simple surface lends itself to a broad range of interesting colors, textures, and patterns that can complement and harmonize with many styles of home and garden.

Running bond   *Jack on jack*   *Diagonal herringbone/jack on jack*

Basket weave   *Herringbone*   *Basket weave/grid system*

Setting bricks in sand

Strike off
2" sand bed
Edging
Temporary guides

1 Strike off the base
To grade the area to be paved, set temporary 2x4 guides inside the edgings defining the perimeter so they're about 3' apart and one brick-thickness below the finished grade. Place dampened sand between the guides, striking it off, about 3' at a time, with a straight piece of lumber. Tamp the sand, then restrike as necessary.

Trowel
Mason's line
Dip to be filled in after removing temporary guides

2 Set the bricks
Remove the temporary guides, using a trowel to fill indentations with sand and smooth. Work outward from a corner, tapping the bricks into place with a mallet. Use a mason's line to help with the alignment.

Bench brush

3 Sand the joints
Spread fine sand over the surface of finished paving. Let it dry, then sweep it into the joints, resanding as needed to fill them. Spray the finished paving with a gentle mist to help settle the sand.

Hand-drilling hammer
Brickset
Scored line

Tap the brickset until you score the brick, then cut it through with a final blow.

CUTTING BRICK

If you want really precise brickwork, or if you're using extra-hard bricks such as "clinkers," you'll need to rent a masonry saw. Softer bricks are easier to cut without a saw. Wearing safety goggles to protect against flying debris, place the brick on sand or earth and score it by tapping a brickset with a hand-drilling hammer, as shown at left. Score all around the brick, then cut it with a sharp blow to the brickset.

Laying adobe pavers

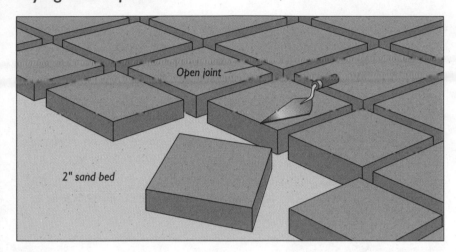

2" sand bed

Open joint

Set adobe in sand
Strike off and flatten a 2" sand bed. Set the adobes as you would bricks, but take extra care that the blocks don't straddle humps or bridge hollows; otherwise, they may crack. Leave 1" open joints between the adobes so you can pack them with sand or earth later.

Borders For Your Adobe

There are several ways to contain adobe paving units once you lay them down. In general, if the surface is flush with the ground, you can simply pack the surrounding soil against the edges of the area to retain the pavers. If the top of the finished paving will be above ground level, consider one of the three edgings illustrated below. Added reinforcing bars are a good idea when working with wood edgings.

Railway-tie edging

Stepped adobe edging

5½"x4"x16" adobe edging

2" sand bed

12"x4"x16" adobe

Adobe blocks

Railway ties

Reinforcing bars

Redwood edging

Pipe or reinforcing bar

Redwood 2x4 edging

2" sand bed

Among the options for adobe edging is adobe itself. As shown above, a stepped adobe edging hugs the paver units while sitting on a larger adobe block for support. Railway ties and redwood also hold pavings firm.

Laying tiles in wet mortar

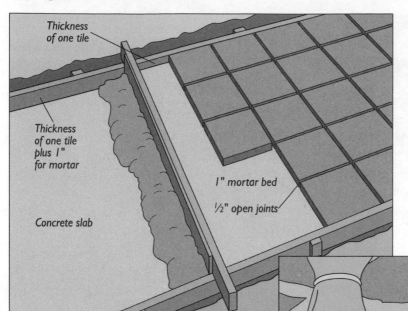

Thickness of one tile

Thickness of one tile plus 1" for mortar

1" mortar bed

½" open joints

Concrete slab

1 Place the tiles
Place temporary edgings over a concrete slab in small, easy-to-work sections. Then lay, smooth, and strike off a 1" mortar bed. Prepare the mortar using a 1:4 cement-sand mix with no lime. Lay the tiles flush with the top of the edgings, which can be removed after the mortar has set. Use wood or special plastic tile spacers to maintain ½" joints between the tiles; remove the spacers before you fill the joints, at least 24 hours later.

2 Fill the joints
Prepare the joint mortar using a 1:3 cement-sand mix with no lime. It should be just thin enough to pour. Form a spout on the top lip of a metal container, such as a coffee can, and pour the mortar into the joints. When it's hard enough to sustain a thumbprint, smooth the joints with a convex tool, such as a broom handle.

Cement-sand mortar

MASONRY CLEANING TIPS

Masonry is not immune to staining. Fortunately, there are products at your local masonry store or home supply center that can clean up most accidents. Always read the label before mixing or applying them and follow all safety instructions. Note: Acid washes (and bleach) can affect surface color. Test them on a small area first.

To remove a mortar smear, use muriatic acid. On concrete, concrete block, and dark brick, a 1:9 acid-water solution is best. Use a 1:14 or 1:19 mix on light-colored brick. Do not use acid on colored concrete, marble, or limestone. First wet the area; then apply the acid with a stiff brush, let it stand for 3 or 4 minutes, and flush thoroughly with water.

Freshly spilled paint can be cleaned up with a rag soaked in the solvent specified for the paint. For dried paint, use a commercial paint remover.

For oil and grease, scatter sawdust or cement powder on the spot right away. If caught in time, the oil and grease can be swept up. If the stain has penetrated, try dissolving it with a commercial degreaser. Residual stains can sometimes be lightened with household bleach.

Rust stains can also be lightened with household bleach. Scrub it in, let it stand, then rinse. A stronger remedy is a pound of oxalic acid mixed into a gallon of water. Brush on the acid, let it stand for 3 or 4 minutes, then hose it off.

Setting flagstone in sand

Level

Rubber mallet

Hand-drilling hammer

Scored line

Brickset

2" sand bed

Lay the stone

Lay the stones in a 2" sand bed as you would for adobe *(see page 243)*. Edgings are optional. Scoop out or fill in the sand as needed to make up for differences in the thicknesses of the stones. Adjust the pattern and the joint spacing as you work, and make sure the area is level; fill the joints with soil. When trimming a stone to fit a pattern, decide where the trim line will be, then mark it. Score the line with a brickset or chisel *(inset)*. Prop the edge to be cut off on a wood scrap, then cut all the way through by striking the brickset.

Laying flagstone in wet mortar

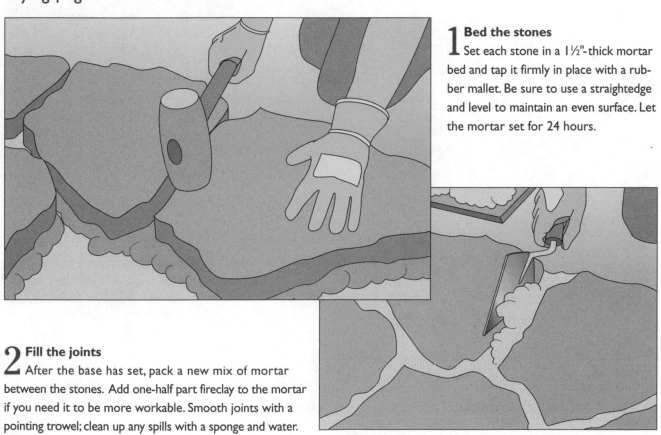

1 Bed the stones

Set each stone in a 1½"-thick mortar bed and tap it firmly in place with a rubber mallet. Be sure to use a straightedge and level to maintain an even surface. Let the mortar set for 24 hours.

2 Fill the joints

After the base has set, pack a new mix of mortar between the stones. Add one-half part fireclay to the mortar if you need it to be more workable. Smooth joints with a pointing trowel; clean up any spills with a sponge and water.

Finishing a Patio in Concrete

A concrete slab patio has its advantages: it's relatively inexpensive and will last for many years. On the other hand, laying a slab can be tricky work, and once it's done, it's very difficult to undo. For the latter reasons, it's a good idea to hire a professional to do the job. However, you might choose to do the site preparation yourself, then get a professional for the pour.

In preparing the site, there are a few things to keep in mind. First, pay special attention to preparing the subbase. Follow the procedure outlined for making a concrete walkway on pages 248 and 249. Divide the area into sections by adding 2-by-4 dividers in a grid pattern, as shown below. The dividers, made of rot-resistant or pressure-treated lumber, allow for settling and expansion of the slab and the exposed top edges act as decorative elements.

One attractive solution to a plain gray concrete slab is cast-in-place architectural concrete paving. This is a job that has to be done by a professional, who can offer you a choice of dozens of colors, textures, and patterns *(see example below)*.

The advantage of architectural paving is the cost: this concrete solution combines the beauty of natural materials with the durability and the relatively low cost of concrete. This material can also be used for walkways and pool decks—and even interior flooring.

ANATOMY OF A PATIO

Architectural paving

Concrete slab (4"-thick)

Divider

Stake every 4'

Gravel bed 4"-6" thick

2x4 forms

Graded subsoil

1/2"x4" expansion joint strip

Mixing Concrete by Hand

Mortar hoe

Mortar box

Use a mortar hoe

To work with 1 to 2 cubic feet of concrete at a time, use a high-sided contractor's wheelbarrow or a homemade or commercial mortar box for mixing, and measure the ingredients with a shovel. First, place the sand in the box and add the cement, mixing well with a mortar hoe (or a flat-ended shovel); add the gravel and mix again. Next, mound up the mixture and hollow the center to form a well, then pour in the water. Work around the hollow, pulling dry ingredients into the water, enlarging the size of the well. Keep mixing until the blend is uniform in color. Note: Air-entrained concrete *(described below)* must be mixed with a power mixer. When working with concrete, wear rubber gloves to protect your hands.

A CONCRETE FORMULA

The following formula will give you good results for most residential footing and paving projects. You'll need to decide first whether you want the basic mix, or one that contains an air-entraining agent for freezing climates.

Basic concrete formula: All proportions are by volume and based on the use of ¾-inch coarse aggregate (stone).

> 1 part portland cement
> 2½ parts sand
> 2½ parts stone or gravel
>   aggregate
> ½ part water

Making air-entraining concrete: Adding an air-entraining agent—a liquid component that creates microscopic air bubbles in the finished concrete—helps concrete resist freeze-thaw damage in colder regions. The agent also makes concrete more workable and easier to place. The extra workability means you can add

less water to a batch, making the finished concrete stronger. For this reason, an air-entraining agent should be used with ready-mix, whatever the local climate. Specify this when you make your order. The amount of agent you'll need will vary by brand, so consult your supplier. If you're using an agent, reduce the sand to 2¼ parts.

When mixing concrete, the sand should be clean construction sand, not beach sand, and the aggregate should range from quite small to about ¾-inch in size. The water you use should be drinkable—neither excessively alkaline

nor acidic, and containing absolutely no organic matter.

To determine how much concrete you need to buy, and to choose the form you want to buy it in, refer to the table below. The figures given are for 30 square feet of finished 4-inch-thick concrete slab and include 10% extra to allow for waste.

If your project is small, mixing by hand is the easiest method. But for large work (or if using an air-entraining agent), a power mixer is the way to go. You'll need an electric or a gas-powered one with at least a 3-cubic foot capacity.

INGREDIENTS FOR A 30-SQUARE-FOOT SLAB (4" THICK)

MATERIAL	AMOUNT
Bulk dry material	Portland cement: 3 sacks Sand: 7.5 cubic feet Gravel: 7.5 cubic feet
Dry pre-packaged mix	25 60-pound bags
Ready-mix	½ cubic yard

Making a concrete walkway

Pointed shovel

String to align trench

Batter board

1 Dig the trench
Use batter boards and string to outline your site, making the outline about a foot wider and longer than the finished slab to allow room for the form boards. Then, using a pointed shovel, remove the turf to the required depth so you can cast the slab on undisturbed soil. Plan to have at least a 4" to 6" gravel base if you have poorly drained or expansive clay soil. Don't cast concrete on topsoil, sod, wood, soft soil or hard rocks.

2 Assemble the form
Nail the form boards to 2x2 or 1x4 stakes spaced 4' apart, using 3½" and 2½" duplex form nails, respectively. Lay out the corners with batter boards and a plumb bob; nail and stake the corners.

Form board

Plumb bob

Gravel base

Stake

Duplex nail

Reinforced splice

BUILDING A CURVED FORM

Gravel

Kerfed plywood

Reinforced splice

Outside stakes

If your design calls for a curve, you'll need to bend some plywood to do the job. This technique works best for gradual curves. Use ¼-inch plywood with the face grain running up and down. Bend it around temporary stakes set on the inside edge of the curve and secure the ends by nailing them to the stakes set on the outside. Add more stakes on the outside, nail the plywood to them, then remove the inside stakes. If the plywood won't curve to your radius, make small saw cuts, or kerfs, across its width as shown.

Extra stakes on the outside of the plywood form reinforce it and ensure that the curve is smooth and stable. Kerfs in the form help you bend the wood.

Level

Board
extending the
width of the form

Spacer

3 Check for drainage

Finished concrete should have about ¼" per foot of a pitch in one direction to allow water to run off. To allow for this pitch, nail one sideboard slightly higher than the other. Then, check the pitch of the form from side to side by placing a level on a long, straight board extending the width of the form; a spacer should be required at one end to level the board (left).

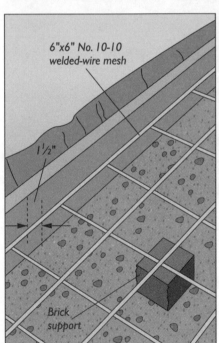

6"x6" No. 10-10
welded-wire mesh

1½"

Brick
support

Square
shovel

Gravel

4 Prepare for the casting

If the slab is to be tiled, reinforce it using steel, usually 6"-square No. 10-10 welded-wire mesh (above, left). Otherwise, use control joints (see page 251). Cut the mesh to size with bolt cutters or heavy lineman's pliers, keeping it at least 1½" away from the sides of the forms. Support the mesh in the

center of the slab on bits of brick. Make sure you have enough helpers and tools, since you shouldn't stop the job until it's done. Dampen the soil or gravel. Start placing the concrete at one corner of the form (above, right) while a helper spreads it out. Push—don't drag—the concrete up against the form and compact it with a square shovel or mortar hoe.

5 Strike the concrete

After you've placed the concrete, level it with a bladed strikeoff (in this case a straight 2x4). Move it slowly along the form in a zigzagging motion. Make two passes this way. It helps if there are two people working together; a third can shovel extra concrete into hollow spaces.

Wet concrete

Darby

Edger

6 Smooth the concrete

You can skip this step on very small projects, but in general, you'll have to smooth the concrete after striking off. Use a darby *(above)*, or a bull float for larger jobs. Start by making flat, overlapping arcs, then straight, overlapping side-to-side strokes.

7 Edge the concrete

Run a mason's trowel between the concrete and the form. Then pass an edger back and forth to smooth and compact the concrete, creating a smoothly curved edge that will resist chipping.

8 Joint and float

Use a 1"-deep jointer with a guide board to make control joints *(right)*. The joints need to be at least one-quarter the depth of the concrete and should divide the area into squares. Jointed sections should never be more than 1½ times as long as they are wide. For a walkway, joints can be made at intervals of 1½ times the width of the slab. Smooth the surface with a wood float *(far right)*, with its leading edge raised slightly. Use a magnesium float with air-entrained concrete.

Guide board

Jointer

Wood float

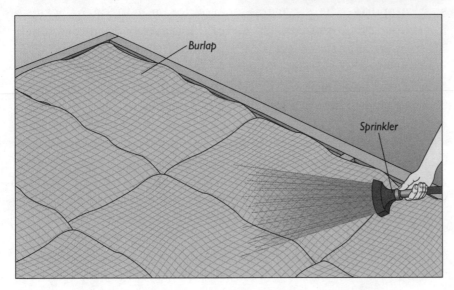

Burlap

Sprinkler

9 Cure the slab

The newly placed concrete needs to be moist-cured to keep its surface from drying too fast and becoming weak. With the forms left in place, cover the firm concrete with burlap and keep it wet with a garden hose. Curing should take at least three days—longer in cold weather. For additional strength and durability, plan to cure your project for a week.

A COBBLESTONE FINISH

Pebbles or cobbles can add a nice touch to a walkway. Lay a ½"-thick mortar bed (regular concrete in cold climates) over the concrete surface. Use stones smaller than 6" in diameter, soak them in water and push them into the mortar until they are buried halfway. Level the stones with a straightedge. Let the mortar set for 2 to 3 hours, then spread another thin layer over the surface, filling in any spaces. Brush away any residual mortar before it sets.

Edging

½"-thick mortar bed

Decorative pebbles

Steps and Stairs

Steps may be a necessity for changing levels, but they also can be an attractive design feature in a backyard. Whatever style or material you choose, take the time to understand the principles of proportions, dimensions, and preparing the base. Then you'll be ready to start work. This section shows you three design options and provides step-by-step instructions for the most commonly constructed type of stairs: stringers covered with wooden treads and risers.

Designing Your Steps

Architects and builders long ago worked out the ideal proportions for steps. As shown on the following page, those proportions translate into a clearly defined relationship between the key elements of step construction: the flat part, or tread, and the vertical element, or riser. Ideally, the depth of the tread plus twice the riser height equals 25 to 27 inches. Thus, the ideal step has a 6-inch-high riser and a 15-inch deep tread.

Dimensions: Divide the rise of the slope (see below) by 6 inches (ideal riser height), the result is the number of steps you'll need. If the answer ends in a fraction, drop the fraction and divide the whole number into the rise of the slope to get the exact measurement for each of your risers.

Wooden steps: For a low-level deck or for easy access from a house, wooden steps are best. Make the stair supports—the stringers—from either 2-by-10s or 2-by-12s. If the steps are more than 4 feet wide, you'll need a third stringer to go between the other two.

Masonry steps: These can be built entirely of concrete or the concrete can be used as a base for mortared masonry units. As shown on page 255, you will need to construct wood forms along the perimeter of the steps; a gravel base may also be required if you are building the steps on poorly drained or expansive clay soil.

Begin by forming rough steps in the earth, keeping the treads as level as possible and the risers as perpendicular as possible. If you are using a gravel base, be sure to allow for the 4- to 6-inch thickness of the gravel bed and the 4-inch minimum thickness of the concrete, on both treads and risers. In severe climates, you may need 6 to 8 inches of concrete, plus a footing that's sunk below the frost line, to prevent damage caused by heaving.

Pour and strike the concrete as for a poured concrete path (page 249). For more weather-safe treads, broom the surfaces to roughen them. Cure as for paving, then install the masonry units, if desired.

MEASURING A SLOPE

With a long, straight 2-by-4, a tape measure, and a level, you can quickly measure the rise and the run of your slope. Place one end of the beam at the top of the slope where the steps will end. Then mark the beam where the steps will begin; this is the run. Raise the beam until it is level, then measure the distance from the bottom of the beam to the point where the stairs will start. You can then calculate how many steps you need.

Carpenter's level

2x4

Run

Rise

STEP PROPORTIONS

Before you can build your steps, you have to determine the riser height—the vertical dimension—and the tread depth, or the front-to-back horizontal dimension. As shown in the illustrations at left, the best proportions for steps are achieved when twice the riser height added to the tread depth comes to between 25" and 27". All the risers and treads in any one flight of steps should be uniform in size.

THREE STEP DESIGN OPTIONS

Building wooden steps

1 Make the foundation

Cast a concrete pad about 4" deep. *(See page 246 for more information on concrete slabs.)* Set J-bolts in the concrete while it's still wet, leaving about 2" exposed. When the concrete has cured, drill holes for the bolts in a pressure-treated 2-by board. Place this kicker plate over the exposed bolts, add washers, and tighten the nuts.

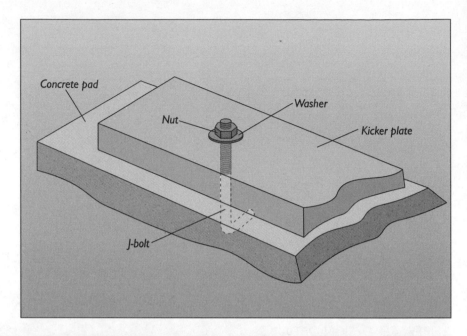

Concrete pad

Nut

Washer

Kicker plate

J-bolt

Stair gauge

Tongue of carpenter's square

Stair gauge

Blade of carpenter's square

Riser

Tread

Notches to be removed

Notch for stringer

Stringer

Tread thickness to be removed at bottom

2 Mark the first stringer

Using stair gauges—devices that screw to a carpenter's square—mark the riser dimension on the tongue of the carpenter's square and the tread dimension on the blade. Line up the gauges with the top edge of the stringer *(above)* and trace the outline of the riser and tread. Mark the rest of the notches. Because the tread's thickness will add to the height of the first step, subtract this measurement from the bottom of the stringer. If you are using a kicker plate, notch the bottom of the stringer to fit around it.

3 Cut and fasten the stringers

Cut out the notches on the stringer with a circular saw, finishing each cut with a crosscut saw. Use the stringer as a template to mark the others. If the ends of the joists are exposed on the side of the structure where the stairs will go,

bolt the top of the stringers to them (above, left). Otherwise, attach stringers to the end joist using joist hangers. Notch stringers to take the connector (above, right). Fasten stringers to the kicker plate with universal anchors or angle irons.

4 Add treads and risers

Nail risers to the stringers first using 3¼" galvanized nails, then nail the treads to the stringers; use two nails at each end of the tread boards. Project each tread 1" beyond the front of the riser to give the stairs a more finished appearance. Space the tread boards with a nail as a guide; if the treads lead to a deck, use the same spacing as you will for the decking. Finally, working under the stairway, fasten the bottom edges of the risers to the backs of the treads.

CONSTRUCTING CONCRETE STEPS

For concrete steps you will need to build forms similar to those used for edgings (page 240). Position 2"-thick lumber so the concrete will be 4" high on the risers and 4" deep on the treads. Level and nail the forms to stakes driven into the ground on the outside of the forms; once the concrete has cured, you can remove both forms and stakes.

After you have placed the concrete, strike and level it, then cure it as you would for a cement walkway (page 250).

Raising a Wall

A garden wall can bestow privacy, muffle street sounds, frame a view, or set off a colorful flower bed. You can choose from a variety of materials to build your wall, but masonry is the best choice when you want a wall that you can build and then forget.

Brick and stone are two of the most attractive options. Both are examples of what is called unit masonry—materials small enough for one person to handle. This section will show you how to build both types of walls from preparing the foot-

ings right up to installing the top brick or stone. They both use double-wall construction: two rows, or wythes, of the building material, tied together with headers—bricks or stones—that run perpendicular to the rows.

Careful selection of the site will contribute to the wall's longevity. Choose a place where drainage is good and the soil is firm. Avoid locating the wall near the root systems of large trees; growing roots can exert a nearly irresistible pressure and may crack your footing.

Preparing the Footings

A strong footing is the key to a long-lasting wall. Dug and poured to the proper depth and width, a concrete footing is extremely strong. If your wall will be higher than the ones shown in this section—roughly 3 feet high—the footing will need to be reinforced.

Before finalizing plans for your wall, check with your local building department about regulations that may apply to your project.

These will specify how close to your property line you can build, how high you can build, whether or not the wall will require steel reinforcing, whether inspections will be necessary, and more.

AN ANATOMY OF A FOOTING
Concrete is the best material for footings. For a freestanding wall, codes usually specify a footing as deep as the width of the wall *(W)* and twice as wide *(2W)*, with the wall centered above. For more information on mixing concrete, see page 247.

Building concrete footings

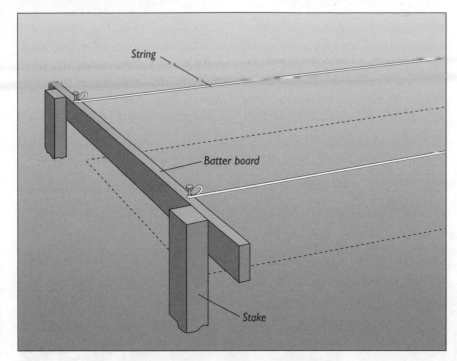

String

Batter board

Stake

1 Lay out the footing and prepare the base

Use strings and batter boards as a guide for the footing trench. (Make the trench about 1" wider and longer than the finished footing will be.) To construct the batter boards, drive in a pair of 2x2 stakes at each end of the trench and nail on 2x4s at least as wide as the trench. Attach strings to mark the sides of the trench. If you happen to dig the trench too deep, let concrete fill the excess; backfill soil will not provide uniform support. If the soil is soft and mucky, dig it out and replace with well-tamped gravel. Footings in cold climates should extend below the frost line to prevent shifting with freezing and thawing.

2x4

1x4 stake

1x2 kicker

1x2 spreader

2 Construct the form

The easiest way to make a footing is simply to dig a trench and cast concrete in the earth. But when the earth is too soft to maintain a vertical side, build a form from 2x4s using the batter board strings as a guide. The form boards should be level, and suported by 1x4 or 2x2 stakes at least every 4". If the earth won't hold a stake, use 1x2 or 2x4 kickers to position stakes back from the forms *(above, left)*. Nail 1x2 spreaders across the tops of the forms *(above, right)* to keep them in place until the concrete is placed; remove them for striking. Steel reinforcements can be supported on pieces of brick. Pour the concrete, level it, and let it cure as you would a concrete walkway *(page 249-251)*. Then remove the forms.

Brick Walls

Once you have had a little practice with the basic technique of throwing a mortar line *(below)*, building a wall can take shape surprisingly quickly. This section will guide you through the construction of a free-standing brick wall. After you have laid out your concrete footing *(page 257)*, you'll move on to laying a dry course and then your first bricks *(page 259)*. Note that a long, low wall may require reinforcing *(page 261)*. Finally, you will learn techniques for corners *(page 262)* and curves *(page 264)*.

Applying mortar

How to throw a mortar line

Learning how to apply the mortar properly is essential to masonry. Place one or two shovelsful of mortar on a wet mortar board. Slice off a wedge and scoop it up with an 8" or 10" trowel. Shake the trowel to dislodge any excess. Bring your arm toward your body and rotate the trowel *(above, left)*, laying mortar about 1" thick, one brick wide, and three bricks long. Practice on the board first. Once the line is thrown, furrow it with trowel point *(above, right)*. Divide the mortar; don't scrape it toward you. The furrow ensures that bricks are bedded evenly and that excess mortar is squeezed out the sides.

CHOOSING A BOND PATTERN

Over the years, masons have developed various patterns for laying bricks. Though all of them are attractive, appearance is not the only factor you should consider. Check with your building department before making your final decision on a bond pattern; if your wall requires steel reinforcing, some bonds may be more adaptable than others.

Common bond
Also referred to as "American bond." Has headers every fifth course; strong and easy to lay.

Flemish bond
Alternate headers and stretchers—bricks laid lengthwise—in each course. Both decorative and strong.

Running bond
Easy to lay. Strong. Mainly used for veneers and single-thickness partitions. Double thicknesses must be linked with metal ties.

Stack bond
Usually used for decorative effect in veneers. Weak; must be liberally reinforced if it is to be used structurally.

English bond
Alternate courses of headers and stretchers. Forms very strong walls. Requires cutting bricks at corners.

Building the wall

Head joint

1 Lay a temporary dry course
Snap a chalk line along one edge of where the bricks will rest on the footing. Lay a single course of bricks lengthwise—stretcher bricks—the full length of the wall. Mark the brick spacing on the footings, allowing ½" spaces for the vertical, or head, joints, as shown.

2 Lay the first bricks
Take up the bricks from the dry course and throw a three-brick mortar line on the footing (page 258). Then load a small amount of mortar onto the end of the trowel and spread it on the ends of the second and third bricks—a process known as buttering. Press the bricks in place with a shoving motion so the mortar squeezes out of the head joints. Use a level to guide you as you tap the bricks into place.

Pencil marks

Backup course

¾ bricks

Ends buttered

Wythe

Header brick

3 Begin the backup and header course
Butter just enough of the inside edge of the first backup brick to seal the ends of the wythes, but note there is no mortar joint between the two courses. Then continue to lay three bricks at a time to finish the backup course. Check the height of the courses with a level, and the width of the wall with a header brick that will run crossways to join the two rows, or wythes, together. Cut two ¾ bricks to begin the second course, then butter and lay three header bricks.

4 Finish the ends

Continue laying stretcher bricks until one end of the wall is five courses high, as shown. (Note that the fourth course begins with a single header.) Use your level as a straightedge to check that this end, or lead, is true on each surface. Now go to the other end of the footing and build another lead, repeating the previous steps.

Level

Header

Mason's line block

Mason's line

Header course

5 Fill in

Stretch a mason's line between the completed leads as shown; keep the line about $1/16$" away from the bricks and flush with their top edges. Then begin laying the outer course. Lay bricks from both ends toward the middle, trimming the last brick if necessary. Shift the mason's line to the back of the wall and lay the backup courses. To build a higher wall, repeat Steps 3 to 5.

6 Planning the cap

The simplest cap is a row of header bricks on edge. Lay them out dry, allowing $1/2$" or so for mortar joints. If the last brick overlaps the end of the wall, mark it, and cut this "closer" with a hand-drilling hammer and a brickset.

Trim line

7 Lay the cap

Throw mortar lines and begin laying the cap. Each succeeding cap brick should be well buttered on its face; check joint thickness carefully as you go. If you have to cut a closer brick, bury it four or five bricks from the end, where it will be less noticeable. When the last brick is laid, check the cap with a level along all its faces.

Closer brick

Reinforcing long, low walls

Long walls can be reinforced every 12 feet with pilasters. These are locked into the wall by overlapping the bricks in alternate courses as shown for a single-wythe wall *(right)* or double-wythe wall *(below)*. Pilasters also serve a decorative function by interrupting the wall's continuous face.

Single wythe

Even course

Odd course

4" wall

Pilaster

Even course

Double wythe

Odd course

8" wall

Pilaster

Adding Corners and Curves

Not all walls are straight: You may need to enclose an area, which will require making a corner, or you may want to add a decorative sinuous curve to your wall.

Each bond pattern requires its own corner treatment and arrangement of closure bricks. Here we show you how to make a corner for a common bond wall *(page 258)*.

Curved walls are an eye-catching option for the backyard builder. They can be built with the help of plywood patterns, as shown on page 264.

Building a corner

1 Lay out the corners
Snap chalk lines, making sure they are absolutely square using the 3-4-5 rule: Measure 3' along one line and 4' along the other. The distance between these two points should be 5'; if it isn't, adjust your lines. Using larger multiples of 3, 4, and 5—such as 6-8-10—will assure even greater accuracy.

Footing

2 Lay the corner lead
After laying out a dry run, as in the first step on page 259, lay the first brick exactly in the corner. Then lay four bricks in each direction. Use a carpenter's level to check level and plumb, as well as the bricks' alignment, as shown.

3 Lay the backup course

Throw mortar lines and lay the backup course as shown. Take care not to disturb the front course, and remember there is no mortar joint between these two courses. Be sure the backup course is level with the first one.

Front course

Backup course

Front course

Chalk line

Pencil marks

¼ closures

¾ closures

4 Start the header course

Take two bricks and cut them into ¾ and ¼ pieces. These are known in the building trade as "closures." Lay them as shown and complete the lead header course.

5 Finish the lead

Now lay the leads for the next three stretcher courses. Note that each of these courses is the same as the first course, except that the fourth course begins with a header. Check the finished lead for accuracy, then repeat these steps for the other corners in the wall. Now fill in the wall between the leads, as shown on page 260.

Header

¾ brick

Closer bricks

6 Complete the corner

Plan and lay the cap (*pages 260 and 261*). Note that the cap course starts flush with one edge of the corner. Lay these bricks first, and then start the other leg of the corner by butting the bricks against the first ones. Use closer bricks as needed (*page 261*). Finally, press or draw a striking tool vertically and then horizontally along the joints to compact and shape the mortar. Remove any excess with a trowel.

MAKING A CURVED WALL

To build a curved wall, cut plywood patterns in the shape of your planned curves. Hold a pattern up to the wall, and set the bricks to match the plywood curves as closely as possible. Check your local code for information on the proper footings and reinforcement.

The distinctive sinuous curve of a serpentine wall is actually an engineering feature: It helps the wall resist toppling and allows you to build thin walls higher than you could otherwise.

Stone Walls

Perhaps more than any other masonry material, stone lends an aura of permanence to a structure. However, because stone walls can't be easily reinforced, building codes tend to frown on stone masonry in earthquake zones, except for low, decorative work.

The kind of stone you choose will depend upon appearance and cost. Sandstone is popular and economical; granite, for a more formal look, is more expensive.

Then decide on the kind of stone work—rubble (rounded, uncut stone) or ashlar (square-cut stone that is laid like bricks)—and whether the wall will be laid dry or mortared. If you choose a mortared wall, you will first have to construct a concrete footing; dry-laid walls may be built directly on the ground. Note that mortar for stone work contains more cement than that used for brick or block: one part cement to three or four parts sand. Make a test batch first.

A few tips will help you during the construction. First, most stone walls should lean inward—toward the center—on both surfaces. This tilting, called batter, helps secure the wall, since the faces rest on each other. One to two inches of batter for every two feet of rise is a good rule of thumb. A dry-laid wall is strongest if it is no higher than the thickness of its base. Stability is enhanced further when you place the largest stones at the bottom. Save some large flat stones for the top course: These will form a protective and decorative cap.

Stone bonding patterns

Depending on the material you choose and the effect you wish to create, stone can be joined in a variety of bonding patterns.

The stone can be laid with or without mortar, and it can be stacked in regular courses, or in random patterns, as you choose.

Untrimmed rubble stone
Whether laid dry (above, left), or with mortar (above, right), place stones so that head joints are staggered, for maximum strength. Crevice plantings give the dry wall a natural look.

Trimmed at the quarry
Roughly squared stones can be laid without regular coursing (above, left), creating an effect similar to a mortared rubble wall. Laid in regular horizontal courses (above, right), the stones resemble ashlar stonework.

Ashlar stone
Square cut can be laid without regular coursing (above, left) for a rustic effect. With coursing (above, right), the result is more formal. In either case, head joints are always staggered.

Building a dry stone wall

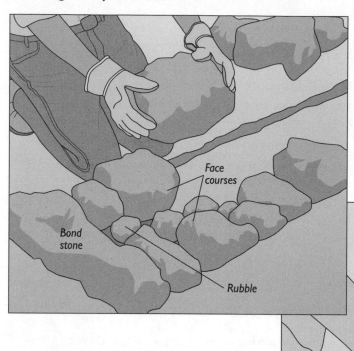

Face courses

Bond stone

Rubble

1 Lay the first course
To help stabilize the wall, lay the foundation stones in a shallow trench; and begin with a bond stone—a stone the width of the wall that acts like a header in a brick wall *(page 259)*. Then start the two face courses, trying to lay the stones flat, as they would occur naturally. Fill in the center with rubble as you complete this and each successive course.

Amount of batter

Batter gauge

2 Lay the second course
Lay stones on top of the first course, being sure to stagger the joints. Stones of each face should tilt inward toward each other. To maintain a proper slope—1" to 2" for every 2' of rise—use a level and a batter gauge made from a couple of pieces of 1x2 as shown.

Hand-drilling hammer

3 Add additional courses
Continue in the same manner, maintaining an inward tilt so that gravity will hold the wall together. Place bond stones every 10 square feet. Fill any gaps with small stones, tapping them in with a hand-drilling hammer; don't tap too hard—driving them too far will weaken the structure.

Putting up a mortared stone wall

1 Start the first course
Make a concrete footing *(page 257)* that extends below the frost line. Then begin the stonework. Be sure the stones are clean and dry, as dirt and moisture interfere with mortar. Lay a 1"-thick mortar bed for the first bond stone and set it in place. Continue as for a dry wall *(opposite page, Step 1)*, dry-fitting stones before mortaring and laying them, then filling in the center with rubble and mortar. Pack the head joints (vertical joints) with mortar after setting the stones.

Footing

Mortar bed

Face courses

Bond stone

Rubble

2 Lay additional courses
For each subsequent course, build up a mortar bed and set the stones in place just as you did to begin. Work slowly, dry-fitting stones before throwing the mortar. You can save mortar by filling large joints with small stones. Check the wall's batter, or inward tilt, as you go *(opposite, Step 2)*.

3 Finishing up
After you've laid a section, use a piece of wood to rake out the joints to a depth of ½" to ¾". Spilt mortar should be wiped up with a wet sponge as you work. Finally, brush away mortar crumbs with an ordinary broom or brush.

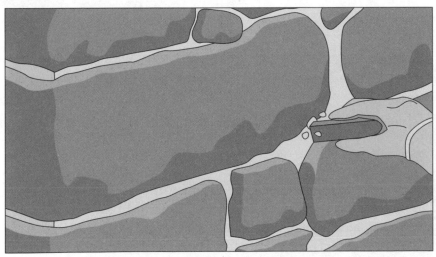

Building a Deck

A deck can take many forms, from a spectacular, multi-level platform for entertaining to a simple tree-shaded structure, perfect for a quiet read. Although building a deck may seem like a daunting task at first, it is actually reasonably straightforward, especially with the assistance of a few helpers. This section provides a basic primer on building your own deck, beginning with a general overview of the process and finishing with more detailed instructions.

ANATOMY OF A DECK

Decks vary in size and complexity but most are just variations on the example shown here: a structure supported by beams, joists, and posts, resting on concrete footings.

Decking

Ledger

Fascia

Joists

Beam

Precast pier block

Rim joist

Post

Cast concrete footing

Deck Materials

Draw up a detailed plan of your deck first, then prepare a list of all the materials you will need. Although everything required is readily available at most home centers, each item has to be considered carefully, whether it is the wood for the deck, the concrete for the footings or piers, or the fasteners and framing connectors that will hold the structure together.

Lumber: Any wooden structure exposed to the elements is a likely candidate for rotting, unless you make sure to take certain precautions. Pressure-treated wood will stand up to the elements for many years. You can build your entire deck with it or just the substructure, and switch to a naturally decay-resistant wood, such as cedar or redwood heartwood, for the most visible part—the decking itself. To vary the look of the deck's surface, choose wider or narrower boards, or consider one of the several decking patterns shown on page 283.

Concrete: Most decks stand on concrete footings and piers. Although working with concrete involves hard physical labor, fairly small jobs are generally manageable. Refer to page 247 for a basic concrete formula and suggestions on mixing

In some cases—when a deck is built on a hillside, for example—the concrete columns need to be reinforced with steel. Consult a professional for this task or if you need to build columns more than 5 feet above grade.

Fasteners: The easiest and cheapest way to attach your deck boards is to nail them in place. Use common nails, or, for greater holding power, deformed shank nails, such as ring-shank or spiral nails.

For corrosion-resistance use hot-dipped galvanized nails, as stainless steel and aluminum nails are harder to find and more expensive.

Although time-consuming, hand nailing will give the best results. An air-powered nail gun (also known as a pneumatic nailer) makes the work go more quickly, but is not suitable for attaching decking, since it tends to shoot nails too deeply into softwoods such as redwood and cedar.

Deck screws can be used instead of nails. They're more expensive, but they hold more securely, eliminate the problem of hammer dents in the decking, and are less likely to be damaged during installation.

Another option is hidden fasteners, such as deck clips; they hold decking in place at the sides.

Framing connectors: Few things are more frustrating than watching an angled nail split the end of an expensive piece of lumber. Metal connectors can help avoid such problems: They not only make it easier to join materials, they also stengthen joints.

Various framing connectors are available, including joist hangers, for connecting joists to a beam or a ledger, and post caps, for joining the beams to the posts. Connectors intended for outside use are galvanized to help prevent corrosion.

Always use the fasteners that are recommended by the connector manufacturer—usually thick, short nails 1¼ or 1½ inches long—to avoid completely penetrating the 2-by lumber you have selected for your deck.

A DECK-BUILDING TOOL KIT

- Butt chisel
- Carpenter's level
- Chalk line
- Circular saw
- Claw hammer
- Electric drill and masonry bit
- Hand saw

- Water level or line level
- Plumb bob
- Reel tape
- Saber saw
- Screw gun or screwdrivers
- Tape measure
- Wrenches

Safety gear
If you are cutting pressure-treated lumber wear goggles, ear plugs, and a dust mask or a respirator. When you are nailing, wear goggles. Rubber gloves will protect your hands from the caustic effects of lime in concrete. Sturdy boots, preferably steel-toed, and a hard hat should be standard construction-site gear.

Combination square
Used to mark and check both 90° and 45° angles. Can also be used to gauge depth; removable sliding head can be locked anywhere along the blade. May include a spirit level for spot-checking level and plumb.

Carpenter's square
For laying out lines and checking square on large stock. Most durable squares are made from steel; because accuracy depends entirely on square's exact shape, store it where it can't fall or be banged and bent by other tools.

A Quick Overview of Deck Building

There are really only six basic steps involved in building a deck, as shown below and on the next page. Once you become familiar with them, you can refer to pages 275-285 where the stages of the process are covered in more detail. Most decks share the same basic structure. Posts anchored to a foundation on concrete footings and piers support beams, which in turn support joists. The deck may be attached to the house with a ledger, which takes the place of a beam and supports one end of the joists. Raised decks require steps, and decks more than 30 inches high should be fitted with a railing.

Building basics

1 Attaching a ledger
Install the ledger, which anchors the deck to the house wall and supports one end of the joists. To fasten the ledger to a solid brick wall or concrete foundation wall, use masonry anchors. Otherwise, fasten it to the house framing with lag screws. Then install flashing and caulk, if necessary.

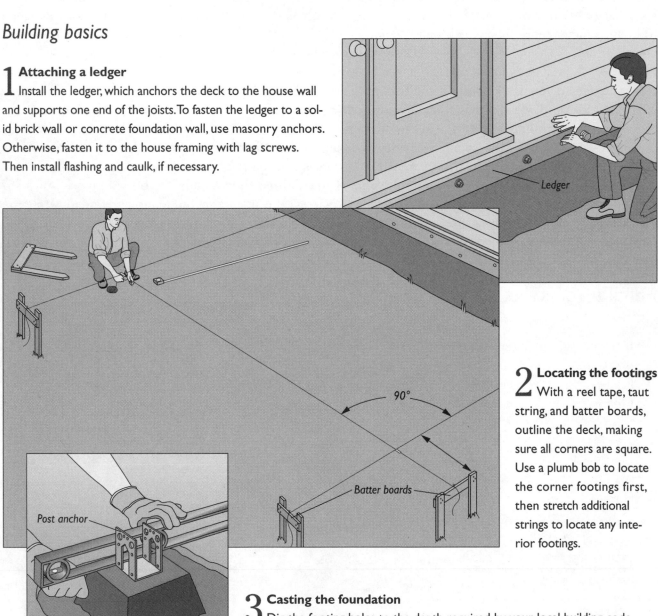

Ledger

90°

Batter boards

Post anchor

Pier black

2 Locating the footings
With a reel tape, taut string, and batter boards, outline the deck, making sure all corners are square. Use a plumb bob to locate the corner footings first, then stretch additional strings to locate any interior footings.

3 Casting the foundation
Dig the footing holes to the depth required by your local building code, then fill the hole with concrete. After a few minutes, when the concrete is stiff enough to support the pier blocks, position them in the concrete, aligning the post anchors with the string lines, and level the blocks in both directions. Allow the footings to cure for several days.

4 Installing posts and beams

Anchor a post on each pier block, plumbing it in on two adjacent sides. Cut the posts to the proper height, then fasten the beams in place with post caps.

Storyboard

Combination square

5 Installing the joists

Starting at an outside corner, use a storyboard, tape measure, and combination square to mark the joist locations on the ledger. Transfer the measurements to the beam that will support the other end of the joists. Install the joists with joist hangers or the appropriate framing connectors.

6 Finishing the deck

Starting at the house wall, lay the deck boards using a nail as a spacer. Let the boards run long, and when you're finished, snap a chalk line along the edge of the deck and saw them to length. Then install the railing, if needed.

Calculating Spans and Spacings

A deck must be strong enough to support certain loads—specified by the building code in your area—so it can safely withstand both regular use and unusual stresses. Strength is a function of the size and type of lumber you use, the span it bridges, and the spacing between structural members.

Loads: Building codes in many areas require that a substructure be strong enough to support 40 pounds of live load (people or snow, for example) plus 10 pounds of dead load (the weight of the construction materials) per square foot (p.s.f). The tables on pages 273-274 are based on this "40 plus 10 p.s.f." load at deck heights of up to 12 feet.

Spans and spacings: A span is the distance bridged by a deck board, joist, or beam, from one support to the next; spacing is the distance between adjacent joists, beams, or posts. Thus, since joists rest on beams, the joist span is the same as the beam-to-beam spacing. The maximum safe spans and spacings depend on the species and the grade of wood used.

Cantilevering a deck: Beams and joists are referred to as cantilevered if they extend beyond the edge of the last supporting post or beam. The cantilevered part of a joist or beam can be up to one-fourth of the allowable span. For example, a joist that spans 12 feet between beams could be cantilevered 3 feet at each

A PROPER SUBSTRUCTURE

Because they determine the ultimate strength or weakness of the support system, spans and spacings are critical to proper substructure design. Sometimes adjustments or extra reinforcements are required—if your deck will be over 8 feet above grade (even if at only one post), for example, or if it must carry unusually weighty loads, such as a heavy planter.

Joist

Decking

Load area

Post

Decking span/joist spacing

Cantilevered distance for joist

Beam

Cantilevered distance for deck board

Post height

Cantilevered distance for beam

Joist span/beam spacing

Beam span/post spacing

end. Thus, cantilevering is a way of increasing the size of a deck without adding more supports. Deck boards can be cantilevered, too, but only by a few inches.

Using the tables: Although decks are built from the ground up, they are often designed from the top down, since the surface will be the most visible part. First decide how you want the deck surface to look, then design the substructure that will give it the support it requires, using the tables on this page and the following one.

The tables are designed to help you calculate the proper sizes, spans, and heights for your deck's structural elements. The figures given are recommended maximums; choose shorter spans, closer spacings, or larger lumber for a more rigid structure. All lumber sizes are nominal, and spacings and spans are measured "on center"—or o.c. Lumber intended for structural applications is graded for strength. In the most common grading system, the grades are Select Structural, No. 1, No. 2, and No. 3, with Select Structural being the highest grade. The tables assume the use of a particular grade of lumber, usually No. 2 and Better.

Finally, code requirements vary from one region to another and may change over time, so be sure to check with your building department before you begin building.

TABLE 1: DECKING SIZES AND SPANS	
SIZE	**MAXIMUM SPANS** (On-center measurements)
1-by lumber laid flat	16"
Radius-edge decking	16"
2-by lumber laid flat	24"
2x3s laid on edge	48"
2x4s laid on edge	60"

This table is applicable for any grade of lumber appropriate for decking. It shows the maximum distance decking can span between joists—or between beams, if you plan to place on-edge boards directly on the beams.

NOTE: For joists supporting diagonal boards, the allowed spacing in the table corresponds to the distance between the joists measured on the diagonal.

TABLE 2: JOIST SPACINGS AND SPANS	
SPACINGS	**MAXIMUM SPANS** (On-center measurements)
16" Joist spacings	
2x6	9'9"
2x8	12'10"
2x10	16'5"
24" Joist spacings	
2x6	8'6"
2x8	11'3"
2x10	14'4"
32" Joist spacings	
2x6	7'9"
2x8	10'2"
2x10	13'

The figures in this table are based on No. 2 and Better joists placed on edge. To determine the correct size and beam-to-beam spacing of joists, you can start with either the joist size or the joist span—the chart will provide the other one.

Determining beam span

This table will help you find the correct span for a given beam size and spacing. If, for example, you want to use 4-by-8 beams spaced 5 feet apart, you will need a post every 9 feet. You may be limited by beam sizes available. If you're using a built-up beam of two 2-bys, for example, you can use the spans indicated in the chart for a 3-by, but this will mean using smaller spans or spacings than necessary. Round the beam spacings down to the nearest whole foot before looking up the span. For more precise figures, consult an engineer.

To determine the post size

Find the joist span—in feet, including cantilever—from Table 2 and the beam span—in feet, including cantilever—from Table 3. Multiply the two figures to determine the load area (in square feet) that each post supports; round up to the next largest load area. Then, consult Table 4 to select a post size that meets the height requirements for your deck. If, for example, you want a deck 12' high, you can use 4-by-4 posts to support up to 72 square feet of load area. In order to make construction simpler, try to use posts and beams of the same thickness. If you'll be designing your deck with continuous posts to support an overhead, consult a professional for the best size of post for the height and load.

TABLE 3: BEAM SPANS

(Maximum on-center measurements based on No. 2 and Better beams placed on edge)

BEAM SIZE	BEAM SPACING								
	4'	5'	6'	7'	8'	9'	10'	11'	12'
4x6	6'	6'	6'						
3x8	8'	8'	7'	6'	6'	6'			
4x8	10'	9'	8'	7'	7'	6'	6'	6'	
3x10	11'	10'	9'	8'	8'	7'	7'	6'	6'
4x10	12'	11'	10'	9'	9'	8'	8'	7'	7'
3x12		12'	11'	10'	9'	9'	8'	8'	8'
4x12		12'	12'	11'	10'	10'	9'	9'	
6x10						12'	11'	10'	10'	10'

TABLE 4: MINIMUM POST SIZES AND HEIGHT

(Maximum on-center measurements based on Standard and Better for 4x4 posts; No. 1 and Better for larger sizes.)

POST SIZE	LOAD AREA (in square feet)									
	36	48	60	72	84	96	108	120	132	144
4x4	12'	12'	12'	12'	10'	10'	10'	8'	8'	8'
4x6					12'	12'	12'	12'	10'	10'
6x6									12'	12'

DESIGNING COST-EFFECTIVE DECKS

You can minimize costs by using larger joists and beams, thus requiring fewer posts and less foundation work. (This will also save considerably on labor if you're constructing the foundation yourself.) To cut down on the amount of lumber used, take full advantage of cantilevering, as described on page 272.

Attaching the Ledger

Installing the ledger is generally the first step in building a deck that is attached to the house because it will be used as a reference point to lay out the rest of the deck.

Choosing the lumber: Ledgers on decks up to 3 feet high are usually made of 2-by lumber: 2x6 or 2x8. Taller decks should have a ledger made of 4-by lumber. Use pressure-treated lumber if the ledger will be close to the ground or in contact with masonry.

Locating the ledger: Position the ledger so the surface of the deck will be at least one inch below the door, to help keep out rain and snow. You'll need to take into account the thickness of the decking and—if the joists will rest on the ledger—the height of the joists.

Note that water can collect between the ledger and the wall of the house. If you have a wood frame house, space the ledger from the wall with washers or install flashing. With a stucco wall, choose flashing, as washers tend to sink into the wall surface.

WHAT'S BEHIND THE WALLS?

Before attaching a ledger to the wood framing of a house *(page 276),* check your basement or crawl space to see what lies behind the outside walls. The ledger needs to be secured to either the band joist *(below)* or the blocking between floor joists *(inset, right).* If the ledger location falls between the floors of the house, attach it to the wall studs.

Joists

Flashing

Blocking

Ledger

Door

Siding

Wall sheathing

Wall stud

Sole plate

Ledger

Floor joist

Subfloor

Allowance for thickness of decking and slight drop

Mudsill

Bolt or lag screw

Washers as spacers

Band joist

Foundation wall

Attaching a ledger

Gap below siding

Brace

Socket wrench

16"

Ledger

Lag screw

To wood framing

Mark a level line indicating the top of the ledger, then brace or nail the ledger in place. Drill clearance holes through the ledger and then a pilot hole into the framing. Remove the ledger and pack each pilot hole with silicone caulk for moisture protection. Run lag screws through the ledger until the points protrude about $\frac{1}{2}$". (The screws should penetrate the framing at least $1\frac{1}{2}$", or as specified by your local code.) If you're not planning to use flashing, slip several large washers onto each lag screw. Working with a helper, line up the lag screws with the holes and tighten them using a socket wrench.

To a masonry wall or foundation

Mark the location of the top of the ledger on the wall. Drill holes for expanding anchor bolts *(inset)* every 16". Tap in the anchor bolts with a hammer. Measure and transfer the bolt locations to the ledger, or hold the ledger in place, level it, and tap it with a hammer to indent the bolt locations on it. Remove the ledger and drill clearance holes through it at the marks made by the bolt tips. Push (or hammer) the ledger onto the bolts; add washers and nuts, and tighten.

Expanding anchor bolt

Washer

Nut

16"

276

Locating the Footings

Once the ledger is in place you can begin marking the locations of the footings. This depends on where the posts will go, which in turn is determined by beam and joist spacing. Use the tables on pages 273 and 274 to work out these measurements, then transfer the rough footing locations to the ground. Then follow the directions below to locate the posts exactly and to be sure the corners of the deck are square. Check by measuring both diagonals across the area you have laid out with strings: They should be equal.

Determining the post locations

Batter boards
String parallel to house
90°
About 18"
Center of corner post

House wall
6'
90°
Ledger
8'
10'
String line
Tape measure
Tape
Batter board

Plumb bob
Post location
String line
Post footing location

1 Set up string lines
Hammer a nail into the top of the ledger in line with the estimated center of the corner post. Set up a batter board about 18" past the location of this post and stretch a string from the nail to the batter board perpendicular to the ledger. To check for exact square, use the 3-4-5 rule *(page 262)*, using a reel tape to measure the diagonal and moving the string on the batter board until the diagonal is exact *(inset)*. Attach the string to the batter board at this point. Repeat to set up a string line on the other side of the deck. Measuring from the house along each line, mark with tape a point corresponding to the center of each corner post. Set up two more batter boards near the two tape marks and stretch another string between them, parallel to the ledger and crossing the original strings at the tape.

2 Marking post locations
Use a plumb bob to transfer the point where the strings cross to the ground; mark the point with a small flag (a large nail through a piece of tape), a stake, or powdered lime. Then measure along the strings and plumb down to mark the other post locations.

Casting the Foundation

Your deck's foundation anchors the entire structure, distributing loads into the ground and protecting posts or beams from direct contact with the earth. The foundation generally consists of a footing that dis- tributes the load underground and a pier that raises the bottom of the post above grade.

The size and depth of footings are governed by code. Cast your foot- ings on undisturbed soil; if you hap- pen to dig too deep, don't put the earth back, just cast the footing deeper. Piers—which may be pyra- midal with a flat top, cylindrical, or rectangular—should hold the post bottom 6 inches above grade.

Placing the concrete

Using precast pier blocks
Cast the footings to the required depth *(left)*, leaving the top of the footing about 1" below grade. When the concrete has stiffened enough to support the piers, position them, then level them in both direc- tions *(below)* and align the post anchors with the string lines.

Post anchor

Precast con- crete pier block

Footing

Post anchor

2x4 support

6"

Stake

Fiber form tube

Footing

Using fiber form tubes
Splay the hole at the tube bottom to let the concrete spread. Suspend the tube about 6" above the bottom of the hole with stakes and supports as shown; it should extend at least 6" above grade. Insert steel rods if necessary and place the con- crete. Smooth the top with a piece of wood and insert a post anchor; align it with the string guides and level it. Fill in the hole around the tube with earth. Cover the top of the tube with newspaper, straw, or burlap and keep it damp for at least a week. Then peel off the tubing that is above the ground.

Installing Posts and Beams

Decks posts are connected to the piers with post anchors. Beams usually sit on top of the posts, connected to them with post caps.

Most deck posts are made of 4x4s, but various other materials can be used, such as larger dimensions of lumber, built-up lumber, steel, or a combination of these.

You can begin to erect posts and beams once the concrete footings have cured for at least a week. Tall posts must be braced to ensure lateral stability. Consult local codes.

If you are using pressure-treated lumber, treat all saw cuts with a brush-on wood preservative such as copper naphthanate.

Post-and-beam assembly

Post cap

Attaching the posts and the beams

Place a post in its anchor on a pier block and mark the final height using a water level (page 291) connected to the ledger. Cut the post to length, attach a post cap, then place it in the anchor. Level the post and brace it temporarily with 1x2s while you nail or bolt the bottom of the post in place. Repeat with the other posts. Sight down your beam to find the crown, if any. When you mount the beam on the posts, place it crown-side up unless the beam is cantilevered at one or both ends, in which case the crown side should face down. Lift the beam into place and nail or bolt it in position (left).

Sandwiched post

Sandwiched beam

Double beam: two 2x6s

4x4 post

4x6 beam

2x6s

4x4 block

Post anchor between 2x6s and 4x4

TWO OTHER POST-AND-BEAM ASSEMBLY OPTIONS

Instead of using post caps to secure the posts to the beams on your deck you can choose one of the two options shown at left. These "sandwich" joints allow the posts to extend above the surface of the deck to support railings, screens, overheads, and benches. If you choose the sandwiched beam design, insert a 4-by block into the post anchor and fasten the 2-by lumber to it.

Installing the Joists

Deck joists spread the decking load across the beams, making it possible to use decking materials that otherwise wouldn't be able to span the distance between beams. Joists are generally made of 2-by lumber and are often the same width as the beams and ledger, as shown below.

Using blocking (*page 282*) to reinforce joists with large spans or wide spacings will keep the joists from twisting or buckling. The need for blocking is determined by local codes, but in general, it's a good idea to block between joists directly over any beams or ledgers. Joists spanning more than 8 feet also need a row of blocking in the middle of the span; joists spanning more than 12 feet need two rows.

The steps that follow show you the process of installing joists, from determining their location to nailing them in place.

Deck with ledger

Decking

Joist hanger

Ledger

Beam

Post anchor

Joist

Post cap

Post

Precast pier block

Footing

STURDY DECK STRUCTURES

Joists either sit on top of beams and ledgers or are connected to the faces of these supports with joist hangers. In many designs, the two approaches are combined, with joists hanging from a ledger at one end and sitting on top of the beam at the other, attached with a seismic anchor. If the joists sit on top of a beam, capping their ends with a rim joist will provide a more finished look and also add rigidity to the overall structure. If you install a rim joist, it can take the place of blocking over the last beam.

Freestanding deck

Decking

Rim joist

Rim joist

Seismic anchor

Joist

Beam

Post anchor

Footing

Precast pier block

Post cap

Post

Positioning the joists

Combination square

Joist location

Ledger

16"

1 Mark joist locations

Starting at one outside corner of the ledger, mark the location of the first joist with an X. For standard 16" centers, hook your tape measure over the end of the ledger or beam and measure 16" to the edge of the next joist; draw a line with a combination square and then an X to indicate which side of the line the joist will fall on. The last interval may be less than 16".

2 Transfer the spacing

Once you've completed the layout on the ledger, transfer the same spacing to the beam opposite, using a storyboard—a marked length of scrap lumber. If you're splicing joists by overlapping them, as described on the following page, the layout on the opposite beam must be offset 1½" to allow for the overlap. Mark the edge of the first joist in from the end at 14½", them mark every 16".

Storyboard

Beam

Scrap piece of 2-by lumber

Joist hanger

Ledger

3 Install joist hangers

To save time, fasten all the joist hangers in place before you install the joists: Position each hanger so that one side of the opening falls on your layout line; the joist's top edge should sit flush with the top edge of the ledger or beam (use a piece of scrap lumber to align the hanger). Nail this side of the hanger to the ledger, then squeeze the hanger so it's snug around the scrap of wood, and nail the other side to the ledger.

Ledger   Joist hanger   Joists

Seismic anchors

Beam   Rim joist

4 Fasten the joists

Measure the distance each joist must span between the beam and the ledger. If the joists will sit in joist hangers at both ends, they can be ⅛" to ¼" inch short of the proper length and still fit. If you find greater discrepancies, measure and cut each joist individually; otherwise, cut them all to the same length.

If the joists will sit in hangers at both ends, simply nail through the hangers into the joists. If the joists will sit on top of the ledger or beam, fasten each joist with a seismic or universal anchor, as shown. Joists should also be fastened to any intermediate beams. If you're installing a rim joist, face-nail through the ends of the joists using three or four 3½" nails at each joist. Any joints in the rim joist must fall centered on a joist end.

Staggered blocking

Face-nailed

Blocking over a beam

Toenailed

5 Install the blocking

Snap a chalk line across the joists at the relevant points, then work your way across the joists, measuring and listing the length of blocking you'll need to cut from joist material. Cut and code all the blocks to correspond to their locations. If you alternate the blocks, staggering them from one side of the chalk line to the other (left), you'll be able to face-nail the blocks; use 3½" nails. When you install blocks over a beam (far left), you can face-nail one end of each block, but you'll have to toenail the other; use 2½" nails.

SPLICING JOISTS

On a large deck, you'll need to splice joists. Splices must fall on a beam; be sure each joist end rests at least a full inch on the beam. If you need to splice several joists, make the various splices fall on several different beams to avoid weakening the substructure.

3" nails

Wood cleats
To maintain uniform spacing, use wood cleats, metal straps, or gusset plates.

Overlapped splice
The overlap method of splicing is easiest, but it breaks up uniform spacing, throwing off the alignment of decking end joists.

Finishing the Deck

Once the substructure is finished, it's time to lay the decking—the most visible part of your deck—and, if necessary, railings and stairs.

For the decking, a simple arrangement is often the best choice—boards that are set parallel, perpendicular, or diagonal to the deck's long axis. These simple patterns create an illusion of size: The eye is drawn beyond the deck rather than being encouraged to focus on the details of the design.

Decking can be fastened to joists with nails, screws, or special clips. Nailing is the cheapest and quickest method, but screws hold better. Fasten deck boards at every support point (joist or beam).

Fastening requirements depend on the lumber: Pressure-treated 2-by-4s and 2-by-6s need two nails at every support point; redwood and cedar 2-by-4s and 2-by-6s need two nails at the ends, and one at all other support points, staggered across the face of the board.

If your deck is higher than 30 inches, you will need some kind of railing. Page 285 shows you how they are built. To add a simple staircase made from wood stringers, turn to page 254.

DECKING PATTERNS

Generally speaking, the more complex the decking pattern, the more complicated the substructure must be to support it. A diagonal pattern requires setting joists closer together; more elaborate designs call for doubling joists at regular intervals to permit nailing of abutting lumber.

Herringbone

Standard

Diagonal

Curved

Mitered

Angled

Planning Joints in Decking

A deck that is less than 16 feet long can be built with no joints in the decking because lumber is available up to 16 feet long; a longer deck will have end joints. Three ways to lay out end joints are shown below.

Random or alternating joints are the strongest, while grouped joints create a pattern that calls attention to itself. For maximum strength, deck boards should span at least three joists without a joint.

Grouped   *Alternating*   *Random*

Installing the decking

1 Fasten the boards
Begin laying decking at the house wall, leaving about a ⅛" gap between the wall and the first board. If the appearance of the lumber permits, lay the boards bark-side up to minimize checking and cupping. If you are using pressure-treated lumber, butt the edges of the boards. When the boards dry, they will contract, creating the required spacing. If you have chosen redwood or cedar boards, space them ⅛" to ³⁄₁₆" apart, using a 3½" nail at each end of the boards as a guide. To keep the nails from slipping down, nail them through a small block of wood *(inset)*. As you fasten the decking, occasionally check the remaining distance to be covered, measuring from both ends of the decking. If possible, adjust the spacing slightly to be able to fit the last board; if a large adjustment will be required, rip the last board to fit.

2 Trim the boards
Snap a chalk line carefully along the deck edges—you can leave the deck boards cantilevered a couple of inches if you wish—and saw along it. A length of wood tacked to the deck as a guide for the saw will ensure that your cut is straight.

Attaching the railings

1 Attach the posts
Cut the posts to length with a circular saw—for 4x4 posts you may have to finish the cuts with a handsaw. If the rails will fit into dadoes in the posts, cut the dadoes now. If you have to notch the decking, mark the notch and then make the cuts with a butt chisel *(right)*. Drill holes for bolts and secure the posts to the deck substructure *(inset)*.

2 Complete the railing
First, add the cap, fastening it to each post with two 3" screws, or 3½" nails. Use the longest lumber available so the cap will be supported by as many posts as possible. At corners, make a miter joint. If the rails are set into dadoes in the posts as shown at left, tap them into place with two 3½" nails. As with the cap, use the longest lumber available. Cut the balusters to length; you can bevel the ends as shown. Then fasten the balusters with one 3" nail or screw at each end.

Stair Railings

Any stairway with more than three risers requires a handrail for people to hold onto. The handrail should be easy to grip; generally a 2-by on edge is best. This means leaving the posts uncapped—cut the ends on angle to shed water and treat the exposed end grain.

Most codes allow only 4 inches between rails (6 inches is acceptable for the triangle under the lowest rail). Measured from the top of the railing to the top front edges of the treads as shown at right, the railing height must be at least 30 inches, or at most 34 inches (check your local building code). Posts should be bolted or lag screwed to the stringers, and never to the stair treads.

Constructing a Low-level Deck

Building a low deck like the one shown below is a quick and easy way to add an outdoor floor to your yard. Because this deck is relatively small—roughly 8 feet by 12 feet—it will fit in a yard of just about any size, providing you with a pleasant garden retreat. It includes most of the basic components discussed previously in Building a Deck. You'll probably want to adapt this plan to suit your exact situation. But if you change the number or length of any of the structural members, consult the charts on pages 273 and 274 for the correct spans, and make adjustments if necessary.

MATERIALS LIST

Use pressure-treated lumber for the structural members; decay-resistant lumber such as cedar or redwood heartwood, or pressure-treated wood for the decking; and corrosion-resistant hardware.

Lumber		
Posts	4x4	– (depends on height)
Beams	4x8	11'9" (2)
Joists	2x6	7' (10)
Decking	2x6	12' (16)
Fascia	2x10	12' (2); 7' 10" (2)
Masonry		
Pier blocks	Precast concrete, with post anchors	
Concrete	12" square footings	
Hardware		
Nails	3½" for decking; nails for framing connectors	
Connectors	Post caps; joist hangers; universal anchors	

On sloping terrain, as shown below, you'll need posts supporting the deck at the low end; cut the posts to the length required to make the deck level on your slope. At the high end, you can place the beam directly on the piers. If the terrain is level, you can omit all the posts, placing the beams right in the piers' post anchors.

To build a higher deck from this plan, increase the length of the posts between the piers and the beams. You can also add a step with 6-by-6 pressure-treated landscape timbers—or place a large flat rock or a concrete slab where you want to access the deck.

A LOW-LEVEL DECK

Plan view (decking)
7'10"

12'

2x6 decking

Plan view (framing)

2x10 fascia

Seismic anchor

Concrete footing

Joist hanger

Precast concrete pier block

4x8 beam

2x6 joists, 16" o.c.

Elevation section

End joist

2x10 fascia

2x6 decking

Post cap

2x6 joists, 16" o.c.

Joist hanger

4x8 beam

Post anchor

Precast concrete pier block

12"

Footing depth, according to code

Concrete footing

Fences and Gates

Good fences make good neighbors, or so goes the old adage. They also make a good backyard even better, transforming the space into a secure, attractive retreat from the outside world. Well designed fences filter the sun's glare, transform a biting wind into a pleasant zephyr, or help mute the cacophony of street traffic, noisy neighbors, or barking dogs. As partitions, they divide the yard into separate areas for recreation, relaxation, gardening, and storage.

This section will help you choose and then build the fence that is most appropriate for your yard. Instructions cover everything from laying out the posts to hanging the gate.

Fencing for Function

Fences serve many more functions than a simple demarcation of your lot's border.

Fencing for protection: Obviously, a fence designed for protection should be tall, sturdy, and hard to climb. But don't forget the effects of psychology. A solid board or panel fence, for example, may be a more effective psychological deterrent than a chain link fence, simply because an intruder can't see what's on the other side.

Protecting children: The type of fence you choose for this purpose will depend on your child's age and fence-climbing ability. Avoid any design that offers convenient toeholds. Smaller wire mesh (2-by-2-inch) is ideal for play yards—its open design allows parents to keep an eye on the children's activities.

Screening for privacy: Give some thought to the design and location to avoid the feeling of a boxed-in space. For example, translucent glass or plastic panels can be used to allow light into the yard yet obscure vision.

Defining outdoor spaces: Low or open fences can physically separate areas while visually preserving the overall size of the yard.

SCREENING AGAINST THE WIND
(Degrees, showing rise in comfort temperature, are expressed in Fahrenheit)

Solid fence
The wind washes right over a solid fence. Protection diminishes considerably at a distance about equal to the fence's height.

Slat fence
Spaced slats, either horizontal or vertical, break up the flow of wind. Up close, the fence offers less protection; temperatures are warmest 6' to 12' away.

Fence with a baffle
A 45° baffle, or tilted ledge, at the top of the fence diverts the downward crash of wind; you feel warmest in the pocket directly below the baffle and up to 8' away from a 6'-high fence.

Baffle angled into the wind
With this design, the greatest protection is close to the fence, but protection extends to a distance equal to about twice the fence height.

COMMON FENCE STYLES

Board

Post-and-board

Post-and-rail

Face panel

Picket

Grapestake

Lattice screen

Wood-and-wire

Building Your Outdoor Fence

After you have settled on a design that takes into account the factors mentioned on page 288-289, it's time to start building. Each of the three stages of fence construction—plot- ting the fence, installing the posts, and then attaching rails and sid- ing—consists of a number of spe- cific steps, which are shown below and on the following pages.

Although fence building doesn't require any advanced technical skills, it's often physically demand- ing, so it's a good idea to enlist the services of a helper.

Plotting a straight fence

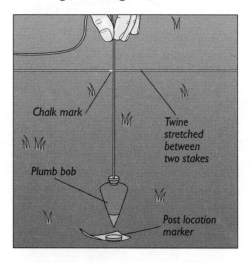

Chalk mark

Twine stretched between two stakes

Plumb bob

Post location marker

Setting up the fence line and marking the posts
Hammer stakes at each end or corner post location, then run a mason's twine or string between them. Mark the centers of the intermediate posts on the twine with chalk. If the twine's low enough, you can just press it to the ground with your finger and mark the spot with a nail pushed through a piece of paper. If the twine is more than a few inches off the ground, use a plumb bob to find the center of the post and set the nail marker in the ground, as shown at left.

Plotting a right angle

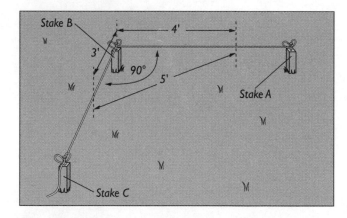

Stake B

4'

3'

90°

5'

Stake A

Stake C

Using the 3-4-5 method
As with setting up a corner for a deck or a brick wall, you can plot a right angle with the help of the 3-4-5 method *(page 262)*. Stretch a string from stake A to stake B, as you would for a straight fence, then stretch another length of twine roughly perpendicular to the first and adjust it until it forms a 3-4-5 triangle. Drive a stake at point C.

PLOTTING A CURVED FENCE

Stake the end points of the desired curve, then drive a stake at the midpoint. Stretch one line between the end stakes, then run a second line at 90° to the first, and drive a 3'-long rod as a pivot point along this line. The farther away from the fence line the pivot post is, the shallower the arc will be, as shown by the red dotted line. Measure cord to reach from the pivot post to an end stake; attach one end to the pivot post and the other to a point- ed stick. Draw an arc in the ground from one end stake to the other *(below)*. Measure and mark desired post spacing for inter- mediate posts by bending a tape measure around the arc.

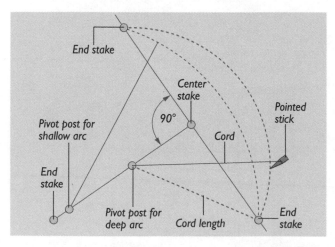

End stake

Center stake

Pointed stick

90°

Pivot post for shallow arc

Cord

End stake

Pivot post for deep arc

Cord length

End stake

Plotting stepped hillside fencing

Descending in steps

Drive the end stakes so their final vertical heights are aligned. Hold one end of a water level next to a point 6" from the ground of the uphill stake. Place the other end against the downhill stake until the water finds its level and determine the height differential—in this case, 2' *(left, top)*. Divide this figure by the number of fence sections to get the drop per section—2' divided by 4 equals 6". Mark the intermediate postholes using twine and a plumb bob, then dig postholes. Set the uphill post to the desired height (6') and mark the drop measurement (6") on the first post. Using the water level, adjust the height of the second post until its top is level with the mark on the first post *(left, bottom)*. Continue in this manner until you set all the posts.

Solutions to Hillside Problems

If your fence line runs uphill, there are two basic ways you can lay out the fence: One is to follow the natural contours of the land; the other is to lay out the fence in steps. In either stepped or contoured fencing, the bottom of boards 6 inches wide or wider should be cut to follow the contour of the hillside; otherwise, unsightly triangular gaps will result where the fence siding meets the ground.

Contour fencing
Picket

Contour fencing
Post-and-rail

Stepped fencing
Post-and-rail

Stepped fencing
Board

Installing fence posts

1 **Set the posts**
Place 4" to 6" of rocks or gravel in a hole 2½' deep—or below the frost line if you live in a cold climate. Compact the gravel with a 2x4, set the post in the hole, then fill it up with earth and gravel (near right). Align and check the post with a level after adding and compacting every 2" to 3" of fill. Slope the top of the fill so water won't pool near the post. For a concrete fill (far right), add 4" of rocks or gravel after setting the post, then shovel concrete around it. As with the earth-and-gravel fill, check the alignment of the post occasionally and tamp the concrete mix, then slope the top of the concrete with a mason's trowel. You'll have about 20 minutes to align your post before the concrete sets; let the posts sit for two days before nailing on rails and siding.

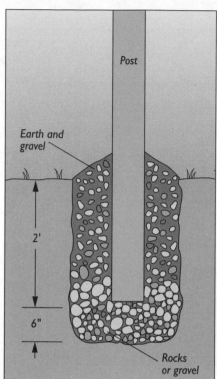

Post

Earth and gravel

2'

6'

Rocks or gravel

Post

Concrete

2'

4"

6"

Rocks or gravel

Spacer

End post

Carpenter's levels make sure the posts are perfectly vertical

Intermediate post one spacer-length away from the twine

2 **Align the posts**
For sections of fence less than 100', a level, spacers, and string are handy for aligning your posts. First set two corner or end posts (above), then cut 2"-long spacer blocks from 1x2s and attach them to the posts about 2' above the ground. Attach twine around the spacers, then level and place intermediate posts so they're one spacer-thickness from the twine. (The blocks will keep the interme-diate posts from touching the string and throwing it out of alignment.) Plumb each post on two adjacent faces as you set it (left). Fill the postholes, making sure the posts are still aligned. If you want a longer fence, you can build it in shorter sections using this method.

JOINERY METHODS FOR ADDING RAILS

Once the fence posts are set and aligned, the hardest part is over. Next, you need to install the rails and siding—boards, pickets, panels, or other material—on the posts. Work carefully: The rails need to be attached firmly to ensure a long-lasting fence.

Many fences use 4x4 posts and 2x4 rails with the siding attached to the rails. But no matter what type of fence you're building, there are a limited number of ways to attach rails to posts. A few of the more common examples are shown here. For contour fencing (page 291), the only two practical methods of joinery are lapping rails over the sides of posts or dadoing rails into them.

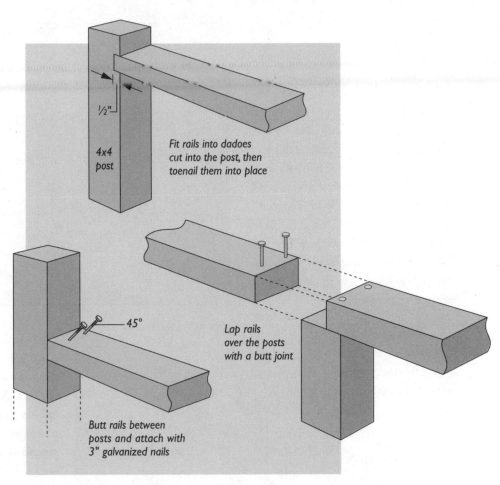

½"

4x4 post

Fit rails into dadoes cut into the post, then toenail them into place

45°

Lap rails over the posts with a butt joint

Butt rails between posts and attach with 3" galvanized nails

Attaching siding

Rail

Post

Siding

String

Carpenter's level

Align the boards

Stretch and level a string from post to post at the height you want the bottom of the siding. Position and level the first board, then secure it in place with nails three times as long as the siding thickness; blunt the nail tips first with a hammer to reduce the chance of splitting the wood. If the rest of the boards fit tightly together, just butt them against each other, as shown at left; otherwise, use a spacer to keep them aligned.

Building a picket fence

1 Plan the fence

Picket fences are usually associated with colonial architecture, but the many styles of pickets and post tops available today let you give your fence its own distinct character. The classic picket fence is about 3' high with 4x4 posts spaced 6' apart and 2x4 rails butted between them. Posts are 5' high—2' below ground and 3' above. Pickets are usually 1x3s spaced 2½" apart. You may want to cut the picket top and post top designs yourself, or have a cabinet shop or woodworker do the work if you have many to do or the design is too intricate.

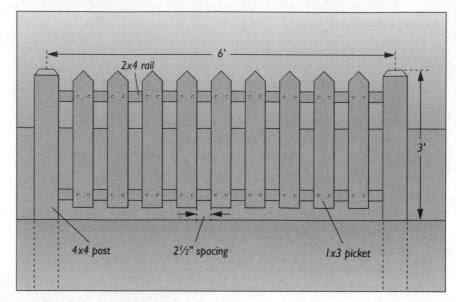

2 Install the posts and rails

Once the pickets and post tops are cut, install the posts and rails *(pages 292-293)*. If you decide to add a kickboard along the bottom of the fence, nail it to the sides of the posts so the pickets rest on top of it *(left)*. The kickboard will touch the ground, so make sure you use pressure-treated or decay-resistant wood.

3 Attach the pickets

To calculate the spacing between pickets, multiply the number of pickets you want by the width of the pickets. Subtract this number from the inches between the posts, then divide the result by the number of spaces (the number of pickets plus one). Rip a picket to this width, to use as a spacer slat. Attach a small 2x4 spacer board, or cleat, to the back of the slat so that when you hang it from the top rail, its top is level with the tops of the pickets. Put the slat flush against the post, then butt a picket against it, aligning the bottom of the picket with the slat. Nail the picket in place with 2¼" galvanized nails. Then use the slat to set the rest of the pickets.

Making a horizontal basket-weave fence

Weave the siding strips

Install the posts and attach the rails to them; you may want to leave the top rail off until you finish weaving the fence. Cut 1x2 nailing strips to fit between the top and bottom rails, then center and nail them to the posts. For siding strips, cut one piece about 2" longer than the distance between two posts. If the siding is too long when it's bent around the 1x1 spacer, cut off about ¼" at a time from one end until it fits between the posts. Use this strip to measure and cut the remaining siding strips, then nail them to the 1x2s, alternating sides (right). Then thread the spacer through the strips, centering it between the posts to create a basket weave (right) and toenail it in place. Finally, fasten the top rail.

Constructing a lattice fence

Attach the strips

Install posts and rails. Paint frame and lath strips, if you wish. Cut strips to length; nail vertical laths to the two rails. Now nail horizontal laths across vertical laths, begin- ning at bottom rail and finishing with the last strip right over the face of the top rail. You can protect and secure the lath ends by nailing vertical strips over the joints.

Building and hanging a gate

1 Build a gate frame

Plan the width of the frame to allow enough clearance space—typically ½" on the latch-post side and ¼" on the hinge-post side. Cut the frame pieces to length and assemble them with a butt joint or the stronger rabbet joint *(inset)*. Use a carpenter's square to ensure that the boards are perpendicular to each other. Then mark the inside corners of the frame on the brace *(right)*. Cut the brace to length, then attach it, nailing through both the horizontal and vertical frame pieces into the ends of the brace.

Gate frame

Brace

Rabbet Joint

First board fastened at hinge side

2 Attach the siding and install the gate

Cut the boards or pickets to size and lay them vertically across the frame, starting flush with the edge on the hinge side. If the last piece is not flush with the frame edge on the latch side, you can start in the middle with full-sized boards and cut or plane the two end boards to fit flush with the frame edge. Mark the position of the boards on the frame, then nail the pieces, starting at the hinge side and using a carpenter's square to check that each board is square to the frame. For plywood or other sheet siding, lay the frame flat over the siding and trace the outside edges of the frame on the siding, then cut the siding and nail it in place. Position each hinge on the gate, mark the screw holes, and drill a pilot hole at each mark. Then attach the hinges to the gate. If the fit is too tight, plane the edge of the latch side as needed.

Installing a gate latch

Positioning a thumb latch

Measure from the edge of the gate to where the hole for the thumbpiece will go. The hole must be long enough to enable the bar to clear the notch in the strike plate when the thumbpiece is raised. Mark the top and bottom of the hole on the gate, drill holes at these marks, and cut out the wood between the holes. Next, slip the thumbpiece through the hole, hold the handle against the front of the fence, and mark the screw holes in the handle onto the fence. Drill pilot holes and fasten the handle in place.

Now position the bar and faceplate on the gate and mark the screw holes. Drill pilot holes and screw the bar and plate to the gate. Finally, position the strike plate against the gate with the bar in its notch and resting on the bottom of the faceplate slot. Holding the strike plate in place, open the gate and mark the screw holes. Remove the plate, drill pilot holes, and fasten the strike plate to the gate *(left)*.

Thumbpiece hole

Bar

Thumbpiece

Faceplate

Handle

Notch in the strike plate

Strike plate

Positioning a self-closing latch

Hold the latch in place on the post and mark the screw holes. Remove the latch, drill pilot holes, and fasten the latch in place. Next, insert the strike into the latch and mark the screw holes on the gate. Remove the strike, drill pilot holes, and screw the strike to the rail *(right)*.

Post

Strike

Latch

Building Overheads and Gazebos

Like a beckoning friend, an overhead or a gazebo invites you to step outside, away from household noise and bustle. It can be a place for quiet conversation, for after-work relaxation, for reading, or for socializing with your friends.

The key is to design a structure that meets the needs of your household effectively and efficiently. To do so, you'll have to keep in mind how the structure will integrate with the style of your home. You may also need to consider the site itself, taking into account factors such as climate and accessibility to your house *(see opposite)*. Whether you want to design and build the structure yourself or you plan to hire a professional, this section will help you understand the entire process, from conception to completion.

The first part of the section includes a basic overview of building an overhead *(pages 300-301)*, followed by a more detailed explanation of the various steps in construction. The section concludes with information on planning and building a gazebo.

ANATOMY
OF AN OVERHEAD

Lath, 1x2, or
2x2

Rafter

Knee-bracing

Beam

Post

The structure of an overhead is essentially the same as that of a deck. An overhead can be freestanding, like the one shown above, or it can be attached to the house with a ledger *(page 276)*. In either case, the structure is supported by a series of posts, which can be continuations of the deck post or rest on cement paving or posts sunk in the ground. If you're adding an overhead to an existing deck, bolt the overhead posts to the deck's substructure, placing them directly above or adjacent to the deck posts. The overhead posts support rafters—the equivalent of joists on a deck. If the overhead is attached to the house, the ledger takes the place of a beam, supporting the rafters directly. Overhead rafters can be left open or they can be covered with any one of a number of materials.

Planning Your Overhead

A good design should take its cue from your home's architectural style. If your house is Victorian, for example, lattice would be an appropriate material.

Though it's not essential that an overhead near the house be built from the same materials as the house, the new structure should blend harmoniously with it, rather than create a jarring contrast. Colors should be complementary, as well.

For a house attached overhead, consider sight lines. When you're standing inside looking out, beams that are too low will pull your viewable horizon down. It's important to plan the height of the overhead so that it doesn't block a pleasing view.

Generally, it's best to ensure that the lowest beam is never placed less than 6 feet 8 inches from the finished floor surface.

Choosing a site: For many overhead projects, the site is predetermined. You may have only one deck or patio—with no intention of building another—and that is where you need shelter from the elements.

If, on the other hand, your site is more flexible or you're developing a comprehensive landscaping plan, consider different locations, evaluating each site in terms of its accessibility from the house, any established traffic patterns from house to yard, views you want to preserve from inside the house, and overall convenience.

By the same token, you'll also want to maximize the assets of your yard. Study its contours, views, the location of trees, and any other relevant elements and factor those into your design.

Sun and weather: Shade is cast at various angles, depending on the time of year and where you live (see map and chart on page 224). If you live in an area that experiences heavy snowfall don't forget to factor in its effects.

If you are planning to have a solid roof on your overhead, for instance, you will need professional advice to make sure the roof will be strong enough to bear the load that snow and ice will put on it during winter months.

MAXIMUM RECOMMENDED BEAM SPANS

The following spans are based on a load of 5 p.s.f. and No. 2 and Better lumber

Beam size	Maximum Spacing Between Beams (or between beam and ledger)	
	12'	16'
2x10	10'	8'
2x12	14'	12'
3x6	8'	6'
3x8	10'	8'
3x10	12'	10'
3x12	16'	14'
4x4	6'	4'
4x6	8'	6'
4x8	12'	10'
4x10	14'	12'
4x12	18'	16'

MAXIMUM RECOMMENDED RAFTER SPANS

The following spans are based on a load of 5 p.s.f. and No. 2 and Better lumber

Rafter size	Maximum Rafter Spacing		
	12"	16"	24"
2x4	10'	9'	8'
2x6	16'	14'	12'
2x8	20'	18'	16'

A Quick Guide to Building an Overhead

The illustrated steps below are intended to give you a general idea of the building sequence for a free-standing overhead. The various structural elements shown in this brief overview—posts, beams, rafters, and roofing—are covered in greater detail in the following pages.

You should also take a look at step-by-step instructions on building a deck (*pages 268-287*). Constructing an overhead is a similar process, from laying out the footings to attaching the decking—or, in this case, the roofing material—except you'll probably spend a lot more time on a ladder. The deck section also contains information on fasteners and connectors such as post caps and post anchors that are commonly used in overheads.

Assembling an overhead frame

1 Set the posts
Set the posts in anchors embedded in a cement slab or in concrete footings or cement piers after cutting the posts to length and nailing post caps on top. Hold the posts vertical and nail anchors to them.

2 Plumb the posts
Place a level on two adjacent sides of each post; secure the post position with temporary wood braces nailed to wood stakes driven into the ground. Repeat with other posts.

3 Attach the beams
Position a beam on top of the posts that will support it. Check that the post is vertical and that the beam is level, shimming it if necessary. Then nail the post caps to the beam.

300

4 Secure the rafters

Set and space rafters on tops of the beams and secure them with framing clips, as shown, or by toenailing them to the beams. If the span warrants, install bracing.

4-foot minimum

90°

5 Brace the overhead

Nail or bolt 1x4 or 1x6 braces, with ends cut at 45°, between beams and posts. Cut the braces long enough so that the beam ends are at least 2' from the post caps. Be sure the structure you create is sturdy and safe.

6 Cover your structure

Cover the rafters with lath, 1x2s, or 2x2s spaced to achieve the desired amount of shading. Finally, nail the roofing material you have selected to the rafters.

Ledgers

Some overheads rely on the use of a ledger to support one end of the rafters at the house. The ledger must be fastened to a masonry wall or to the framing of a wood frame house. If you have a one-story house, you'll fasten the ledger to wall studs, or if the overhead falls just under the house roof, you can attach the ledger to the roof rafters. On a two-story house, you can attach the ledger to the floor framing as shown below. Locate the middle of the ledger about 6 inches below the interior floor level. To transfer this measurement to the exterior wall, use a window or door sill as a reference point.

Securing the ledger: Fasten the ledger to the house as you would a deck ledger (page 276). First you'll need to brace or nail the ledger temporarily at the desired height; make sure it's perfectly level. For a wood frame house, drill lag screw holes into the framing every 16 inches as shown and screw the ledger in place. For a masonry wall, use expanding anchor bolts at the same intervals.

Keeping the rain at bay: Unless the ledger is protected from the rain by the eaves or by its own solid cover material and flashing, you'll have to prevent water from accumulating in the joint between the ledger and the house To do this, space the ledger out from the wall with washers. Or you can protect the ledger with aluminum or galvanized sheet metal Z-flashing.

ATTACHING A LEDGER TO A TWO-STORY HOUSE

Interior of the house

Floor to sill

Floor joist

Band joist

Exterior wall

Floor to sill plus 6"

Lag screws staggered every 16"

Ledger

Carpenter's level

Top of ground-level door

Ledger fastened to house wall

Metal rafter hangers

Beam

Metal post cap

Post

Rafters

Covering

Posts

Overheads are most commonly supported by posts of solid or built-up lumber, steel, or a combination of the two. A variety of post styles is shown below.

Wood posts are made of dimension lumber or timbers. Another alternative to standard lumber is to work with decay-resistant treated poles, available from your lumber or landscaping center. Wood posts that will be within 6 inches of the ground or in contact with concrete should always be made of pressure-treated lumber.

Attaching the posts: Posts can be mounted directly on a slab, using a post anchor, as shown at right. If you're combining the overhead with a deck and designing the two at the same time, the best system of support for the overhead is to continue the posts supporting the deck upward to support the overhead as well *(page 279)*.

Overheads can also be attached to the substructure of an existing deck; however; this may put strain on the deck structure that it was not designed to handle. In order to transfer the weight of the overhead directly to the ground, design it so that the overhead posts fall directly over or adjacent to the deck posts below. (If, however, the overhead posts penetrate through the decking, attach cleats to the sides of the posts to support the ends of the deck boards.) If the design of your overhead does not allow you to position the posts in this way, you should consult a professional to determine

Post — Existing slab
Metal post anchor
Prepunched holes for nails
Expanding anchor bolt

whether the beams or joists can support the weight of the overhead in the middle of their spans.

When attaching overhead posts to the deck substructure, drill holes for through bolts and use four $\frac{1}{2}$-inch bolts.

POST POSSIBILITIES

Treated poles.
Decay resistant. Avoid recycled poles: They may have been treated with creosote, a harmful chemical.

Prefabricated column

Built-up lumber
Can be used instead of solid lumber for decorative effect.

Solid lumber
Can be surfaced, rough, or resawn. Routed grooves or trim add decoration.

Beams

Beams can be made of solid lumber or built up from lengths of 2-by lumber nailed together with ½-inch pressure-treated plywood spacers in between to form a beam 3½ inches square—the same as the actual size of a 4-by post.

Beams generally sit on top of posts, but they can also mesh with them in any of the ways shown on page 279. To fasten the beam to the post, use a metal post cap or one of the two methods shown below. Hoisting a large beam atop a post

over your head demands considerable strength; get help for this stage of the construction. One method is to slip short lengths of 2-by-4 under each end and use the pieces of wood as convenient lifters that several people can grip.

POST-BEAM ASSEMBLIES

Lag bolt

Half-lap joint

Cleat

Decorative cleats

Rafters

Most overheads have rafters of one kind or another, either level or sloping. Rafters must support their own weight over the open space without sagging or twisting, and they must also support the added weight of the covering. Consult the span table on page 299 to determine the proper size and spacing of the rafters.

In a freestanding overhead, rafters are typically supported by beams at each end. If the rafters are sloped, use seismic anchors, as shown at right. In most cases, one standard anchor is adequate. However, in high wind or in seismic areas, a second one may be required diagonally across from the first one—consult your building

department. If you choose the standard anchors, you'll need to notch the rafters to fit; this can be avoided by using a double-sided anchor. Fitting sloping rafters involves making an angle cut at each end.

In an attached overhead, the rafters are fastened to the house at one end. This can be accomplished in any of the ways shown opposite. The best connections are made with metal framing connectors. You can use joist hangers to hang the rafters from the ledger, but for sloping rafters you would have to notch the rafters; instead you can use special rafter hangers as shown on the previous page. (If the rafters will sit on top

RAFTER-TO-BEAM CONNECTIONS

Rafter

Double-sided seismic anchor

Beam

Notch

Standard seismic anchor

Rafter

Illustrations courtesy and copyright Simpson Strong-tie Co.

Knee bracing

Wood frame overheads normally require knee bracing, especially if they are freestanding. You can start by building the overhead without the bracing; then, check the stability of the structure and add knee braces if necessary. The simplest type of knee bracing is shown below (right). Mark individual braces in position and cut them on the ground. Nail them in place temporarily, then drill holes for lag screws or bolts into the posts and beams. Fasten the braces permanently. To prevent rot, avoid designing braces with the end grain exposed to the rain in a horizontal position.

Decorative options

Brace hidden behind lattice

Framing with lattice panel on top

Decorative brace

Lag screw

Simple knee bracing

Vertical end grain

³⁄₁₆" space for drainage

90° maximum

of the ledger, attach them with seismic anchors in the same way as you would attach rafters to a beam.)

For a level overhead, attach the rafters to the beams—or the ledger and beam—the same way you would attach joists to beams in building a deck *(page 281)*.

Rafters can be spliced over beams in the same way as with deck joists *(see page 282)*. Long rafters usually need blocking to prevent twisting or buckling; consult your local codes. For rafters longer than 8 feet, install staggered blocking in the middle of the span *(page 282)*. For rafters shorter than 8 feet, a 1-by fascia nailed across rafter ends is adequate.

RAFTER-TO-HOUSE CONNECTIONS

Joist hanger

Rafter hanger

Ledger

Overhead rafter

Ledger

Ledger

Overhead rafter

Seismic anchor

Overhead rafter

Roofing Your Overhead

Once you have erected the overhead structure of posts, beams, and rafters, you need to add the finishing touch: the appropriate cover material. When you select roofing, be sure the materials you choose will create the environment you want. One material may turn a patio into an oven because of restricted air circulation. Another may offer welcome shade in summer, only to darken an otherwise sunny room in winter. Garden supply centers can supply you with material suitable for your home's climate and appearance.

Overhead covers can be of two types: open or solid. Generally, open-style covers are made from wood, but the wood used can range from thin lath to standard lumber sizes. Other materials are shown opposite. Using lightweight materials such as fabrics or bamboo allows the overhead cover to be removed before the onset of winter. Of these materials a more permanent option is corrugated plastic; it's easy to install and provides light protection against rain.

Lath and louvers, made of wood, are two of the most popular choices for overhead covers. Instructions are included for installing both types starting on this page.

Creating shade: If you are working with lath or boards, you'll have to determine the right spacing and direction for them to create the amount of shade you're trying to achieve. You'll also have to be sure you don't exceed the allowable spans for the materials you're using. Remember that wood thickness and spacing can vary enormously: Thin lath laid flat won't cast as much shade as thicker stock.

Lath or boards can be laid flat or set on edge, as shown below. Laid flat, they will let in more sun in the early morning or late afternoon but block more sun at midday. The direction you should choose to run the lath or boards depends on what time of day you need maximum shade. If you want the greatest relief from the sun at noon, plan to run the material east-west; if you want more shade in the early morning and late afternoon, run it north-south.

Building a lath cover

1x3 frame

Rafter

Cleats

Making preassembled panels

To reduce the time you need to spend on the rooftop, you can assemble panels on the ground and then fasten them in place as a unit—just be sure the rafters are straight enough to receive the panels without a struggle. You can make the panels in practically any size, but about 3x6 feet is the optimum for lightweight material. Face-nail the roofing material to a frame of 1x3s. Attach cleats to the faces of the rafters and fit the panels in place. You can face-nail the panels to the inside of the rafters, or you can leave the panels unfastened for easy removal and cleaning.

Varying the height: The height of a lath-style overhead will affect the amount of light that falls on your deck. The higher the overhead, the more diffused the light becomes. Conversely, the lower the overhead, the sharper the striped shadows will be on the deck surface.

Suitable spans: To avoid sagging and warping, be conservative on the distance your material must span. For common lath, 2 feet is the maximum; 1-by boards can span up to 3 feet, but 2 feet is better. With 1 by 2 or 1-by-3 stock laid on edge and with 2-by-2s, you can span 4 feet without too much sagging, but boards may warp or curve a bit.

A GALLERY OF OVERHEAD COVERS

Spaced lath is easy to install.

Spacer

Rafter

Corrugated plastic panels are often used for patio overheads.

Panel overlap

Woven reed provides an interesting texture.

1x2s

Rafters

Blocking

Egg crate is open to the sky but gives a sheltered feeling.

Toenail blocking to rafters

Grommets

Shade cloth is available in different weaves that provide 20 to 90 percent shade.

Screw eyes

Lattice panels can be purchased or you can make your own in the pattern of your choice.

1x2 ledger

Angled louvers made from 1-by boards offer an extra element of sun control over the lath overheads shown on page 306. Adjustable types can give you almost any degree of light or shade you want throughout the day; fixed louvers can block the sun during a particular time of the day when it's unwanted.

As shown at right, the more you tilt the boards, the fewer pieces you'll need. But if you try to spread them too far, you'll diminish the amount of reflected light that can shine through. For a pitched roof, don't forget to add the angle of the pitch to the angle of the sun's altitude when figuring louvers.

Louvers are generally made of 1-by-3s, 1-by-4s, or 1-by-6s not more than 4 feet long. The narrower the pieces, the more closely they will have to be spaced.

Instructions below and opposite tell you how to make both fixed and adjustable louvers. Adjustable louvers are more time-consuming to make. If you don't want to attempt the precision work involved, consider buying a ready-made system or having a professional do the job for you.

Installing louvers

Fastening fixed louvers

Fixed louvers can be built in place—nailed directly to rafters—or they can be built in modular sections and then fastened in place in the same way as the vertical boards shown on page 306. Shown at right are three different ways of fastening louvers to their supports. NOTE: If you make stepped cuts in the rafters, be sure the width of the rafter at its narrowest point is not less than specified for the span.

Constructing adjustable louvers

In the home-built design shown at right, louvers fit into a frame fastened between rafters. They pivot on metal pins and washers. A 1x2 attached to the bottom of the louvers with eye screws controls the angle. Build the modules separately and then fasten them between rafters. Cut the louvers slightly shorter than the spacing between the sides of the frame to allow them to pivot while remaining tight enough to stay in place. For metal pins, aluminum nails with the heads clipped off work well.

Metal pin
and washer

1x6 frame nailed
between rafters

1x6 louver

Rafter

Hole
for pin

Rope   Eye screw   1x2

5½"

Solid Roofing

Solid roofs are designed to shed rain and snow. Materials you can install yourself include shingles, wood shingles and shakes, siding, asphalt roll roofing, aluminum panels, and aluminum shingles. The pitch of the roof will depend on the materials chosen, as will the base that is installed under your roofing material. Shown here is a typical solid roof of asphalt shingles. The shingles are installed over a base of plywood sheathing and a layer of roofing felt.

Other options for a solid roof are plastic or glass. These materials can maxi-mize light, view, and shelter. But, when improperly designed, a plastic or glass roof can act as a heat trap or create a condensation and drip problem.

Because of the weight of solid roofing materials and the snow they collect, solid roofs should be designed by a professional.

For a colorful and lightweight roof, you may want to consider outdoor fabrics. Various types are available, including acrylic, cotton duck, vinyl-coated canvas, and vinyl-laminated polyester. You can design a fabric roof yourself, but be sure to take in the covering in the winter so it doesn't become loaded with snow.

Ridge

Asphalt
shingle

Hip

Sheathing

Roofing felt

Planning a Gazebo

When you think of a gazebo, you may imagine an elaborately detailed summerhouse for entertaining guests or a simple garden retreat where you can relax and watch the setting sun. Or your mind's eye may envision a more contemporary, sophisticated design.

Although gazebos come in a variety of shapes, they often feature a hexagonal or octagonal design like the model shown below in the anatomy view. Building the structure, with its foundations, posts, and beams, is basically the same as building an overhead. The main difference is that all gazebos are freestanding, whereas overheads occasionally make use of a ledger strip. For information on beam and rafter spans, see the charts on page 299.

Building a roof for a hexagonal or octagonal gazebo is the trickiest part of its construction, and is dealt with more fully on pages 312-313.

Finding a site: Like any other independent element in your backyard, a gazebo should be considered in terms of the existing traffic patterns and the intended use of the structure. If you plan to use it as a reading spot, for example, your gazebo will probably see more use if it is located some distance away from your children's play area. On the other hand, as an entertainment center for barbecues and parties, your gazebo might serve better if it is centrally located and easily accessible from your house. Of course, there may also be legal restrictions to consider, such as setback and height limit. Contact your local building department.

ANATOMY OF A GAZEBO

Like an overhead, a gazebo is typically supported by a foundation: either a concrete footing and pier or a concrete slab as shown at right. A sill of treated 2-by lumber is fastened to the slab with expansion anchors at least ½" in diameter. The posts are fastened to the sill with post anchors. The tops of the posts are secured to the beams by joist hangers; alternatively, you can toenail through the beams into the posts. Knee braces ensure a more rigid structure. The rafters radiate outward from a central hub, and are joined to the top ends of the posts. The gazebo may be covered with either solid or open roofing (page 307).

Center hub
Solid roofing
Open roofing
Rafter
Beam
Knee brace
Wall panel
Post
Rail
Post anchor
Concrete slab
Treated sill

Scale drawing: A good scale drawing of your yard will enable you to visualize how the gazebo will fit into its surroundings. Even if you're planning to turn the project over to a professional, it's still a good idea to prepare a base map of your yard similar to the one shown on page 226, with such features as direction of prevailing winds, existing trees and location of the house and any other structures on your property. You can create a plan for your own gazebo based on the anatomy opposite, or you may wish to go with an existing plan. Pages 314-315 feature plans and a cutting list for an elegantly simple design.

CHOOSING GAZEBO KITS

If building your own gazebo from scratch sounds a bit overwhelming, you may want to consider a gazebo kit. Several companies manufacture gazebos that you can purchase in kit form, complete except for the foundation. You construct the gazebo on a slab, deck, or foundation of piers or crushed stone. For some types, assembly—with a helper—takes a weekend or two and requires only basic tools and skills.

Depending on size, material, and style, kits are available from as little as $500 to as much as $20,000; most are in the $2,000 or $4,000 range. This is often less than the cost of having a custom gazebo designed by a professional builder, even if you buy the kit and pay a carpenter to assemble it.

Buying a gazebo kit can be a major investment, so shop carefully. Check that connections are made with galvanized or brass hardware, and that machining is carefully done so assembly is relatively easy. Details, such as railings or bracing, are worthy of close scrutiny. Also be sure to read the assembly directions beforehand to see if they're easy to follow.

A gazebo kit takes a lot of the guesswork out of building your own structure. The kits can normally be assembled with hand tools and are as elaborate as your pocketbook allows.

Find out whether the gazebo is made from redwood or cedar heartwoods or from less-expensive pressure-treated lumber. Can the wood be finished naturally or does it have to be painted?

Also, make sure you know what's included in the price. Who pays for delivery? This is important, because a gazebo may weigh 1,500 pounds or more. Is flooring and floor framing included? What about benches, screen,

and steps? Many kits allow you to choose between open railings or lattice panels and other similar details.

If you're not able to see an example of the gazebo, ask the company for some names of customers. They can tell you whether they were satisfied with the company's service and the quality of the workmanship.

Here are a few tips to keep in mind:
- Plan the site carefully; remember that most kit gazebos are permanent once they're assembled.
- Be certain to anchor the gazebo properly; otherwise a heavy wind might blow it over.
- If you put the gazebo on a concrete slab, make sure that you pitch the slab for rain runoff.
- Follow the manufacturer's instructions closely, paying particular attention to the building sequence and to techniques for anchoring the gazebo, fastening joints, and finishing.

Roofing Your Gazebo

Gazebos may have open or solid roofs. Since many are octagonal or hexagonal in shape, roofing poses some special challenges. The roof rafters of these structures meet at a center point, where they are fixed to a hub. (Typical hubs are shown opposite.)

Fitting sloping rafters in place can be quite tricky for a novice. The best method is to cut one rafter to fit, then use it as a template to mark and cut the rest.

If you need to splice rafters, you can use board lumber gusset plates, butting the ends of the rafters together over a supporting beam. Two pieces of 1-by lumber of the same width as the rafters and about 18 inches long are then nailed on both sides of the splice. You can also join the members using manufactured metal splice plates. Remember that in a gazebo there is usually no ceiling to hide the underside of the roof, so for the sake of appearance, metal plates are less conspicuous.

To prevent twisting and buckling, blocking may be required between

SHEATHING OPTIONS

Solid roofs require sheathing to support the shingles that actually resist the rain or snow. Asphalt shingles require both plywood and roofing felt (right), while wood shingle can should be laid over open-sheath roofing (below).

With plywood sheathing, you might consider using a higher grade, one-side-good plywood, because the underside of the sheathing is usually visible from inside the gazebo.

The solid roof usually begins with a layer of plywood sheathing, fixed to the roof with 2-inch common nails for plywood up to ½" thick, and 2½-inch nails for ⅝"or greater thickness. A layer of 15-pound roofing felt is then laid down with the appropriate overlaps as shown. Asphalt shingles then complete the roof.

An open-sheathing roof starts with solid rows of 1x4s at the eaves, secured with 2½-inch nails. The rest of the boards are arranged with gaps separating them; a scrap piece of 1x4 can be used as a spacer.

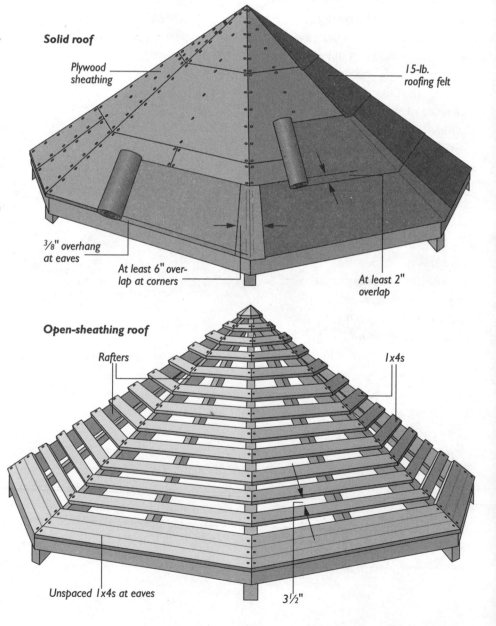

Solid roof

Plywood sheathing

15-lb. roofing felt

⅜" overhang at eaves

At least 6" overlap at corners

At least 2" overlap

Open-sheathing roof

Rafters

1x4s

Unspaced 1x4s at eaves

3½"

the rafters. Your local building code may require certain specifications.

While rafters are usually thought of as just a part of the roofing substructure, they can also add a decorative touch to your gazebo. Some possibilities are shown at right.

An open roof and a solid roof are built in essentially the same way up to the point that the rafters are installed. After that, you can add the roofing material for an open roof (lath strips, for example), or you can install solid roofing materials. Two sheathing options are described on the opposite page.

In building your roof you will also have to take into account its pitch, which refers to the vertical rise against a standard horizontal distance of 12 inches. The term 4-in-12 tells you that the roof rises 4 inches for every 12 horizontal inches. The steeper a roof's pitch, the better it sheds water.

Asphalt and wood shingles are designed for roofs with a 4-in-12 or greater slope. Shallower pitches can support these materials with additional underlayment.

DECORATIVE RAFTER CUTS

HUB STYLES

Four-sided hub

4x4 trimmed to a point

Recessed lag screw

Toenailed

Eight-sided hub

45° cuts   60° cuts

Eight-sided hub   Six-sided hub

Manufactured hub for kit

Overhead: Open Gazebo

A grove of lanky cedar trees provides a dignified setting for a gazebo designed for entertaining. Groups of four cedar posts support the open rafters and the two built-in benches.

Posts for a gazebo can be fastened to the deck's substructure, or the deck's posts can be made longer. For this gazebo, the posts continue down beneath the gazebo's decking, where they're anchored in footings. At each corner, built-in planters between the posts add seasonal color. A series of 1-by-2s wrap around the post tops, creating texture and visual interest. Trim is fitted to the bottom of the posts at deck level.

The 2-by-6 rafters, trimmed with 1-by-4s nailed to each side, cross at the ridge. Both rafters and trim are fitted together with angled half-lap joints. For more information on building an overhead, such as a gazebo, turn to page 298.

turn to page 298.

MATERIALS LIST

Designed for cedar heartwood, corrosion-resistant hardware.

LUMBER

Posts	4x4
Beams	2x8
Rafters	2x6
Ridge boards	2x6
Trim	1x4 for rafters; 1x2 for tops of posts; 2x3 for bottoms of posts
Benches/planters	2x4 seat boards; 1x6 trim

HARDWARE

Nails	1½" for 1-by trim; 3" for 2-by trim; 3½" for rafters to beams
Bolts	½"x7" machine bolts
Other	Galvanized steel liner for planter

This airy gazebo's sophisticated design, uncluttered lines, and natural finish perfectly complement its serene setting.
Architect: Robert C. Slenes and Morton Safford James III for Bennett, Johnson, Slenes & Smith

THREE-DIMENSIONAL VIEW

2x6 rafters

Angled half-lap joints (rafters and decorative 1x4s)

Decorative 1x4

2x8s

1x2s, spaced 1½" apart

2x3 trim, mitered, nailed to post

4x4 posts (extension of deck's posts or fastened to deck's substructure)

½"x7" machine bolt

2x4 seat boards

Planter with galvanized steel liner; drain holes at bottom

4x4 short connector post, decoratively cut

1x6 trim

Elevation

16"

30°

8'

Plan view

Benches

2x6 rafters, with 1x4 trim, 2' o.c.

4x4 posts

12"

2'

10'

2'

12"

12"   2'   3'   3'   2'

10'

Index

316

Acknowledgments

The editors wish to thank the following:

Adair County Cooperative Extension Office, Columbia, KY

Al Root Company, Medina, OH

American Association of Variable Star Observers,
    Cambridge, MA

Aquasculpture, St. Laurent, Que.

Jon Arno, Troy, MI

Bat Conservation International, Austin, TX

Ben & Jerry's Homemade, Inc., South Burlington, VT

Bomanite Corporation, Madera, CA

Building Officials and Code Administrators International,
    Country Club Hills, IL

Celtic Advertising, Inc., Brookfield, WI

Conservation Technology, Inc., Baltimore, MD

Datalizer Slide Charts Inc., Addeson, IL

Garden Concepts, Inc., Glenview, IL

General Housewares Corporation, Terre Haute, IN

Gaetan Gilbert, Chambly, Que.

Huffy Sports Company, Division of Huffy Corp.,
    Waukesha, WI

Marcod, Inc., Boucherville, Que.

David Nanasi, St. Laurent, Que.

National Concrete Association, Herndon, VA

National Horseshoe Pitchers Association, Franksville, WI

National Presto Industries, Inc., Eau Claire, WI

National Spa and Pool Institute, Alexandria, VA

Mario Pagnoni, Methuen, MA

United States Badminton Association, Colorado Springs, CO

United States Croquet Association, Wellington, FL

USA Volleyball, Colorado Springs, CO

**The following persons also assisted in the preparation
of this book:**

Chantal Bilodeau, Normand Boudreault, Lorraine Doré, Joan Beth
Erickson, Caroline Joubert, Jenny Meltzer, Giles Miller-Mead, Heather
Mills, Mathieu Raymond-Beaubien, Rebecca Smollett, Britta Swartz

Picture Credits

4 Saxon Holt
5 (upper) Comstock
5 (lower) Jay Graham, Graham Photography

ENJOYING BACKYARD LIFE
6, 7 Saxon Holt
8 Bill Ross
9 (upper) Philip Harvey
9 (lower) Peter Christiansen
10 Jay Graham, Graham Photography
11 (upper) Balthazar Korab
11 (lower) Comstock
12, 13 Comstock
13 Philip Harvey
14 (inset) Victor Budnik
14 Balthazar Korab
14, 15 Philip Harvey
15 George M. Sangrik
16 Stephen Marley
16, 17 Tom Wyatt
17 Balthazar Korab
18 Philip Harvey
24 Peter Christiansen
25 (both) Peter Christiansen
26 Peter Christiansen
27 Stuart Watson (3)
28, 29 Weber-Stephen Products Co.
30 (upper right) Weber-Stephen Products Co.
30 Robert Chartier (3)
31 (left) Weber-Stephen Products Co.
31 (right) Peter Christiansen
34 Peter Christiansen
35 Peter Christiansen
36 Norman A. Plate
37 (left) Robert Chartier (3)
37 (upper right) Paul Hammond
38 Norman A. Plate
39 (upper) Robert Chartier (4)
39 (lower) Chris Shorten
40 Comstock
41 Peter Christiansen
42 Tom Wyatt
43 Peter Christiansen
44 Peter Christiansen
45 Peter Christiansen (3)
46 Don Normark
47 Courtesy: International E-Z Up, Inc.
48 Peter Christiansen
49 (upper right) Peter Christiansen
49 Norman A. Plate (2)
50 Norman A. Plate
51 (upper) Weber-Stephen Products Co. (4)
51 (lower) Darrow M. Watt
52 Noel Barnhurst Photographer

54 (upper right) Peter Christiansen
54 Weber-Stephen Products Co. (2)
54 (lower left) Norman A. Plate
55 Tom Wyatt
56 (upper left) Don Normark
56 (lower right) Balthazar Korab
57 (left) Norman A. Plate (4)
57 (right) Don Normark
58 (upper right) Jessie Walker
58 (lower left) Richard Nicol
59 Saxon Holt
60 (inset) Norman A. Plate
60 Bill Ross
61 Robert Chartier
62 Norman A. Plate
63 Norman A. Plate
64 Norman A. Plate
66 Peter Christiansen
69 (both) Norman A. Plate
82 (upper) Stephen Marley
82 (lower) Tom Wyatt
84 (upper) Norman A. Plate
84 (lower) Courtesy: Infratech Corporation
85 (left) Norman A. Plate
85 (right) Jack McDowell
86 (inset) Don Normark
86 Kathy Brenzel
91 Peter Christiansen (5)
91 (lower right) Peter Whiteley
92 Saxon Holt
93 Thomas C. Boyden (3)
93 (lower left) Saxon Holt
94 Franz Guyana/Masterfile
96 (left) Merlin D. Tuttle/Bat Conservation International
96 (right) Jim Kennedy/Bat Conservation International
98 (inset) Saxon Holt
98 Balthazar Korab
99 Tom Wyatt
100 Courtesy: Wardley Corporation
104 Norman A. Plate
105 (upper) K. Bryan Swezey
105 (lower) Momatiuk, Eastcott/Woodfin Camp & Associates
106 (upper) Richard Fish
106 (lower) K. Bryan Swezey
107 (upper) Courtesy: National Spa & Pool Institute
107 (lower) Tom Wyatt
108 (upper) Courtesy: National Spa & Pool Institute
108 (left) Tom Wyatt
108, 109 Jessie Walker
110 Courtesy: National Spa & Pool Institute

111 Zigy Kaluzny/Tony Stone Images
112 Jessie Walker
113 Courtesy: Hutch Sports USA
114 (left) J. Taposchaner/Masterfile
114 (right) Courtesy: Huffy Sports Company
118 Courtesy: Sporting Goods Manufacturers Association
119 Courtesy: Hutch Sports USA
120 Chris Shorten
121 Courtesy: Hutch Sports USA
122 Courtesy: Hutch Sports USA
123 (left) Erwin C. Nielsen
123 (right) Frank Siteman/Tony Stone Images
124 Courtesy: Hutch Sports USA
125 (both) Mario Pagnoni, The Joy of Bocce & Masters Press
126 B. Bachmann/Reflexion
127 Courtesy: Gaétan Gilbert
128 Jack Zehrt/Masterfile
129 (upper left) Roberta Voleary/National Museum of Science & Technology
129 (upper right) Courtesy: Datalizer Slide Charts, Inc. & Sonia Di Maulo
129 (lower left) Courtesy: Orion Telescope Center
129 (lower right) Courtesy: Swift Instruments
131 Stephen Cridland
132 Peter Christiansen
133 Darrow M. Watt
134 Darrow M. Watt
138 Darrow M. Watt
140 Darrow M. Watt
142 Stephanie Rausser
144 Stephanie Rausser
145 Stephanie Rausser
146 Darrow M. Watt
148 Darrow M. Watt
150 Stephan Cridland
151 (upper left) Comstock
151 (lower right) B. Bachmann/Reflexion
152 Glenn Christiansen
153 (both) Andy Freeberg
154 (both) Darrow M. Watt
156 Florian Werner/Masterfile

GARDENING FOR PLEASURE
158, 159 Comstock
160 Ken Straiton/First Light Associated Photographers

BUILDING IN YOUR BACKYARD
222, 223 Jay Graham, Graham Photography
224 Philip Harvey